Zoning Rules!

THE ECONOMICS OF LAND USE REGULATION

WILLIAM A. FISCHEL

Cambridge, Massachusetts

© 2015 by the Lincoln Institute of Land Policy

All rights reserved

Third printing, July 2018

Library of Congress Control Number: 2015940857

ISBN 978-1-55844-288-7

Designed by Westchester Publishing Services

Composed in Janson by Westchester Publishing Services in Danbury, Connecticut.
Printed and bound by Puritan Capital in Hollis, New Hampshire.
The paper is Rolland Enviro100, an acid-free, 100 percent PCW recycled sheet.

MANUFACTURED IN THE UNITED STATES OF AMERICA

Zoning Rules!

*To my students,
from whom I have learned so much*

Contents

Preface ix

CHAPTER 1 1
Land Use and Land Economics

CHAPTER 2 27
The Structure and Administration of Zoning Laws

CHAPTER 3 69
Judicial Supervision of Land Use Regulation

CHAPTER 4 129
Fiscal Zoning and Economists' View of the Property Tax

CHAPTER 5 163
The Economic History of Zoning

CHAPTER 6 219
The Coase Theorem, Land Use Entitlements,
and Rational Government

CHAPTER 7   261
Zoning and Suburban Development

CHAPTER 8   289
The Politics and Economics of Metropolitan Sprawl

CHAPTER 9   328
Remedial Strategies for Excess Regulation

References   369
- CASES   369
- SECONDARY SOURCES   371

Index   401

About the Author   417

About the Lincoln Institute of Land Policy   418

Preface

Zoning has shaped American cities since 1916, when New York City adopted the first comprehensive ordinance. The title of this book expresses my thesis that zoning should be thought of as an active force rather than a background rulebook that is occasionally glanced at by developers and public officials. When landowners have plans to change the use of their property, they must first consult the rules in the local zoning ordinance. The rules are not immutable, but neither are they paper tigers that crumble at the whim of developers.

Zoning Rules! is the successor to the book I published 30 years ago, *The Economics of Zoning Laws* (1985). Enough has changed in the political arena of land use regulation as well as in the scholarship about zoning that I thought that a new title was in order. My own views have shifted as well, not least because I have written three other books about local government in the meantime: *Regulatory Takings* (1995), *The Homevoter Hypothesis* (2001), and *Making the Grade* (2009). The roles of property law and constitutional doctrine figure less in the present work than the demands of local residents, especially homeowners.

From my historical inquiries about its origins, zoning now looks to me more like a bottom-up institution. The development and spread of zoning are less about the planning profession—a necessary but not sufficient ingredient—and more about the changes in transportation technology that have made homeowners eager to try a new approach to controlling conditions in their communities. Modern proposals to reform zoning will go awry unless they understand the concerns that brought about the acceptance of zoning and its spread in the twentieth century.

One of the lessons I learned from my 1985 book on zoning is that many readers approached it selectively. It has been on many college and university reading lists, but almost always as selected chapters. Even I have used it that way in my course in urban and land use economics at Dartmouth. The present work is organized to form a sequential and (I hope) coherent narrative, but most chapters have been composed to be read independently. (Chapters 6 and 7 are best paired, as are chapters 8 and 9.) This creates some redundancy that I hope the reader of the entire book will forgive. The following outline of the themes of each chapter may also help readers who navigate the book outside the sequential box.

The law and institutions described in this book are almost entirely from the United States. My international students at Dartmouth, however, have had little trouble adapting this knowledge when undertaking research about urban regulations in their home countries, which have included Australia, Canada, China, Denmark, Finland, Germany, Lithuania, Singapore, and Thailand. This adaptability makes me suspect that the economic behavior that drives American zoning has shaped institutions in other nations as well.

Outline of the Book

Chapter 1 offers an overview of land use in the United States. Its most important observation is how little land is used for urban and other built-up activities. We are not about to run out of land for farming or other rural uses. Nonetheless, I do argue that excessive suburbanization—sprawl—is an important problem. Urbanization is a critical part of a productive and growing economy, and the major benefit of urban life is that people can work and live in close physical proximity to one another. Zoning and related land use controls are necessary to manage the intimacy of urban life, but they also can be applied so strenuously that we become strangers to one another.

Chapter 2 describes how zoning works and the recent trends in land use regulation. I emphasize here that zoning is not a single-valued constraint. It is a complex, locally generated web of regulations, and cutting any single strand is not likely to compromise its overall strength. I also defend the role of the often-maligned board of zoning appeals on the ground that local knowledge is critical to sensible land use decisions. The major trend in land use regulation since 1970 has arisen from the initiatives undertaken by the states and the federal government. In the few instances where they have displaced local authority, state and federal regulations have tilted zoning mostly toward more restrictiveness. They have seldom made local governments accept developments that local residents do not want. The starting point for discussions about land use policy still has to be the local zoning map.

Chapter 3 reviews judicial supervision of zoning and related matters, focusing on decisions of the U.S. Supreme Court. In contrast to my earlier work, this book places less stock in the courts as agents for promoting rational land use. The main reason for this change in emphasis is that intelligent land use decisions require a degree of local knowledge that is difficult to transmit to judges far removed from the facts. I demonstrate this by closely examining one of the earliest zoning decisions of the Court, *Nectow v. Cambridge*, 277 U.S. 183 (1928), in which the Court made a dubious decision because it did not understand the neighborhood involved or the effect of new automotive technology. The Court's saving grace is that it has been reluctant ever since to become the national board of zoning appeals. The chapter also reviews the influence of the regulatory takings doctrine, which would have governments pay compensation to developers frustrated by unreasonable regulations. The Court has prevented states from abolishing the doctrine, and it has established broad parameters that deter some extreme regulations, but it has otherwise not been inclined to develop a robust and clear standard for when it should apply. Despite concerns by planners and environmentalists about recent decisions that limit land use exactions, no one should expect the Court's hands-off attitude to change.

Chapter 4 shows how closely integrated zoning is with other local government functions such as property taxation, municipal infrastructure, and public schools. The focus of the chapter is a debate among economists about how to think about the property tax. I show that zoning has the capacity to make the local property tax into a fee for public services, which implies that it is not really a tax at all. The fiscal powers of zoning are sometimes clouded from economists' view because zoning is also used by local governments to promote other objectives such as job growth and preservation of pleasant environments. This chapter also challenges the notion that suburban communities are invariably hostile to social and economic diversity within their borders. Diversity may actually be a local public good, and communities' use of "exclusionary zoning" can be seen as a device to rationalize fiscal transfers to the poor rather than avoid them altogether.

Chapter 5 offers a new history of zoning as a "bottom-up" movement rather than the conventional story about the progressive planners and pioneering lawyers who created its intellectual infrastructure. Zoning is the product of popular government; in this instance, the elites who developed it were the servants of the people. The cause of zoning's amazingly rapid adoption and spread in America was the expansion of low-cost freight trucks and jitney buses in the 1910s. As a result, suburban homeowners could no longer rely on the distance of their neighborhoods from the city center and from rail lines to keep industry and apartments at bay, and they quickly embraced an institution that had few antecedents in American law. The major shift in zoning was the rise of growth controls in the 1970s. I argue that this was largely the result of the rapid construction of the interstate highway system in the preceding decade, as well as the 1970s inflation in home values, which transformed owner-occupied homes from consumer goods into investment goods. The growth control movement is critical to understand because of evidence that it is contributing to the national segregation of the poor from the rich and reducing access by workers to high-productivity urban areas in the Northeast and West Coast sections of the United States.

Chapter 6 uses graphical expositions of economic principles to develop an analytic framework for zoning. As in my 1985 book, the core of this framework is the Coase theorem. Land use regulation favors the interests of existing community residents, but developers can bargain with local officials to change zoning. The possibility of rezoning and the blandishments of developers present an opportunity cost to local officials and make them aware of the demands of prospective community residents and businesses. I explore in this context the regulatory takings doctrine, which would make governments pay for excessive regulations. The doctrine's drawback is not, as some critics argue, that governments are incapable of responding to an economic cost if they have to pay for the consequences of regulation. The problem (as argued in chapter 9) is that the doctrine itself can be applied in so many other situations that popular government would drown in its demands.

Chapter 7 applies the Coase theorem approach to the process of community development. It focuses on a paradigmatic town, Acton, Massachusetts. Like many other Boston suburbs, Acton shifted from accommodating development in an orderly fashion in the 1950s to implementing growth controls in the 1970s and 1980s. The graphical model to examine this transformation is borrowed from the local public finance literature on the Tiebout model. The shift from developer-influenced zoning to growth controls was facilitated by the legal tools of the environmental movement and the expansion of legal standing to nongovernmental organizations and individuals. An important insight from another article by Coase is how irreversible "conservation easements" help local governments commit to a growth control regime. While such policies are rational for each suburban community, they can be collectively problematic, as argued in chapter 8, for the economic and environmental health of the larger metropolitan area.

Chapter 8 examines the problem of excessive decentralization—sprawl—in a metropolitan context. A major cause of sprawl is growth-control zoning in desirable, close-in suburbs, which sends developers out to the farther reaches of the metropolitan area to create "edge cities" and excessively low-density residential development. The chapter considers two alternative approaches to dealing with sprawl, one epitomized by Portland, Oregon, and the other by Houston, Texas. Portland's urban growth boundary does appear to contain sprawl, but it may have the side effect of monopolizing the urban housing market and retarding overall regional growth. Houston is the only large city that lacks zoning. It continues to grow exuberantly, but its low housing prices may reflect the risks of homeownership in an unzoned city. I advance a middle ground for zoning, the "good-housekeeping" model, as a path between these two extremes.

Chapter 9 addresses how zoning might be restored to the "good-housekeeping" model and away from the excesses of growth controls. I had in previous work supported the regulatory takings doctrine as a means of promoting local decisions that paid attention to the demands of outsiders. The theoretical virtues of regulatory takings, however, are in this chapter brought face to face with the extreme difficulty of administering this legal doctrine and containing it within reasonable bounds. The alternative that I promote is to reduce the demand for growth controls. The most promising way of doing this is by changing federal income tax rules that subsidize housing relative to other investments. Reducing excessive investment in owner-occupied housing is likely to be the most effective means of tempering the anti-growth syndrome that has caused excessive sprawl and promoted a lopsided distribution of income and wealth within and among America's metropolitan areas.

I gratefully acknowledge the support of the Lincoln Institute of Land Policy and Dartmouth College for a sabbatical leave during which much of the work on this book was done. With respect to my intellectual debts to individuals and other institutions, I am a hopeless bankrupt. Joan Youngman read the manuscript and provided helpful comments. Specific comments by individuals are acknowledged in the text, but I will single out here those of Bethany Berger, Peter Buchsbaum, Peter Ganong, Alex von Hoffman, Gideon Kanner, Nicholas Marantz, Danny Shoag, and Michael Wolf. The book's dedication to my students is heartfelt; their papers and class presentations over many years have filled gaps in my knowledge and often provoked me to look in corners I would otherwise have ignored. My wife, Janice G. Fischel, as always was encouraging and helpful, but for this book she made a specific contribution: its title!

Hanover, New Hampshire
March 2015

CHAPTER 1

Land Use and Land Economics

> In the United States there is more space where nobody is than anybody is. This is what makes America what it is.
> —GERTRUDE STEIN, *THE GEOGRAPHICAL HISTORY OF AMERICA*, 1936

The fundamental premise of this book is that land use controls are best analyzed as collective property rights under the control of economically rational voters. The present chapter is devoted to some tasks preliminary to developing this theme. The first of these is to outline some facts about land use in order to set the parameters of what is to be regulated. The focus is on urban development and population pressure on land resources. Here, my major conclusion is that we are in no danger of running out of land for nonurban purposes due to population growth or development. The second task of this chapter is to review some elements of land economics. In order to comprehend the role of public property rights in allocating land, one must understand the basic forces by which private land uses are determined. The most powerful and least clearly understood of these is urban agglomeration economies.

1.1 How Much Land Is Urbanized?

A persistent concern about urbanization is that, left unchecked, it will "pave over" America's farmland. An advocacy group, the American Farmland Trust, declared on its website, "Every minute of every day, we have been losing more than an acre of agricultural land to development." To put this claim in perspective, I have for several decades posed the following thought experiment to my students in urban economics: Divide the current United States population into households of four persons and house them at the density of one acre per household. What percentage of the total land area of the 48 contiguous states would be taken up? I explain to my students that an acre is approximately the size of a football field without the end zones, but I offer no other data. I ask them to write down a response before I poll them in order to reduce conformity bias.

The answers have been amazingly consistent over the years. Each group's guesses range from over 90 percent to less than 10 percent, but the median guess is almost always between 30 and 40 percent. Nearly everyone offers guesses considerably above the correct answer: 4 percent. I have also posed this question at academic and policy forums on land use and zoning, and the responses are usually the same. The only two exceptions are academic geographers and commercial developers. The geographers' average guesses are extremely high, on the order of 50 to 70 percent, and the developers get it almost exactly right, with median guesses of less than 10 percent.

What explains the consistently high guesses? I have talked with students about this, and the misperception could be the result of two factors. One is the projection of personal experience onto a larger stage. Most Americans live in suburban areas. As the distinguished rural geographer John Fraser Hart (2001) has noted, "Each one of us can think of rural areas that we have seen converted to urban uses. We yield to the perfectly normal human temptation to assume that our observations and experiences are typical, and we project them to the status of Universal Truths" (540). (Hart later concludes, "There are good and compelling reasons for concern about the expansion of urban areas into the adjacent countryside, but attempts to block or control it cannot be justified on the grounds of loss of good cropland/farmland" [542].) The other factor is a systematic bias in public sources of information. Farmland preservation has a remarkably strong press because of nostalgia for rural life and aesthetic norms ("amber waves of grain") and because tracts of suburban housing have long been derided in popular culture as "little boxes made of ticky tacky," as the Malvina Reynolds song would have it.

One may object to my heuristic calculation. Average household size is smaller than four (it was 2.60 in 2010), and other activities besides housing need to be counted. The facts, however, show that my simple calculation is not far off as a measure of development's encroachment on rural land. A number of modern studies (some discussed below) that use remote sensing devices and geographic information systems (GIS) make it clear that the fraction of land that is in any realistic sense urban or built-up remains remarkably small, usually on the order of 3 to 4 percent of the non-Alaska U.S. land area.

An objection to these figures is that they do not indicate the *rate* at which rural uses are converted to urban purposes. One well-publicized study indicated that this rate had increased alarmingly in the 1970s (National Agricultural Lands Study [NALS] 1981). The alarm turned out to be false. I subsequently did a study of the data used by NALS and showed that the methods used were not credible (Fischel 1982). Julian Simon and Seymour Sudman (1982) came to the same conclusion as I did, and the more sober-minded researchers at the U.S. Department of Agriculture eventually backed us up (Thomas Frey 1983). The lack of credible data to support the farmland preservation cause made it difficult for the NALS people (who went on to found the American Farmland Trust) to convince Congress to nationalize the cause of farmland protection (Tim Lehman 1995).

The issue of urban and suburban development can be put in perspective by looking at table 1.1, which shows the major classes of land use for the 48 contiguous United States. (Including Alaska would increase land area by about one-fifth, most of it in the forest and rural parks category: Half of the land area of the National Park System is in Alaska. Hawaii is too small to

TABLE 1.1
Major Land Uses in the Contiguous United States, 2007

This table ranks land uses, from unarguably open spaces (top) to clearly developed areas (bottom). The last two categories, urban areas and transportation zones, seem to comport with what most people think of as developed land, making it 4.6 percent of the total 48-state area.

Forests (30.4%) and Rural Parks (5.8%) =	36.2%
Grassland Pasture and Range =	32.3%
Cropland (active and reserved) =	21.5%
Miscellaneous Areas (swamp, desert, bare rock, unclassified rural) =	3.6%
National Defense (military bases and reserves) =	1.2%
Farmsteads and Farm Roads =	0.6%
Rural Transportation Zones (highways, railroads, airports) =	1.4%
Urban Areas (includes urban transportation) =	3.2%
Total of 48-state land area (1.89 billion acres) =	100.0%

Source: U.S. Department of Agriculture, Natural Resources Conservation Service. 2007. National Resources Inventory (NRI), http://www.ers.usda.gov/data-products/major-land-uses.aspx.

Notes: Entries in the "Special Use" category of the NRI, which include rural parks, national defense, rural transportation, and farmsteads and farm roads, were assigned to separate lines in this table. The NRI "Miscellaneous" category appears to be a residual classification (especially "unclassified rural"), and its "desert" and "bare rock" categories do not include most of the arid and mountainous areas that the NRI classifies as forest and rural parks and rangeland.

move any of the decimal points.) The table shows that 90 percent of American land is in three indubitably rural categories: forests and parkland, pasture and range, and cropland. Should an "Earth probe" from an alien planet crash in a random spot in the United States, it would be unlikely to hit any human habitation.

One hazard in looking at table 1.1 is a tendency to view each category as if it were fixed for all time or uniquely suited for its present purpose. This is not true, as but one example will show. From the beginning of the twentieth century, cropland expanded from 319 million acres to a peak of 478 million in 1949; it then declined to 443 million in 1964. In response to unusual increases in international grain demands (chiefly from Russia), farmers expanded cropland to 470 million in 1978. And then it declined again, to 408 million acres, in 2007. But the decline did not occur because the land came to be used for urban or other developed purposes.

Most of the reduction in cropland has resulted from conversion to other rural uses, most commonly pasture or forest land (Hart 2001). The American Farmland Trust's alarming figures cited at the beginning of this section neglect this source of "loss," which is entirely reversible. Indeed, during the five-year "loss" of 34 million acres of cropland between 2002 and 2007, the combined categories (1) forest and (2) pasture and range (the first two lines of table 1.1) *increased* by 45 million acres. During the same period, the category for urban areas, which is based on U.S. Census data (which by those dates had adopted consistent definitions based on geographic information systems) expanded by a total of 975,000 acres, or an average of 175,000 per year. (The Farmland Trust's alarming figure of an acre per minute "loss" to development would work out to more than 525,949 acres per year and cannot be taken seriously even if all urban development were at the expense of farmland.)

A much better, though not repeating, study was done by Marcy Burchfield et al. (2006), who used aerial and satellite images from the mid-1970s and early 1990s to get a fine-grained look at the process of suburbanization. The authors found that "only 1.9 percent of the [coterminous] United States was built upon or paved by 1992. Two-thirds of this was already in urban use by 1976, while the remaining one-third was developed subsequently" (588).

Well, this is good news and bad news. Good because the 1.9 percent is even lower than most measures of urban development. We are not in danger of paving over America. Nonetheless, cities are indeed spreading out more rapidly than before. (Keep in mind that not all of this expansion is on farmland.) How else could one-third of all detectable urban development in 1992 have occurred in a mere 16-year period? That is, while it took hundreds of years of settlement to arrive at the 1976 figure for urban land coverage, it took only 16 more years to increase it by one-third. (Note, however, that ongoing development fills in at least some of the spaces within the already developed area [Richard Peiser 1989].)

Sprawl—the mildly pejorative term for excess suburbanization—does appear to be a problem. My point here is that the problem is not about running out of farmland in any aggregate sense. Sprawl is an urban problem and, in an indirect way, an environmental problem (from excessive energy consumption and greenhouse gas production), but not a food problem. Chapter 8 will deal with sprawl in more detail, but its bottom line is that sprawl is largely caused by the excesses of local land use regulation. Among the excesses is zoning land for agriculture when it would be better used for urban development. One of the greatest promoters of sprawl is, paradoxically, the urge to preserve farmland.

1.2 U.S. Census Definitions of Urban Areas

In order to evaluate urban land use and its trends, it is necessary to understand some official definitions. The most widely used classification for urban data has been the Metropolitan Statistical Area (MSA), which is the basic unit for understanding American urban statistics. To be included in an MSA, an urban area must have a population of at least 50,000 people in one or more central cities. The MSA includes these cities *and* the *entire area* of surrounding counties that are economically linked to the central city. (The exception is the New England states, where only surrounding towns are included.) About 84 percent (as of 2010) of the U.S. population lives in MSAs. Another 10 percent of the population lives in a more recent urban classification, the Micropolitan Statistical Area. (It is abbreviated μSA, the Greek *mu* being a handy substitute for the Roman M.) The μSA has a core city or cities of at least 10,000 plus the surrounding county or counties.

The common element in all of these measures is the county. Every state is blanketed with counties or county equivalents, such as parishes in Louisiana, boroughs in Alaska (not to be confused with the small municipalities so named in New Jersey and Pennsylvania), and Virginia's 39 independent cities (cities not subject to separate county government), plus the independent cities of Baltimore and St. Louis. Because MSAs and μSAs include so much rural area, they are not appropriate for measuring population density. A better measure of urban land is the Urbanized Area (UA). The UA is the built-up, contiguous part of an MSA. This does not mean just the central city of the MSA; rather, the UA includes surrounding suburbs, but its extent is based on population density rather than political boundaries. The density criteria for being included in a UA are not too demanding: A suburban housing development that has one house for every two acres can be included so long as it is adjacent to the rest of the UA.

In addition to Urbanized Areas, which have a population minimum of 50,000, the census for the year 2000 collected data on "Urban Clusters" for areas with centers that have between 2,500 and 50,000 people. Every Micropolitan Area (minimum population 10,000) has an Urban Cluster at its core, but, somewhat confusingly, some Urban Clusters are so small (less than 10,000 but more than 2,500) that they are not necessarily within MSAs or μSAs.

The reason for including the smaller places is that 2,500 was the minimum population for the Urban Place, for which data are available back to the first U.S. census in 1790. The problem with the Urban Place was that it sometimes included too much territory, as it once counted everyone within a municipality regardless of how rural, and it often ignored built-up areas that were not within a municipality. The shift away from the Urban Place to the Urban Cluster, whose baseline density now defines all Urban Areas, has been facilitated by high-quality satellite images and the development of geographic information systems. The U.S. Census Bureau deserves credit for adapting its collection methods to modern remote sensing technology, and its inventory of American urbanization is now highly inclusive (it does not miss much that is arguably urban) and reasonably limited (it does not count much rural land as urban). Thus the 3.2 percent of the 48 states' land area that is now classified as urban in table 1.1 is a reasonable representation of urban settlement, which contained 80.7 percent of the U.S. population in 2010. We do not use up much land, and we are certainly not as a nation running out of farmland.

1.3 City Size and Urban Agglomeration

Most people are accustomed to talking about the distribution of population among urban areas as if it were linear. We refer to "big," "medium," and "small" cities. In fact, however, the distribution of urban areas by size class is nonlinear and highly skewed. The distribution of population by size can be

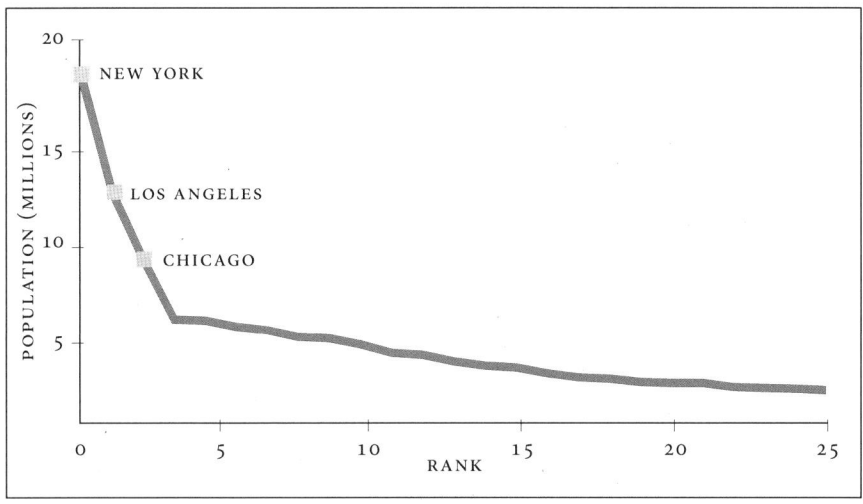

FIGURE 1.1 Population Rank and Size of the 25 Largest U.S. Urbanized Areas, 2010
Source: U.S. Bureau of the Census, Largest Urbanized Areas, 2012. https://www.census.gov/dataviz/visualizations/026/508.php.

seen in figure 1.1, which plots the 25 largest UAs from largest to smallest. The plot approximates a rectangular hyperbola, not a straight line. In urban texts, this relation is called the rank-size rule, and it is found to apply to a remarkable degree both across time and across countries (Rosen and Resnick 1980).

A consequence of this skewed population distribution is that aggregate population data for urban areas will be dominated by the largest ones. Figure 1.1 shows how exceptional New York, Los Angeles, and Chicago are compared to UAs elsewhere. The big three contained about 40 million people, which, in 2010, was over 15 percent of the U.S. urban population and about 13 percent of the entire U.S. population.

The skewness of the distribution also complicates evaluation of land use policies. Bigger cities almost always have higher housing prices; the more people who are squeezed in a given area, the greater the scarcity of land. Many studies of zoning's effect on housing prices compare cities with strong regulations to those with weak regulations, often limiting the sample to "large cities." But as the rank-size rule indicates, a large city is not a useful term of art. Portland, Oregon, which has strong growth boundaries (as discussed in chapter 8), has been said to have high housing prices, but no higher than those of San Francisco. But the Portland urban area has a population that is less than one-half of the San Francisco urban area. Given that housing price elasticity with respect to urban area size is about 10 percent (Edward Glaeser 1998), Portland should have housing prices that are 10 percent *lower* than those of San Francisco, and both cities should have prices lower than those of Chicago, which is twice the population of San Francisco. (Chicago housing prices are actually lower than prices in either place, which is indicative of the regional variation in housing prices discussed below in chapter 5.)

Big cities do not just have more people than small cities. They are different in a number of ways that are important to keep in mind when studying the effects of land use controls. First and foremost, average worker productivity—and thus average wages—are higher in bigger cities. An urban area with twice as many workers pays wages that are about 10 percent higher than the wages that similar workers would earn in the smaller area. Wages in big cities are higher because workers are more productive when they operate in close physical proximity to one another, and a competitive labor market results in higher pay. (The benefit of higher pay is largely offset by the aforementioned higher housing prices, so not every worker will want to move to the biggest city.)

The proximity effect is illustrated by a conversation I had with a friend some years ago. Phil is a lawyer with a central-city Boston firm. He lives in the suburbs and was complaining about his commute. I said to him, "Phil, you're a partner in the firm. Why not just have the offices relocated to the suburbs to be closer to you?" (I would guess most other partners' commutes would be reduced, too.) Phil looked at me as if I had suggested that he fly to the moon. He replied simply, "Out of sight, out of mind." His firm depends on frequent contact with clients, and the contacts have to be up front and personal. He has to know not just how their businesses are doing but also how their kids are faring in school and how their tennis games are going—my examples of building social capital among adults—if he is to maintain the level of trust that being a lawyer or most any other well-paid professional requires. (This, by the way, is why residential colleges and universities have little to fear from competition by online courses. If the means of mastering a course of study at a distance were a threat to universities, they would have been put out of business by Gutenberg.)

Proximity effects are generally promoted by high densities. Because many firms benefit from proximity, developers build tall buildings in a small area to accommodate the demand to be close. The land on which skyscrapers rest is much more costly than land just a few miles away. Buildings themselves are physical manifestations of an algebraic term, the capital/land ratio, which will be important for analyzing the effect of zoning in urban areas. Their dramatic size—as in the skyscraper—can sometimes lead students into a kind of circular reasoning: The buildings are tall because the land is costly, but it is the costly land that induces the developer to put up tall buildings. The true source of both phenomena (expensive land, tall buildings) is that businesses and related activities are more productive when they are close together.

Proximity or density effects are part of what economists call "agglomeration economies." The other major aspect of agglomeration is size itself, which I illustrate with the career of another friend, a New York surgeon named Keith. He is one of the world's best within his specialty. If you have the type of cancer he operates on, you should go see him, even if you live many miles away. He is among the best not just because he is a well-trained, smart, hardworking, and dexterous guy, but because he developed his skills in a surgical market that is so large (the New York area) that he sees many patients per day to operate on one type of cancer. As a result, there are almost no variations of this disease that he has not seen and, in many cases, published scientific papers about. Many smaller-city surgeons may have the same kinds of intellectual and manual skills that Keith does, but few would be able to match him for experience. Smaller town docs have to fill up some of their time doing a variety of surgeries.

The context in which I have illustrated these two types of agglomeration effects makes them seem entirely comparative, explaining why wages and land prices and housing costs are higher in Boston and New York than in Worcester and Albany. But this can obscure the role of cities as engines of economic progress generally. Maps of the world showing the economic well-being of countries match rather closely with maps showing the extent of urbanization of populations. (The few exceptions are lightly populated nations that are mineral rich.) Urbanization does not simply parallel prosperity. As Jane Jacobs has explained in *The Economy of Cities* (1969), invention and application of technologies are cooperative and serendipitous processes that occur most frequently in places where many people meet in close proximity to one another. Edward Glaeser (2011), who is also a Jacobs fan, has persuasively argued that societies that manage to accommodate these interactions are destined to be more prosperous than those that discourage immigration to cities and unduly restrict the upward climb of buildings at their cores.

Land use regulations are, of course, intended to discourage some types of immigration and the upward climb of many buildings. It would be a mistake to condemn them for this, since some types of immigration (of, say, junkyards to residential areas) and some building sizes are economically as well as aesthetically inappropriate for some settings. The multistory Soviet-era "panel buildings" that still blight the suburbs of Eastern Europe come to mind, as does the mile-high residential tower that Frank Lloyd Wright envisioned but never built.

The normative problem is to balance the desire for regional prosperity and the "quiet enjoyment" of one's residence and neighborhood. As I will argue in later chapters, the issue is not likely to be resolved by a higher government's command to local governments to accommodate new development, even if the command is accompanied by offers of compensation. Zoning and related land use regulations are the most jealously guarded local prerogatives, and attempts to override them are likely to be resisted or subverted. The better way, I shall argue, is to facilitate voluntary transactions between communities and would-be developers and to reduce the importance of home values in most residents' financial portfolios.

1.4 Urban Land Trends in the Rest of the World

This book is almost entirely about land use regulation in the United States, but this section gives a nod to urban trends in the rest of the world. My task is facilitated by a remarkable study called *Atlas of Urban Expansion* by Shlomo Angel et al. (2012). The core of the book consists of 120 maps of a sample of larger urban areas (that is, with populations over 100,000) along with corresponding economic and demographic data. The maps were generated by satellite images taken roughly ten years apart, centering usually on 1990 and 2000. The most striking conclusion (to me) is that suburbanization and reduced urban density are worldwide phenomena. All but 16 of the 120 urban areas on every continent grew outward and reduced their overall population densities in the last decade of the previous millennium, even as almost all of them grew in total population.

This is not to say that urban population densities are similar across the world. The American cities in the atlas's sample generally had the lowest densities, ranging from about 20 to 30 persons per hectare. (A hectare is about 2.5 acres, so this would be about eight to 12 persons per acre.) European cities have densities on the order of two or three times that figure (with wide variation). The highest densities are in the cities of Africa and eastern and southern Asia, with persons per hectare amounting to between 200 and 400, or more than ten times that of comparably sized American cities. In a separate essay examining the same data, Angel, Sheppard, and Civco (2005) reported statistical tests used to examine the differences in densities. The most important and consistent variable that explained variation in density is the material prosperity (GDP per capita) of the nation in which the city was located. Richer countries have lower-density cities. The decline of the crowded urban tenements that so concerned American reformers like Jacob Riis in the early twentieth century may have had less to do with housing legislation than with the growing prosperity of the nation. Families with rising incomes demand more housing, and developers are willing to respond.

The point that Angel et al. emphasized in their study is the high rate of urbanization in developing nations. The cities of Asia, Africa, and South America are the vessels of economic development in their nations, but their recent rate of development appears to be much more rapid than that of the Euro-American cities of the nineteenth and twentieth century. Angel and his coauthors warn that the developing nations need to accommodate these rapidly urbanizing and suburbanizing cities with plans that reserve transportation corridors and public spaces before private developments make them excessively difficult to obtain. They caution, on the other hand, that attempts simply to halt urbanization are both unlikely to work and likely to have adverse effects on economic development and the eventual condition of the cities. Faced with the inevitability of growth and suburbanization, perhaps what is needed is a "smart sprawl" plan that accommodates this trend with the sensible policies that Angel and his coauthors recommend.

My favorite historical example of futile restrictions were the many monarchical commands to restrict development around the city of London, as related by Robert Bruegmann (2005). An institution within the area not to be developed was the Church of St. Martin in the Fields. I had heard the name of the church from the recordings of a music group, the Academy of St. Martin in the Fields. I had always envisioned the person of St. Martin standing in the fields and blessing wildlife in the manner of St. Francis. Sadly, "in the fields" refers to the location of the church, not the saint. The church was originally built in what was then regarded as a remote area, much like the Manhattan apartment house called the Dakota, which was built on the edge of the wilds of what is now Central Park. The fields around the London church have long been converted to urban uses despite royal edicts. A tourist can now view St. Martin in the Fields in Trafalgar Square, in the heart of the city that engulfed it.

1.5 Land Rent and Land Taxes

The price of land, computed per unit of time, is usually called rent. Rent can be confusing because the same term is sometimes applied to income from all real property such as apartments and commercial space. It is also used by economists to describe the income from an asset whose supply curve is perfectly inelastic (such as Picasso drawings) or any profits in excess of those required by a firm to continue in business. The latter usage is often called "economic rent." Here I use "rent" in its classical sense: as income derived from selling the services of a unit of land, independent of the services of capital or labor.

Most prices of vacant lots or agricultural plots are not pure rents. There are two causes for the divergence between market prices and rents. The first is that land quality is influenced considerably by past and current investments. Drainage, soil management, grading, utilities, and transportation access are investments that contribute to the value of the asset. Separating these contributions to value from pure rents is very difficult for individual parcels. The second cause is that land prices reflect landowners' market-seeking and risk-bearing activities. Seldom is the most valuable use of land in urban areas evident to the casual observer. Identifying such locations for investments and assuming the risk of loss if one is wrong are important entrepreneurial functions. The reward for such activity is often at least part of the capital gain made by reselling the land at a higher price. Thus, even without any tangible physical investments, land prices may include more than just the classical notion of rent.

The usual discussion of land rent in economics texts proceeds by drawing a vertical supply curve (S_C) and a conventional demand curve, as shown in figure 1.2. The vertical supply curve is sometimes confusing. For any given parcel of land, the supply is completely inelastic, since land cannot be moved. For all land taken together (that is, the stock of land), the supply is also inelastic: As Mark Twain quipped, they aren't making any more of it. (This is true only in the sense of location, not dry and buildable land, which has been abundantly supplemented in most major cities of the world by filling parts of their bays, harbors, lakes, and rivers.) But for land to be used for a particular

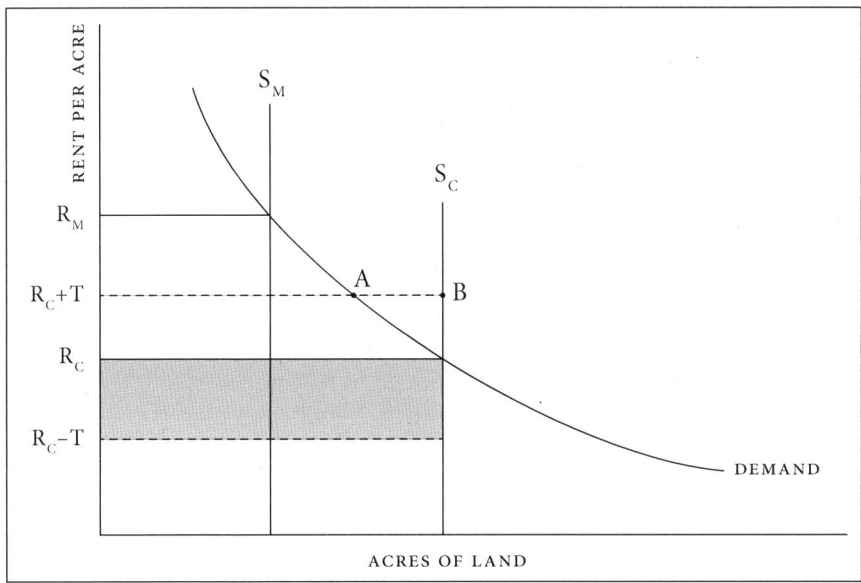

FIGURE 1.2 Supply and Demand and Taxation of a Fixed Stock of Land

purpose, the supply curve is not vertical. As mentioned earlier, prices for wheat and corn rose dramatically in the 1970s, and the demand for cropland shifted to the right, raising its price. This encouraged farmers to convert other land to cropland, as shown in figure 1.3 (p. 14). The upward sloping supply curve does not contradict the vertical supply curve of figure 1.2, since having more acres of cropland reduces the number of acres for some other use (typically forest and grazing land) by the same amount.

The distinction between a tax on all land and on particular uses is helpful in understanding some aspects of land use policy. Economists agree that a tax assessed on specific parcels of land or on immutable characteristics of land (such as "all land within New Hampshire") will be borne entirely by landowners and not shifted to other parties. Precisely because of this incidence, the tax is also efficient: The revenue that the government gets will exactly equal the revenue that the landowners lose. They cannot remove their land to another jurisdiction. Nor can they avoid the tax burden by selling the land, because buyers will offer a lower price as a result of the tax, reflecting the continuing obligation to pay taxes on it. Landowners can no more pass the tax onto tenants than they can pass on the cost of an operation

14 CHAPTER 1

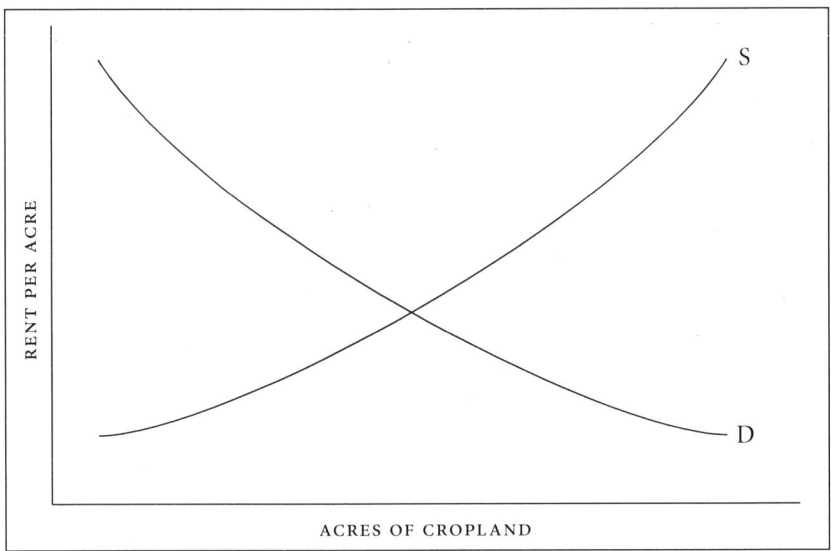

FIGURE 1.3 Supply and Demand for Farmland

for their mothers. (When there is inflation, either exigency may be used by landowners to justify an increase in nominal rents.)

Figure 1.2 demonstrates the previous point graphically. A tax of T dollars per acre of land applied to all parcels making up S_C (say, all land within a 20-mile radius of Pittsburgh) will generate revenue indicated by the shaded area. It will not reduce the supply of land for any use. If landowners were to respond by increasing rents to $R_C + T$, as in figure 1.2, a surplus of land (the line segment $A-B$ in the figure) would develop, because the demanders of land would substitute other factors of production for land (for example, building two-story houses instead of one-story houses). This surplus would be eliminated only when landowners reduced rents to R_C. Competition among landowners would ensure that this occurred.

The efficiency characteristics of the land tax just described are sometimes misconstrued to be applicable to *any* type of land tax. Many taxes on land are assessed at different rates according to use. An example is the widespread practice of assessing agricultural, forestry, or open space at a smaller fraction of value than that of developed land (Bowman and Mikesell 1988; Anderson and England 2014). The supply of land for these purposes is at least somewhat elastic, so the owner can avoid some land taxes by choosing the use to which the land is put. This does not mean that such tax systems are wrong; their very purpose may be to encourage the supply of land for one purpose and to discourage some others. But as such, the classical model of the incidence and efficiency of land taxes cannot be applied.

1.6 Why Not a Land Tax?

The previous section indicated both the virtues and drawbacks of a land tax. The chief virtue (at least to economists) is its efficiency: Land will not go anywhere if you tax its income or value at a high rate. Owners of land essentially just have to shrug their shoulders and pay; they cannot alter their economic behavior in response to high rates. Economists call this a "nondistorting" tax, and many give an approving nod to the nineteenth-century reformer Henry George (1879) for his vigorous advocacy of such a tax. For example, a theoretical model by Richard Arnott and Joseph Stiglitz (1979) found that a land value tax whose revenues are dedicated to local infrastructure and services will result in a more efficiently developed city—a result dubbed the "Henry George theorem."

If economists like this tax so much, why does it seem so rare in practice? One reason is administrative. The difficulties of disentangling land value from present and past owners' contributions of capital and labor are not just theoretical (Steven Bourassa 2009). In order to apply a land tax to a parcel, the value of the parcel must be assessed by a public official. Assessors are essential in administering the most widely used form of local taxation, the property tax. Property taxation is typically applied to all private real property within a jurisdiction. "Real" property, also called "realty" (as opposed to the portable or disembodied "personalty" [*sic*]), consists of land and buildings and other features that are not intended to be moved when its owners depart the scene. Most land of any value within a community already has something attached to it and is already subject to taxation.

To administer a land value tax, local assessors have to distinguish the value of a home or office building from the value of its underlying land. For many assessors, this task makes as much sense as trying to separate the value of the first floor of the house from the second floor. (Practicing assessors said as much in Daniel Holland [1970].) The building and its land are intimately related—that is what makes them collectively "real" property—and they are almost always sold as a unit. The sales of vacant lots in some communities, occasionally resulting from "teardowns" of existing homes, offer some basis for comparisons on which land values could be assessed (Dye and McMillen 2007). But vacant land is often so special in its situation (there may have been some unusual reason it remained vacant or the previous building was demolished) that assessors are naturally skeptical of using it as a basis for assessing other land.

One way of dealing with administrative and assessment problems is to tread lightly into land value taxation by adopting a hybrid model called the "split rate" system. The general idea is to tax land at a higher rate than buildings. This does not eliminate any of the aforementioned assessment issues, but it does make errors in assessment less important. If assessors underestimate the value of land on some properties, they may implicitly make it up on building valuations, and vice versa. The advantage of this system is that it makes clear to property owners that their property taxes will not rise very much if they add a new room to their house or add a floor to their office building. As more development takes place, land values rise generally, and tax collections increase, all without discouraging investment in structures.

Does the split rate tax work as advertised? The state with the largest collection of municipalities that have adopted the split rate tax is Pennsylvania, and it has not gone unnoticed by scholars of property and land value taxation. Several econometric studies have been done to see if the Pennsylvania cities that have adopted split rate taxation have done better economically, as measured by new construction, than those that have not. Most of the studies find that the split rate tax system seems to promote more construction and general prosperity. The magnitudes are not overwhelming, but the positive direction is consistent (Oates and Schwab 1997; Banzhaf and Lavery 2010).

The main problem with this evidence is its limited political success. It looks like split rate taxation is an economic winner. If so, why is it that more cities in Pennsylvania have not adopted the system? Since 1913, Pennsylvania's constitution has allowed cities to adopt a split rate system. (The previous constitutional objection to it was the uniformity requirement in property taxation.) The number of cities that have done so, however, is not large. As of 2000, 18 cities had adopted a split rate system. (Pennsylvania has more than 2,500 municipalities.) The two largest cities with the split rate, Pittsburgh and Scranton, adopted it in 1913. All of the rest have adopted it since 1975, when the class of municipalities that were permitted to opt for the split rate system was expanded. (Several cities adopted it at the urging of Georgist advocate Steven Cord [1983].)

The discouraging news is that cities that adopted the split rate seem to be moving back to the uniform property tax assessment system that prevails in the rest of the state (and in all other states). Five Pennsylvania cities dropped from the list between 2000 and 2006, and there have been no new additions (Banzhaf and Lavery 2010). The most distressing reversal was that of Pittsburgh in 2001, since its split rate system has been extensively studied and generally been given some credit for promoting the city's comeback after the steel industry declined so much in the 1970s (Oates and Schwab 1997). Pittsburgh voters nonetheless rejected their longstanding tax system after a countywide reassessment revealed to voters that a small and a large home in the same neighborhood could have the same land values and thus pay close to the same amount of taxes (Bourassa 2009). But such disparities are inherent in any system of land value taxation and are indeed one of its supposed virtues, according to economists. The owner of the small house is not discouraged from building more rooms, as would be the case under a normal property tax system. Popular feelings about the fairness of property taxes—people in larger houses should pay proportionately more—seemed to have trumped such issues.

Or maybe not. Perhaps the reason most American communities do not embrace land value taxation is that they have turned the regular property tax into something like a land tax. The neglected aspect of property taxation is the management of the property tax base by means of zoning. As I shall argue in chapter 4, zoning allows municipalities to tailor the type and intensity of development it allows. If a community permits only office buildings not higher than five stories in a commercial zone (a common enough requirement), and office buildings of that size are in fact an efficient use of land in that zone, a tax on land and buildings in that zone is pretty much the same as a tax on land alone in that zone. The main exception to this rule arises when there is little demand to build, say, office buildings anywhere in the city. Most of the cities in Pennsylvania that adopted the split rate tax system, which is essentially a subsidy for building, were older, built-up cities and boroughs that were losing much of their employment base. For cities in decline, not taxing buildings can be a good strategy to help reverse the decline.

1.7 Government Land Ownership

The largest landowner in the United States is the federal government. It holds title to nearly one-third of the nation's land area (a quarter of the 48 contiguous states' area and most of Alaska). Its holdings outside Alaska are largely in the dry and mountainous areas west of Denver. The per-acre value of this land, with the exception of some mineral holdings, is not large. Most of the valuable farmland is now in private hands, and most urban land is likewise privately held.

At one time, of course, the federal government or the colonies owned nearly all of the land. (Here I adopt the Eurocentric view of ownership and decline to examine aboriginal claims.) The disposition of this land was a major focus of political debate throughout the nineteenth century (Marion Clawson 1968). Questions of private ownership and monopoly were constantly raised. Federal policy was originally aimed at selling land for revenue purposes. Later, land policy was more deliberately designed to fulfill the Jeffersonian ideal of a nation of independent yeoman farmers. One need not admire the policy or its consequences in order to agree that the idea of fee simple ownership of land was consciously chosen; it was not an accident of history, as is sometimes asserted.

Nor was the way American land was laid out an accident. After the American Revolution, the U.S. government assumed control of nearly all of the land west of the Appalachian Mountain chain. The Louisiana Purchase nearly doubled the size of what became known as the public domain. Driven by republican principles that lauded widespread ownership of land and by the need to obtain revenue to pay its debts, the federal government embarked on what may have been the biggest land sale in world history.

To facilitate the sale of public land, almost all of it was divided up into squares that measured six miles a side (Andro Linklater 2002). These "townships" were then divided into square-mile "sections" and further into acreage-size subsections (the acres of "the south forty" in many a Western movie). Even Texas, which was not subject to the U.S. Public Land Survey—it had been an independent country—adopted a state lands survey that functioned very similarly. The western provinces of Canada undertook similar surveys.

This massive, top-down enterprise had some disadvantages. The system that it replaced (and that continued to be used in states formed from colonies before the American Revolution) was the "metes and bounds" survey. This was the generic, "bottom-up" method of acquiring land titles. Claimants would measure off the land they wanted to buy, often using natural features such as streams and mountain ridges for boundaries, then register their claim with state or local authorities.

Metes and bounds had the advantage of respecting natural boundaries. The straight-line township and range system ("ranges" being part of directional designations, though land areas are called only "townships") ignored natural boundaries, and so farmers often plowed furrows that ended short of a more natural turning point. It was possible to modify the grid. Thus, towns that developed along riverbanks or railroads that did not parallel the east-west, north-south grid sometimes adjusted their town sites to parallel the river or railroad so that intracity roads would not have to cross the border too often. In rural areas, farmers could purchase or swap land with neighbors to make more sensible layouts. But the persistence of the grid lines, still clearly evident from the air or satellite mapping pictures, suggests that the original legal boundaries had staying power.

The great advantage of the grid system was that it made land easily saleable. Once the land had been surveyed—a massive but durable public investment—it was relatively simple for the government to dispose of it. A buyer could indicate that the parcel wanted was the southeast quarter section (160 acres) of the 17th section of the township designated T10N, R5S of the sixth principal meridian. The local land office could check to see that it was not previously sold or reserved for the school fund, and the transaction could be consummated without much difficulty. Equally important was that the land could be resold again and again without incurring further surveying costs. In contrast, the metes and bounds system was often irregular in its survey methods and deed registration, and the possibility of conflicting claims from generations back haunted every transaction. Abraham Lincoln said that his father emigrated from Kentucky, which was surveyed by metes and bounds, to Indiana (surveyed by the public lands system) because of the difficulty he encountered in obtaining clear title to land in Kentucky (David Donald 1995).

More systematic evidence of the advantage of the standardized survey is provided by Gary Libecap and Dean Lueck (2011). They found that a large area of Ohio called the Virginia Military District, located between the Scioto and Little Miami Rivers, had been settled under the metes and bounds system of Virginia. (The district was not used for military purposes but as a reward for Revolutionary War veterans, most of whom sold their land vouchers to others.) The rest of Ohio had been divided for sale under the standardized township and range method that became the rule for the rest of the new territories of the United States. Libecap and Lueck obtained detailed census and economic records from locations on either side of the Military District's borders to see how the adjacent areas fared over time. Both areas had similarly varied topography (some level, some hilly) and a similar mix of early settlers, most of whom were initially from other parts of the United States and from Germany.

Libecap and Lueck calculated that the standardized survey added considerably to farmland values. Flat land in a rectangular survey area sold for 25 percent more than similar land in the metes and bounds area (the Military District) in 1860. Interestingly, the premium was smaller for hilly areas because the more nuanced metes and bounds survey method allowed for holdings that made more geographic sense. More remarkable is the persistence of the differences in farmland value and other indicators of economic development—population density and manufacturing employment—right through the twentieth century. The legacy of grid-style land measurement is surprisingly large, and, as Libecap, Lueck, and Trevor O'Grady (2012) show in another paper, apparently appreciable in other nations of the world. Economists such as myself are often critical of top-down government initiatives that impose uniformity across the nation, but this seems to be an instance in which it worked pretty well.

1.8 Does Feudalism Still Govern European Planning?

The reader might ask what Libecap and Lueck's finding has to do with modern land use regulation, which began in earnest in the United States in cities, not rural areas, and developed robustly only after about 1910, long after the Public Land Survey was done. The answer has to do with how easily land can be sold or otherwise transferred. The American rectangular survey system is not the only difference between the United States and much of the rest of the world. Developable tracts in the United States can be easily purchased by an amateur land developer. Even in the states carved from the original British colonies, where metes and bounds still prevail, rural land is owned in fee simple. This means that a single party (individual, family, or business) can arrange the sale. Fee simple ownership was in fact one of America's chief attractions for land-hungry European immigrants (James Ely 1992). In England and most of Europe, there is a distinct possibility that a would-be buyer of land will have to deal with the claims on the land of many parties, several of whom may not even be known to the would-be buyers and sellers of land.

The European pattern is the legacy of centuries of feudalism, in which fee simple ownership of land was the exception rather than the rule. Dan Bogart and Gary Richardson (2008) note that under English feudal landholding, a "complex spectrum of overlapping privileges (common, communal, clerical, feudal, familial, statutory, and royal) enforced by an array of courts (manorial, county, clerical, and royal) pertained to most plots of land" (1). Bogart and Richardson go on to describe periodic parliamentary efforts to cut away these impediments to modern development, and they commend the resulting adaptability. But the process of clearing up feudal law did put Parliament in the center of national land policy, and many of the traps for unwary developers of rural land remained in place. As a result, conversion of English rural land (and most probably that of other nations with feudal legacies) to urban uses is not a job for unsophisticated developers.

The modern manifestation of feudal inhibitions on rural development is that the pattern of suburbanization in Europe is distinctly different from that of the United States. I have noticed this looking out of the window of airplanes over the years (as did Robert Bruegmann 2005), and I have confirmed it with more systematic tours of American and European cityscapes via Google Earth. An example I do for my students is to compare suburban land use in Cleveland, Ohio, and Frankfurt am Main, Germany, which have similar population sizes and are surrounded by farmland subject to similar weather conditions, thus making the pattern of rural land comparable.

Set the eye elevation at about 20,000 feet at the center of the city, tilt up a bit, and "fly" out to the suburbs for 20 miles. In the Cleveland area, the density of housing and other buildings declines gradually. Farmland eventually appears, but it is almost constantly interspersed with low-density housing and business structures that are most probably not farm related. The Frankfurt flight looks far different. There is a distinct line between the city and surrounding farmland. The farmland is almost entirely without on-site habitation or buildings. There are many suburbs, but these show up as islands of buildings whose density appears to be almost as great as that at the edge of the main city itself.

Europe has plenty of suburbanization, but most suburbs appear to have grown up around ancient towns and grown outward in high-density accretions. The European suburban pattern looks like so many beads of mercury scattered about the big city, while the American pattern looks like a blob of molasses spread out at continuously declining depths away from the big city. The European pattern has some benefits and some drawbacks compared to that of the United States. The benefits of the compact suburbs are that residents have a walking community; they do not have to get into cars to visit neighbors or get some groceries. Most European suburbs also appear dense enough to be able to support public transportation to get to the central city for work or pleasure.

The drawback for European suburbs is that homes in these compact villages offer much less interior and exterior space. American suburbs usually require car-based commuting, but they offer the compensation of homes and yards that are more spacious than those closer to the city center. European suburbs look a lot like miniature central cities but with longer travel times to get to work if the residents work outside their village, as most surely do.

I have long been curious about the source of this difference between North American and European city land use patterns. The usual explanation is that land use regulation in the United States is local, while in Europe land regulation, especially conversion from rural to urban use, is controlled by the national government or the state-size subnational government. This begs the question of how such systems developed, a question too large to address with more than some hints and suspicions on my part. Centuries of wars surely contributed to the centralization of power (as they have to a lesser extent in the United States), but that by itself does not explain why the national government should adopt a compact-growth policy. Indeed, I argue in chapter 8 that in the United States, larger-area governments are apt to be more favorable to development than smaller communities.

A more likely explanation is that European rural land has always been difficult to convert to urban uses because of its legacy of feudalism. A British book on rural land development indicated that it is even difficult to determine who owns a given parcel of rural land (Goodchild and Munton 1985). The impediments to converting rural land to urban uses very likely tilt the political tables in favor of less development. American rural landowners know that their land can easily be sold for a profit if the demand arrives sometime in the future, and they form a political force against regulations that would prevent them from profiting. European rural owners are a less cohesive force politically because their opportunities to profit are difficult to realize without a great deal of negotiation with the many potential claimants to their land. In Europe, political forces that oppose development are more influential because development-minded rural landowners do not have much fight in them.

1.9 Monopoly Ownership?

Concentration of farmland ownership in a few hands could lead to a monopoly. The increasing average size of farms and the growth of holdings of land by large corporations have worried some for this reason. But as vast as these land holdings can be, they must be evaluated in terms of the land market of the entire country, and perhaps of much of the rest of the world. In this broader market, even the largest holdings of agricultural land amount to infinitesimal fractions of the possible substitute sites (James MacDonald 2011). Only a national cartel enforced by government sanctions—which is what agricultural price supports enforced by inducing farmers to set aside cropland amount to—can have any effect. Even this program does not work very well as a price support, since farmers then substitute other factors of production, such as machinery and fertilizers, for land.

Monopoly of land for urban uses would seem more likely than monopoly for agricultural or forestry uses. In a single metropolitan area, an owner of undeveloped land would need to control far less developable land to affect the price of land for new housing, especially if it were concentrated in the suburbs. There is no evidence, though, that such concentration exists in any metropolitan area. It is true that the land development industry, particularly for housing, has become more concentrated (Tsuriel Somerville 1999), but these developers typically have to amass many parcels from independent owners, and they seldom hold on to them for long because of the carrying costs. As a large-scale developer once remarked to me, "Land eats money."

A confusion that seems endemic in the land use literature is the identification of land rent with monopoly returns. This confusion may stem from the modern usage by economists, who classify all supernormal returns, such as those a monopolist might get, as "economic rent." Monopoly returns and land rent are quite different, though. In figure 1.2, the supply of land was denoted by S_C. Its competitive return is R_C, and no single owner dares to charge more, lest tenants flee to other sites. If only one owner controlled all sites, this owner could artificially restrict their supply to, say, S_M, which would result in greater revenues. As section 7.9 will demonstrate, however, even a government-enforced monopoly on land is complicated by land's durability and the difficulty of convincing current buyers that more supply will not be released in the future (Ronald Coase 1972).

Land rent is often referred to as "unearned" income. This does not mean that the income is the result of no *previous* exertion or forbearance on the part of landowners. They or their forebears may have labored and saved for a long time to acquire title to the land. The sense in which rent is "unearned" derives not from a theory of deservingness but from the already observed quality of fixed supply. There is no current activity that the landowner can undertake to increase the land's rent.

1.10 Land and Inequality

Monopoly power is not the only concern about concentration of land ownership. Many worry that unequal private ownership of land contributes to inequality of income and wealth. There are two statistical issues here. First, how unequally held is land? Second, is income from land a large fraction of national income? Unfortunately, we can offer only tentative answers to both questions. Most aggregate data fail to separate the value of physical capital from the value of land. The much-discussed work on inequality by Thomas Piketty (2014) lumps land ownership with capital ownership.

We do know that ownership of real estate contributes less to inequality than does ownership of other assets, especially corporate stocks (Edward Wolff 1983). A large fraction of land's value is in owner-occupied housing and farms. Although most residential parcels are small, their location in urban areas usually makes them disproportionately valuable. Nearly two-thirds of all households own their homes, and most farms are owner-managed, even when the nominal form of ownership is corporate. Land ownership in the United States is widely dispersed, if not equally distributed. "Rental income of persons," the closest category for annual land rent in the national income accounts, is less than 5 percent of GDP, but this does not count corporate holdings or the capital gains (or losses) that accrue to homeowners and other owners of land. Nonetheless, this number suggests that redistribution of land or national taxation of land rents would not equalize the distribution of income and wealth to a significant degree.

While land ownership itself does not appear to contribute much to inequality, it is possible that land use regulation does. Inequality due to regulation has two dimensions, which will be examined more closely in later chapters. The first is the long-standing concern about exclusionary zoning in the suburbs. This is said to bottle up the poor in the central cities and deny them access to better housing and public services, most notably the better public education offered in suburban schools (Anthony Downs 1994; Jonathan Rothwell 2012). The second is more subtle and recent. It appears that the rise of land use regulation in the 1970s has reduced migration from low-income *regions* of the United States to higher-income regions. This seems to have contributed to the rise in income inequality in the last 40 years (Ganong and Shoag 2013). This topic will be an organizing principle of my account of the history of zoning in chapter 5.

1.11 Conclusion: Malthus's Paradox and Robert Frost's Question

Thomas Robert Malthus is famous for articulating what economists now call "the law of diminishing returns." Successive inputs of labor and capital added to a fixed factor of production (namely, land) will eventually result in smaller and smaller additions to total output. Given a fixed quantity of natural resources, any positive growth rate of population is bound to result in a standard of living (output per person) that is not sustainable.

Most economists shrug and talk about technological progress when Malthus's grim projections are brought up. The world has become much more populous (by a factor of about seven) since Malthus published in 1798, and most of the world's diet and other indicators of standard of living have improved considerably since then (Robert Fogel 2004). But a more direct challenge to the principle of diminishing returns is the general success of cities. Cities occupy a very small part of the earth's surface, and people and buildings have been crowding together in them at an increasing rate. Yet the impact of population growth on the growth of urban output per capita seems to be positive. Societies with more urban populations are more prosperous than others, and the biggest cities generally have the highest standard of living. The power of agglomeration economies is a source of the technological progress that has kept the Malthusian wolf at bay.

The survey of land use in this chapter indicates that there is no danger that development will impinge on the stock of land for nonurban uses. We are not running out of farmland. Even India and China, which have more than a third of the world's population, are in no danger of running out (Ausubel, Wernick, and Waggoner 2013). The latter part of this chapter points out that land has substitutes and that land rent is only a small fraction of the national economy. This may provoke some readers to wonder why I have written a book about land use controls. The answer is that although the amount of *land* may not be crucial, the way we *use* it is, especially in urban areas.

Let me close with the basic problem of land use regulation. The productive advantages conferred by urban agglomeration economies are so strong that they can overpower other aspects of urban life that people value. The profit from adding more buildings and workers can often seem like a good reason to sacrifice just a little more street space, take away just a little more of the afternoon sun, add just a few more vehicles to the streets, make the block just a little less safe, reduce air quality just a smidgen. The cumulative effect of such private decisions can yield an urban environment that is a good deal less healthy and pleasant for its citizens unless governing institutions can put some brakes on uncoordinated private activity. In the next chapter, I will describe the main regulatory institutions that people have developed to tame and channel the economic energy of the city. These institutions, however, have the capacity to be too exclusive, a topic that will be explored at considerable length. We economists always have two hands, balancing benefits and costs. The larger problem in land use is to balance the competing goals of people in urban areas or, as Robert Frost put it in the poem "America Is Hard to See," "how to crowd and still be kind."

CHAPTER 2

The Structure and Administration of Zoning Laws

My approach to zoning holds that it should be thought of as a collective property right exercised in ways that can be analyzed by the tools of economics. The problem with this approach is that no law simply grants property rights in land to the community authorities. As will be argued in chapter 5, zoning evolved from a popular demand for community stability, not from a well-established body of law. State legislatures and courts did not consciously reassign the "use" stick in property from private owners to public control. (Scholarship on property law subdivides its essential characteristics into three metaphorical sticks: exclusion, use, and transferability.) As a result, the structure and administration of zoning laws require special attention to glean the ways in which property rights have been modified. A subsidiary mission of this chapter is to persuade economists in particular to pay attention to the flexibility and evolutionary quality of zoning and to refine their theoretical models and empirical inquiries accordingly.

The other point of emphasis in this chapter is the political nature of zoning. Many social scientists seem to assume that zoning is a technical matter of drawing maps and writing planning documents. On this basis, they either endorse it as a wise means of "internalizing externalities" or condemn it as a wooden-headed constraint on sensible developments. Both views overlook that zoning is the product of local political activity. Planners propose, but the voters dispose. The descriptive material in this chapter sets the stage for the political models that are developed and deployed in chapters 6 and 7.

The most important land use innovations in the last 30 years have come from institutions that compete for local municipal control, including private community associations, state and regional regulatory bodies, and federal agencies. These are considered here mainly to the extent that they affect local zoning. My general conclusion is that they have altered zoning, usually in the direction of making it more difficult to get development done. Nonetheless, the strongest hand in "the zoning game" (to invoke the title of Richard Babcock's 1966 collection of insightful zoning stories) is still held by local governments.

2.1 Zoning Basics: Strands in the Web of Regulation

Zoning is the division of a community into districts or zones in which certain activities are prohibited and others are permitted. The most obvious manifestation of a zoning law is the (now) multicolored map, with each color indicating a zone keyed to a designation such as SR-1, GR-2, or B-1, which indicates what sort of development is permitted in each geographic zone. A simplified zoning map is shown in figure 2.1. The abbreviations usually have some intuitive content. Thus, "SR" typically means free-standing, single-family residences, and the number following indicates something about minimum lot size. Thus SR-1 might be restricted to single-family homes on

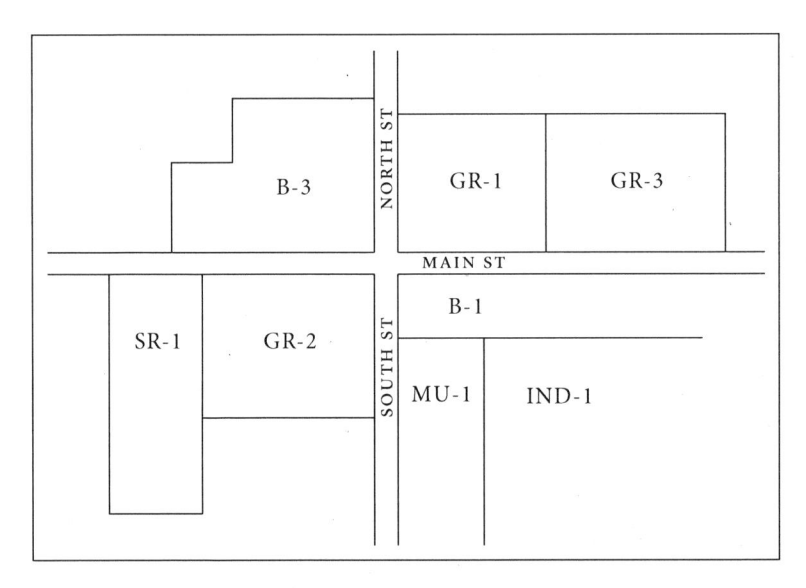

FIGURE 2.1 Simplified Zoning Map

one-acre lots. "GR" usually means general residence, allowing some multifamily structures; "B-1" could be neighborhood (as opposed to regional) business; and "MU," mixed use, might enshrine a prezoning mix of business, residence, and institutional uses. There is no uniform letter code, however, that facilitates comparisons across communities.

In the text of most modern ordinances, a section for each zone, say GR-1, will indicate permitted uses as well as height limits and dimensional and placement requirements for buildings. Early ordinances sometimes applied dimensional and usage rules by separate overlays, so that height restrictions, for example, were delineated separately and might apply across several use zones. Emily Talen (2012) has written a book that vividly traces the evolution of zone requirements over time, using historical illustrations. In it, she demonstrates (and laments) that American zoning districts have become more exclusive, forestalling mixtures of commercial and residential uses, and that dimensional requirements have increasingly favored automotive transport over pedestrianism. Ordinances have also become more complex and verbose. The text of the original New York City zoning resolution of 1916 is 12 pages long, a length now exceeded by more than a factor of ten by ordinances of small towns such as Hanover, New Hampshire.

In any case, someone interested in what is allowed on a particular parcel can identify its zone on the map and then go to an official document, the zoning ordinance, in which permitted uses are listed. It used to be somewhat difficult to locate zoning maps without a trip to city hall, but nowadays almost all jurisdictions make them available online along with the text of their laws. Some cities have sites that allow the user simply to plug in an address to learn what zone the property is in.

The place to look for zoning, by the way, is city hall, not the county courthouse (unless the county does the zoning). A property deed, normally kept by the county, will indicate ownership and (one hopes) the obligations and entitlements to which previous owners of the land have agreed. Such burdens could include covenants with neighbors, membership obligations in a community association, and easements that allow strangers to drive or walk on part of the property. But the existence of zoning and other public constraints are not usually memorialized in deed records. Zoning can be changed without notice or consent of the owner, and so recording changes in deeds would be impractical.

Zoning is one of the community's "police powers." These comprise all of the legal regulations that govern everyday life, not just those that are enforced by a police officer. In local government law, the police power is one of the trinity of powers that distinguish governments from private organizations, the other two being the authority to tax and the power to take property under eminent domain (Robert Ellickson 1982). All three involve the coercive power of the state. Eminent domain must be accompanied by "just compensation," while exercises of the police power do not, and the line between the two is largely refereed by the courts. (To anticipate the extensive discussion of this issue in chapter 3, I will note that the courts generally side with an expansive view of the government's police power and seldom require that landowners burdened by new restrictions must be paid for their losses.)

The municipality's authority to use the police power is derived from the state government. In a legal sense, all local governments are "creatures of the state" and require its permission—or at least not the state's opposition—to conduct their legal business (Richard Briffault 1990). Permission is usually not difficult to obtain in a nation in which state legislatures are elected by contiguous geographic districts that have some congruence with municipal borders, rather than by statewide party lists. In most cases, a special enabling act, patterned after a standard act promulgated in the 1920s (and discussed in more detail in section 4.5), gives the locality the power to zone. States can augment this authority. The "Quiet Revolution," famously named by Fred Bosselman and David Callies (1971), in which a few states took over some traditionally local land use matters, was an extension of state regulation (usually without displacing local controls) and did not raise fundamental constitutional issues.

It is important for economic research into the effects of zoning laws to recognize that they are not single-valued constraints. That is, a community's laws cannot be characterized just by a single height requirement or minimum lot size, not least because there are many zones in each community. Zoning constitutes a web of regulations that communities can use to control almost all aspects of development. For example, one cannot look at minimum lot size, which is the workhorse of suburban zoning, and dismiss it by assuming that an owner can put any number of buildings on a three-acre lot or that a developer can just build upward to escape the lot-size constraint on building size.

Along with acreage requirements and use limitations, every zoning law will have height limitations. (After encountering two studies that purported to compare a sample of cities with and without height limits, I went online to check the cities' ordinances and could not find one that lacked a height limit.) Height limits in the central area of larger cities are often expressed as maximum "floor area ratios" or FAR, which are the cumulative square footage of floor space divided by the square footage of the lot. An FAR of 4 will allow four stories with no uncovered land or (more normally) eight stories with half the land uncovered by structures. The law will also prescribe positioning rules, such as the minimum setback distance from the front of the building to the street and to neighboring lots. Undeveloped lots usually have road-frontage requirements that also keep new buildings at a distance from one another.

Many communities have additional rules about parking requirements, soil quality (for septic systems and drainage), and shapes of lots, which prevent developers from utilizing their subdivisions in overly creative ways. For example, minimum lot size calculations might exclude the area in wetlands or on steep slopes. A more inventive restriction to discourage oddly shaped lots calculates the allowable minimum buildable area as that which falls within a continuous circle within the boundaries of the parcel. (For an inventory of the varieties of zoning constraints in Massachusetts, see Amy Dain [2005], from whom I learned about the internal-circle rule.)

The effect of minimum lot size on density can be difficult for social scientists to observe by inspection or remote sensing. Developers of a 100-acre tract subject to three-acre zoning often want to cluster the 33 permitted homes in order to conserve on infrastructure and perhaps to create a more village-like community, which can make it more attractive to home buyers (Paul Asabere 2014). Many communities accommodate this scheme with cluster zoning, and the resulting group of 33 homes appear to be on relatively small lots, say a third of an acre each for each home, and thus altogether appear to use only 11 acres of land. In this scenario, the remaining 89 acres will usually not be built upon in the present or in the future. Instead, because of the zoning and subdivision process, the acreage will remain in common ownership of the buyers (via deed restrictions or conservation easements) or perhaps be deeded to the municipality as permanent open space. Such deals often modify the constraints of the original three-acre zoning in sensible ways, but the use of clustering in these instances does not promote metropolitan-area density. Scholars who examine actual density patterns by maps and geographic information systems (GIS) need to be aware that the apparently high density of some neighborhoods is offset by perpetually preserved open space nearby.

Zoning cannot be personal in its designations. It cannot designate that the Smith family gets to do something that the Jones's cannot. Zoning exceptions such as variances (discussed in section 2.5 below) typically run with the land, meaning that buyers of property acquire the benefits and burdens of the sellers. If Mr. Smith gets a variance for a home business and sells his property to Ms. Jones, she is normally entitled to the benefit of the variance. Time limitations on exceptions and periodic reviews of conditions may, however, have much the same effect as granting them to particular persons.

Ordinances cannot mention income, ethnicity, or race of prospective occupants as a criterion. One exception to the rule against using personal criteria is age. Municipalities can zone for retirement communities that have a minimum age requirement. This can be controversial when the rule's purpose seems largely to minimize the number of school children, but it has long been permitted in most states (Gregory Richards 1982). Another exception is a limitation on the number of unrelated people who can share a single-family house. Such limitations are sometimes adopted by communities that want to limit the rental of homes by multiple college students and by suburbs that want to prevent parents in low-quality school districts from relocating their children to friends or distant relatives in better school districts. The legality of such restrictions varies by state (as discussed below in section 3.17), and the U.S. Supreme Court in *Belle Terre v. Boraas*, 416 U.S. 1 (1974) has largely allowed the states to go their own ways on such issues.

2.2 Which Type of Local Government Does the Zoning?

The United States is unusual among nations of the world for the decentralized nature of its planning and zoning. International observers marvel at the number of jurisdictions that are empowered to establish zoning. A British observer claimed that the United States has "40,000 local governments which administer zoning" (J. Barry Cullingworth 2002, 1). His numbers may be on the high side; my estimate of local governments that have zoning authority is about 25,000 (William Fischel 2001, 23). In any event, Cullingworth found the high numbers to be cause for despair: "The social scientist who attempts to impose a scheme of order upon this abundant variety must surely fail" (2002, 1). I will leave it to the reader to decide whether my attempt in the present work to impose "a scheme of order" is successful.

Virtually every general-purpose local government in the United States has the authority to adopt zoning and related police-power regulations. (Special-purpose governments such as water districts and school districts do not zone.) Which forms of government zone, then, simply depends on what types of government are important in the area. (The unique case of Houston, the only large city in the United States without comprehensive zoning, is sufficiently interesting to deserve a longer discussion in the context of metropolitan structure in chapter 8.) But this begs the question of which governments are important—a question that turns out to be a historical one related to differences among regions rather than among states. As I demonstrated in my book about school districts (Fischel 2009b), the geographic pattern of local governments (not just school districts) in the United States was largely determined by two factors: rainfall and race.

In rainy and not-too-mountainous areas, rural population settlement in the eighteenth and nineteenth centuries was sufficiently dense (initial settlers were farmers) that it was economical to form many local governments and cover almost the entire state (or what became a state) with them. Counties had a minor role in local government in these states. As a result, in the dirt-farming North (stretching eastward from the 100th meridian, which vertically bisects the Dakotas, and north of the Ohio River), most rural areas adjacent to cities were governed by a lattice of small towns and rural townships that had general-government powers to tax, spend, and regulate public life. Annexation of rural communities by the bigger city, which was common in the nineteenth century, became rare in the North after about 1920 (Jon Teaford 1979). As the urban population spread out in the twentieth century, the formerly rural township or small town became a suburb and adopted zoning. (I argue in chapter 5 that the availability of zoning is a primary reason that suburbs stopped consolidating with larger cities.) As a result, cities in the North are surrounded by dense networks of suburbs, which, in the nineteenth century, had usually been distinct small towns and townships.

The exceptions to this pattern occurred mainly in the arid and mountainous West, which I will call the inland West, and in the South. The inland West is the area west of the 100th meridian and east of the coastal valleys of California, Oregon, and Washington. Eastern-style farming was precluded in the inland West by the scarcity of rainwater or by mountainous terrain. Cattle ranching and forestry, which require extensive land holdings, resulted in widely spaced homesteads. As a result, the inland West lacked sufficient rural population to form a dense network of towns and school districts. City expansion more often annexed rural land in the West, and the remaining county land was controlled by rural voters.

In the South, which actually had more rainfall and higher rural population densities than the North, disfranchisement of blacks kept the density of the enfranchised rural population low. Whites' wariness of black participation in local government also shifted power to the state and its local administrative vehicle, the county (Horace Mann Bond 1934). In effect, racial anxieties made the South more like the low-population-density areas of the West. As a result, counties in the South and in the inland West assumed most local government functions and continue to have an important role in zoning outside of larger cities. This is important because, for reasons discussed in chapter 8, rural county governments have generally been more accommodating to development than other types of government (Michelle Anderson 2012). Thus, differences in local government can be understood in terms of the type of agriculture prevalent in the nineteenth century. Northern farmers, western ranchers, and southern planters each produced regionally characteristic patterns of local government that still influence which unit of government does the zoning, even in urban areas.

Because counties are considered unorganized territory (except where municipal powers are specially granted them by the state), cities in the South and West can expand their territory by annexation of county territory adjacent to their limit. To make preannexation development conform to city standards, cities in these areas often have extraterritorial controls on land not yet annexed. Thus, even if their surrounding counties have few land use controls, the territory nearest the city is often subject to urban rules.

In sum, almost all urban and suburban areas have zoning, and the number of rural communities that have no zoning is diminishing. Even those that lack zoning cannot be said to be completely open to development. In most cases, an unzoned community that is confronted by plans for some unwelcome development can legally forestall it by hastily enacting an interim zoning law. Those with permissive ordinances may use permit moratoria to give them time to adopt a more restrictive ordinance. The major legal restriction on moratoria is that they have some scheduled termination date, but the finish line can be moved pretty often. For these reasons, we may practically assume, without even investigating the existence of particular ordinances, that all general-purpose governments in urban, suburban, and exurban (rural but near cities) areas have zoning and that they can change their zoning laws either to accommodate or to deter developments. It often appears that the only time developers have a true "vested right" to develop is after they have literally established that right in the concrete of a building's foundation.

2.3 Up and Down the Zoning Pyramid

The original zoning laws from the early twentieth century conceived of a hierarchy of land uses to be protected. At the pinnacle was residential use, especially the single-family home. The hierarchy was most obvious in the older, "cumulative" zoning regulations. In these, commerce and industry were prohibited in most residential zones, but residential uses were permitted anywhere. This is no longer typical of modern local ordinances, in which homes are prohibited from being built in industrial areas, just as industry is prohibited from locating in residential zones. W. L. Pollard (1931) indicates that this modern practice was intended to protect industry from nuisance suits by residents who moved in after industry was established.

The idea of uses exclusive to each zone is subject to modern scholarly criticism. For example, Rick Hills and David Schleicher (2010) criticize the use of exclusive-use zones designed to retain jobs in dying urban industrial districts by preventing factories from converting to residential use. They see it as a strategy that is more costly than straightforward subsidies. Sonia Hirt (2014) both demonstrates and questions the American preference for free-standing single-family homes over other residential forms, a preference not found elsewhere. There is also a movement, inspired by the urban theorist and activist Jane Jacobs (1961), to facilitate a finer mosaic of uses in urban neighborhoods, which the exclusive-use approach hinders. Form-based zoning, which emphasizes contextual conformity of buildings rather than designation of specific uses, has become popular in the urban planning literature, where it is called "transect" zoning (Duany and Talen 2002; Nicole Garnett 2013). Some modern zoning ordinances feature a few "mixed-use" zones that judiciously mix commerce and residential development. Additionally, some redevelopment in proximity to urban transit stations is designated "transit-oriented development" or TOD. Protection of residential uses from other economic activities nonetheless remains the default rule almost everywhere.

The image of a hierarchical pyramid of land use is probably responsible for the original use of the term "downzoning." Before about 1970 (and especially in the eastern states), downzoning meant reclassifying land for more intensive use such as apartments or offices or industry. A downzoned parcel was moved down on the pyramid of land use, which usually resulted in an increase in its value. The modern usage, which apparently originated in California, denotes just the opposite: Downzoning land means it can be used only for less intensive purposes, such as single-family houses on larger lots. The "down" in "downzoning" now everywhere refers to the usual reduction in value from the newly restrictive regulations. The linguistic judgment of the marketplace has displaced that of the early planners.

Implied by this terminology of new regulations (as in downzoning and its opposite, upzoning) is that zoning designations can be changed by the municipality. Most zoning laws have considerable staying power over time—wholesale rezonings or brand-new laws that alter district lines are unusual—but almost every zoning ordinance is amended annually and sometimes more often. The power to fine tune an ordinance is critical to practical administration, as conditions do change and the wording of older laws can have unintended consequences that require a response. The possibility of change is also important to the interaction between developers and the rest of the community, both of whom are aware that new laws can modify a current map that looks too restrictive or too permissive. Social scientists as well as attorneys advising clients need to be aware that existing zoning maps are not the final word for gauging community preferences.

2.4 "Grandfathering" Preserves Existing Uses, Mostly

When zoning ordinances do change, they often leave in their wake buildings and lot configurations that were formerly consistent with the zoning regulations (if there were any) but that are now nonconforming with respect to new regulations. Early twentieth-century zoning laws required that nonconforming uses would have to be discontinued once the new ordinance took effect (Kathy Kolnick 2008). As described in more detail in section 5.13, this draconian rule was modified but not entirely abandoned within a few decades. The general rule nowadays is that nonconforming uses are "grandfathered" so that they do not have to be discontinued. (The term is in wide use despite its unsavory origins, which referred to laws by which Southern blacks were disfranchised for failing literacy tests, while their equally illiterate white neighbors retained the right to vote because their grandfathers could, prior to Emancipation, vote before the test was imposed.)

Grandfathered land uses do not, however, enjoy a free pass. They are often subject to special restrictions on future expansions. A nonconforming grocery store within a residential neighborhood would not be able to leverage its grandfathered status into a larger-sized supermarket. Especially noxious nonconforming uses might also be subject to the common law of nuisance and be discontinued or at least modified as a result. (Nuisance law is discussed in section 2.14 below.) Discontinuance of offensive nonconforming uses is sometimes required after a period of years deemed by statute to be sufficiently long to have amortized the original investment (Michael Berger 1992). Amortization statutes seem drastic when taken by themselves, since no compensation is offered under the police-power rationales for them. When seen as a compromise between perpetual grandfathering and immediate discontinuance of a nuisance, however, they seem less arbitrary. In any case, the practice of amortization has become rare, perhaps because modern environmental and health regulations have tamed the more noxious nonconforming uses and as a result, made their persistence more acceptable to the community.

The practice of grandfathering has some notable effects on land use regulation. One is that developers sometimes catch wind of an impending change in zoning regulations that are adverse to their interests. They hustle to get their projects going so that they will be grandfathered under the new rules. For example, Roger Sanjek (1998) described how developers bought many properties in the New York Borough of Queens in 1980s in anticipation of downzoning. The new owners sought to demolish old houses and quickly build new ones that utilized the more permissive old regulations. Such opportunism is often forestalled both by the many stages of review that larger projects are subject to, during which municipal officials can slow things down, and by the problematic economies of getting financing for premature developments that may not yet be marketable. (Sanjek noted that despite opposition by developers, "half of Queens" [328] was downzoned by 1993.)

Public officials who contemplate newly permissive regulations may also be wary about doing so if they know that they cannot easily correct their mistakes. When I was chair of the Hanover, New Hampshire, zoning board, I once proposed that a local sign ordinance be liberalized to help local business owners, and the change was accepted by the voters as one of the routine annual housekeeping amendments. The resulting proliferation of sandwich-board signs has given me pause, but any effort to undo the liberalized ordinance would be complicated by the claim by business owners that their signs were grandfathered. (Christopher Serkin [2009] advances this and other arguments against grandfathering.)

The most important political consequence of grandfathering, though, is that zoning can be made much more restrictive without incurring the wrath of resident voters. A large-scale downzoning of rural land from a three-acre minimum lot size to a ten-acre minimum would be a very hard sell if current rural residents with houses on smaller lots had to acquire additional land in order to meet the new lot size. A proposed height limit of two stories would be difficult to pass if current owners of three-story homes had to cut off the top floor. And of course most observers would think that grandfathering in these cases is reasonable. But the practice does allow political insiders (current residents) to impose costs on outsiders (prospective residents), which most of the insiders do not have to endure. If the costs of restricting new housing and other development had to be spread around among currently enfranchised voters, communities might be more circumspect about establishing such restrictions.

2.5 The Zoning Board: A Study in Misrule?

The establishment of zoning rules and any substantial changes to them are carried out by the local legislative body, which is often subject to a local plebiscite. Quotidian adjustments in existing zoning (variances and special permits) are delegated to the zoning board of adjustment (sometimes called the board of zoning appeals), whose members are untrained residents appointed (usually) by municipal legislatures. Adjustments are needed even though most zoning categories list uses that are allowed "as of right," meaning without zoning board review. Other uses are permitted by special exception, often granted by the zoning or planning board with strings attached and thus called a "conditional use permit." For example, a general residence zone might allow one- and two-family homes as of right, while requiring that construction of apartment houses with more units be allowed only by special exception. In general, designated special exceptions are presumed to be granted if specific criteria are met. This sounds permissive, but one of the specific criteria is often that the use not adversely affect the "character of the neighborhood," which often invites open-ended discussion and negotiation with established residents of the neighborhood.

A proposed use or a dimensional exception not listed as permitted or conditionally allowed requires a zoning variance. A landowner who has an oddly shaped lot might petition for an exception to the set-back requirements for a front porch, and the zoning board might permit this usage if the criteria for a variance are met. Such criteria usually demand that the property have some unusual characteristic—a steep slope or a marshy area—that makes conformity especially difficult; they also usually stipulate that the variance would still be consistent with the rest of the neighborhood and not conflict with the purposes of the ordinance. Sometimes an owner will petition the board to allow a change in use, say, to open a small grocery store in a rural residential area. Use variances tend to be viewed more skeptically by zoning boards than dimensional variances, and the landowner might better go to the planning board to start the rezoning process (as described in section 2.7 below).

From 1987 to 1997, I served on the Hanover, New Hampshire, zoning board, chairing it for my last five years. The most enduring lesson I learned from this service was how much actually visiting the site in question matters. Our board would take testimony from applicants, abutters to the land in question, and the public at large. In the week between the hearing session and the deliberation session, board members would travel individually (group travel required public notice as a meeting) to the location of the proposed project and tramp around the lot and the neighborhood. Though its resident population is only 10,000, Hanover is a busy employment center, and its land area (48 square miles) is the size of Boston, so locations were sometimes unfamiliar.

Site visits could change our views of the case enormously. At one hearing, an applicant showed charming pictures of his antique-car hobby and sought a variance only to park some storage trailers. A site visit revealed that he actually harbored a private junkyard, which was entirely prohibited in the town. (Neighbors had not previously complained because the junkyard had been there before their homes were built, and the owner was a nice guy—two extralegal criteria that nonetheless explain many land use nonconformities.) In another case, a wetland setback where a barn was proposed seemed on our visit to be as high and dry as any location in Hanover. (Wetland definitions do not actually require water to be evident [Royal Gardner 2011].)

I mention the importance of local knowledge because there is a large literature on zoning boards, most often by attorneys, which finds fault with their decisions. Among the earlier and better known critiques was titled, "The Zoning Board of Adjustment: A Case Study in Misrule" (Dukeminier and Stapleton 1962). The chief "misrule" was the willy-nilly issuance of variances for business signs in Lexington, Kentucky. This irregularity seems to have been cured in recent years by tighter procedures and legislation, according to law professor Kathryn Moore (2011), who actually served on the Lexington zoning board. She nonetheless concluded that "a more difficult problem to correct, is the Board's tendency to make decisions that seem fair and practical rather than technically legally correct" (520). That tendency is widespread.

A more recent study of "misrule" was by an attorney who statistically examined variance decisions in five New Hampshire towns, one of which was Hanover, during the years 1987–1992, when I was on the zoning board. His chief finding was that variances are disproportionately granted if abutters to the applicant's property do not object (David Kent 1993, cited with similar studies in Robert Ellickson et al. 2013). To which most board members would say, privately and with palms up, "Nu? Who knows better than the neighbors whether the variance will have an adverse effect?" The practice illustrates the recurrence of an early, grass-roots approach to land use regulation, which required landowners who proposed nonconforming uses to obtain permission of local property owners. The practice was struck down as unlawful delegation of the police power in several early cases such as *Eubank v. City of Richmond*, 226 U.S. 137 (1912), but most local zoning boards informally operate as if it were still in effect. (The cases that preceded New York's first-in-the-nation ordinance of 1916 were typically based on ordinances that applied only to parts of the municipality.)

Mr. Kent, the New Hampshire critic of zoning boards, neglected to point out that four of the five towns in his sample have administrative officers who could discourage applicants with weak cases. (Hanover's certainly did.) It is possible that what looked to Kent like overly permissive decisions by the zoning board had first been vetted by the zoning administrator, resulting in what social scientists call "selection bias" toward applicants with strong cases. Kent also reported (accurately) that during the period of his study, the New Hampshire Supreme Court overturned ten towns whose opponents appealed their granting of variances. (Some advice to board chairs who want to stay free of judicial appeals, as Hanover did while I was zoning board chair: Be publicly respectful of all opinions, even when—especially when—they seem unreasonable to you.) The court reversals seem to support Kent's conclusion that local boards were prodigal in their awards of variances. However, a 2001 decision, *Simplex v. Newington*, 145 N.H. 727, changed the court's previous zoning variance criteria, on which Kent had relied as the source of proper variances, and instituted a less exacting standard that more closely reflected actual practice. (A similar evolution in judicial review of variances in Wisconsin is described, though also with lawyerly disapproval for zoning board discretion, by Alan Madry [2007].)

Legal error is not practical error, much less ecological or economic harm. While articles critical of zoning boards mention the possibility of variances degrading neighborhoods, even anecdotal evidence in support of that contention is scarce. Without visiting the site in question, it is often extremely difficult to tell whether the variance was warranted by legal, practical, or economic criteria. An underappreciated study by law professor David Bryden

(1977) established this more systematically. Bryden examined scores of Minnesota lakeshore variances for the positioning of buildings and septic systems (for on-site disposal of human waste). He had no part in granting them. His analysis led him to conclude that what looked like a travesty of zoning board permissiveness from the legal point of view in almost all cases made perfectly good sense to local board members who were acquainted with the details of the sites in question.

For example, variances allowing homes to be built closer to the lakeshore, which by themselves seemed to have been issued with little regard to the state's standard setback criteria, were granted mainly to allow septic systems to be even farther from the lake than state regulations required. The local officials knew the sites and made what Bryden inferred were appropriate trade-offs between the serious risk of septic-tank pollution of water bodies and the less-consequential (in their minds) aesthetic concerns about building set-backs. (Katherine Moore [2011] also found that the occasional deviations from formal zoning rules that she examined in Lexington, Kentucky, had no adverse effects on the neighborhoods.)

This is not to say that zoning boards are faultless. They may be swayed by popular opinion or by slick presentations. Some members can be, in my experience, petty busybodies. Though I never had reason to suspect corruption on my board, I sometimes thought that personal sympathies flavored some members' votes. But even the least sophisticated zoning boards have an asset that is almost never available to appellate judges or statistical analysts: They know from personal experience at least the neighborhood and usually the specific site. In zoning as in other aspects of life, a large portion of success is just showing up.

2.6 Planning Boards and Delphic Master Plans

The planning board is in most places distinct from the zoning board. Both are usually appointed by the local legislature, though sometimes either office may be elective. In all but very small communities, the zoning board and the planning board are supported by a professional staff of city planners. The planning board draws up and periodically amends a general statement of the goals that are to be implemented by zoning and other local legislation. This statement is called the "master plan" or the "comprehensive plan," and the mantra of zoning is that it should be done "in accordance with a comprehensive plan." Most communities do have a planning commission and a master plan.

But often the planning commission and master plan came *after* the first zoning ordinances were enacted. The city of Euclid, Ohio, whose zoning was the first to be upheld by the U.S. Supreme Court in 1926, did not adopt a master plan until 1994 (Ruth Knack 1996). Some small communities that have zoning continue to operate without a master plan.

The lack of formal planning before zoning may be attributed to two factors. First, the per capita cost of a professional planning consultant may be substantial in rural communities on the edge of an expanding metropolitan area. Such communities often find that they want to enact or amend a zoning law in response to the proposal of a large development. In their haste, they often forgo the niceties of formal planning.

Second and more important, most courts have been unwilling to deem a zoning ordinance invalid simply because the community lacked a formal master plan. They interpret "in accordance with a comprehensive plan" as requiring only that all of the community, rather than selected parts of it, be zoned (Charles Haar 1955). Community-wide zoning must embody a plan of some sort, judges reason, even if it is not written down. The existence of a master plan is often helpful to the community in that it provides evidence that the community did not act arbitrarily (when it is accused in court of having done so), but the plan itself has little force of law.

Both of these factors have been changing gradually. The federal and state governments have provided grants to communities to be used for planning, and so the costs to those communities have been reduced. Some federal programs that send funds to local governments are contingent on the existence of local planning and zoning. The courts have also become more hostile to zoning changes that are not backed by master plans. Communities have thus been encouraged to avoid charges that they are undertaking illegal "spot zoning." The term is more connotative than denotative, as no one knows at what scale a rezoned area becomes a mere spot on the zoning map, and some individualized rezonings actually make the lot more consistent with uses in the surrounding area and the master plan. Again, knowing the site and its history makes a difference.

The movement toward encouraging a formal planning process seems to have been engendered by conflicting motives. One concern has been that zoning is not sufficiently restrictive and that more planning is necessary to take into account longer-range environmental effects. Thus communities were encouraged to plan in order to preserve sensitive environments and conserve natural resources (William Reilly 1973). My impression is that communities have mostly succeeded in doing so. The other concern has been that zoning is too restrictive, especially with regard to exclusion of lower-income groups. Several states have adopted legislation requiring communities to plan for their share of the region's low-income housing. It was hoped that planning could induce communities to open their gates a little wider (Daniel Mandelker 1976).

Most planning documents written since 1970 seem to reflect both of these concerns. But master-plan statements are so broad as to make them unhelpful to advocates who would deploy them in "opening up the suburbs" (per the title of Anthony Downs's 1973 book) to more intensive development and city-like diversity. The breadth of the purposes of zoning as stated in such plans makes it difficult to isolate one motive as a controlling factor. The community master plan may devote a section to the need for low-cost housing, but the actual creation of zoning for it may be overshadowed by concern for protecting the environment, preserving historic areas, preventing farmland conversion, and reducing traffic congestion (Ellickson et al. 2013, 779–84).

The Delphic pronouncements and undifferentiated lists of most master plans provide something for every community interest but no ranking of which is to come first. The status quo of current development patterns is thus protected by a web of goals, each strand seemingly reasonable and flexible but collectively unbreakable. As an antidote to this, Rick Hills and David Schleicher (2011) recommend remedying local planning's exclusionary bias through a "zoning budget" for larger cities in which downzonings are matched by equivalent upzonings (permitting more units). Their proposal would balance unpopular uses among various neighborhoods by assuring existing residents of a given neighborhood that they will not become the invariable object of unpopular land uses. Their plan has more precision than "fair share formulas" that allocate unpopular land uses among neighborhoods and whose success has been limited (Ellickson et al. 2013). But relying on malleable, something-for-everyone planning documents to form a base for regulating zoning changes, as Hills and Schleicher (2014) propose in a later article, seems overly optimistic.

2.7 Rezoning and Subdivision Regulations

A developer who seeks to have some land rezoned for a more profitable use starts with the planning board. (Section 6.9, however, suggests that starting with the neighbors is sometimes the better strategy even though not legally required.) She must convince the board that the new designation, say for mixed-use commercial and residential, is in the public interest. It will help if this proposal seems consistent with the master plan. Planning staff will consult with other municipal officials (in the fire department, the public works department, and so on) to see if their missions can accommodate the effects of the proposal. Advisory boards such as the historic commission and conservation council will also be notified and invited to opine on the proposed development. If the developer gets the planning board's approval, she must then convince the local legislature to approve the rezoning, again after public hearings. The city council's approval in many cases may require affirmation by a local plebiscite. (Local voters may also reverse the council's disapproval of a rezoning proposal, though this is less common.) Rezonings are thus possible and sometimes not all that controversial, but in cases involving major changes, there are a number of hurdles that only determined developers with patient bankers and savvy lawyers should undertake to get over.

And savvy lawyers make a difference. I once attended a statewide conference on zoning at which three attorneys made presentations. Two were okay, but the third grabbed my attention. He went from topic to topic in a logical and persuasive way. I would jot down a note about what he said, but then say to myself, "But what about this issue?" The attorney would then address the issue, as if I had asked out loud. After the conference adjourned, I approached him and said that my town was looking for new counsel, and if he was interested I could recommend him to the selectmen. He smiled and said he actually had only one client, and that was taking all his time. I asked if he could tell me who the client was. He replied, "I work for Walmart."

Within a zoning district, developers who seek to build several new structures on more than one lot are usually subject to subdivision regulations. In order to proceed with their projects, developers must meet certain requirements set by the planning board, even if the proposal is consistent with the zoning regulations. The planning board thus serves two ends of the community development time spectrum: composing long-term master plans and dealing with the nitty-gritty of specific projects. The zoning board, as described above, occupies the intermediate time-horizon by reviewing requests for variances and special exceptions.

Subdivision regulations often demand that the developer put in roads, sidewalks, sewers, water mains, utility lines, and recreation areas. New infrastructure is normally deeded to the municipality, an exchange that both parties deem desirable. (The developer typically does not want to foist the obligation to maintain streets on prospective buyers except where a gated community is involved.) Although subdivision regulations are codified so that the developer has some idea of what to expect, both the developer and community authorities benefit from some ongoing negotiation of how best to proceed within the often broad parameters of the law. Unlike the zoning board, which has a judge-like function in reviewing exceptions to the zoning law and thus cannot bargain too closely with applicants, the planning board has a freer hand to negotiate with developers of sizable projects. The negotiations may involve payments to the community, which are called "subdivision exactions" (sometimes codified as impact fees), as an alternative to having the developers themselves build infrastructure obligations or offsite mitigation projects for a major subdivision.

A variation on subdivision regulation is the Planned Unit Development (PUD), in which the developer and community authorities negotiate every feature of the project. (Many of these developments will have their own internal, private governing structures for residents and property owners, as discussed below, but prior to construction, it is the developer who does the negotiation.) While PUD negotiations allow for more community discretion, they also permit more opportunity for the developer to strike deals and compromises with the authorities. It is not clear why PUDs are not more common, given their general advantages for the developer and community authorities. It is possible that nearby established residents are wary of how the negotiated PUD will turn out and for this reason resist their establishment on the zoning map. Having a nearby vacant lot designated for single-family homes or even commercial use offers neighboring homeowners more security than having it zoned "make an offer and then negotiate."

The importance of subdivision regulation is that it enables the community to force the developers to pay for at least some of the community infrastructure occasioned by development. (What can be demanded is the subject of some recent U.S. Supreme Court decisions discussed in section 3.26.) There is, however, a substantial difference between these regulations and zoning. Zoning is a more powerful device because it permits the community to exclude many uses altogether. Under subdivision regulations, developers must bear certain costs, but having done so, they usually have the right to build. Under a valid zoning ordinance, developers do not have the right to erect any structure not in conformance with the zoning district, regardless of what they are willing to pay. The community may refuse any attempt to alter a valid zoning ordinance, while it may not heap arbitrarily burdensome subdivision exactions on permitted uses. (To anticipate a theoretical discussion in section 6.5, zoning protects the community by a "property rule"—the right to "just say no"—while subdivision regulations protect it by something closer to a "liability rule," which gives developers the go-ahead if they are willing to pay for the costs their projects gives rise to [Calabresi and Melamed 1972].)

2.8 Building and Housing Codes Are Less Contested than Zoning

Rather than prescribing the developer's contribution to community infrastructure, which is what subdivision regulations do, the municipal building code designates the standards for materials and procedures to be used in new structures. These codes may require specific materials for pipes for water and sanitation flow, insulation of a particular quality, and the use of fireproofing and sprinklers in certain areas. Such regulations can add to the cost of any structure, and they have been criticized for retarding the use of new building technologies and raising housing costs (Listokin and Hattis 2005), though the magnitudes seem modest by comparison with zoning, whose effects on housing costs will be discussed in chapter 5.

Building codes have not generated the same kind of controversy as zoning. This may be because the costs to be borne by the developer are more specific. Most communities adopt some variation on national building codes, and their uniformity and technical nature discourage much negotiation between developers and community authorities. And codes do have an upside. A recent article found that building codes in Florida that reduced the hurricane hazards to nearby buildings (much wind damage is caused by unsecured debris blown in from neighboring properties) resulted in 4 to 12 percent higher housing values in jurisdictions that adopted them (Dumm, Sirmans, and Smersh 2012).

Housing codes differ from building codes in that the housing codes apply to existing structures, while the building codes usually apply only to new construction or substantial renovations. Housing codes set standards for the continuing maintenance of units, such as having hot water available and ensuring that stairs are in good repair. They have reversed the common-law presumption, which prevailed until the 1970s, that renters take their accommodations "as is" and have no warranty of habitability (Stuart Banner 2011).

Housing and habitability codes are thus mainly constraints on rental housing units, and they are most controversial when the community imposes rent controls. When rents are limited, landlords have an incentive to reduce maintenance, and so housing codes can be a way to force them to keep up their rental units. Efforts to make landlords comply with these codes, however, tend to be only partly successful. Studies of rent control in Cambridge, Massachusetts, between 1970 and 1995 showed that much of the rental housing stock became measurably run down, if not illegally substandard, during its duration (Autor, Palmer, and Pathak 2012).

2.9 Urban Growth Boundaries Are Mostly in the West

An indirect constraint on development, which can vary significantly in importance, is the community's willingness to provide municipal infrastructure such as roads and water and sewer lines. Communities may limit development by refusing to extend water or sewer lines to certain areas or by refusing to annex unincorporated areas adjacent to them, which would deny new developments access to municipal services. This is an especially important constraint in areas where septic tanks and individual wells are not feasible, which is usually the case in the arid regions of the western United States. (The option of on-site wells in well-watered states of the eastern United States may explain why low-density exurban development is more prevalent there [Marcy Burchfield et al. 2006].)

Control by infrastructure management has bloomed into a concept called "urban growth boundaries," which prevent almost all development outside a designated area. These boundaries are most viable in places where a single unit of government, such as that of a large city or a city-county combination, controls most of the developable land in its metropolitan area. If there are multiple governments, all that a single jurisdiction's urban growth boundary will accomplish is what planners call "leapfrog development": In this scenario, developers skip over the out-of-bounds area and into a more hospitable jurisdiction. The growth boundary of Boulder, Colorado, which is among the oldest in the nation (circa 1970), appears to have stimulated the growth of nearby towns that have declined to coordinate their land use policies with the city. A majority of workers in Boulder commute from outside the city, and its expansive greenbelt no doubt makes their commute longer and perhaps a bit more scenic. (Pendall, Martin, and Fulton [2002] survey the growth boundary literature and offer case studies of Boulder and two California cities.)

One major city, Portland, Oregon, has largely succeeded in avoiding the leapfrog effect of an urban growth boundary. Portland achieved this by having the state legislature establish an independent, metropolitan-wide governing structure ("Metro") that could veto local zoning decisions of the many otherwise independent cities that make up the metropolitan area (Mildner, Dueker, and Rufolo 1996). This untouchable cartel—its governing board is elected along lines that do not correspond to municipal boundaries, which immunizes it from local politics—does indeed promote the high-density infill development that is said to be the solution to urban sprawl. Portland and Houston, which has no zoning or growth boundaries, represent opposite land use regimes and will anchor discussion of metropolitan structure and suburban sprawl in chapter 8.

2.10 Besieged Localism?

Zoning is preeminently the product of local initiative. It started that way a century ago (as I will describe in chapter 5, which disputes the usual story about Progressive-era elites), and it has stayed that way. In one sense this is remarkable, in that the legal and institutional forces that are described below appear to be more powerful than local governments. Municipalities lack constitutional status, the taxable resources of the federal and state governments, and a commonality of interest (suburbs are often said to be at odds with central cities and with each other). Higher governments can displace local zoning if they want to. Municipalities are regarded as "creatures of the state" in legal terms.

Wear and tear on local zoning comes not just from higher government. The foundations of localism, the city block and the suburban neighborhood, are subject to centrifugal forces that estrange them from the cities and towns of which they are a part. The next sections will describe and evaluate these political forces.

The pressures from above can be divided into categorical regulations, in which the impact on local zoning is incidental to the main purpose of the state and national legislative goals, and preemptive regulation, in which the higher government intentionally substitutes its rules and procedures for those of the local government. My main points in what follows are that local governments retain the trump cards in most of the important zoning decisions. Where municipal authority has been displaced, the effects of both the higher government interventions and local decentralization movements have been to make zoning more exclusive.

2.11 NEPA and the Clean Water Act Led the Way

The vast majority of higher government interventions have been put in place since 1970, when the environmental movement established its federal beachhead with the National Environmental Policy Act. NEPA requires federal agencies to conduct environmental impact studies for their development activities. Since federal money is often involved in local projects such as airport development, low-income housing, and road construction, the developers of these projects must conduct such studies. This gives individuals or groups who object to these developments an opportunity to challenge the adequacy and conclusions of environmental impact statements. The challenges may end up in court, where the opponents may obtain substantial concessions from the developer or even halt the project altogether.

NEPA and its state counterparts, along with the Endangered Species Act and the Clean Water Act, are part of the "standing revolution" in land use law (Clifford Holderness 1998). Prior to the 1970s, dissenting individuals and groups dissatisfied with a development that was duly approved by local authorities did not have legal standing to challenge the decision. At the time, the result of such challenges was that "neighbors usually lose" (Norman Williams 1974). After NEPA and other post-1970 national and state laws went into effect, court interpretations of these statutes expanded their scope well beyond developments that required permits from the higher-level government. Thus, parties other than developers and public officials gained an opportunity to modify and sometimes stop developments that would have sailed through under pre-1970 legal and administrative laws (Stewart Sterk 2011).

It is worth noting, though, that NEPA also filled a gap in popular land use regulation. Property that is owned by the federal government is exempt from local land use regulation, as is property owned by state governments unless the state legislature modifies the rule (Ellickson et al. 2013, 832–37). The federal government's vast holdings of public land, national forests, and parkland are typically far from cities, so their land use activities affect relatively few people. But federally owned property in or near urban areas is also exempt from local review. Federally funded developments such as public housing, scientific laboratories, military bases, federal offices, post offices, and especially highways, do affect nearby residents, and NEPA's review requirements allow local residents an opportunity to voice their opinions as they had been unable to do before.

The construction of the interstate highway system, which began in 1956, was perhaps the most important factor in giving rise to NEPA. Using eminent domain to push through urban neighborhoods, the federally financed highway system took little account of its impact on the residential quality of life. The citizen groups that sprang up to fight it—Jane Jacobs headed one in New York—were the advance guard of the environmental movement (Raymond Mohl 2004). The standing that NEPA gives to citizen groups can be thought of as an indirect way for localities to influence otherwise unregulated federal land uses.

Besides the general legal standing that NEPA offered to citizen groups, the Clean Water Act pushed the federal government into an active role in state and local land use management. Regulation of navigable waterways by the federal government was established in the nineteenth century under the Commerce Clause of the Constitution. Many controversies back then involved local damming of rivers for waterpower. The Clean Water Act of 1972 expanded this traditional federal regulation to include "any discharge" into the waterways and extended the definition of "waters of the United States" to include wetlands. Wetlands were not just swamps, marshes, and bogs. They included ground that, though usually dry, was saturated long enough to support vegetation typical of wetlands. Black ash trees are a characteristic species of wetlands in the northeastern United States, and that is how I learned (from a specialist) that the apparently dry lot I was inspecting for the Hanover zoning board was part of a wetland and hence out of bounds for development under our ordinance.

The regulations that require municipalities to protect wetlands usually do not come directly from the federal government. The Clean Water Act designated two unlikely bedfellows, the U.S. Army Corps of Engineers, which traditionally engineered and policed navigability, and the new U.S. Environmental Protection Agency (EPA) as the wardens of wetlands. (The source of this awkward marriage was disagreement between the House and Senate, as explained by Royal Gardner [2011].) The EPA allows states that meet its criteria to administer the act, and states in turn require that wetlands be given due consideration in local zoning matters.

Zoning approvals are thus subject to a secondary veto power. The developer of a site that is partly within a wetland is well advised to build only on the upland part, and the owner of a site that is entirely within a wetland may be able to do little more than watch the characteristic wetland vegetation grow. Wetlands regulation is not entirely prohibitive. Developers can offer mitigation plans that allow them to selectively fill wetlands for urban purposes, and the Corps sometimes allows deals in which developers will create or improve an alternative wetland to replace the one they are filling. Nonetheless, wetland regulation is often a sticking point for developers and another opportunity for third parties to intervene in the process.

Wetlands regulation is also unusual in that its reach is so extensive. This is because most cities developed along some form of navigable water, and those that did not usually grew up as centers for rain-fed agriculture. Other federal regulation has more indirect effects on local zoning. The Clean Air Act defines standards for air pollution and requires states and localities to develop plans to meet them. This certainly influences the location of businesses such as dry cleaners and gas stations. But attainment of air quality standards seldom requires the municipality to rezone particular tracts. The Endangered Species Act has a more direct effect on land use decisions and is something of a wild card to use against developers (Barton Thompson 1997). The presence of endangered butterflies and birds have forced the modification and sometimes abandonments of many projects. In a similar vein, various state and federal acts that protect historic sites and promote farmland preservation have stymied many projects.

2.12 Federal Preemption Is Gingerly Applied

The national legislation described in the previous section made no attempt to preempt local decisions in a direct sense. The most intrusive of them, the Clean Water Act, operates as a kind of "overlay zone," in which additional constraints are added to development in the local residential or businesses districts (for example) that happen to be in wetlands. But the Clean Water Act does not insist that any particular zoning designation be changed to meet federal goals.

During the mid-1970s, it seemed possible that the federal government would establish something analogous to a land use planning commission, if not a national zoning board, which would have a more direct effect on local land use. Senator Henry Jackson of Washington held hearings and drafted legislation to promote national regulation. Neither house of Congress approved the bills that would have moved in this direction. A similar effort in the early 1980s to get the national government involved in preserving agricultural land was also beaten back. Jerold Kayden (2000) summarized the overall outcome in the title of his article, "National Land-Use Planning in America: Something Whose Time Has Never Come." (See also Tim Lehman 1995 and

Sidney Plotkin 1987.) The more salient federal interventions in local land use have focused on specific uses rather than attempting to establish general authority. The major incursions are discussed in the bulleted sections below (borrowed largely from the indefatigable Patricia Salkin [2012]).

- Federal flood insurance regulations dating from the 1970s have required local governments to have some zoning in place to reduce flood hazards for homeowners to be eligible for federal insurance. This was not literally preemptive, but it was effectively so because commercial lenders are reluctant to give mortgages for homes in flood plains if they are not insured. Almost all communities have complied with the federal requirements. This has not generated much controversy largely because flood plain zoning is not difficult to do and is not especially restrictive. Communities that want to allow development in flood plains can continue to do so as long as certain precautionary construction standards are met. On the other hand, communities that want to restrict development can use the flood plain as another reason to do so.
- Group homes for the disabled are a protected category under the provision of the Fair Housing Act and the Americans with Disabilities Act. These protections come into play most often when an agency or entrepreneur seeks to build or modify a single-family home in a residential district to house people with disabilities. The federal legislation is an ace to trump local restrictions on the number of unrelated occupants and on structural limitations that would impede the building's use by the disabled. The main controversies arise when the clientele to be served is disabled by reason of drug or alcohol dependence.

I do not include laws pertaining to handicapped access in this category, as they are general construction standards applicable to any location, sometimes in surprising places. My favorite application was the requirement of a wheelchair access ramp into an Appalachian Mountain Club cabin in the White Mountains National Forest of New Hampshire, which is accessible only by a five-mile trail over which no wheelchair-bound travelers could venture on their own. An advocacy group actually did stage a "wheel in" for the cabin, but the beneficiaries were carried most of the way by able-bodied volunteers so they could make their triumphal roll up the cabin's ramp (*New York Times*, August 17, 2000).

The federal group-home regulations are episodically controversial, but they do not alter local decision-making in any fundamental way. The legislation calls for "reasonable accommodation" of the protected category, not blanket exemption from regulation. Some municipalities attempt to prevent the concentration of group homes in a single area so as not to create a group-home ghetto. While most agree with the general aspiration of the Americans with Disabilities Act to ensure that the benefits of living in a pleasant, well-zoned community are available to the disabled, there is some legal push back against anti-concentration ordinances (Daniel Mandelker 2011).

• The placement of cell-phone towers must also be given reasonable accommodation under the federal Telecommunications Act of 1996. Zoning cannot be used to ban communications towers outright, and regulating them because of concerns about the effect of radio waves on health is forbidden. But the subsequent case law indicates that cities and towns have hardly lost all of their power to control tower placement, though denials must be based on "substantial evidence" and are not granted the same deference as ordinary zoning decisions (Kathleen Ruane 2012).

Cell-phone tower placement generally does not require eminent domain, as many alternative sites may be feasible, but service coverage does require their placement in many communities that may not be so welcoming. In adopting the Telecommunications Act in 1996, Congress was repeating a cycle of preference for new network technologies that were enjoyed in the nineteenth century by railroads and telephones and in the twentieth by pipelines and airports, among others (Fischel 1995). These preferences were granted not just because of corporate lobbying. Most ordinary citizens were eager to have railroads and electric power available even if they preferred not to have the facilities in their back yards. Indeed, the prospect of gaining better cell-phone service is at least an implicit compensation for putting up with some unsightly towers. The federal nudge to local zoning does not seem so alarming when viewed from this perspective.

• Religious institutions are subject to local zoning, and the Religious Land Use and Institutionalized Persons Act (RLUIPA), passed by Congress in 2000 to succeed the Religious Freedom Restoration Act of 1993, is by far the most controversial of federal forays into local land use decisions. As Patricia Salkin (2012) summarizes the act, "Section Two provides in part, [that] 'no government shall impose or implement a land use regulation in a manner that imposes a substantial burden on the religious exercise of a person, including a religious assembly or institution, unless the government demonstrates that... [the regulation] is in furtherance of a compelling governmental interest.'" The latter condition, requiring the local government to show a "compelling government interest," is quite different from the usual judicial test for the legality of a restriction on private development, which is highly deferential to local authorities (as described in the next chapter). The two acts were passed in response to U.S. Supreme Court rulings upholding local regulation of churches. Much of the controversy about them has to do with which branch of government, the Supreme Court or Congress, has the final say about the First Amendment's religious freedom guarantees.

In contrast to large cell-phone towers and halfway houses, religious institutions are generally welcome in most communities. The evidence that they were singled out for exclusion is thin (Stephen Clowney 2007). The problem with RLUIPA is that many churches, synagogues, and mosques are in residential areas. Religious institutions often have auxiliary activities that are arguably related to their mission but nonetheless look (and sound and smell) like commercial uses. Outdoor concerts, education facilities, food service, and retirement homes can be backed by nonreligious institutions and subject to local regulation, but RLUIPA gives the same activities a leg up if the sponsor has a religious affiliation.

With the exception of RLUIPA, though, Congress has trod gingerly into local zoning matters when it is explicitly addressing them. What looks like a big stick of federal command is usually softened by words like "reasonable" and by standards that involve local feedback. Concerns about a federal takeover of local prerogatives seem overwrought, especially in light of the defeat of the modest federal land use bills in the 1970s and early 1980s. The more important federal influence on local zoning has been indirect. Environmental, water quality, and endangered species legislation has provided a means for individuals and groups to modify local zoning decisions.

2.13 The Double Veto Undercuts the Smart Growth Movement

In the late 1960s and early 1970s, state legislatures began reasserting their police-power authority over the use of land. This took a number of forms. A handful of states (Vermont and Oregon most prominent among them) set up statewide regional land use commissions (David Callies 1994a). These commissions reviewed many of the decisions of local governments for their regional impacts. Other states established similar commissions, but only for a special area of the state. Examples include New York's Adirondack Park

Agency, New Jersey's Pine Barrens Commission, and the California Coastal Commission. A third approach has been state establishment of metropolitan federations to coordinate land use policies among the many local governments that constitute most large urban areas. Well-known examples are the Minneapolis and St. Paul Metropolitan Council, as well as the assumption of land use powers in the Miami, Florida, area by Dade County and the subsequent formation of a unified Miami/Dade municipal organization.

Despite their appearance, these new agencies have not greatly supplanted local autonomy (Callies 1994a). The local governments within the regions covered by the agencies seldom give up the power to zone and regulate subdivisions. The chief impact of the agencies is to provide a "double-veto" power to residents who oppose a particular development (Fischel 1989a; Scott Bollens 1992). Hearings before regional boards take evidence both from interest groups such as the Sierra Club and from local individuals who feel that their views were not given sufficient weight in the initial local decision. If the proposed shopping center passes the local zoning and planning board, it may still be rejected by the regional or metropolitan commission. It seldom works the other way. Few of these commissions have told local governments that they must accept developments that they do not want.

The double veto system continues to spread. The 1970s saw the rise of what were labeled "growth controls," or what is less aggressively termed "growth management." Traditional zoning laid out zones for various uses but did not attempt to slow down the rate of development in any of them. Growth controls added a temporal dimension to the spatial zoning map. Because growth controls were often adopted in places where demand for development was strong, zoning permits were prized, and communities could demand that developers offer a variety of compensatory benefits to the community (Douglas Porter 2008).

Growth management schemes were typically the product of local initiative, not statewide commands. The variation on growth management that arose in the 1990s was called "smart growth." (A brilliantly preemptive term: Who could be in favor of "dumb growth"?) The architectural movement related to it is "the new urbanism," which seeks to promote a higher-density living environment mixed with commercial and employment uses and connected by a variety of transportation modes. (The avatars of the movement are architects Andres Duany and Elizabeth Plater-Zyberk [with Jeff Speck, 2001].)

My introduction to new urbanism came from a talk at Dartmouth at which a speaker (a Duany associate) showed a local ideal of the new urbanism. It was a view of the urban part of South Royalton, Vermont, which is near Dartmouth and is familiar to me from my stints teaching at Vermont Law School, which is located in the village. The town does not have zoning (I confirmed that the speaker did not know that); if it did, the picturesque and somewhat irregular layout of the town would surely not have developed as it did. Although critical of traditional zoning, most smart-growth advocates seek to bend local regulations to accommodate more density rather than throwing zoning out altogether. (I would add that new development in South Royalton is now subject to statewide environmental review, so even without zoning, it is unlikely that its spontaneous "new urbanism" pattern could be reproduced elsewhere in town or in any other place in Vermont.)

Smart growth seeks to facilitate new urbanism in two ways. One is to deter exurban development with urban growth boundaries and (if necessary) very low-density zoning of undeveloped rural areas. The idea is to deter leap-frog development beyond the growth boundary. The second is to promote infill development by rezoning and otherwise enabling the higher-density development that promotes walking and use of public transit over automobiles. Both of these involve state or regional plans that can override local preferences.

Overrides are always difficult to effect, especially when they attempt to force localities to rezone to accommodate infill development that is not welcome (Anthony Downs 1994). So most of the state programs that address smart growth involve incentives. Examples are subsidies for local infrastructure such as bike paths and relatively toothless demands that local comprehensive plans include various smart growth components (Gregory Ingram et al. 2009; Kurt Paulsen 2013). Generally speaking, it is much easier to convince localities to preserve open space (the first prong of smart growth) than to get them to accept higher-density development.

Several states have attempted to preempt local authority over the location of especially noxious but necessary projects such as hazardous waste dumps. (These are designated by one of the better acronyms that populate the literature: LULUs—locally unwanted land uses.) This should be easy to do under the theory that local governments are mere creatures of the state, and constitutional objections to preemption have usually not succeeded. Despite their inferior legal status, though, local governments retain substantial control. State legislators who represent local districts are induced to intervene on behalf of the aggrieved city. Such intervention, along with other forms of grass-roots activism have generally succeeded in squelching various pre-emption schemes that seek to override local vetoes (Michael Wheeler 1994). Even carefully worked legislation that offers compensation to affected communities generates substantial opposition, which, in turn, usually upends the arrangement.

2.14 Nuisance Law and Right to Farm Embody Contradictory Impulses

Municipal land use controls have competition from a class of devices that are even more decentralized. These include the traditional law of nuisance, conservation easements, private covenants, and private community associations. For the most part, all of these operate independently of municipal zoning. That is, they apply regardless of whether the area on which they operate has zoning. They cannot trump zoning by allowing something prohibited in the municipal ordinance, but they can impose additional restrictions. Nonetheless, there is often in practice a symbiotic relationship between zoning and its private-law alternatives (Christopher Serkin 2010).

Nuisance law is the branch of tort law that deals with specific harms by one activity on another nearby. The law of nuisance was a predecessor of zoning, but it is not a land use control in the modern sense. A nuisance is defined as a specific activity, and it must be shown to exist and actually cause some harm before a court will decide the case. It becomes a land use control only as a result of the effect of spatial proximity of incompatible activities, such as hog farms and most anything else.

Nuisance law has largely been superseded by zoning and other police-power controls. (For a highly regarded article urging more reliance on nuisance and private law, see Ellickson [1973].) The reasons for this include the somewhat narrow definition of what constitutes a nuisance, the lack of prospective control, and the high cost of litigation. More important than these, I suspect, is that zoning allows communities to control activities that no court has ever found to constitute a nuisance. In other words, zoning represents a far more generous distribution of entitlements to the community than does nuisance law, even though nuisance law does not require the community to pay compensation.

The other problem with nuisance law is that of "moving to the nuisance." The classic modern case, *Spur Industries v. Del Webb Development*, 494 P.2d 700 (1972), arose when the developer of a retirement community in the Phoenix area set up downwind of a cattle feed lot operation (owned by Spur) that had been in operation long before. The new residents of the retirement village were offended by the rich rural smells and attendant vermin and sought a court injunction to have it discontinued.

Many non-lawyers are surprised to learn that the law of nuisance favors the newcomers in this case. Moving to the nuisance is not by itself a defense for the perpetrator of the nuisance, notwithstanding its priority in time. Economists also disparage the "first-in-time, first-in-right" principle because it creates incentives for landowners to opportunistically plant what they know will be problematical uses in advance of the regulations or to lazily ignore neighborhood changes that they should anticipate (Donald Wittman 1980). The novel twist in *Spur Industries* was that the Arizona Supreme Court required Del Webb, the home developer, to pay for the relocation costs of Spur Industries. (This was a rare application of "liability rule" protection, discussed in section 6.5.) This case has not gained much of a following in other courts, but its result presaged the widespread modern "right to farm" legislation, which protects preexisting agricultural operations from nuisance suits and rezonings by newly arrived suburbanites (Adelaja and Friedman 1999).

Regardless of the common-law rule, popular opinion seems to favor the first-in-time users, as was also suggested by the previously discussed rule (section 2.4) about grandfathering preexisting nonconforming uses. An unforeseen use of right to farm (and grandfathering in general) is the possibility of using opportunistic threats to create or perpetuate a nuisance so as to get a rezoning. The classic case involved a frustrated motel developer who established a pig farm on his property in Stowe, Vermont. He deliberately piled manure upwind of the neighboring landowners who had opposed him, as described in *Coty v. Ramsey Associates*, 149 Vt. 451 (1988). A similar instance occurred when the owner of an eyesore garage near my home in Hanover candidly told me (in an email!) that she would not sell or repair the garage because she was using it to persuade neighbors to support her request for a favorable rezoning of other property she owned in the immediate area. She told them she would fix it up only if she could get the rezoning. She has so far not succeeded, and reports about similar efforts by developers to use noxious farm activities to leverage favorable regulatory treatment indicate that such tactics usually backfire. The Stowe pig-farm saga ended badly for its protagonist (Ramsey) in that he was denied his permit to build a motel and had to remove the offending manure from his faux farm and pay damages to his neighbors.

2.15 Covenants and Residential Private Governments Compared to Zoning

Another major alternative to public land use control is the protective covenant. In this category I include, as a lawyer might not, all private agreements between landowners. These include a remarkable variety of legal devices, generally called "servitudes," which illustrate the extent to which property rights can be divided and sold. (An informative overview and defense of some of their ancient rules is found in Stewart Sterk [1985].) One can acquire air, mineral, and travel rights on another's land. Neighbors can agree to restrict architecture, landscaping, or conditions for occupancy. The former practice of using covenants to restrict ownership by race probably contributed to the disrepute into which they fell for many years.

One of the practical objections to protective covenants is the difficulty of changing the rules if conditions that motivated the original agreements change unexpectedly. For a homeowner to alter the conditions of the covenant to allow, say, a home business office, would normally require unanimous written consent of all those subject to the covenant. I cannot resist a local story to illustrate this. A homeowner in a rural area of Hanover built the roof of his house to a height that exceeded that allowed in the subdivision's covenants. (It was okay with the zoning in that district.) He called each of his neighbors asking if they would agree to an exception. All agreed except one. "You don't remember me, do you?" he began ominously. (My quotes here are for narrative effect.) "I was a developer in a nearby town, and you opposed my development. And I'm not going to sign off on the exception." The owner sued, claiming spite was not a legitimate reason to oppose the exception, but he lost. The judge pointed out that the owner had been fully informed of the rules, and the roof was dismantled and reconstructed to conform to the original covenants.

An alternative to the covenant is the "residential private government," the most common forms of which are condominium and homeowner associations (Uriel Reichman 1976). The private government has the same function as ordinary covenants, but instead of obliging each property owner to enforce them, the obligations to administer and enforce them are vested in a property owners' association. This association, which the original developer sets up, can then alter, usually by a supermajority of owners rather than by unanimity, various constraints and obligations contained in the original covenants. Thus, for instance, an obligation to clear snow outside one's unit might be offloaded to a professional manager and financed by association dues. The association also maintains an ongoing governing board, usually selected by vote of the property owners, to maintain common areas and enforce (and grant exceptions to) rules that all property owners originally agreed to.

Some observers regard zoning and private covenants as essentially the same thing, since they are directed toward the same types of issues. Indeed, the land use regulations imposed by private associations are often considerably more detailed and extensive than zoning rules. This has not discouraged the development of private associations. As Robert Nelson (2005) has shown, they have grown immensely since 1970. Nowadays it is rare to find a development of more than a handful of homes that does not have some form of private governance. It should perhaps go without saying that privatizing zoning does not seem to reduce the heat with which the rules and rulings are contested. Nelson also suggested that private community associations would eventually replace municipal zoning, but in the case of Florida, at least, Rachel Meltzer and Ron Cheung (2013) found that associations generally supplemented local zoning restrictions rather than supplanted them. In economists' language, private regulations and public zoning seem to be complements, not substitutes.

There are two crucial differences between zoning and private covenants (including those administered by associations). The first is that covenants cannot be *established* without the consent of all of the owners of the original land. I emphasize consent in the establishment of the community rather than the consent of those who subsequently buy into the community because buyers in zoned communities can be said to have at least implicitly consented to the regulations in place insofar as there were other communities in which they could have lived. For covenants, consent usually means that a single developer acquires all the land and then unilaterally imposes covenants and a governing structure on all of the lots she expects to sell. The buyers must agree to accept this structure and so can be said to consent to them. Given that there is almost no room for modification of the terms at the point of sale, buyers' consent is more of a legal formality than a considered bargain.

But there is still an important difference between covenants and zoning. In setting up the association and the covenants, the initial developer has to think about the configuration of restrictions that will maximize the collective value of the property. Those restrictions that would put off many buyers would be rejected at the outset. The developer also has to think about neighborhood effects. For example, the developers of Columbia, Maryland, a large planned community between Baltimore and Washington, had to think about the mix of rental and owner housing and the location of commercial activities and their intensity (Richard Brooks 1974). In such cases, some residential value might be sacrificed because the commercial value is higher. On the other hand, too much retail might excessively reduce the value of adjacent residential property.

The situation for municipal planners who lay out a zoning ordinance is somewhat different. While they will consider whether a commercial district will adversely affect nearby homes, they might discount the interests of business owners if the homeowners were politically dominant. If the potential commercial land is not owned by politically active residents, the cost of zoning it for a less valuable use such as open space may not be evident to decision-makers. As will be discussed presently, the opportunity cost of zoning might be perceived in the form of fiscal, convenience, or employment benefits from certain types of activities. But on its face, zoning for less intensive uses appears to be cheaper than it does for private community developers.

The other crucial difference in private community development is that the developer can maintain a majority of votes in the governing association and thus avoid the problem that economists call "time consistency" and everyone else calls "keeping your promises." In most cases, one vote is assigned to the owner of a lot in a private community. Owners of more than one lot thus have more than one vote, unlike residents of a municipality, where every adult has no more than one vote. But the more important distinction is that in private communities, developers assign themselves three votes for every unsold lot. Thus, developers can maintain control of community associations until three-quarters of the lots have been sold. They do not have to worry that initial association members might change rules or insist on development patterns that might frustrate their initial plans. In effect, the voting scheme forestalls the downzoning problem that bedevils later development in many suburban communities (Vernon Henderson 1980).

2.16 Historic Districts and Neighborhood Conservation Districts

The main problem in establishing private community associations is getting the consent of all the landowners. This is why almost all such associations are set up by a single developer who owns a large tract rather than by a consensual pact among neighboring landowners. Retrofitting an already-developed neighborhood with a private community association is next to impossible. Yet some neighborhoods have reason to want them. Residents may believe that other city residents or special interest groups may have more control over local zoning and that the dominant faction might want to shoehorn some unwanted activity in their midst (Fischel 2012a). This diversity of preferences is most likely to be found in older cities and larger (county) jurisdictions, where the body politic is more demographically diverse and development-minded interest groups have more sway than in small suburbs. I have found an example of a neighborhood that was granted the legal right to veto zoning changes proposed by the city, as described in *Bellevue v. East Bellevue Community Council*, 138 Wash.2d 937 (1999), but they are not common and rest on legally shaky ground. Court decisions such as *Seattle Title Trust Co. v. Roberge*, 278 U.S. 116 (1928), generally disfavor delegating zoning authority to neighborhood property owners.

One answer for protection of particular neighborhoods is local representation on city councils and on zoning and planning boards. Electing city officials by contiguous wards rather than in at-large elections gives neighborhoods more control over land use decisions (James Clingemeyer 1993). Another way to insulate neighborhoods from unwanted zoning is to create historic districts that correspond to the neighborhood. Although the historic preservation movement originally centered its attention on individual monuments, it soon spread to entire neighborhoods. Most of these designations are generated by the neighborhood itself, and often a special vote of property owners and residents within the proposed district is necessary to create the district (Thomas Merrill 2010).

Once created, historic districts regulate much more than most zoning ordinances do. New developments and even minor changes such as window replacements are subject to review by a neighborhood board. Only after review by the historic commission can a proposal begin to go through normal zoning and planning review. Although the latter review board does not necessarily have to accept the historic commission's decisions, it is rare for them to be rejected. Historic districts thus operate as another example of the double-veto system that state land use regulations add to municipal regulation, except that in this case the potential veto arrives prior to municipal review rather than afterward.

There are two problems with using historic districts as armor for an anxious neighborhood. One is that at least some of the buildings (not all) have to have some historic value. Actually, this is not all that demanding. The usual standard is that buildings should be at least 50 years old and be good examples if not exemplars of their period. Even with fairly elastic standards, though, many urban neighborhoods would find it difficult to qualify.

The more problematic aspect of historic designation is that existing neighborhoods that seek protection from change may get too much protection. Minor alterations that are acceptable to every other owner in the district may nonetheless be blocked by the historic district commission. The governing body of the historic district often includes residents of the neighborhood, but it is largely composed of citizens and professionals who actually want to preserve the historic quality.

The answer to these two problems is the neighborhood conservation district (Adam Lovelady 2008). Although the term "conservation" traditionally suggests natural resources, what is really being conserved is the existing character of the neighborhood. The neighborhood need not be historic. It only has to have some common characteristic that seems worthy of preservation. A style of architecture, not necessarily ancient or distinguished, is often enough. Sometimes the district is defined by its street layout or proximity to a park or school. Lack of historical or architectural significance actually confers an advantage in that proposed changes do not have to be reviewed by experts on history or architecture. Governance and review of land use changes are done by locally selected committees, which are more likely to be sympathetic to practical alterations such as windows and doors than historic commissioners would be.

The revolutionary aspect of neighborhood conservation districts is that they operate very much like private community associations, but they do not require unanimous consent of the property owners. The rules for forming such a district vary a great deal by state, but none that I have encountered requires unanimity of property owners, as formation of a residential private government would. In this respect, the districts are similar to other submunicipal bodies such as business improvement districts and charter schools. Neighborhood conservation districts are not, however, empowered to collect dues or assessments (as business improvement districts are), and their decisions can be reversed by city authorities (which skirts the delegation problem), though that seldom happens. (Suggestions for forming more elaborate sublocal governing associations besides those described above can be found in George Liebmann [1993], Robert Ellickson [1998], and Robert Nelson [1999].)

Just why cities allow this selective secession from their regular land use controls is not entirely clear. That city planners are wary of them is suggested by the elaborate reports and surveys that must be conducted in order to form neighborhood conservation districts. Perhaps allowing a district is just simpler than rezoning the area. Creation of some districts is often occasioned by sudden development of a permitted use that turns out to be offensive to the rest of the neighborhood, such as building a huge mansion in an otherwise modest area. Like the residential private governments surveyed by Meltzer and Cheung (2013), neighborhood conservation districts appear to be complements to zoning, not substitutes for it. In high-value residential areas, homeowners seem to want more protection for their existing neighborhoods rather than less.

2.17 Conservation Easements: Zombie Zoning

Private landowners can limit future development on their own land by giving a conservation easement to a third party. The third party, often a conservation institution organized for this purpose, such as the Nature Conservancy, then has the responsibility and legal authority to regulate development in the future according to the terms of the easement. Development is usually restricted to less than that allowed by zoning. Conservation easements have grown rapidly since the mid-1980s (Jeff Pidot 2005). Gerald Korngold (2012) sees them as a valuable private alternative to coercive public regulations like zoning, but they do present some complications.

Conservation easements are difficult to reverse. In order to qualify for a federal tax deduction for the donation, the easement must be perpetual. The U.S. Internal Revenue Service adopted this rule mainly to forestall the possibility of a donation being a simple tax avoidance scheme, wherein owners get deductions for easements they later reclaim. (Even so, more than a few easement donations end up benefiting an adjacent property owned by the donor, so that the net cost of the easement is low.) Perpetuity creates at least two difficulties. The owner of the easement (usually a land trust) must monitor it for a long time (or pass it to others who will), and the original purpose can get lost over time. The other problem is that it is very difficult to alter the easement to accommodate unforeseen events. It may turn out that the tract subject to the easements is not useful for its original purpose of, say, wildlife protection, because the wildlife have disappeared for other reasons. A later owner who would want to build a recreation area instead would find it exceedingly difficult to remove the easement's restrictions (Jessica Owley 2011).

The perpetual nature of most conservation easements is, however, useful for other purposes. Zoning that allows cluster development (as described in section 2.1) leaves the property owner with a great deal of open and potentially developable space. The local government often seeks to forestall further development by insisting that the owner establish a conservation easement. Such an easement would tie the hands of future planners who might want to rezone it for more intensive use. Developers negotiating with planning boards about issues such as wetland protection might also be required to donate easements to protect the wetland or to provide substitute wetland protections in other places. And many rural residents who worry that the rural or agricultural zoning might be changed sometime in the future often seek to acquire farmland or open space easements to assure themselves (and future buyers of their property) that things will not change.

The more problematic side of conservation easements is their tax treatment for donation purposes. An owner of a large tract of land can get several substantial tax benefits from a conservation easement. The value of the easement is deductible from federal and (most) state income taxes as a charitable deduction. The donation also reduces any estate taxes. A few states (Virginia and Colorado) also grant substantial state tax credits for donations, which in many cases actually result in net financial gains for the donor, especially since the credits can be transferred to other parties.

The largest donor benefit, however, arises from establishing inflated values of the easement donations for tax purposes. Federal tax regulations require a professional appraisal, but donors are allowed to select their own appraisers (Pidot 2005). Anyone familiar with litigation involving real estate valuations knows that both sides can find an appraiser whose methodology will support their conflicting claims. These biases are ameliorated in courts of law by having two opposing parties whose attorneys can question the quality of the other's appraisal and examine witnesses.

The IRS procedure involves none of this. The donor's appraiser is subject only to the remote possibility that the IRS will bring a charge of fraud against the donor (Erin Gisler 2009). Not only are these substantial tax expenditures a fiscal burden on the state and federal governments, but they also can be costly to the local government in terms of reduced property tax revenues (Korngold 2007). Overall they encourage a kind of private zoning process that is not subject to local review and is costly to all levels of government in terms of tax revenues foregone. And, as will be argued in chapters 7 and 8, their widespread use by developing suburbs contributes to lower than optimal population densities and urban sprawl.

2.18 Planners or Politics?

The establishment of zoning and similar land use regulations is clearly the function of the local governing body. So too are major alterations in the zoning laws. It is important to emphasize this point, because some theories of zoning seem to suppose that zoning is established by an independent authority whose goal is the efficient use of land. Economists often invoke a hypothetical "benign planner" in their normative models. Some of the planning literature seems to suggest as much by painting a picture of a farseeing planning office attempting to correct the misdeeds of the private market or to supplant it altogether.

The idea that planners and the planning profession in general should control zoning stems from movements early in the twentieth century. One placed a great deal of faith in the ability of technically trained people to solve social problems. City planning was to be part of a technocratic process, removed from partisan politics and pressures (Robert Nelson 1977). The other attempted to remove municipal decisions from party politics, which were regarded as a source of *The Shame of the Cities* according to Lincoln Steffens (1904). Together, these movements gave us the professional city manager and the nonpartisan elections of many local governments.

Despite this tradition, zoning is an eminently political process, and it may be the most important municipal function in many communities. The most common reason for municipal incorporation of suburbs is to control zoning (Richard Cion 1966; Fischel 2001). Most of the modern planning literature recognizes this. Professional planners whose ideas of good planning and zoning are at odds with those of elected officials who appoint them usually have little job security.

This is not to say that planners are unimportant. Insofar as they are often the main source of technical information, they can use this position to further their own goals. Their role is often considerable in the higher layers of land use review by state and regional governments, such as those in Oregon and Vermont. The aforementioned study of the Lexington, Kentucky, zoning board found that the lay board members accepted the great majority of professional planners' recommendations concerning zoning variances (Moore 2011). But it seems possible that the planners did a good job of divining the board members' preferences as well as the applicable law in each case.

2.19 Conclusion: *Euclid* Is Dead; Long Live *Euclid*

"Euclidean zoning" is a famous play on words in a field that is apparently desperate for some signs of lightheartedness. As will be discussed in section 3.3, the United States Supreme Court in 1926 put its imprimatur on zoning in the case of *Euclid v. Ambler*, 272 U.S. 365 (1926). The zoning law of the village of Euclid was not the first in the nation (a distinction that belongs to New York City's 1916 ordinance), but it was the first to come under review of the U.S. Supreme Court, and the Court saw that it was good. Because Euclid's entirely typical zoning map involved the geometry of city streets and more-or-less linear zone borders, the conventions of map-based zoning began to be called "Euclidean zoning," particularly by commentators who sought to upend those conventions.

Non-Euclidean zoning involves such novel devices as Planned Unit Developments, overlay zones, transferrable development rights (allowable density moved from one zone to another), transect zoning (controlling density rather than use), and mixed-use zones. These last I would call "Jane Jacobs" zones because of her advocacy (as mentioned earlier in section 2.3) of mixing residences and light commercial uses. Their common non-Euclidean element is that they are harder to indicate on a map than traditional zones such as single-family residential, multifamily residential, and business and manufacturing. Moreover, the Euclidean tradition sees collective controls as being solely those of the municipality. The latter part of this chapter has described several higher government interventions that complicate local development decisions. I also outlined new private-governance structures and procedures that allow developers and seated residents to make rules for their own neighborhoods.

The thrust of this chapter has been that non-Euclidean innovations have not significantly displaced municipal zoning. Even Donald Elliott (2008), a thoughtful critic of traditional zoning, reminds readers that "most non-Euclidean improvements explicitly or implicitly rely on Euclidean zoning as a backstop" (130). To the extent that zoning reforms have altered local practice, it is almost always in the direction of making a pro-development community less able to realize its plans. (Transect zoning, which regulates by location and size but not use, would appear to be an exception, since it does not specify uses, but, as Nicole Garnett [2013] points out, the detailed negotiations that it calls for at almost every stage of development would filter out incompatible uses, as does a similar practice in Europe, according to Sonia Hirt [2012].)

Calling the higher government reviews of zoning decisions a "double veto" system, as I did in a previous section, actually has a quaint ring to it. In many communities, especially those that are very attractive to developers, the number of potential vetoes has risen to several integers. The municipal zoning ordinance is nonetheless the first and usually most important stop for almost any developer with substantial plans.

The Euclidean map also remains preeminent. Indeed, where one's property sits on that map is one of the most crucial determinants of its value as a residence, business, or nonprofit institution. A change in zoning to a more intensive use can often increase a parcel's value by orders of magnitude. That fact alone indicates that the mantra of real estate valuation, "location, location, location," is substantially influenced by local zoning. Zoning has long been a dynamic institution, and reports of its demise have been greatly exaggerated.

CHAPTER 3

Judicial Supervision of Land Use Regulation

> In many cases that come before us at the appellate level, we really do not know what the facts are.
>
> —JUDGE JAY PLAGER, *ENVIRONMENTAL LAW* (1995)

The person who best understands the nature of zoning is a practicing lawyer with a client. The client may be a developer, a landowner, a municipality, a neighbor to a proposed development, or (much less frequently) an outsider who wants to live in the community. In all cases, the question is: What entitlement do I have to the use of some property? If I am a developer, can I build on it? If a municipal official, how much or how little can I regulate it? If a neighbor, can I prevent it from being developed or alter it to protect my property's value? If an outsider, how can I get the community to rezone it to accommodate housing that members of my group might buy?

This chapter reviews many of the considerations that lawyers face in determining these entitlements. There are so many works on the subject by lawyers that it is hardly the comparative advantage of this book to add to them. (The work on which I have most relied is the casebook of Robert Ellickson, Vicki Been, Roderick Hills, and Christopher Serkin [2013], which provides especially insightful commentary.) Instead, I shall attempt to describe some of the more important judicial principles and practices, especially their interpretation of constitutional protections, so as to point out their economic implications.

The present chapter is largely descriptive. The most discussed constitutional concept is the Fifth Amendment's conclusion that property may not be "taken without just compensation." Its application to regulation (as opposed to outright acquisition) simultaneously attracts litigants and worries land use officials. To an economist, the obligation to pay for regulation would seem to impose a price on excess regulation, and this chapter will evaluate the extent to which such a discipline is effective. The normative basis for using the Takings Clause will be taken up in chapters 6 and 9, which consider (respectively) the economic logic and the administrative costs of the "just compensation" remedy.

My overall conclusion in the present chapter is that claims regarding the constitutional rights of landowners to develop their property are long on rhetoric and short on results. What look like robust constitutional doctrines favoring property rights are costly to vindicate in the face of determined opposition. Even when development-minded landowners enjoy the support of municipal officials, the modern growth of legal procedures and the expansion of entitlements for nongovernment organizations can make development a difficult process. For reasons I hope to illuminate, courts of law have been loathe to insert themselves in local controversies.

3.1 Conflict Resolution: Local Politics or the Courts?

The previous chapter indicated that the land use powers granted to local governments by state zoning enabling acts are broad and subject to a great deal of local discretion. This sets the stage for conflict between the local government and owners and users of the land that is regulated. Such conflicts may be resolved by the political process. If local officials offend enough owners and users of land, they may be voted out of office and replaced by those who are more sympathetic to the goals of their constituents.

The other method of conflict resolution is to go to court. Litigation about land use regulation occupies a larger portion of state court time than would seem to be justified by the modest fraction of income derived from land in the Gross Domestic Product accounts. Although the exact fraction is contested, rental income from all land amounts to about 5 percent of the GDP, which is considerably less than, for instance, the transportation sector's 10 percent or health care's 18 percent. There are two reasons for land being a special source of litigation. One is land's immobility and the other (related) reason is political feedback.

A city that establishes onerous regulations on, say, the sale of alcohol may cause its purveyors to move to a different location, which may well have been the reason for the regulation. When regulation's intent is not to drive the business away, both sellers and buyers of alcohol (and related businesses like restaurants and hotels) may be unhappy to see the regulated industry depart. Officials who adopt an unpopular regulation will find their tenure in office shorter than they may have hoped.

The mobility discipline—the prospect that those subject to regulation will depart—can even work when those subject to regulation have no direct political influence. The Old Order Amish, a religious sect renowned for their adherence to horse-and-buggy technology, refuse to participate in politics or legal controversies. When legal changes threaten their way of life, they move to other states. But Amish settlements are the objects of tourism in Pennsylvania, Ohio, and Indiana, and non-Amish business people who rely on tourism are staunch defenders of the Amish. The have frequently persuaded state and federal officials to grant the Amish exceptions to environmental and labor regulations to keep them from leaving (Donald Kraybill 2001).

Many other land use regulations are not subject to this discipline. Undeveloped land that is downzoned to allow only low-intensity activities will lose much of its value, but its owners have no way of recouping that value by moving to another jurisdiction. Of course, the would-be developer of the land can move elsewhere, but the landowners or the developers who did not have sufficient foresight to purchase the land with a contingency clause for appropriate zoning cannot recoup anything by relocation. Land's immobility is the economic answer to the title question of Eduardo Peñalver's article criticizing judicial solicitude for real property, "Is Land Special?" (2004).

Because of the fixed location of land and other difficult-to-move ("real") property, its owners are apt to be closely involved in local government. Throughout the nineteenth century, this meant that enterprising business owners and farmers were the dominant factions within most American localities (Hardy Wickwar 1970). But as homeownership began to be the dominant form of urban housing in the twentieth century, the most numerous owners of land in almost every city were residential homeowners.

Homestead land is typically held for quiet enjoyment, not entrepreneurial reasons. Thus, the interests of owners of land who were eager to develop it or use it for nonresidential purposes were subordinated to the interests of homeowners in most American suburbs (Fischel 2001). By the twenty-first century, the land use policies of an increasing number of central cities, including New York, also began to be influenced by homeowner interests (Been, Madar, and McDonnell 2014). Homeowners may have owned stores and factories, but their places of business were now often in a different town from the one where they resided and voted. The division of owners' interests combined with the fixity of location made it more difficult to resolve land use disputes by the ordinary give and take of politics. Thus, the courts became an important forum for resolution of land use disputes by the middle of the twentieth century.

3.2 State Courts Share Common Ground on Zoning

Zoning is the product of state law, which might make one think that there are 50 distinct sets of rules. There are, but it is not necessary to study in detail the laws of every state to make useful generalizations about land use regulation. The formal underpinning for this broad approach was the widespread adoption of the Standard State Zoning Enabling Act (to be discussed in more detail in section 4.5), which was first promulgated in the 1920s. But much of zoning law's regularity among states and localities is behavioral. Voters and public officials learn from the mistakes and successes of other places, and planning professionals are nationally mobile and attuned to worldwide trends. The particular applications of zoning are endlessly varied, but the overall framework—the primacy of maps, local political control, multifaceted regulations, the possibility of change, and citizen participation—is remarkably uniform across the nation.

The source of uniformity of judicial zoning decisions is similar to that of statutory regularities, as just described. Court opinions are not coordinated with other states by anything like a model statute. Instead, the coordination comes from the state constitutional provisions that litigants invoke, and these are similar throughout the states. The similarities among state constitutions are in part the historical product of congressional review of proposed constitutions at the time they were admitted, but most migrants to western territories were happy to copy the constitutions of the states from which they came (Paul Gates 1968; Andrew Morriss 1995).

Cross-state similarities are also promoted by the method of common-law adjudication, which seeks to fit the controversy at hand into templates based on previous decisions. The most authoritative previous decisions are, of course, those of the state's own court or (where relevant) those of the U.S. Supreme Court. But where in-state precedents are not quite on point, the common law encourages judges to look to other state courts' decisions. (The term "foreign precedent" usually refers to other states.) Since land use law generates a substantial and continuing body of decisions, it is possible to think of the states as generating a national framework for zoning. Courses in land use in law schools in Maine, Washington, Arizona, and Florida can all be organized around the same casebook.

A common national framework does not, however, preclude important variations among the states in their pattern of decisions. (Dennis Coyle [1993] offers insightful analyses of the variations; see also Ellickson et al. [2013].) The California Supreme Court was noted (some would say notorious) for its systematic undermining of developers' interests beginning in the 1970s (Joseph DiMento et al. 1980). Pennsylvania is regarded as a pro-developer state, a reputation shared with Illinois. New Jersey's Supreme Court has been especially aggressive in combating exclusionary zoning, a practice that has gathered many admirers in the academy but few imitators on the benches of other states. To the extent that these differences can be thought of as "natural experiments" (and not the inevitable product of geographic or historical factors), they can be useful to economists in evaluating the effects of various zoning regimes. But for now the "state courts" will be regarded as a single collective entity.

A variation among the states that is sometimes mentioned is their adherence to "Dillon's rule." John Dillon was a judge and commentator who advanced the idea that delegations of state authority to local governments should be closely reviewed by the courts (Dillon 1871; Joan Williams 1986). The counter to Dillon's narrow view was that of Judge Thomas Cooley (1868), who inferred from the Constitution a right to local self-governance that states should not interfere with. Both men wrote before the invention of zoning enormously expanded local government's powers and implicitly embraced Cooley's vision (Carol Rose 1989; Fischel 2001). A Brookings Institution study found little evidence that application of Dillon's rule actually inhibited zoning initiatives (Richardson, Gough, and Puentes 2003). But state judges who cannot find a better reason to overturn a local ordinance will still sometimes refer to Dillon's rule and thereby encourage researchers to compare regulatory outcomes in "Dillon's Rule" states to those that supposedly lack this protean doctrine.

A possible reason for similarities among state courts may be attributed to the role of the U.S. Supreme Court. Because state and federal constitutional pronouncements about property are similar, the supremacy of the federal courts can bring a good deal of uniformity to them. It certainly does in matters concerning freedom of religion and criminal procedure, among the many aspects of the U.S. Bill of Rights that have been deemed by the U.S. Supreme Court to be incorporated by the Fourteenth Amendment as rights that states (not just the federal government) may not abridge.

Because both the Fifth and Fourteenth Amendments are protective of property rights, there is textual justification for an active federal role. Yet the Supreme Court has been reluctant to take zoning cases, for reasons suggested in later sections. Even when it has taken them, it has left far more discretion to the states (including both courts and legislatures) than it has in situations involving other constitutionally protected rights. Indeed, the Court often seems more influenced by an apparent consensus among the states. This is not to say that its pronouncements are unimportant. Even when the U.S. Supreme Court indicates that states may go their own ways, the few decisions it does hand down have normative and political influence beyond their exact holdings, as will be demonstrated by the grandmother of the zoning cases, *Euclid v. Ambler*, 272 U.S. 365 (1926).

3.3 *Euclid v. Ambler*: The States Get in Line with Zoning

The city of Euclid is an independent suburb of Cleveland, about ten miles northeast of the city's central business district. In the early 1920s, Euclid was still a largely undeveloped residential community (then called a village), with most of its land in farms or open space. It nonetheless anticipated that it would soon by engulfed by the suburban expansion of the adjacent city of Cleveland. In 1922, Euclid adopted its first zoning ordinance, based largely on the New York City ordinance of 1916. That a tiny suburb (population under 10,000) could take New York's ordinance as its model surely indicates how elastic zoning can be. Though proponents of zoning conceived of the ordinance as regulating city land use, it quickly spread to the suburbs, and the city of Euclid was not unusual, as a contemporary survey confirmed (Newman Baker 1927).

Euclid's 1922 zoning map is available at the city's website, and it looks sensible. Industry and commerce are zoned next to the two railroads that split the community and along the major thoroughfares, and residential zones are near Lake Erie (on the northwest side) and in the low hills on Euclid's southeast border. As is the case with most other municipalities, Euclid's map built on preexisting patterns of development and anticipated subdivision activity. Zoning's innovation was the regularization of expected development, not the creation of an idealized city plan.

But Euclid's zoning did not satisfy everyone. The new ordinance zoned part of the property owned by the Ambler Realty Company for residential use only, as shown in figure 3.1, adapted from the city's original map. (The

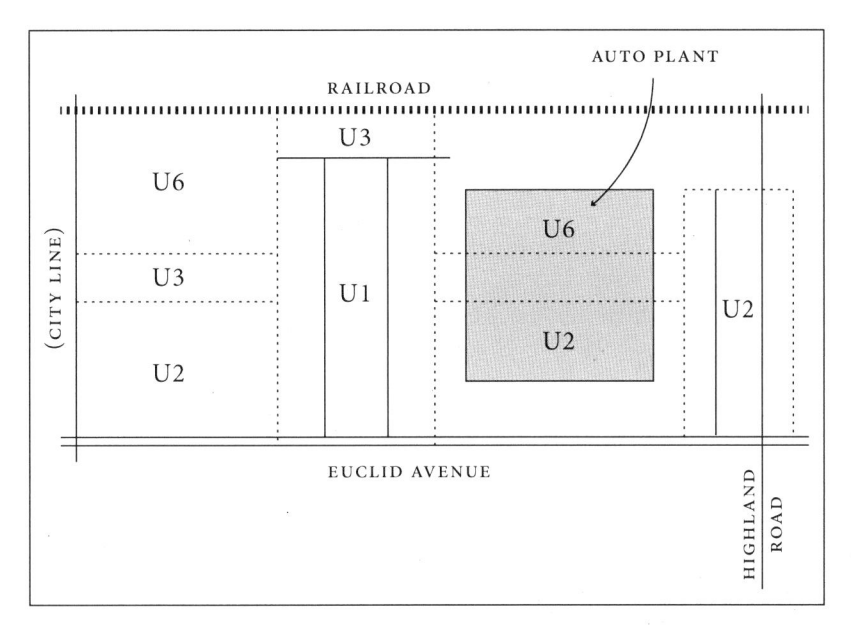

FIGURE 3.1 *Euclid v. Ambler* **Site Map**

tract owned by Ambler contains the shaded area designated "auto plant," a subsequent development whose history will be described presently.) The village's planners hoped that the part of Ambler's tract (and others) that abutted Euclid Avenue, designated "U-2" on the map, would continue the high-end residential development that seemed to be stretching toward it from the city of Cleveland. Ambler, on the other hand, had purchased the property in the expectation of selling it for industrial use.

Ambler argued—and its argument was not seriously contested—that zoning exclusively for residential use reduced its property's value to about a quarter of its previous, unzoned value. I would actually contest this finding. Ambler had attacked the constitutionality of the entire ordinance, so the village's attorney did not bother to get an appraisal of Ambler's holdings. The basis for my suspicion that Ambler's land was not seriously devalued is that Ambler also owned the parcel adjacent to the one in question and was developing it for residential purposes, not industrial ones (Michael Wolf 2008). The tract was the U-1 (single-family) subdivision in figure 3.1, to the left of what became the auto plant. Had the alleged 75 percent reduction in value been realistic, it is difficult to see why Ambler would not have developed the property right next to it for industrial uses as well before the adoption of the zoning ordinance. (It could have been that Ambler was developing worker housing along with its expected industrial use, but this would have made sense only in an isolated community where workers had to live near their jobs, not in a metropolitan area with easy commuting by streetcar and motor bus.)

Ambler's case against Euclid's zoning was tried in Federal District Court of Northern Ohio before Judge David Westenhaver. Ambler invoked the Fourteenth Amendment's Due Process and Equal Protection Clauses as well as the Takings Clause of the Fifth Amendment. In what is now called a "facial challenge" to the ordinance, Ambler's counsel sought to have Euclid's zoning struck down entirely. Judge Westenhaver obliged. He added to his opinion what some commentators now regard as a prophetic pronouncement: "[T]he result to be accomplished [by Euclid's law] is to classify the population and segregate them according to their income or situation in life" (*Ambler v. Euclid*, 297 F. 307, 316 [1924]). Concerns about zoning's exclusionary possibilities are not new.

Euclid's federal trial court loss drew the attention of zoning's national defenders, especially those in New York, whose ordinance Euclid had imitated. If Euclid's ordinance had been struck down in its entirety, New York's and many others were in peril. The Ohio village appealed to the U.S. Supreme Court. The village's feisty attorney, James Metzenbaum (who also chaired Euclid's zoning commission, which drew up the ordinance), appeared to have lost the case at oral argument. But Metzenbaum convinced the justices to allow further briefs and a second oral argument—both unusual concessions by the Court. With considerable help from a brief by one of zoning's national pioneers, Alfred Bettman, Euclid got a hole-in-one on its Mulligan round. Drawing analogies to nuisance law, the U.S. Supreme Court ruled that zoning was a legitimate exercise of the police power so long as it had some "reasonable relation" to the promotion of the purposes mentioned in the Standard State Zoning Enabling Act—namely, health, safety, morals, and general welfare.

Zoning's national advocates were pleased to have won in court, but what most got their attention was that the author of the opinion was Justice George Sutherland, who, like several others on the Court, was willing to question the merits of much economic legislation; he later became famous as a foe of New Deal legislation (Hadley Arkes 1994). In his *Euclid* opinion, Sutherland broke with his conservative brethren and gave local zoning his qualified approval. Sutherland's opinion is widely regarded as having pushed most of the wavering state courts, which could still rule against zoning on state constitutional grounds, into the position of approving zoning.

3.4 The Cautionary Example of New Jersey

One brave court, the Supreme Court of New Jersey, continued its opposition to the zoning-enforced separation of residential and commercial uses even after the *Euclid* decision. In *Oxford Construction v. Orange*, 137 A. 545 (1927), the New Jersey court insisted, as it had in other cases, that construction of facilities that the court viewed as being innocent of harmful effects should be given building permits notwithstanding an otherwise legitimate zoning ordinance. (Oxford had sought to build an apartment building in a single-family zone in the city of Orange.) The court's intransigence (or principled stand, depending on your point of view) appears to have been the last straw for the residents of that most suburban of states. Within a year, New Jersey voters overwhelmingly approved a state constitutional amendment specifically endorsing the kind of zoning of which the court had disapproved.

In a later case, *Lumund v. Rutherford*, 73 A.2d 545 (N.J. 1950), the New Jersey court briefly reviewed the history of its zoning decisions and as much as admitted that the 1927 court had been trumped by the amendment:

> The courts of this State were reluctant to recognize zoning insofar as it sought to divide a municipality into districts for various uses, such as residential, mercantile and industrial. Such use zoning was considered to be an unreasonable exercise of the police power.... That attitude continued in our judicial opinions for several years until October 18, 1927, when an amendment was made to the [state] Constitution...

That New Jersey's 1927 constitutional amendment was aimed at previous court decisions was also indicated by an editorial in the June 1927 *National Municipal Review*, which urged passage of the amendment: "Readers will recall New Jersey as the horrible example of a state whose courts have been consistently negative respecting the broader aspects of zoning" (353).

A similar popular reaction to judicial hostility to zoning seems to have occurred in Georgia. In *Vulcan Material Co. v. Griffith*, 114 S.E.2d 29 (Ga. 1960) a judge made the rueful (and hyperbolic) claim that he was unable to protect private property from zoning burdens because of constitutional change: "But the people by their votes amended or changed this constitutional guardianship of private property, and in the process stripped their judiciary of power to protect it, as had theretofore been the case. By the constitutional change the people voluntarily subjected their property to the unlimited control and regulation of legislative departments" (*id.* at 31–32). The *Vulcan* opinion does not mention the specific date that zoning was enshrined in the Georgia Constitution, but a case that it cites, *McCord v. Bond* 165 S.E. 590 (Ga. 1932), notes that Atlanta and several other cities were given constitutional authority to zone in a 1927 amendment, and authority was later extended to most other jurisdictions. Nineteen twenty-seven was a good year for zoning.

My reason for drawing attention to these cases is to caution reformers against putting too much hope in the judiciary to make wide-ranging reforms of zoning. We have zoning not because Alfred Bettman turned the tide in *Euclid* or because Justice Sutherland forgot his conservative values. (I argue elsewhere that his endorsement of zoning was actually consistent with the view of local government endorsed by Sutherland's mentor at the University of Michigan Law School, Thomas M. Cooley [Fischel 2001].) We have zoning because a large majority of voters almost everywhere want it. Chapter 5 will offer a theory of why zoning did not appear until the 1910s (newly inexpensive trucks and buses played a large role), but the remainder of the present chapter will review the judicial decisions that have tried to rein in what many regard as zoning's excesses and shortcomings.

3.5 Racial Zoning Was Struck Down

Before addressing post-*Euclid* zoning jurisprudence, it is worth a look back at an earlier zoning decision that almost everyone now agrees the Supreme Court got right: *Buchanan v. Warley*, 245 U.S. 60 (1917). Following the lead of Baltimore, Maryland, the city of Louisville, Kentucky, as well as several others had adopted a zoning law that explicitly attempted to segregate blacks from whites by neighborhood (Garrett Power 1983). Such efforts had been triggered by the "great migration" of southern blacks to cities in the early twentieth century, a move that provided them with both job opportunities and opportunities to be excluded from the housing market. The exclusionary laws were pressed by modern progressives who often excoriated the profit-driven activities of landlords who would rent to blacks (David Bernstein 1998).

Under Louisville's ordinance, property owners in a city block occupied by a majority of whites (as most presumably were) could not sell or rent to blacks. To make the racial zoning law sound neutral and presumably to address the "separate but equal" criterion endorsed by the Supreme Court in *Plessy v. Ferguson*, 163 U.S. 537 (1896), owners of property in neighborhoods that were majority black could not sell or rent to whites, either. The stretch for neutrality extended to exceptions: Black servants who lived in the homes of whites were exempt from the exclusion rules, and white servants who lived in the homes of their black employers were likewise allowed to stay. No estimate was provided as to how many homes fit the latter category.

The Kentucky Court of Appeals had little trouble upholding what we would now characterize as racial apartheid as a reasonable exercise of the police power. South Africa's apartheid system was actually a model that Louisville, among other American cities, had studied, according to Benno Schmidt (1982). The purpose of the law, according to the Kentucky court, was "to prevent conflict and ill-feeling between the white and colored races."

The U.S. Supreme Court reversed the decision. Unanimously. Justice William Day's opinion stressed that the Fourteenth Amendment of the Constitution had been motivated in part because newly freed slaves had been subjected to laws that deprived them of the right to own property. The Court conceded that it was powerless to alter racial attitudes that caused "ill-feeling" by whites, but Louisville's law involved an abrogation of property rights, and that was one area that the Court did have the authority to control.

Buchanan v. Warley is nowadays regarded as correct but quaint for its property-oriented reasoning, but in its day, its holding was remarkably effective in halting the spread of legally compelled segregation schemes. Even southern state courts fell into line and struck down laws similar to those of Louisville (Bernstein 1998). One virtue of the Court's focus on property rights was that it gave a remedy to parties in a good position to enforce it—namely, owners of property in the jurisdiction. While some owners might be intimidated by white neighbors into withholding sales or rentals from blacks, others would find the higher rents and prices offered to be irresistible, and the residential segregation plan would fail. (White real estate interests were important allies of the National Association for the Advancement of Colored People in opposing these laws, according to Garret Power [1983].) Had the Court's remedy been given to prospective tenants or buyers, as modern federal fair-housing statutes do, any attempt to undermine Louisville's racial law effectively would have required continued litigation by the newly formed NAACP (which had contrived the case) and diverted much of its resources from other activities.

3.6 Private Covenants as Substitutes for Racial Zoning

The other reason for public acceptance of *Warley* was that private substitutes were available to discourage blacks from buying or renting in white areas of both the South and the North. The least violent of these was the private covenant, in which blacks as well as Jews, Italians, and other unwelcome minorities could be excluded. Because covenants did not involve the active participation of the state (as zoning did), the U.S. Supreme Court did not find them similarly offensive until *Shelley v. Kramer*, 334 U.S. 1 (1948), which finally held that the use of the courts to enforce such restrictions was state action and thereby constitutionally unacceptable. (*Shelley* is still regarded as a remote outlier in the Court's "state action" jurisprudence, which it uses to establish boundaries for litigation based on the Fourteenth Amendment.)

Private covenants were not, however, a perfect substitute for racial zoning. As I argued in section 2.15, creating covenants in built-up neighborhoods is extremely difficult. Holdouts are common, as are the difficulties of merely locating property owners. (See also Carol Rose's [2004] historical review of the practice for evidence of difficulties specific to racial covenants.) Covenants are easiest to set up in greenfield developments (which were previously open land) in new suburbs, where a single owner does not have to deal with holdouts. Since blacks in the early twentieth century were usually migrating to the built-up parts of central cities (where they could walk to work or use public transportation), fearful urban whites could not easily establish covenants. Even when one white neighborhood overcame the "free riders" who wanted to retain the right to rent or sell their property to whoever made the highest offer, racial covenants covered only that neighborhood, not those that bordered it.

Evidence for the limited effectiveness of covenants is that many communities that already had substantial coverage by private covenants (not necessarily related to race or ethnicity) were nonetheless eager to adopt zoning. The preamble to Euclid's 1922 zoning ordinance mentions the existence of private covenants on much of its territory, and several nearby communities with covenants also adopted zoning (Gerald Korngold 2001). Suburban demand for zoning persisted long after racial zoning had been struck down, so it seems unreasonable to suppose that ordinary zoning was motivated primarily by a desire for racial segregation. Zoning was eagerly embraced by cities in the North that were not affected by the Great Migration and where, as a result, racial concerns were minor.

The Court's holding in *Warley* caused considerable consternation and anxiety among zoning's advocates, even those without obvious racial animus (Power 1983). The decision played a role in the later lower court decision in *Ambler v. Euclid*. Judge Westenhaver used *Warley* to fortify his reversal of Euclid's zoning law, even though Euclid's ordinance made no reference to race. He reasoned that if the Supreme Court disallowed zoning that prevented blacks from occupying land next to whites, it should also disallow zoning that prevented industry from occupying land in residential districts. The unsavory but commonly understood implication of this argument was that having black neighbors was at least as offensive as having industrial neighbors. To zoning's advocates, it looked like the Court might extend its invalidation of Louisville's apartheid ordinance to general zoning schemes.

But the Supreme Court's property-based approach to *Warley* made it easy to distinguish ordinary zoning from Louisville's scheme. The *Warley* Court emphasized that the right to acquire and dispose of one's property was a core principle of the Fourteenth Amendment. Without it, recalcitrant southern states might be able to reinstitute a close substitute for slavery by holding blacks in a property-deprived state of peonage. The Louisville ordinance at issue in *Warley* clearly interfered with both acquisition and disposition. Nothing in Euclid's ordinance or any ordinary zoning ordinance interfered with the alienation of property. Ambler's undeveloped acreage might have become less valuable as a result of its being zoned in part for residential (rather than industrial) use, but Ambler could nonetheless sell its land to anyone, and the buyer would have the same rights (or lack of rights) that Ambler did.

As it turned out, the *Warley* decision did nothing to turn back the tide of zoning, and racism remained a deeply embedded aspect of American land use (Massey and Rothwell 2009). But *Warley* did keep explicitly apartheid regulations off the books and thus facilitated African Americans' gaining an urban toehold during the early twentieth century, in contrast to the banishment of blacks from cities in apartheid South Africa (Higginbotham, Higginbotham, and Ngcobo 1990). The growing political influence of African Americans in the big cities of northern states was an important catalyst for American civil rights legislation in the 1960s (Gerald Rosenberg 1991).

3.7 Euclid's Zoning Was Durable

According to the online *Encyclopedia of Cleveland History*, Ambler's property was actually rezoned for industrial use during World War II as an aircraft-parts manufacturing plant. (It is shown on the overlay on the site map in figure 3.1 as the "auto plant.") One can imagine that Ambler Realty or its successor in title lobbied for the zoning change to accommodate the national emergency. The industrial site at 20001 Euclid Avenue was converted after the war to an automobile body assembly plant, and in the 1970s the plant was used for other automobile-related manufacturing. After the plant was shut for good in 1993, the building was repurposed for (among other tenants) "the Sports Plant," which offers a variety of indoor recreation activities by the city and various private organizations.

The Ambler tract's history illustrates the flexibility—for better or for worse—of zoning compared to private covenants, which surely would have stood in the way of the tract's conversion from residential to industrial during wartime. Focus on the Ambler property's industrial transformation, though, gives a somewhat misleading view of Euclid's land use regulation. The most remarkable aspect of Euclid's twenty-first century zoning map is how much the present version (available on the city's website) looks like the original 1922 map.

Industries rose and fell; an interstate highway bisected the community; the population grew from 4,000 to 48,000. Yet Euclid's modern ordinance still has most of the same lines dividing zones U-1 (single family), U-2 (two-family), U-3 (multifamily), and U-4, U-5, and U-6 (commercial and industrial zones). The lines run along the same streets in most cases. Even the classification abbreviations (U-1, and so on) are the same as the original (and different from most modern ordinances). Euclid is not an affluent suburb (the affluent have moved still farther away from Cleveland), but, for better or for worse, it is hard to believe that the city would look the same today if it had not adopted zoning in 1922.

3.8 *Nectow v. Cambridge*: Telescopes under a Microscope

The Supreme Court reaffirmed zoning in several cases soon after *Euclid*, with the supposedly archconservative Justice Sutherland writing for the majority in *Goreib v. Fox*, 274 U.S. 603 (1927), and *Zahn v. Board of Public Works of Los Angeles*, 274 U.S. 325 (1927). Sutherland's embrace of zoning was not a temporary lapse in attention or change in his values. But in 1928, when the Court took another case that originated in Cambridge, Massachusetts, Justice Sutherland's opinion gave the complaining landowner a victory. In *Nectow v. Cambridge*, 277 U.S. 183 (1928), a real estate developer named Saul Nectow objected

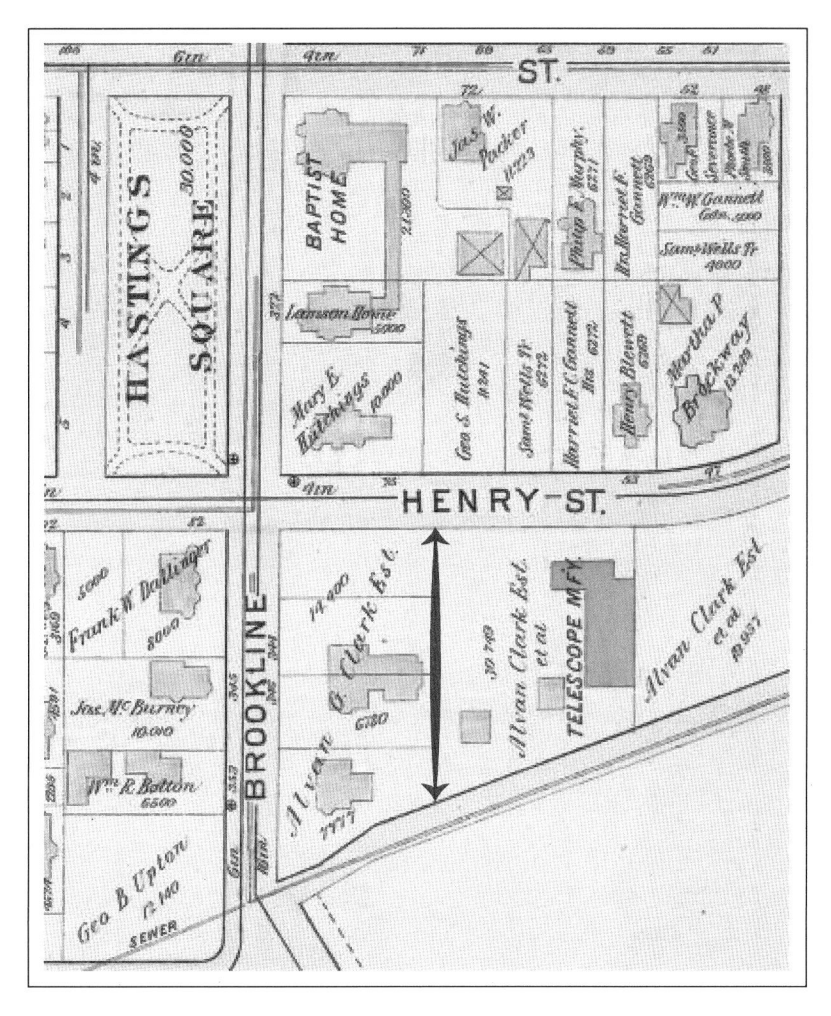

FIGURE 3.2 *Nectow v. Cambridge* Site Map
Source: G. W. Bromley and Co. *Atlas of the City of Cambridge, Massachusetts*. Philadelphia: G. W. Bromley and Co., 1903.

to the city's zoning of part of his property for residential rather than industrial use under its original 1924 zoning law. The Cambridge zoning looks like a smaller-scale version of the one that applied to Ambler's property in Euclid in that only part of Nectow's tract was zoned residential.

Figure 3.2 shows a map of the property at issue as it appeared in 1903. The trapezoidal tract in the lower right part of the map, to the right (east) of Brookline Street (which I take as running north-south), was owned at that time by the estate of Alvan Clark. Some background on Clark and his telescope factory is necessary to understand the nuances of the controversy.

Alvan Clark was born in 1804 and made a living as an artist specializing in portraits. (Details of his life are given in the biography of his company by Warner and Ariail [1995].) The development of photography diminished the demand for portraits, and in 1846 Clark began grinding lenses for telescopes, for which his artistic eye and manual skill were well suited. His business prospered such that in 1860 he bought the tract of land shown in the bottom-right quadrant of figure 3.2 and built his factory and the larger of the two houses that fronted Brookline Street. He built a second home to the south of the original in 1874. The two smaller squares next to the factory may have indicated the telescope test-mount and another outbuilding, but they did not figure in the controversy. (Maps and property records that I have relied on are available online at the Cambridge Historical Commission's site, http://www2.cambridgema.gov/historic/library.html. Especially useful are Christopher Hail's Cambridge Buildings and Architects database and the Bromley Atlases of various dates.)

Clark was joined in his business by his two sons, Alvan Graham and George, and they and their families lived in the two homes on Brookline Street, the larger of which was a two-family house. The Clarks specialized in refractive telescopes, the type that require a finely polished lens to focus the light of a distant object, rather than reflective telescopes, which use concave mirrors for focusing. Together they fashioned many of the most famous telescopes of their time, including those at the University of Chicago's Yerkes Observatory and the Lick Observatory of the University of California. The Clarks' numerous astronomical discoveries (including the companion star of Sirius) and instrument advances garnered them honors from heads of states and academic institutions.

The two homes along Brookline Street were especially convenient for the three Clark families, given their occupation. Almost everyone walked to work in that period. Their very short commute to work enabled the Clarks to do nighttime tests of their telescopes on the special mount they had constructed between their homes and the factory. It also allowed them to safeguard their valuable lenses. The senior Clark had an alarm system that connected the factory with his bedroom.

The factory itself used steam power for its machines, but it was actually a fairly modest affair. The larger telescopes were made to order, and the Clarks employed no more than a dozen skilled craftsmen and mechanics. Their operations probably had little adverse effect on the nearby neighbors. Warner and Ariail (1995) describe the factory's grounds as "covered with grass and beds of flowers. The factory itself was an unpretentious two-story brick structure, about forty feet long by twenty-five feet wide, with an ell of the same width and thirty feet long" (17).

Alvan Clark died in 1887, and his two sons continued to run the business. But they died relatively young (within ten years of their father), and longtime employees ran the business on behalf of the surviving families. In 1901, the Clark estate incorporated the business, and its principals apparently chose not to live in the Clark houses on Brookline Street. Telescopes continued to be manufactured on the site until 1936, when the factory was razed, but the business had slowly declined as improved reflective telescopes displaced the refractive telescopes in which the firm specialized. Sometime before 1916, the Clark estate sold the entire tract to William P. Abbott, who, in turn, sold it to Saul Nectow in 1920. The Clark telescope business continued producing instruments at the site until 1933 (presumably as lessees), when it was bought by another company, which in 1936 moved all operations to a site in Somerville.

The two Clark houses on Brookline Street met an earlier fate. According to the master appointed by the Massachusetts court (whose pivotal role in the case will be described presently), the houses had been rented and were not well maintained. According to Cambridge property records, Nectow had the southerly house on Brookline Street torn down in 1921, and he demolished the main house in 1925, the year after the city's first zoning law was adopted.

3.9 Cambridge's First Zoning Law Divided Nectow's Land

Nectow acquired the tract when Cambridge, like many other cities, was considering its first zoning law. In 1918, as part of a general overhaul of its constitution, Massachusetts added a clause, Article 60, which authorized zoning. The clause was not controversial, nor was it a response, as it was in New Jersey (described in section 3.4 above), to a series of hostile court decisions. Massachusetts decisions that later mentioned Article 60 actually suggested that it might not have been needed to legitimize zoning, and the commentator reporting its adoption regarded it as an "obvious" response to urban problems (Lawrence Evans 1921, 222). The state legislature approved a general zoning enabling act in 1920. Cambridge was not the first city in the Commonwealth to adopt a comprehensive zoning law, but it was not far behind others with its 1924 ordinance.

According to my online research, two Cambridge newspapers, the *Tribune* and *Chronicle*, had an average of seven or eight articles per year on zoning from 1919 to 1923 (and none before). These reported on the numerous public meetings that preceded zoning's adoption. Arguments for zoning emphasized the need to prevent the invasion of industrial and commercial uses in residential neighborhoods. At one meeting in 1921, the city assessor, one of three speakers, urged the protection of property values: "We have seen factories creep into residential districts and stores misplaced, thereby depreciating the valuation of the surrounding real estate" (*Cambridge Chronicle*, December 3, 1921).

Once zoning was adopted, Cambridge drew lines to divide residential from commercial and industrial property. Like those of other zoned cities, the lines followed existing uses where they had been established. If a neighborhood was predominantly residential, it was zoned to stay that way, with nonconforming uses allowed to persist but not expand. (Section 5.11 will discuss Los Angeles's earlier attempt to expel nonconforming businesses.)

The zoning line at issue in *Nectow* divided the Clark parcel between residential and industrial districts. Cambridge drew the dividing line on the north-south border between the lots with the two large houses and the lot with the telescope factory. I have superimposed a double-arrow line on figure 3.2 to indicate the border's placement. Parcels on both sides of Brookline Street were zoned residential, as were all of the lots north of Henry Street.

To the south of Clark's parcel was more industrial land (its buildings are not shown on the map in figure 3.2). Until 1913 the south parcel was used by the Norcross Construction Company, but in that year it was developed by the Ford Motor Company as an assembly plant for Model T cars and trucks. The Ford plant still stands but has been repurposed many times—once as a facility for the Polaroid Corporation—and is now a high-tech business incubator owned by the Massachusetts Institute of Technology, whose main campus is about a mile to the northeast.

The new Ford plant undoubtedly increased the demand for nearby land by businesses that supplied the plant. As nearly as I can tell, Saul Nectow was a one-shot land speculator in Cambridge. His name appears on no other property records of the period, and his main occupation seems to have been that of a manager and sometime-owner in the New England leather and shoe industry. Before zoning was adopted, Nectow entered into a contract to sell the entire parcel (including vacant lots to the east of the telescope factory) for $63,000 for industrial purposes. The would-be buyer backed out, however, when he learned that under the zoning ordinance, the lots along Brookline Street could be used only for residential purposes.

3.10 Nectow Gets a Friendly Master in Court

Nectow's attorneys were surely aware that a facial attack on the entire ordinance would be unproductive after the *Euclid* decision. Mr. Nectow complained instead only about the zoning as it applied to his own land. He diligently objected to the zoning classification when it was passed and requested an exception from the city's building office. (Zoning boards of appeal had not yet become established by all ordinances.) All to no avail. He then took his grievance to the court system.

In *Nectow v. Cambridge*, 260 Mass. 441 (1927), the state's highest court upheld Cambridge's zoning classification, just as it had done in recent challenges to other cities' zoning. Perhaps because the court conceded the case was "close to the line" (*id.* at 448), it went to the trouble of appointing a special master—a nonjudicial expert—to conduct an on-site investigation. (There appears to have been no lower court trial.) The court's summary of the master's report reads as if it had been commissioned by Mr. Nectow, who sought to have the residential designation overturned.

The master pointed out that the nearby Ford plant was, as the Massachusetts court put it, "noisy, and ... sometimes run at night" (260 Mass. at 444). A railroad siding divided the two properties, and soap-manufacturing factories in the vicinity emitted "bad odors." (Modern visitors may not realize that Cambridge was an industrial town well into the twentieth century, and MIT students of the 1950s were said to have been accustomed to pungent odors from industries near the campus [*MIT Technology Review*, December 21, 2010].) A new warehouse used by a grocery company had recently been built on the eastern part of Nectow's industrially zoned property, which Nectow had sold for $30,000 after his earlier deal had fallen through. He retained, however, the lots containing the telescope factory and the now-demolished homes on Brookline Street.

The view by the master from Brookline Street to the east and south must have been bleak, lacking the now-demolished houses and the "grass and beds of flowers" that the Clarks had nurtured during their occupation as telescope makers. The master found that "no practical use can be made of the land in question for residential purposes, because, among other reasons herein related, there would not be adequate return on the amount of any investment for the development of the property" (260 Mass. at 445). Most damning to Cambridge's classification was the master's conclusion: "I am satisfied that the districting of the plaintiff's land in a residence district would not promote the health, safety, convenience, and general welfare of the inhabitants of that part of the defendant city, taking into account the natural development thereof and the character of the district and the resulting benefit to accrue to the whole city, and I so find" (*Id.* at 445).

Although the Massachusetts court conceded that "it is difficult if not impossible to differentiate the material and dominant characteristics of the automobile factory and the plaintiff's other adjoining land from those of the locus [the house lots along Brookline Street]" (260 Mass. at 444), the justices unanimously held for the city. The court did not specifically disavow the master's report, but it noted (correctly) that "The locus, so far as it ever has been improved, has been devoted exclusively to residential purposes" (*id.* at 447).

The court mentioned that the city had plans (not then finalized) to widen Brookline Street, which would reduce the depths of the residential lots from 100 feet to 65 feet, and then anticipated an objection by stating, "If it is thought that the locus is too narrow, there is nothing to prevent the plaintiff from adding to the depth of the locus by land from his remaining tract" (260 Mass. at 447). Zoning of the remaining tract was for "unrestricted" use. In the cumulative zoning that Cambridge and many other cities initially used, residential structures could be built in industrial areas, though not vice versa. The court also gave a shrug to the necessity of line drawing: "If there is to be zoning at all, the dividing line must be drawn somewhere" (*id.*).

The U.S. Supreme Court took the master's remarks as more authoritative than the decision of the Massachusetts court, and in a five-page opinion it sided with Mr. Nectow, who then got the zoning line that he wanted. One hopes that he savored his win, for it was the last time the Court did anything like it for the rest of the century. The Court declined to decide another zoning case until the late 1960s, and even after that, the sparse landowner victories never followed the *Nectow* line.

Reading the *Nectow* opinion, one can perhaps understand why later courts have not accepted similar cases. The justices spread out a map of Cambridge showing its zoning classifications, and on the basis of a report by a special master whom they did not appoint and with whom they had no apparent contact, they decided to overturn the Cambridge planning board's decision as to where to draw a line on that map.

The master's conclusion that "no practical use can be made of the land in question for residential purposes" seems wrong. The Massachusetts court noted that the locus was worth $8,000 as zoned for residential. That was not a trivial amount in 1928—it was more than three times the average U.S. family income—and it can only have derived from the prospect of some viable residential use. The master himself noted that the rest of the residences in the neighborhood, to the west of Brookline Street and north of Henry Street, were "all in good condition and well kept" (260 Mass. at 619).

But why wasn't Brookline Street a more reasonable dividing line, as the master apparently believed? City streets are poor borders for dividing industry from residences. It is usually better for the industrial activity to face the backyards of the adjacent homes (as Cambridge's original zoning had required) rather than fronting them across the street (as they did after *Nectow* was decided). Residences do have fronts and backs, and most owners put more effort into decorating and maintaining their front facades and lawns.

A front entrance that faces an unattractive use across the street loses much of its "curb appeal," as modern real estate salespeople would put it. Having an ungainly neighbor adjacent to the back yard instead permits the homeowner to adopt mitigation strategies, such as high fences, shrubs, and strategically placed outbuildings, which would be less practical (or not allowed) in the front yard. Cambridge's original zoning did impose some costs on Nectow, but it surely would have conferred nontrivial benefits on the immediate residential neighborhood, contrary to the master's categorical conclusion.

3.11 Looking Forward and Backward from the Nectow Site

Nectow's disputed land lay vacant until 1947. It is now occupied by a low-rise MIT warehouse at 350 Brookline St. (MIT acquired the building after it was built.) The structure and its parking lot cover the entire area formerly occupied by the Clarks' homes and their factory. The MIT warehouse is not a neighborhood asset, but neither is it an eyesore. (I have visited the site, and Google Earth's Streetview does it justice.) Trees and shrubs are planted in the shallow setbacks to partly shield the view from homes across the street. Most of the homes shown on the 1903 map are still there. The warehouse's entrance, loading dock, and parking lot are on the east side of the building, away from the residential fronts of Henry Street and Brookline Street.

It is possible that the building's low rise and discreet operation are the product of conditions subsequently put on the original "unrestricted" industrial zone by the City of Cambridge. Current zoning of the building and a mile-long slice of industrial territory to the northeast encourages the conversion of grandfathered industrial uses to mixed-use residential. Progress on these conversions may be slowed by Cambridge's eagerness to include developer-subsidized affordable housing in the area. It is not impossible, though, that a century after *Nectow*, the disputed property will again become residential.

My discoveries about *Nectow* foreshadow my thesis about the origins of zoning (Fischel 2004a), which I will advance at greater length in chapter 5. The master appointed by the Massachusetts court concluded that Nectow's industrial classification would not harm public welfare "taking into account the natural development thereof and the character of the district" (260 Mass. at 445). In this respect, the master was assuming that the industrial district would inevitably spread into adjacent residential neighborhoods.

My thesis is that invasions by industry and commerce into residential districts changed from being occasional episodes to becoming so frequent as to amount to pervasive risks. The cause was the rapid development of low-cost motor freight in the early twentieth century, which liberated business from ties to central business districts. Industry no longer had to be located on the waterfront or the railhead because motorized trucks could haul freight more cheaply than horse carts. (The ironic marker of the transportation revolution was the Nectow property's industrial neighbor, a new Ford assembly plant.) Cambridge and many other cities had good reason to believe that protection of residential properties could no longer rely on traditional nuisance rules and ad hoc regulation.

Zoning would not have been acceptable to American voters in an earlier era because business owners and workers lived near their place of employment. People like the Clarks (owners of the telescope factory) had a dual stake in having their residence near their business. The obvious one was that living next door saved on commuting costs and enabled them to monitor their business more closely.

The more subtle stake was that factory owners were not eager to conduct their business in such a way as to reduce the value of their homes. Had the Clarks wanted to install a noisier machine in the factory, the value of their residences (if sold separately) would be reduced. Even if they did not mind the noise, they might have been more sensitive to the concerns of their neighbors and would thus have had an extra incentive to mitigate the spillover effects of the factory's operations. The Clark family was active in Cambridge social circles and was held in high regard (Warner and Ariail 1995). Their residential neighbors had direct access to the firm's owners, and the web of social and business relations could restrain adoption of noxious manufacturing processes.

After the Clarks died, the factory's owners no longer lived nearby, and industrial expansion into residential neighborhoods was facilitated by the same motorized vehicles that allowed all factory owners to live farther from their jobs. Multiply this by the rapidly growing number of automobiles and trucks in America, and it is easier to understand why the impersonal mechanism of zoning displaced informal methods of dispute resolution. *Nectow* turned out to be no more than a speed bump in urban America's rush to zoning.

I cannot leave *Nectow* without addressing a darker possibility about the abuse of zoning. The Massachusetts court mentioned that Cambridge was planning to widen Brookline Street along the block fronting Nectow's land. The city had not yet done so (it was widened after the case), but it is possible that the $8,000 in valuation for the residentially zoned land was established for purposes of taking the property by eminent domain. The Massachusetts court did not mention a source for the $8,000 value, but it did indicate that this figure represented a substantial reduction in value from the industrial classification.

Using zoning to deliberately devalue property that is coveted by the highway department has long been disapproved by the courts in almost all jurisdictions. But it is difficult to determine motives for zoning and rezoning. The master appointed by the Massachusetts court did not raise the possibility of devaluation, even though he addressed (and dismissed) the claim that the residential zoning was intended simply to create a park or open space.

In any event, government agencies that can show that a devalued property was rezoned for a more innocent reason are normally given the benefit of the doubt, even if the effect is to make the land cheaper to acquire. As I have endeavored to demonstrate, Cambridge's original zoning did have a "rational basis," to adopt the deferential term that is now used by the courts to avoid making decisions in cases like *Nectow*. Cagey calculation by the city to reduce eminent domain costs does not seem likely in this very early exercise of zoning. However remote, though, such lingering possibilities do indicate that even in its earliest stages, zoning presented issues of local knowledge that continue to vex those who would use the courts to supervise its excesses and shortcomings.

3.12 The Evolution of Constitutional Clauses: Due Process

The word "property" is used sparingly in the United States Constitution. It is protected (along with life and liberty) from deprivation "without due process of law" and from taking for public use without just compensation in the Fifth Amendment. The Fifth Amendment's protections (and the rest of the Bill of Rights) were originally regarded as applying only to the national government, though most states had similar provisions in their constitutions. The Tenth Amendment reinforced the principle of state sovereignty.

The hands-off-the-states view was revolutionized by the Civil War. The post-bellum Fourteenth Amendment became the foundation for Congress and the Supreme Court to enforce the federal Bill of Rights against state actions rather than just federal ones: "No state shall make or enforce any law which shall abridge the privileges or immunities of citizens of the United States; nor shall any state deprive any person of life, liberty, or property, without due process of law; nor deny to any person within its jurisdiction the equal protection of the laws." There are thus three main clauses upon which litigants in zoning issues can base their cases: due process, equal protection, and just compensation; the last is also referred to as the Takings Clause or the Eminent Domain Clause.

Since plaintiffs often invoke several clauses simultaneously, it can be difficult to distinguish one from the other. Appellate courts are not always careful to say which clause (or, sometimes, which constitution) they are basing their decision on. Part of this may be inevitable, since the clauses are closely related both in text and in purpose. I shall nonetheless try to differentiate them below.

Legal treatment of due process is divided into two parts: procedural due process and substantive due process. The first asks whether the legislative or administrative body in question followed the rules in processing the claim of the plaintiff. In zoning cases, this means inquiring whether appropriate notice was given, whether hearings were held, and whether permits were issued on schedule. The rise of open-meeting legislation, which entitles the public to attend and record meetings of public officials, has often tripped up local authorities, but because the due process remedy is usually confined to a "do-over," such errors seldom undermine zoning laws. Substantive due process, on the other hand, asks whether the rules themselves are reasonable, at least in the eyes of the judge. A developer challenging the zoning of land exclusively for, say, farmland may argue that the law itself is not reasonably related to the purposes of the police power to promote the general welfare of the community. This is a substantive question.

As applied to zoning, substantive due process has seldom provided relief for aggrieved property owners or developers, especially after the 1930s, when the Supreme Court adopted a highly deferential view of New Deal legislation. The main test is whether the regulation has a rational basis or a reasonable relation to the traditional police-power purposes of zoning: promotion of the health, safety, and general welfare of the community. ("Morals" was originally included in this list but has fallen out of favor.)

The catch-all phrase is "general welfare," and it is not a term of art. It is as broad as it sounds. Almost any legislation that might enhance local property values could count as general welfare. Most courts decline to review what should count as general or welfare, deferring almost invariably to what the local statutes assert or even what might be inferred from them.

The trickier part of general welfare and, hence, judicial review of it, concerns geographical inclusiveness. The default unit is the borders of the jurisdiction adopting the zoning laws. Sometimes disputes with neighboring municipalities will raise the question of whether cross-border effects must be considered, as when a new shopping center might generate unwanted traffic and noise in a neighboring municipality. Such issues have become less salient since the 1970s, when, as described in section 2.11, state and federal environmental regulations and sometimes statewide and regional agencies became the forums in which local cross-border disputes were addressed. I have suggested in other work that many intermunicipal spillover issues are resolved informally by norms of reciprocity that are endemic to municipalities that must deal with one another on many issues and for a long time to come (Fischel 2001).

In applying due process scrutiny, a further distinction is also sometimes made between administrative decisions and ordinary legislation. Many laws set up a specialized board, such as the National Labor Relations Board, to administer their provisions. Courts are inclined to scrutinize the decisions of the administrative body more carefully because, goes one theory, parties who lose from administrative decisions have fewer political roads available for correcting the decisions than they do in legislative matters, where coalitions and log-rolling compromises are possible.

Whatever the merits of this distinction, it is actually more difficult to apply to zoning (Carol Rose 1984). Municipalities often lack any strict division between legislative and executive (administrative) branches. Zoning and planning boards can be thought of as administrative, but they also set the agenda for policy changes, and elected officials often serve as board members or, in smaller towns, constitute the entire board. Elected city councils are surely legislators, but the city's chief executive, the mayor, often sits as a member of the council or is chosen from it. City councils can change zoning laws, which is clearly a legislative function, but they also often tailor the changes to particular parcels, which looks more like an administrative procedure. Judicial hostility to spot zoning is perhaps based on this distinction, but the fact that spot zoning (legislative) looks a lot like a zoning variance (administratively granted by the zoning board) highlights the difficulty in treating local government procedures in the same fashion as those of the state or national government.

3.13 Equal Protection within a Zone, Unequal Outside It

Equal protection implies, at minimum, that the law applies impersonally to everyone. A law might pass muster on due process grounds but still deny equal protection. It could advance a legitimate public purpose but be applied unequally. Equal protection thus affords landowners some protection from arbitrary treatment. The community cannot allow Jones to build in a district in which it has denied permission to Smith, assuming that both had planned to erect similar structures under similar conditions. But it does not protect Smith from being treated differently from Jones if they own property in different zoning districts, provided that the community can withstand Smith's due process charge that it drew the district lines arbitrarily and capriciously. For reasons indicated in the previous discussion of *Nectow v. Cambridge*, courts are unlikely to help an aggrieved landowner in such cases.

The adventurous use of the Equal Protection Clause is to argue that outsiders who are excluded by a zoning ordinance are being treated unequally. (This has sometimes been characterized as expanding the geography of the "general welfare" to include the larger metropolitan area, as advocated by Gerald Frug [1999].) This is an outgrowth of the attempted expansion of the Equal Protection Clause in the 1960s in the wake of civil rights movements.

The federal courts have not been hospitable to such claims with respect to land use. In *Warth v. Seldin*, 422 U.S. 490 (1974), a diverse group of plaintiffs from outside the community alleged damage from the exclusiveness of the zoning ordinance of Penfield, New York, a suburb of Rochester. They were denied standing to sue because the Supreme Court decided that they could not show harm specific to themselves, as an owner of property within Penfield might have done. In *Arlington Heights v. Metropolitan Housing Corp.*, 429 U.S. 252 (1976), the court declined to rule that the denial of a rezoning for a low-income housing project in an all-white Chicago suburb was invalid merely because the ordinance had the effect of excluding many blacks from the community.

These cases effectively closed off the use of the Fourteenth Amendment's Equal Protection Clause as a basis for attacking exclusionary zoning. The Court's ruling that the plaintiffs had failed to show racially discriminatory *intent* on the part of the Arlington Heights authorities set up a nearly impossible barrier for this type of litigation to surmount. (A subsequent suit based on federal civil rights legislation was successful in inducing Arlington Heights to accept the housing project.) The Supreme Court has declined to rule that housing is a fundamental right, and it has backed away from declaring income a "suspect classification" on the same order as race or national origin. Both of these moves preclude the "strict scrutiny" of the suspect legislation, which usually results in reversal of the legislation. In brief, the court decided to maintain its traditional noninterventionist attitude toward local zoning decisions. This parallels the U.S. Supreme Court's role in school finance decisions. Plaintiffs in *San Antonio Independent School District v. Rodriguez*, 411 U.S. 1 (1973), alleged that the unequal financing (from property taxes) of schools was a violation of the Equal Protection Clause, but the Court held that such issues were for the states to decide.

A few state supreme courts, most notably New Jersey's, have not been so reticent with respect to exclusionary zoning. The New Jersey courts have accepted, on state constitutional and legal grounds, nearly every argument that the federal courts have rejected or avoided. The landmark case was *Southern Burlington County NAACP v. Mount Laurel*, 336 A.2d 713 (1975), in which the New Jersey court found that the township of Mount Laurel, a suburb of Philadelphia, was guilty of exclusionary zoning, to the detriment of outsiders in general and the poor in particular. The court ordered all New Jersey communities to revise their zoning regulations to insure that housing was affordable to all segments of society (Henry Span 2001).

The township of Mount Laurel did not eagerly comply with the court's order, and the New Jersey Supreme Court decided to take extraordinary measures to get it and other communities to comply in a later version of *Mount Laurel*, 456 A.2d 390 (N.J. 1983). It set up a lower court to hear claims against communities and to grant a "builder's remedy" that ordered communities to rezone. To get the remedy, builders themselves had to subsidize the low-income housing, making this a sort of tax on market-rate housing (James Mitchell 2004). This remedy was sufficiently controversial that the New Jersey legislature took over the task by forming an independent body, the Council on Affordable Housing, to set standards for *Mount Laurel* compliance and to adjudicate claims.

The efficacy of this and a related legislative initiative in Massachusetts, colloquially referred to as the anti-snob zoning act, will be evaluated in section 9.17. (My conclusion there is that they help the plaintiffs at bar but encourage a backlash against all development, ultimately making the whole region's housing less affordable.) Most other state courts, however, have not followed New Jersey's lead. *Mount Laurel* is noted widely and approvingly, but in terms of altering zoning practices, it did not become, as Professor Norman Williams hopefully proclaimed it would, "the new *Euclid*" for residential housing types (Williams 1974 [1980 suppl. 66.13a]).

3.14 Taken without Just Compensation?

The Takings Clause requires that the government pay for the resources that it takes for public use. (It used to be the *Taking* Clause, but the plural form of the gerund has become dominant since about 1990 by the same inscrutable process by which *data* has become a singular noun.) The easy application is land acquisition for a public road or structure. Even though the project meets the due process criterion that it is reasonably related to a public purpose, the agency cannot simply expropriate the land. In the context of zoning, a taking might be found if a regulation so restricted the use of one's property that it might be deemed analogous to expropriation. The demarcation of this point has long vexed courts and commentators. For now, it will suffice to note that in practice, substantial decreases in property values due to changes in zoning laws are routinely upheld without compensation. As noted above, the *Euclid* court was not bothered by Ambler's (dubious) claim that its land had lost three-quarters of its value.

Takings differ from equal protection in two respects. First, a taking may be found even though the law does not seem to have been the result of any invidious distinction among individuals or distinct classes of persons (for example, by race or sex). Second, a violation of equal protection would always require that the ordinance be suspended; a finding that a government action was a taking would allow the government to continue the action if it was willing to pay just compensation.

Due process is preliminary to a taking. In principle, judges first ask whether a law meets due process criteria; if it does not, the community is told to get rid of or modify the law, and no inquiry into a taking is necessary. But a law might pass muster on due process grounds and still be ruled a taking. A court could rule that an ordinance that zoned an area for "open space" was reasonably connected to police-power purposes, but nonetheless the burden on landowners of not being able to develop at all might be great enough to constitute a taking for which they would have to be compensated.

The distinction between due process and takings had for years been muddled by a dictum in the U.S. Supreme Court's decision in *Agins v. Tiburon*, 447 U.S. 255 (1980). The Court did *not* hold that Agins's property had been taken by the downzoning that had prevented him from building his home on a lot that had long been zoned for housing. But the Court did state that one of the tests for a taking would be that the city of Tiburon's law did not "substantially advance a legitimate government interest" (*id.*, 260). Such a finding, however, would indicate a failure to meet the traditional due process criterion. It would require invalidation, not monetary compensation. About 25 years later, the Court in *Lingle v. Chevron USA Inc.*, 544 U.S. 528 (2005), explicitly corrected this confusion between due process and takings. The Takings Clause, it must be kept in mind, is a right to a particular remedy—just compensation. The obligation of governments to behave rationally must be found, if found it can be, in the Due Process Clause.

Constitutional doctrines that apply to zoning rise and fall in favor. Before the 1930s, the Due Process Clause was invoked most often by both state and federal courts when they wanted to protect businesses or landowners from what the judges considered unreasonable or unfair regulations (James Ely 1992). Its use was considerably curtailed during the Great Depression, as the Supreme Court acquired new members more in sympathy with the New Deal and government regulation generally.

The Takings Clause has to a large extent succeeded to the role formerly occupied by the Due Process Clause. The traditional application of the Takings Clause focused on expropriation and physical invasions of private property. The case that is now regarded as the lodestar of regulatory takings, *Pennsylvania Coal v. Mahon*, 260 U.S. 393 (1922), was originally discussed in the legal literature as a due process case. The city of Scranton had adopted a regulation that forbade the mining of coal beneath urban properties in such a way as to cause damage to structures on the surface. (Surface rights and underground mineral rights were often separately owned.) This made the mining of coal beneath most of the city impractical, and the mine owners sued the city for having taken their property rights by regulation. The city won in state court, but the U.S. Supreme Court in *Pennsylvania Coal* held for the mine owners. Justice Oliver Wendell Holmes famously opined for the majority that "The general rule at least is that while property may be regulated to a certain extent, if regulation goes too far it will be recognized as a taking" (*id.* at 416).

How far "too far" is has been debated ever since, but the remedy of just compensation for regulation is nowadays the centerpiece of modern land use controversies. Had *Euclid v. Ambler* been heard in the 1970s, the plaintiffs probably would have played up the alleged devaluation of Ambler's property by Euclid's ordinance and sought just compensation rather than invalidation.

3.15 Free Speech and Property Rights

The First Amendment is sometimes invoked in controversies involving zoning of movie theaters, bookstores, churches, and outdoor signs (Shelley Saxer 1998). (Religious institutions are discussed below.) Among the more direct clashes between property rights and free speech was a decision by the California Supreme Court in *Pruneyard Shopping Center v. Robbins*, 153 Cal. Rptr. 854 (1979), which the Supreme Court upheld in 447 U.S. 74 (1980). Students seeking signatures on a political petition had set up in a public area of the shopping center, which is located near San Jose. (The center is unusual in that much of its common area is not enclosed; covered but open arcades connect most of the stores.) The center's managers asked them to leave, which they did, but the students subsequently sued on the grounds that their right of free speech had been violated.

Owners of the Pruneyard demurred, noting that their shopping center was private property, not a public forum, and that adequate alternatives for political petitioning existed nearby. The California Supreme Court agreed with the students, holding that the center had become a de facto public forum. In the same ruling, the California court denied that requiring a temporary occupation by political petitioners would amount to a taking of property. The U.S. Supreme Court held that the U.S. Constitution was not so elastic as to require private owners to allow unwanted political activity on private property, but it also held that state supreme courts could go beyond their rulings in these matters as long as their doing so did not derogate other Constitutional rights. Just what to do when one protected right—speech—ran into another—private property—was not profitably discussed.

In 2004, Dartmouth students Smita Reddy and Emily Liu investigated what had happened after *Pruneyard* for a project in my course on law and economics. Digging into the legal literature, Reddy and Liu found that only a few other state courts had imitated California's approach, and even those states usually allowed only certain types of political activity. They also permitted shopping center owners to restrict the time and place occupied by petitioners. The time-and-place limitations appear to be effective in discouraging most political activity. California had by 2004 slightly narrowed Pruneyard's application (free-standing stores were exempted), but the basic holding still applied.

To check its relevance in California, Reddy and Liu visited the Pruneyard over Thanksgiving break and innocently asked where they might petition. Security guards firmly told them that doing so was not allowed, nor were there any procedures to obtain permission. Reddy and Liu then contacted the chairs of the Democratic and Republican parties in Santa Clara County (where Pruneyard is located) and asked them whether they had any interest in collecting signatures in the shopping center. The chairs indicated they did not, since voters were not responsive and actually sometimes hostile to their efforts in shopping centers. Public sidewalks were much more conducive to petitioning. I would add that I had never seen a political petitioner inside a shopping center in the four separate years when my wife and I lived in California since 1980.

Shopping center owners certainly do not like *Pruneyard*, but the decision has not resulted in the havoc that they feared. The restrained outcome is partly due to the equivocal nature of the decision, which permitted shopping center owners to adopt "reasonable" conditions. These have turned out to be a formidable roadblock for most would-be political actors (Suzanne Schiller 2000). Perhaps more important for the quiet outcome is that one side of the controversy, shopping center owners, have an ongoing stake in controlling their property. Annoyed or fearful shoppers translate directly into reduced sales and rents.

The other side of the entitlement, would-be political petitioners, represent largely unorganized, diffuse interests or, like the political parties, have only episodic demands for the space and are concerned about their image with the voters. Organization like the American Civil Liberties Union can aggregate some of the diffuse interests, but once the lawyers have gone away, a shopping center's managers can tweak the rules to control the outcome, given that the court gives them a rule of reason in their defense. The "rule of reason" seems so favorable to them as to perhaps justify the Pruneyard's security guards' belief that petitioning was simply not allowed.

The lesson I take from this outcome for other zoning controversies is that legal remedies need to be mindful of which parties have an ongoing stake in the outcome and whether that stake will make the remedy stick. Efforts by state courts to make more low-income housing available in suburban locales are resisted by an entrenched group, preexisting homeowners, who have a strong and continuing interest in the value of their homes. On the other side are potential beneficiaries of low-cost suburban homes, most of whom are not even aware of any particular location in which they might live or of potential allies. Advocacy groups such as the NAACP and various fair housing associations can overcome some of the cost of organizing, but they require allies such as for-profit developers who are willing to persist in overcoming the many hurdles of local zoning. (Recall that I had drawn a similar lesson from *Buchanan v. Warley*, where the U.S. Supreme Court crafted a remedy against apartheid-like zoning that gave profit-making landlords the entitlement to rent to whom they pleased.)

3.16 Neighbors' Cases

Economists tend to think of only one kind of court case in zoning conflicts: This is when landowner-developers sue community authorities for refusal to accommodate their proposals. Such cases are known in the zoning literature as "developers' cases." There is, however, another type of suit called the "neighbors' case." This distinction, drawn most clearly by Norman Williams (1974), is crucial to understanding zoning cases. In neighbors' cases, the zoning authorities are sued for having allowed some development that residents near the project believe will be detrimental to their interests. Neighbors may thus sue over variances, special permits, or rezonings for property near their own.

The existence of neighbors' cases draws attention to the facts that zoning is the exercise of governmental authority and that a government's actions may often displease at least some of its constituents. Within most communities, protection of neighbors from unfavorable decisions by zoning authorities is offered by the political process and the procedural rights of neighbors in zoning decisions, who must be notified of hearings about proposed legislation and administrative decisions and be given an opportunity to be heard. Perhaps as a result, most neighbors' cases in the past did not succeed unless there was some violation of the foregoing procedures.

The adage that "neighbors usually lose" has a hollow ring to it these days, not because of changes in the legal status of neighbors, but because the number of procedures that local authorities must go through has increased greatly since 1970. Increased procedures have been occasioned by both statute and judge-made law. (I discussed these at length in chapter 2 and for that reason will mention them only briefly here.) Premier among new statutory procedures is the Environmental Impact Statement (EIS). Although an EIS is required at the federal level only for government projects (a list of which is longer than one might think, since it includes projects even partially financed or licensed by the government), several states, including California and New York, require them for almost any local project. The cost of the EIS and the delay from subsequent administrative and legal challenges give neighbors a powerful entitlement.

The second source of neighborhood power is the multiple layers of review of local decisions that have been put in place since the 1970s (John Carruthers 2001). A variance or rezoning may be granted by a local authority, but in many states, it is necessary for projects to pass review by a regional or statewide body, which can also veto the project as a result of neighborly testimony as well as on the ground of more formal standards.

3.17 Local Governments Usually Prevail in Court

Before the 1970s, the general *Euclid* view that courts would not intervene in procedurally proper local land use decisions was not seriously challenged in the federal courts. The *Nectow* decision, which redrew Cambridge's zoning boundary, was never repeated. Indeed, except for a minor decision involving discontinuance of a lake-like gravel pit on Long Island, *Goldblatt v. Hempstead*, 369 U.S. 590 (1962) (ordinance upheld, without compensation), the Supreme Court stayed out of zoning almost entirely. When it got back in through cases involving equal protection and due process, the Court continued its deference to local decision-makers, making *Nectow*, with its close attention to a local zoning map, more isolated than ever. A brief rundown of recent cases (some already mentioned in this and the previous chapter) follows.

Belle Terre v. Boraas, 416 U.S. 1 (1974), ruled that the village of Belle Terre, a Long Island suburb near a state university campus, could regulate home occupancy by family relationship, effectively excluding rental of single-family homes to college students. This decision was modified in *Moore v. City of East Cleveland*, 431 U.S. 494 (1977), in which the court struck down the city's narrow definition of "family," which excluded grandchildren who apparently had moved there to take advantage of the city's better school system.

This pair of cases illustrates some of the Court's ambivalence about zoning, but it is arguable that *Belle Terre* has the more lasting influence. Ellickson et al. (2013) find that only four states (albeit big ones), California, New York, Michigan, and New Jersey, have departed from *Belle Terre* by holding that personal associations may not be so regulated under their state constitutions. The Court's rhetoric and the opinion's author may have swayed some courts. Justice William O. Douglas, who was both an environmentalist and a civil libertarian, wrote the majority opinion, and wags referred to *Belle Terre* as "*Douglas v. Douglas*." He let his environmentalist leanings prevail in language often repeated in defense of large-lot suburban zoning: "The police power is not confined to elimination of filth, stench, and unhealthy places. It is ample to lay out zones where family values, youth values, and the blessings of quiet seclusion and clean air make the area a sanctuary for people" (416 U.S. at 9).

Whether Douglas's "sanctuary for people" included poor people was the subject of a pair of cases that attempted to pry open suburban zoning by using the Equal Protection Clause (Lawrence Sager 1969). Both were unsuccessful. As mentioned in section 3.13, *Warth v. Selden* (1974) and *Arlington Heights* (1976) were cases in which the Court declined to involve itself in local zoning. The two cases were part of a general resistance on the part of the Court against using the Equal Protection Clause as a lever for redistribution of income and wealth, but they are also consistent in terms of the Court's reluctance to second-guess local land use decisions.

The Supreme Court in *Eastlake v. Forest City Enterprises*, 426 U.S. 668 (1976), upheld a Cleveland suburb's practice of requiring referenda for rezonings of individual properties, reversing the Ohio Supreme Court. This case not only upheld local authority, but expanded it beyond the bounds that the locality's state supreme court deemed acceptable. The adoption of zoning ordinances and major amendments has long been put to voters in many jurisdictions, but parcel by parcel approval by the electorate had been rare.

Ballot-box zoning has long been frowned upon by commentators as lacking the procedural and information resources that boards and legislatures have access to (Callies, Neuffer, and Caliboso 1991). The *Eastlake* decision gave the green light to an expanded role for citizens in the zoning process, and this role, in turn, was an element reducing the supply of housing and other developments (Samuel Staley 2001; Mai Thi Nguyen 2007). The drawback of plebiscites is not so much that the preferences of the electorate are different from those of their elected officials. As explained in Fischel (2005), the problem is that anonymous voters have less reason to keep commitments to previously made plans than do public officials.

Young v. American Mini Theaters, 427 U.S. 50 (1976), upheld Detroit's use of zoning to limit concentration of pornographic movie houses. Previous cases had held that cities could not ban such establishments entirely, and thus many cities attempted to reduce their concentration instead—an anti-red-light-district strategy. (A more nuanced approach to city regulation of subnormal activities is discussed in Ellickson [1998].) The Court's deference to the deconcentration burden, justified on the basis of the adverse neighborhood effects of such establishments rather than the content of their protected expression, is yet another example of the pattern of its deference to local control of land use.

Boerne v. Flores, 521 U.S. 507 (1997), upheld the zoning ruling in the city of Boerne, Texas, that prevented a church in a historic district from expanding. This garden-variety holding was the occasion for the Court to strike down congressional legislation that gave religious land uses greater protection from local regulation than secular uses. (One of my students found that the city and the church later came to a compromise that allowed the expansion.) Congress responded by passing (unanimously) the Religious Land Use and Institutionalized Persons Act (RLUIPA) in 2000.

The act gave the same extra protections to churches as had been granted under the previous legislation but enforced them by congressional spending power (withholding funds to communities that did not comply) rather than the Fourteenth Amendment, which the Court had decided in *Boerne* was solely the province of the judicial branch. As I discussed in section 2.12, RLUIPA represents an important imposition of federal authority on what are mostly local land use decisions, despite lack of evidence that churches are unduly burdened (Stephen Clowney 2007). But it seems to have come about as a byproduct of a contest between the Supreme Court and Congress over which branch has final say over the Constitution (Salkin and Lavine 2008). In the present context, *Boerne* stands for bland confirmation of the Court's deference to local decision-making in land use issues.

3.18 Regulatory Takings Superseded Substantive Due Process

Against this backdrop of failures on the part of pro-development plaintiffs, a new doctrinal approach to land use regulation was put forward. The concept of regulatory takings had been around since at least 1922 (when *Pennsylvania Coal* was decided) and arguably even earlier (Eric Claeys 2003). The rise of the Takings Clause was caused not just by the failure of landowners to win under due process and equal protection. After 1970, the financial stakes got larger both because regulations became more widespread and stringent and because real estate values grew faster than the rate of inflation. (Both issues are reviewed in more detail in chapter 5.) Besides this, an intellectual movement within the law schools began to address the problematic aspects of judicial review of land use regulation.

The Due Process and Equal Protection Clauses provide little textual basis for reviewing land use regulations (John Hart Ely 1980). The Takings Clause has two distinct advantages. The first is that the U.S. Constitution and those of the states do mention property as something to be protected. The second, emphasized by Robert Ellickson (1977), is that it offers a remedy, just compensation, that seems more flexible than the injunctive relief (a court order to do or refrain from doing something) that would follow from an adverse decision along due process or equal protection grounds.

The remedy of just compensation is called "damages." Non-lawyers should note the "s" at the end, which is used for both singular and plural, denoting dollar amounts to be awarded by a court. The actual pain and loss lacks the "s" at the end of "damage." Damages for injury or for expropriated property are almost always approximated by the market value of what is alleged to have been lost by the plaintiff as determined by a judge, a jury, or an administrative panel.

The remedy of damages for regulatory excess has a practical advantage over injunctive relief. While no regulatory body likes to have its rules reversed by a court, compliance does not usually affect its budget too much. Indeed, in zoning regulations, some regulating bodies may drag their feet or even deliberately subvert compliance by adopting another regulation that ostensibly cures the faults of the one found to be illegal but burdens the complaining landowner just as much.

This is not just a theoretical possibility. When the Pennsylvania Supreme Court held that a township had illegally excluded apartments in *Appeal of Girsh*, 263 A.2d 395 (Pa. 1970), the township turned around and rezoned some land for apartments. But it was not the land owned by the complaining landowner, who undertook the considerable cost of litigating the case. In this instance, the state court did fix the problem by requiring the township to rezone the plaintiff's land (*Casey v. Warwick Township*, 328 A.2d 464 [Pa. 1974]).

Pennsylvania is unusual, if not unique, in its willingness to give successful plaintiffs a "curative order" to rezone. And that is actually the approach that advocates of takings jurisprudence find problematical. The Pennsylvania Supreme Court is not in a good position to second-guess local decisions. (I have more favorable things to say about this court's approach in section 9.17.) The Takings Clause approach, its advocates say, gives the local government a choice. It can rezone as the successful plaintiff desires, or it can pay damages for the burden incurred. If the township thinks Mr. Girsh's land really is inappropriate for high-density use, let them purchase the development rights. This happens all the time in other contexts—development rights are purchased and transferred as conservation easements—so the remedy is hardly foreign to the law.

Another virtue of just compensation is that delay by the offending agency becomes costly. The most notorious evidence of this is the statement by a California land use attorney, James Longtin (1975), who was instructing municipal attorneys in how to handle adverse judgments: "If all else fails, merely amend the regulation and start over again" (192). This cynical advice was noted by Justice William Brennan in his dissent in *San Diego Gas and Electric v. San Diego*, 450 U.S. 621 (1981). Brennan used it in support of his view that the Court needed to review the California Supreme Court's apparent disdain for the damages remedy of the Takings Clause. (The principles behind Brennan's dissent are discussed in section 9.10 below.)

3.19 Just Compensation as a Check on Zoning Enthusiasm

The appeal of regulatory takings to economists is that it makes regulators pay close attention to the economic consequences of their actions. A city council that is considering the planning board's proposal to downzone undeveloped rural residential land from a three-acre minimum lot size to a ten-acre minimum lot size will think harder about it if landowners who are adversely affected by the downzoning will be owed compensation for the reduced value of their property. This does not necessarily mean that the proposed regulation will not pass. The council could decide that the value of the regulation as judged by reduced municipal services costs or perhaps by the gain in home values in the rest of the community makes the payout worthwhile.

An example of this apparent calculation was presented in a recent student paper about Indian Hills, Ohio. (The student is Elizabeth Blackburn, Dartmouth class of 2015.) The city is an affluent suburb of Cincinnati, it is zoned for large lots, and it is almost exclusively residential. Its school district corresponds to the city's boundary except for a few small areas that are part of an adjacent township. One undeveloped parcel in these areas was a former gravel pit, which a developer sought to buy. The aim was to put up high-density homes whose appeal would be enhanced by being within the Indian Hills School District. Aside from adding pupils to the schools and eroding the tax base, the city worried that the new development would add to traffic congestion in its residential areas, since the main access roads to the development were through Indian Hills. But because the parcel was outside the city, Indian Hills had no regulatory authority to make the proposed development conform to the large-lot standards its residents were held to. So the city bought the parcel, outbidding the developer (and not using eminent domain), and turned it into a public park.

Before discussing the takings cases I should alert the reader that there is a literature among law professors that holds that compensation either will not deter regulators or will deter them so much that even sensible regulations would not be adopted (Daryl Levinson 2000; Bethany Berger 2009). I will deal with these and related objections in section 6.13, in which I concede that they have some merit but are mostly unconvincing in the local land use setting. What actually makes the regulatory takings doctrine economically problematic is excessive entry of claimants and the institutional inability of courts to draw an appropriate line between compensable and noncompensable regulations, as I will discuss in chapter 9.

3.20 Historic Preservation: Lead Us Not into Penn Station

Penn Central Transportation Co. v. New York City, 438 U.S. 104 (1978), upheld the city's designation of Grand Central Terminal (owned by Penn Central) as a historic landmark and thus frustrated its owner's plan to build a skyscraper in the air space above the old terminal. The city's law had been inspired by the demolition of another New York landmark, Penn Station, and preservationists were determined not to lose another. I view this as a zoning case even though the designation of the terminal was initiated by a special historic district commission rather than through the usual zoning and planning channels. The proliferation of special regulatory districts undermines the ability of cities to make deals with developers and neighborhood groups, but in the present case, it seemed clear that an obligation to compensate would come from the city's fiscal resources, and the city council could adjust the historic district's mission accordingly.

Early advocates of historic preservation had assumed that restrictive regulations like those applied in this case would have to involve some quid pro quo to pass judicial scrutiny (John Costonis 1974). The city was not about to offer monetary compensation—this was the era of near-bankruptcy for New York City—but it did give Penn Central what are called "transferrable development rights" (TDRs), as recommended by Professor Costonis in his article, so that the railroad company could sell or utilize its air rights elsewhere in the neighborhood. The company argued that TDRs fell short of "just compensation." New York's highest court (the Court of Appeals) held for the city, and the U.S. Supreme Court affirmed. The latter made note of the TDR program but also sidestepped its implications, since the terminal's owners had attacked the ordinance's constitutional validity and not specified their losses.

The U.S. Supreme Court did nonetheless offer guidance by describing the circumstances that would lead it to find that just compensation was due. Justice Brennan's opinion outlined a "multifactor balancing test" to determine whether an otherwise valid police-power regulation shaded into a taking of property for which compensation was due. The factors are: (1) the "economic impact" of the government action, (2) the extent to which the action "interferes with distinct investment-backed expectations," and (3) the "character" of the action (438 U.S. at 124).

These factors, which have become the lodestar of most judicial inquiries, offer some promise for curbing government enthusiasm for regulation, but the parameters are wide (Steven Eagle 2014). A regulation that has no "economic impact" is generally one that private owners will not complain about. But because almost all new regulations have some adverse economic impact, this criterion alone says almost nothing about how much restraint on economic activity is sufficient to trigger a compensation requirement.

"Distinct investment-backed expectations" seems more promising as a guide. One would think that if the original owners of Grand Central Terminal had actually contemplated building something on top of their elaborate, Beaux-Arts structure when it was built and had actually made some concrete investment to facilitate its future plans, frustration of this plan would require compensation. In fact, the original structure had incorporated extra columns and supports in contemplation of building additional stories over the terminal (438 U.S. at 115, n.15). But that was in 1909. The passage of years and development of new technology made these particular investments redundant, and the tower that was proposed by Penn Central's owners did not make use of that investment. Even so, the forward-looking activity by the original builder (Cornelius Vanderbilt, who owned the New York Central Railroad and whose statue adorns the entrance of the terminal) should have counted for something.

Perhaps this standard would apply to new regulations that halted an otherwise legal project in the middle of construction, but the investment-backed expectations standard has not proven to be much of a deterrent to rapid changes in regulation. And it may be just as well. As economists have pointed out (Blume, Rubinfeld, and Shapiro 1984, to be discussed in section 9.6), landowners could use the rule to game the system inefficiently by beginning development too early solely in order to protect themselves against regulatory change or perhaps solely to extract compensation where it might otherwise not have been due.

The "character of the action" standard is the murkiest, but Justice Brennan's example of something that would require compensation under this was specifically the physical invasion standard. He illustrated this with a case involving an invasion of airspace, which might arguably fit the denial of construction in the airspace above the railroad terminal. The case he cited, *United States v. Causby*, 328 U.S. 256 (1946), involved interference by low-flying military aircraft with the quiet enjoyment of property (by Mr. Causby's chickens) rather than foregone opportunities for development. Physical invasion is an easily comprehended extension of the traditional exercise of eminent domain, in which the government takes title to the property and thus can physically occupy it and exclude others. An action that does not take title but causes owners to be unable to exclude government agents, the general public, or uses inimical to their interests (such as the water of a rising government dam) has long been deemed compensable.

The physical invasion standard was later reinforced by *Loretto v. Teleprompter*, 458 U.S. 419 (1982). Mrs. Loretto objected to the installation of a cable-TV box, as required by law, on the exterior of her Manhattan apartment house. Reversing the New York Court of Appeals, the Supreme Court held that she was entitled to just compensation. The case caused much perplexed head-scratching among commentators and gave rise to the adage "the smaller the stakes, the more likely the Court will require compensation." Mrs. Loretto's apartment house was hardly devalued by the rooftop cable-TV installation, which was about the size of the proverbial bread box. (Later compensation was set at $1.00.) The government action that more substantially devalued her property was New York City's rent control regulations, but the Court has routinely brushed aside takings challenges to their application, even where the tenant ends up effectively owning most of what was formerly the landowner's property (*Yee v. Escondido*, 503 U.S. 519 [1992]; Werner Hirsch 1988).

The *Penn Central* majority opinion admits that "this Court, quite simply, has been unable to develop any 'set formula'" for takings, and it concedes that its rules look like "essentially ad hoc, factual inquiries" (438 U.S. 104, at 124). This language seems to allow state and lower federal courts to use a balancing test in ways that are about equally favorable to private plaintiffs as they are to government defendants. One might expect that the outcome of the cases would fall more or less equally between plaintiff (property owner) and defendant (government) victories. To the contrary, the vast majority of lower-court opinions that invoke the *Penn Central* balancing test hold for the government defendants. Surveys of decisions that have invoked *Penn Central* find that they overwhelmingly reject regulatory takings (Adam Pomeroy 2012). Most of the cases surveyed were in federal court, but the state courts are, if anything, even less inclined to invoke *Penn Central* to give a landowner a rare victory (David Callies 1999). In short, the supposed three-factor balancing test of *Penn Central* should not cause a jurisdiction contemplating a more restrictive land use regulation to think much about the economic costs of its actions.

3.21 The California-Federal Standoff Began with *Agins v. Tiburon*

A series of U.S. Supreme Court cases that reviewed California decisions created the expectation that the Court would set a more robust standard for regulatory takings. The cases turned out to be little more than an attempt by the U.S. Court to see to it that the California courts (and those of some other states) did not simply read the "just compensation" remedy out of the Takings Clause. To have decided this line of cases differently would have reduced the perceived cost of regulation to government agencies, but the actual outcomes did not raise the bar much above the less-than-stringent

Penn Central standard. I will discuss one of these cases to give a sense of the municipal behavior that I think a just compensation requirement might properly temper. (Other cases are discussed in my book on *Regulatory Takings* [Fischel 1995].)

In 1968, Dr. Donald Agins, a dentist, bought an undeveloped, five-acre tract of land atop a ridge in Tiburon, California, a city just north of the Golden Gate Bridge in San Francisco. He planned to build a home for himself and finance some of its cost by subdividing the remainder of the land for other homes. Residential development in Tiburon had been gradually moving up the ridge from the edge of the bay, and Agins's proposal looked like a continuation of that trend.

In 1972, the city decided it wanted to preserve the top of the ridge as open space. I have visited the site, and it is easy to understand why both the city and Dr. Agins would covet the sweeping views of San Francisco Bay and its environs. The city's voters approved a bond issue to purchase the land by using the power of eminent domain. However, the appraised value of the land had risen so rapidly (for reasons related to Marin County's regulatory revolution, as described in section 5.23) that the city gave up. It instead changed its zoning laws so as to limit Agins's ability to build. Agins sued for compensation for what he argued was a regulatory taking.

Agins's loss in the California courts was not surprising, as these courts had a long history of deferring to local government regulatory actions (Joseph diMento et al. 1980). What was novel about the case was that the California Supreme Court took the occasion to openly declare what many had begun to infer from its decisions: Compensation was not legally available for regulatory takings under any circumstance. The only remedy would be injunctive relief.

The U.S. Supreme Court took the case, but in *Agins v. Tiburon*, 447 U.S. 255 (1980), it simply sidestepped the state court's selective excision of the final three words of the Fifth Amendment from the U.S. Constitution ("nor shall private property be taken for public use *without just compensation*"). The U.S. Court simply affirmed the California Court's decision on the grounds that no regulatory taking had yet been proved, since Agins had not exhausted the administrative process necessary to attempt to develop. But it was plain that the U.S. Court was not pleased with the direction of the California court.

If the U.S. opinion in *Agins* was a shot across the bow, the California court did not heed it. The matter was finally joined in *First English Evangelical Lutheran Church v. County of Los Angeles*, 482 U.S. 304 (1987). The church's summer-camp buildings had been destroyed by one of those hundred-year floods that seem to occur more than once a century, and the county passed a flood plain ordinance that forestalled reconstruction of the camp. The church sued for just compensation, which the California courts denied, and the U.S. Court finally held that damages had to be considered as a remedy if there was a taking. Moreover, the clock for calculating damages had to start from the moment the final denial took place, which made it risky for the county simply to delay amending the regulation.

One would think that in view of this decision by the highest court in the land, California jurists would line up and salute and amend their ways. Not so. Like sulky children who have been chastised but are not chastened, the California courts admitted that damages were available if a regulatory taking was found, but they almost never found any regulation to be a taking. This strategy started with *First English* on remand. The California trial court simply ruled that no taking had taken place, and the church failed to get the decision reversed on appeal.

3.22 Moving to the Taking? Not in This Court, *Palazzolo*

Other states have taken a different approach to tamping down litigation on regulatory takings. Several have held, sometimes without quite saying so, that an owner who acquires property after a regulation is established has no legal right to challenge the regulation (Steven Eagle 1998). The idea that simple notice of the regulation's existence should disable the claims of new buyers originated in California in *HFH v. Superior Court of Los Angeles County*, 542 P.2d 237 (Cal. 1976), but it was not directly addressed by the U.S. Supreme Court until *Palazzolo v. Rhode Island*, 533 U.S. 606 (2001).

Mr. Palazzolo wanted to develop his barrier-island property, which was subject to wetlands regulation that had been adopted while he owned the land. He later reincorporated his development firm and transferred the property to the corporation, which meant that he was essentially selling it to himself. The Rhode Island Supreme Court held that by purchasing his land (the second time) after the regulation was in place, Palazzolo lost his right to receive just compensation for the new regulations. In effect the state court argued that if you "move to the taking" you have no one to blame but yourself.

The argument has some superficial attractiveness. Buyers should be aware of both the benefits and burdens that come with a property. A buyer who wants to build a store in a residential neighborhood should know enough to look at the zoning regulations before she closes on the property, and it would be uncontroversial to deny her just compensation if the regulations forestalled her plan. But the previous owner would not have had a claim to build a store, either. The buyer stands in the same legal position as her predecessor in title. If there is a regulation that might be a taking of property, the first owner's claim can be no better or worse than that of the second.

It may be that the first owner's claim is not very strong or is costly to adjudicate in court, and the buyer will appropriately reduce the price she would pay for the land. But such a private calculation cannot by itself serve as the basis for diminishing the right to compensation. If it were, then a buyer who naively (or strategically) paid no discount for the regulated property would have a better claim for compensation than one who purchased at a realistic discount. (I discussed this at greater length in *Regulatory Takings* [Fischel 1995].)

In any case, the U.S. Court in *Palazzolo* disallowed the moving-to-the-taking argument, though not without some ambiguity created by the several concurrences that precluded a clear majority opinion. *Palazzolo* could thus be considered a case in which the Court did make a rule that made it more likely that government would have to pay for excessive regulations. This should be seen as precluding a proposed path, not changing traditional practice. As Gregory Stein (2012) found in his evaluation of *Palazzolo's* later impact, most courts that, prior to *Palazzolo*, had invoked the purchase-with-notice rule applied it as a redundant make-weight. Even without this rule, most of those plaintiffs would have lost. As did Mr. Palazzolo, who did not succeed in getting his permits after the case was remanded to the Rhode Island courts.

The importance of *Palazzolo* was the road not taken. Had the U.S. Court affirmed the Rhode Island Supreme Court's argument, it would surely have emboldened many state courts to adopt the rule as a primary brake on takings claims. For instance, the Court's rousing endorsement of ballot-box rezoning in *Eastlake v. Forest City Enterprises* has led to the expansion of initiatives even in states whose courts were skeptical of the practice (Kevin Wagner 2010), though several state courts, deploying their own constitutional provisions, continue to hem in the practice (Callies, Neuffer, and Caliboso 1991).

3.23 Which Way to the Federal Courthouse?
You Can't Get There from Here

Although *First English* and *Palazzolo* did nudge some state courts away from paths that would have forestalled just compensation for regulations, the Court has not followed up with stronger measures. It is not in principle difficult to move land use cases into federal court. Even if there is no direct federal question or diversity jurisdiction (where one of the parties is from another state), Section 1983 of the post–Civil War era Civil Rights Act offers a conduit into federal court for litigants who believe their civil rights—which include the "life, liberty, and property" in the Fourteenth Amendment—have been deprived by state action. Yet the Supreme Court has moved in exactly the opposite direction. Starting with *Williamson County v. Hamilton Bank*, 473 U.S. 172 (1984), the Court erected complex procedural barriers to getting takings cases into federal court (Berger and Kanner 2004).

Two barriers are worth mentioning because they illustrate a larger problem with regulatory takings. One requirement for getting into federal court is that property owners have a final decision by the government agency regarding their dispute. A landowner who is denied a permit to build an apartment house by the local planning board cannot simply take that denial to court. She must apply for a reconsideration of her plan or a variance. If denied this, she must submit other, less intensive plans for consideration, and if these are denied or, more likely, approved only with stringent conditions, she must show that the conditions make the project economically infeasible.

The other roadblock is exhaustion of remedies, which refers to judicial proceedings. According to the *Williamson County* rules, the aggrieved developer must go to a state court, get a decision there, and then go through all appeals within the framework peculiar to that state. If she gets a final denial from the highest state court, then she might be able to apply for federal review. (A decision is thus "ripe" for federal court consideration if the plaintiff has obtained a final administrative decision *and* exhausted her state court remedies.) However, if the state court denies her appeal on the grounds that no taking has occurred under state law, the federal court can rule that there was no denial of Fourteenth Amendment rights. The U.S. Court generally declines to overrule the state court on the question of whether a taking has occurred. With few exceptions, the only way a developer can get into federal court is if the state court offers no possibility of compensation even if it finds that a regulatory taking has occurred.

It is easy to see how even mildly competent state and local regulators could structure proceedings so that almost no claims could get into federal court. Local officials can adopt multiple levels of discretionary review, which have proliferated in any case, and adopt the rule of "never say never" to an applicant. Always come back next month with a slightly amended proposal. State courts can similarly behave so as not to preclude another round of litigation.

The applicants' legal budget, not to mention their project's financing schedule, will eventually force them to give up the chase. The authors of a leading land use casebook ask, "In light of the hostility shown to land use cases... when is it appropriate for a lawyer to file a land use challenge in federal court?" (Ellickson et al. 2013, 263). They do not offer a definitive answer, but the subsection in which the question appears is titled simply, "Malpractice?"

I have made this seem like cynical calculation on the part of local officials who just do not want to reach the day of reckoning, but there are more innocent reasons for the procedural demands as well. The applicant may have deliberately submitted a proposal that he knew would not be accepted so as to get the authorities to settle for a more reasonable-sounding proposal on the next round. And even nonstrategic applicants can be impatient with reasonable rules or just not understand the process. There is no reason for federal courts to have to sort them out.

The U.S. Supreme Court seems to have erected these barriers to litigation in federal courts for prudential reasons. Land use regulations and conditions vary enormously around the country. As I have previously emphasized, especially in the discussion of *Nectow v. Cambridge*, the reasonableness of each party's claims is hard to assess without the local knowledge that is difficult to transmit to higher courts. Moreover, the federal courts have a great deal of other business that presses upon them. The elected board of trustees of the Village of Hoffman Estates, Illinois, inexplicably derailed a previously approved plan by developers. The developers sued the trustees but lost their case in state court, and they sought to vindicate their due process rights in federal court. In his opinion denying such access, Judge Richard Posner, one of the progenitors of the law and economics movement, candidly wrote: "If the plaintiffs can get us to review the merits of the Board of Trustees' decision under state law, we cannot imagine what zoning dispute could not be shoehorned into federal court in this way, there to displace or postpone consideration of some worthier object of federal judicial solicitude" (*Coniston v. Village of Hoffman Estates*, 844 F.2d 461, 467 [1988]; for a scathing critique of Posner's opinion, see Richard Epstein [2007]).

3.24 Thou Shalt Not Steal: The Gospel According to *Lucas*

As of 1990, the federal standard for regulatory takings can be summarized briefly: Plaintiffs had to bring their cases in the state courts, not the federal courts, as long as the state courts allowed the possibility of obtaining a monetary remedy, however remote in practice, for excessive regulation. Damages had to be clocked from the moment a final decision was made, but this was of little consequence in disputes where no damages were awarded. State and federal cases were largely governed by the *Penn Central* test, which was another way of saying that the plaintiff almost always lost. The only clear constraint on the states was to disallow regulations that required physical occupation by the public or by a collateral agent such as inundation from a government-sponsored dam. (Controversies about exacting concessions for a permit for development will be considered in the next section.)

Lucas v. South Carolina Coastal Council, 505 U.S. 1003 (1992), added another federal parameter to the regulatory takings doctrine. David Lucas owned two building lots along the coast in a resort area north of Charleston, South Carolina. The vacant lots were among the last remaining in a successful, high-end residential development called Wild Dunes, which Lucas had been a partner in developing. Shortly after Lucas purchased the two lots from his partners, South Carolina enacted a coastal protection act intended to push development back from the beach. The law's effect was to eliminate the possibility of any permanent development on Lucas's two lots.

I discussed in an earlier section the procedural convolutions that landowners must go through in order to get their cases heard by federal (and many state) courts. The first is to get a final decision from the governing body, and finality normally includes having applied for a variance from the rules. Just how many variances must be applied for is not clear, but it is at least one. The South Carolina legislation that weighed on Mr. Lucas simplified his appeals by specifically providing for no variance procedures. I do not know why the legislature disallowed them, but it is consistent with the general hostility to zoning variances in the legal literature. Planners and lawyers worry that the untrained locals on the board empowered to grant exceptions will be so generous as to undermine the purposes of the legislation.

As I pointed out in my discussion of zoning variances in section 2.5, the evidence that variances do any economic or ecological harm is almost nonexistent. The outcome of the *Lucas* case is a point in my favor on this issue. A local board empowered to grant variances to South Carolina's otherwise reasonable idea—do not build so close to the ocean—would have received a request from David Lucas to allow an exception. The board members would have taken a site visit, as I did in November 1994 when I happened to be in South Carolina for a meeting, to look at the properties and learn more about the neighborhood. The two lots, which were still vacant at the time of my visit, were separated by a large square-shaped house (with about 4,000 square feet of interior space). On either side, up and down the coast for at least a mile, almost every shoreline space was filled with similar houses or condominium developments. All of these structures were grandfathered by the regulation, though they were burdened at the time by a rule that prevented their reconstruction if they were substantially destroyed by a storm. Mr. Lucas's lots were like two missing pickets in a long fence of development. (Photos showing this are on my website, http://www.dartmouth.edu/~wfischel/lucasessay.html.)

Had the Lucas lots been in an otherwise undeveloped area, or even one that was just partially developed, a local board would probably not have granted a variance. The resistance to encroaching on the coast has to start somewhere, after all. And zoning boards still surprise me sometimes, but it would have been a major shock if the hypothetical land use board on Isle of Palms had not granted Lucas a variance to build something more or less like the homes of scores of his neighbors.

Lucas got a judgment in his favor from a local trial court. The judge, who may have had some idea of what the coast looked like, held that the regulation amounted to a taking of property. The court's award of $1.2 million was reversed by the South Carolina Supreme Court, which held that no taking had occurred. The legislature had crafted the coastal zone protection act in the language of "harm prevention," which under traditional criteria did not require compensation (Ellickson 1973). Uses deemed harmful to the public can almost always be forestalled without warranting just compensation.

The U.S. Supreme Court reversed and reinstated Lucas's claim. Its holding identified a categorical exception to the usual deference to regulations accorded by the *Penn Central* rules. It holds that if the regulation eliminates "any reasonable economic use" of the property, it can be justified as noncompensable only if the banned use was deemed harmful under "background principles" of state law such as the common law of nuisance. The extent of these "background principles" has been much debated in the legal literature on the case (Joseph Sax 1993; Patrick Hubbard 2007), but Justice Antonin Scalia's invocation of "background" may have been intended to forestall what he perceived to be the manipulation of language by the legislature to insulate its regulatory scheme from the Takings Clause.

3.25 *Lucas* Did Not Hobble Environmental Legislation

I should point out that having no "reasonable economic use" is not the same as having no economic value. A highly regulated parcel may be sold for some value to a buyer who expects the regulation to change sometime in the future to his advantage. Given such expectations, courts cannot use economic value as a basis for their decisions, since value itself depends in part on how they are expected to rule. A court that declared that Lucas's lots retained some economic value (as I suspect they did) and thus ruled that the regulation need not be compensable would have further reduced the parcel's value. "Economic use" makes more sense because it alludes to an external standard that is not itself determined by adjudication.

The *Lucas* decision caused a great deal of consternation among environmentalists and planners. David Callies, who had previously coauthored a book that downplayed the importance of the takings issue (Bosselman, Callies, and Banta 1973), wrote *Preserving Paradise: Why Regulation Won't Work* (1994b), which warned that Hawaii's preservation regulations were at risk as a result of the *Lucas* decision. The *Lucas* rule also again raised the issue of "conceptual severance," which involves attempting to slice property rights in such a way as to make any regulation seem like a taking (Margaret Radin 1988). The requirement that my house must be set 15 feet back from the street makes that 15-foot strip of land valueless if one conceives of it as being severed from the rest of the lot. Courts usually do not accept this argument and instead consider the effect of the regulations on the "parcel as a whole," which means pretty much what it sounds like. (Just as "conceptual severance" describes a view too narrowly focused, the "parcel as a whole" can be stretched to include too much area—possibly even entities not owned by the plaintiff—as discussed by Steven Eagle [2011].)

The consternation about *Lucas* does not seem warranted by the path of regulation since the case was decided in 1992. Hawaii remains a paradise for natives, tourists, and land use regulators, as David Callies (2010) later conceded. Zoning and environmental regulations have prospered and grown all around the nation. There is no evidence of a downswing attributable to *Lucas*. This is partly because the Court has not been hospitable to attempts to expand the *Lucas* doctrine to get a categorical rule about planning delays. A concerted effort to get a specific rule about "temporary" delays that lasted several years was unsuccessful in *Sierra-Tahoe Preservation Council v. Tahoe Regional*

Planning Agency, 535 U.S. 302 (2002). (Prospects for modifying this decision seem remote given that the lead appellate lawyer for the victorious planning agency was John G. Roberts Jr., now Chief Justice of the United States.)

The other reason *Lucas* has had only modest effects is that it is not difficult to tailor regulations so that some economic use remains. The most expedient way to assure that possibility is to install some variance procedures in the legislation. The absence of a variance procedure that would have allowed commonsense regulators to give Lucas an exception for his two lots triggered a court decision that is now known as the *Lucas* exception.

It is not that novel an exception—many courts before *Lucas* would not have countenanced regulations that eliminated all economic use (Neil Komesar 2001)—but it did draw attention to the possibilities of regulatory excess and has made planners and environmentalists more aware of the consequences of regulation. In this publicity sense, then, *Lucas* does represent an additional economic constraint. Had *Lucas* been decided otherwise, more zoning and related land use laws would be passed without even a nod toward their cost to private landowners. (I shall discuss the aftermath of the decision—the state settled the case by buying the land, which it then sold for development—in section 6.14, which more formally addresses the choice between regulation and outright acquisition.)

3.26 Do Exactions Mitigate Takings or Create Them?

The general reluctance of the Supreme Court since *Nectow* to examine the content of local regulation may account for the peculiar (to an economist) group of cases in which the Court has overruled regulatory exchanges. Even governments with considerable sensitivity to landowner concerns are apt to adopt regulations whose otherwise reasonable application will seem unreasonable in particular cases. If the regulation is so burdensome as to eliminate all reasonable economic use, the landowner might be able to get relief under the *Lucas* doctrine by demanding that the government pay for the devaluation, assuming the regulation is not justified by the common law of nuisance or other "background principles" of state law.

But in most cases some scintilla of economic viability remains for the parcel that is heavily regulated. Indeed, one way to assure that some constitutionally acceptable use is available is to grant small exceptions to the regulation. In either case, the possibility of negotiation means that there are still mutually beneficial gains from trade to be had. The developer gets an exception that improves the value of his land, and the government gets something—parkland, a trail, a better intersection, or just cash with which to reduce local property taxes or spend on general community improvements—that makes it better off, too.

Before embarking on a discussion of the U.S. Supreme Court's puzzling exactions cases, it is worth noting that economists have not provided especially helpful guidance regarding exactions and impact fees. Most analyses at least initially conceive of these payments as if they were taxes, like sales and income taxes (Altshuler and Gómez Ibáñez 1993; Skidmore and Peddle 1998). After all, they involve payments from private parties to government agencies. But exactions are quite different from taxes insofar as taxes have to be paid regardless of whether you get the benefits of whatever activity they finance. Households that do not have kids in school nonetheless have to pay property taxes; people who are pacifists still have to pay income taxes. (I will consider this issue more in the fiscal zoning discussion of chapter 4, in which I argue that the local property tax is actually more like an exaction.)

Exactions are different in that the private party can decline to pay them if she is willing to forgo the development permit. She will still have her land, subject to whatever regulation is legal, and can keep her money. If she wants a permit to develop the land, she pays the exaction. Economists' confusion on this simple point has contributed to the erroneous view that exactions are anti-development devices. That is simply not true, as Burge, Nelson, and Matthews (2007), Joseph Gyourko (1991) and (eventually) Altshuler and Gómez Ibáñez (1993) demonstrate. The underlying regulations from which exactions purchase relief may be anti-development, but the bargaining that exactions facilitate reduces their sting. The economic studies that find that communities that use exactions raise housing costs overlook the deeper issue. Communities that employ exactions have to have regulations that are more restrictive than those of most other towns. Otherwise the developers would be unwilling to pay exactions, since they could move to another jurisdiction. It is a city's underlying regulatory climate that makes its housing prices high.

The three U.S. Supreme Court decisions that have limited the scope of exactions have nonetheless been cheered by development-minded landowners and the advocacy groups that often fund the litigation. In *Nollan v. California Coastal Commission*, 483 U.S. 825 (1987), the Court struck down a proposed exchange of regulatory relief for a public benefit. The commission, established as a result of a statewide voter initiative in 1972, regulates land use along the entire coast. (It does not supplant local regulations except where the locals want to do something more intensive than the commission would like, so the effect is an example of a "double veto" structure described in section 2.13.)

In *Nollan*, the commission proposed allowing previously established beachside homeowners to build larger structures in exchange for allowing the public to have pedestrian access to the beach on the ocean side of their properties. In effect, the Coastal Commission asserted control of the air rights above the homes, which had the purpose of preserving public access to views of the ocean. It then offered to exchange some of the public's air rights for the owners' right to exclude people from the beach. Private owners did not have to surrender their beach-exclusion rights (several of Mr. Nollan's neighbors had done so previously), but then they had to continue living in smaller dwellings than they might have liked. (The smaller dwellings were, as in almost all new regulatory regimes, "grandfathered" and could remain in their original condition but not expand without the commission's approval.)

The *Nollan* Court struck down the commission's demand on the grounds that the right given up by the landowner—exclusion of the public from the beach—did not have anything to do with the right given up by the commission—control of the height and bulk of buildings. The term used by the Court for the necessary relationship was "nexus." A regulatory bargain that involves exchanging one property right for another was considered a taking of property if the two rights bore an insufficient nexus to one another.

3.27 *Nollan/Dolan* Nolens Volens

It is not necessary to plumb the depths of the term "nexus" because two subsequent decisions make it evident that the Court simply does not like some regulatory bargains and will grab whatever legal language is handy to limit them. In *Dolan v. Tigard*, 512 U.S. 374 (1994), the Court struck down a condition imposed by the city of Tigard (a suburb of Portland, Oregon) in exchange for a permit to expand a hardware store, owned by Frances Dolan, within the setback to a floodplain. The terms demanded by the city were that Mrs. Dolan donate land along the creek for a public bike path. The Court accepted the city's "nexus" rationale, which was that the bike path would alleviate additional traffic caused by the expanded store, but held that the burden of the bike path requirement was not proportional to the entitlement that the city gave up—a floodplain setback. The Court held that henceforth regulatory bargains must exhibit a "rough proportionality" between the value of what the state gives up (the setback regulation) and the value of what the landowner gives up, in this case the strip of land for the bike path. (In my review of these two cases in *Regulatory Takings* [Fischel 1995], I argued that "rough proportionality" made more sense than "nexus" as a safeguard to landowner interests.)

Most state courts adjusted their decisions to these cases without too much difficulty. Some bargains were struck down under the happily rhyming *Nollan/Dolan* test, but it is likely that many of them would have been found wanting under independent state constitutional interpretations. As Ellickson et al. point out (2013), many state courts had limited the scope of exactions under the doctrine that the locality was applying an unauthorized tax. And the "rough proportionality" test of *Dolan* had been explicitly distilled from the practice of many state courts, so its application was hardly foreign to many of them.

Dolan did add a new obligation for governing agencies, though. Instead of requiring that the plaintiff landowner prove that the government's demands are unreasonable, the burden of proof for "rough proportionality" was shifted to the government. How many potential exchanges were undone by this is not known, but the salience of *Nollan* and *Dolan* was probably diluted by the continuing barriers to federal courts created by the *Williamson County* procedural rules, which make it extremely difficult to get a regulatory takings claim into federal courts. For almost two decades, the Supreme Court did not take another exactions case.

In 2013 the more-or-less manageable—if not entirely reasonable—parameters of exactions jurisprudence were set adrift in the wetlands of central Florida. The facts of *Koontz v. St. Johns River Water Management District*, 568 U.S. ___ (2013), reveal a fairly common exactions process. Coy Koontz owned a 14.9-acre tract near Orlando that was undeveloped but adjacent to a major highway intersection. Most of the land was designated wetlands and was part of the drainage system of the meandering St. John's River, Florida's longest. Koontz and the district began negotiations that would allow him to develop some of his land. Among the options that the agency suggested was that he could develop 3.7 acres if he would contribute money to finance wetland improvements elsewhere in the area—in the same drainage system but several miles away. Another option suggested was that Koontz develop just one acre and dedicate the rest of his parcel to wetlands, with no off-site contribution.

Koontz cut off negotiations and won a verdict at trial that these "demands" (whether they were demands or options is not clear) violated the *Nollan/Dolan* rules. The Florida Supreme Court reversed, and the U.S. Supreme

Court in turn reversed the Florida Supreme Court. The U.S. Court concluded that the *Nollan* nexus may have been satisfied (it was a wetland for wetland deal) and that the *Dolan* disproportionate burden was not obviously violated. It instead added to the *Nollan/Dolan* standard the rule that the demand for *money* (to buy the off-site wetlands) was itself an unconstitutional exaction.

A not-unreasonable reading of this decision puts all transactions between developers and regulators at risk, since it is rare for such transactions not to involve a requirement that the developer pay for something, usually in the coin of the realm, but if not, with some activity (hiring a backhoe) that is certainly translatable into a dollar value. (Ellickson et al. [2013] briefly put a more positive spin on *Koontz*, suggesting that its allowance for money as property makes the *Dolan* rough-proportionality test easier to meet.) It is somewhat peculiar that this case is characterized as a regulatory taking, since the Court did not find that any particular regulation was unconstitutional. The *Koontz* majority instead maintained (as in *Nollan*) that the demand was an "unconstitutional condition" in that the district's demand for money (for the wetland mitigation) would have resulted in Koontz having to accede to regulations on his own land, which might otherwise have been compensable.

The classic "unconstitutional condition" (as discussed in *Nollan*) is a government demand that someone surrender a constitutional right in exchange for a discretionary government benefit. The government cannot demand that a public library employee refrain from criticizing the chief of police in exchange for her continued employment. Nor may a crop subsidy be withheld from a farmer who publicly disagrees with government policies. Note that these types of conditions apply to situations in which no one expects bargaining to occur. Librarians do not routinely expect that they have to bargain about constitutional rights to keep their jobs. But bargaining has for years been a widespread and widely accepted part of land use regulation, so its review in *Nollan*, *Dolan*, and *Koontz* is more problematic.

No one can deny that some demands look like extortion, but the tests that the Supreme Court has proposed—nexus, rough proportionality—seem as likely to inhibit ordinary negotiations. The Court's view that an unconstitutional condition had been imposed merely by suggesting a payment (among other possibilities) by Mr. Koontz to obtain a permit seems to make almost any negotiation suspect. Just how the *Koontz* facts will be distinguished from the everyday horse trading that goes on between planners and developers remains to be seen. Lee Fennell and Eduardo Peñalver (2013) find that *Koontz* is even more puzzling and doctrinally unmoored than *Nollan* and *Dolan*, which at least gave some parameters (nexus and rough proportionality) to guide nervous regulators.

3.28 Do the Anti-Exactions Cases Reduce or Raise the Cost Regulation?

My organizing theme in examining takings cases has been their economic effect on the behavior of governments as land use regulators. Do the decisions make governments pay more attention to the effects of their behavior? The *Lucas* and *Loretto* decisions raise the cost of adopting regulations in certain situations by insisting on payment in the event of elimination of economic use or physical invasion. The *Penn Central* doctrine raises some small risk that payment will have to be made, but the government has little to fear if it allows at least a smidgen of value and does not appear to be operating in bad faith. But once a regulation clears those hurdles, as most do, what cost does the government face in maintaining it indefinitely?

The economists' answer is opportunity cost. As I will elaborate in chapter 6 with regard to the Coase theorem, the government can be thought of as "owning" the regulation, but if it can exchange it with the landowner, both can be made better off by the bargain. A development-minded landowner who wants to escape a burdensome regulation can offer something of value to the government, and such offers raise the opportunity cost to the government of keeping the regulation in place. To the extent that bargaining is inhibited, the opportunity cost to the government of *maintaining* the regulation is reduced, not increased. By adding to the transaction costs of bargaining, the Court in the three exactions cases appears to be entrenching regulations.

At the American Planning Association convention that I attended in 2014, several panels were held to advise planners on how to respond to *Koontz*. A few commentators offered the nearly hysterical advice that planners should simply stop talking with developers. Do not even let them in the room to talk about modifying a regulation, lest something you say could be construed as demanding an unconstitutional condition in return for a permit. (*Koontz* seemed to feed this anxiety insofar as the regulators offered a menu of choices for mitigating wetland loss, not a final demand that Mr. Koontz pay to restore off-site wetlands.) But even the more sanguine assessments of the impact of *Koontz* were that bargaining will be more hazardous to regulators.

Their anxieties might not turn out to be justified. Developers with good reputations might be trusted to offer deals that they will not go to court on, though choosing to negotiate only with some developers could raise equal protection issues. (An acquaintance who had worked in public housing development in Boston assured me that experienced developers rarely go to court, as they know that the city will not deal with them again regardless of the outcome.) Perhaps the state courts will not follow *Koontz* very closely, knowing that *Williamson County*'s procedural demands make it difficult to move cases to federal court. If *Williamson County*'s demands are softened, the Supreme Court might modify its holding when it realizes that adjudicating these types of cases will take up all its time. It has happened before when the Court in *Louisville & Nashville Railroad v. Barber Asphalt Paving*, 197 U.S. 430 (1905), found that reviewing the conditions of special assessments, which are similar to exactions, overly taxed federal judicial resources (Ellickson and Tarlock 1981). But generally, *Koontz* and the *Nollan/Dolan* doctrines seem to march in the opposite direction that economists would like to see by lowering the opportunity cost of maintaining inefficient regulations.

Here is the caveat that might explain why the Court keeps poking at this issue: My conclusion that the exactions cases lower the cost of regulation stems from a view that the adoption of regulations is independent of the opportunity to get some money from selling them. If one considers the position of a government that is contemplating the costs and benefits of adopting more stringent regulations, it could be that one of the benefits that is at least implicitly considered is that exceptions can be sold and used to replace revenue that would otherwise have to be raised by taxation.

This scenario is not entirely fanciful. Fred McChesney (2001) describes Illinois legislators' "fetcher bills," which are intended not to be passed but to induce ("fetch") campaign contributions from parties who would be harmed by their passage. Jerold Kayden (1991) argued that New York City's "incentive zoning" amounted to "Zoning for Dollars," as he titled his article. I have shown that the law at issue in *Pennsylvania Coal v. Mahon*, the granddaddy of regulatory takings (described in section 3.14), was adopted not to protect homes from falling into coal mines—the mining companies did not want that to happen and fixed things when it did—but to force all local mining companies to pay an exaction-like tax to repair damage previously done by irresponsible (and judgment-proof) mining companies (Fischel 1995).

It is also possible that the availability of revenue would attract nongovernmental actors to oppose developments just to obtain payments by sharing in the exactions. Such organizations might lobby officials for more stringent land use regulations in order to obtain side-payments (Vicki Been 2010). If these motives were important, then the Supreme Court's anti-exactions cases could be seen as raising the price of *adopting* new or more stringent regulations by making the financial reward for doing so more difficult to obtain. In short, the Court does not want land use law turned into tax law.

The possibility of extortionate motives for regulation, however, seems pretty remote in the three exactions cases just discussed. The California Coastal Commission, whose exactions were challenged in *Nollan*, got its authority from a statewide initiative, and it seems doubtful that the voters had in mind that the new regulations would be currency to obtain other public goods. Indeed, expressing the thought might have made the initiative less palatable to many voters. The floodplain setback regulations on the Dolan property in Tigard, Oregon, were applied generally and look very much like regulations promulgated in many other parts of the nation. The Florida wetlands preservation regulations at issue in *Koontz* were part of national environmental legislation, and my guess is that most of its proponents would be dismayed to have its protections bargained away. There is plenty of trade in wetlands, though, much of it like that which the St. Johns River Water Management District tentatively proposed (Royal Gardner 2011).

So the evidence of fiscal opportunism in the three prominent cases seems almost nil. Nor does it appear that California regulators after *Nollan* just said something like, "Aw shucks, let's ease back on regulations if we can't wring any cash out of them." (I was cited in the *Koontz* dissent for having said as much in my 1995 book.) The prospect of a court making regulations inalienable seems as likely to encourage as discourage their adoption, but I think the vast bulk of regulatory initiatives would not be affected. Under the circumstances, the Court's exactions decisions run counter to the economic idea that takings jurisprudence makes governments face a higher cost for regulation.

3.29 Conclusion: It's the Regulatory Baseline that Counts

It may be that the Court's real concern in these three cases has more to do with the extremity of the regulation rather than with the proposed exchanges. I have visited the sites of all of the cases (after the decisions), and they all appear to be, at least at first sight, a bit dubious. In *Nollan*, the California Coastal Commission's prohibition on expanding buildings was justified by commission documents and the lower court that upheld the regulation as preventing a "psychological barrier" between landward citizens and the view of the ocean to which they were constitutionally guaranteed access. In fact Mr. Nollan's two-story home does not block the view from the Pacific Coast Highway any more than the lower structures, since most of them are fronted by apparently legal six-foot fences over which this bicyclist could not see the ocean.

The floodplain at issue in Tigard, Oregon, is along a modest-sized stream called Fanno Creek. It floods now and then, and among the uses at risk was the bike path that the city of Tigard wanted to build. (Mrs. Dolan's property was a missing link to connect two already built segments at the time of litigation.) The store expansion that was proposed to encroach on the setback seemed no more at risk than several other buildings nearby. The proposed bike path did get built, by the way, as did the store extension. The city seems to have found the resources to buy the land as well as the huge out-of-court settlement it felt necessary to pay Mrs. Dolan when the subsequent jury trial appeared to be going badly.

I also visited the Koontz tract near Orlando in November 2013. I was not the only trespasser to tramp across the tree-covered land. There were several informal trails, and I came across two separate encampments with a homeless person in each one. On one of them, which was near the area that Koontz had proposed for development, a middle-aged woman whom I encountered had been living in a barely concealed tent for several years. She assured me that the place does flood periodically and that she had to hoist her belongings up on her cot to avoid getting them wet.

What had made me curious about this was that a large apartment complex had been built just south of the Koontz tract, and it appeared to be in the same watershed. The complex can be seen on Google maps at the telling address of 1300 Waterford Woods, Orlando, Florida. I had stopped there before traipsing through the Koontz tract and learned that it was financed with tax credits to be used for low-income housing. I asked the homeless woman I met later why she did not live there, as she certainly would have qualified as a low-income person. She explained that her last landlord evicted her and her boyfriend after she had called the police in response to the boyfriend's domestic violence, and an eviction record foreclosed her access to public housing. I left her with some guilty cash and my feeling that maybe Florida could improve its housing policies.

I relate these personal accounts to make a point about how difficult it is to actually figure out what is going on in many cases without a fair degree of local knowledge. There is a further point in this. I was able to visit the sites in question and form at least some opinion about the merits of the regulation in question. What I have not been able to do is hear the conversations that might have gone on between the regulators and the landowners.

The California Coastal Commission may indeed be prone to overreaching. I have met a former chair and thought that she seemed overly dismissive of landowner concerns. (For more direct evidence, see Babcock and Siemon [1985], who detail the high-handed tactics of the Coastal Commission director they dealt with as advocates for property owners.) But maybe Pat Nollan (occupation: municipal attorney) had conspired with his neighbors to stand as the last holdout on Faria Beach, thus making the concessions of beach access by all his neighbors to the commission amount to nothing.

It is possible that Coy Koontz and his father (also named Coy) were being jerked around by the St. Johns River Water Management District, but it is also possible that they were being jerks themselves, or at least not taking sufficient account of the district's responsibilities to deal with their land and be faithful to their mission. The Waterford Woods project south of the Koontz tract stands as a potential rebuke to the water management district's solicitude for wetlands, but perhaps its developers settled for the same kind of deal that Koontz rejected and paid for wetlands to be preserved elsewhere. It is difficult to know the details of bargaining, let alone to distinguish at a distance cheap talk from intransient demands.

My admonitory point here is one I have made before (Fischel 1995): If the Supreme Court wants to help redress the balance between landowner rights and regulatory obligations and make governments perceive that there is some cost to adopting extreme regulations, it needs to look to the substance of those rights, not the manner in which they are exchanged. As Neil Komesar (2001) has argued, the information demands of this task are so great that the Court is unlikely to take up this task. The intentionally vague standards of *Penn Central* and the byzantine procedural rules of *Williamson County* suggest that the Court shares Komesar's view.

My survey in this chapter leads me to conclude, however, that many of the Court's decisions have stood against the tide of problematical regulation that would have followed from a contrary position. *Buchanan v. Warley* nipped formal apartheid in the bud, and the hands-off decisions in *Arlington Heights* and *Warth v. Selden* may have induced Congress and the states, whose remedial powers are greater, to confront racial and exclusionary issues with the Fair Housing Act. The Court has not stood in the way of national housing legislation and state-court inclusionary zoning schemes. The *Loretto* and *Lucas* decisions do establish some boundaries—physical occupation and loss of all economic use—for regulators, and *First English* and *Palazzolo* do prevent adventurous state courts from draining the Takings Clause of its last drop of remedial punch. The endorsement of ballot-box zoning in *Eastlake* made long-range deal-making more difficult, though, and the Court's attempt to supervise bargaining between regulators and landowners in *Nollan*, *Dolan*, and *Koontz* does not appear to be a helpful way to rationalize the web of local regulation.

CHAPTER 4

Fiscal Zoning and Economists' View of the Property Tax

The previous chapter described the judicial parameters on the use of zoning. The message there was that the seemingly clear commands of the Constitution translate in practice to a loose set of constraints on local government discretion. The present chapter asks whether people on the ground actually use zoning to pursue coherent local goals. The way I approach this is to address a specific question about zoning that is at the heart of a long-standing controversy about the nature of property taxation, a question that will seem odd to non-economists: Is the property tax really a tax?

Economists agree that if localities can conduct "perfect zoning," which effectively makes all real estate development decisions subject to a review that balances the developments' benefits and costs to the community, then the local property tax can be converted into a benefit tax, which lacks the efficiency losses that come with most other taxes. This chapter argues that American zoning is closer to this ideal than many economists think. The practice is often difficult to detect because zoning serves several objectives besides fiscal prudence.

The larger theme of this chapter is that zoning is not simply a supplement to municipal activity. Modern cities cannot be analyzed as if road building, parks, public safety, and schools were put in place, and then, by the way, we adopted a zoning ordinance. Zoning has been around for a hundred years. Once it became available to protect existing uses and guide development, the system of roads, parks, public safety, and schools have all been framed by land use regulation. The tax base itself is subject to discretionary development. Urban economics and local public economics texts need to start with this framework, not tack it on as a trailing chapter. Law professors Rick Hills and David Schleicher (2014) have made a parallel claim about zoning's role in property law. Public law, of which zoning is a central element, is actually more important for property lawyers to understand than common-law rules concerning such matters as adverse possession and title conveyance. Jonathan Levine (2006) is in the vanguard of planning professors who also see zoning as an integral part of urban development.

4.1 Order without Zoning?

As I will discuss in the next chapter, zoning and related land use regulations began in the United States early in the twentieth century and spread rapidly. Almost all American urban municipalities and counties now have zoning regulations. The question for this chapter is how much traction does zoning actually have? A counterexample may put this question in perspective. In a famous article, Ronald Coase (1960) used cattle trespass as a hypothetical example of the effect of legal rules. In rural areas where both cattle ranching and crop farming are viable, cattle must be kept from invading cornfields and other areas that might attract them.

Two rules to control the animals are available. Ranchers can put up fences to keep roaming cattle out of fields (or actively herd them to accomplish the same goal), or farmers can put up fences around their crops to keep out cattle (or actively police their boundaries to deter cattle trespass). Coase's objective in his article was to show that it did not matter for economic efficiency whether the farmer was legally obliged to fence out cattle or the rancher was legally obliged to fence them in. If initial legal liability can be reassigned voluntarily and deals are easy to make and enforce, the same result will occur regardless of who has the initial entitlement.

I will apply Coase's framework to bargaining between developers and municipal officials who control zoning in chapter 6, but right now I will point to a different issue that Robert Ellickson raised. Maybe the legal rules—fence-in or fence-out—do not actually govern cattle trespass. Ellickson did field research in Shasta County, California, where legal rules had recently been changed so that owners of free-roaming cattle were now liable for cattle trespass in areas where they had formerly not been. He found to his surprise that the legal rules did not matter much at all. Traditional ranchers and their neighbors adhered to self-generated rules of behavior that required, in a nutshell, that ranchers always take care of their animals, regardless of the law. Victims of cattle trespass, for their part, almost never resorted to legal remedies. They deployed instead informal, measured sanctions on cattlemen who violated local norms. Ellickson expanded his inquiries into the relevance of property law in other dimensions and produced a now-classic book, *Order without Law* (1991).

4.2 Property Taxes and Zoning

So does zoning actually control private land use decisions, or is it, like cattle trespass law in Shasta County, just an appendage that only crops up occasionally? The title of this book, *Zoning Rules!*, certainly suggests the former position, but the reign of zoning could be deficient in certain dimensions. The particular issue examined in this chapter is whether zoning allows communities to control the composition of its property tax base. Here is a brief explanation of the relevance of that question. As described in section 1.6, economists in the tradition of Henry George (1879) have argued that a tax on land is a better tax than general property taxes. Higher tax rates on land do not cause owners to remove it from the jurisdiction or modify their decisions about how to use it.

Of course, a higher tax rate on land will make owners of land poorer (assuming they had not anticipated the higher rate before they bought the land), and their poverty might cause them to undertake less development than they had previously planned. Unhappy landowners might decide to sell their land in that case, and the buyers would pay a lower price for it as a result of the higher annual tax burden. But the buyer's decision about what to do with the land will not be affected by the tax. If constructing and operating a medical office was the ideal use for the land (it's near a hospital), then the same office will be built regardless of how much the land was taxed.

Now consider a tax that generates the same revenue as the land tax but is applied only to structures themselves. The owner of the raw land in this case sees that her tax depends on how big a building she puts up. Instead of erecting the medical building, she uses the land as a parking lot, which has lower value and lower revenues. The medical office (if one is built at all) might be built in another jurisdiction that has lower taxes on buildings.

The economic loss from using land less intensively than is optimal (as the medical building was assumed to be) or pushing activities to less efficient locations (as the displaced medical building was, as it requires longer trips to visit the hospital) is called the "deadweight loss" or "excess burden" of the tax. The tax revenue itself is not a deadweight loss, since what one party (the taxpayer) loses, the receiving party (the government) gains and can use to finance public goods. The deadweight loss is a cost that arises from a lose-lose situation: The taxpayer does not get her building where she wants it, and the government does not get as much tax revenue from a parking lot. (For a real life, though minor, example of deadweight loss, see the example in section 4.8 below about "hairy cattle.")

4.3 Incentive-Compatible Property Taxes

Urban planners might wonder how much difference deadweight loss matters for the overall form of the urban area. The answer is that public finance and urban form are closely related. For one thing, an anemic tax base—one easily avoidable and hence laden with deadweight loss—will be unable to finance the urban public services that support well-planned cities. For another, property tax avoidance often makes for bad planning. Medical office buildings ought to be built near hospitals, not miles away just to reduce property tax payments. Economic efficiency and sound urban planning are often corresponding principles.

How might communities overcome the economic and planning distortions of a property tax on buildings? A land tax is an obvious answer, but land taxes in the United States are seldom used, perhaps because of the administrative costs of separating the value of land from the value of improvements, as mentioned in section 1.6. The impatient reader, perhaps aware of local tax revolts, might ask, why tax real estate at all? Why not have a local sales or income tax instead of taxes on buildings or land? (These alternatives are discussed in Ebel and Petersen [2012].) Then the owners of land could make development decisions without the distorting taxes on buildings and without assessors having to make guesses about the difference in value between land and structure.

Yet the property tax survives. One reason is that taxation of property is incentive-compatible, to use an economic term that actually means what it sounds like it means. Taxation of local property provides the right incentives for those who decide how much to tax, what to spend the revenue on, and how generally to govern (and zone) the community. Public decisions under local property taxation are more efficient because the decision-makers (ultimately, in my view, the voters) have to think about the consequences for all property values within the community, not just a single lot (Edward Glaeser 1996). Because the property tax base is long-lasting, property taxation also induces decision-makers to think more about the future than they would with a sales or income tax.

Consider a jurisdiction that has a sales tax instead of a property tax. It must decide whether a commercial zone should have office buildings or shopping centers. The office building is presumed to be better because it adds more value to the land and because it is less annoying to neighbors, having less traffic, noise, and odors than a shopping center. Under a property tax regime, the office building would have obtained zoning approval. But if sales taxes are the main source of local revenue, the shopping center has a better chance of being approved, even though it is less valuable and has the effect of reducing nearby residential property values, because the center generates more sales tax revenue (Paul Lewis 2001). Of course, neighborhood protest at zoning and planning hearings might forestall the shopping center, but residents in parts of the community not near the proposed center would generally be in favor of something that added to the local treasury. This is also true for a property tax, but the net gain to the rest of the community from the less-desirable shopping center would be smaller because of the devaluation of nearby homes.

Property taxation without zoning does not work very well. A history of zoning in Weston, Massachusetts, one of the more stringently zoned communities in the Boston area, mentioned that its original estates were founded by wealthy families who had fled Boston when the city adopted a high property tax in the late nineteenth century (Alexander von Hoffman 2010a). Zoning had not yet come to Massachusetts (or any place else). Rich folks could avoid the consequences of unexpectedly high property taxes by selling their Boston homes, which would then be broken up into apartments suitable for lower-income people. This would both lower the tax assessment on the building and spread the tax burden among a number of tenants rather than having it on a single owner. Boston might be poorer as a result, but the escaping plutocrats could reduce their losses by relocation.

If Boston had had a zoning law that prevented people from subdividing mansions into apartments (as most modern ordinances do), the rich owner would have needed to find some other rich owner to buy the mansion if he wanted to avoid the higher tax. The prospective buyer would notice the higher property taxes and refuse to buy unless the price was lowered considerably.

Faced with this fact, the original owner might decide to stay where he was, just as he might calculate under a pure land tax.

Of course, there were many other reasons that people might move to the suburbs besides tax avoidance. City services might be deteriorating, or suburban locations might be easier to reach because of commuter rail service or streetcars, which were proliferating at that time in Boston. But without zoning, higher property taxes created another incentive to move to the suburbs. One of zoning's functions can be thought of as trying to reduce property tax avoidance by making any structure's use difficult to change. It is not quite a tax on land, but if a land tax is too difficult to administer, zoning to control property owners' behavior could be the next best thing. The wealthy emigrants to Weston eventually made sure that the problems they left in Boston stayed there. As an early Weston planning document quoted by von Hoffman (2010a) puts the matter, multi-family homes were excluded because they attracted "a class of tenants who add nothing to the revenues of the town, but who, on the contrary, become the cause of increased expense in all departments" (31).

The problem of controlling erosion of the property tax was also evident in Pittsburgh around the time of zoning's beginnings. The Pittsburgh Committee on Taxation (1916) was convened to study local property taxation, but soon found it necessary to take a wider view. Under its section on zoning (which the city did not have at the time), the committee's report urged that the city take a cue from New York, which had just adopted the first zoning law in the nation:

> If Pittsburgh is to continue to raise practically all its revenues by taxing real estate values, steps must be taken to prevent the needless destruction of those values and to stabilize and promote their increase in every way possible.... Should we any longer tolerate sky-scrapers of unlimited height which steal the light and air from their neighbors, or permit the building of public garages, factories or apartments in splendid residential neighborhoods? (20)

Pittsburgh could have adopted an income tax instead of a property tax. A high local income tax, however, encourages emigration from the jurisdiction because there is less penalty for leaving, even if zoning prevents changes in the use of property. Suppose a community with uniformly good housing raises an income tax. Variation in incomes typically exceed variation in property values within communities. Wealthy doctors might live in the same neighborhood as not-so-wealthy professors in similarly valued houses. A switch to a local income tax could induce the wealthy doctors to sell their homes to professors without suffering much of a capital loss. When the doctors head for places with lower income taxes, the original community loses tax revenue that it might have been able to keep if taxes were on property rather than on income.

This may explain why local income taxes are rare. The primary examples are some school districts in Ohio, and as John Spry (2005) and Joshua Hall (2006) demonstrate, school districts are sensitive to the migration possibilities of their residents and limit the use of the tax accordingly. Income taxes in Ohio are used mainly in large rural districts where migration out of the district is less likely; rates have also excluded nonlabor income so as not to push millionaires out of the school districts.

4.4 The "New View" Challenge

My view of how zoning makes the property tax efficient is controversial among economists. I hasten to point out that it was not my idea. Bruce Hamilton (1975) developed it when we were both graduate students at Princeton. His idea built on that of Charles Tiebout (1956), in whose view local governments could be thought of as business-like suppliers of public services. Potential residents would "vote with their feet" for the service mix (schools, security, parks, infrastructure) they wanted. Wallace Oates, who was a young professor at Princeton at the time, had brought attention to Tiebout's model by showing that homebuyers actually paid attention to differences among communities (Oates 1969). Towns with better services had homes with higher prices, while higher property taxes reduced what buyers were willing to pay.

One criticism of Tiebout's model was that it did not sort out potential free riders (Buchanan and Goetz 1972). People could build modest homes in good school districts and pay less in property taxes but still get the benefit of the schools. Hamilton proposed an elegant but ruthless solution to that problem: Localities would use fiscal zoning to make sure that homebuyers would have to pay enough for housing to generate the property taxes that would pay for the schools. What I will show is that zoning as an institution is capable of configuring barriers to entry to avoid free-riding on local public services.

The scholar with whom I have been paired in opposition (by Thomas Nechyba 2001) is George Zodrow (2001). The view of the property tax that Zodrow has espoused in excellent economics journals has been called the "new view" of the property tax, which was originally developed by Peter Mieszkowski (1972). What is new about the new view is its larger scope. Rather than just being a local tax on real estate, which was the old view, the new view points out that the property tax is so widespread that much of it could be viewed as a national tax on real estate capital. (New-view people agree with everyone else about the land-value component of property taxes, which nowadays accounts for about a third of real estate values.) After all, almost every jurisdiction has property taxes, and real estate accounts for more than half of the capital stock, so a good part of the property tax could be seen as a national tax on capital.

I am not going to work out the implications of the new view. My task here is to respond to a challenge that Zodrow has proposed. He and coauthor Peter Mieszkowski have conceded that the Tiebout-Hamilton view is correct if—and this is a big if—zoning is effective enough to be able to charge every potential entrant into every community for the public service costs that they incur (Mieszkowski and Zodrow 1989). They call such a condition "perfect zoning," and, as the label implies, they doubt that it applies in many places. In a later article, Zodrow (2007) laid down the rules for a study that would convince him that perfect zoning was in fact in force. Such a study would entail "the admittedly onerous task of conducting a detailed property-by-property study to determine the extent to which the zoning requirements impose binding constraints on marginal housing consumption decisions" (513).

4.5 The Standard State Zoning Enabling Act Regularized Zoning

I am not sure that Zodrow was entirely serious about a "property-by-property" study, but there's something that seems almost as compelling called the Standard State Zoning Enabling Act (usually abbreviated the SZEA) of 1924. An enabling act is, in this context, a delegation of powers by the state legislature to localities. Zoning laws had originally been adopted in several cities without specific authorization from the state. New York City's 1916 ordinance was the first, but many others followed in rapid succession. The purpose of the SZEA was to remove an important question about zoning's legality. Some state courts had held that such local legislation was *ultra vires*, meaning "beyond their powers," and the SZEA made it clear that localities did indeed have regulatory powers that applied to land. It also helped to promote legal uniformity so that planners, developers, and attorneys would not have to learn the rules of each state and community from scratch.

The SZEA was drafted by a distinguished panel of engineers, lawyers (especially Edward Bassett and Alfred Bettman), and city planners (including Frederick Law Olmstead Jr., son of the designer of New York's Central Park), who were assembled for the task by Herbert Hoover, then the U.S. secretary of commerce. It was not federal legislation. Creation of municipal governments and delineation of their powers are exclusively the business of state governments. (Federal court cases about zoning do not concern the legitimacy of its existence; most are about its effect on constitutionally protected rights or congressional legislation.) The SZEA was a "model" act that any of the (then) 48 states could adopt in order to promote zoning.

The SZEA reflected several years of state and local experience with zoning and related land use controls. At least a dozen states had written their own enabling acts before the SZEA, and its contents were widely known before its official 1924 publication date (Stuart Meck 1996). Bassett, Bettman, Olmstead, and the rest of Hoover's committee were not brainstorming about a novel concept. Zoning evolved by experimentation with a number of different regulations. A formal zoning board of appeals was added as cities found that existing officials were not up to the task. Not all early rules survived. For instance, early zoning required the elimination of previously existing but now-nonconforming uses. As section 5.13 will show, public uproar about the actual application of this requirement resulted in the current rule that such uses are "grandfathered" and not subject to removal. Planners proposed, but the public disposed.

A remarkable aspect of the SZEA is that nearly every state adopted legislation that was either taken verbatim from this model statute or was heavily influenced by it. This in itself would make the SZEA unusual in the history of state government, as most model acts are either ignored or substantially modified by the states that adopt them. The enduring popularity of the SZEA stems from the broad powers that it grants to local governments coupled with a lack of compulsion for any community to adopt it. Communities whose voters worried that zoning would undermine their rights could ignore it, while those that valued its benefits could embrace zoning and tailor it to their circumstances.

There seems to be no better way to convey a sense of zoning's broad powers than simply to reprint the first three sections of the act. These sections are about one-fifth of the entire act, the rest being devoted to procedural matters such as how to adopt an ordinance and legally defend it.

Section 1. Grant of Power.—For the purpose of promoting health, safety, morals, or the general welfare of the community, the legislative body of cities and incorporated villages is hereby empowered to regulate and restrict the height, number of stories, and size of buildings and other structures, the percentage of lot that may be occupied, the size of yards, courts, and other open spaces, the density of population, and the location and use of buildings, structures, and land for trade, industry, residence, or other purposes.

Section 2. Districts.—For any or all of said purposes the local legislative body may divide the municipality into districts of such number, shape, and area as may be deemed best suited to carry out the purposes of this act; and within such districts it may regulate and restrict the erection, construction, reconstruction, alteration, repair, or use of buildings, structures, or land. All such regulations shall be uniform for each class or kind of buildings throughout each district, but the regulations in one district may differ from those in other districts.

Section 3. Purposes in View.—Such regulations shall be made in accordance with a comprehensive plan and designed to lessen congestion in the streets; to secure safety from fire, panic, and other dangers; to promote health and the general welfare; to provide adequate light and air; to prevent the overcrowding of land; to avoid undue concentration of population; to facilitate the adequate provision of transportation, water, sewerage, schools, parks, and other public requirements. Such regulations shall be made with reasonable consideration, among other things, to the character of the district and its peculiar suitability for particular uses, and with a view to conserving the value of buildings and encouraging the most appropriate use of land throughout such municipality.

4.6 The SZEA Endorsed Fiscal Zoning

No economist should overlook the fact that section 1 of the SZEA delegates to the municipality the power to control virtually every aspect of private development. The size of a lot, a building's height, configuration on the lot, and contribution to overall population density, and its use for "trade, industry, residence, or other purposes" are, without reservation, all subject to community control. Nor is there any requirement for compensation for regulations that might be especially burdensome, though compensation is not precluded, either.

Section 2 of the SZEA does put some limitations on community discretion. Within zoning districts, regulations have to be uniform. As Sonia Hirt (2012) points out, American uniformity requirements were a big selling point for early proponents of zoning. Uniformity gave the appearance of equal protection of the laws for property owners and served as barriers against favoritism and corruption. A *New York Times* article of June 22, 1922, endorsed within-district uniformity as well: "But these differing regulations are the same for all districts of the same type. They treat all men alike."

American uniformity requirements within each zone are offset by the community's almost unlimited discretion as to the number and configuration of zoning districts. Unlike the European presumption of mixed use, retail stores may not (without a variance) be allowed in American residential districts. But American communities can sketch in a retail business district near enough to residents to create almost the same proximity effect. The American SZEA's section 2 also authorizes community control not just at the time of development but also during "reconstruction, alteration, [and] repair" of buildings. Zoning authority does not stop when the initial building is completed.

The powers granted to local governments are directed to particular purposes in section 3 of the SZEA. The section starts with an apparent procedural limitation, requiring a "comprehensive plan," but all this means in practice is that a zoning map must cover the entire community, not just a fraction of it. Comprehensiveness distinguishes zoning from nuisance law and private covenants. Nuisance law applies case by case and offers only retroactive remedies for unneighborly activities. Covenants require consent of each property owner, which would be prohibitively costly to obtain where there were more than a handful. Zoning cuts through the transactions costs of universal agreement by authorizing the local government to regulate each property regardless of the owner's consent.

The "purposes in view" of section 3 list what the SZEA's drafters—reflecting urban experience—had in mind. Fiscal considerations are clearly paramount as indicated by phrases about "safety from fire, panic, and other dangers" and "adequate provision of transportation, water, sewerage, schools, parks, and other public requirements." It is difficult to imagine a more permissive charter for fiscal zoning than the SZEA. Its open-ended invitation to regulate may account for the durability of this model act, which still forms the core of most zoning legislation. When regulations not specifically mentioned in the act were proposed, there was little need to go back to the state legislature to amend or expand the enabling act's list.

An early bottom-up innovation, which the SZEA embraced, was an appointed zoning board, which could grant or withhold variances and special exceptions. Their role in smoothing the application of uniformity within districts to the historical and geographical realities of urban life can be contentious, but boards from the outset were regarded as "that original and ingenious institution devised to cover a multitude of sins" (Ernst Freund 1929, 144). It should be understood, however, that zoning boards cannot change laws or alter districts. Only the local legislature or, in many towns, the voters at large, can amend or rewrite a zoning ordinance.

In the 1970s, lawyers were concerned that some innovations of the era, such as regulating the timing of growth, allowing the transfer of development rights, and establishing historic districts, would be at legal risk (Fred Bosselman 1973; John Costonis 1974). Litigation did follow their establishment, but few decisions successfully challenged the regulations as straying from the state enabling act. Even if they did, the state legislature was often persuaded to authorize the supposedly *ultra vires* innovation to the satisfaction of the local governments.

The provisions of the Standard State Zoning Enabling Act are a powerful but only partial response to Zodrow's challenge about the effectiveness of zoning. The act shows, I believe, that local governments in the United States have available to them all of the tools to undertake fiscal zoning. Some economists might object that the SZEA offers only quantity controls, not a true pricing scheme. Economists generally regard price incentives, such as those created by taxes and subsidies, as superior to quantity controls, but quantity controls can get the same results. Zoning encompasses some price mechanisms such as impact fees and subdivision exactions, which will be discussed in section 4.9, but its primary mechanism is the establishment of broad and detailed controls over the physical configuration of development.

4.7 Zoning Need Not Be Strictly Observed to Be Effective

There is no doubt that fiscal zoning is possible, but the next question is, do communities actually do it? It could be that the tools are left on the shelf or used ineptly. This and the following sections will address these issues.

Almost all members of zoning boards (I served on one in the 1990s) can give examples from their neighborhood of activities that violate zoning rules: woodsheds within the setbacks, driveways wider than allowed, homes occupied by more than three unrelated people. (As described in section 3.17, the last rule is controversial in that it was often applied in communities with attractive school systems in order to limit enrollments, but college towns use it to keep student housing out of residential areas.) Some of these exceptions reflect the grandfathering of previously existing nonconforming uses, but even these could be thought of as undermining the strict application of fiscal zoning principles. Indeed, one can find numerous exceptions to strict adherence to private property rights. This article opened with a bow to Robert Ellickson's field work about cattle trespass in Shasta County, California. He found that the formal rules of trespass law were largely supplanted by local norms. If a group of scholars investigating private property started in Shasta County, they might easily conclude that a trespass rule was not much of a constraint. The same could be said of zoning rules.

But the exceptions to both property law and zoning law are, well, exceptions. They are important in that exceptions are useful to prove the rules. ("Prove the rule" originally meant explore or probe the rule, not provide a logical proof.) Ellickson's initial inquiries were a springboard to developing a more general theory of social control, one in which legal rules were relevant chiefly in high-stakes controversies and among distant strangers. This is likewise true of zoning exceptions. Minor zoning violations are often tolerated among close neighbors. (Most enforcement is the result of citizen information, not active policing.) In many states, a long-standing, harmless zoning violation can eventually receive legal blessing (and thus not complicate real estate sales) even if it had not been given an official variance. Many zoning boards seem to operate on the pick-up basketball rule of no harm, no foul. If the neighbors do not object to the proposed variance (or better, if they support it), it is often granted despite the niceties of the ordinance.

All of these are what I would call "intimate exceptions" to property law and zoning law. Instead of invoking the law, neighbors tailor their relations around norms of reciprocity. This helps to keep administrative costs—such as consulting with lawyers—low, which may be why most of the complaints about the exceptions in the literature are by attorneys.

The intimate exceptions could add up to a large fraction of the rules, but they do not add up to a large fraction of the developable space, nor do they add up to a judgment that fiscal zoning is ineffective. In Ellickson's Shasta County, local norms were not relevant when the stakes were high and when strangers were involved. Large-scale invasions by an opportunistic (and out-of-state) rancher were met with calls for legal remedies, and when a stray cow was hit by a motor vehicle with catastrophic results, lawyers were not disdained. Use of a home in a residential district as a commercial auto-body shop will bring the zoning administrator to the door, and a court injunction and day-by-day fines will follow if the shop is not soon shut down.

I have been on a board that required a homebuilder who knowingly violated the setback rules to dig up the foundation that he had already poured, and he did so. An unintentional violation of a skyscraper height limit in New York City resulted in the owner having to remove 12 nearly complete stories (Simon Elkharrat 2012). (The city could have granted a waiver, but a Manhattan neighborhood group, Civitas, headed by former city parks commissioner August Heckscher, insisted that the letter of the law prevail [*New York Times*, March 29, 1989].) Major zoning violations are usually obvious, and noncompliant owners face many penalties, not least of which is that the lenders for would-be buyers of their property may demand that flagrant zoning violations must be remedied in order for the buyers to qualify for a mortgage.

4.8 Is It Worth Zoning in Great Detail?

Disbelievers in fiscal zoning could concede that zoning law offers the opportunity for controlling development but still contend that none of this actually affects the "marginal housing consumption" that George Zodrow is concerned about. Margins are small units, and controlling all of them would be problematic. When I wrote a comment on the relationship of zoning to property taxation (in response to Mieszkowski and Zodrow 1989), I opened with a story that illustrated this problem:

> A few years ago I was driving through the rural town of Orford, New Hampshire, about twenty miles from my home in Hanover. Orford has unusually high property taxes because it proudly chooses to have its own high school, whose graduating classes number a few dozen, rather than send its children to less costly regional high schools. On this trip, I noticed an unusual herd of cattle along a rural road. The steers had a long, shaggy coat. The farmer was nearby, so I stopped to ask about the unusual breed. He explained that they were Scottish Highland cattle, which do not have to be kept in a barn in the winter. He did not want to build a barn, he volunteered, because then his property taxes would go up.
>
> There you have it: the deadweight loss of the property tax is hairy cattle. (Fischel 1992, 171)

Actually, one might reasonably ask what kind of deadweight loss there is in hairy cattle. A few years later I got to know the farmer who owned the cattle, and he took me on a tour of his farm (still without a cow barn) and explained the economics of Highland Cattle. He raised them primarily for breeding stock, which were usually sold to survivalist homesteaders in Alaska and other remote areas. Cattle that did not meet his breeding standards were "put in the beef program," as he delicately phrased it. He gave me a sample of meat to take home, and my wife roasted it. It was tough and had an aftertaste of liver. The deadweight loss of hairy cattle (and perhaps a cost of being a survivalist) is not very tasty beef.

The town of Orford, where I spied the hairy cattle, did not then have zoning, a distinction enjoyed by eighteen other rural towns in the state. (New Hampshire has 234 towns and cities.) But even with zoning, cattle owners would still have had pretty much the same incentives to avoid property taxes and could have done so under all but the most draconian zoning scheme. The Town of Draco's ordinance might read something like, "for every animal unit there shall be four square meters of barn built to the standards set out in section 104B, subsection 38A." It would probably not be beyond the powers of zoning to make such a rule, but it would be unlikely that a rural community, where landowners and farmers are important political actors, would actually do so.

The same problem of micromanagement of construction arises even in many thoroughly zoned cities and towns. As Zodrow (2007) points out (quoting Helen Ladd 1998), "No one would disagree that the property tax would distort decisions about minor expansions and repair that are beyond the purview of the zoning authority but not the tax assessor" (512). Actually, those are my words; because of the opaque editing of the volume, writings of the commentators (of which I was one) were mixed with those of the principal author, Professor Ladd. So I have long conceded that for small-scale decisions, the property tax could have some deadweight loss. It is possible that tax assessors do not notice these small changes, either. Reassessment occurs only every few years, and the statistical methods that are used in mass appraisals have fairly crude indicators of building quality. But the point remains: Within the zoning envelope (the maximum height, setback, and floor area permitted in the district), there are discretionary decisions about maintenance and expansion that might be discouraged by the property tax.

My main point about minor construction decisions, however, is that we should consider the administrative costs of making institutions do their job when evaluating zoning and property taxation. The institution of private property is not seriously impugned by the fact that there are everyday exceptions that are too costly to police. Employees routinely use company photocopy services for private use; children often take shortcuts across private lawns on their way to school; department stores that combat "shrinkage" of their inventory too vigorously might excessively shrink their customer base and their pool of employees. Zoning laws could make every property decision subject to public review, but in most cases it seems hardly worth the effort. (I learned from a student paper that some German cities actually do zone every structure for its current characteristics [confirmed by Sonia Hirt 2012], so that every change is subject to public review, and this seems also to be the case for exterior modifications of buildings in American historic districts.)

4.9 Which Margin? Holistic Development Projects

The margin at which zoning's fiscal control is most important to communities is new construction and redevelopment. At these decision points, the local government almost always has some say in the formation of its tax base. Developers who propose projects that have large public service costs without offsetting tax benefits are well-advised to make some additional arrangements to satisfy public authorities.

These arrangements can be difficult for scholarly observers to detect. The developer of a housing project might offer a public park as compensation for the additional congestion caused by the project. If that is not enough, she might include some commercial development to add to the tax base. She might accede to financial exactions and pay impact fees as part of the deal.

Such side payments are fairly routine and usually uncontroversial, but after they are put in place, they become fiscally invisible. That is, five years or so after the project was built, the property tax payments from each house do not seem to pay for the services that can be fairly attributed to each household. But that calculation overlooks the previous payments—the in-kind compensation of the park, the payments from the new commercial development that was tied to the rezoning, and the exactions for new sewerage and roads—that were part of the decision-making process by the community authorities. (I will address the adverse effect of judicial constraints on exactions when marginal costs are rising in section 7.7.)

To make serious judgments about fiscal zoning, scholars need to evaluate zoning in a more holistic context. That context includes more than the aforementioned side payments. It also includes the situation of individual communities. For example, it may be that an important local public good is not yet subject to congestion by newcomers. Some years ago I was driving through Wyoming and listening to a radio program featuring two candidates for mayor of a nearby town. Both candidates were outdoing themselves in promising to attract more residents. The stated reason was that they wanted to build up the tax base so they could pave the town's dirt streets. More recently, many small towns in America's Great Plains are eager to attract new residents in order to have more children in local schools, which would otherwise be shut down and replaced by a distant regional school (Timothy Egan, *New York Times*, December 1, 2003).

More commonly, fiscal issues are made invisible by attention to employment concerns or their seemingly opposite concern, protection of neighborhood ambiance. In larger metropolitan areas, fiscal concerns usually take precedence over employment issues because the employers can locate in a number of different towns. It usually makes little sense for a small suburb to make much effort to attract firms to boost local employment, since most of the beneficiaries of their efforts will be workers who live elsewhere. A new automobile assembly plant would provide jobs to the larger area. In suburbs that are a small part of a larger metropolitan area, it is mainly the fiscal benefits that count.

But a small, declining city that is distant from other employment centers might find that the jobs such developments offer might be worth some sacrifice on other fronts. The city council might decide that it is worth the extra downtown congestion they will have to deal with. If the new developments are fairly benign in this respect, the city might be willing (surely with a prod from the developer) to give up something on the fiscal side and grant property tax abatements. The city might even provide the employer with new local infrastructure that is financed by general taxes rather than exactions. This is a situation in which it appears that the city is giving away fiscal benefits, which is seemingly the opposite of fiscal zoning, but the city may well be calculating that on net it will improve its fiscal health. After all, if the city cannot attract employment, it is likely to endure a deteriorating residential property tax base. (A good example of small towns' concern with jobs is the placement of prisons in isolated areas that are eager to get jobs, as described by Eric Williams [2011]).

An important institutionalized approach to promoting industrial redevelopment is tax increment financing, known by its pugnacious acronym, TIF. Communities that want to promote development can designate an area in which additional property tax revenues (the "tax increment") from the new development can be used to finance the development and its infrastructure. The city continues to collect property taxes at the old, pre-redevelopment level until the project is paid off, after which normal property taxation resumes. The idea is that the community will not lose too much money in the short run but will gain a redeveloped area, with its better infrastructure, jobs, and tax revenues, in the long run.

The economic efficacy of TIFs is debated in an extensive evaluative literature (Weber, Bhattaa, and Merriman 2007; Greenbaum and Landers 2014), but my main point here is that TIFs are also calculated land use decisions. The community uses its regulatory powers as well as its (abated) fiscal powers to attract industry. Consequently, the commercial and industrial side of the property tax base, which account for almost half of all revenue, appears to be largely open to negotiation between the city council and footloose firms, which can easily choose among several cities. Nearly every state has programs that allow localities to negotiate some form of property tax relief. The best evidence for this comes from sources that decry the excessive use of tax incentives, mostly because city councils have difficulty distinguishing between businesses that are truly footloose and those that are thoroughly anchored but feigning flightiness (Kenyon, Langley, and Paquin 2012). Public economists are surprisingly opposed to competition among communities in this realm, but that may be due to the incentive for political opponents to dwell on bad results. The good results are more difficult to detect because a city that successfully lands a large employer creates substantial wage benefits for regional workers, not just those who work for the firm itself (Greenstone, Hornbeck, and Moretti 2010).

It should also be emphasized that regulation of commercial and industrial property is relatively uncontroversial. Regulation of housing development can bring complaints from housing advocates, state legislatures, and the courts, but detailed regulation of nonresidential property is routinely accepted. As I argued long ago in my Ph.D. dissertation (summarized in Fischel 1975), such acceptance allows the substitution of regulation for taxation. A firm that would not pay enough in property taxes to compensate the community can be made to pay in-kind or monetary exactions. This happens also in residential development, but the practice is subject to more criticism as exclusionary zoning, a problem nonresidential development seldom faces.

Concern about local employment and its flip side, the adverse neighborhood effects of business and industry, means that local concern about property tax revenue is nested in a larger set of local objectives. It is similar to a retail store's concern about preserving its inventory of goods, which is nested in its larger concern about profits. Store managers will sacrifice some of their stock if additional protective measures will alienate too many customers and employees. City managers, who are at least as faithful to their constituents as the managers of business corporations, rationally trade off one margin against another, and that can make property tax issues appear to be less than central.

4.10 Community Heterogeneity and the Tiebout-Hamilton Model

My defense of fiscal zoning has so far focused on its ability to mold the process of development and redevelopment. To the extent that the community can do that, it has the capacity to make the property tax on capital have nearly the same characteristics as a tax on land. The land tax's virtue is that landowners cannot shirk from paying it by removing the land from the jurisdiction. Zoning makes the building (capital) component of the property tax difficult to shirk as well.

There is another aspect to fiscal zoning that the Tiebout-Hamilton model entails and that is even more controversial. This model proposes that residents can shop around among communities to get their most-desired mix of public services. This shopping trip results in property tax payments that are essentially a fee for services.

Of course, all taxes could be thought of as a fee for government services in the sense of Justice Oliver Wendell Holmes's dictum about taxes being "the price we pay for a civilized society." What makes the Tiebout-Hamilton model different is that the local government services obtained by every resident have the same quality as private goods. The economic sacrifice a family makes to purchase the package of local streets, schools, parks, and sewer systems is valued at the same rate as its sacrifice for other goods such as a piano. (For economists, this means that the ratio of the marginal utility of the public goods to their price is the same as the ratio for all other goods, also known as the Samuelson [1954] efficiency conditions.) In the standard economic discussion of public goods, meeting this condition is impossible for public services because new consumers cannot be excluded from them in the way that they can be conditionally excluded (if they do not pay) from ordinary goods like pianos.

The previous sections have argued that zoning provides the exclusion mechanism to make the Tiebout model work. But economists have a further objection to the application of the zoning process. If it works so well, why do we see diverse communities where we (economists) would expect to see homogenous ones (Calabrese, Epple, and Romano 2012)? Diversity is a problem for economic models for two reasons. One is that in most models, the demand for public goods is assumed to be strictly income-elastic. Rich people are willing to spend more on good schools and clean streets than poorer people—an unattractive but not unreasonable generalization that, at any rate, makes the economic model mathematically tractable.

The other problem with diversity is that even if demand were not sensitive to income, the "tax-price" that people with different incomes would pay is different. People who live in smaller houses with low assessments end up paying less in taxes, but they get the same amount in public services. This causes them to vote for more services than they would pay for in the private market. For the opposite reasons, rich people are "overcharged" for local services and thus get "too little" for their money. Both heterogeneity and different tax-prices seem to violate the efficiency conditions that the Tiebout-Hamilton model proposes.

Heterogeneity of income raises a question of perspective. In the view of many reformers, suburban communities are far too homogenous. "White bread" suburbs prevent access to the poor and minorities who live in central cities and who cannot obtain the better educations and safer neighborhoods that those suburbs provide. Economists such as Anthony Downs (1994) specifically blame zoning and allied practices for this outcome. It is not, as some other urban economists have argued, the result of a natural process of housing development. In one sense, then, the suburban reformers are allies with the economists who argue that zoning works effectively. The twist is that the reformers regard the outcome as quite undesirable.

On the other side of the coin are economists who point out that most communities, even the suburbs, are a lot more heterogeneous than the Tiebout-Hamilton model would lead one to expect (Pack and Pack 1977; Joseph Persky 1990). There are plenty of poor people in the suburbs, and rich people do not all congregate in the same municipalities. One can find a few examples that border on perfect homogeneity of housing (mostly because the land area is so small as to constitute only a single neighborhood), but most suburbanites live in communities where they can easily rub shoulders with fellow residents who have twice or half their income.

One way to reconcile these different views of residential sorting is to invoke a widely shared degree of myopia on the part of land use planners, who do not foresee that general income growth will make people demand larger homes and better public services to complement them. Thus, they undertake rational fiscal zoning based on current economic conditions, which allow for smaller homes and lower impact fees than would be warranted under a long-range view that sees today's mansions become tomorrow's middling homes as newly wealthy people buy ever-larger houses. Because this myopic view is periodically updated for new developments, which then are more costly than the old ones, the community comes by stages to be more heterogeneous even though that was never the goal of any particular generation of planners and the public that supported them. Even if zoning becomes more restrictive, older substandard uses are grandfathered. In short, the history of community development makes a difference.

4.11 (Limited) Community Diversity

I certainly agree that history matters for community development, but that complicates the benefit view of property taxes that I espouse. So I advance here an additional public good that helps along the benefit view—namely, the demand for "(limited) community diversity." There are two aspects to the phrase in quotations. Community diversity is desired by many homebuyers. I impute this demand to homebuyers from their apparent demand for it in their children's colleges and universities (Caroline Hoxby 2000). Highly selective institutions could easily fill their ranks with full-tuition-paying students whose academic credentials are excellent and whose parents are rich. Colleges instead reserve some fraction of their scarce spaces for lower-income and minority students and finance the scholarships in large part with higher tuition payments on the well-to-do families.

I once shared the view that this practice was the product of top-down social engineering. Colleges engaged in affirmative action for students and employees to satisfy or at least to preempt their federal masters. But that pressure, if it was ever much of a threat, has long since abated, and colleges still want to create diversity. American colleges compete vigorously for students and faculty, so they have to make themselves attractive to them. Almost all of the selective colleges list diversity as a goal, and most seem willing to trade off other objectives to achieve it. The reason is that prospective students demand diversity. Diversity is a public good because it depends on the fraction of the disadvantaged population in a geographic area (college or municipality) and cannot easily be obtained by purely private actions on the part of students or households. (This claim is related to theories that hold that local governments can undertake some redistribution of wealth for the benefit of those who pay for it as well as those who receive it [Hochman and Rodgers 1969; Marc Pauly 1973; Plotnick and Winters 1985].)

The more direct evidence in support of a public demand for (limited) diversity is the experience of Massachusetts. In 1969 the legislature passed what was commonly called the "anti-snob zoning" law. It seems to have been tit-for-tat legislation. Suburbs had supported a school desegregation law that affected only the larger cities, and city representatives combined with progressive state legislators to pass a bill to make the suburbs more receptive to low-income housing (Sharon Krefetz 2001). The law requires that communities that have less than 10 percent of their housing stock designated as "affordable" (by regional income and housing-price standards) be subject to state-imposed modification of their zoning to allow qualifying moderate-income housing. The law has long been controversial, especially in the suburbs, and it is not toothless, as Lynn Fisher and Nicholas Marantz (2014) have demonstrated.

In 2010, Massachusetts voters were presented with a statewide initiative to abolish the anti-snob-zoning law, which has come to be known by its less-judgmental statutory designation, "40B." Since a majority of the state's voters live in cities that are subject to 40B oversight, I expected that the initiative would pass handily. Instead it failed by a convincing margin, with 58 percent of the voters opposing repeal of 40B. Only Plymouth County (between Boston and Cape Cod) had a majority of votes to repeal.

The map in figure 4.1 below, generously provided to me by Nicholas Marantz, shows the pattern of voting. In one sense, it is predictable in that the suburbs were in favor of abolishing 40B. But a closer look indicates that only 42 of the state's 351 municipalities, most in the far-suburban reaches of Boston, actually mustered majorities against 40B. Most of the other suburbs, along with all of the larger cities and truly rural areas (in the west) voted to retain 40B.

Despite opposition to individual 40B projects from neighborhoods and often communities, it appears that voters are reasonably satisfied with the (limited) obligations that the law imposes. It is possible that other factors affected the vote. State and local officials strenuously and publicly opposed the initiative, and it is possible (though I think unlikely) that voters suspected that without 40B, the Massachusetts courts would impose even more severe obligations on the suburbs, as New Jersey's had. Nonetheless, when invited in the privacy of the ballot box to reject 40B, voters declined.

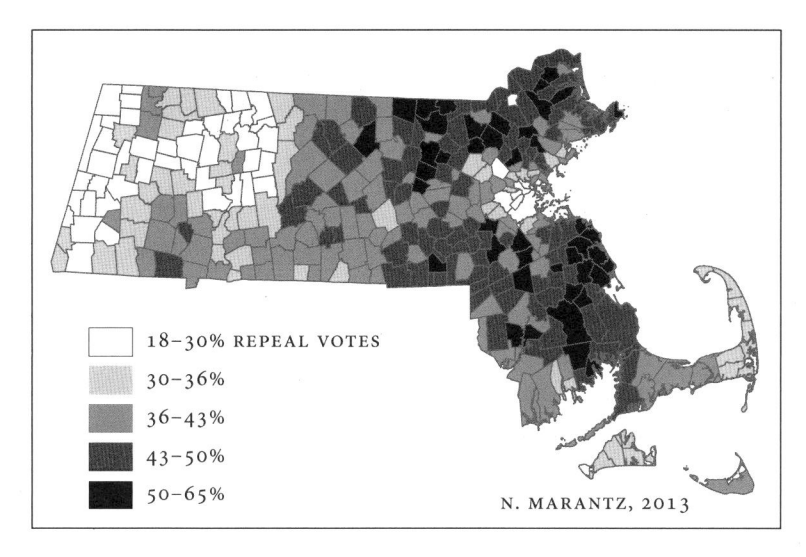

FIGURE 4.1 Massachusetts Town Votes to Repeal 40B, the Anti-Snob Zoning Act, in 2010
Source: Drawn for the author by Nicholas Marantz, University of California, Irvine.

The other aspect of "(limited) community diversity" is the (limited) side. I put the word in parentheses because it is generally not spoken or explicitly written. Sometimes it is alluded to in calls for regional "fair-share" schemes to distribute low-income housing among communities, but it is mostly kept quiet because it evokes notions like quotas, tokenism, and gentlemen's agreements. The anxiety that gives rise to the demand for limits on diversity is what Thomas Schelling (1971) called "the tipping point." Modest degrees of diversity (which would still usually exclude or severely limit public housing and mobile homes) add to the value people place on their community, a value usually reflected in the price of homes.

But if diversity diverges much from the regional average, it becomes a liability rather than an asset. If the fraction of low-income housing increases from, say, 10 percent to 20 percent, middle-class homeowners worry that prospective buyers of their largest asset will project that increase into the future and shy away from the community. Homeowners and home buyers are forward looking, and the most usable projection is what has happened in the recent past. Some existing owners may panic and sell at low prices to escape even lower prices in the future, and where this happens, the community has tipped into a downward slide in value.

Zoning allows communities to provide (limited) diversity within the community. Local control offers the extra insurance that diversity will not exceed the unspoken tipping point that would repel many homebuyers. To the extent that it is successful, diversity zoning can explain why communities can engage in fiscal zoning while at the same time appear to defy its principles by allowing or even encouraging some housing to be built whose additional tax revenues will not cover the additional cost of local public services.

4.12 The Special Position of School Districts

School districts look like a problem for fiscal zoning. Taxes earmarked for local schools account for about two-thirds of all property taxes paid. Property taxes account for almost all of school district revenues aside from the (often larger) revenue obtained from state and federal grants, and locally generated taxes are usually the only source of discretionary funds. Almost all school districts are governed by boards that are elected separately from general municipal government, and school boards have no authority to appoint local land use boards. School district boundaries frequently wander outside of municipal and county boundaries, and consolidated districts often encompass more than one municipality. Even if municipal zoning were dedicated to preserving the fiscal status quo by restricting construction that would bring more students, its regulatory geography would in many cases fail to reach a project that would send their taxpayers larger school-tax bills. By the same token, the regulators who do have control over the areas in question could easily turn a blind eye to the fiscal consequences of a child-rich development, since costs would mostly fall on voters in another jurisdiction (Ross, Hall, and Resh 2014). In short, school districts look like the exception that consumes the fiscal zoning rule.

In our national survey of the overlap between school districts and municipal and county boundaries, Sarah Battersby and I (reported in Fischel 2009b) found that the divergence between boundaries was more apparent than real. In New England and New Jersey, district and municipal boundaries almost always correspond. There, consolidated districts involve combinations of municipal boundaries, and financing the schools is usually done on a proportional-use basis—more students, more taxes—so that in a fiscal sense, each municipal tub rests on its own base. The New England model (as I call it) prevails in much of the rest of the urban Northeast. In the South, the pattern tends toward countywide school districts (as in Florida, Maryland,

and Louisiana) or large urban districts surrounded by suburban county districts (as in Atlanta and Nashville). But in these same places, the county also regulates most of the developable land, so that zoning jurisdictions and school districts overlap closely. The pattern in the West is more mixed, but even there, we found that most of the urbanized population lived in a district that had substantial overlap with municipal boundaries. When suburban development spreads into the unincorporated county firmament in the West, the preexisting school district lines form obvious boundaries along which to form municipalities.

That the school board is elected separately from the city council makes no difference for land use policy in the political model of local governance that I espouse, which is that both elected bodies represent the interests of a majority of resident voters, the most active of whom are homeowners (Fischel 2001). Indeed, service on the school board is often a precursor to service on a city council or other municipal office. In the many instances in which land use ordinances and their amendments are put to the voters, the correspondence is obvious. Studies have shown that elected municipal officials adopt policies that are quite similar to those adopted in otherwise similar jurisdictions by the voters themselves (Salvino, Tasto, and Turnbull 2012).

Even if one does not accept the majority-rule voter model, most of its alternatives also point to some correspondence of interests across governing bodies. If it is bureaucrats who dominate politics, both school superintendents and municipal managers will be interested in preserving their tax base in order to increase their power and advantages. If it is special interest groups such as employee unions, preservation of revenue sources is something both school boards and city councils will be interested in. That one can invent scenarios in which there is a failure to coordinate is not sufficiently persuasive to overcome the fact that pretty much the same people who elect school boards also elect city councils.

4.13 School Children as Fiscal Menace

Another argument against fiscal zoning is the simple observation that local officials allow structures likely to house children who could attend the local schools. By most calculations, a family with children is a net fiscal drain on the community. A recent article calculated that the main subsidy to local education was not from high-income to low-income households, but from the tax payments by households that had no children currently in the school system, which account on average for about two-thirds of all households (Kurban, Gallagher, and Persky 2012). (Their result should, by the way, chasten the usual back-of-the-envelope calculation of fiscal impacts of new housing, which usually attributes one or two kids per household, when the number per unit at any given time is now about one-third the assumed number over the life of the taxable unit.)

Kurban et al. appear to show that a two-thirds majority of the voters must be fiscally irrational. They have no children but still fail to vote down all school budgets (beyond that mandated by state law), and they still allow zoning that permits at least some residential development. A community that zones for any but retirement homes is *prima facie* evidence that fiscal zoning cannot be an operative motive, since new houses bring in children and less tax base than is needed to pay for their education. Indeed, the fact that any sentient adult consents to conceive and raise children is surely evidence against basic economic rationality. Even if we neglect the outlay on direct expenditures for food, clothing, entertainment, and education of the young, the time cost of raising children is immense. Think of those hours wasted attending teacher conferences, going to soccer games, watching school plays....

Of course I am not serious. One of the main reasons for having children in an urban society, say sociologists who are not afraid of outrageous questions, is that children connect us to the rest of the world (not to mention other generations) better than most other means (Robert Schoen et al. 1997). I took the connections argument one step further to ask why voters seem reluctant to abandon local public schools in favor of a privatized system involving education vouchers (Fischel 2009b). Formal education, after all, is not a public good in the classic sense of non-exclusion or non-rivalry, as the robust system of private schools that are attended by about 10 percent of the nation's children clearly demonstrates. The publicness of local public schools, I argued, is that it augments the location-specific social capital of parents and so reduces the cost of citizen-provided, local public goods. Public schools are the main way that adults in modern urban societies get to know other adults outside of their workplace. (I used to get what I called the bobble-head effect when I first presented this at seminars, in which young adults of child-rearing age began to nod vigorously. I actually obtained more empirical evidence for the hypothesis than that, though none more memorable.)

So the view of children as a fiscal sump to be avoided requires a model of human behavior that is far too selfish. Even the classical, bare-bones economic theory of consumer behavior posits an atomistic household in which the utility of one member is the utility of all. And even as children among native-born Americans (and indeed in most high-income societies) have become more scarce, support for education, at least as measured by spending per pupil, continues to grow. For a community to regard school children mainly as fiscal liabilities is like saying one should avoid good music, international travel, or fine food because you might acquire an expensive taste.

There is also a more selfish reason for communities to welcome families with school children. Study after study finds that the quality of schools is one of the most important determinants of home values in suburban areas (Haurin and Brasington 1996). Communities cannot have good schools unless they allow families with children. This elementary proposition is often hidden in studies that look only at the cost effects of new development. The benefits of an attractive community held together by the ties that bind the parents of schoolmates are entirely overlooked. But in fact, the benefits of local school spending are usually larger than the costs, if their net effect on housing prices is any gauge (Kang, Skidmore, and Reese 2012). Public schools seem to add more to the value of communities than would be justified by purely economic calculations, which usually involve comparing the cost of public education to that of private education.

The school-tax issue reflects a more general problem in evaluating property taxes. Surveys of public attitudes about taxation often conclude that the property tax is "The Worst Tax," as Glenn Fisher (1996) titled his book. (Fisher did add a question mark to his title, but he did not consider the tax in the benefit-forcing context considered in this chapter.) But that is not the appropriate evaluation for the property tax if the thesis of this chapter is even partly correct. The property tax is almost always a local tax, and it is closely tied to financing particular services, especially schools. Income and sales taxes are general revenue taxes usually used by states and national governments, and they are tied to no particular public good. Without asking about what the property tax actually purchases, surveys direct voters only to the highly visible, inconvenient-to-pay aspects of the tax and not to the public goods that voters get to consume and control. (And the surveys most scholars refer to actually show that after 1979, the income tax was disliked at least as much as the property tax [Rabin, Hildreth, and Miller 1989].)

Of course, there are diminishing returns to spending on local schools as well as other good things. It would be imprudent for any community to suppose that the benefits of having school-age children can be had without a cost. Even the most child-friendly community might balk at a large project that would suddenly flood the school district and cause overcrowding before more facilities could be built. Oversize districts and crowded schools are potential detriments to school quality and to the fiscal health of the community. Community authorities might reasonably employ their land use levers to demand that larger-scale developments contribute something extra, beyond anticipated property tax revenues, to build schools. That does not alter the fact that most communities continue to behave as if schools and the children who attend them are a community asset as well as a fiscal liability. As I have emphasized in this chapter, fiscal zoning is a nested part of a more general hypothesis about municipal objectives and the means of achieving them.

4.14 The Rural and Big City Exceptions and Delayed Capitalization

The model of political economy that I have espoused in the *Homevoter Hypothesis* (Fischel 2001) holds that homeowners are the dominant faction in local government politics. Owner-occupied homes provide both consumer services (housing) and an undiversified, durable investment (house and land) that is sensitive to what local governments do. As a result, homeowners monitor local government activities and discipline local officials whose actions jeopardize home values. This makes them especially leery of land use proposals that would have adverse fiscal consequences for the community.

Homevoters are most numerous in the suburbs. Indeed, the modern residential suburb was invented primarily to serve homeowner interests (Robert Fogelson 2005). As of 2010, a bare majority of the population of the United States live in suburbs, but a good fraction (about a third) still live in central cities, and about 15 percent live in rural areas. Homeowners are less influential in the latter two places but for different reasons. (The behavioral typology of local government is explored at greater length in chapter 8.) Officials in large cities are attentive to homeowners, but they also pay attention to development and employer interests. Indeed, Harvey Molotch (1976) emphasized developer interests in his famous theory of city development, which he characterized as a "growth machine." Cities also have a larger proportion of residents who rent rather than own. They have the full panoply of land use regulations, but regulation often serves goals other than simply protecting the value of single-family homes. Employment issues and renter protections are given more emphasis than they would in most suburbs. While developer interests are no longer as strong in big cities as they once were, their role is still prominent in bigger cities and counties because they can help fund political campaigns for city offices. Suburban politics is simpler and more transparent.

It would be wrong, though, to dismiss central cities from the fiscal zoning model. I argued earlier in this chapter that fiscal zoning has to be evaluated as a unit in a nest of objectives of the local polity. In central cities, fiscal zoning is deeper inside the nest than in the suburbs, but it is still there. Few central city mayors will be unconcerned about erosion of the tax base from a project even when the project might also provide employment benefits and reward important interest groups. And neighborhood groups are also powerful within most cities. They are likely to become more important in those cities that have become "consumer cities" in the phrase of Glaeser, Kolko, and Saiz (2001), who found that many cities had become attractive for reasons not closely related to employment but because they offered desirable amenities to high-skill workers.

Rural areas are different from suburbs and cities because of their larger stock of undeveloped land. This has two consequences. One is that owners of undeveloped land—often farmers or ranchers—have a bigger say in local affairs, especially about land use regulation (Thomas Rudel 1989). Their bigger say makes them more skeptical of the virtues of zoning, since it may interfere with their plans to develop their multiacre parcels at some time. But it does not shield them from the concerns that animate zoning in more suburban locales. Nearby development by other property owners may have adverse effects on their own plans. Projects that would degrade the fiscal condition of the area would also be unwelcome. Most rural townships (in the East) and counties (in the South and West) now have zoning, and so they possess the devices that enable the local government to manage the future property tax base (Michelle Anderson 2012). Fiscal zoning may be less of a priority in rural areas, but it is not absent altogether.

The other effect of a large stock of undeveloped land is that the benefits and costs of local decisions are less likely to be capitalized in the price of existing houses. If some exogenous event causes suburban property taxes to be reduced or local services to get better (say, via an unexpected court decision), the town becomes more attractive and more people want to live there (Byron Lutz 2015). Because most suburbs have already developed to a large extent, and local zoning prevents much infill development, such happy events cause existing home values to rise. But in rural areas, where there is plenty of land available, the more favorable fiscal circumstances (lower taxes) will cause more homes to be built, thus dampening the demand for existing homes and allowing for only modest increases in the price of existing housing. The Lutz result seems to suggest that fiscal zoning is ineffective in rural areas. But that is because our eyes are trained on the owners of developed land, typically homeowners.

What *is* capitalized in rural areas from an unexpected shift in demand for housing is the price of *undeveloped* land, and fiscal zoning is part of this story. To see this, consider a rural community in which some of the land parcels have houses (containing resident voters) but most other parcels are undeveloped. Furthermore, suppose that the undeveloped land is owned by a majority of community residents. (They are mostly farmers who expect eventually to sell their land for development.) They have an interest in establishing zoning that will maximize the value of their property, which includes the homes in which they live and their undeveloped land.

In order to attract homebuyers, the enterprising farmers will zone the land in such a way that it is consistent with fiscal probity, separating incompatible uses and excluding fiscal losers. (Chapter 7 describes this process in a slightly more formal model.) The development takes place, and the value of their original homes does not rise, since the new homes that are being built are pretty much perfect substitutes for the preexisting homes. But of course there is an enormous capital gain to be had here in that formerly undeveloped land (the farmland) has become more valuable. The capitalization effect of effective fiscal zoning is reflected in the value of newly developed land rather than in existing homes.

4.15 Enterprising Communities Need Land Use Regulation

The rural-to-urban transition can be facilitated by zoning. Take, for example, the experience of Dairy Valley, California, now the Los Angeles suburb of Cerritos. Dutch dairy farmers had settled the area when it was well beyond the urban fringe of Los Angeles. As residential development crept toward them in the 1950s, the farmers, who were a majority of voters, worried that newcomers would not appreciate the odors and operations of concentrated dairying. The farmers initially attempted to exclude residential development by incorporating their town and adopting extra-large-lot zoning. But opportunity cost soon beckoned, and they decided to rezone for suburban residential use. Zoning facilitated an orderly transition, and the substantial capital gains that the farmers harvested from selling their feedlots for house lots enabled them to relocate their farms elsewhere (Carol van Kampen 1977). The benefit of the rezoning was capitalized in the farmers' land values, not in the homes of the newcomers.

A similar process was at work in a more contemporary setting. The Walt Disney Company bought land in Florida and developed the town of Celebration, which was built incrementally over a period of years (Frantz and Collins 1999). The town was entirely master-planned so that early homebuyers would know what to expect in later stages of development. Early residents could not change the plan because Disney held a majority of the votes in the community association (which was not an unusual arrangement). During the early years, a shift in demand for homes in Celebration (as a result of lower interest rates, for example) would not affect the prices of existing homes (owned by residents) because the Disney Company would speed up development of new homes. After Celebration was entirely built out, increases in demand for homes there would increase the prices of all homes. Adherence to the Disney master plan (the private zoning) preserved the value of homes in all stages, but only after the community was complete would an unexpected shift in demand cause an increase in existing home prices. The value-preserving benefits of effective zoning (or the Disney master plan) were operative at every stage of development, but they were only easily detectable after the supply of new homes was exhausted.

The subtlety of capitalization is relevant to another zoning issue. A number of national and regional studies have indicated that excess growth of housing prices has been caused by increased zoning restrictions (Glaeser, Gyourko, and Saks 2005a). (I will argue in chapter 5 that these restrictions were largely the result of demand shifts, not different legal regimes.) But housing prices have not gone up in other areas of the country—chiefly the South and the Midwest. This has led some economists to conclude that zoning is effective only in a few parts of the nation, such as California and the Northeast. But this conclusion overlooks the fact that the higher prices in the latter areas are driven by differential demands to locate there. Zoning can drive up housing prices only as long as there is excess demand for existing units, and then only when the supply of new sites is severely limited.

But limiting the total amount of development is hardly the only zoning objective. Growth controls were a post-1970 development. Even before the growth-control movement started driving up housing prices, fiscal zoning was clearly operative in that it was able to preserve public services from congestion by overdevelopment. This is one of the implications of Wallace Oates's (1969) much-cited study of property-tax capitalization. His New Jersey sample was taken from the 1960 census, in the pre-growth-control era. Without zoning to control fiscal free riders, it is unlikely that any community could have capitalized the benefits of better-than-average schools or lower-than-average property taxes. The communities in Oates's sample were fully developed, and that enhanced the capitalization effect (Hilber and Mayer 2009), but something has to be in place to prevent subdivision of existing homes by developers who would take advantage of the fiscal advantages in high-service or low-tax communities. That something is zoning.

4.16 Conclusion: Is the Local Property Tax Really a Tax?

Taxes are involuntary payments to the government for which no specific benefit is promised, other than staying out of jail. The definition begs many fine distinctions, of course. Social security "contributions" (that is the "C" in FICA, the Federal Insurance *Contributions* Act, on your pay stub) entitle one to social security benefits at some time in the future. But outside of the offices of Health and Human Services in Washington, they are regarded as taxes. Paying them is not optional, and the benefits are only loosely related to the amount paid. (The progressive earmarked benefits, however, appear to inform the public's view of the system and thus makes the tax's regressiveness more acceptable [Colin Campbell 1969].)

Property owners similarly have no choice about paying their taxes (though property-value assessments can be appealed), and the money they pay to the local government is used to provide services for which the taxpayer gets no earmarked benefit. But this view overlooks activity *prior* to the payment of the taxes. You do not have much choice about making your monthly mortgage payment, even if your house is no longer satisfactory, but few would regard mortgages as a tax. You volunteered for this home-owning commitment, and you could have kept renting.

In the United States, most people choose their municipality and school district in the same sense that they choose to purchase property and assume mortgages to finance it. Indeed, for most people the choice of buying a house is closely bundled with the community in which the property is located. But this would be true even if local services were financed by a local income tax. What the present chapter has argued is that the community itself—its elected and appointed officials, more or less responding to established residents—actively shapes and manages the property tax system in a way that would be difficult to do with any other tax base. Local land use regulation constrains the wholesale tax-avoidance behavior that bedevils most other potential tax bases. Supplemented by revenues from impact fees and by negotiated exactions from developers, fiscal zoning makes most development pay its own way. Apparent exceptions to this behavior arise chiefly because communities trade off fiscal security for other objectives such as employment or (limited) income redistribution.

In a 1992 paper in which I first defended this position, I added to it my then-recent hypothesis (Fischel 1989b) about the cause of California's Proposition 13, which severely limited property tax and the growth of assessments. Prop 13 looks like evidence in support of a general aversion to property taxes, but I took it as an example in support of my view that local property taxes are more like fees for local services. Prop 13 was caused, I argued, by the California Supreme Court's decision in *Serrano v. Priest*, 135 Cal. Rptr. 345 (1976), which required that school spending could not vary among districts on the basis of variation in local tax bases. The legislature's implementation of this plan in 1977 meant that most local property tax payments were no longer related to local schooling, which made the property tax into a statewide tax.

As I have argued in several articles (best summarized in Fischel 2004b), the voters rationally responded to this exogenous event (the court decision) by embracing an initiative that severely limited the property tax. If the schools have to be state-funded, the voters seemed to be saying, let the state use something other than the property tax. If I am right about this, the connection between the *Serrano* decision and Prop 13 is evidence in support of the fiscal zoning model. Voters had formerly regarded their property taxes as a fee for (mostly) school services, and they had used fiscal zoning to protect their property tax base. When the state, per the *Serrano* decision, commandeered local property taxes to pay for school finance equalization, voters scrapped the property tax system for schools.

My explanation for Prop 13 has become the conventional wisdom among scholars of local public economics. The conventional wisdom attracts critics, and I have addressed the concerns of the two most articulate, Kirk Stark and Jonathan Zasloff (2003) and Isaac Martin (2006), in my 2004b and 2009a articles, respectively. I do not think of my *Serrano*-Prop 13 theory as having been proved. It wins mainly by default: There are no other plausible theories to explain Proposition 13 within the intellectual space of modern political economics. Its relevance is chiefly grounded on the durability of Prop 13. Despite the enormous mischief it has caused in California, Prop 13 is the most untouchable political topic, the "third rail" of California politics. It is likely to persist, I submit, as long as the rigorous demands of the *Serrano* decision persist. For the time being, Prop 13 can be viewed as the logical consequence of attempting to make the property tax into a true tax.

School district lines still are strongly capitalized in California, perhaps because homebuyers now value student peer effects more than differences in school spending, which are now negligible (Brunner, Murdoch, and Thayer 2002). Test scores, not spending, are now the school district markers that homebuyers care about. Local governments now favor commercial land uses that generate more sales taxes rather than higher property values (Burnes, Neumark, and White 2011). Housing developers are asked to finance more infrastructure and pay more in exactions and impact fees (Dresch and Sheffrin 1997). And a larger fraction of local public services are now provided in the private sector in the form of homeowner associations (Ron Cheung 2008). Private school enrollments among high-income families have risen significantly since the passage of Prop 13 (Brunner and Sonstelie 2006). Rather than creating the more egalitarian system desired by the *Serrano* plaintiffs, more affluent Californians have removed themselves from the public sector and left the rest of the population to attend overcrowded schools and put up with severely constrained public services. Viewed in light of this experience, the local property tax and fiscal zoning might not be as inefficient and regressive as they are often made out to be.

CHAPTER 5

The Economic History of Zoning

This chapter develops an economic theory of the history of zoning over the entire twentieth century. Zoning began in the 1910s with ordinances in Los Angeles and (most clearly) in New York City in 1916. It was remarkable for its rapid spread all over the country. Thus, this history is less about the particulars of individual cities and more about larger economic and social trends. I emphasize the development of low-cost, over-the-road transportation as the primary cause of zoning in the 1910–1930 period. The informal methods and traditional legal rules that homeowners formerly used to control unwanted development were overwhelmed by industrial and apartment developers who were made footloose by the motor truck and the jitney bus.

The other major shift in zoning history occurred in the 1970s, when the growth-control movement was born and spread almost as rapidly as zoning originally did, though its effects were regionally selective. I argue that a combination of modern forces induced this change, but the most important was the 1970s period of inflation, which helped transform housing from a consumer good to an investment and thus gave rise to a political class I have called "homevoters." (A formal analysis of land use regulation that uses an "overlapping generations" model—an economic version of history—that comes to a conclusion similar to mine is that of Ortalo-Magne and Prat [2014].)

The assessment of fiscal zoning in chapter 4 offered a mixed normative verdict. Zoning grants community residents an entitlement to control what happens in their environs. This security is especially valued by homeowners, who have an unusually large and vulnerable asset that is at risk from neighborhood change. The upside is that zoning probably makes for more efficient provision of local services and better neighborhoods than would be available without it. The downside is that zoning can go too far and prevent economically desirable increases in density and hinder what many people regard as the desirable mixing of socioeconomic groups within communities. While I do concede that many communities might want to have some diversity within their community, many readers would balk at the "(limited) diversity" that I think they achieve and insist that the "limited" be deleted along with my coy parentheses.

5.1 Exclusionary Zoning Retards National Migration and Income Convergence

The issues of suburban exclusionary zoning were well known when I first started writing the predecessor of this book in the early 1980s (Fischel 1985). What is new and compelling 30 years later is evidence that the excesses of American land use regulation have more problematical effects than even its most severe critics suspected. Zoning is not simply retarding the mobility of the poor from central city to suburbs. According to an important study by Peter Ganong and Daniel Shoag (2013), land use regulation is retarding the mobility of low-income people within the entire nation. They show that for the first two-thirds of the twentieth century, states of the union were converging in their average levels of income. The convergence was not caused by richer states becoming poorer. Both rich and poor states had growing real incomes, but poor states were becoming richer faster.

Most of this convergence was caused by migration of people from poor states to richer states. Families from relatively poor Oklahoma moved to richer California (to invoke the dust-bowl migration memorialized in John Steinbeck's *Grapes of Wrath*) or, to use Ganong and Shoag's example, from Mississippi (the poorest state) to Connecticut (the richest). Ganong and Shoag demonstrate that this convergence was the result of directed migration, not random resettlement. The poor aimed at the richer states. In a sense, Ganong and Shoag have shown that the famous "great migration" of southern blacks to northern cities in the early twentieth century was part of a general movement of the poor to richer places. In *The Warmth of Other Suns* (Isabel Wilkerson 2010), the three African Americans who epitomize the great migration left the South for New York, Chicago, and Los Angeles not just to escape racial segregation but to improve their economic position. The populations of poorer states grew less rapidly than that of richer states, and incomes in poorer states started to catch up with those of the richer states.

This sounds like merely a reshuffling of the poor. Although Ganong and Shoag do not emphasize this interpretation, other urban economists such as Edward Glaeser (2011) and Enrico Moretti (2012) have argued that the skills that make people richer in high-income places are contagious. It is not just that a poor taxi-driver from New Orleans moves to Seattle and gets better fares. He, or at least his children, end up getting more education and training, and they find better careers. The story of immigrant success is commonly told on an international scale, but it applies within the nation as well. Geographic mobility is an important channel for economic and social mobility.

Ganong and Shoag show that rising housing prices have substantially reduced America's intranational tradition of moving to opportunity. Like some other researchers, they have found that high housing prices repel potential workers from regions (Raven Saks 2008; Young, Varner, and Massey 2008) and that this pattern is strongly associated with land use regulation (Gyourko, Mayer, and Sinai 2013). But Ganong and Shoag have gone beyond these findings in two important respects. First, they see a strong temporal association between housing prices and land use regulation by region. Many scholars do not appreciate that housing prices throughout the United States were fairly similar among regions in the 1950s and 1960s. Bigger cities had higher prices, of course, and nicer suburbs had higher home values than less nice suburbs (especially if "nice" reflected school quality), but housing in California, which is currently the persistent leader in housing prices, used to be no more expensive than it was in comparably sized urban areas in the Midwest and the Northeast (Case and Shiller 1990; Thomas Thibodeau 1992).

Ganong and Shoag tie the rise in housing prices in California (and the rest of the West Coast) and in the Northeast to land use regulation in a clever way that allows them to see how the regulatory constraints evolved over time. They searched the decisions of every state supreme court from the 1920s to the present for the phrase "land use." Dividing the number of cases that simply mention "land use" by the total number of decisions gives an indication of how important the issue is relative to other states and to other time periods in the same state. ("Zoning" gave similar results.) States that increase land use regulation should find that they have a relative increase in litigation, and indeed this indicator of litigation is strongly correlated with modern surveys of land use restrictiveness that were established by scholars at the University of Pennsylvania (Gyourko, Saiz, and Summers 2008, discussed in section 8.13).

The advantage of the method used by Ganong and Shoag is that they can go back to early in the twentieth century to see how the stringency of regulation has evolved in each state.

They find a strikingly close relationship between the growth of housing prices on the East and West Coasts, on the one hand, and the 1970s explosion of land use litigation in those states, on the other. Just as housing prices in California, Oregon, New Jersey, and Massachusetts were rising steeply, their land use litigation was taking the same trajectory. These states (as exemplars of their regions) were not leaders in land use litigation before 1970, when housing prices were more or less the same everywhere.

Ganong and Shoag then develop a model in which the post-1970s housing inflation affected migration. High prices have a differential effect in that they deter low-income immigrants more than high-income movers. (They call these groups "low-skill," meaning those with no more than high school diplomas, and "high-skill," referring to those who have college degrees, but the groups themselves are no different from those termed "low-income" and "high-income.") Potential migrants calculate not just the expected wages from moving to Oregon; they subtract from this the extra housing cost that living in Portland would entail. This differential affects everyone, of course, but housing is a smaller fraction of consumer expenditures for high-income people. As a result, high housing costs selectively exclude low-income people.

The selective exclusion is their answer to a paradox attributed to Yogi Berra, who observed that a restaurant was so crowded that no one goes there anymore. If San Francisco is "too expensive," why does anyone live there? The answer is that coastal housing prices have not decreased because the people who do not go there anymore are the poor. Not that the rich get off without a penalty. As Enrico Moretti (2013) points out, the increasing differences in household income between residents of the coasts and the rest of the nation is more apparent than real because higher regional housing costs reduces spending on other things, even for the rich.

This is the same charge that reformers have for years brought against the suburbs, but in this case the "suburbs" are in the affluent, economically dynamic metropolitan areas of the United States, the majority of which happen to be located on either side of the country. The consequences of this regional exclusion, though, seem more normatively dire. Ganong and Shoag offer calculations that suggest that almost a third of the decrease in American economic inequality up to 1970 (when American incomes were, by historical standards, most equally distributed) can be accounted for by migration of workers from poor states to rich states. Moving to opportunity was an important source of income equalization for the first two-thirds of the twentieth century. That migration trend has nearly stopped as a result of increased land use regulation in the high-productivity areas.

The rest of the present chapter is devoted to explaining how this state of affairs came about. It is motivated in part by a comment Peter Ganong made in passing. I have been something of a cheerleader for Ganong and Shoag's article since it appeared as a working paper in 2012, and Peter mentioned that he was further encouraged by its favorable reception by policy-makers in Washington, DC. I have watched for 40 years as one federal commission after another addressed the problems of exclusionary zoning. The commissions have had almost no effect on zoning practice. In fact, as I argued in chapter 2, Washington has more often been part of the problem than a solution. An important reason for this is that zoning's origins and development are neglected by economists and misunderstood by planners. When its history is considered at all, zoning is thought of as being the product of high-level experts and Supreme Court judges who stepped in when the adverse effects of urban life finally became intolerable. I hope in the following sections to explain that this is not so. My objective is to unearth the conditions that brought forth zoning in the 1910s and then growth controls in the 1970s in order to point to more effective roads to reform.

5.2 The Supply-Side Bias of History

Histories of institutions are usually beholden to the supply side of the story. In researching my book on the development of the American school system (Fischel 2009b), I found that most histories of education took as their primary sources the writings of state superintendents of schools and their advocates in early academic departments of education. Annual reports by the superintendents conveniently aggregated the doings of the multitude of school districts and pedagogical conferences. Professors and deans of schools of education were the contemporary sources whose commentary modern scholars leaned on to explain why one-room schools gave way to the consolidated school districts that now dominate education delivery systems.

Such sources, however, have a supply-side bias. Superintendents such as Horace Mann and education-school leaders like Elwood Cubberley almost invariably advocated for school consolidation. So when consolidation finally arrived, it seemed natural for latter-day historians to infer that it was advocacy from these quarters that caused it. The role of the demanders of education, parents with school-age children and voters in local school districts, was slighted not so much for lack of interest by historians as for lack of a consolidated, contemporary source of what parents thought. (My theory, summarized in Fischel [2014], is that parents decided that consolidated schools were acceptable after the economic payoff for a high school education made it a worthwhile investment, and one-room schools were rightly deemed inadequate to prepare their kids for high school.)

A similar bias affects views of how zoning developed and spread. The suppliers of zoning theories, city plans, and legal documents usually left a record of their thinking. Planners and lawyers and civil engineers had outlets for their ideas in professional journals, legislative hearings, and conference proceedings. The documents they drafted are available for review by modern historians, who are well advised to study them. Much of the history of zoning, then, is replete with attention to those who headed the zoning movement, such as Alfred Bettman, Edward Bassett, James Metzenbaum, and Justice George Sutherland (Haar and Wolf 2002).

The other side of the story, what I call the demand side, constitutes the voters in municipalities that adopted zoning. Advocates of zoning could not make even the first step without the approval of voters or their duly elected city and town councils. In more than a few cases, initial zoning laws (and, later, their numerous amendments) had to be put to a municipal-wide vote. A fuller account of zoning needs to look at why voters decided that zoning was a good idea.

This chapter will show that a majority of urban Americans decided they needed zoning because the development of motorized trucks and buses delivered industry and apartment houses as unwelcome neighbors to single-family areas. Industry and business had formerly been confined to areas near ports, railroads, and streetcar lines because of the high cost of overland freight and passenger transportation. It was not so much Henry Ford's inexpensive Model T automobile that threatened residential neighborhoods. It was the modifications of the Model T in the form of jitney buses and motor trucks that induced homebuyers and their agents, large-scale homebuilders, to embrace zoning.

In what follows, I will allude to a general model of the supply and demand for zoning. Supply and demand analysis is a convenient way of aggregating and identifying a highly diverse set of social forces. The economic terminology is justified, I submit, because the prices and quantities of an important economic asset, the single-family home, drove the development of zoning. (Chapter 7 will be more formal about this, but formality at this point would brush away too many potentially important social and economic factors.)

5.3 Homeownership Instigated Zoning's Rapid Rise

Zoning started in the United States just after 1910. Many cities already had ordinances with some zoning-like features in the nineteenth century (Raphael Fischler 1998a). Almost all of these, however, addressed particular issues within the developed area of the city rather than designating uses throughout its area. Concern about fires motivated attempts to regulate building materials. Widespread construction of steel-frame skyscrapers in the late nineteenth century induced cities to adopt light-and-air regulations such as maximum height requirements. Some cities also adopted residential districts that forbade certain noxious businesses—livery stables were a special target—and, occasionally, multifamily homes.

Zoning in the 1910s represented an important break with the selective regulations of the past. The new features were the comprehensiveness of the zoning map and the law's presumption that single-family residences were to get the most protection. Every square inch of the city or town was made subject to zoning, not just certain sections, as had been the case in earlier land use regulation. Some zoning districts may have been permissive either by law or by practice, but there were no unzoned districts. Comprehensive zoning did not, as planners often lament, emerge from a comprehensive plan. But in the process of designating every acre of land to be within one zone or another, the city could now control the future use of its land. Prospective regulation freed the city authorities from having to react to neighborhood land use conflicts with ad hoc regulations or the cumbersome and uncertain process of nuisance litigation.

The presumption that single-family districts are to get the most protection is now so widespread that we seldom ask why it should be so. In other political settings, where one works is at least as important as where one lives, and the services of rental housing are no less important to their occupants than those of owner-occupied housing. Yet the single-family, owner-occupied home appears to be the object of most solicitude in nearly every zoning ordinance. The occasional exceptions that put business purposes at the top, such as the City of Industry in Los Angeles County, California, are sufficiently unusual as to seem bizarre. (I visited Industry several years ago, and its scrubbed-street lifelessness gave me the queasy feeling of having stepped onto the set of a science fiction movie.)

The attraction of citywide zoning was the security it gave to early twentieth-century homebuilders and homeowners. Once zoning was adopted, builders and buyers were no longer completely uncertain whether the nearby tract of undeveloped land or the one ripe for redevelopment would be put to some use that was incompatible with their own. Homeowners and builders could read in a public record what the zoning allowed and forbade, and they knew that if a developer sought to change what was allowed, neighbors and other citizens would have some influence on the political process by which the change was considered.

Since I wrote my original article advocating this historical chain, other accounts of zoning's development have come forth. They emphasize the preexisting conditions of the community, such as the prezoning density of population, to explain why land use regulation became more or less exclusive over time (Jenny Schuetz 2008; Glaeser and Ward 2009; Jonathan Rothwell 2009). The present account does not gainsay (or affirm) those accounts. But none of them addresses what I regard as the singular fact about zoning: Before 1910, there was not a single zoning ordinance in the United States. By 1930, it had spread to all sections of the country, not just the big cities or areas undergoing racial change. It is this rapid, nationwide institutional change at this particular time that requires explanation. If density of population or rural settlement patterns had determined zoning's initial establishment, its development would have been spread over a longer period of time.

5.4 First Is Not Important: Zoning Spread Like Wildfire

Most accounts give New York City's 1916 ordinance the honor of being the first comprehensive zoning law, in that it included the whole city in some zone or another (Seymour Toll 1969). It is clear, however, that many other American cities were developing similar ordinances at the same time (Marc Weiss 1987; Fischler 1998a). Had New York not been first, several other cities were poised to take the title.

It seems unlikely, then, that zoning was the product of circumstances in one particular place. Nor, I submit, was it the brainchild of planners who had embraced the City Beautiful Movement, progressives who supported scientific management of government, or lawyers who argued for an expansive view of the police power. The roles of planners, progressives, and lawyers were, I believe, supply responses to a popular demand for zoning. This popular demand did not initially manifest itself through direct democratic means. (Those came into play later in the century.) It was filtered through housing developers, who, I shall demonstrate presently, found that they could sell homes for more profit if the community had zoning.

Focus on large cities such as New York and Los Angeles for zoning's origins tends to cause modern scholars to overlook the fact that zoning quickly spread to the suburbs and small towns in metropolitan areas. Zoning suburbanized by the 1920s and spread rapidly (Sam Bass Warner 1972). Eight cities had zoning by the end of 1916. By 1926, 68 more cities had adopted it, and between 1926 and 1936, zoning was adopted by 1,246 additional municipalities (Robert McKenzie 1933; Toll 1969). The National Bureau of Standards survey by Norman Knauss (1933) concluded that 70 percent of the U.S. population was subject to zoning, though not all of cities listed had comprehensive laws.

The village of Euclid, whose zoning ordinance was the occasion of the U.S. Supreme Court's landmark decision to uphold zoning's constitutionality in 1926, was a young suburb of Cleveland at the time of the legal challenge. (Section 3.3 discussed *Euclid v. Ambler*, 272 U.S. 365, in more detail.) Euclid's victory cleared the way for zoning in almost all of the state courts, which had been about evenly split on the constitutionality of zoning up to 1926. As I described in section 3.4, a few courts like New Jersey's continued to resist the zoning tide for a year or two, but the New Jersey Supreme Court's anti-zoning decisions were reversed within a year by a state constitutional amendment. That New Jersey's constitutional amendment was so quickly and easily adopted in that most suburban of states (its two largest central cities, Philadelphia and New York, are outside the state) is testimony to the suburban enthusiasm for zoning from the outset.

Zoning also spread to the more remote suburbs. Weston, Massachusetts, for example, was far removed from the urban bustle of Boston but nonetheless felt moved to adopt zoning in 1928. The spread of the automobile was an important impetus for regulation. As Alexander von Hoffman (2010a) observed, "the planning board set its main goal: to protect Weston's 'distinctive character' as a 'quiet, beautiful country village.'" Implementing zoning would allow the town to keep pace with the changes spurred by motor vehicle traffic and counteract "the problems of public garages, oiling stations and the small manufacturing industries which [were] creeping into towns all over the state" (32).

The conventional explanation for the creation of zoning invokes the increasing interdependence of urban land uses that arose after the dawn of the twentieth century along with the need to deal with incompatible uses by means other than traditional nuisance law and private covenants. This claim is seldom closely argued, which is just as well. Accounts of urban conditions in the eighteenth and nineteenth centuries leave little doubt that the nuisances and near-nuisances that were said to give rise to zoning were much worse in the past (Jack Larkin 1988; William Cronon 1991; Joel Tarr 1996). If it was mainly negative externalities that gave rise to zoning, American cities would have had it decades if not centuries before its actual inception.

Nor is it credible that no one had thought of zoning before it was imported (at least as an idea) from Germany, whose cities had adopted it around 1880. Regulation of land use, albeit in a less than comprehensive way, goes way back in American history (John Hart 1996), and the extension of regulation to include all land seems like a logical next step. Many eighteenth- and nineteenth-century American cities, not just Washington, DC, were laid out in detail by their founders, so urban planning was not new (John Reps 1965).

5.5 Streetcar Suburbs Set the Stage for Zoning

A crucial precondition for zoning was the spread of a mechanically powered, intra-urban transportation system. Prior to 1880, most people walked to work in American cities. Horse-drawn streetcars mounted on fixed rails existed in many larger cities before the Civil War, but they were slow, environmentally problematical (from the manure), and limited in their hauling capacity. As a result, the rich tended to live closest to their jobs, since long walks were tiring as well as time consuming (LeRoy and Sonstelie 1983; Todd Gardner 2001).

The development of electric-powered street railroads in the 1880s made it possible for urban workers to live in exclusively residential districts and commute daily to their jobs in the central city. Streetcar lines in the United States grew from 3,000 miles, all horse drawn, in 1882 to 22,500 miles of mostly electric lines by 1902 (Brian Cudahy 1990). As the streetcar lines were constructed, homebuilders responded to the housing demands of people who could afford the not-inconsequential commuting fares, and the rich started to move to the suburbs. Some suburban developers actually built and subsidized streetcars routes specifically to promote their own building lots (Gerald Korngold 2001).

Homeowners did not, however, immediately adopt zoning upon moving to the suburbs. The best known history of early suburbanization along trolley lines is Sam Bass Warner's *Streetcar Suburbs: The Process of Growth in Boston, 1870–*

1900 (1962). Warner offers a detailed account of the development of Boston's close-in suburbs as the streetcar lines were laid outward from Boston's core. He describes the construction of homogenous neighborhoods by a highly fragmented, decentralized building industry. Small-time developers built and marketed tracts of homes whose neighborhoods look as if they had been subject to the uniform standards of a zoning law, yet zoning was nowhere in sight. Private covenants were used later in the period (Korngold 2001), but they typically applied only to the original subdivider's parcels and cannot by themselves account for the uniformity that existed across subdividers' parcels.

Other observers of development in the streetcar era (1870–1910) have also remarked on the apparent orderliness of suburban development. Andrew Cappel (1991) describes the outward development of New Haven, Connecticut, in the pre-zoning era. The uniformity with which New Haven's homes were set back from the street, a hallmark of later zoning laws, is striking. (For alternative views on the zoning history of the much-studied city of New Haven, see Stephen Clowney [2005].)

Using more quantitative methods, Daniel McMillen and John McDonald (1993) examined the land use patterns and property values of Chicago just before it adopted zoning. Their calculations led them to conclude that the patterns that zoning subsequently enforced cannot have raised land values, as zoning's proponents argued it would, since land uses before zoning looked pretty much like those after zoning. If zoning is concerned, as its many proponents claimed, with promoting neighborhood uniformity and thus preserving property values, it is not clear why any city would have adopted it during zoning's heyday.

Cappel (1991) suggests a reason why land use patterns in the pre-zoning era did not mix apartments and commercial establishments with single-family and duplex homes. The impetus for New Haven's suburbanization was, as in Boston, the electric streetcar line. Apartment houses were almost always built near them to take greatest advantage of the convenience they offered tenants. Streetcar lines were also a major determinant of development in early twentieth-century Minneapolis–St. Paul, with density of housing rising substantially within walking distance of the lines (Xie and Levinson 2010). Streetcars could not carry large amounts of freight, so only less-noxious commercial developments, such as retail stores, were pulled out of the central city. Heavy industry remained concentrated around wharves and railheads.

Because apartments and commercial activity tended to be located near the streetcar lines, their immediate neighborhoods were rather mixed (Alexander Von Hoffman 1996). But it was easy for builders of one- and two-family homes to avoid these areas. Residential developers had only to build single-family homes a few blocks away from the streetcar tracks. Moreover, the location of streetcar lines and their stations was subject to public review, and both Cappel (1991) and Charles Cheape (1980) found that homebuilders and organized homeowners used their political muscle to prevent streetcar intrusion into residential or prospectively residential areas. Control over the location of streetcar lines, in other words, was a substitute for zoning.

5.6 Trucks and Buses Undermined Informal Controls

In his New Haven study, Cappel found that, in addition to controlling the streetcar lines, homeowners and homebuilders relied on a web of informal agreements, mutual understandings, and ad hoc resort to the law to enforce the patterns that zoning later dictated. (A similar pattern was found in Brookline, Massachusetts, a near suburb of Boston, by Ronald Karr [1981].) Since interlopers and uncooperative developers were only occasional phenomena, they could be handled by neighborhood norms. Close observers of land use dwell on the importance of these relationships even today as supplements and sometimes substitutes for land use law (Thomas Rudel 1989; Robert Ellickson 1991). The original residents of American streetcar suburbs seemed to have been doing okay without zoning.

I submit that Henry Ford broke up this cozy arrangement. It was not the automobile that did it. Ford's low-cost Model T, which appeared in 1908, actually made it easier for middle-class suburban residents to avoid living near the streetcar lines, as single-family housing developers filled in the land between the spokes of streetcar lines that radiated from central business districts. It was instead the bus and the motor truck, which came into use soon after the automobile, that undermined the security of suburban single-family residences.

The truck liberated heavy industry from close proximity to downtown railroad stations and docks. It allowed manufacturers to take advantage of lower-cost land in residential districts. Leon Moses and Harold Williamson (1967) fixed the date of the motor-truck revolution in the 1910s, just as zoning was beginning its meteoric rise. They found that displacement of horses by trucks in Chicago reduced the cost of freight hauling by about 50 percent during the 1900–1920 period. They concluded that "the introduction of the motor truck had a greater impact on core area firms than those already outside the core" (215) and thus promoted within-city decentralization of industry. The lower cost transport mode was eagerly embraced by firms in other cities. The number of registered trucks in the United States doubled about every other year between 1905 and 1920 (U.S. Bureau of Census 1975).

Factories' newfound ability to relocate was soon also appreciated by zoning advocates. In a pamphlet of essays on zoning published by the American Civic Association (1920), its field secretary wrote, "The motor-truck has enabled the indifferent or the blackmailing industrial concern to threaten to locate its factory in the heart of the loveliest of law-decorated suburbs. Formerly a factory had to be near a railroad, but that is no longer necessary" (6).

The motorized passenger bus, another extension of the automobile, likewise liberated apartment developers from close proximity to the trolley tracks in the 1910–1930 period. Construction of fixed-rail streetcar lines peaked in 1906. One reason was the rise of the motorized minibus, as we would now call it. As the headline of a March 21, 1915, article in the *New York Times Magazine* announced, "Jitney Bus Wins Favor Quickly; Several Thousand of the Nickel Motor Cars Are Now in Operation Throughout the United States." By the early 1920s, jitneys and larger buses had begun to replace electric streetcars.

Streetcar companies themselves began to use buses to supplement and, in lightly traveled suburban areas, supplant trolley lines (Schaeffer and Sklar 1975; Christine Boyer 1983; these sources should dispose of the old canard that elimination of the Los Angeles trolleys was the product of an automakers' conspiracy.) Instead of having apartment builders following the rails, the buses could be depended upon to follow the apartment builders. Buses could be subjected to public regulation like that of the street railways, and many cities discouraged jitney service in favor of more regular buses, but the lower cost of changing a bus route made it more difficult for homeowners in a particular neighborhood to control them.

5.7 Homebuyers Worried about Nonconforming Neighbors

Newly footloose industrial and apartment development created a problem for homeowners and the developers who catered to them. Suburban land was cheaper than that in the center city or near the trolley lines. A lot in a single-family neighborhood could now be developed profitably for low-cost apartments. Low-income apartment dwellers could use jitneys to get to work and do other tasks. For this reason the 1915 *Times* article (cited in the previous section) noted the opposition to the free-wheeling service was not just from streetcar interests: "Realty associations are backing up the protests of the traction [streetcar] people on the ground that the prosperity and extension of the street car service go hand in hand with the development of real estate, which is not fostered by these jitney men."

Suburban neighborhoods of the streetcar era lacked zoning. Single-family neighborhoods looked as if they were zoned because of the adoption of local norms by practical homebuilders. But Cappel (1991), as well as Marie Boyd (2013), reported that by the 1920s, homeowners in New Haven began to worry that the boom in apartments facilitated by the new transportation media would overwhelm the pre-zoning institutions that had protected their neighborhoods. This looks to me like a demand-side explanation for New Haven's first zoning law, but Cappel (1991) nonetheless regarded the city's zoning as having been foisted on an otherwise contented population by political and planning elites who wanted to put the city in the progressive vanguard.

Comments from other sources in the 1920s, however, indicate that invasion of residential districts by nonconforming uses was regarded as a serious problem by homeowners. Stanley McMichael and Robert Bingham's respected real estate treatise, *City Growth and Values* (1923) offered two chapters (of 36) on the new institutions of zoning and planning. The authors, a real estate professional and an attorney in Cleveland, discussed the pros and cons of zoning. Among its most prominent advantages was protection of home values, especially in the suburbs, because zoning forestalled the threat of apartments and commercial and industrial uses from settling in the neighborhood.

By way of illustration of this possibility, McMichael and Bingham displayed two pictures of residential neighborhoods invaded by a natural-gas storage tank and by a warehouse in the pre-zoning era. That this sort of problem was endemic at the time is suggested by a Harvard professor's mention of it in his widely used municipal government textbook (Chester Hanford 1926) as well as by several state supreme court opinions that upheld zoning at the time (Martha Lees 1994). In my research on the 1927 *Nectow* decision, described in chapter 3, I found indications of similar concerns in Cambridge, Massachusetts. Christine Boyer (1983) confirms that such incompatible uses were "commonplace anomalies in the American city of the 1920s" (156). This may explain why, in a later econometric study, Dan McMillen and John McDonald (2002) found that Chicago's first zoning ordinance in 1923 raised residential land values more than commercial values. They suggest that "residential landowners valued the insurance that zoning provides against future intrusions of conflicting commercial land uses" (63).

William Munro, a Harvard government professor who had become vice president of the National Municipal League, pointed out the reciprocal advantages to both residents and businesses of legally enforced separation by zoning:

> With a city entirely zoned, they [realtors] could assure purchasers of residential property that their neighborhoods would never be encroached upon by business, while on the other hand, zoning would give business property a touch of monopoly value. Accordingly the signs went up on vacant lots: "Zoned for business," or "Zoned for apartments," with the definite implication that such action on the part of the public authorities had resulted in giving the property a higher and more assured value than it would otherwise have. (Munro 1931, 203)

The anxiety that footloose businesses created for homeowners and homebuilders soon trumped the ideology of private property at the highest levels. In his *Euclid* opinion, Justice Sutherland raised the possibility of apartment invasion of single-home districts. His mention of apartments is all the more interesting because the plaintiff had not even complained about restrictions on apartments. (Ambler Realty had wanted to sell the land for heavy industry.) Sutherland brought up the apartment issue on his own (though amicus briefs had addressed it) and famously characterized the apartment building as "a mere parasite, constructed in order to take advantage of the open spaces and attractive surroundings created by the residential character of the district" (272 U.S. at 394). It is possible, of course, that jurists and commentators were being influenced by ideas, such as those of the City Beautiful movement, rather than by everyday observation. Yet accounts of the effects of zoning's adoption suggest otherwise. In his review of American attitudes toward zoning in the 1910–1930 era, Raphael Fischler (1998b) quotes many contemporary sources to show that protection of single-family homes was paramount from the outset.

New York was pressed by mercantile interests, especially the Fifth Avenue merchants, to adopt zoning to prevent the spread of industry and apartments into its exclusive shopping areas (Toll 1969; Warner 1972). A late nineteenth-century effort by the Vanderbilts to protect their upper–Fifth Avenue enclave by purchasing potentially offending properties did not succeed. Even the extraordinary wealth of the Vanderbilts and their friends was not enough to keep ahead of commercial and apartment developers without the force of zoning. (A *New York Times* headline called it "The Battle Money Couldn't Win: The Vanderbilts and Their Battle Over Fifth Avenue," June 12, 2014.)

Although the city's zoning protections were initially weak, Fischler's (1998b) quotation from the *New York Times*, October 22, 1916, suggests that homeowners were quickly responding to the new assurance:

> Barely three months after the enactment of the zoning code [of 1916], an optimistic headline in the *New York Times* proclaimed: "Home-Coming Season in Murray Hill—Interesting Changes in Old Center; Many Former Residents Moving Back from Uptown—Zoning Act Removes Fear of Business Invasion." (185, n. 29)

5.8 Developers Demanded Zoning to Supplement, not Replace, Covenants

Fischler describes how protective covenants had been designed to shield the fashionable Murray Hill section in New York City from commerce and apartment development. Covenants succeeded for a time, he noted, because "time honored custom" had prevented commercial development at the edges of Murray Hill (1998b, 185, n. 48). The timing of the breakdown of this custom coincides with the development of trucks and buses. After commerce and apartment development began to invade the district, homeowners needed public controls.

Murray Hill's experience may shed light on a modern argument about private covenants as an alternative to zoning. Some commentators have advocated covenants as if they had been overlooked when zoning started out (Bernard Siegan 1972). Judges were sometimes hostile to covenants (Ellickson 1973), but developers nonetheless did employ them extensively (Robert Fogelson 2005). The problem was that they did not cover enough land area. Nonconforming uses were placed on the borders of well-planned, covenanted subdivisions, to the detriment of the homebuyers.

Perhaps as problematic as the vulnerable borders of covenanted land was that covenants seldom controlled an entire municipality. This meant that the fiscal fortunes of homebuyers were left uncertain. A developer of upscale homes could reasonably fear that an adjacent tract of land might be dedicated to downmarket housing. Even if there were no direct spillovers, prospective buyers in the upscale area would worry about whether their taxes would rise or public services decline if the rest of the land in the municipality were developed for lower-valued properties.

The attention to municipal expenditures and the property tax base in the Standard State Zoning Enabling Act of 1924, as described in section 4.6, also makes it clear that the progenitors of zoning were thinking well beyond the borders of individual neighborhoods, where property might be protected by covenants. Indeed, there is evidence that covenants and zoning developed side by side in some places. In an account of the development of the Cleveland area after the *Euclid* decision, Gerald Korngold (2001) points out that three nearby communities were developed by a single owner and made subject to comprehensive covenants. The municipalities were nonetheless also subject to zoning, and, as if to press home that the two devices are complements rather than substitutes, the covenants were legally administered by the mayors of the three towns. The Ohio suburbs were not unique in this respect. As Fogelson (2005) points out, zoning's early advocates such as Edward Bassett regarded zoning as an important supplement to covenants because zoning could control more territory and deal with border effects.

Marc Weiss (1987) observed that the developers who pioneered large-scale residential subdivisions in Southern California in the pre-zoning era were the prime movers behind the adoption of zoning regulations in Los Angeles. Developers found that voluntary covenants were insufficient to protect their property's value from incompatible uses on their borders. J. C. Nichols, whose famous Kansas City "country club" residential developments were subject to covenants from 1907 onward, was an early and active advocate of zoning (William Worley 1990).

Far from being something foisted on unwilling developers, zoning was actively promoted by developer organizations at the national level. Commerce Secretary Herbert Hoover was induced by the homebuilder lobbies to promulgate the Standard State Zoning Enabling Act of 1924, which, as described in section 4.5, became the nearly universal template for zoning in America. (Hoover's action looks like a top-down or supply-side account of zoning, but Weiss [1987] makes it clear that the initiative came from developers who were responding to anxieties about neighborhood stability expressed by their prospective customers.)

Developer support for zoning was not based on starry-eyed faith in the capacity of planners. Zoning was regarded with some suspicion by homebuilders, and its advocates were careful to warn developers and real estate professionals to use their political influence to keep zoning within reasonable bounds (Worley 1990). They also took a larger view, according to Weiss, about the possibility that some of their own parcels might be adversely affected by zoning. Developers believed zoning "would maximize aggregate land values, and stabilize values at each location, but would not maximize values everywhere" (1987, 101).

But in the end, developer support for zoning was founded on the need to induce homeowners to invest their savings in a large, undiversified asset. An early zoning advocate pointed out that "'So long as undesirable properties could encroach upon an area in which good residences and good income-bearing properties were already established, there would be no stability or trust in real estate as an investment'" (quoted in Charles Cheney 1920, 33). As planning historian Christine Boyer (1983) points out, zoning was seen as a way to provide "an insurance policy that the single-family home owner's investment would be protected in stable neighborhood communities" (148).

When I gave an oral presentation of this chapter in a seminar at Universitat Pompeu Fabra in Barcelona, Professor Fernando Gomez raised an objection. I was presenting the development of zoning as an example of popular democracy (more on that to come), but Weiss's California example looked very much like the public-choice model of interest-group legislation. Large-scale developers were (and are) a powerful interest group, and they spearheaded the adoption of a national standard for zoning. I had to concede to Gomez's point. Developer groups could overcome the transaction costs of political organization better than homeowners, who were organized only (if at all) by neighborhood. My defense of the majority-rule model is that after developers started zoning, it became very popular with homeowners. The New Jersey experience, described in section 3.4, of a statewide plebiscite to change the constitution to permit zoning in 1927 is evidence of this. Even if developers had wanted to reverse course on zoning, it would almost certainly have been politically impossible.

5.9 Zoning Perpetuated Metropolitan Fragmentation

The motor vehicle's paternity of zoning led to another offspring, the fragmentation of American metropolitan areas. It is well known and, among many academics and planners, regularly decried, that most large American metropolitan areas are overseen by scores and sometimes hundreds of local governments. The fragmentation reflects the bottom-up approach to local government that has prevailed through most of American history.

Less well known is that for much of the nineteenth century and up to 1910, suburban governments were formed and soon after went out of existence as a result of consolidation with an adjacent, growing central city. Jon Teaford's (1979) masterly review of suburbanization from 1850 to 1970 found that until about 1910, it was common for an expanding central city to consolidate with (and thus politically absorb) its incorporated neighbors as well as to annex adjacent unincorporated territory. The 1850–1910 period was characterized by exuberant incorporations of individual suburbs around growing cities followed by sober incorporation into the larger body.

After 1910, however, a different pattern emerged and began to be the rule by the 1920s (Teaford 1979; Kenneth Jackson 1972). Central cities found that their incorporated suburbs were much more reluctant to give up their independence and consolidate with their large neighbors. In addition, territory that was formerly unincorporated (as part of the county) became more difficult to annex. Residents of unincorporated areas began to consider annexation by the newer suburbs or incorporation as an independent municipality, with no intention of eventually merging with the central city. This was a major change in the governance of American urban areas for which urban historians have what I regard as only partial or ad hoc explanations.

I submit that it was the institution of zoning that gave rise to the newfound reluctance of suburbs to merge with their larger neighbor (Fischel 2001). Prior to zoning, independent suburbs had to regard urban development and its attendant public costs as inevitable as the tides. There was little to prevent a residential structure from being converted to commercial use, to keep the single-family structure from being subdivided into smaller apartments, or to stop the vacant lot from being occupied by a high-rise apartment building. Few private covenants would cover sufficient territory within the municipality to afford private control over development.

Given their lack of control over development, suburbs found the blandishments of central-city suitors attractive. As suburbs began getting urban uses and urban densities, their residents began demanding urban services. Crime and traffic would overwhelm small-town police forces, and the formally organized, larger forces of the big city were better trained and equipped for the tasks. Demand for water for domestic use and fire prevention in suburbs often exceeded local capacity, which was in most places already chancy and irregular. Many central cities had deliberately acquired excess capacity as bait for their outlying areas.

After zoning became popular in the decade around 1910–1920, suburbs no longer had to view development as inevitable. A small town could control its land use and fiscal destiny in the face of urban development. Consolidation no longer looked so attractive, and suburbs began cooperating with one another to provide water and other basic services with scale economies, which had previously been the monopoly of the central city. Zoning thus allowed suburbs to remain independent indefinitely, and this surely encouraged many more to incorporate. It is not coincidental that in Chicago, "Eighty-nine new suburbs—nearly all enforcing a strict separation of land uses—were incorporated over the course of the decade" after zoning became established in Illinois in the 1920s (Schwieterman, Caspall, and Heron 2006, 28).

Support for the influence of zoning on municipal independence can be seen in histories of municipal incorporation activity. Accounts of twentieth-century municipal formation by Jon Teaford (1979; 1997), and Gary Miller (1981), as well as my own investigations into 1990s incorporations in the Seattle area (Fischel 2001), indicate that twentieth-century incorporations were most often motivated by resident's desire to control land use and related fiscal issues. This does not mean, of course, that each new city was a suburb that wanted to stop development. There were plenty of pro-development municipalities. But even in them, the residential districts were carefully separated from the fiscally profitable commercial and industrial areas.

Development in metropolitan areas of western and southern states often occurred in "unincorporated" parts of a formerly rural county. The county almost always stepped in to provide zoning as development took place. In many of the modern municipal incorporations, however, control over land use was an issue because the county government's zoning was too pro-development, especially in its inclination to rezone formerly single-family areas for apartment units (Richard Cion 1966; Michelle Anderson 2012). Because of their larger size, which made it more difficult for voters to know candidates' positions, county governments were more often responsive to developer interests and thus were regarded as excessively permissive by owners of homes in existing neighborhoods.

5.10 Homeowners Dominated Politics in the Suburbs

So far I have argued that zoning arose because new modes of transportation allowed people to separate where they lived from where they worked. The development of motorized buses and trucks undermined traditional means of protecting neighborhoods. Zoning was preferred to (or added to) covenants because it protected the borders of covenanted land and could protect the municipal tax base and control service demands. The ability to control land uses in turn made it attractive for suburban municipalities to maintain their independence from the central city. The last piece of the puzzle is why homeowners—as opposed to renters, developers, employment interests, and bureaucracies (including planners)—should have taken over as the primary political group whose interests are promoted by zoning.

The detached, owner-occupied home is at the top of the zoning pyramid in nearly all zoning laws. Early illustrations of this hierarchy actually drew pyramids with single-family homes forming the apex. The primacy of homeownership remains so widespread that we hardly think of it as something requiring explanation. Yet there is no theoretical reason why other uses of land should be regarded as less important. Apartment dwellers are as much citizens as home dwellers; property ownership has not been a requirement for municipal voting for more than century. And the economic interest that owners and employees have in commercial and industrial properties are at least as considerable as in their homes. How did homeowners get the zoning game rigged in their favor?

I submit that the urban transportation revolution that replaced walking with motorized transport led to a less obvious political revolution (Fischel 2001). When people walked to work, they had to live close to work. This usually meant that their homes were within the same municipality as their jobs and businesses. In this respect, most urban workers in the walking cities were like most farmers, who still live where they work. Commercial farmers are of two minds about prospective development: It disrupts their home and business life, but it also provides opportunities for financial gain. Rural communities are for this reason still more inclined to give pro-development forces a fair hearing (Pendall, Wolanski, and McGovern 2002; Michelle Anderson 2012).

Up to about 1920, residents of towns and cities also lived close to their place of work. Even if they commuted (mainly on foot), work was not far away and seldom politically isolated in another municipal jurisdiction (Alexander Von Hoffman 1996). One of my great-grandfathers was a baker in Phillipsburg, New Jersey, circa 1900. He lived with his wife and five daughters above his shop, and his employees lived nearby simply because it otherwise took too long to get to work in a pedestrian and equine transportation system. This proximity made for mixed feelings about local development. The prospect of a new warehouse in the neighborhood would have an adverse effect on residential amenities: more noisy traffic, potentially dangerous materials, increased risk of fire. But the new warehouse could also bring in more customers for the bakery and perhaps serve as a convenient place to store inventories. A proposal to systematically segregate commerce and industry from residences would not generate much enthusiasm. Even the employees of Jacob Ottenbacher's "steam bakery" who lived in the area might have felt the same way. (Bread baked in ovens heated by steam pipes was more uniform than loaves from open-fire ovens.) The warehouse's inroads on their residential amenities were at least partially offset by the prospect of more secure employment in a more profitable businesses.

People who moved to independent suburbs and then commuted daily via train, trolley, bus, or car no longer had that binocular vision (Michael Danielson 1976). The city was where they worked, but the suburb, the locus of their residential wealth, was where they voted. Residential amenities—and prevention of anything that smacked of disamenity—became paramount in the eyes of suburban voters. My great-grandfather moved to a suburban home soon after he bought his first motor car.

We know from present-day studies that the value of owner-occupied homes is greatly affected by what local governments do (Wallace Oates 1969; Hilber and Mayer 2009). Improvements in schools, neighborhood safety, and public parks all raise the value of owner-occupied homes. Conversely, increases in local taxes, local pollution, and ugly billboards all reduce home values.

It is worth a moment to consider how financially problematic an owner-occupied home was at the beginning of the twentieth century—and remains to the present. An investment advisor whom you have consulted looks at your middle-income portfolio and tells you that you should put almost all of your liquid assets in a single investment. It is not a diversified mutual fund; it is a single firm, and the firm makes only one product in a single location. It has a great upside in that its returns are almost entirely untaxed under federal and state income tax laws, and it insures you against rent increases by the landlord. But its asset value is subject to a multitude of risks. Not least are those from the neighborhood and the single municipality in which the firm is located. Bad events next door, down the street, at the school district, and in city hall can put your life savings in a tailspin.

The "investment advisor" in this case is a developer or realtor who is trying to sell you an owner-occupied home. Both of you know that you can insure the home from the risk of physical breaches such as fires and burglary, but there is almost no insurance against neighborhood and municipal problems. Few homeowners can self-insure by diversifying their other assets for the simple reason that they do not own much besides their house (Andrew Caplin et al. 1997). As a result, homeowners have a powerful financial as well as personal incentive to pay attention to local government land use policies. (The home-value insurance plans promoted by Robert Shiller and Allan Weiss [1999] are tied to metropolitan-area price indexes and, as discussed in section 9.15, cannot be used to insure against localized risks.)

As suburbs formed and became a permanent part of the metropolitan area after 1910, homeowners were motivated to take over local government, or at least the regulatory apparatus. Urban homeownership was growing rapidly in the early twentieth century, especially in the suburbs (Robert Barrows 1983). Homeowners were numerous and highly motivated, and since they lived in contiguous districts and sent their kids to the same schools, the transaction costs of political organization were lower for them (Fischel 2006). Having staked their life savings in their communities' character, homeowners became a major force in local politics. They supported zoning, which had originally been proposed by homebuilding developers, and they made their homes the primary object to be protected.

This did not mean, of course, that job-creating business was unwelcome in the community. To the extent that it paid local taxes in excess of the additional cost of local services it required, business was welcome in suburbs if its neighborhood effects were not too noxious or it could be sequestered in a nonresidential area of the town. But the mechanism by which the public was persuaded to accept industry was no longer tied to the voter's employment or investment in the business, as it was in the walking city. Public decisions about industrial zoning now focused on helping to pay property taxes and mitigating spillover effects that might reduce home values (Teaford 1997).

5.11 Planners or the People? The Showdown in Los Angeles

The apparent simultaneity of supply-side efforts by planners and demand for zoning by homeowners presents an identification problem: Which was the primary mover, the planning establishment or the homeowners? One way to determine the more important factor is to consider an element of zoning that the planners wanted and initially obtained, but that was subsequently rejected by the public. If the demanders trump the suppliers, the hand goes to the demand side.

The instance is in fact important and current. The planners who promulgated zoning regarded the zoning districts as seriously flawed if any nonconforming uses were allowed to persist (Lawrence Veiller 1916). They consistently proposed that nonconforming commercial and industrial uses be expelled from residential neighborhoods. Expulsion was required regardless of how long the nonconforming use had been there or whether it had arrived long before the residences. A brief grace period to facilitate relocation of the activity might be allowed, but no compensation was to be paid.

Lest one think that this was but a passing fancy of the early stages of zoning, I would point out that the idea of terminating nonconforming uses has never faded away. Planners of New York's pioneering 1916 ordinance thought that oversize skyscrapers (more than five stories, according to one planner) ought to be torn down (Keith Revell 1992). The principal author of New York's ordinance, Edward Bassett, did not disagree but thought it would be politically imprudent for the ordinance to insist on removing existing buildings. He nonetheless wrote that "non-conforming uses should be placed under a constant pressure to become conforming through time and changes" (American Civic Association 1920, 10). Another leading planner, Harland Bartholomew (1939), succinctly stated his thesis in the title of his article, "Nonconforming Uses Destroy the Neighborhood." A *Stanford Law Review* student note (1955) advocated termination of nonconforming uses. A modern expression of the same idea, though more nuanced in its application, has been advanced by law professor Christopher Serkin (2009).

American courts agreed with the idea of uncompensated termination without much dispute. The leading case—Frank Michelman (1967) called it (and thus helped make it) "the undying classic" (1237)—was *Hadacheck v. Los Angeles*, 239 U.S. 394 (1915). John C. Hadacheck had built a brick-making facility in a rural part of Los Angeles County seven years before the city of Los Angeles annexed territory containing his property. (My account relies heavily on an excellent dissertation by Kathy Kolnick [2008].) Hadacheck had moved to his initially rural site specifically to avoid conflicts with his residential neighbors. His business had been expelled from a previous site nearer to downtown by a 1902 ordinance, adopted in response to the objections to his operations by his residential neighbors, who included the owner of the *Los Angeles Times*.

Hadacheck moved his operations about a mile west to an eight-acre site southeast of the corner of what is now Pico and Crenshaw Boulevards. Although the case does not mention it, this decentralization was likely facilitated by what a 1908 article in the *Brick and Clay Record* headlined as "Motor in a Brick Yard," picturing a freight-carrying truck and noting that its ideal use was "for local delivery of brick" (358). Hadacheck's new site was at the time outside the boundaries of the city of Los Angeles. However, he did not move far enough. His new neighborhood became filled with homes soon after he built his facility. After the new residents petitioned that the area be annexed by the city, the city's "districting" laws—the precursor to its comprehensive zoning law—designated the area as exclusively residential in response to the demands of neighbors who had recently moved there.

The city required Hadacheck (and another brickyard nearby) to discontinue operations. He refused, noting the large investment he had made and the considerable drop in value of his property if it were to have only residential use. Expensive and difficult-to-move machinery had been installed on the site, and deep pits from which the clay for bricks had been mined rendered the site problematic for alternative uses. Kolnick (2008) found that sometime afterward Hadacheck's land was actually developed as mixed (single-family and apartments) residential. However, she did not say what Hadacheck was paid for land or what remediation was necessary in order to build on it. (I have been to the site, and no trace of his operation is evident.) In any case, both the California and United States Supreme Courts upheld this ruling without a dissent, with the U.S. Supreme Court blandly declaring that "there must be progress."

Hadacheck has long intrigued me for two reasons. One is that it seemed to involve a zoning controversy in Los Angeles that arose several years before New York's supposedly first-in-the-nation zoning ordinance of 1916. Los Angeles was not yet a huge city—in 1910 its population was only about 320,000, compared to New York's nearly five million at the same time—but it was growing rapidly because of internal migration, especially from the Midwest. Indeed, the major industry in Los Angeles at the time was residential development. Why has Los Angeles not been regarded as the mother of American zoning?

Kolnick's answer is that the zoning to which Hadacheck was subject was not comprehensive or citywide. Indeed, the word "zoning" was not used. Neighborhoods would petition the city to be placed in an exclusive residential district either because business had invaded the area or because residences were (as in Hadacheck's case) now moving to areas where industries had come first. The city government became especially responsive to these requests after its first experience with the local voter initiative, which was a novelty at the time. But the Los Angeles districting process was done piecemeal, and the entire city was not covered with districts. Indeed, the city itself was rapidly growing in area (by annexation) as well as in population, so comprehensive zoning would have been especially difficult to undertake. New York's title for first in the nation in 1916 was based on the comprehensiveness of its zoning map, which designated the entire city—whose five-borough borders had been set in 1900—for some zone or another. Los Angeles did not get around to that until 1921.

5.12 Zoning Was Not Based on Nuisance Law

The more pressing question for my present purpose is why the *Hadacheck* precedent had not led to a general rule that allowed nonconforming uses to be expelled without compensation, as the fathers of zoning had clearly desired and the courts were comfortable with allowing. One reason *Hadacheck* is not a clear guide is that it looked like a nuisance case. If that was all it was, then the fact that the brickyard had to be moved despite its precedence would not be especially unusual. First in time does not establish an entitlement to continue a nuisance under common law principles. As Richard Epstein (1985) succinctly explained, Hadacheck had been granted an implied but temporary easement by neighboring landowners to conduct a nuisance that did no damage as long as the land nearby was vacant. Once neighboring landowners developed their property for residential use, the brickyard was obliged to leave.

The problems with the nuisance theory of *Hadacheck* are two. One is that both the California Supreme Court and the U.S. Supreme Court did not treat it as a simple nuisance case. *Hadacheck* was a test of the police power, not the common law of nuisance. (W. L. Pollard [1931], an early defender of zoning, specifically emphasized this distinction.) The difference is that under the police power, the city of Los Angeles could have designated Hadacheck's neighborhood as an industrial zone, and Hadacheck would have been protected from the wrath of his neighbors. In fact, the city did have to create such zones, as I will discuss presently. The other problem is that *Hadacheck* was preceded by two cases that also tested the city's districting regulations. The other two were not uses that would have been considered nuisances.

Ex parte Quong Wo, 161 Cal. 220 (1911) involved the creation by local petition of a residence district near downtown Los Angeles, on Flower near Seventh Street. Quong's was one of more than a dozen Chinese hand laundries (no power machinery was employed) that were affected by the 1911 ordinance.

They had long been interspersed with homes and other commercial buildings, as indicated on the map constructed by Kolnick (2008). Quong Wo had operated in the area for more than 14 years but was ordered to close his business. He declined and was arrested (as Hadacheck was in the later case) and appealed his conviction to the California Supreme Court, which upheld the ordinance and the conviction. (The arrests were less traumatic than they might sound; both Quong and Hadacheck sought to be arrested because they could then appeal on the basis of *habeas corpus* and get a quicker resolution of their complaints.)

Chinese hand laundries would not have met almost any traditional definition of nuisances, and several of Quong Wo's neighbors testified that it was inoffensive (Kolnick 2008). Prejudice against Chinese surely informed earlier laws against Chinese businesses (as described—and overturned—in *Yick Wo v. Hopkins*, 118 U.S. 356 [1886]). But anti-Chinese prejudice was declining in Los Angeles. As the city's population swelled with non-Chinese immigration from other states, the resident Chinese became such a small minority that they did not affect native Americans' wages. The laundries in this case were just laundries, not symbols of the "yellow peril" that American labor unions feared, and the California court simply treated the laundry issue as a test of the breadth of municipal discretion on the police power and did not mention nuisance issues at all.

The third case (second in time) was *Ex parte Montgomery*, 163 Cal. 457 (1912). It involved a lumber yard located at North Avenue 61 and North Figueroa Street, which was also required to discontinue operations as a result of a newly adopted residential district. It was possible that some nuisance-like activities occurred in lumberyards at the time, but they surely could have been abated without requiring that the business be entirely removed. The more remarkable aspect of Montgomery's specific circumstance was that the lumber yard was adjacent to a railroad (the Santa Fe), across which was a commercial neighborhood. It hardly seemed out of place, and the California Supreme Court specifically noted that a lumberyard was not a per se nuisance.

5.13 The People and Prudence Overruled *Hadacheck*

One would think that the court losses by Hadacheck and the other two would have been the end of the controversy. The planners had had their way, and the highest courts of the state and the nation had given uncompensated removal of nonconforming uses their unqualified support. New York zoning advocate Lawrence Veiller (1916) happily approved of this proceeding. Indeed, in the 1920s, the Illinois courts briefly declared that the "grandfathering" of previously established nonconforming structures was illegal, thereby seeming to require expulsion of nonconformers (Schwieterman, Caspall, and Heron 2006). (The Illinois court's reasoning was that grandfathering would preserve a local monopoly.) But of course anyone familiar with zoning law knows that this was not the end of the story. In fact, Mr. Hadacheck would nowadays likely prevail, though his brick-making might be scaled back by environmental laws. Nonconforming uses are now handled with kid gloves (as described in section 2.4) and normally are allowed to persist.

Yet *Hadacheck* is still good law (Joseph diMento et al. 1980), and it has never been reversed—at least not explicitly. De facto reversal has, however, occurred, and there are two reasons for this. One was popular revulsion to the law. According to Weiss (1987) as well as Kolnick (2008), Hadacheck's case and the other two were causes célèbres. It just did not seem fair to ordinary observers that established businesses could be eliminated by the stroke of a pen. The same popular feeling has emerged as modern "right to farm" laws (discussed in section 2.14). Such laws protect preexisting uses against nuisance suits (and sometimes zoning changes) that arise when residential neighborhoods are built around farms. The new neighbors find the smells and sounds of agriculture are not to their liking, but the "right to farm" laws stay their hands. This is despite common-law principles that disfavor the "moving to the nuisance" defense that right-to-farm supports.

Aside from popular perceptions of fairness, the city of Los Angeles faced a practical problem. Although the biggest business in Los Angeles in the early twentieth century was residential development, both the city council and voters were aware that some industrial and commercial developments were essential for longer-term employment. Most of the immigrants who flocked to southern California's amenable climate needed jobs, many needed services, such as those of Chinese laundries, and homebuilders did require bricks and lumber. But residential development was proceeding so rapidly that Hadacheck's problem cropped up time and again.

The answer to the problem was the exclusive industrial (and later commercial) zone. The impetus for the industrial district was the fear that the city would be unable to attract industry. As Kolnick (2008) observed, "Though the California state and federal courts had declared it constitutional to require what were considered as nuisance businesses to be removed from residence districts, an anti-industry reputation was one the city council and civic organizations were at pains to avoid" (254). City council members were aware that nearby cities were attracting industry with promises of exclusive districts. El Segundo brought in a refinery and established worker housing nearby (both still visible south of LAX airport), having apparently been able to persuade the refiner that the business would not be chased out in the manner of Hadacheck's.

Within industrial zones, businesses could be more secure. They were not exempt from nuisance litigation, but that was not what caused the problem. What had been problematical was the residential development around established businesses and the subsequent demand for an exclusive residential district. People who moved to a designated industrial zone, by contrast, could be told that they did not have the right to demand removal of offending businesses.

Los Angeles initially struggled to determine the location of its industrial zones. Centered on the Los Angeles River (east of downtown), the initial district was fitfully expanded to accommodate industry and divided into degrees of offensiveness, with the worst being placed farthest from the residential areas. The city council had no stomach for actively removing residents from the industrial zone, but it appears that they left of their own accord over time, and at least those who owned property profited from the sales.

Kolnick's more remarkable finding, however, was that most of the firms that had been officially banished from residential zones actually did not leave. Hadacheck did depart, but most of the Chinese laundries remained for many years, probably at least as long as the ordinary lifespan of an urban business (about five years). Other banned businesses were often in place years after the exclusive residential area had been established. Kolnick found no official record of their being granted exceptions (and she was an assiduous researcher); instead, it seems that after a while controversies over expulsions simply died out.

Although most of zoning's national advocates continued to decry the persistence of nonconforming uses, most seemed to accept that it was politically difficult to dislodge them. Some attempted to justify their acceptance of nonconforming uses by claiming that the California courts were extreme in their deference to the police power. But the bland and unanimous acceptance of California's practice by the U.S. Supreme Court in *Hadacheck* suggests that, however extreme California may have looked initially, there would be no interference from the federal courts.

Most state courts as well as many commentators continue to regard grandfathering previous uses as strictly a matter of noblesse oblige or political necessity on the part of local jurisdictions. Many have accepted the concept of an "amortization period" during which nonconforming uses are granted a temporary reprieve from discontinuance. But even amortization periods have gone out of fashion, leaving most previously existing nonconforming uses in place (Serkin 2009). Chicago bravely adopted a new ordinance in 1957 that called for discontinuation of nonconforming uses after an amortization period, but it was "eventually deemed a failure" (Schwieterman, Caspall, and Heron 2006, 113).

This seems to be a case in which the leaders of zoning called for a practice that the public was unwilling to accept, even though the courts either endorsed the practice or tolerated it. For this reason, the continuing practice of grandfathering nonconforming uses supports a "bottom-up" theory of zoning's development. The special status of nonconforming uses is largely contrary to the "supply side" represented by planning advocates and theorists. Grandfathering has been integrated into zoning practice for such a long time that most planners now regard it as entirely natural, but that natural feel is actually illustrative of the power of what I call the "demand side" of zoning.

5.14 From 1920s Good Housekeeping to 1970s Growth Controls

The land use revolution that began in the 1910s did not happen all at once. Zoning required considerable fine-tuning to cover unanticipated contingencies. For example, the original 1918 enabling act in Massachusetts allowed for regulation of "buildings" but not structures such as walls and signs (Lawrence Evans 1921). (It was soon rectified and brought up to the standards of the Standard State Zoning Enabling Act.) Even after the *Euclid* decision upholding zoning in 1926, early zoning laws encountered constitutional and political hurdles that took time to overcome (Ernst Freund 1929; Keith Revell 1999). Up to the late 1940s, state courts were often solicitous of the rights of development-minded landowners (Richard Babcock 1966; Norman Williams 1982). The Great Depression and World War II slowed real estate development almost everywhere, so the full impact of zoning was not felt until after World War II.

The Federal Housing Administration (FHA), created during the Depression, in fact encouraged zoning in all but name, though it seems too much to claim, as Andrew Whittemore (2012) does, that the FHA rules caused Los Angeles and other cities to adopt low-density zoning. Kolnick (2008) shows convincingly that early zoning in Los Angeles was the product of indigenous homeowners' demand. The federal government was just conforming to the underlying demand for neighborhood security for single-family housing. In any case, nearly all municipalities within the developed parts of metropolitan areas had zoning by the 1950s.

The main criticism of zoning in the 1950s and 1960s was that it excluded the poor. In a 1953 article, Charles Haar pointed out the obvious exclusionary intent of minimum house-size standards, which were popular in New Jersey at the time and which courts generally upheld. (Minimum house-size rules are no longer common, but other regulations concerning lot size and coverage accomplish the same goal.) Even in the late 1960s, when two parallel federal commissions addressed zoning issues, the primary complaint was about suburban zoning's effect on the *mix* of housing within individual communities, not constraints on metropolitan or regional supply (National Commission on Urban Problems 1968; President's Committee on Urban Housing 1969).

Federal commissions that addressed zoning after 1970 have, in contrast, made overall housing prices a major focus (President's Commission on Housing 1982; Advisory Commission on Regulatory Barriers to Affordable Housing 1991). The U.S. Department of Housing and Urban Development actually institutionalized this concern with a program to overcome regulatory barriers. Its ineffectiveness was inadvertently confessed when, for a time, the department published a "Strategy of the Month" to suggest how local barriers could be overcome. One wonders why, if the department had an effective strategy, it would need to come up with a new one every month.

For the balance of the present chapter, however, I want to address a question that must precede reform efforts. Regardless of its normative effects, why did land use regulation and housing prices suddenly take off in the 1970s? James Metzenbaum, who wrote Euclid's 1922 zoning ordinance and successfully defended it in court, later characterized it in his treatise on zoning as municipal good housekeeping: "Zoning does no more than apply the rules of good housekeeping to public affairs. It keeps the kitchen stove out of the parlor, the bookcase out of the pantry, and the dinner table out of the bedroom" (Metzenbaum 1930, 6).

The good housekeeping idea of separating uses applied well into the 1960s, even if some cities' idea of a tidy municipality was one that lacked racial minorities and poor people. But something changed around 1970. The study by Ganong and Shoag that was the touchstone for the opening of this chapter is among the best to have established that land use regulation experienced a discontinuity at that time. For readers with a less quantitative bent, I present below linguistic evidence of this quantum leap as well as a suggestion of its causes.

5.15 When Did Zoning Constraints Shift? Evidence from Ngrams

The Google search engine offers a free site called the "ngram." It graphically tracks the frequency of use of words and phrases over a designated period of time, say from 1900 to 2000. The words and phrases that are entered are gleaned from the millions of books that Google has scanned in major libraries. This archive does not include newspapers, but it does include journals, trade magazines, and government documents as well as traditional monographs like the one now in the reader's hands or on the screen. An ngram can give one a reasonably accurate feel for the rise and fall of a concept as well as the relative importance of two or more concepts represented by a word or phrase.

For example, the ngram (all for "American English") that pairs *Milton Friedman* and *John Maynard Keynes* for the period 1940 to 2000 is given below in figure 5.1. As one can see, Keynes led Friedman until about 1968, and Friedman's lead peaked in 1981. Both declined after that and nearly converged by 2000. This roughly tracks the relative positions of *monetarism* (whose modern apostle was Friedman) and *Keynesianism* in public discourse. Friedman and monetarism became ascendant in the 1970s and early 1980s, when peacetime

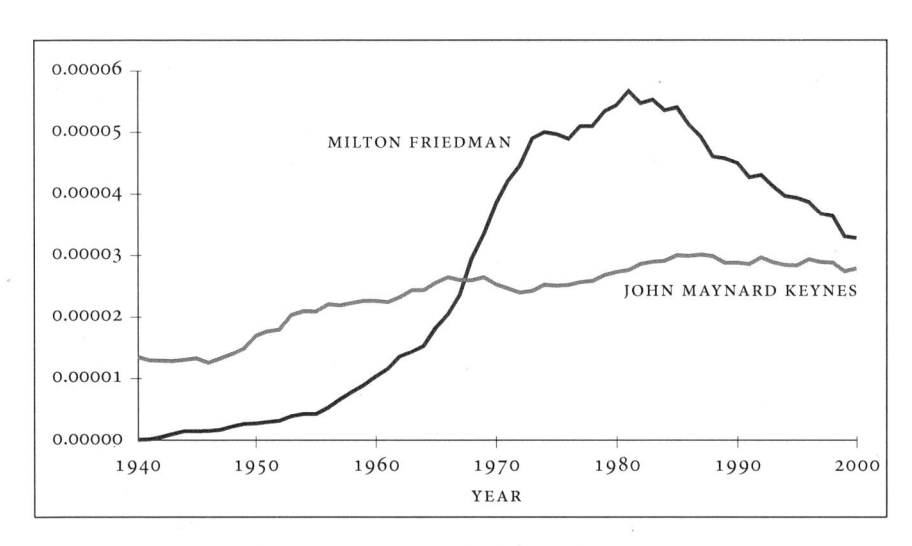

FIGURE 5.1 Ngram for John Maynard Keynes and Milton Friedman
Source: Adapted from the Google Ngram Viewer.

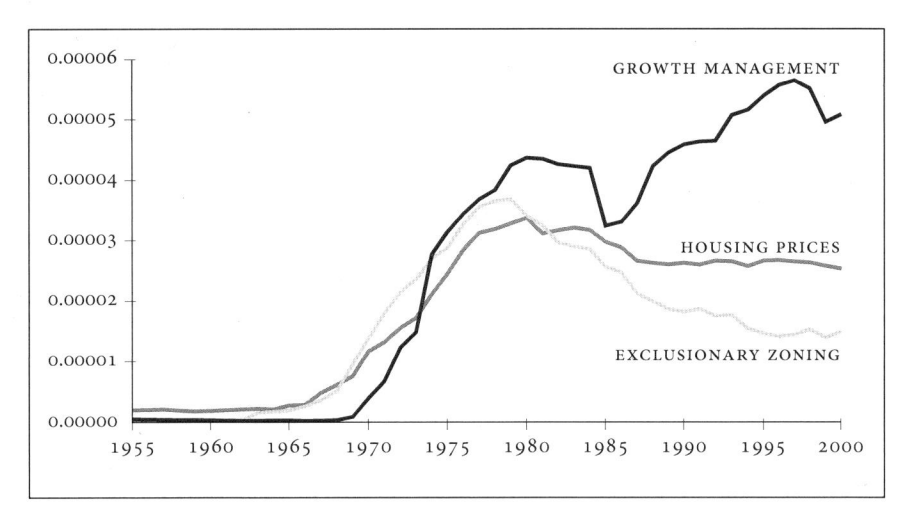

FIGURE 5.2 Ngram for Zoning Terms and Housing Prices
Source: Adapted from the Google Ngram Viewer.

inflation became the focus of concern, and monetarism declined as inflation declined in the late 1980s and 1990s.

Figure 5.2 shows the ngram for the terms "housing prices," "exclusionary zoning," and "growth management." (The term "growth control" has some scientific and engineering uses, which makes it less suitable as a marker for public discourse about land use issues.) Growth management is clearly the dominant of the three terms (it also picks up some scientific applications), but the most important observation is that all of the terms were nearly unused before 1970. Before 1970, housing prices were not an object of much attention, and the terms "growth management" and "exclusionary zoning" were hardly used. In other ngrams (not shown here), the acronym "NIMBY" also gains currency in the 1980s, as do "regulatory takings" and "urban growth boundary," all of them nearly absent before 1970. Other terms related to the growth-control movement that show dramatic increases in usage are "farmland preservation" (starting in 1973), "wetland protection" (1970), and "smart growth" (1993). Of course, not all ngram terms increase over time. "Trolley cars," for example, peaked around 1918 and then declined steadily except during World War II; references to other dated forms of transportation, such as "express train" and "ocean liner," also showed decreases.

The remarkable thing about suburban growth controls is that they represent a discontinuity both in language and in practice. Almost absent in the fast-growing 1950s and 1960s, they became widespread in the 1970s, arriving with a speed that rivaled the initial adoption of zoning in the 1910–1930 period. Their strong correlation with housing prices is, of course only suggestive of a causal relationship.

My original reasoning about the surge in zoning was that unprecedented peacetime inflation that began in 1973 had something to do with it (Edwin Mills 1979; Fischel 1985). Inflation made new development of the same sort of housing that already existed in the community more of a fiscal burden. Previous residents had financed municipal capital expenditures (water and sewer and streets) at low interest rates. New development required infrastructure that was more costly and could be financed only at interest rates made higher by inflationary expectations. Using the previous methods of financing infrastructure would raise all property taxes, not just those of newcomers. To avoid assuming a greater fiscal burden, I suspected, existing suburban residents tightened their zoning requirements.

This particular story about inflation no longer persuades me. (Inflation's role in creating more demand for zoning via higher housing prices will be explored below.) As I will demonstrate in chapter 7, exactions and impact fees could easily have handled the higher costs of new development, so that zoning would not have had to become any tighter. Legal authority for such fees had long been in place (Heyman and Gilhool 1964), though the Supreme Court's exaction jurisprudence (reviewed in section 3.26) seems to cut back on this since the 1980s. More important, since the mid-1980s we have had nearly three decades of much lower inflation and nominal interest rates than in the 1970s and early 1980s, but zoning and the housing-price differentials that appear to arise from zoning regulations do not seem to have let up.

As mentioned at the beginning of this chapter, we now seem to have a long-lasting differential in housing prices across regions: The West Coast and the Northeast have persistently higher home prices than other regions (Karl Case 2007). These differences did not exist in the 1950s and 1960s. It was not differential rates of population growth that caused the new price differentials, either. The population of California, the 1970s leader in the growth-control movement, grew much more rapidly in the 1950s and 1960s, but its housing-price differential did not rise before the 1970s (Gyourko and Voith 1992; Fischel 1995). Southern states that grew rapidly in the 1970s as a result of the migration of manufacturing to the "sun belt" did not experience housing price inflation (Glaeser and Tobio 2008). In my survey of the growth-control literature, I found little evidence that zoning policies affected metropolitan housing prices before

1970 (Fischel 1990). Something besides the higher nominal cost of infrastructure seems to have induced a sea-change in zoning behavior in the 1970s.

5.16 Central City Problems Do Not Explain Growth Controls

Perhaps it was the growing problems of American central cities that caused suburbs to raise their drawbridges even higher. Court-ordered busing to desegregate city schools (which suburbs were mostly able to evade) was an important reason for whites to leave the city, as the careful work of Leah Boustan (2010; 2012) has shown. The growing urban crime rates of the 1960s and 1970s, manifested most dramatically in race riots, were also a reason for people to want to leave for suburban locales. One study estimated that in the 1970s and 1980s, large American central cities lost one resident for every violent crime committed (Cullen and Levitt 1999). It is tempting to look at the tempestuous urban events of the late 1960s and early 1970s as causes of a shift in demand from ordinary zoning to growth controls.

These explanations are not entirely satisfactory for several reasons. Crime has been declining everywhere, especially in the largest cities, since 1990 (Kneebone and Raphael 2011). The trend has contributed to a reversal of their population declines, and several of the largest central cities have grown since the 2000 census (Glaeser and Gottlieb 2006). Selective relaxation of school desegregation orders has also caused some relocation of whites to cities that were subject to more stringent orders before (Kane, Riegg, and Staiger 2006). But neither trend appears to have affected suburban zoning at all. It may, of course, be too soon to tell. Perhaps exclusionary zoning will eventually be reduced as people get the word that crime is down everywhere and neighborhood schools actually serve neighborhoods. But for now, neither of these trends seem to correspond with changes in suburban land use policies. Instead, the back-to-the-city migrants seem inclined to adopt the anti-growth land use policies of the suburbs (David Schleicher 2013; Been, Madar, and McDonnell 2014).

The other difficulty with the "flight to the suburbs" explanation is that the flight had been going on fairly steadily throughout the twentieth century, starting even before the Wright brothers invented that other flight (Mieszkowski and Mills 1993). The rate of suburbanization as represented by population density gradients seems to have been fairly steady for almost a hundred years. (This was masked in the pre-zoning years by central city annexation of many suburbs and later by the slowdown in housing construction from 1930 to 1945.) Even if the 1960s represented a surge in departures from central cities, such a surge would not have required a change in zoning policies for most suburbs. They had been happy to accommodate middle-class, single-family housing from 1945 to 1970. Some were pickier than others, but all had the same zoning tools available to them during that time. A surge in demand for middle-class housing might have filled up some suburbs more rapidly, but within most metropolitan areas, semirural townships, exurban county areas, and small towns were available to absorb the spillover.

5.17 Better Explanations for the Rise of Growth Controls

My hypothesis is that events around 1970 changed both the supply and demand for land use controls in ways that made the controls more restrictive. Much of this change had to do with the democratization of the process of adopting and altering land use regulation. During the 25 years after World War II, up to 1970, zoning and almost all other land use regulation were regarded as if they were done by an insular municipal guild. Local officials drew up zoning laws, and local appointees administered them. Elected officials were reasonably faithful to what they perceived to be the preferences of their constituents, and once they made their decisions, there was little further debate.

Under this regime, the impact of zoning on suburban development was mitigated by the large variety of jurisdictions, each of which was able to set its own policies. If Scarsdale was not eager to have more residential or commercial development, then developers could head to the more accommodating suburb of New Rochelle. Most importantly, if the local government of New Rochelle wanted to adopt *pro-development* policies, there was little that a minority faction within the city or anti-development groups outside of the city could do about it. For this reason, courts typically upheld community decisions if they wanted to retard development *or* if they wanted to promote development (Norman Williams 1974). Zoning thus had little impact on metropolitan housing patterns. Apartment and commercial developers who were shut out in one municipality simply rolled up their blueprints and shopped around for another town more willing to cut a deal.

Around 1970, however, economic and social trends arose that made suburbs as a group more exclusionary. I will divide these factors into new demands by suburban homeowners for exclusion and a supply-side of the story about additional methods to facilitate exclusion. The primary *demand* factors were (a) the growing suburbanization of employment (as opposed to just residences) resulting from the construction of the interstate highway system; (b) the expansion of equalitarian legal principles that derived from the civil rights movement of the 1960s; and, most importantly, (c) the sudden growth of housing values (partly endogenous to other factors) in the portfolio of homeowners. The chief elements that facilitated the *supply* of exclusion were (a) the expansion of legal standing to opponents of development; (b) the federalization of the environmental movement that dawned on the national scene in 1970; and (c) state legislation that established multilayered review of many projects that were formerly regarded as entirely local.

While I will focus below on the (already broad) aforementioned factors, it must be understood that larger social and political trends were at work at the same time. These include an irregular but general growth in affluence that gave rise to a demand for more spacious homes and lots and outdoor recreation in suburban areas. Along with growing affluence came a greater regard for individual rights that made citizens less inclined to accept the wisdom of public officials. The latter is best summarized by the popular bumper sticker motto, "Question Authority." Never mind that the slogan invites the paradoxical retort, "Who are you to tell me to question authority?" Opinion polls showed a distinct and consistent decline in Americans' respect for government authority in the 1970s and 1980s (Nye, Zelikow, and King 1997).

5.18 The Second Transportation Revolution

As interstate highways were built in the 1960s, jobs began to follow residents to the suburbs at an increasing rate (Glaeser and Kahn 2001). Suburbs with sufficient amounts of vacant land and residents eager to have help paying their property taxes accommodated this influx with the oxymoronic "industrial park" and other zoning innovations (Jon Teaford 1997). In one sense this form of suburbanization was a replication of the first era of zoning in the 1910–1930 period. Trucks and buses had made it possible for industry and apartment houses to decentralize to the suburbs, increasing the threat of annoying neighbors and inducing homeowners to demand zoning.

By the 1960s, changes in manufacturing technology required continuous processing in single-story buildings instead of lofts. Construction of the interstates induced manufacturing jobs to relocate to the open spaces of the farther suburbs. The highways enabled suppliers to get their materials to manufacturers on a "just-in-time" schedule, and they also enabled workers to drive their cars from multiple locations, not just those around the job center. A related development of the 1960s was the rise of containerized shipping, in which freight could be loaded into a standard-sized steel box that could be moved by truck, railroad, and ocean freighter without disturbing the goods inside (Marc Levinson 2006). The development of motorized trucking in the 1910s had released the auxiliary functions of manufacturing from the downtown ports; the 1960s container box released the entire manufacturing operation from the need to locate portside.

The decentralization of metropolitan employment meant that workers no longer needed to live near a single central business district. This undermined the classic urban-economics conception of jobs in a central city surrounded by successively higher-income rings of suburbs. The shift in jobs to the suburbs was dominated by less-skilled occupations. Glaeser and Kahn (2001) demonstrate that the high-skilled "knowledge industry" jobs became more concentrated in city centers, even as they note that the high-skilled workers continued to reside in the suburbs. Once blue-collar jobs suburbanized, low-income workers who had formerly resided close to central cities to conserve on commuting costs now had to find jobs in the suburbs. Indeed, for those poor without automobiles or confined by racial prejudice to the central cities, the "spatial mismatch" between jobs and homes became a real concern (Holzer, Ihlanfeldt, and Sjoquist 1994).

Although the suburbs had been zoned for decades, administration of the rules up to the 1960s was often flexible (Babcock 1966). Farmland in a developing suburb was often initially zoned as a temporary "holding zone" for multi-acre residential lots. Landowners and civic leaders expected such land to be rezoned to smaller lots as development pressure arose. The new development was not much feared by existing homeowners because it was expected to include more of the same types of homes that were already there. But as jobs decentralized, the supposedly "natural" factors that had established the high-income suburbs—the greater pull for the rich of cheaper suburban land compared to their larger suburban travel cost—started to break down. Urban economists began to question whether income and travel cost could explain as much about suburbanization as they originally thought (William Wheaton 1977).

Ownership of automobiles grew from 59 percent of all households in 1950 to 82 percent in 1970. The difference in travel costs among income groups was reduced primarily to the opportunity cost of time, which is lower for the poor. Urban miles traveled by passenger vehicles grew by 73 percent between 1960 and 1970, a higher rate of growth than in any previously recorded decade (U.S. Bureau of Census 1975). As jobs for both rich and poor became decentralized, the working poor were almost as inclined to live in a distant suburb as the rich. In urban-economics terms, expansion of automobile ownership flattened the rent-offer curve (what people would pay for locations near the center of the city) of the poor faster than that of the rich.

At the same time, quality of life became a more important issue for existing suburban homeowners, since they, too, were less tied by location near the central city. In the multi-nucleated metropolis, urban jobs are almost equally far from any given suburb. Bruce Hamilton (1982) showed that by the 1970s, actual metropolitan commuting patterns looked almost random when compared to the theoretical suburb-to-central-city paradigm. Communities had come to be chosen more for quality of life than for commuting convenience.

5.19 Civil Rights Law Drove Suburbs to General Exclusion

The civil rights movement of the 1960s had a profound but subtle effect on suburban land use decisions. As I described in section 3.5, the incipient use of zoning to segregate races by neighborhood or community had been struck down in 1917 in *Buchanan v. Warley*. Maintenance of segregation by the use of private covenants, which were in any case an incomplete substitute for racial zoning (since holdout landowners could sell profitably to blacks), had been legally undermined in 1948 by *Shelley v. Kramer*. What was new in the 1970s were the federal and state fair-housing laws that made it more costly to keep blacks out by private discrimination and by informal means, such as racial steering by real estate agents.

Anything that looked like racial zoning was almost never tolerated by the courts. Zoning could, however, be used to reduce potential contact between races, or between high- and low-income people, by the superficially neutral expedient of insisting on large lots and single-family homes in residential districts (Sheryll Cashin 1999). Racial anxieties could not, of course, be mentioned in any public document as a reason for the ordinance. Local officials learned quickly to expunge any such language. And, in my opinion, race has only been part of the anxiety of established suburbanites. Christopher Berry (2001) found no evidence that fully zoned Dallas was more segregated than unzoned Houston. Zoning in Vermont and New Hampshire, two states with minuscule fractions of racial minorities, does not look much different from zoning in heterogeneous New York and California. Exclusion is far more an income-based, class issue (Lee Fennell 2001).

The heirs of the 1960s civil rights lawyers recognized that the issue of the 1970s was not just inequality among races, but economic inequality generally. They brought legal tools to bear on what they perceived as the maldistribution of wealth created by suburbanization. The new legal targets were no longer just segregated schools and overt racial discrimination in housing. They were now inequalities in school spending and property tax resources (Coons, Clune, and Sugarman 1969), as well as zoning laws that made it especially difficult to build private and public housing for the poor in the suburbs (Lawrence Sager 1969). The legal attack on local property tax financing of schools and the assault on exclusionary zoning were undertaken for the same reason: to open the advantages of suburbs to the less affluent.

As an aside, I would note that the attacks on local school finance systems have had much greater success than legal attacks on exclusionary zoning. Almost half of the states have had plaintiff victories in the school finance area, and even where suits have been lost, states have responded defensively by centralizing school finance and making differences in property tax bases less important (Bradley Joondeph 1995; Rueben and Murray 2008). Yet there is almost no evidence that reduced property tax differentials have reduced exclusionary zoning.

The foregoing changes that began in 1960—decentralized jobs and civil rights liability—shifted suburbanites' demand for zoning. The poor were knocking at their gates, and public-interest lawyers were poised to man the battering rams. Zoning's older means of exclusion, which overtly favored single-family homes and discouraged apartments, was newly vulnerable to legal attack. The *Mount Laurel* decisions in New Jersey in 1975 and 1983 served notice that deference to municipal exclusivity, once formerly warmly endorsed by the New Jersey courts and most others (Williams 1974), was now under siege (Haar 1996). Even though *Mount Laurel*'s aggressive legal remedy (court-mandated rezoning) has not been widely copied, the sentiments it embodies are shared by courts in almost all states, and that keeps suburban homeowners wary.

The suburbs' response to the threat of having more low-income neighbors was to adopt the seemingly neutral policy of restricting all development, not just that for low-income people. (Section 9.16 describes studies supporting this view.) The rubric for doing so was "growth management," which became, as Norman Williams (1982) put it, "a major movement in the 1970s—apparently springing up spontaneously in local areas all over the country" (235). Faced with the curtailment of selective exclusion, localities began to opt for general exclusion. The first communities to adopt growth controls were generally those with upscale homeowners that had recently experienced growth (Protash and Baldassare 1983). Moreover, the courts seemed untroubled by the practice, as shown by the *Mount Laurel* court's often-cited 1983 dictum:

> Finally, once a community has satisfied its fair share obligation [a fraction of the region's low-income housing], the *Mount Laurel* Doctrine will not restrict other measures, including large-lot and open area zoning, that would maintain its beauty and communal character. (*Mount Laurel II*, 456 A.2d at 421)

Adopting larger lot and "open-area" zoning, two mainstays of growth management, had the drawback of sacrificing some fiscally profitable commercial development. For many homeowners, however, that was a fiscally acceptable trade-off. If attracting industry meant having to take the people who worked there, better not to seek it. New commercial development and high-value housing, moreover, were becoming less fiscally profitable in many states as property tax-base sharing formulas for financing schools were put in place (Justin Ross 2013).

5.20 Environmentalism Supplied a Neutral Ideology for Exclusion

I have so far described two factors that led suburbs to demand more general exclusion of development: decentralization of jobs and legal imperatives to accommodate the poor. Yet anti-growth politics were not easy to supply. Important changes in zoning such as growth controls require a unifying ideology to get them implemented (Ellickson 1989). Economic advantage is a powerful private motivator, but it plays poorly in public discourse. It is considered gauche (I have tried it) to mention in a public meeting that a particular public policy will raise or lower home values, even though what is acceptable to mention—traffic, crime, walkable streets, local pollution—pretty clearly maps onto home values. Something less obviously selfish is required to get other community residents to rally around the cause.

The early-twentieth-century idealization of the single-family home as a font of virtue in a dangerous urban world is said to have helped unify a potentially disparate group, homeowning residents, into a purposeful political force (Martha Lees 1994; Rafael Fischler 1998a). Home-and-hearth ideology helped state and federal judges, typically drawn from the same social spectrum as suburban homeowners, to suspend their scruples about the new zoning laws' effect on segregating people by their station in life and their derogation of traditional property rights.

Judge Westenhaver, who wrote the lower court opinion in *Euclid v. Ambler*, was not alone in his concern (disregarded by the Supreme Court) that the effect of zoning would "classify the population and segregate them according to their income or situation in life" (*Ambler v. Euclid*, 297 F. 307 [1924]). Nonetheless, zoning was widely embraced in the 1920s by a public for whom these concerns were overridden by the growing belief that single-family homes—and not apartments (then equated with pestilent tenement houses)—were the sources of civic virtue. One could also interpret this position as an extension of the Jeffersonian belief that yeoman farmers (owners, not tenants) were the proper foundation of a democratic republic. The single-family home could be thought of as the farm without the fields attached.

In the 1970s, however, a new ideology was needed to justify the suburban shift from selective growth to reduced growth. Home-and-hearth ideology, after all, applied to the poor as well as the middle class, to the owners of condominiums and mobile homes as well as to owners of standard single-family houses. The environmental movement of the early 1970s offered a seemingly new and compelling ideology to justify a more general exclusion of development.

Adaptation of environmentalism to suburban demands required some fancy footwork. Environmental ideology that inspired the national legislation of the 1970s was actually poorly suited to local zoning. The inspirations for the National Environmental Protection Act (NEPA) were catastrophes that had little to do with local decisions. The events of 1969 that were said to inspire Earth Day—the Santa Barbara oil spill and the fire on the Cuyahoga River in Cleveland—were at most incidental to local zoning, and almost none of the early agenda of environmentalism focused on local decisions. Indeed, the whole idea of Earth Day, first held in 1970, was to direct attention to national and global problems that transcended local boundaries.

Yet environmentalism was soon bent to the service of land use regulation. Much of the "limits to growth" literature, which was conceived on an international scale as a computer-simulation project, was quickly adapted to the particulars of local land use. One of the authors of the *Limits to Growth* study, Donella Meadows, who was resident at Dartmouth for much of the time, was especially influential in efforts to promote local activism. "Think globally, act locally" became the unofficial mantra, and acting locally typically meant preserving open space from the bulldozer (Meadows 1991). Farmland preservation, which fits somewhat uncomfortably into an environmental agenda (outside the suburbs, commercial farming methods are criticized by environmentalists), was nonetheless also embraced as a means of shunting development to other communities (Peterson and Yampolsky 1975; Kline and Wichelns 1994).

5.21 The "Quiet Revolution" Empowered NIMBYs

As I mentioned in a previous section, overall metropolitan development in the 1920–1960 era was not much affected by zoning because of the variety of local governments in place. For every suburb that was dedicated to exclusionary zoning, there was a not-too-distant town that was more than willing to accommodate development. The pro-development communities were either dominated (for a time) by landowner and developer interests, or they had started out poor enough (as, say, formerly isolated factory towns) that middle-income housing and apartments looked fiscally attractive to them. Where an affluent suburb might reject a middle-income development because of its impact on local schools, a lower-income suburb might see the same proposal as the road to educational salvation. Variety among the suburbs—still falsely presumed to be "homogenous"—ensured that market-driven development had a place to go.

Municipal autonomy in zoning was undermined in the 1970s by several trends that have grown out of the environmental movement. The more universal trend was the empowerment of neighbors who were dissatisfied with the pro-development decisions of their own local government and its bodies. The legal outcome up to the 1970s had been that neighbors usually lost when making these challenges (Williams 1974).

The environmental legislation of the 1970s, by which I mean both NEPA and its state-law equivalents and related legislation, empowered private citizens to bring litigation against their own local governments in a different legal setting than the old "neighbors cases" (Bernard Frieden 1979). Courts, whose judges shared the same environmental attitudes as middle-class homeowners (just as 1920s judges shared the ideology of hearth and home) were more sympathetic to claims that the local decision had failed to account for environmental impacts than they had been to seemingly selfish claims that neighbors' home values were at risk.

Simultaneous with the new empowerment of neighbors was the development of state and regional authorities whose mission was to deal with regional issues. Dubbed "The Quiet Revolution" by Bosselman and Callies (1971), this movement attempted to transcend localism in order to deal with issues that spilled over from one municipality to another. (Section 2.13 discussed other aspects of this movement.) Land use was embraced as one of the regional issues, but regionalism faced (and continues to face) a political problem. As Teaford (1997) showed, regionalism was rejected after the 1920s because proposed regional governments would supersede local zoning. Individual cities wanted both the right to reject development and to promote it as they pleased. Smaller municipalities are willing to cooperate on many levels with their neighbors, but ceding control over land use within their own boundaries continues to be a major sticking point for metropolitanism (Frug and Barron 2008).

The regional governance arrangements that began to be formed in the 1970s found a workable compromise. Instead of giving the regional authority plenary power over land use, the systems that evolved were almost all of the "double-veto" variety (Frank Popper 1988). The local municipality retained the power to exclude uses, but it gave some of its power to permit them to the regional authority. A real estate developer had to jump through the regional authority's hoop as well as the local authority's. If he missed either jump, he was out of the running.

In Vermont, for example, the Hartford Planning Board approved a housing development near an interstate highway exit, but the regional planning commission, set up by the state under Act 250, sided with a neighboring landowner whose objections had been overruled by the municipal planning board, and withheld its approval (*Valley News* [Lebanon, NH], August 2, 2013). (Scott Milne, the frustrated developer, ran for governor the following year and nearly upset the incumbent.) The regional authority, however, cannot make the local authority accept a proposal that the locals had rejected. The double-veto structure distinguished the Quiet Revolution from earlier regional proposals that would preempt both positive and negative local decisions, and that made the new arrangement acceptable to the increasingly anti-development suburbs.

I submit that neighbor empowerment and double-veto systems, in conjunction with local application of environmental laws, changed metropolitan development patterns after 1970. Pro-development communities, which had formerly been the suburban safety valves for higher-density uses, were less able to accommodate lower-income housing and other less-than-popular developments. The fact that the objections to the new development came from a small minority of its own residents or from people who did not live in the community, as at a regional land use hearing, was now less relevant. A minority of insiders or organized outsiders now could stop or at least delay and modify (mostly by proposing fewer units) development in communities that had previously offered developers one-stop regulatory shopping.

One should not be entirely censorious of this trend. It is possible that the empowerment of neighbors rectified an unjust situation, wherein majoritarian preferences subsumed the well-being of a defenseless few within the community. Putting the necessary but unlovely land use in the poor neighborhood or in the poor community is a classic example of what the 1990s "environmental justice" movement sought to rectify (Richard Lazarus 1992). It is also possible that intermunicipal spillovers sometimes went unaccounted for by those who made land use decisions. Indeed, social scientists have hypothesized a "beggar-thy-neighbor" syndrome, in which a municipality deliberately zones for fiscally profitable but polluting industries along its downwind or downstream borders (Daniel Ingberman 1995).

I say "it is possible" in these cases because the evidence for them is surprisingly slim, especially when compared to the intellectual freight they are made to bear. (They were the rationale for the 1970 decisions that federalized environmental legislation [Daniel Esty 1996].) Studies of zoning board decisions have found that they have been remarkably sensitive to immediate neighbors' objections, even before neighbors carried the threat of federal environmental lawsuits in their back pockets (Nicolaus Tideman 1969). Modern searches for systematic examples of "environmental racism" have mostly come up short (Vicki Been 1994). Likewise, the few documented beggar-thy-neighbor examples turn out on closer inspection to look more like mutually advantageous deals than one-sided opportunism (Fischel 2001).

One reason for optimism in these cases follows from the same logic whereby most homeowners try to be civil to their neighbors even if they do not like them. Careless or opportunistic behavior invites retaliation in kind. The numerous and long-term interactions between municipal neighbors cautions the opportunistic types to think about long-term consequences (Clayton Gillette 2001). The municipal norm may not be "love thy neighbor," but "respect thy neighbor" is closer to the truth than the opportunistic hypothesis would have it.

5.22 Interstate Highway Construction Fueled Anti-Growth Organizations

In section 5.18 and in the article on which this chapter is based (Fischel 2004a), I argued that the development of the United States interstate highway system shifted the demand for exclusionary zoning by making both industry and apartment developers footloose. This was a continuation of the automotive revolution that started the first wave of zoning in the 1910–1920 period. Readers and seminar participants have generally found my explanation for the earlier zoning revolution more convincing than the second. One weakness in the interstate highway story is that the interstate did not introduce a new mode of transportation—it relied on already ubiquitous automobiles and trucks. The other is that an alternative source of opposition to growth was the environmental movement and the suite of legal tools that enabled nongovernmental agents and ordinary citizens to put up additional hurdles to growth, as just described in the previous sections.

I want to suggest that the application of the environmental movement to land use regulation was at least partly caused by the interstate highway system. Environmental concerns and the ideology that organized them long predated the 1970s. Most organizations that promoted environmentalism, however, had little to say about urban and suburban areas. The issue with which the Sierra Club was concerned was preservation of wilderness areas, almost all of which were far from cities. Pollution-control legislation did concern cities, but successful movements to control smoke from coal-burning factories was largely generated by local and state governments. Pittsburgh managed to clean up its notoriously smoky downtown through state and local initiatives. President Truman declined to support federal legislation in what was regarded as a state and local issue (Roy Lubove 1969). The federal government was involved in environmental issues primarily in national forests and public lands in the West.

Histories of the interstate highway system often point out that it was the greatest public works project in history. What these usually laudatory claims often overlook is that it was arguably the most locally disruptive transportation system every put in place in the United States. Ordinary roads, even fairly wide roads, do not divide communities in the same way that a limited-access highway does. Their detractors sometimes refer to the interstates as the American version of the Great Wall of China. But the Great Wall was *intended* to keep people from crossing it. (Having hiked along the Great Wall, I would add that it seems safer for a pedestrian to cross it nowadays than to dash across even a lightly traveled interstate.) Interstates do allow passage across them at selected overpasses and underpasses, but these are, in urban terms, widely spaced. If you want to divide one part of a community from another, it is hard to beat the design of an above-ground, limited-access highway. Robert Moses, New York's "master builder," was most reviled for his expressways that cut through neighborhoods in the Bronx (Robert Caro 1974), but limited-access highways were cutting through neighborhoods everywhere in the 1960s and creating political backlash throughout the country (Raymond Mohl 2004; Earl Swift 2011).

The closest parallel to the construction of the interstates was the development of American railroads. They, too, divided communities—the "other side of the tracks" is a disdainful term derived from the division—but their effect was moderated in important ways. Grade crossings were something local governments and often individuals could build to reconnect neighborhoods divided by the railroad. Spanning a divided highway, on the other hand, is a major capital investment requiring the participation of multiple levels of government. The national railroad system was built relatively gradually from about 1830 to 1890, a span of 60 years. The 42,000 miles of interstate highways were mostly built in about 16 years, between 1956 to 1972. That works out to an average of 2,625 miles per year, almost the distance from Washington, DC, to Los Angeles, California, every year for 16 years. Many people's lives were disrupted in a short period of time.

Interstate routes had been subject to a great deal of planning by federal officials dating from the 1930s. (Earl Swift [2011], whose work I lean on generally, specifically demolishes the idea that President Eisenhower, for whom the system is named, had much to do with the idea.) But unlike the railroads, the interstate routes involved little negotiation with local officials and neighborhood groups. Most urban railroads required some level of local input, and their routes in larger cities were the subject of considerable negotiation. The railroad companies could bully and deceive, but they required the cooperation of local officials on many fronts, such as location of stations, which imposed some limits on their behavior.

The interstates were financed almost entirely by the federal government. They required the cooperation of state highway officials, but these road engineers did not have to seek the cooperation of local officials. Indeed, one of Earl Swift's major points is how surprised highway officials were at the opposition that eventually did develop in the late 1960s and early 1970s. Highway engineers conceived of the urban sections of the interstates as the cure for every city's traffic congestion problem; they expected to be hailed as saviors rather than invaders. In reading Swift's account, I was also struck by how little highway planners expected the highways to change basic location patterns. They expected cities to grow but not decentralize to the extent that the interstates caused. Nathaniel Baum-Snow (2007), estimated that "one new highway passing through a central city reduces its population by about 18 percent" because city residents can move to the suburbs (775).

The construction of the interstates engendered what have come to be known as "freeway revolts." As the "freeway" name implies, they started first in California, where pre-interstate highway construction engendered widespread opposition by nongovernmental groups. Of course, many government projects of the era generated local opposition. Public housing projects have never been popular in residential neighborhoods, and waste disposal facilities are unpopular almost everywhere. But these types of projects lacked the qualities that made opposition to interstates more widespread. Public housing usually required some local government input, and waste facilities could be relocated in the face of opposition.

It was difficult to relocate a limited-access highway route, and opponents had few local government channels that led to effective opposition. Local zoning, for example, does not apply to state or federal government projects. So freeway opponents had to resort to nongovernmental organizations, and environmental groups were best positioned to overcome the usual free-rider problems that local organizers face. Thus environmentalism became the primary vehicle by which the highway juggernaut could be resisted. Environmental organizations' new urban role swelled their membership and gave them new direction as stewards of city and suburban environments rather than just the Sierra Nevada and other remote areas.

5.23 California Freeway Revolts Sunk the Growth Machine

It is not my contention that opposition to freeways was the sole source of the sudden rise in urban environmentalism and opposition to suburban growth in the 1970s. The passage of national environmental legislation in 1970 and its enthusiastic seconding by the judiciary were occasioned by many events. And freeway revolts were just one example of the empowerment of protest groups. The baby boom generation was coming of age and had experienced models of protest from the civil rights movement and opposition to the

Vietnam War. Freeway revolts were further manifestations of the same distrust of government authority.

An article in the *Journal of Urban History* by Louise Dyble (2007) described the process by which Marin County, which lies at the north end of the Golden Gate Bridge from San Francisco, became one of the earliest and most durable examples of growth control in the nation. California highway builders saw the federal 1956 interstate highway program as an opportunity to build new bridges and freeways into the county, whose sole direct road connection with San Francisco was (and still is) the Golden Gate Bridge, built in the 1930s. With the initial and enthusiastic support of a majority of Marin County's elected officials, highway officials proposed several new routes that would improve commuter access to San Francisco and the East Bay and at the same time open up Marin's undeveloped area along the Pacific Ocean to recreational users.

The proposed highways generated unanticipated opposition. After a number of noisy public hearings, state officials backed away from their plans. Professor Dyble did not end the story there, however. After recounting the rout of the highway officials, she went on to describe how the new coalition of anti-highway groups became a permanent force in Marin County politics:

> For the first time, opposition to a major transportation project represented the entire spectrum of interest groups and localities in the county. It was not the typical array of property owners in the immediate vicinity of the proposed route, who were generally loud but easily dismissed as self-interested. Nor was it the tiny (if influential) conservationist elite that had participated in previous efforts to stop bridge and highway construction to preserve parkland and scenery. Rather, it was a broad segment of Marin society representing cities and neighborhoods throughout the county, even those not directly affected by construction. Under tremendous public pressure, mayors and city council members had abandoned the growth machine, and soon county-level politics would be transformed, as well. (49)

The transformation Dyble described caused pro-growth officials to be replaced by anti-growth candidates in all public offices, including representatives to the state assembly and senate. Plans that had been drawn up to make the Point Reyes National Seashore the "Jones Beach of the Pacific," as one elected official described it, were dumped, as was the pro-growth legislator, who may not have known that Jones Beach in New York was an accomplishment of Robert Moses. Revised land use plans by both the county and its (few) incorporated cities ensured that the state's projections that Marin County's population would grow to nearly 800,000 by 2020 would never be realized. (Population in 2010 was 250,000.) Transportation planning shifted away from highway construction to public transportation and finally to simply denying transportation improvements at all on the rationale that any improvements would bring population growth. Marin County voters repeatedly rejected taxes that would have funded an extension of the commuter-oriented Bay Area Rapid Transit System, and BART still has no rail connections to Marin.

The unifying element of the revolt was home values. Public officials before the freeway revolt had been sensitive to homeowners' concerns, but they regarded further development as necessary for the region's overall economic health and, not least, the expansion of the local tax base. The freeway revolt created an organizational focus that put home values at the front of the political queue. Environmentalism was the ideological vehicle, but the true objective was something else. As Dyble summed up her analysis of the political turnabout,

> A close look at the dynamics of regime change in Marin reveals that power in the county shifted only when the real value of exclusivity, open space, and natural beauty became clear to property owners. Marin's celebrated environmentalism was founded on the value of real estate. (59)

5.24 Inflation and the Rise of Homevoters

Home values themselves became a larger fraction of most families' financial portfolios in the 1970s because of inflation. I had in a previous section dismissed inflation as a cause of fiscal prudence by municipalities—negotiated exactions could make up the difference between property taxes paid and infrastructure costs of new development—but here I will argue that inflation had an important but indirect effect on the demand for growth controls.

The reason was that inflation combined with the mortgage-interest tax deduction substantially reduced the effective mortgage rate for homebuyers (James Poterba 1984). To understand how this happens, consider a couple who has $50,000 to invest. They are currently renting a nice home with a value of $250,000. The family could buy stocks and bonds and continue to rent. The interest, dividends, and capital gains on the financial investment would represent the gross return, and that return would be subject to federal and state income taxes. The rent they pay would not be tax deductible.

If the household alternatively invested the $50,000 for the down payment to buy the $250,000 home, the gross returns on their investment would be the housing services they would get—what they would have had to pay if they were renting. However, this return would be invisible to the government, because they would now be paying it to themselves. If the home rose in value to $300,000 and they received a capital gain, they would not have to pay any additional tax in most circumstances. If inflation goes up, the value of the untaxed capital gain increases, since inflation-driven capital gains on other assets—not homes—are subject to taxation. Thus for high-income families, owning a home became much more attractive in an inflationary regime.

The graph below (figure 5.3), taken from work by my colleague Jon Skinner (1994), shows the dramatic increase in capital gains from housing. (Housing prices show almost exactly the same pattern.) Before the 1970s, housing was a

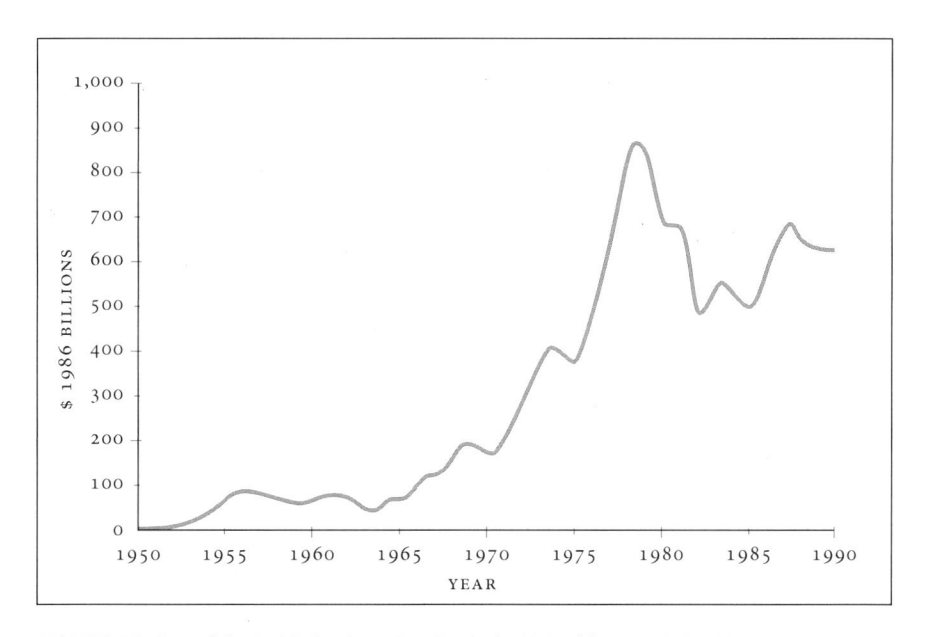

FIGURE 5.3 Annual Capital Gains from Housing in the United States, 1950–1990
Source: Adapted from Skinner (1994).

large part of the American household portfolio, but it was a fairly stable amount. Homeowners could not expect their home to be a growth stock. If they wanted to save for retirement or to help pay for their children's education, they were well advised to put their money in stocks. The 1970s changed that calculation. As Skinner opens his article, "Between 1955 and 1970, the share of owner-occupied housing in total household net wealth hovered around 21 percent. In the nine years between 1970 and 1979, housing wealth climbed to 30 percent of net wealth" (191), which was the highest up to that time in the twentieth century.

The rise of housing values as a source of wealth had effects that were different from a similar rise in the stock market. Stocks are held by a much smaller fraction of Americans, and even those who hold them have little control over them, since they are usually part of a diversified portfolio of mutual funds and retirement accounts. An owner-occupied home, however, is largely undiversified, and (partly for this reason), owners try to devise means to protect and enhance its value. This principle was the foundation of my book, *The Homevoter Hypothesis* (2001).

The twist I add in the present work is that homevoters became much more caring about their major asset beginning in the early 1970s. This shift in attention to home values meant that any potential threat to those values—not just their level, but their trajectory of increase—would draw homeowners' attention. Home values are sensitive to neighborhood conditions, and as home values increase relative to other assets, homeowners rationally become more watchful of changes in their neighborhood. If a home accounted for only 10 percent (say) of your wealth, a 10 percent decline in its value would not occasion much angst. But if the home rises in value such that it accounts for 50 percent of your wealth, well, maybe it is worth attending the neighborhood meeting about the proposed development down the street.

To envision this, consider what I would call the "Antiques Roadshow" effect. On this popular TV show, ordinary people bring antiques whose value they do not know and get on-air appraisals. Some of them get appraisals well in excess of their expectations. Those who do, I imagine, take a great deal more care transporting and storing their old clocks and candlesticks. Instead of tossing the items in the trunks of their cars as they did on the way in, they lovingly wrap the treasures and maybe have a companion look after them on the way home, where they store them in a cool, dry closet instead of the humid attic or moldy basement. More valuable assets get more attention and care.

A community's quality of life soon became as important a determinant of home values as other location-specific attributes such as commuting time. As a result, homeowners became ever more watchful of zoning changes that might affect that quality of life. Protection of home values was the common denominator that overcame ordinary residents' passivity. The formerly relaxed accommodation of development of the 1950s, when most community residents were content to allow municipal officials to deal with zoning, began to be replaced by a watchful electorate that crowded meetings and signed petitions to bring rezonings to a vote. The multi-acre minimum lot sizes and farmland categories that had formerly been regarded as temporary "holding zones" solidified into a permanent cast that kept the poor and higher-density development at bay.

My inclination in talking with economists has been to privilege the rise in housing prices as the key to the growth-control movement. This is because it has a self-perpetuating and infectious quality. Rising housing prices make homeowners into watchful wardens of their community. The success of initial exclusion brings an unrealized capital gain, which in turn breeds even more concern about land use issues. Housing inflation also has an easily identifiable exogenous cause, the unprecedented peacetime inflation that started in 1973.

I do think that housing inflation is key to galvanizing the demand for regulation. That does not mean that the supply-side factors I have identified—urban environmentalism, double-veto legislation, enhanced standing for outsiders—were simply called forth in service of enhancing homevoter demands. Even in the absence of these demands, they could have been brought about by democratic institutions responding to the demands of activist constituents. Other demand factors such as resistance to interstate highways and civil rights activism also seem to have had lives independent of housing prices. As causes of the rise of growth controls in the past 40 years, they almost surely had a complex interaction with general inflation.

5.25 Summary and Conclusion: Interest over Ideology

Most histories of zoning emphasize the supply side of the story. Planners, lawyers, and public officials got the idea that land use regulation was a good idea, and, in the spirit of the time, progressive elites with their scientific management principles foisted it on the public. This chapter has leaned against the scholarly wind and emphasized the demand side of the story. Public officials respond to the interests of their constituents, and public ideologies such as city beautification, hearth-and-home, and environmentalism come to the fore when they serve the interests of property owners. The property owners of the nineteenth century who were politically dominant were owners of businesses. Homeowners were not dominant back then because older urban transportation technologies—mainly the legs of humans and horses—required that they live close to their place of employment.

Once people could live farther from their work, their local political loyalties became divided, but unequally served, and the place where they voted was their place of residence. As trucks, buses, and cars replaced rail-bound modes of transportation, suburban residential districts could no longer rely on nuisance law, informal pressures, control of rail routes, and piecemeal covenants to protect their residential investments from incompatible uses. Zoning was a response to potential insults to their homes from near-nuisances transported to their neighborhoods by footloose trucks and buses.

The second land use revolution was caused by a conjunction of events in the late 1960s and the 1970s, none of them specifically local. They can be divided into demand and supply factors. The interstate highways made everyone footloose, including businesses and the poor, which undermined the role of transportation cost in keeping undesired development out of the more distant suburbs. The rapid and often ham-handed construction of federally funded divided highways in urban areas was also an important catalyst to the anti-growth movement. The increase in automobile ownership and accompanying traffic congestion in suburbs as well as cities made established residents wary of all new development.

With jobs moving to the suburbs and workers following them, the selective exclusion of apartments and other low-income housing opportunities became a more salient issue in the 1960s and 1970s. Attempts by civil rights lawyers to "open up the suburbs" were answered by a usually subtle backlash that promoted general exclusion rather than selective exclusion. The growing environmental movement of the era, which had not previously paid much attention to urban issues, provided a convenient rationale to support general exclusion of development by maintaining open space and (less consistent with environmental principles) preserving farmland. The federalization of environmental legislation in the 1970s and the establishment of multilayered reviews of development, exemplified by the double veto of the Quiet Revolution, supplied the tools to implement the new demand for general exclusion.

The nationalization of environmentalism and the rise of citizen power were not initially local, but they did provide a new supply of regulation that powered the anti-growth machine. As in the initial development of zoning in the 1910s and 1920s, the courts of the 1970s were largely followers of public opinion. In this respect, I am backing away from my previous focus on judicial initiative, especially in California, as a source of anti-growth leadership (Fischel 1995). Judges could have slowed the path of general suburban exclusion, as Pennsylvania's did (James Mitchell 2004), and the California Supreme Court's rapid shift to an anti-development stance continues to make the Golden State an outlier on the anti-development spectrum. But most judges seem to have been following a national shift in public opinion, or at least in the opinions of the educated class from which judges are drawn. In any event, the tools judges had at their disposal to limit growth controls were either too weak (the case-by-case injunction) or too strong (the regulatory takings doctrine, as I will discuss in chapter 9) to have stemmed the tide of democratic opinion. Where courts have vigorously deployed equal protection doctrines, as in the New Jersey *Mt. Laurel* cases, they have accelerated the suburban drive to preserve open space and thus drive up housing prices generally (Schmidt and Paulsen 2009 [discussed in section 9.16]; Thomas Rudel et al. 2011).

In sum, the three *demand* factors that led the 1970s growth control movement were (a) the growing suburbanization of employment (as opposed to just residences) resulting from the construction of the interstate highway system and the spread of containerized shipping; (b) the expansion of equalitarian legal principles that derived from the civil rights movement of the 1960s; and (c) the sudden growth of housing values in the portfolio of homeowners. The three elements that facilitated the *supply* of exclusion were (a) the expansion of legal standing to opponents of development; (b) the federalization of the environmental movement that dawned on the national scene in 1970; and (c) state legislation that established multilayered review of many projects that were formerly regarded as entirely local.

My emphasis on the democratic demand for zoning should caution against pointing fingers at particular states and cities as perpetrators of exclusion. Ganong and Shoag (2013), whose work formed the motivating introduction of this chapter, found that states in the Northeast such as Massachusetts and New Jersey, and those on the West Coast, such as California and Oregon, had increased regulations that drove up housing prices. But the regulatory frameworks from which growth controls emerged in these states were equally available in all other states. And even with a strenuous regulatory regime in place, housing prices do not rise much unless there is a shift in demand to locate in particular metropolitan areas. Indeed, the demand for creating a regulatory framework would be weak in places where the demand for housing was also weak. We need an explanation for why urban areas in the Northeast and the West Coast became so attractive to the college-educated.

Glaeser et al. (1992) suggest that cities with more employment diversity were causes of this type of growth, and Moretti (2012) emphasizes higher education and quality of life. Just why these factors should not have developed elsewhere in the nation is not clear. I have some preference for external factors such as the worldwide increase in demand for high tech (hence the West Coast boom) and financial services (hence the Northeast boom), which attracted the highly educated to places that had specialized in these industries.

What is interesting is that the 1970s "sunbelt" increase in manufacturing and worker immigration did not generate a local growth control movement in the South. I will explore the political reasons for different parts of the nation responding differently to increased demand for housing in section 8.12. A fragmented local government and the availability of voter initiatives, both lacking in the South, are key factors. For now, the lesson of an endogenous demand for regulation is that the cure for exclusionary zoning cannot just be to limit the supply of regulation. The demand for regulation, chiefly caused by excessive attention to home values, may be the missing link to reforming zoning.

CHAPTER 6

The Coase Theorem, Land Use Entitlements, and Rational Government

This chapter offers a formal structure with which to analyze land use controversies. The first part introduces the Coase theorem and applies it in the context of a controversy between neighbors. I develop the entitlements diagram in this highly localized context and then expand it to include local public goods. The expansion to include local government decisions requires a model of governance that relies on someone called the "median voter." I then consider the evidence that median voters are economically rational in that they respond to changes in the "tax price" of public expenditures. The evidence is most controversial in the case of compensation for regulatory takings. I conclude that local governments and the zoning laws they enact are no less economically rational than their purely private cousins, modern American business corporations.

6.1 There Goes the Sun: The Miami Beach Hotel's Problem

Two resort hotels stand side by side in Miami Beach, Florida, as shown by the diagram in figure 6.1, a schematic as seen from a boat on the Atlantic Ocean, looking west. The one to the north (direction is important here) is the Eden Roc, a spectacular architectural confection built shortly after its southern neighbor, the Fontainebleau. In 1959, the owner of the Fontainebleau is erecting an addition on the north side of his property, indicated as FB tower in figure 6.1. When completed, the addition will be so tall that it will

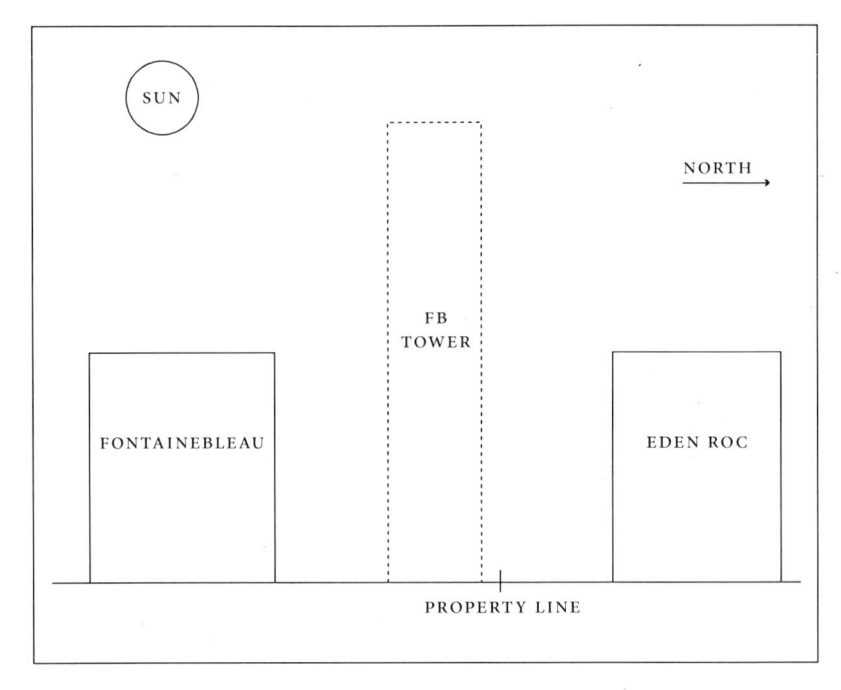

```
                    ┌─────────────────────────────────┐
                    │                                 │
                    │    ╭───╮                        │
                    │   ( SUN )                       │
                    │    ╰───╯      ┌┄┄┄┄┄┐           │
                    │               ┊     ┊           │
                    │               ┊     ┊      NORTH│
                    │               ┊     ┊      ────▶│
                    │               ┊     ┊           │
                    │               ┊ FB  ┊           │
                    │               ┊TOWER┊           │
                    │    ┌────────┐ ┊     ┊ ┌───────┐ │
                    │    │        │ ┊     ┊ │       │ │
                    │    │FONTAINE│ ┊     ┊ │EDEN ROC│ │
                    │    │ BLEAU  │ ┊     ┊ │       │ │
                    │    └────────┘ ┊     ┊ └───────┘ │
                    │               PROPERTY LINE     │
                    └─────────────────────────────────┘
```

FIGURE 6.1 Miami Beach Hotel Site

block the rays of the sun from reaching the pool and sundeck of its neighbor, the Eden Roc, during much of the day in the winter months.

The owner of the Eden Roc goes to court to get an injunction that will prevent the addition from being completed. One of his claims, the one that is the focus of this example, is that his southern neighbor is violating the doctrine of ancient lights. In English common law, a property that has enjoyed access to the sun's rays for a long time is entitled to enjoy it in the indefinite future. This entitlement is alienable, however, meaning it can be transferred to another party or modified so as to benefit someone else. The Eden Roc claims that the Fontainebleau is about to take its entitlement to the sun's rays without its permission. Attorneys for the Fontainebleau reply that the common-law doctrine of ancient lights might have applied in Old England, but this is the United States, and owners of property can build as high and wide as they like.

The conflicting claims to legal entitlements are indicated on the horizontal axis of figure 6.2 as point 1 ("full sun") and point 5 ("no sun"). The points can likewise be characterized as "no building" (point 1) and "biggest building"

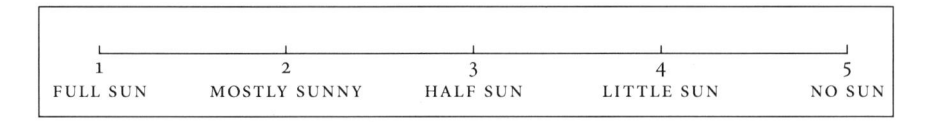

```
|----|----------|---------|-----------|--------|
| 1  |    2     |    3    |     4     |   5    |
|FULL SUN|MOSTLY SUNNY|HALF SUN|LITTLE SUN|NO SUN|
```

FIGURE 6.2 Possible Legal Entitlements to Sunlight

(point 5). The points in between are modifications of these extremes, with point 2 being "mostly sunny" or "small building," point 3 being "half sun" or "medium-size building" and point 4 being "little sun" or "big building." Legal entitlements are often characterized as extremes such as point 1 or point 5 in part because it is difficult to specify exactly what modification constitutes an in-between entitlement such as "half sun" (counting night time? cloudy days? summer or winter?). But it is not difficult for two adjoining landowners to specify a configuration ("a four-story building 150 feet wide") that involves minimal sun blockage, so the intermediate points such as 2, 3, and 4 are reasonable examples of a continuum of possible architectural possibilities.

Figure 6.3 modifies figure 6.2 by adding a vertical component called "dollars per entitlement." What is shown by each rectangular portion under the stepped line are the successive valuations to the Fontainebleau of moving from point 1 to point 2, point 2 to point 3, and so forth. These are the marginal

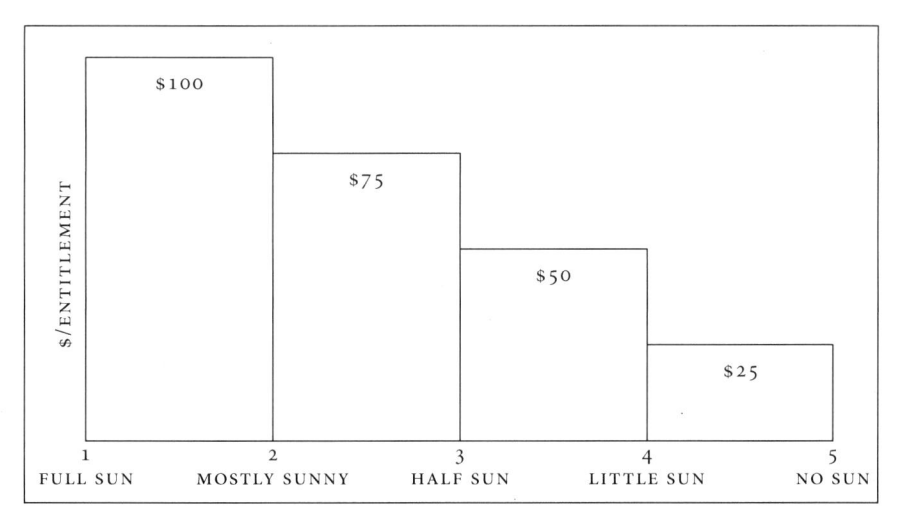

[Bar chart: $/ENTITLEMENT on vertical axis; horizontal axis from 1 FULL SUN, 2 MOSTLY SUNNY, 3 HALF SUN, 4 LITTLE SUN, 5 NO SUN. Bars: $100, $75, $50, $25 descending.]

FIGURE 6.3 Fontainebleau's Valuations of Rights to Build and Block Sunlight

valuations to the prospective builder of the new addition, the Fontainebleau, of being legally entitled to build successively larger structures. The first rectangle, whose area is $100 (million, if you will) could represent the value that the hotel puts on being able to put up a four-story building as opposed to none. The second rectangle ($75) could represent the value of putting on an additional four stories (for eight in all) to the proposed building. The number of stories is arbitrary in this example; the real issue is how much sun it blocks.

6.2 Valuing Sunlight Entitlements

The stepped schedule in figure 6.3 is what I will call the marginal benefit (MB) curve for the development-minded party, in this case the Fontainebleau. The total economic value or benefit of any given entitlement is determined as the sum of each marginal benefit unit read from left to right. Thus the total benefit to the Fontainebleau of prevailing in the litigation and having the alleged doctrine of ancient lights soundly and irrevocably rejected is measured as the sum of each marginal benefit from point 1 to point 5, or $100 (for going from point 1 to 2) plus $75 (point 2 to 3) plus $50 (point 3 to 4) plus $25 (point 4 to 5) equals $250.

The example here reifies the entitlement as a building of so many stories, but what is valued here is not the physical traits but the permission by the state courts to do something and the promise by the state to enforce the exercise of that power against other parties. So entitlement point 4 acquires a value of $225 in comparison to point 1 because the state of Florida and its institutions will not prevent the Fontainebleau from putting up a "big" building (but not the "biggest" of point 5) and will use the law to prevent the Eden Roc or anyone else from hindering its construction.

The values under the MB curve are not the same as the value of the building itself, which requires other resources besides legal infrastructure. But the general shape of the MB curve is derived from the profitability of potential buildings of various size: the potential revenues from use as hotel rooms or other purposes less the costs of construction and operations. The MB schedule slopes downward in this example, so that the second rectangle from the left side, going from four stories to eight stories, is smaller than the first rectangle, even though that was defined as adding the same number (four) of stories as the first. This is just because of the law of diminishing returns. The extra stories on a building usually entail higher construction costs than the lower stories because the upper stories add weight to the structure, which must be supported from below, and more stories add to the need for wind bracing, which also must be applied to the whole building. Extra stories also reduce the amount of rentable floor space because of the need for extra elevators and fire safety equipment. So the value of an entitlement to add a twentieth story on the structure is usually less than that of the tenth story.

There is an exception to this generally diminishing value. People who occupy hotel rooms (and apartments and office buildings) often like the longer and less obstructed views from the upper stories of taller buildings. So the generally downward slope of the MB curve in this example (and some others) could for a time be interrupted by an upward slope, where the higher revenue from the demand for nice views overcomes the higher cost of construction. But I would argue that this is usually temporary. The view from the twentieth floor is not a lot better than that from the thirtieth, and it does involve extra elevator stops for the tenant as well as higher construction and operating costs for the owner. In any case, all that is required to set up my example is that the MB curve eventually turns negative and that it intersects the opposing party's MB curve during its downward phase.

Which brings us to the opposing party in the present battle for entitlements, the Eden Roc. It has a demand for the unobstructed sunlight it enjoyed when it originally erected its now-immovable (as an economic proposition) building. On the south side of its property, toward the Fontainebleau, it placed its swimming pool and sundeck, assets that are quite valuable to it and that would be devalued by any blockage of the sun. My assumption is that there are degrees of blockage that result in different levels of devaluation of the Eden Roc property. Starting on the right side of the entitlements diagram as drawn in figure 6.4, the Eden Roc's pool and sunbathing area is always (during the winter—high tourist season) in the shade of the monster building that the Fontainebleau can put up under entitlement 5, the zero ancient-lights entitlement. The Eden Roc is willing to pay, by my supposition, $120 to get some relief (to point 4) from the everlasting shade. It would be willing to pay another $80 to go from point 4 to 3 to get still more sunlight, and yet another $60 to go from point 3 to 2, and another $20 to get from point 2 to 1.

The value of these entitlement points is net of the costs of mitigating their gain or loss. The Eden Roc could relocate its pool and sunbathing area to other corners of its property, and, to get ahead of the story, in fact it did build another pool elsewhere on its limited-size lot. But the relocation was costly, and the new pool is obviously (to me, as a visitor) poorly placed for the hotel

224 CHAPTER 6

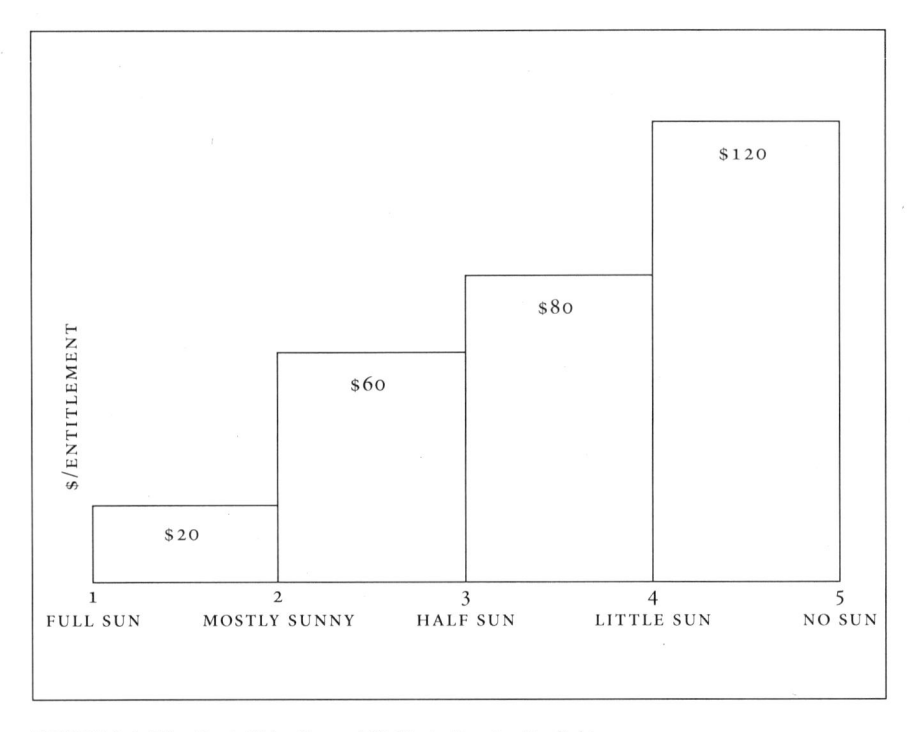

[Bar chart showing $/ENTITLEMENT on the y-axis and sunlight categories on the x-axis:
1 FULL SUN: $20
2 MOSTLY SUNNY: $60
3 HALF SUN: $80
4 LITTLE SUN: $120
5 NO SUN: (no bar)]

FIGURE 6.4 Eden Roc's Valuations of Rights to Receive Sunlight

guests. The two qualifications here are that the value of these entitlements is given in part by the cost of relocation options and that relocation is costly given the initial placement of the hotel.

It is also possible that, as was the case for the MB curve for the Fontainebleau, the Eden Roc's schedule is not always downward sloping from right to left. Perhaps the extra sun gained from point 4 to 3 is valued more than the initial amount of sunlight gained from point 5 to 4. Although I find this unlikely, the only claim needed for the following analysis is that the marginal value of sunlight eventually diminish and that the MB curve for the Eden Roc cross the MB curve of the Fontainebleau while both are on their downward slide to the horizontal axis. (Actually, one or the other "curve" could be a horizontal line; the key is that neither be upward sloping where they intersect or the proposed equilibrium will be one extreme or the other.) If the lines do not intersect at all—both schedules fall to the horizontal axis before touching the other—then there is no conflict and no controversy. This

6.3 The Coase Theorem and Entitlement Exchange

A few years ago I met a former student who said that he did not recall much from his introduction to economics, but he did remember that when two lines crossed one another, something important was going on and you should pay attention. Figure 6.5 is the juxtaposition of figures 6.3 and 6.4 except that it is smoothed rather than stepped. This smoothing is actually a bit controversial these days in the field of law and economics, with some scholars insisting that property is best thought of as consisting of discrete lumps rather than continuously divisible entitlements. Without passing judgment on that controversy right now, I am presenting the smooth economics curve version of property entitlements to point the way to economic analogies.

The MB curves are now labeled with arrows on top as reminders of which direction the two parties prefer. The FB (Fontainebleau) curve is read

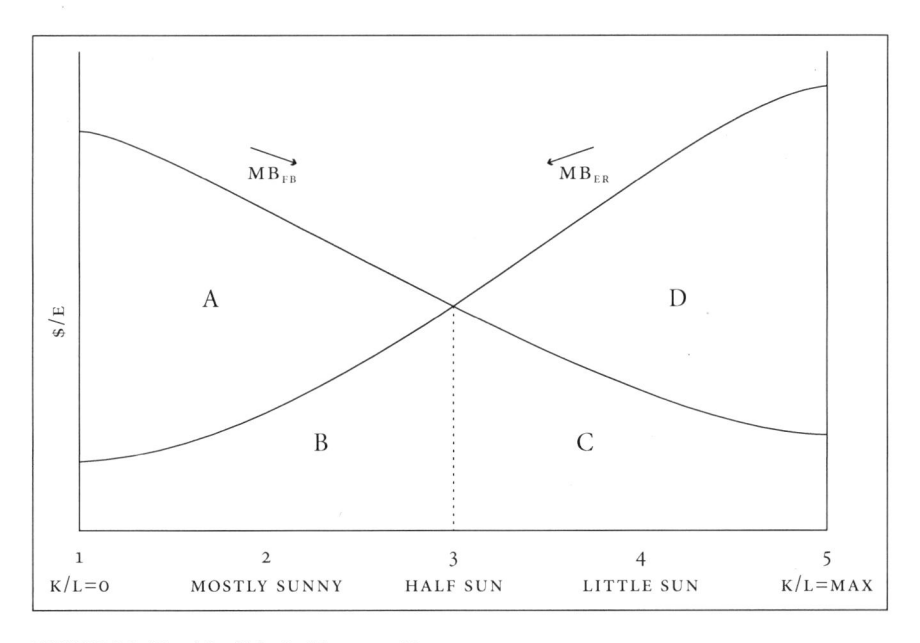

FIGURE 6.5 Hotel Sunlight Entitlements Diagram

from left to right, and the most preferred initial entitlement for the Fontainebleau is point 5, which allows for the biggest building and pretty much blocks all of its neighbor's sun. The most preferred initial entitlement for the Eden Roc is point 1, full sun for its original pool and sun deck and no building by its south side neighbor. The court battle between them, *Forty-Five Twenty-Five v. Fontainebleau*, 114 So. 2d 357 (Fla. App. 1959), will determine which party will get its preferred entitlement.

Now we step back from the fray and ask a seemingly existential question: Does it really matter which party prevails in court? It certainly matters for the parties involved. One will be happy and the other will be sad. But after they get over that, there is business to be done. Suppose that the Eden Roc (whose address is 4525 Collins Avenue, from which it takes its dull corporate name) prevails and is awarded the right to sunlight. Big party at the Eden Roc. Afterwards, the owners of the Fontainebleau come over, hats in hand, and say, can we make a deal here? We have these big plans for a tower (point 5), but we can scale it back to a moderate size (point 3). Eden Roc's executives check back in a few days and say okay to point 3, provided the Fontainebleau pays the Eden Roc enough to compensate for the moderate loss of their sunlight. Since the MB curve of the Fontainebleau is above that of the Eden Roc between points 1 and 3, it is possible to make a deal.

The Eden Roc will settle for no less than the amount represented by area B in figure 6.5, which is the value of the sunlight entitlements it gives up. Note that this implies that the MB curve of the Eden Roc, which is read from right to left, is actually a marginal cost curve to the Eden Roc when moving from left to right. A benefit forgone is a cost in the relativistic world of economics, so from the viewpoint of the Fontainebleau's emissaries, who need to pay good money to the Eden Roc, it looks like a rising marginal cost curve.

However, there seems to be a complication. The Eden Roc, sitting there in the catbird seat, points out that there is no reason it should have to settle for just being compensated. It sees that the Fontainebleau would be left with a surplus (profit or rent, whatever you want to call it) represented by area A if all it had to pay was area B. So the Eden Roc bargains for some of amount A. In principle the Eden Roc could get almost all of area A, since the scenario here is what economists call a bilateral monopoly—two parties with no other place else to go. In a competitive market, where there were other places to expand its hotel, the Fontainebleau could keep most of A by threatening to build elsewhere.

In any case, though, economic theory predicts that the two hotels' owners will make a deal and move from point 1 to point 3. They will not move any farther to the right because the MB curve of the Eden Roc is above that of the Fontainebleau in that region: The value of sunlight lost by the Eden Roc is greater than the value of extra stories of the Fontainebleau's hotel addition. This possibility is why I kept calling the court's decision in this case the *initial* entitlement. It is just a starting point for bargaining and exchange.

The less obvious proposition in this thought experiment is to ask what would happen if the court had decided on the opposite position, denying that the English doctrine of ancient lights had any currency in America, and granting victory to the Fontainebleau, as it in fact did. Now the initial entitlement is point 5, in which the Eden Roc has no right to access to sunlight and the Fontainebleau can build the biggest building. Now the victory party is held in the bar of the Fontainebleau, and the Eden Roc's owners are the supplicants. But clearly (from the diagram, at least), there is room to make a deal.

The Eden Roc values a move from point 5 to point 3, limiting the Fontainebleau's addition to a moderate height, by the dollar amounts represented by D plus C in figure 6.5 (the area under the ER's MB curve between points 5 and 3). The Fontainebleau values this limitation on its building only by the dollar amount represented by area C, so a mutually advantageous trade can be made. There is nothing in theory to say how much of amount D (Eden Roc's surplus) Fontainebleau can gouge out of its neighbor, so we cannot know the precise amount that will be paid, but if the two parties are just interested in making money, they will move to point 3 and a moderate-sized tower will be built.

Observe what just happened. Economic principles of an ordinary sort—the presence of conflicting uses of property (sometimes called "externalities"), the desire to make money (or not lose it), and willingness to make a deal—showed that the initial legal entitlement duly established in court made no ultimate difference in how resources were actually deployed. This is the unqualified version of the Coase theorem, which was derived from a 1960 article by Ronald H. Coase. The term "theorem" was applied to it in a textbook treatment by George Stigler (1966), who was among the famous Chicago economists who initially did not believe it to be true. Coase argued his case using a pithy numerical example rather than any diagrams or mathematics, and that approach invited considerable doubts. But Stigler, Milton Friedman, and other Chicago luminaries were eventually won over, and Coase's article became one of the founding documents of modern law and economics.

It is important to understand that the Coase theorem's demonstration of the irrelevance of the initial legal entitlement does not mean law is irrelevant.

Establishing some initial entitlement is usually a critical precondition for bargaining and exchange. And exactly which initial entitlement is important to both parties: One will be elated by victory and the other disappointed and poorer by loss. If the outcome is unexpected, windfall gains and losses affect the wealth of the parties involved. But not that much. If the Fontainebleau had lost, its value as an enterprise would be lower, and it might be less able to finance even the modest-sized tower that the previous example proposed would be efficient to build. In a world where it is easy for businesses to buy one another and get financing, though, this disability would be transient. Another hotel owner would buy the Fontainebleau (for a lower price that reflected its loss) and take up negotiations with the Eden Roc. Indeed, one could conceive of a hotel-takeover entrepreneur buying both hotels and then simply doing the most profitable thing, which is build the modest-sized tower. This is called the "merger solution" in law and economics, and its invocation is a sort of "game over" condition when modeling conflicts among land uses.

6.4 Pareto Optimality and Transaction Costs

An aside on some normative nomenclature is in order at this point. An efficient outcome in this case is one that is "Pareto optimal," or just plain "optimal." That means that it is impossible to make any further exchanges of entitlements that can make both parties better off. At point 3 in figure 6.5 (directly below the intersection of the two curves), any possible gains to the Fontainebleau of building higher are less than the losses to the Eden Roc from loss of sunlight. The result is the same for making the proposed building smaller—the gains to the Eden Roc of extra sunlight are less than the losses to the Fontainebleau from a smaller building.

Optimality describes a static condition, but it can also be expressed in terms of potential gains. All voluntary exchanges that move in the direction of a Pareto optimal outcome are called "Pareto superior." At point 2, for example, the Fontainebleau can compensate the Eden Roc for its extra loss of sunlight, and if it does so, the move to point 3 is Pareto superior. When all Pareto superior moves are exhausted, the two parties have achieved Pareto optimality.

The most important and partly implicit assumption in the hotel example is the absence of transaction costs. These are the costs of making a deal. Without anything to hinder a deal between the two parties, they will always end up at the same point (point 3 in figure 6.5), and the outcome will always be

Pareto optimal. It is possible to define transaction costs as anything that would prevent the parties from making an exchange that would be mutually advantageous, which makes the Coase theorem a tautology. And in fact it is a tautology, which may be why it was so difficult to grasp initially. The use of the Coase theorem, as Coase (1988) himself took pains to point out, was not that we will always get to the same efficient outcome. Its usefulness is that it offers a different approach to the economic problems of public life.

It is not enough, Coase argues, to simply call the shadow that a building casts upon its neighbor an externality and then devise ways to tax it or regulate it. Coase's approach suggests that we first ask about the nature of transaction costs that impede the parties themselves from reaching a socially satisfactory outcome. And in raising the question of transaction costs, Coase hoped that economists would consider a number of different institutional arrangements before recommending a policy. For example, if it is easier for prospective builders of hotel towers (like the Fontainebleau's) to make the necessary transactions to assure that their northern neighbors' legitimate concerns about shadows are taken into account, then some doctrine akin to "ancient lights" might be a good policy.

On the other hand, if prospective victims of shadows can easily anticipate the sensitiveness of their operations (the pool and sun deck of the Eden Roc) and can without much trouble take steps to avoid the problem (by placing them at a greater distance from the south lot line), then the doctrine of ancient lights can be safely rejected, as it in fact was. This exercise is an example of trying to identify the "least cost avoider" of a potentially harmful (to another party) activity, and it is now almost routinely invoked in economic analyses of tort and property law (Guido Calabresi 1961; Robert Ellickson 1973).

Despite the enormous influence of Coase's article, there is no widely agreed upon classification of transaction costs. Most frequently mentioned are the administrative costs of invoking the legal system to establish entitlements and then to cement the deal. In the hotels' case, any compromise that moved beyond the initial entitlement would require that attorneys draw up a covenant that specified what was to happen (or not happen) and that they legally bind the agreement to the publicly recorded deeds to the two properties. The reason for placing the agreement in both deeds is to make the agreement "run with the land." This means that later purchasers of either property will know what their rights and obligations are. If the agreement was only a personal contract between the current owners of the hotels, subsequent owners might feel free to ignore it.

The other big transaction-cost category is information (Harold Demsetz 1969). Potential transactors would want to know in the hotel case not just the profitability or loss of profitability from the whole range of sunlight-blocking entitlements but also the other party's costs or benefits. In everyday transactions, this is not much of a problem because many other people are buying the same thing. The problem is magnified for episodic transactions such as buying real estate, and so you rely on evaluations of other experts such as building inspectors as well as personal visits. But even these magnitudes are small compared to the exercise supposed in the example of the two hotels, which hinges on some difficult-to-value qualities such as the effect of shade on prospective vacationers' demand to pay for rooms.

The difficulties entailed in evaluating many alternative scenarios may account for the tendency for controversies involving property to settle on a few simple outcomes as default points. In the hotel case, the judge could grant entitlements somewhere in between the extremes of a right to full sun and no right to any sun. But the extremes are obvious even if not obviously desirable, and the judges might reasonably assume that the parties are in a better position to modify the outcome. The advantages of having standardized entitlements and avoiding the complexity of tailored arrangements is addressed in the legal literature about the *numerus clausus* principle (Merrill and Smith 2000). (The Latin term comes from Roman law, which offered a finite number of classifications for property categories.)

A third category of transaction cost that seems relevant to this case is willingness to bargain. The example supposed that both parties were profit-maximizing hotel owners who could easily put aside the animosities of their legal wrangling and, after judgment was rendered, come to the bargaining table to rectify the possible inefficiencies of the ruling. Coase himself usually used conflicts involving commercial activities, in which the motive to improve one's economic position is reasonably assumed. He actually invoked this very controversy as an example of conflicts among businesses that might be resolved by private exchanges (Coase 1960).

6.5 Holdouts and the Property Rule/Liability Rule Distinction

The case on which my paradigmatic example rests is famous outside of legal circles in large part because the owners of the hotels were *not* entirely motivated by profit. They were parties to a personal feud. Ben Novack (FB— I am going to attach the relevant hotel abbreviation to the owners' names to help keep them straight) and Harry Mufson (ER) had previously been business partners in developing resort hotels in Miami Beach. Novack went his own way in building the Fontainebleau. He hired a famous hotel architect and designer, Morris Lapidus, to create what at the time was regarded as an over-the-top luxury hotel.

Either because of a business disagreement or because of a poorly received practical joke that Mufson played on Novack, the two had a bitter falling out (John Glatt 2013). Mufson subsequently bought the vacant parcel just north of the Fontainebleau, hired the same architect (Lapidus) who had worked for Novack, and built an even fancier (though smaller) hotel, the Eden Roc. In retaliation, Novack built the 14-story northern addition. Aside from shading the Eden Roc's pool, Novack's spite wall (as everyone called it) was left almost entirely windowless, and the concrete side facing the new Eden Roc was for many years left unpainted.

After it became apparent that the building in progress was going to shade his hotel's pool, Mufson (ER) brought suit against the Fontainebleau and got a preliminary injunction from the trial court. The Florida court of appeals (the intermediate court) reversed, famously reiterating that American jurisdictions had rejected the English common-law doctrine of ancient lights. Mufson (ER) had also sought the aid of the City of Miami Beach, which accommodated him by hastily amending its zoning law to forestall Novack's (FB) behavior. Alas, that was a bit too hasty. The Florida court held that the zoning amendment was adopted without the required legal notice and public hearings, and it ordered the city to issue a building permit to Novack (FB). The more famous opinion, which rejected the "ancient lights" theory, was occasioned by Mufson's (ER) last-ditch effort to find something in the common law to stop the travesty that was being erected as revenge by his former business partner.

The special nature of these facts makes it a strange case with which to introduce Coasian bargaining, which presupposes economically rational parties going about their profit-maximizing business. Given the enmity with which the Fontainebleau's tower was started, it is almost certain that the Florida court's ruling determined the final outcome. If Mufson had won (and ancient lights protected the Eden Roc), the tower would not have been built. Given that Novack (FB) had won, it was inevitable that the tower was going to be completed. Novack was motivated by a desire to harm Mufson, not (it would seem) to maximize the value of the Fontainebleau.

In newspaper parlance, my use of this controversy is "burying the lead," that is, starting with one lead—happy commercial compromise—but ending with a contradictory story. My excuse for this, other than starting with an arresting story, is that it highlights the often idiosyncratic nature of property disputes. One of my favorite land use picture books is titled *Holdouts!*, compiled by real estate developers Andrew Alpern and Seymour Durst (1984). It consists mainly of photographs of New York City buildings (mainly in Manhattan) whose owners obviously resisted the blandishments of a developer of a much larger structure that now towers over their buildings. The Russian Tea Room, a venerable restaurant at 150 West 57th Street, is a famous example: It is a low-rise building flanked by enormous skyscrapers (one of which houses Carnegie Hall), whose developers fruitlessly negotiated with the owners of the Russian Tea Room.

One cure for holdouts is the use of eminent domain, the power by which a government agency (or a private developer who is lent the power of eminent domain by the government) can force a holdout to sell provided the owner is paid just compensation. Because "just compensation" normally amounts to the market value of the property, holdouts in the situations illustrated by *Holdouts!* would not receive compensation for their idiosyncratic valuations. Alpern and Durst actually published *Holdouts!* as a plea to allow the use of eminent domain by private developers. Former New York mayor John Lindsey wrote an introduction that more-or-less endorsed the idea. The book's initial effect on this reader was to cheer for the stubborn owner of the little house or restaurant who would not sell. The adverse national uproar over *Kelo v. City of New London*, 545 U.S. 469 (2005), in which the U.S. Supreme Court upheld the use of eminent domain on behalf of a private owner to take Ms. Kelo's "little pink house," suggests that my reaction was widely shared. (The *Kelo* case is discussed more in section 9.5, where the sympathetic reaction to Ms. Kelo's loss is contrasted to the public's indifference to uncompensated regulatory takings.)

The nature of eminent domain's powers was discussed in another classic of law and economics, "Property Rules, Liability Rules, and Inalienability: One View of the Cathedral," by Guido Calabresi and A. Douglas Melamed (1972). In contrast to the question asked in the Miami Hotel case, which was what initial entitlement each owner had to build a tower or remain in the sunlight, Calabresi and Melamed asked a subsequent question: How should those entitlements, once granted, be *protected* from someone else who covets them? The article's title straightforwardly states three options. (The "one view of the cathedral" subtitle refers to their modest admonition that their view is only one way of examining an important institution. Further views are by Krier and Schwab [1995].)

"Property-rule protection" is, as the name implies, the ordinary position from which an owner faces a would-be purchaser: The owner can name the price and other terms. It is the right to "just say no" to those who want your land or other property. Property rule protection is implicitly what I assumed in describing the possible transfers of sunlight rights between the owners of the Eden Roc and the Fontainebleau. At point 1 in figure 6.5, which permits the Eden Roc to have full sun, the owner of the Fontainebleau (Mr. Novack) had to persuade Mr. Mufson (the Eden Roc owner) to allow him to block any sunlight. Under the assumed values in figure 6.5, the Eden Roc owner would have to be paid at least the sum represented by area B to leave him no worse off. But because Mufson (ER) is assumed (as part of zero transaction costs) to know everything about the value that Novack (FB) puts on obtaining entitlement point 3, Mufson can extract from Novack the surplus amount represented by triangle A as well.

Property rule protection can also be illustrated from the opposite entitlement, point 5 in figure 6.5, in which the Fontainebleau is granted the right to build as large a structure as it pleases. Now the owner of the Eden Roc must beg the Fontainebleau not to build so tall. While being reasonable (moving to point 3) costs the Fontainebleau only area C, the owner of the Fontainebleau can potentially extract amount D as well. A property rule puts owners in the driver's seat in any negotiations and protects them from having to give up any idiosyncratic value (not shown in figure 6.5). But it also allows owners to extract other people's surplus, and, in a world with only slightly greater than zero transaction costs, the attempt to extract a surplus from buyers may result in a failure to come to terms.

Failure to make otherwise viable, value-increasing exchanges results in deadweight loss. In figure 6.5, the deadweight loss from failure to make a transaction if the initial entitlement were point 5 would be area D. Area C is not counted because that is what the Fontainebleau keeps as a result of being at point 5 rather than point 3. Area D is deadweight loss because it represents the excess value of point 3 over point 5 that neither the Fontainebleau nor the Eden Roc gets if the entitlement is stuck at point 5. For similar reasons, if the entitlement were assigned to the advantage of the Eden Roc at point 1 and no trade could ensue, the deadweight loss would be area A in figure 6.5.

If we think that transaction costs are especially high in this situation, the Calabresi-Melamed liability rule approach might give better results. Liability rule protection is a lesser protection of one's property entitlement. You still own it, but you must give it up if someone makes you an offer that some third party (a judge or a panel of assessors) believes is reasonable compensation. The term "liability rule" comes from the monetary damages that are paid in accident law, so it is usually synonymous with the loss that someone suffers. In the hotel example, liability rule protection for the Eden Roc would work this way. The Eden Roc is entitled to full sunlight (point 1 on figure 6.5). It can sell this right (it is not inalienable, the third protection Calabresi and Melamed consider), but its owner cannot "just say no" to an offer that covers the cost to the hotel (the consequences of more shade from their neighbor). In this case, the Fontainebleau will pay amount B to the Eden Roc, leaving it in no worse an economic position than before. All of the surplus of the exchange, area A, would go to the Fontainebleau, but the Eden Roc would not be worse off.

Liability rule protection could also be applied to the opposite initial entitlement, point 5, in which the Fontainebleau gets to build the maximum sun-blocking tower. The judges in the actual case could have awarded (as they did) the Fontainebleau the right to build and block the sun but (as they did not) protect that right only by a liability rule. In this counterfactual instance, the Eden Roc could have paid the Fontainebleau for the loss of any value to reducing the size of its tower. The Fontainebleau could not have held out for more (some or all of area D) or refused to trade at all, options it had under a property rule.

6.6 Spite Fences and Efficiency

Liability rule protection generally is commended by law and economics scholars (including Calabresi and Melamed) when transaction costs are inherently high. The most compelling case of high transaction costs arises when there are multiple parties involved, so that it is especially difficult to aggregate preferences and get unbiased information. This situation clearly is not present in the hotel case, where the conflict involves just two parties who have pretty good information about one another. The real transaction cost is that the two owners hate each other, and at least one of them, Novack (FB), wants to do harm to his former partner, Munson (ER).

We could analyze this situation by adding to the Fontainebleau marginal benefit schedule Mr. Novack's willingness to pay to harm his former partner. In this case, the "efficient" outcome is the maximum height of the building that was actually achieved. However, it seems doubtful that this is actually efficient. If it were, the Coase theorem would say that if Novack (FB) had not won the case, he would have paid Mufson (ER) for the damage he wanted to inflict. But this makes no sense. Novack's purpose in undertaking this monster wall was to harm Mufson economically. Like a reverse altruist, Novack had his utility increased by the reduction in Mufson's utility.

It is probably best to think of the feud between the principals in this case as one giant transaction cost, something to be overcome rather than respected. The tower itself probably added little to the value of the Fontainebleau. (I have actually stayed in the tower, having been stranded at the hotel for several days after a conference as a result of the events of September 11, 2001.) The blank wall that faces the Eden Roc means that the tower suites in the Fontainebleau are denied a view on the north side, reducing its rental income. I could locate no other hotel in Miami Beach that lacked windows on all sides on which views were possible. (Yes, I looked during the extra time I had in Miami Beach after 9/11.)

It is interesting that both owners lost control of their hotels within a few years as a result of bankruptcies. One wonders whether such colorful personalities made for unstable management—John Glatt (2013) does not paint a flattering picture of either man—although bankruptcy is hardly unknown among hotel owners. More to the point is that by 2012, the Eden Roc built its own tower on its south lot line, presumably having obtained a zoning variance and the cooperation of the now-corporately owned Fontainebleau. The new Eden Roc tower remedies the blank-wall look of the Fontainebleau's tower and takes advantage of the north-facing view, but it does not remedy the shade cast upon the still-extant but now second-string swimming pool of the Eden Roc.

Spite fences are frowned upon in American common law and prohibited by many statutes (Stewart Sterk 1987). At the same time, most have exceptions that permit spite fences (and spiteful trees) that are incidental to some productive purpose. In these cases, liability rule protection against the supposedly spiteful activity might be helpful. The payment of compensation would not include the spiteful value, since the disinterested parties that make up the market for hotel properties have no use for spite.

6.7 The Transaction Costs of Public Goods

In my 1985 book that is the predecessor of this work, I developed the Coase theorem framework by using a local controversy that I had investigated and written an article about (Fischel 1979). It involved a developer of pulp mills (the raw material of paper) who had purchased an option to buy land in Walpole, New Hampshire, which is about 50 miles south of my home in Hanover. The pulp mill developer needed to get the town of Walpole to rezone the land to accommodate the proposed mill, and the firm conducted an extensive campaign to convince local voters of the mill's merits. The selling points included increased employment, substantial property tax payments, and a ready market for timber. The mill asked for a straw vote to test the sentiments for a rezoning. It initially got a favorable reaction, but when it presented more extensive plans, another vote was taken in Walpole and the mill proposal was defeated. The mill developers, Parsons and Whittemore, instead chose an isolated location in Monroe County Alabama (just north of Mobile), where the plant still operates.

In my 1985 book, I presented the framework with which the Florida hotel controversy was analyzed above to consider alternative Coasian ways by which the pulp-mill controversy might have been resolved. (In the present work, I have reversed the directional units of the horizontal axes, so that more intensive use—bigger hotel, larger pulp mill—is on the right side of the diagram, which is the more conventional way in economics of representing supply and demand.) The formal logic is the same in both the hotel and the pulp mill controversies, but the Miami hotel case involved only two parties, while the Walpole pulp mill raised issues that are clearly local public goods. The proposed mill would have changed the air quality in the vicinity as well as caused additional traffic and visual disamenities. Many people would have been affected, not just immediately adjacent property owners.

The Coase theorem would seem not to apply readily if public goods are involved. The problem of public goods as presented by Richard Musgrave (1939) and Paul Samuelson (1954) is that such goods cannot be withheld from people who do not pay for them. Overhead fireworks are visible to all in the vicinity. A fireworks entrepreneur who sought to obtain a payment from potential customers would have a difficult time of it. Even if it were possible to identify all potential viewers in the relevant area, many people would decline to pay for the display even if they enjoyed looking at them. They would calculate that enough others would pay to make it viable, and then they could "free ride" on the service by looking up at the sky at the appointed time.

Free-riding applies to the Coase theorem as well. A developer with the right to build a locally undesired pulp mill might be persuaded by a group of citizens to head for the wilds of Alabama instead of a small town in New England. But when the local committee that negotiates the deal comes to nearby property owners to collect the monies necessary to finance the covenant, many beneficiaries will decline to pay, hoping that enough other people (or a benign foundation) will make the sacrifice. (I assume here that negotiating would be with property owners who might want to host the mill and that the deal would "run with the land" so that any other mill developer would be excluded as well.)

The difficulty that independent property owners have in organizing is sometimes said to be a justification for the usual rules of zoning, which place the burden of persuasion on the individual developer rather than on the diffuse residents. This is not the right justification, though, for it overlooks that the same problem is at work when the developer has to persuade residents to accept a zoning change that has, we shall presume for this example, economic benefits well in excess of its costs. Now the developer has to persuade a large number of property owners to accept some form of compensation. If each of them can veto the deal (as is normally the case if they have property rule protection), then at least some will strategically hold out to get more money than most other people would consider to be a fair deal. These holdouts are the mirror image of free riders. The holdouts may scuttle many otherwise efficient proposals because the developer's negotiation costs will rise.

A better justification for privileging existing residents in zoning is the same as giving people the right to vote where they live rather than where they work. Most people's homes and neighborhood give them considerably more consumers' surplus than their place of employment. Much of this consumers' surplus comes from long-time associations with nearby households, which is a form of agglomeration economies. Entitling promoters of nonresidential uses with the right to develop land in residential neighborhoods would undermine surplus value that individuals put on their land by causing some of them to move away (beyond the usual forces that make Americans mobile). Requiring the residents to buy out the developer would draw down this surplus and, because of cooperation problems among residents, often result in value-reducing development. The better strategy to avoid economic loss is thus to bias the outcomes of neighborhood change in favor of the status quo of existing neighborhoods, as most zoning laws indeed do.

6.8 A Case Study of Rezoning in West Lebanon, New Hampshire

Having offered a justification for a regulatory regime that favors homeowners, I will now consider an example in which this right was modified by the efforts of a single developer. This is an intermediate step between the purely private controversy, exemplified by the Florida hotels, and the larger public controversy, which deals with community and regional land use regulations, which will be examined in the next chapter. The instance here involved an experienced commercial developer, David Clem, whose acquaintance I made after he succeeded in changing the land use regulations on a particular parcel of land in Lebanon, New Hampshire. (A map and description can be seen on his website, http://www.riverparkwestlebanon.com/.) The 38-acre parcel is largely a greenfield. It had one commercial building (an auto parts dealer) when Mr. Clem bought it, which was demolished before the rezoning effort began.

The original zoning allowed for low-density residential development on most of the parcel. There had been no prior efforts to build in conformity with the existing zoning. Clem was the owner of Lyme Properties, whose most notable developments were biotech research complexes in Cambridge, Boston, and nearby cities. Having sold off his Boston-area holdings before the real estate crash of 2007, Clem planned to retire and divide his time between his Texas ranch and the area around his alma mater, Dartmouth College. But he could not resist one more development effort, and so he bought the land in Lebanon and tried to get it rezoned for a mix of offices, retail space, and residences, with a focus on the kind of biotech research firms that he had successfully developed in the Boston area.

Figure 6.6 represents a stylized entitlements diagram to illustrate Clem's problem. Its axes are similar to those in the figure for the Florida hotel controversy. On the horizontal axis, the far left side allows no development—the capital/land ratio is zero—while the far right side allows as much development as physically possible (K/L = max). The marginal benefit schedule for Clem, MB_{Clem}, slopes downward from the left vertical axis. The MB schedule hits zero (the horizontal axis) at some point short of the maximum intensity because of its location in the corner of a small town in a lightly settled area.

COASE THEOREM AND LAND USE ENTITLEMENTS 239

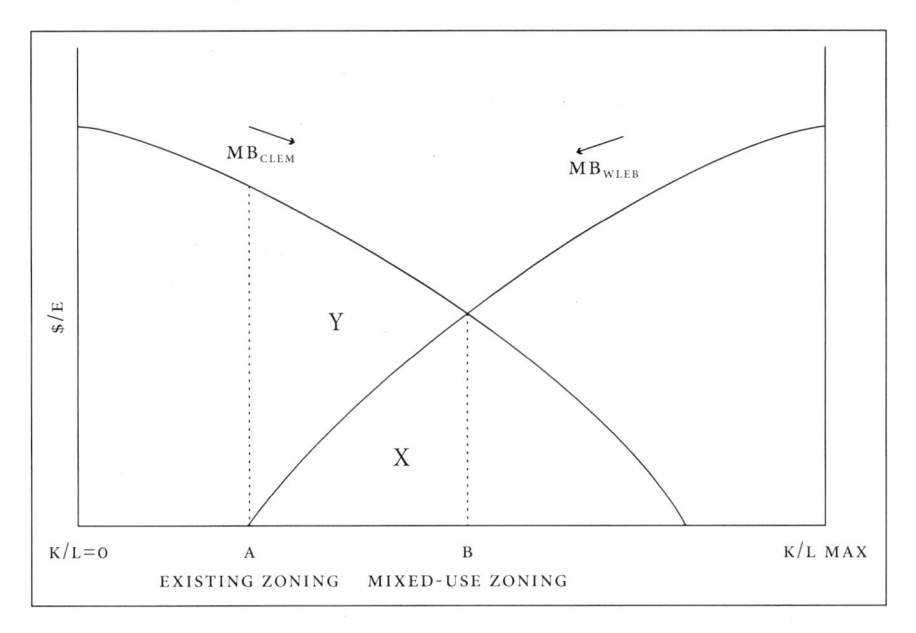

FIGURE 6.6 Zoning Entitlements Diagram

Building structures that are larger or closer together generate no additional profit after some point.

The marginal benefit schedule for the other side of the controversy is designated MB_{WLeb}. It is more complicated than in the Miami Beach hotel controversy. The potential spillovers from a mixed-use development affect many people. Those most obviously affected are the residents who are in the immediate neighborhood of the project. On the south side of Clem's parcel is a residential neighborhood. Its mostly single-family homes are modest but well-kept. Across the road is a newer neighborhood of single-family homes, which were built by a single developer; this neighborhood has a community association. Both of these neighborhoods would be directly affected by potential noise, traffic, and loss of open space (viewable but not physically accessible without the owner's permission) from increased development.

Parties more distant from the site might also be affected by more intensive development. The rest of the city of Lebanon and the adjacent towns of Hanover, New Hampshire, and Hartford, Vermont (whose commercial and railroad center is White River Junction, directly across the Connecticut

River) would endure some additional traffic from a larger development. New jobs in Clem's development would pull new employees into the region and require more school expenditures and municipal services as a result. The city of Lebanon would get compensation for its inconvenience by the expanded commercial tax base (which Clem states would more than offset the school costs from the project's additional housing), but other towns would not. However, new employees from biotech firms would likely purchase or build homes somewhat more valuable than average and thus would be less likely to cause a fiscal burden. In any case, as I argued in chapter 4, all of those towns have the zoning tools to protect their fiscal affairs.

Despite the apparent net fiscal benefits, most public officials and the planning and zoning staff of the city of Lebanon were opposed to rezoning the land to accommodate Clem's project. The opposition had less to do with the merits of the project itself than its inconsistency with the city's master plan, which directed commercial and industrial development to other areas of the city. Clem could have built in other areas that were already zoned for his proposed use, and the city regarded his proposal as a form of spot zoning.

Much of the appeal of the West Lebanon parcel, however, was that it was not in a commercial zone. The proposed biotech firms need to attract highly educated workers, and one of their nonwage attractions is a pleasant work environment. In the Cambridge-area sites that Clem had previously developed, the urban amenities of a university community provided the attraction. In rural New Hampshire, the main amenities were a pleasant natural environment. The western edge of the parcel abuts the Connecticut River, and views of the river and access to it would enhance its value to firms as well as residents who would locate there.

6.9 How to Get Your Rezoning: Start with the Neighbors

Clem might have tried to convince the city's planning board that its master plan should be changed and then get the city council to change the zoning. Lebanon is a city, not a town, so zoning changes are not necessarily brought to a citizen vote. Instead, Clem started from the bottom and worked his way up. After buying the site and having preliminary plans drawn up, he personally went to the immediate neighbors and explained what he was up to. More importantly, he asked for their opinions and indicated a willingness to modify his plans in response to their concerns. Along with his personal contacts, he set up a website and started a blog to show his proposal to the larger community. He held several community meetings not just to tell people what he wanted to do but to get feedback from them about what they wanted. He used "clickers" (electronic devices by which people can anonymously respond to questions) to encourage audience participation and get hard data about neighborhood sentiment.

Clem learned from these sessions that residents in the area were most interested in getting some access to the Connecticut River. The neighborhood to the south of his property adjoins the river but does not have access to it because of steep slopes and because it is private land. Clem's land has an area that slopes gently down to the river's edge and allows easy pedestrian access. He decided that the neighbors would be much happier with his development if he shared this access—which was to be a selling point for his commercial tenants and residential units—with the neighborhood outside of his holdings. He promised that access would be guaranteed by a local land trust and that necessary roads and paths open to the public would be built as part of the project.

In terms of figure 6.6, Clem wanted to improve his entitlements by moving from A to B. The neighborhood would have resisted this because it would lose residential amenities worth amount X, the area under MB_{WLeb}, the marginal benefit to the West Lebanon neighbors between A and B. Clem's riverfront donation appeared to compensate them for this loss. His net gain from this exchange was the area indicated by Y on the diagram. It is the increased value of his land by having it rezoned from entitlement A (low-density residential) to entitlement B (mixed use). The total value of that move to Clem is area X plus area Y, but he had to give up an amount equal to area X (not to mention other transaction costs) in order to get his rezoning.

Donating river access to the city was probably the least costly way for Clem to get the neighborhood on board with his project. It had the virtue of "running with the land," so that if any neighbors moved away, they could point out to prospective buyers of their homes the benefits of nearby river access. It also was a collectively consumed good. It is possible (he did not try this) that Clem could simply have paid his neighbors cash to support his project. Even if this were legal (I am not sure), it would have invited invidious comparisons among neighbors ("How come you got the same as me, when I'm more affected by this project?").

A cash payment would also have the drawback of not running with the land. The project has taken years to develop, and departing residents would have taken their money with them as they left. Newcomers would ask, what's in it for me? Clem could say, you got a lower-priced home (if in fact there were unpleasant spillovers), so don't complain. But there is no way to disable newcomers from opposing the project despite their awareness of the previous deal. They cannot alienate their right to public expression or access to the political process. The advantage of a public donation like the river-access easement is that existing residents and newcomers get equal and ongoing compensation for supporting—or at least not opposing—the project.

Lebanon city officials nonetheless continued to oppose the rezoning. This was nothing new to Clem. After graduating from Dartmouth in 1971, he began graduate study in city planning at MIT in Cambridge. While still in school, he successfully ran for a Cambridge city council seat and got himself on the ordinance committee, which was tasked with reexamining the city's zoning laws. There, he acquired intimate knowledge of how planning and zoning worked. After he lost his council seat in the next election (he may have been insufficiently enthusiastic about rent control, then a popular cause in Cambridge), he finished his graduate studies and began his career as a developer. He found that his knowledge of zoning and how citizens responded to changes in it was vital for getting projects going. His firm, Lyme Properties, built several of the most successful biotech research complexes in the area, including the Genzyme Center at Kendall Square in Cambridge and the Center for Life Sciences in Boston.

Clem approached Lebanon's zoning in the same hands-on way that he had in Cambridge. He did not rely solely on consultants and attorneys to deal with regulatory affairs. After the city turned him down at a particular stage, he used a little-noticed provision in the city's laws that allowed him to get his project voted on by the city's residents. Plebiscites are often frowned on in the literature as "ballot-box zoning" (Samuel Staley 2001). The usual complaint has it that developers go through all the city's hoops but then get shot down by voters who know little about the merits of the proposal. But the story here was almost the opposite. Lebanon voters overwhelmingly approved the rezoning despite opposition from the city's planning department and a majority of city councilors.

6.10 Homevoters, Median Voters, and the Tax Price

The previous example looked at how an enterprising developer managed to get a rezoning despite opposition from local officials. This section is going to look at local officials more sympathetically. They are in most cases (I argue) reasonably faithful representatives of voters within their jurisdiction. They are the agents who help overcome the free-rider problem in local public goods. The way free-riding is dealt with is for the government to take responsibility for providing the public good and collecting involuntary payments (taxes and fees). There are, of course, many intermediate associations, such as Chambers of Commerce, Rotary Clubs, volunteer fire departments, and Lions-Elks-Moose-Eagles clubs that promote local cooperative ventures, but their roles are largely supplementary.

Given the many local governments in the United States, the provision of these goods looks like a market to many economists (starting with Charles Tiebout 1956) despite the involuntary nature of taxes and local regulation. Rather than focus on the market-like qualities of household mobility—"voting with their feet"—and municipal competition (as described in chapter 4), this section and those following investigate the economic models by which political decisions about taxes, spending, and regulation are made at the local level, all with an eye as to whether the Coase theorem applies to governments as well as private corporations.

My view is straightforward and seemingly naive. In most local governments, the preferences of the majority of voters are catered to indirectly by elected officials or sometimes directly implemented by a plebiscite. Moreover, under most conditions, the majority knows its own interest and votes accordingly. Since the majority of residents in most communities own their own homes, they have a long-term outlook because they know that prospective buyers will care about the quality and cost of local services. To use a term I invented at the turn of the century, "homevoters" will embrace local policies that improve their net worth and resist those that do not (Fischel 2001).

When asked to consider a new or expanded local public program, homevoters consider what economists call the "tax price" of the program. This is simply how much they will have to lay out in extra tax payments (usually property tax payments) if the proposed project is adopted. Voters hear this often enough in news stories: "A new library for the school will increase the taxes on a $200,000 home by $40 per year for 20 years." The $200,000 home is usually chosen as being one that the typical voter might own, and I will personify that owner as "the median voter." (I neglect renters here because they comprise a low proportion of voters in most suburbs, but where they are influential, they seem somewhat less inclined to perceive the cost of additional spending than homeowners [Wallace Oates 2005].) Strictly speaking, the identity of the median voter could change according to what personal qualities cause people to vote. Dog owners might care more about the proposed dog park than the school library, but because most local policies affect property values even if most voters do not have kids or dogs, lining people up from low to high home values is a reasonable default position.

The idea of a single median voter is very convenient for economists who study the public sector. The economic theory of individual choice in a resource-constrained world works well for choices about private goods, where mine and thine are clearly distinct. Adding up preferences to determine demand is easy (conceptually) for private goods. But public goods cannot be similarly aggregated. We do not know how to add the preferences of the Smith family to the Jones family to get their joint demand for overhead fireworks displays, since the Smiths see exactly what the Joneses do. But if we make the leap that Smith and Jones chose the same local *government* over some other possible locations in the urban area, we can infer their joint demand for public goods from the person who occupies the middle of the preference spectrum, the median voter (Duncan Black 1948). The median voter enables economists to avoid the problem of interpersonal comparisons of utility by representing the "community" as a single person. This does not mean that everyone will agree about local policies, but it does mean that the choice of local policies can be analyzed through the otherwise individualistic axioms of economics.

The median voter's decision about what and how much the public sector should spend is determined by the tax price she faces. The tax price is different from the tax rate. In the numerical example just given, the community's additional tax rate is $40/$200,000, or .0002 percent. If the same household's overall annual tax payments were $4,000 (including all expenditures, not just the school library), the property tax rate is 2 percent. If another community with the same number of taxpayers (neglecting nonresidential property) but with a median voter whose home was valued at $400,000, the tax price would still be $40 for the new library, but the additional tax rate would be only 40/400,000 or .0001 percent. Tax prices are independent of how big or small the average home's value is in the community, but average tax rates clearly are not. Differences in tax rates are not the same as differences in the tax price.

Economists consider the tax price to be the main influence on the median voter and hence the political decisions that the town will have to make when considering how much to spend on local public goods. The typical way that the tax price is represented is in figure 6.7, which has private goods on the vertical axis and the local public good on the horizontal axis. The budget line

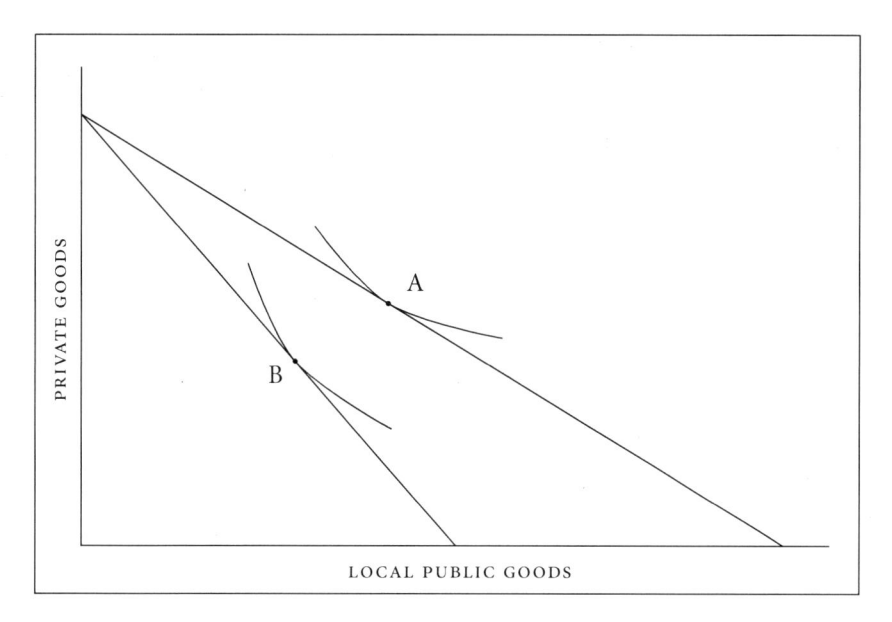

[Figure 6.7: Tax Price of the Median Voter — graph with axes "PRIVATE GOODS" (vertical) and "LOCAL PUBLIC GOODS" (horizontal), showing budget lines and indifference curves with tangency points A and B.]

FIGURE 6.7 Tax Price of the Median Voter

indicates the choices available to the median voter. The public good itself in this case is represented as the median voter's share of a public good such as, say, school expenditures or sidewalks. The slope of the budget line is the tax price of the public good. The slope pivots out (for a lower absolute value) if the good itself is more public than private (so that it is shared by others) or if the tax base is expanded by having more real estate that does not also consume any of the local public good. In most cases, having more commercial and industrial property or vacation homes, which do not come with children to attend schools, also causes the local tax price to decline. The median voter is assumed to be decisive in choosing the level of public goods. The tangency of her highest indifference curve is represented by point A in figure 6.7.

6.11 Local Democracy Works

The model espoused here has many critics who question its relevance. The mildest critics claim that voters do not pay sufficient attention to elections and politics for this model to describe local behavior. The oxymoronic term "rational ignorance," apparently coined by Anthony Downs (1957), says that voters do not learn much about political topics because they do not expect their single vote to influence the outcome of any election. Almost no election is determined by a single vote, so even caring voters are inclined to pay little attention to public events. The especially low turnout in most American local elections seems to support this idea.

In contrast to public concern about the decline in American voters' participation, many economists wonder why people vote at all. The Downsian pessimism has been carried to its (current) limits by Bryan Caplan (2007), whose survey of voter knowledge and opinions leads him to conclude that it might be a good thing if even fewer people voted. This adds to the pessimism engendered by traditional theories of the limitations of voting, the most famous of which is the voting paradox variously discovered by the Marquis de Condorcet, Charles Dodgson (the author of *Alice in Wonderland*), and Duncan Black (1948). It shows that voting among issues A, B, and C by voters X, Y, and Z (or any larger group) could result in the voters first choosing A over B, then B over C, but not, as elementary rationality would seem to have it, A over C when their pairing was voted on. Kenneth Arrow (1951) took this paradox as an element of his pessimistic and famous "impossibility theorem," which casts doubt into the very foundations of liberal democracy.

As the old seminar joke would have it, democratic voting seems to be one of those things that works in practice but not in theory. But there actually is a theory that supports the collective rationality of voters. It has a somewhat disjointed provenance but is normally attributed to Condorcet (again!) as rediscovered and elaborated by Duncan Black et al. (1958). (It was also rediscovered without apparent knowledge of its predecessors by James Surowiecki [2004] and dubbed "The Wisdom of Crowds.") The theory supposes that the majority of voters have some information about issues and candidates and that this information is more likely to be true than false. If this is true and voters are not systematically misled or subjected to group-think cascades of misinformation, voters are likely to choose policies that work in their own interests. (Black called this the "jury theorem," which is somewhat misleading, since jurors deliberate as well as vote and have to get to unanimity, not just a majority. Hélène Landemore [2012] offers a more nuanced discussion of the connection between majority voting and knowledge than I have space for here.)

Here is how I think collective wisdom works. A new fire station is presented to the voters as a way to increase safety and reduce fire-insurance costs, thus in effect paying for itself (without increasing tax rates) from higher property values (Caroline Hoxby 1999). But it could also amount to a wasteful boondoggle, causing taxes to rise with few offsetting benefits. Few voters in a local referendum would take the trouble to read all the arguments for and against this proposal, but there is enough newspaper and online chat for many to form some opinion. The majority vote will, according to Condorcet's jury theorem, most likely accurately predict which proposition is true. Since voters would normally vote according to what they think is in their interest, the median voter (the majority) will most likely make the correct decision.

Critics of this upbeat proposition about democracy point to the limiting assumptions of the theorem. The most critical (in my mind) is that the information voters have is not systematically distorted. Back in chapter 1, I demonstrated how systematically wrong most students were about how much land is urbanized. The "median voter" in my class was off fairly consistently by a factor of almost ten, thinking that between 30 and 40 percent of the nation is occupied by urban land instead of between 3 and 4 percent. But I also conduct some other experiments in my class to show that the median voter model works adequately if there is no systematic bias. The median student guesses about the width of the classroom, how many seats it has, the distance to the dining hall, and the instructor's height are all spot on. (In support of skeptics like Caplan, I must report that some students think I am six-feet-six and others think I am five-feet-five when I am really exactly six feet tall, a height that in one instance was guessed by no one but that the "median voter" had exactly right.)

It is also important to understand that the median voter who has such wisdom is not an actual person. A few years ago, I figured from housing and income data that I was the median voter in Hanover, New Hampshire. That would not have justified the selectmen's canceling elections and referenda and just asking me what I would like the town to do. The median voter's wisdom falls out of a statistical distribution, not a single person's knowledge. (But maybe my median position explains why I like it here.)

6.12 Evidence Supports the Median Voter Model

Whether the median voter's guesses about the merits of a new fire station are sufficiently biased by the fire department's propaganda is an empirical issue. Studies indicate that the median voter model has considerable explanatory power in local government. A substantial body of evidence finds that the level of local public goods is sensitive to the tax price (Borcherding and Deacon 1972; Gramlich and Rubinfeld 1982; Silva and Sonstelie 1995; Jonah

Rockoff 2010). I will offer a description of two related studies by Nathan Anderson (2006; 2011) that explore some sources of variation in tax prices and voters' balanced response to them.

The Minnesota legislature in 1996 made some statewide changes in how various classes of real property could be assessed and thus how much taxes they would generate for the local government. One of the changes decreased the assessments on vacation homes, whose owners typically cannot vote in the jurisdiction and generally do not have children in local schools. After the 1996 reform, year-round residents of communities thus had to shoulder a larger proportion of local property taxes, which means that the local tax price had risen.

Anderson examined the impact of this higher tax price on local public finance decisions. The elasticity of demand for local public services is a much-studied issue in public economics. Many studies have concluded that the elasticity of demand is relatively low. Voters appear not to be significantly swayed by how much they have to pay for local public services. However, most of these estimates are from cross-section studies, which have inherent econometric limitations, mainly because people have sorted themselves into communities where taxes and spending matched their expectations. (This is also probably why average voter turnout in local elections is low: Residents who have chosen the community do not disagree very much.) The new Minnesota policy that Anderson examined upset those expectations. The implementation of the policy was fairly rapid, and Anderson was able to use data from shortly after the policy was implemented, so there was not too much movement between districts. He found that voters who faced higher tax prices cut local expenditures considerably, suggesting a nearly unit-elastic demand for public services.

The main drawback of Anderson's vacation-home paper is that communities with a lot of such property are themselves unusual. It is not clear how widely applicable they are. In a follow-up study, Anderson (2011) addressed this by using another Minnesota tax policy change. The new legislation caused a reclassification of commercial property so that it added less to local tax bases, which also caused the local tax price to rise. Commercial and industrial property are much more widely distributed than vacation property, so the results are more relevant to a wider range of communities. Anderson again found a high tax-price elasticity, almost the same as for the vacation home sample. Both of these changes can be represented in figure 6.7, which shows the median voter's tax price. The reduction in taxation for commercial property caused the homeowner's private-public budget line to become steeper. If the previous equilibrium was at point A, the new equilibrium (after the tax price rose) was at point B, which is represented as southwest of point A. The higher tax price resulted in an equal percentage reduction in consumption of public goods and in private goods.

6.13 The Tax Price Response to Regulatory Takings

So it is clear that communities respond to changes in the prices of public services and that they do so in directions that seem rational to economists. This supports the underlying political theory of local public economics, which is that local officials are generally faithful conduits of the preferences of local voters, and that the latter respond to price changes pretty much the way that other institutions do. This contention has been questioned by some legal scholars, best represented by Daryl Levinson (2000).

Levinson's argument is fairly straightforward. Governments are not like businesses in their response to higher costs or other economic penalties because government decisions are political. Political leaders are responsive to voters and interest groups rather than stockholders and managers, and so their response to external stimulus is going to be much less certain and perhaps even the opposite of what one would expect. Considerations other than profit and loss, such as moral obligation and constitutional imperatives, are likely to complicate government behavior more than their private counterparts.

Levinson's position is quite the opposite of that which I adopted in the *Homevoter Hypothesis* (2001) and in the present work. State constitutions classify local governments as municipal corporations along with business corporations, and not without reason. Local governments have always been much like businesses and were important agents of economic development for most of their history (Eric Monkkonnen 1988; 1995). In the twentieth century, the governance of municipalities has become dominated by homeowners, and because they have so much of their net worth wrapped up in their homes, they become especially watchful of local affairs. Homevoters are if anything too aware of external events that may adversely affect the local budget and regulatory apparatus. Their skittishness about developments that have the slightest chance of devaluing their homes has earned a widely known acronym, NIMBY, for "not in my back yard."

A major concern that motivated Levinson was regulatory takings. As he notes, many law-and-economics scholars have invoked the Takings Clause as a more efficient way of reining in what they see as the excesses of land use regulation. But if governments do not respond to external financial incentives such as monetary damages, this doctrine seems useless and perhaps even perverse. Landowners would get damages and taxpayers would foot the bill, creating deadweight loss from higher taxes, but regulations would not change. Alternatively, government agencies might simply abandon their regulatory roles when faced with the prospect of damages. Neither outcome seems consistent with the law-and-economics and Coasian view of land use regulation advanced in the present chapter.

The latter outcome—drop the regulation in the face of damage awards— seems to have been what happened in Oregon. In 2004, Oregon voters approved Measure 37, an initiative that called for compensation for land use regulations. Owners of property who had acquired title before current land use regulations had been put in place were eligible for compensation for any devaluation created by the regulation. Government agencies could award compensation and keep the regulation in place, or they could rescind the regulation as it applied to the property in question and avoid making any payment.

Thus Oregon offered an experiment on the efficacy of the just compensation remedy that scholars such as Robert Ellickson (1977), Richard Epstein (1985), and the present author (Fischel 1995) have advocated. Our position is not that regulation should always be discouraged. The just compensation principle is not simply about justice, though it is that, too. It is also about economic accountability. A downzoning or other new restriction that confers benefits on nearby homeowners should be capitalized in higher home values, and the higher values provide a base for general taxation to compensate the landowners. A regulation that does not provide such benefits to nearby homeowners (or other recognizable beneficiaries) appears to fail the efficiency test and should not be adopted.

Law professor Bethany Berger (2009) set out to examine the results of Oregon's experiment. She found that the requirement of compensation for regulation did indeed have an effect. About 7,000 claims were made by property owners during the nearly three-year period that the law was in effect. But only one resulted in payment of just compensation by a locality, which was then able to keep its regulation in place. The other 6,999 or so all caused the government, usually a local government, to rescind the regulation as it applied to the property in question. The new compensation requirement did change the behavior of the government, but not in the nuanced way that advocates (at least this advocate) would have expected. Even if regulations were randomly adopted, *some* of the new regulations had to have had benefits in excess of costs. Yet statistically zero governments decided to keep any of the challenged regulations.

Oregon's experiment is cautionary, but one should keep in mind the special conditions that prevailed there. The first is the extremity of Oregon's regulatory apparatus, as documented by Sara Galvan (2005). The Portland area is famous for its stringent urban growth boundary, which has been in effect since the 1970s. One can actually see it from Google Earth without any political boundary lines turned on. (More on Portland in chapter 8.) Its visibility is the product of a nearly complete prohibition on development that is not agricultural or forestry-related outside of its limits. Because it is administered by a regional body, Metro, which is not accountable to any particular local government, municipalities outside of the growth boundaries are powerless to grant exceptions. As Galvan explains, court review of exceptions is hobbled by procedural rules that are unusually hostile to development-minded landowners. The extremity of the regulations are evident not just in the Portland area. Oregon's statewide restrictions on even rural land use are famous and controversial.

6.14 Substitution of Regulation for Taxation

The extremity of Oregon's regulations and the response to suddenly having to pay compensation for them can be analyzed with a standard device from microeconomics. Figure 6.8 is an "isoquant" diagram, which is normally used to illustrate the response of a firm to changes in the prices of two different inputs that it uses for making its product. For example, the firm chooses to produce 100 widgets with various combinations of labor and capital, the exact combination depending on the relative prices of those inputs. The "firm" that is depicted in figure 6.8 is a local government, and its "output" (Q) is a pleasant environment for its residents. The two inputs depicted here are physical acquisition of land (financed by local taxes) on the vertical axis and uncompensated police-power regulations (which do not require taxation) on the horizontal axis. The curved isoquants themselves represent constant amounts of "pleasant local environment." Isoquants farther from the origin are ever more pleasant communities. At Q_2, the residents have more parks, walking trails, bike paths, and pleasant vistas than at Q_1.

The curvature of the isoquants represents the ability of the community to provide these outputs with either regulation or with expenditures. A footpath,

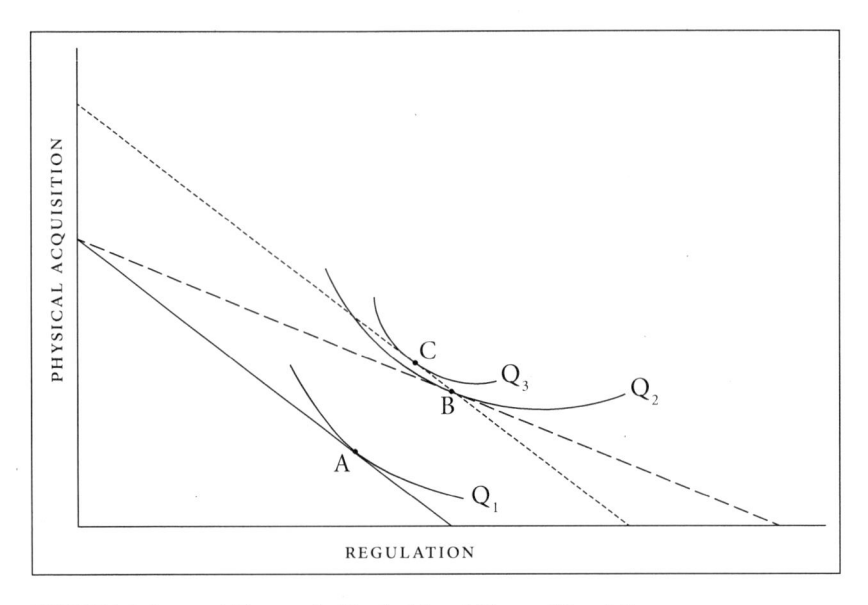

FIGURE 6.8 Isoquant Diagram for Physical Acquisition and Regulation

for example, will normally require that the government acquire the land and build and maintain the trail, all involving expenditures. But it might instead simply require that landowners tolerate trespassers over certain routes, which would save the taxpayers the cost of acquiring the land. The government could then use the money it saved to build footbridges and trail markers. Because the local voters do not have to pay as much, they will choose more trails and have higher quality amenities, Q_2 instead of Q_1. Similarly, the locality might want to preserve pleasant hilltop vistas by buying the land outright (or just the development rights) from owners whose buildings might block the view, or it might simply adopt regulations for development in hilly areas that have much the same effect. (This trade-off describes the behavior of the city of Tiburon, California, which gave rise to the case of *Agins v. Tiburon* discussed in section 3.21.)

The isoquant trade-off can be thought of in other dimensions. The famous geographer Gilbert White (1945) developed the basic idea (without using the economics diagram) to consider optimal use of inputs to control damage from floods. Governments can spend the taxpayers' money and use eminent domain to build flood-control dams upstream from vulnerable populations. Or they can control the vulnerability of downstream populations by adopting flood-plain regulations to reduce the damage of occasional floods. This is not an either-or situation; for any degree of flood-hazard reduction, the least costly policy will involve both regulation and dam building (Allison Dunham 1959). White's work was the basis for the national flood protection and insurance programs put in place after World War II. (The effects of a similar trade-off in protecting watersheds from development are described by Dehring and Depken [2010], who document the redistribution of wealth from watershed property owners to water consumers by uncompensated lot-size regulations.)

The choice that a cost-conscious community will make between acquisition and regulation will depend on the relative prices that it perceives. If a regulation is seen as having the same cost as acquisition, so that the solid budget line in figure 6.8 has a slope of minus one, then the optimal combination might be represented by point A, which is tangent to isoquant Q_1. Some regulation will be adopted and some land will be acquired in providing the given level of amenity.

It is important to understand that the regulation here does not involve payment for the cost of regulation to particular landowners. It nonetheless is shown to have the same opportunity cost as buying the land. The major pressure is political. Landowners have political clout to see to it that regulation is not overly burdensome. They might accept uncompensated regulation because they know that their property's value will be enhanced by it, and payment of compensation would require increased taxes that will both burden their property and perhaps cause the community to forgo the benefits of the preserved open space. Even if the landowners do not constitute a majority in this scenario, they may benefit from the respect of other residents such as old-timers. As I will argue in section 8.2, newcomers want to fit in with their adopted community and often defer to the interests of old-time landowners. There is also some opportunity cost in terms of foregone property taxes from the regulated land, though many communities regard this as small compared to the fiscal and amenity benefits of open space.

The informal political internalization of the cost of regulation is less likely when landowners and residents form distinctive groups with different interests and few regular interactions. A community whose residents live in homes on small lots may not have any reciprocity of interest with the owners of rural land within their borders. This seems to have been the case in Oregon. At one time, its cities had a common interest with its rural landowners insofar as forest products (for instance) were processed in urban areas. As cities became less dependent on this relationship, forests began to look more like recreation areas than tree farms, and preserving them for recreational use became more important. The outlays needed to purchase rural land, however, are daunting, and so uncompensated regulation looked more attractive. As rural residents lost influence in the state legislature (especially after the Supreme Court's reapportionment decisions in the 1960s), the political cost of regulation was reduced. Ideologies that cast the formerly normal use of nearby rural land for housing development as subnormal behavior—sprawl—made it easier to disregard the interests of landowners near cities as well as those in more remote areas.

Dismissing the interests of rural landowners can be thought of as having reduced the price of regulation, as shown by the dashed (– – –; not dotted .....) budget line in figure 6.8. The new equilibrium choice of inputs is represented by point B. It involves much more regulation than point A, and it gives the political majority—largely city dwellers—a higher level of environmental quality, Q_2.

Landowners might be willing to pay for exceptions to the most onerous regulations, which might give urban residents the opportunity to extract revenue from such exceptions. This is the scenario that I suggested in section 3.28 might be the basis for the U.S. Supreme Court's anti-exactions decisions. Both parties could presumably be made better off from such exactions. As I mentioned earlier, courts might worry then about the possibility of governments downzoning property just to get paid to upzone it later. In terms of figure 6.8, the perceived budget line (the dotted ..... line) would thus be shifted outward so it is parallel with the original budget line but passes through the regulated outcome, point B. (This is because there is another set of indifference curves in an Edgeworth box, which are not shown here and which represent the landowners' preferences, and movement from B to C is a movement to the contract curve that also passes through point A.)

Because the government can turn its original regulatory choice, point B, into cash to acquire land, this actually makes the regulation efficient in that the government now faces the correct opportunity cost. The community thus chooses something like point C, which involves the efficient combination of spending and regulation, given that the community is now "wealthier" for having taken the regulated property. I discussed this as the "Kozinski paradox" (Fischel 1991) after the federal judge whose opinion expressed it as a reason to strike down mobile-home rent control in *Hall v. Santa Barbara*, 833 F.2d 1270 (9th Cir. 1986). Allowing mobile-home owners to cash in on the value created by rent control reduced their inefficient incentives to stay put just to enjoy rent control. (*Hall* was later reversed in *Yee v. Escondido*, 503 U.S. 519 [1992].)

Exactions aside, the substitution of regulation for expenditure in figure 6.8 seems generally in line with the Oregon situation. And it explains why so few regulations resulted in compensation after Measure 37 was adopted. Measure 37 could be thought of as snapping the budget line back from the dashed (----) budget line in figure 6.8 to the solid budget line. Since regulation had been considerably underpriced (as indicated by the dashed line), rational public officials substituted regulation for expenditure. Once the cost of regulation became apparent by the obligation to compensate, they rationally rescinded the regulations rather than pay to maintain them. This "snapped back" the choice from point B to point A.

This "snap back" is similar to what happened after the U.S. Supreme Court's 1992 decision in *Lucas v. South Carolina Coastal Council*, as I described in section 3.24. The Court held that the elimination of all reasonable use of Mr. Lucas's two lots by the Coastal Council warranted a claim for just compensation. So the Coastal Council (through the state attorney general's office) negotiated to purchase the two lots to settle the case. Now that it owned the vacant lots, which sat along the ocean flanked by scores of other houses, the Council sensibly decided to sell them to the highest bidder who wanted to build homes on them. Plaintiff David Lucas (1995) wrote that this exposed the hypocrisy of the council, which had allowed no economic use as long as the loss was pinned on him. My view, which I reported in *Regulatory Takings* (Fischel 1995) and in a web essay whose photos show the new houses, is that this simply reflects the change in relative prices perceived by the Coastal Council. When regulation is cheap, rational agents will use a lot of it; when it becomes costly, they will respond by using less.

Getting back to Oregon, my use of Measure 37 to demonstrate the effect of relative prices is not to say that it actually provided the correct opportunity cost. Measure 37 swept all regulations into the same basket when at least some provided reciprocal benefits to the complaining owners. It also arbitrarily excluded landowners who had purchased their property after regulations were in place. (Although they presumably paid less for their land with regulations in place, the price also reflected some probability that they could eventually use it more intensively.) Measure 37's plan of compensation also did not take into account the deadweight loss of taxation and other transactions costs, which even a community of cooperative landowners might consider in choosing between regulation and expenditure. All in all, Measure 37 should be taken as a marker of the public's frustration with Oregon's disregard for landowner rights—not a well-considered plan for just compensation.

6.15 Measure 37 Was Too Temporary to Test the Tax Price

The analysis in the previous section compressed all regulations into a single box, all equally effective or ineffective. In reality, some regulations make more sense than others in producing environmental quality. Measure 37 did not distinguish between low-value and high-value regulations. Any devaluation was deemed compensable, even if the public got benefits well in excess of its costs. Yet in all instances but one, the regulations were rescinded rather than compensated. One cannot just blame Oregon's overall regulations, even if they are more extreme than those of other states, for the lack of compensation in all but one instance.

To explain this, one needs to consider the transition from one regulatory regime to another from the point of view of land use regulators. Measure 37 did not apply just to regulations adopted after it was passed in 2004. If it had, proposed regulations could have undertaken the benefit-cost analysis that economics-oriented proponents of compensation commend. Measure 37 applied to all regulations that were adopted after any given owner acquired property. Many elderly owners had held their land for a long time, and thus many regulations at issue had been adopted without much concern by governments that they would have to pay for them.

Regulators' reliance on lack of compensation was well founded in the Oregon Supreme Court's decisions. As Sara Galvan (2005) explained, not only did the court uphold almost all regulations and participate in the procedural disfranchisement of landowners, the court had actively suppressed a previous political effort to adopt compensation. Measure 7 was an initiative that passed in the year 2000 and looked much like Measure 37 in 2004. The Oregon Supreme Court struck it down almost immediately on the dubious grounds that it affected more than one constitutional clause. (Is there any constitutional change that could not be argued to affect more than one clause?) This history is relevant to Measure 37 because it, too, was immediately challenged in court, and less than a year after its passage a trial court found it unconstitutional.

Now, if one were a local public official in Oregon after Measure 37 passed, would you be inclined to set up a system to raise taxes to compensate complaining landowners? It is not trivial to do so, as appraisals must be made from before and after the regulation is established. Many prior regulations would have become obscure, as would their effect on current valuations. Bethany Berger's (2009) detailed description of the one instance in which compensation was paid demonstrates how difficult it was to do—and how ungrateful was the landowner who ultimately got compensated. Even before the trial court made its ruling, most officials had reason to think there was a good chance that the Oregon Supreme Court would eviscerate Measure 37. Public officials would have undertaken to set up compensation mechanisms for naught if that happened. It would seem more sensible for them to take a wait-and-see attitude, hoping that the courts would bail them out.

But then the unexpected did happen. The Oregon Supreme Court actually reversed the trial court and upheld Measure 37 on January 10, 2006, more than 14 months after it passed. The court's decision did not, however, cow the regulators into submission. Instead, it galvanized Oregon's environmental community, which immediately began promoting another initiative, Measure 49. Having been hammered by the voters for their extreme regulations, the regulatory community (epitomized by the "1,000 Friends of Oregon") did what political scientists have for years recommended and predicted. They moved toward the political center to appease many of the voters they had previously alienated.

Measure 49 standing by itself looks like a pro-property rights bill. It allowed landowners with Measure 37 claims to develop at least some of their property (three homes as of right, up to ten if devaluation could be proved), an idea that had been strenuously resisted by Oregon land use authorities for more than 40 years. Although it specifically undid Measure 37's damages remedy for all past regulation, it did enable suits for compensation for prospective regulations, which perhaps some future scholars will examine as a more reasonable test of the regulatory takings mechanism.

Measure 49 was passed on November 6, 2007, with 62 percent of the votes, about the same margin as Measure 37 had three years earlier. Public officials surely suspected that it had a good chance of passing. Stories about inappropriate developments enabled by Measure 37 were widely disseminated. Public opinion quickly shifted after the effects of that poorly drafted law began to be felt. (A cynic might suppose that officials surrendered their regulations to generate public opposition, but large payments of public funds to compensate owners would surely have had the same effect on public opinion.) Had officials begun to set up an apparatus for paying compensation after the Oregon courts upheld Measure 37, almost all of their work would have been for naught. Given the costs of setting up compensation and the dim prospects for using it for more than a year or so, it is less surprising that Measure 37 induced so little effort at compensation by government officials.

6.16 Compensation in Larger Contexts: Highways and the Draft

There are more positive examples of the effect of compensation on government behavior. California and the federal government reformed their eminent domain rules for acquiring highway rights of way in the 1960s (after a lot of highways had been built). The new rules for compensation raised the tax price of highways insofar as they had to cover (among other things) relocation expenses for tenants displaced by highways and for businesses whose inventory had to be moved. Careful econometric studies by Joseph Cordes and Burton Weisbrod (1979; 1985) showed that highway authorities responded as economics would predict. The new rules raised the cost per mile and thus reduced the amount of highways built. The higher price did not end all highway construction, of course, but it did slow it down and perhaps made highway planners more selective in their choice of routes. I would add that, given the "freeway revolts" of the 1960s described in section 5.22, this outcome was probably in line with what much of the public actually wanted.

Another example of the effect of compensation on government behavior is the military draft. The military draft operated for most of the period 1941–1973, when it was replaced by an all-volunteer military. Military pay for draftees had been well below their civilian wages. The draft could be thought of as a taking of young men's right to select an occupation with less than full compensation. I researched the effect of the end of the draft to explore how a large government agency (in this case, the Defense Department) would respond to the need to pay the market value of the resources it used (Fischel 1996). The answer was clearly in line with what economic principles would predict. The army (the branch that relied most on conscripted labor) substituted capital for labor once labor became more costly. Soldiers were paid more and were employed less often for low-value tasks such as dishwashing. High-tech machinery was introduced for both military and administrative purposes.

This substitution of capital for labor confirms that even a government agency as large as the Defense Department could respond rationally to a change in resource prices. The transition, by the way, was not entirely smooth. Army personnel policies had been developed when the draft was in effect. For most army leaders, conscripted labor looked cheap unless it involved the son of a member of Congress. It took a few years for the military to realize what a labor market looked like. But after it got used to hiring personnel at the going wage rate, the military was pleased with having an army of volunteers rather than conscripts. Well-paid soldiers had higher morale and performed better, and turnover and the need to train new recruits were reduced. The occasional calls to restore the draft do not originate from within the military. (For a worldwide review of economic issues raised by conscription and a discussion of whether it makes governments less inclined to go to war—it does not appear to—see Poutvaara and Wagener [2006; 2011].)

6.17 Conclusion

This chapter has made a case for applying the tools of ordinary economic analysis to government land use regulation. It began with the Coase theorem, which shows that land use issues can be framed as legal entitlements that can be exchanged, just like ordinary commodities. The Coase theorem was then extended to consider the assignment of entitlements and their exchange when one of the parties is a government and at least some of the entitlements are public goods, equally available to many people. This raised the question of whether the government representing numerous people could be modeled as an economically rational party. The answer is yes, though it requires a model in which some character called "the median voter" takes the place of the rational consumer or firm manager. It appears that the median voter does respond to the tax price of local public goods.

The responsiveness of voters to the tax price is of special interest in land use matters because of the takings issue. Some commentators question whether making governments pay "just compensation" for excessive regulation will make them respond in economically rational ways. The answer appears to depend on whether a compensatory regime is expected to last for a long time. Brief experiments in compensation are apt to be viewed as not worth investing the time and effort to respond along the lines that economists would expect. Indeed, this qualification on rational behavior would seem to explain many of the experimental results that motivate behavioral economics. The "offer-ask" disparity, which states that people require more money to part with a good than they would spend to acquire the same good, tends to diminish (but not disappear) with repeat play. Subjects learn with experience that it makes sense to sell the chocolate bar or mug they have been given (as part of an experiment) for an amount not much in excess of what they would pay for it in the store down the street (Plott and Zeiler 2005).

The same thing seems to have happened over time with land use entitlements. When I wrote the original version of this book in the early 1980s, the idea of exchanging land use entitlements for other goods was anathema to most environmentalists. It was regarded as a mixture of immorality, impracticality, and unconstitutionality. But eventually it became acceptable to do so, at least in some situations. Experience with the Clean Air Act's tradable emissions showed that commodification could lead to better air quality than many programs that directly regulated the sources of pollution. The barriers to trade in zoning entitlements are formidable because of the number of parties who might be affected, but outraged alarm at the very idea is a diminishing problem.

CHAPTER 7

Zoning and Suburban Development

The previous chapter made a case for the relevance of the Coase theorem and related tools of microeconomic analysis in zoning controversies. The analysis there, however, involved a single developer who managed to get a single parcel of land rezoned. There was no big picture of how the community as a whole arrived at its policies. The present chapter will extend the analysis to an entire community that has many development-minded landowners and evolves over time. It offers a case study as a microcosm of the national history of zoning presented in chapter 5 and an extension of the microeconomic tools from the property-rights theories examined in chapter 6.

My goal is to explain what happened over the last 50 years that caused zoning to move from the "good-housekeeping" model to the "growth-control" model that prevails today. The historical pivot identified in chapter 5 was the burst of inflation in the early 1970s, which transformed owner-occupied homes from domiciles to assets and increased the demand for growth control. The acceleration of suburbanization caused by the interstate highway system also shifted this demand for suburban exclusion, and environmental legislation provided the tools to accomplish this. The land use history of the town of Acton, Massachusetts, embodies all of these trends.

7.1 Acton, Massachusetts, Began with Conventional, Developer-Friendly Zoning

Alexander von Hoffman has been studying the history of housing development in the nineteenth and twentieth centuries for most of his 30-year career. Based at Harvard's Joint Center for Housing Studies, von Hoffman has focused on the development of Massachusetts cities and towns. In three separate papers, he examined the history of land use in three Boston suburbs: Weston (von Hoffman 2010a), the most affluent town in the state; Arlington (2006), a close-in, working-class suburb; and Acton (2010b), a more remote, mixed-use community. All these papers relate a history of regulation that starts from local elected officials adopting and controlling most aspects of land use regulation to a more decentralized, citizen-driven process that imposes onerous and largely effective burdens on new development. The projections of population growth based on 1950s zoning in all cases were far higher than has come to pass or is likely to occur.

My focus is on the town of Acton because it seems most typical. Von Hoffman's history starts from a pre-zoning point and recounts the town's adoption of a full range of development controls. Like most New England towns and suburbs, Acton has a town meeting form of government, with an elected council called the board of selectmen, a professional town manager, and a citizen legislature called town meeting. Town meeting is less important than it sounds (attendance is usually low), but its tradition does encourage citizen participation in town affairs. Most important changes in land use are voted in plebiscites in the form of referenda whose content originates with elected and appointed officials or citizen initiatives that can bypass the planning and zoning process.

Acton was largely a rural town until after World War II. It had long enjoyed commuter rail service to Boston, but most of its residents did not regard themselves as suburbanites. Development pressure started in earnest when postwar highway building brought Acton within easy driving distance to Boston and the suburban technology firms that developed along the circumferential highway, Route 128. The town adopted zoning only in 1954. Under its original ordinance, three-quarters of the town's undeveloped space was zoned for single-family homes on what are known as "builders' half acres" of 20,000 square feet. (An acre is 43,560 square feet, but modern subdividers often use 40,000 as a decimal approximation.) Under its original ordinance, Acton did have scattered areas zoned for industry and commercial development, but attracting the burgeoning electronics industry, which was a goal of several nearby towns and cities, was not high on its priorities. Apartments were allowed in industrial and commercial zones and in a few others along the major roads, but Acton's initial zoning clearly contemplated development as a moderately low-density suburb of single-family homes.

Developers and town officials enjoyed a friendly relationship during the 1950s. Developers willingly acceded to town-imposed conditions for roads, water lines, septic systems, and drainage. Under this regime, planning consultants in 1961 "projected that Acton, whose local population then just exceeded 7,000 people, would eventually contain between 40,000 and 45,000 residents" (Von Hoffman 2010b, 9). Acton did double in population to slightly less than 15,000 in 1970, but thereafter its growth slowed considerably to less than an average of 10 percent per decade. With a population of about 22,000 in 2010, it is unlikely that Acton will get anywhere near the 45,000 residents that even its original "suburban sprawl" zoning had envisioned. At 45,000 residents, the gross density of the town would have been about 2,000 persons per square mile, which, by way of comparison, would still have been less than the nearby suburb of Wellesley, which in 2010 had a density of 2,700 per square mile and a median household income that was even higher than Acton's. (I should note that the 1961 population projection probably assumed a household size somewhat larger than that which prevails today, so the shortfall of population is not quite as large as it might appear.)

While Acton does have a few town centers with historic homes and small shops, most of the population is now spread out in subdivisions that are widely separated by private and public open space. Most residents must use cars to commute, shop, or go to school and community events. A commuter rail line to Boston has a station in South Acton, and it is popular as a park-and-ride stop for Acton residents and some of those who live in other towns. Acton does have three small town centers with some commercial activity and a few highway commercial strips, but the majority of the population lives in small, exclusively residential neighborhoods.

7.2 Growth Restrictions Came from Citizen Participation

Acton's path from what was originally expected to be a moderate-density suburb to an enduringly semirural suburb came through a number of local, grass-roots initiatives and was facilitated by changes both in state and federal law and in state court decisions. Although most changes were driven by some proposed development, no single event can be said to have slowed growth from the path projected by its original zoning.

During the 1960s, newcomers who had supposed that they were buying into a rural town became dismayed by the pace of development. This motivated a series of downzonings beginning in 1963. A residential district that covered 30 percent of the town was rezoned from the half-acre minimum lot size to full (builder's) acres of 40,000 square feet. In 1966, half of the main residential district was downzoned again, this time to minimum lot sizes of two acres. The most restrictive zoning category, agricultural conservation, was established first in 1975 in previously residential (but not yet developed) zones. The agricultural zone prohibits all residential uses and was expanded so that by 2005 it occupied about 10 percent of the town's land area.

In the 1960s, rapid construction of highly visible apartments along the town's main thoroughfare presented "an appalling sight" to townspeople "who viewed Acton as a rural-looking or upper-middle-class suburb" (Von Hoffman 2010b, 11). This led in 1968 to a town vote to prohibit apartments in industrial zones and to tighten review of apartments elsewhere. In 1970, a large proposed townhouse development that met existing zoning requirements was nonetheless subjected to additional restrictions on the number of units as a result of popular pressure. The developer sued on the grounds that he had applied for permits under previous regulations, but in a landmark decision, *Bellows Farms v. Acton*, 364 Mass. 253 (1973), the Massachusetts Supreme Judicial Court held that the new regulations were acceptable.

Massachusetts law had up to that time generally recognized landowners' right to proceed with development according to rules that prevailed when permits were first applied for. The court's decision in *Bellows Farms* was regarded as a major change throughout the state. Indeed, the Massachusetts courts were generally sympathetic with new local land use restrictions, not least, one suspects, because their members were drawn from the likes of Actonian activists. The local lawyer who won the case for Acton with a creative argument—a vested right to build apartments does not say *how many* apartments—was later appointed to the state's highest court.

In 1964, Acton voters declined to fund a sewer project endorsed by the board of selectmen that would have facilitated higher-density developments than reliance on septic systems. On-site, individual septic systems were something of a problem for developers because much of the town's landscape is wetland (like that of many New England towns) and thus problematic for on-site waste disposal. Yet this limitation was modest compared to those that arose in the 1970s. In 1972, the Massachusetts legislature presented exclusionary suburbs with a gift—perhaps not unexpected—with a sweeping wetlands protection law that prohibited most wetland disturbance without getting approval from first the local government and then the state. Local agencies were encouraged not just to prevent development in wetlands but also to establish setbacks from the wetlands in which development could be restricted. Like many other towns, Acton adopted setback requirements that exceeded those required by the state in the 1990s. Wetlands are a pervasive legacy of the last glacial period for most New England towns, and the 15 percent of Acton's area they occupy understates the likelihood that they will be a contentious part of development processes because of the added setback area.

Acton supplemented its regulatory controls with outright purchases of conservation land, which removed it entirely from development. Purchases had begun before zoning, but they were expanded considerably with a town-voted bonding authority in 1974. Total purchases amounted to 8 percent of the town's land. This is actually a modest fraction compared to nearby towns such as Weston (20 percent) and Lincoln (34 percent). It does not, however, include land subject to private conservation easements, much of which was established under the cluster zoning approach that began in early 1980s.

Cluster zoning allowed developers of, say, a 20-acre parcel in the R-4 zone (one-acre minimum lot) to place all of the 20 allowable homes on a contiguous plot of five acres (or so) as long as the remaining 15 acres were preserved as open space. Clustering relieved the developer of some infrastructure costs—shorter roads, sidewalks, and water lines—and it sometimes reduced wetlands conflicts by including wetlands in the undeveloped area. Conservationists and residents who wanted to preserve open space liked this, too, though some grumbled about allowing developers to use the otherwise-unbuildable wetlands portions as part of their initial minimum lot size calculation.

Clustering and the three village centers that gave similar allowances for development near existing concentrations of population were the two instances of pro-development innovations that Acton took on. But neither of these changed the gross density of the town, since the unused land had to be subject to conservation easements or some other nearly irreversible arrangement (like common ownership by a neighborhood association) that forestalled further development. Clustering may have enabled more development insofar as it defused some of the anti-development sentiment among neighbors and other town residents, who might have otherwise spearheaded a drive to adopt even larger minimum lot size requirements.

7.3 Local Developers Lost Their Clout

Von Hoffman's history of Acton was the product of many personal interviews as well as archival research. One advantage of the town's relatively late adoption of zoning (1954) was that many people recalled incidents that gave some indication of why regulations were successively modified toward restrictions. The most commonly given reason for resisting development was the expectation that the town should not change much after residents had moved there: "In the 1960s and 1970s, Actonians' revulsion to development focused especially on their desire to retain the town's 'rural character'" (Von Hoffman 2010b, 13). This informed the successive downzonings, agricultural zoning, purchases of conservation land, and cluster zoning.

The town's wetlands regulations, one the most contentious issues developers faced, did sometimes raise spillover issues for existing neighbors, but they also were a convenient hook to oppose development in general. Fiscal issues concerning municipal costs were sometimes raised as a reason to slow development, but what chiefly drove the property tax rate were public school expenditures. They were rising as the school system expanded, but new development had little to do with that. Acton has unusually good schools, and long-time residents found it profitable to sell their homes to families with children. (On a visit to Acton, I spied a real estate firm by the name of "Good School Realty," which, according the *Boston Globe*, March 13, 2013, was founded by a Chinese immigrant to help others locate the best school districts in the area.) Particular fiscal issues seemed to be subsidiary to preservation of open space.

Most of Acton's post-1950 homes were developed on parcels that had been owned by a variety of landowners, many of whose families had lived in the town for generations. Von Hoffman's narrative followed the successive developments of a family named Sweeney, whose paterfamilias had decided to give up an unprofitable dairy farm in favor of development. The older Sweeney had no problem with the initial zoning and planning regulations in developing his first subdivisions in the 1950s.

Although von Hoffman does not say so specifically, longtime residents like the Sweeneys may have had some influence on the initial zoning or at least had their interests looked after by those who drafted it. Even when landowners are a minority in a community, my impression is that newcomers are not eager to defy their expectations without some additional stimulus. (An account consistent with this is Thomas Rudel's [1989] fine-grained study of the regulatory evolution of a Connecticut town.) Descent from an old-time family confers some status in most towns, and communal activities that involve informal reciprocity protect otherwise vulnerable interests. New residents are shy about changing the rules on zoning when those adversely affected send their kids to the same school, coach the soccer team, operate a snowplow service, or just say hi at the post office.

As the town developed, though, the informal interactions that kept regulation in check were eroded. Perhaps inevitably, community relations become more impersonal as a town grows. The old-time farmer becomes just a developer; the schools multiply (Acton went from one elementary school to four) so that landowners' social influence is dissipated; commuting residents spend less time in town. The gradual erosion of small-town character undermined the status of previous landowners. Referring to the landowner who was developing his ancestral farm in stages, Von Hoffman (2010b) writes, "Musing on the irony that the homeowners in his family's first subdivision opposed his latest project, Sweeney commented, 'Paradoxically, I sell to people who become my enemies'" (17). Asset motivation may have had some play, too. Over the period Sweeney operated, 1954–2005, the initial homes he sold had become enormously valuable, and protecting that value became a goal that may have overridden neighborly relations.

Von Hoffman did not choose to study Acton because it represented an outlier in terms of growth restrictions. Acton actually seemed fairly typical of developing Boston suburbs during this period. If anything, Acton was a little more accommodating to growth than others. Its 2010 gross density was actually higher than all but one of its immediate neighbors, Maynard. While every community's development path is heavily influenced by its history and geography, the land use changes that shaped Acton were shared by many other communities with which von Hoffman was familiar.

Von Hoffman indicates in several places that a new land use device that was successfully used in one town, especially neighboring Concord, was picked up in Acton. Indeed, the entire Boston-area market has become a laboratory for studies of the effects of land use regulation on home prices and other economic indicators (for example, Evenson and Wheaton 2003; Zabel and Dalton 2011; Glaeser and Ward 2009). On the other hand, there does not seem to have been any conscious coordination of land use policies that an economist could point to and say that this looked like a cartel. The regional planning organizations or powerful counties that sometimes undertake cartel-like activity (such as agreements not to compete for fiscally profitable developments) in other metropolitan areas seem almost absent in Massachusetts and New England generally. The only regional activity undertaken by Acton that von Hoffman mentions is the establishment of a regional high school with neighboring Boxborough.

7.4 A Tiebout-Style Model of Community Development

This section begins the development and discussion of a simple economic model that characterizes the sequential development of a suburban town like Acton, Massachusetts. The model is in the spirit of Charles Tiebout (1956), who proposed that the efficient level of local public goods could be achieved by having many communities among which prospective residents would "vote with their feet." The present model focuses on a single representative community and describes its development rather than examining the metropolitan system as a whole. (Chapter 8 will look at zoning in a metropolitan context.)

Figure 7.1 represents the cost of maintaining a fixed amenity throughout the development of a suburban community. (Early versions of the model are Sonstelie and Portney [1978] and Fischel [1978].) The community is entirely residential, and each household is expected to own its own home. All residents commute to a nearby central city for jobs and commercial purchases. The homes are required by zoning to have identical amounts of capital, so the demand is actually for buildable lots. The community has a fixed amount of land, and it can neither annex new territory nor subdivide itself into more than one community. The amenity is a shared public good that is subject to congestion. One can think of a system of parks and roads, but the more general amenity is "community character."

The average cost of maintaining the amenity is the classic U-shaped curve from introductory courses in economics, and the analogy is deliberate. In microeconomics, it is traditionally assumed that average costs of production for a firm initially decline because of the division of labor and other scale economies. Eventually, however, size becomes a liability for the firm, the law of diminishing returns sets in (in the short run, some factor of production is fixed), and cost per unit goes up.

The community's U-shaped average cost in figure 7.1 is different in two important respects. For an ordinary firm, it is output that varies on the horizontal axis. For the municipality as shown here, it is number of consumers of the output that varies. N is for households (actually, building lots for households), not levels of output. The "output" here is the community

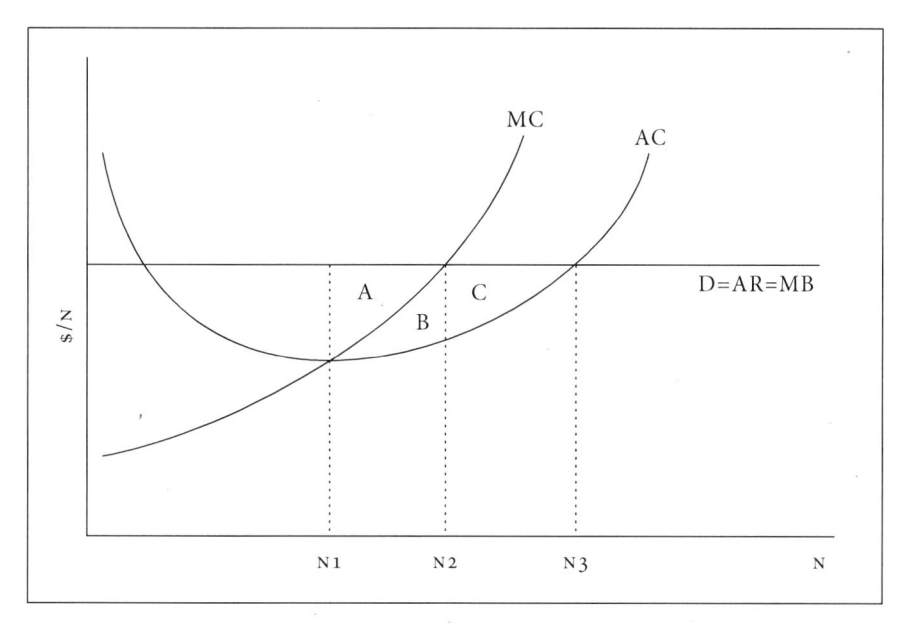

FIGURE 7.1 Community Development Costs in Perfect Competition

amenity level, and it is held fixed for present purposes. The reason for this is that in the Tiebout model, each community specializes in a particular set of amenities, and households select the community that best fits their preferences. (A close analogy to "voting with one's feet" is selecting a residential college to attend.) The town of Acton, for example, is but one of scores of suburban and exurban towns in the Boston metropolitan area.

The shape of the AC curve in figure 7.1 is determined by the nature of congestion costs. As more people move in, the parks, roads, and schools become more crowded, and the marginal cost of providing the amenity begins to rise, eventually dragging the average cost up with it. In a private market, this would result in more firms entering the market, forcing any given firm to operate at the minimum of its average cost curve. But municipalities in most metropolitan areas occupy a fixed amount of land area, and this condition is embedded in the fixed boundaries assumption adopted here. As a practical matter, municipalities in urban areas can neither expand nor cut themselves into smaller parts. Their "fixed factor" is the land within their boundaries, and so they are forever operating in the cost structure of the short run, as depicted in figure 7.1.

The cost of providing the municipal expenditures that maintain the preset level of amenity is shared equally among the resident homeowners. A uniform property tax on home values is the source of municipal revenue, and, since all homes are the same in this model, each home pays the same amount. It is possible to charge owners of undeveloped land special assessments to cover the fixed costs that give the average cost curve its initial downward slope. It is also feasible to charge builders of new homes monetary exactions and impact fees, the amount of which will be controversial and discussed presently. In general, then, the bowl-shaped AC curve represents the ongoing payments by existing homeowners for the municipal expenditures necessary to maintain the community's amenity level. (I have chosen not to draw both an average fixed cost and an average variable cost curve in figure 7.1 because the major points in this chapter do not depend on the difference between them.)

The community whose development costs are depicted in figure 7.1 is but one of many similarly situated in its metropolitan area. For this reason, the demand for locating there as opposed to some other place is, in this baseline model, perfectly elastic. Hence the demand curve is a horizontal line, and for any additional residents the marginal revenue equals average revenue equals the marginal benefit of building one more home in the community. (The case of a community that apparently has market power will be considered presently.) However, the number of communities within the metropolitan area is fixed. This is the second difference from the standard model of a competitive firm. No community has any "market power" vis-à-vis the others, but entry of municipalities into the business of providing local services is limited. One could suppose that there are new communities available outside the metro area, but they are so distant from the center that no one can live in them and still have a job in the city. What this implies is that location rent (determined by proximity to the big city) and fixed boundaries keep the perfectly elastic demand by homebuyers *above* the minimum average cost of providing amenities.

7.5 Congestion and Political Control of Community Development

This section describes the development of the community over time. There are three actors in the development drama: landowners, potential homeowners, and resident homeowners. The property of landowners may have been farmed, ranched, or forested, but its proximity to a growing city now makes subdividing it for houses profitable. These owners are assumed to want to develop their land at some point, and "landowners" will be interchangeable with "developers" in this discussion. In the previously discussed case of Acton, the Sweeney family, which turned from farming to development, is the paradigm of this party. The second group, potential homeowners, make up the demand for location in the community. They are assumed to live outside of the community and have no way of knowing that they might want to live there and hence have no political influence. Their only influence is from their potential dollar votes, which they exert most directly on the aforementioned landowners. The third group is composed of resident homeowners who own their homes but no other land within the community and have no plans to subdivide their property. (This model is similar in spirit to the more formal models by Hilber and Robert-Nicoud [2013], and Ortalo-Magné and Prat [2014].)

Resident homeowners and those landowners who live in the community select the public officials in the community, including members of the local legislature and (through them) the planning, zoning, and other land use boards. I am going to ignore the enfranchisement of renters in this analysis because they are a small minority of residents in most suburbs. They are also ambivalent about development. They would be allied with resident homeowners in desiring lower levels of congestion of public amenities, but they may be allied with development-minded landowners if they want to obtain more housing or become homeowners. These effects are small on net because renters realize that reducing congestion will make the community more attractive and result in higher rents, which are a cost to them but a benefit to established homeowners (the value of their homes rise). Renters also realize that the depressing effect on prices of any additional housing built in the community will benefit the entire metropolitan area, not just renters in a particular community. In any case, renters are a small fraction of the voting population in almost all developing suburbs.

The problem of optimal community size in this situation is analogous to that of highway congestion. Up to some "design capacity" (roughly speaking, the number of vehicles that can go the speed limit), urban freeways have no congestion costs. Once traffic increases (as during rush hour) and the design capacity is exceeded, the average cost of congestion rises. The marginal cost is above the average in this situation, meaning that entrants to the freeway impose a cost on existing users of the road by slowing them all down. This cost is an externality in that the entrants make their decisions on the basis of the speed of cars in front of them (the average cost), but not their effect on slowing down those behind them. The theory of optimal transportation tolls starts from this elemental problem and attempts to make new users perceive the marginal cost rather than the average cost of congestion.

The peak-load use of highways usually plays out daily. You encounter congestion every morning on the way to work, and it is a fact of life over which you have no control. The congestion issue in land development is different in that it is played out over a long period of time and can be anticipated. Users of busy urban freeways have no ability to limit access by others to the highway. Owners of developable land and early homeowners (the local political actors) do have some control over subsequent congestion of community facilities.

The model assumes that potential buyers of homes in the community—the people whose bids make up the demand curve—are aware of potential congestion costs within the immediate neighborhood of the home they are interested in. They would resist buying homes there without some assurances that the neighborhood would not be overdeveloped, but they cannot foresee the course of development of the community as a whole until they have purchased a home and become resident voters. Potential residents can be reassured by the existence of municipal zoning, but until they become residents, they do not have any control over how zoning will play out over time. It is the playing out over time that is the interesting problem.

7.6 The Goldilocks Dilemma

As a technical matter, the optimal community size, in terms of the number of households (N) in figure 7.1 is N_2. This is the "just right" Goldilocks point. At this point the marginal cost of providing (or preserving) community amenities is just equal to the marginal benefit received by the last home built there. At a lower number, say N_1 (at the bottom of the AC curve), the marginal benefits (given by the demand curve) of additional homes exceed the marginal costs. At a higher number, say N_3 (where AC crosses the demand curve), the marginal costs exceed the marginal benefits. N_3 is like the congested highway that is not subject to an optimal toll, while N_2 is analogous to the traffic after the (largely theoretical) optimal toll has been imposed.

If the owners of undeveloped land in the community cooperate with each other *and* can maintain control of the development process (rather than cede it to new resident homeowners), then they would generally zone the community so as to get to N_2, the optimal level. Although it might profit some landowners to allow more than N_2, they are collectively aware that forward-looking potential homebuyers would resist buying in a community in which there was no commitment to restrain development to something like the Goldilocks point. A zoning ordinance that committed the community to N_2 would be necessary to attract buyers and maximize the total value of land, even if some individual parcels might still be profitably developed after N_2 was reached. This is generally consistent with the rhetoric of those homebuilders who originally advocated for zoning back in the early twentieth century, as noted in section 5.8. They believed zoning "would maximize aggregate land values, and stabilize values at each location, but would not maximize values everywhere" (Marc Weiss 1987, 101).

The reader might notice that N_2 is the same as the Coasian efficient equilibrium point in the last chapter, except that here the "bargaining" is among a large number of landowners who are disciplined by the anxieties of potential homebuyers. To see this more clearly, suppose that a single owner had all the land in the community. There are in fact many instances of corporate developers building entire communities, though seldom on as much land area as a New England town. Large-scale developers who plan to sell to forward-looking homebuyers need to convince potential buyers that they will not exceed the Goldilocks point while at the same time making sure that they do not give up their (the developers') ability to get to that point.

To get these dual assurances, private community developers draw up master plans for the community, impose detailed covenants, conditions, and restrictions (the "CC&Rs" of real estate) on individual lots, and establish a self-governing community association. (An example is the Disney-developed town of Celebration, Florida, discussed in section 4.15.) Voting in the association is usually one vote per lot owner except that the developer holds three votes for every unsold lot. This allows the original landowner to control the association until three-quarters of the lots are sold. Changes in the master plan and the association's constitution usually require a supermajority of members, so the developer's extra votes do not permit her to change the master plan without the cooperation of actual homeowners. The master plan and the voting arrangements serve as two-sided commitment devices to ensure that N_2 can be reached but not exceeded. Uriel Reichman (1976) described these legal rules, which Vernon Henderson (1980) explored in a formal economic model.

Henderson's general conclusion was that development controlled by a single developer was likely to result in communities whose size was at least locally optimal. In most real-life communities, however, undeveloped land is owned by a number of different landowners, and they may not be entirely cooperative with one another. Some may have disparate visions for the community, some may want to sell their land sooner than others, and some may be absentee owners without close ties to the community. If such a varied group of landowners kept control of zoning throughout the community's development, lack of cooperation among them could lead to shifting land use rules that end up with a community of size N_3. Some developers might be able to grab some extra land rents, indicated by area C in figure 7.1, but this would be at the expense of previous homebuyers, who had expected development to stop at N_2. Beyond N_3, the benefits of living in this particular community (the horizontal demand curve) are actually less than the annual tax cost (AC), and even myopic homebuyers would shun the place.

As the reference to "myopic" homebuyers indicates, getting to a bad (overdeveloped) result here depends on initial homebuyers having less than perfect foresight. Homebuyers worry most about the immediate neighborhood, and they do take into account the community's general zoning. But until they live in the community for a while, it is difficult for them to assess plans for other neighborhoods, let alone the possibility that planning undertaken by landowners may be changed later by those who have not developed their land. Thus, initial buyers have reason to be concerned about zoning controlled by original developers in that it could be opportunistically changed sometime in the future to the homeowners' detriment.

7.7 The Homeowners Take Over Zoning

At some point in the development process, resident homeowners will learn enough about their community to want to take over the zoning and planning from the original political actors, who are attuned to landowner interests if not themselves development-minded landowners. Private community developers can forestall this takeover by the aforementioned rules governing community associations, but in public communities, each resident has the same number of votes, and changes in the rules cannot usually be forestalled by contractual devices. The changing of the guard may be gradual or it may occur suddenly as the result of some obvious threat to homeowner interests. (One threat that occurred nationwide was the rapid construction of the interstate highway system in the 1960s, as described in section 5.22.) I assume that the homeowner takeover occurs around the time the community reaches the average-cost-minimizing level of development, N_1 in figure 7.1.

At N_1, the commonly shared community taxes are at their minimum for the level of amenity homeowners originally selected their community. If homeowners have taken the municipal reins *before* the community reaches N_1, they will have an incentive to encourage new development, because new residents add to the tax base without causing offsetting increases in congestion costs. Up to N_1, more is merrier, or at least reduces taxes for existing homeowners.

Understanding the political economy of what comes next requires identifying the source of profits to owners of developable land. In figure 7.1, potential profits of selling an additional home site are the vertical difference between the demand "curve" (horizontal line in this case) and the marginal cost of preserving community amenities. Thus, the total potential profits to developers of going from N_1 to N_2 in figure 7.1 is the sort-of triangular area A. This assumes that the newcomers (those who constitute the extra households between N_1 and N_2) are made to pay their marginal costs and know about it in advance. (This a reasonable assumption, since it involves easily observable out-of-pocket costs, not some vague future liability.)

But if every community member is expected to pay AC in property taxes, by what mechanism are the newcomers (beyond N_1) expected to pay an amount higher than AC? One answer is land use exactions and impact fees. These are typically assessed on the developer, not the prospective buyer, but from a development perspective it does not matter who pays it as long as it is not deducted from the newcomers' property tax bills (and it is generally not). As development gets closer to N_2, the impact fees and exactions get larger until, just at N_2, there is no more profit left for the developers, and they cease building homes. Thus, the amount that is paid in exactions from developer-landowners is the triangle of area B in figure 7.1.

The previous scenario is the nice one—established members of the community just want newcomers to pay their full freight. Indeed, it is another manifestation of the Coase theorem, which holds that which side possesses the initial entitlement does not matter for the ultimate outcome. On the one hand, if development-minded landowners had controlled zoning and been able to restrain opportunistic behavior by their fellow developers, the community would also get to N_2. On the other hand, shifting control of development to existing residents yields the same result as long as the residents have no trouble (no transaction costs) agreeing how much exactions to charge for development beyond N_1 so as to get to N_2. (As noted earlier, N_2 is on a larger scale the same as the Coasian bargaining equilibrium attained by individual developers in section 6.8.)

The discussion of the U.S. Supreme Court's exactions decisions in chapter 3 (following section 3.26) may be relevant at this point. In the three cases discussed there, the complaining landowners seemed to have been treated differently from other landowners in the same community. In particular, people who owned land prior to the challenged regulatory regime did not seem to have had to give the public beach access (*Nollan*) or a bike path (*Dolan*) or quite so much off-site wetlands (*Koontz*). It is possible that the plaintiffs were being treated unfairly by some standards, but the analysis in the present chapter suggests that owners of essentially identical parcels of land should be treated differently at different stages of community development. All of the lots on the horizontal axis of figure 7.1 are the same, but the developers of the lots later in the process, after N_1 has been reached, should pay more than the earlier developers. The MC curve does not start pushing up average costs until there is some congestion.

Of course, if a single developer were selling lots and had committed herself to N_2 in advance, all lots would sell for the same price because she anticipates the higher marginal costs and prices accordingly. Indeed, even when there are many developers, the resale value of all homes will be the same after equilibrium is reached. But before that point, efficiency considerations dictate what appears to be discriminatory pricing for newcomers after costs begin to rise. Disallowing the exactions or impact fees will cause the existing community, which controls the zoning process, to want to remain at an inefficiently small (and low density) stage of development.

7.8 The Monopoly Zoning Scenario

It would appear from my opening account, however, that Acton's initial zoning, which would have resulted in a town of about 45,000, was something that successive residents worked against. In terms of the Goldilocks diagram of figure 7.1, where N_1 is too low, N_3 is too high, and N_2 is "just right" (marginal benefit equals marginal cost), it appears to me that Acton is considerably closer to N_1 in what we would call an *ex ante* sense. That is, if a developer had controlled all of Acton's land, and the market for homes was competitive, and the developer was able to commit himself and all buyers to a town-wide plan, N_2 would have been the ultimate population.

The optimal population of Acton might have changed over time, of course. The discovery that wetlands had environmental benefits would have steered some development away, though cluster development could have maintained overall densities. Growth of income among potential homebuyers would have caused them to demand larger homes, though it is not clear that this would have required larger lots than the half-acre minimum that was initially adopted for most of the town. (And if modern buyers did demand more acreage, it is worth keeping in mind that a half-acre minimum does not prevent developers from building on lots larger than half an acre.) And as mentioned earlier, nearby Wellesley was developed to a density similar to that of Acton's original zoning, and Wellesley remains a highly desirable, affluent community. (Wellesley is slightly closer to the central city, Boston, so higher density would be predicted by the standard, zoning-free urban economics model, but its higher income is not.)

The previous sections presented a political scenario in which the community had no market power. My purpose in making this assumption was to make the economic analysis analogous to that of a competitive firm and move quickly to the more interesting issue of who controls the politics. The politics was evolutionary, moving from control of land use by local development-minded landowners who were aware that prospective buyers had some demand for zoning, to control by resident homeowners, who were mainly interested in protecting their investment from excessive development. The situation in this and the following sections is changed to give the community some market power, presenting it with a downward sloping demand curve. (Monopolistic zoning is the main case analyzed by Robert Ellickson [1977] in his classic analysis of suburban growth controls. A more formal analysis is by John Quigley [2007].)

The monopolistic community is illustrated in figure 7.2 with the classic case of a straight-line, downward-sloping demand curve and a rising marginal cost curve. In the monopoly case shown in figure 7.2, the community sees the marginal revenue curve (MR) as being below the demand (average revenue) curve. The reason is that existing homeowners realize that new homes will be competition for their existing homes and reduce the price for which they could eventually sell them. The monopoly community's profit-maximizing number of households that are permitted is N_1, at the point where MR = MC, and it earns profit π. (N_1 is not necessarily at the minimum AC, although it is drawn that way here, but it will always be lower than N_2.) The profit could manifest itself as exactions in excess of the costs imposed by development. The money could be used to lower local taxes or provide public amenities in excess of those originally expected by the original homeowners.

The other "profit" is the higher price of preexisting housing. This requires that there was a previous zoning regime that did not involve a zoning monopoly,

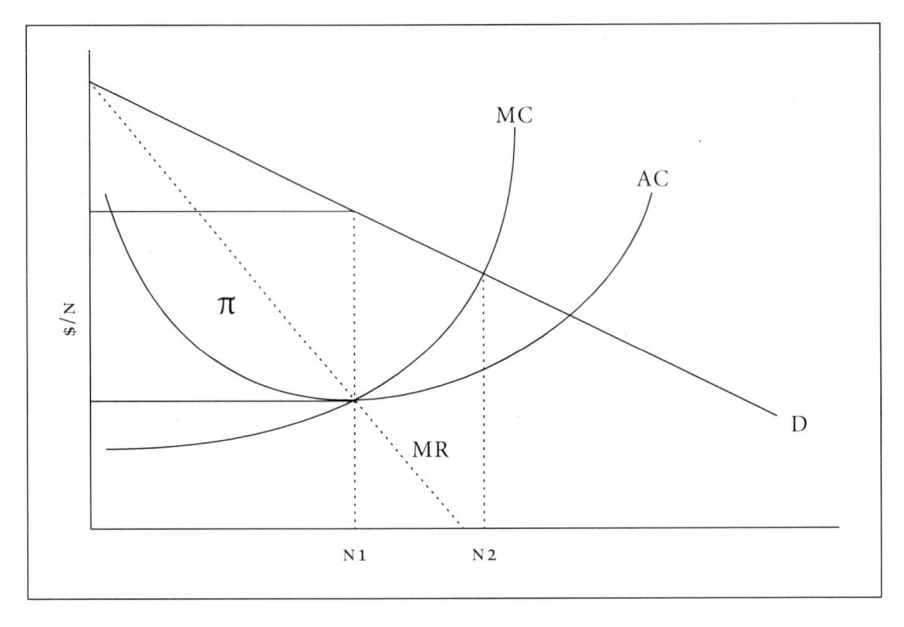

FIGURE 7.2 Community Development under Monopoly Conditions

in which developer-generated zoning (adopted to assuage the concerns of buyers) limited expected housing development to N2. The developers were sufficiently numerous that they could not form a cartel to perform what the community is assumed to do here. Moreover, a developer cartel is illegal, but a community-generated monopoly is not. The arcane legal rule that exempts community politics from antitrust laws is called the Noerr-Pennington doctrine and is discussed by Stuart Deutsch (1984). Municipal exemption from antitrust was briefly threatened in the 1980s, but Congress intervened to preserve local government immunity (Brent Kinkade 1992). (Immunity even protects established retail owners who use the zoning process to keep out Walmarts and other potential competitors [Pugh and Lucas 2012].)

When the zoning regime switches from developer control to homeowner control, the limit on new housing to N1 is presumably a surprise to the local market, and existing homeowners get a capital gain. The element of surprise that produces the capital gain is that neither developers nor homebuyers know that a monopoly regime is in store. (If they did, the developers would have charged higher prices to begin with.) As in the competitive case described in previous sections, homebuyers are aware of the existence of zoning, but only after they have actually lived in the community will they have a hand in guiding development. Just what events created the surprise limitations on development is considered in section 7.11 after a side-trip to visit a peculiarity of a monopoly on land.

7.9 Zoning Monopolists Must "Waste" Land

The monopoly zoning story is not as simple as that shown in figure 7.2. The first complication is that the land that is withheld from development, the difference between N_1 and N_2 in figure 7.2, is still sitting there. Unlike the monopolist in a market for ordinary goods, who simply makes less of the stuff so as to sell what he does make at a higher price, the local government monopoly does not actually produce land. It is already there, waiting for permits to be issued. So a zoning monopolist who "under-produces" permitted lots in the current time period has land left over that could be permitted in a later period. Buyers who are offered homes in the earlier period might worry that after they have paid top dollar for their place in the monopoly, the community will turn around and sell off some of the reserved land. Competition from new construction would cause the early buyers to suffer capital losses. Contemplating that scenario, early buyers may end up declining to buy at all if they cannot protect their investment.

In "Durability and Monopoly," Ronald Coase (1972) analyzed the problem just described (though he did not address zoning). A monopolist with a pile of durable stuff will have a difficult time convincing early buyers that they will not be played the fool at a later time, when the monopolist decides to sell off what remains. Skeptical buyers will hold back in the first place, that will force the original price down toward the competitive price, and monopoly profits will never materialize.

Coase did not pose this situation to argue that monopolies of durable assets were ineffective. His main point was that a would-be monopolist has to devise ways to convince his earlier buyers that the price will stay high. One such device is available from the art world. Sculptors who worked with materials that could be easily reproduced, such as bronze castings, would publicly "break the mold" from which the originals were cast and thus assure buyers that only a limited number would be sold. (Many people who see Rodin's "The Thinker" in several different places are surprised that it was cast several times and that each is considered an original.)

Land regulations can "break the mold" in a variety of ways. The most obvious is large-lot zoning whose requirements exceed the demands that most buyers actually want. Many studies indeed show that the second or third acre in most three-acre zones (common in the fancier suburbs that are in scarce supply) is worth much less than the first (Pollakowski and Wachter 1990; Glaeser and Gyourko 2003). In my tightly zoned town, a nonconforming but grandfathered one-acre lot (subdivided before the area was downzoned) sells for almost the same as a nearby three-acre lot. Once they are developed, multi-acre lots are almost impossible to subdivide because of opposition to rezoning from neighbors. In many cases, the large lots are actually concealed by clustering of the structures, with the remainder of the land held in common and generally unavailable for future development.

Another technique, more costly and also more difficult to reverse, is to subject undeveloped land to conservation easements, which are typically designed as perpetual and are extremely difficult to undo. (Christopher Serkin [2010] describes how public conservation easements were established in Marlboro, Vermont.) Communities can require development-minded landowners to impose conservation easements on the land that is not directly used for housing development, and the tax benefits can mitigate the sting of restrictive zoning. (Donors of easements can get substantial tax deductions both from current income and estate taxes, as described in section 2.17.) Even if the easement is not explicitly required, the developer might volunteer it as a way to get permit approvals. The perpetual easement gives both the community and residents of the new subdivision additional assurance that further development on the low-density parcel is forestalled by a process not subject to future municipal discretion. (Another benefit to established residents of Massachusetts communities is that conservation land is not counted in the state's formula for determining the amount of "affordable housing" that all towns are obliged to accept [Sharon Krefetz 2001].)

7.10 Using Inclusionary Zoning to Cement Monopoly

Another way for the community to exercise monopoly power is to impose additional burdens on homebuilders beyond the usual exactions and impact fees. One common way a community with market power can do this is called an "inclusionary zoning" requirement. A typical example would be for the developer to be required to produce one unit subsidized (by the developer) for every four "market-rate" units that were built and sold. This is in effect a tax on homebuilders, which results in their producing fewer homes in total (both market rate and subsidized) and so maintains the higher prices of existing homes (Schuetz, Meltzer, and Been 2011). The inclusionary requirement is different from simply allowing the developer to build more modest units and selling or renting them at a market rate. The required subsidy is the difference between what would have been the inclusionary unit's unconstrained market price and the amount the developer is actually allowed to charge.

The question is why this form of exaction is used instead of straightforward impact fees on developers, whose funds could be used to benefit existing residents. One relatively benign answer is that communities have what I called in section 4.11 a demand for "(limited) community diversity." Many communities have a genuine desire not to become entirely homogenous. My coy parentheses around "(limited)" are intended to indicate that a community's professions of openness are subject to a desire to keep this diversity within acceptable bounds, whose rationale is not officially spoken but widely understood. For a community that has achieved substantial market power by virtue of its highly restrictive zoning, inclusionary zoning offers a way to achieve (limited) diversity, especially if it is under some political or judicial pressure to do so. Just rezoning some of its land for moderate-size housing would not get much diversity. The moderate-size homes in a desirable community would be bid up in price almost immediately, and, because most initial zoning envelopes are somewhat loose, owners would gradually expand the homes so that the community would become homogeneous anyway.

The advantage of inclusionary zoning for the community is that it both dampens demand by developers to build regular units, thereby keeping up the prices of existing units, and it permanently creates affordable housing. The permanence comes from resale controls or tenant income requirements that keep the units from being sold or rented at market rates. A third benefit to the community is that the developer of the market-rate homes usually has to mix them with the inclusionary units. This reduces some of the NIMBY problem, since the immediate neighbors to the lower-income units are not there to complain (they have not yet bought), and the developer has an incentive to make the inclusionary units as nice as possible in order not to scare off the potential buyers of the market-rate units.

A potential advantage of inclusionary units would be to provide municipal workers with housing closer to their jobs (and thus permit the community to pay them less), but most inclusionary programs cannot discriminate in that manner and often take applicants by lottery or off long waiting lists. Resale price controls on inclusionary units do present some problems in that owners of inclusionary units may neglect maintenance if there is a binding price ceiling on their units—why fix the pipes if we will get the maximum allowable price anyway?—but homeowner-association obligations and contractual allowances to recover costs for repairs and improvements can deal with this particular moral hazard.

7.11 The Source of Monopoly Power

There is some empirical evidence that government structure affects zoning behavior. Studies by Louis Rose (1989) and James Thorson (1996) find that government structure—whether municipalities are many or few in a given metropolitan area—does have an impact on housing prices, presumably through regulatory constraints. These studies explain some of the variation in housing prices across the country. What is not explained is the sudden upsurge in land use regulation in the 1970s and why it has had the strongest effects in the Northeast and on the West Coast. The Northeast in particular has highly fragmented government in its metropolitan areas. The four largest municipalities in the Boston urbanized area account for less than 10 percent of its land area. If any region should conform to the "competitive local government model," it would be the Northeast. (The Upper Midwest likewise has fragmented local government.) The regions in which suburban governments (typically counties) occupy the largest fraction of their urbanized area are in the South and the inland West. (Historical and climatic reasons for this variation were described in section 2.2.) Such areas would presumably have the most monopoly power over land use, yet they are generally considered pro-growth and have lower housing costs.

A more likely cause of the uncoordinated rise of monopoly-like growth controls was the upsurge in home values caused by the interaction of inflation and federal income tax laws (James Poterba 1984), as described in section 5.24. This housing price inflation was unprecedented in American history. Possessing a nice home in a good neighborhood, with good schools, safe streets, and pleasant amenities was always desirable. But when homes were a modest part of most people's portfolios, it was difficult to interest homeowners in efforts to deter remote threats to their value. Homevoters became much more concerned about their major asset beginning in the early 1970s. This shift in attention to home values meant that any potential threat to those values—not just their level, but their expected increase—would draw homeowners' attention. (Other studies have also found that land use regulations are endogenous to housing demand [Byron Lutz 2015; Albert Saiz 2010].)

The rise of the homevoter class was, I submit, the prime mover for the cartelization of the housing market. But this begs the question of how so many towns and cities were able to coordinate their efforts to restrict housing supply. The monopoly zoning story seems generally consistent with economic theory, but I must say I have never encountered anyone in favor of downzoning actually say they favored the action because it would result in monopoly profits or even add to their home values. (The developer who got the rezoning described in section 6.8, David Clem, did tell me that some neighbors of his proposed mixed-use project worried that new homes would depress demand for their homes, and he cut back on their number for that reason.) I have seen hints of it, of course—you cannot have an economics Ph.D. and miss the undertone of some discussions—but it just does not seem like a powerful public motivator.

However, it is important to build models on what people do, not what they say they do. Business leaders seldom say in public that they are eager to maximize profits, but economic models that assume otherwise have little predictive power. Even organizers of blatant cartels rationalize their price-preserving efforts as needed to "stabilize the market" and "prevent cut-throat competition" and "preserve the industry's reputation for quality." When I first learned as a young faculty member on the Dartmouth admissions committee that the Ivy League participated in a cartel to fix financial-aid awards, I naively asked, "Isn't this illegal?" I was assured in tones that varied from soothing to indignant that it was fine because preserving institutional resources was for the greater good of the students. Soaking the richer applicants (by disallowing scholarships based on academic promise rather than financial need) allowed the schools to subsidize applicants from lower-income backgrounds. (Caroline Hoxby [2000] confirmed that it actually accomplished this.) The U.S. Justice Department eventually got wind of this arrangement and obtained a consent decree to halt the information-sharing about individual awards that was key to the cartel.

7.12 Cartel Creation by Higher Governments

After zoning became widespread in the 1920s, most local governments had been reluctant, despite much cajoling, to join regional governments that would control land use (Jon Teaford 1979). The prospect of a regional government controlling zoning was always a deal-breaker. In one sense, this consideration seems to work against the monopoly motive. A metropolitan-wide government that controlled land use everywhere would have considerably more monopoly power than any of the smaller constituent communities that it replaced. (The possibility that Portland, Oregon, has accomplished this will be considered in chapter 8.) But ever since zoning became widespread, localities have been loath to surrender their land use powers to higher level governments.

The problem as most municipalities see it is that a larger government might make communities or neighborhoods accept some developments that they would otherwise be able to exclude under purely local zoning. As I described in section 5.21, the compromise that has become accepted in many states is the "double-veto" system. By empowering the higher authority only to veto a locally approved project (rather than also empowering it to approve a locally opposed project), the double veto adds to the market power of the community by forestalling the options of developers. Although this can also be regarded as a way of simply dealing with formerly neglected intermunicipal spillovers, state and regional land use authorities gradually became more influential in all aspects of what had been formerly local decisions (David Callies 1994a).

In the purely competitive case depicted in figure 7.1, there were no monopoly profits, because the demand curve was flat. But because of the finite and inflexible number of communities within desirable locations, it was possible for the community to shift some of the landowners' development profits (land rents) to the initial homeowners. Opportunities to grab some development rents were most compelling when the community grew to such a size that services for new development began to cost more because of facilities congestion. (This would occur between points N_1 and N_2 in figure 7.1.) I had argued that the community, now dominated by existing homeowners instead of development interests, could cover the rising costs with exactions and impact fees and ad hoc transfers from developers who wanted to get their projects done.

Before 1970, most of these negotiations involved just two parties, the developer and the community authorities. The relative bargaining skills would determine how much of the rent that was available would be obtained by either side. Professional expertise would favor the developer, while knowledge of local conditions might favor the community boards. But once a deal was made, the project would get under way without much further review.

The environmental revolution of the 1970s changed all that. As a result of federal and state legislation and court decisions, most development proposals of more than modest scale were subject to additional review. This meant not only that developers had to deal with more parties, but that the number of people at the table was actually uncertain. Requirements for an environmental impact statement opened the door to private individuals and groups who might arrive near the end of settlement talks and require that they begin all over again (Stewart Sterk 2011). Developers began to complain about "greenmail," in which an environmental group would demand payment (often in the form of land dedications but sometimes just cash) to forestall tying up the project in court in a fight about wetlands or the adequacy of the environmental impact statement (Bernard Frieden 1979).

Higher governments, once relatively passive in local negotiations, were required by new legislation to become more active in the permitting process. Open-meeting laws forestalled some bargaining by making "cheap talk" offers and counter-offers too costly for public officials and developers to engage in. The cost is that a "let's suppose" offer of building a new playground in order to get the development going, even if it is just a feeler for what officials might accept, becomes more difficult to back away from when it is made publicly. It might also run afoul of the U.S. Supreme Court's exactions decisions, as described in chapter 3.

7.13 Exclusion Spread to Other Towns

Now, the reader should know that all these 1970s reforms convey some benefits to someone. And they arguably can improve the quality of development that does take place. If all that the new entitlement holders obtain from their improved position is some share of the developers' profits, there is no substantive harm done in any case. But nearly every serious assessment of the new process regards it as slowing development and reducing the number of units that are ultimately built (Katz and Rosen 1987; Kahn and Matsusaka 1997; Paul Gottlieb et al. 2012).

More important for the present argument, these procedures slowed development in almost every community, not just one or two. Frustrated developers previously could just roll up their plans and hike to a nearby community that was more welcoming. Now they found that all of the alternatives were becoming more wary of development. Even communities that had resisted adopting growth controls and had then found themselves facing more rapid development began to slow the process down. Von Hoffman's (2006) study of development in the formerly pro-development city of Arlington, Massachusetts, found that developers who had been shut out of the better suburbs (such as Acton and Weston) were soon discovering that the supposed infill communities had begun to adopt growth restrictions. The demand for location in every community became more inelastic as a result, even though each community maintained its own regulations.

In terms of the community development process, this shift in attention meant that previously acceptable amenity levels—on which the AC and MC curves of both figures 7.1 and 7.2 were drawn—were now too low for most homeowners. In the original Tiebout (1956) model, this would mean no more than an increase in the number of communities with higher amenity levels. But in my version (the more realistic one) of the Tiebout model, the number of communities is fixed. So every community tries to increase its amenity level, which raises its average cost of providing public services in figures 7.1 and 7.2. This shifts the marginal cost upward, and hence, for a given demand curve (flat or sloped), the optimal size of the community will be lower. Put another way, the easiest way to protect one's newly valuable house is to limit growth.

In looking for sources of monopoly power, one might consider the homebuilding industry itself, which has evolved from a welter of small builders to one in which, in many parts of the nation, firms like Del Webb, Hovnanian, and Toll Brothers put together large-scale projects involving hundreds and sometimes thousands of units. As was mentioned in section 1.9, a national survey by Tsuriel Somerville (1999) found evidence that homebuilders in some metropolitan areas appear to be "monopolistically competitive."

Maybe this structural change could account for the rise in home values as opposed to regulatory constraints. But probably not much. It is important to distinguish homebuilders from landowners, whose ability to withhold land from the market gives rise to monopoly power. Homebuilders do need to own land, but they do not want to hold it very long. In any case, homebuilder holdings are small compared to the amount of available land in most suburban communities. Somerville also found that homebuilders were generally more competitive in areas in which regulations were stringent and local governments were relatively small. As just mentioned, the Northeast meets both of those criteria and thus has more homebuilder competition, yet this region has (along with the West Coast) the highest housing prices in the nation.

7.14 Conclusion: Acton Redux

The model advanced in this chapter started with the proposition that it really should not matter for community development whether it is controlled by a single developer, a cooperative consortium of developers, or the initial residents who seize the zoning process as the community develops. Coasian bargaining and low transaction costs cause outcomes to be the same. In the last case, community residents set up a system of exactions and impact fees to cover public expenditures not covered by the normal use of property taxes. It certainly matters to developers whether they have to pay such fees, but my baseline view is that the size of the fee was just a struggle over land rents. It did not affect the ultimate allocation of resources.

The reason for setting up the model this way was to explore what phenomena could have changed the baseline outcome. It is abundantly clear that development in suburban communities after the 1970s was considerably less intensive than originally planned. But there is not a lot of literature on why things changed. My explanation for the sea-change in attitudes toward development was the unanticipated inflation in housing values in the early 1970s. This made homeowners wary of development that could slow the upward trajectory of their homes' values, and it helped homeowners overcome the organizational costs of opposing development. Large-scale highway development abetted both the rise in suburban housing prices (by making suburbs more accessible) and providing dramatic occasions for homevoters' organization. The newly formed national and state environmental regulations were seized as devices to overcome the control that development-minded landowners originally held in their communities.

Most of the causes just listed have abated. Inflation has not been a serious problem since the early 1980s, highway construction has been much lower than it was in the 1960s (in part because of new rules adopted in the 1970s), and the adoption of environmental regulations seems to have plateaued. If these were reasons for higher housing prices, why have they not come down? I exclude here the national housing price crash brought about by the financial meltdown of 2006–2007. The national housing bubble and its bursting may have been influenced by growth-control regulations (Jansen and Mills 2013), though the evidence seems less than conclusive on this (Glaeser, Gyourko, and Saiz 2008; Thomas Davidoff 2013). In any case, prices in the high-demand areas are headed back up, and the differential in prices between the coasts and the rest of the United States persists. There does not seem to be much evidence that communities are loosening their land use regulations to any significant degree.

Most of the newly installed regulations—especially conservation easements—are difficult to reverse. More importantly, there is little demand to reverse them on the part of homevoters. Let me illustrate this with a family story. By wild coincidence, my son and his wife recently purchased a single-family house in Acton, Massachusetts, the history of which anchored the model of this chapter. The price my son and his wife paid for the Acton house in 2014 was actually slightly less than it had been sold for ten years earlier. But the amount is still a huge fraction of their financial portfolio, and I would expect that they will be as watchful about land use decisions that might affect their home's value as their fellow Actonians were when housing prices were going up. (They both participate on town volunteer boards.) Only if real prices fell to levels that prevailed in the 1960s and they had little prospect for excess capital gains in the future would homeowners' financial incentives for municipal watchfulness be diminished seriously. Even then, the institutional and intellectual apparatus that support current land use regulations would hardly disappear.

CHAPTER 8

The Politics and Economics of Metropolitan Sprawl

This chapter addresses the macro problems of local zoning. It starts with a stylized political characterization of government in metropolitan areas and considers how the local politics of zoning differ among big central cities, small suburbs, and rural townships and counties. This simple model offers the basis for explaining exclusionary zoning, metropolitan sprawl, and regional income sorting. The chapter next considers some variations on this model, which are epitomized by the growth boundaries of Portland, Oregon, and the rejection of comprehensive zoning by Houston, Texas. While both have some merit in combating the problems of local zoning, each has some drawbacks that undermine its respective paradigm.

Finally, the chapter asks why zoning regulations vary so much by region of the United States. I argued previously (chapter 5) that restrictiveness is largely the product of the demand for housing itself. High productivity regions attract affluent people who want more land use restrictions to protect their valuable assets. This is only a necessary condition. The other condition is that local homeowners control the political process. They do so in the high-demand Northeast by virtue of their control of small local governments, where homeowners prevail easily over developers. In the high-demand West Coast, homevoters prevail because of the availability of the voter initiative, which trumps the otherwise pro-development activities of counties and larger cities. The proof of this was the migration to the sunbelt as a result of the 1970s energy crisis. Home values and regulatory indexes stayed low because most states in the South lack both responsive local governments and the voter initiative for land use.

8.1 Rube Goldberg's Sprawl Diagram

The comic artist Rube Goldberg is famous for his cartoons of fanciful devices that accomplished simple tasks in complicated ways. Most of the diagrams used in this book are the antithesis of that idea, I hope. I normally want to show complicated ideas in simple ways. But when I started to redraw the diagram that illustrated the sprawl principle from my 1985 book, it came out looking more like a Rube Goldberg contraption. Rather than fight this outcome, I've decided to embrace it in figure 8.1 and hope that readers are willing to summon their inner Rube and follow along.

Figure 8.1 shows a cross section of how urban economists look at a city. The city is circular with a central business district (CBD) at the center. What is shown on the vertical axis is the capital-to-land ratio, denoted K/L. (Urban economists more often show land prices per acre on the vertical axis, which follows the same general shape, but the K/L ratio illustrates regulatory issues better.) The ratio represents both the average height and land cover of buildings of all types. The city spreads out more or less the same in all directions, so the horizontal axis shows just one direction and measures the distance from the CBD. The horizontal axis is sliced into three types of municipalities, the central city (or cities like the twins of Minnesota), the suburbs (all gathered together here as one but assumed nonetheless to be numerous), and rural townships or counties at the outer "exurban" edge of the city.

The starting point for the sprawl discussion is the downward sloping solid line in figure 8.1. It starts high in the central city, visible in the CBD as skyscrapers and then diminishes as one moves away from the center to apartment houses, commercial buildings, row houses, and perhaps some older, close-together single-family neighborhoods. As the journey outward crosses into the suburbs in this baseline scenario, the buildings get less tall and more widely separated. But in the baseline story, there is no discontinuity created simply by crossing a municipal border. The only indicator of hitting "the suburbs" is that the street signs might look different and the police cars have another city's name on them. Continuing through the suburbs, the density of buildings continually diminishes until a rural township or county line is encountered.

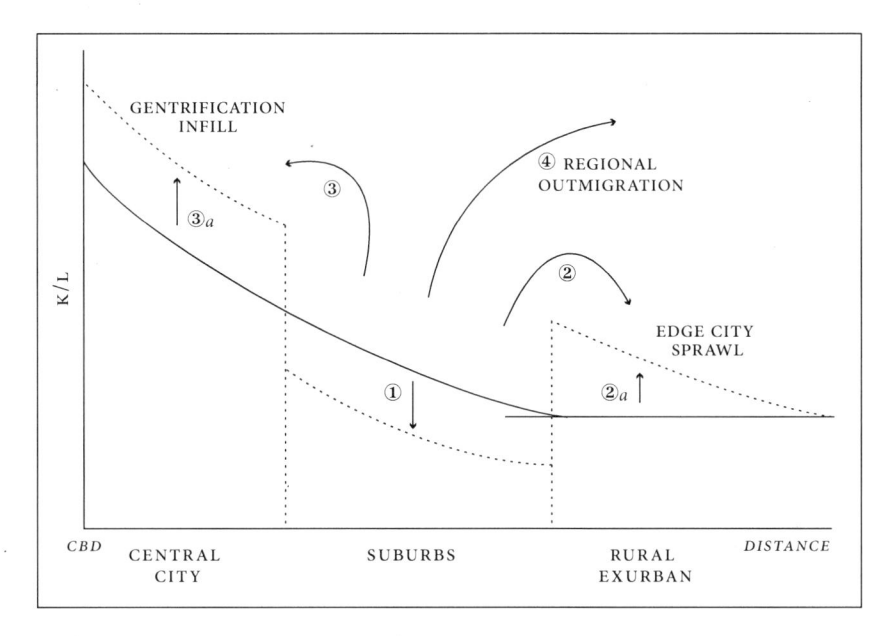

FIGURE 8.1 Metropolitan Sprawl from Suburban Downzoning

Beyond the outer edge of the suburbs, in the exurbs, the land becomes rural. The solid horizontal line indicates farms (or forests or deserts, depending on where in the United States this is) that are not dependent on urban location. In reality, the rural exurban area continues low-density urban settlement in the rural area. I drew in the solid horizontal line to indicate a visually dominant land use, not an absence of homes or businesses.

The solid baseline is what I call the "efficient" distribution of buildings and people in the city. It has land use regulations, but they are of the "good-housekeeping" variety that simply segregates incompatible land uses without affecting their overall distribution within the metropolitan area. (There is more to the real-world baseline that will be discussed presently, especially the subsidies to housing and underpricing of transportation, but I want to continue to the diagram first.) The city is suburbanized but in a continuous way such that suburban borders do not matter. It is the continuity of the K/L ratio that matters in the baseline case.

Next, figure 8.1 is modified by the sequentially numbered arrows and the broken lines. Arrow 1 indicates that "the suburbs" downzone their land before it is fully developed. The new K/L ratio falls to the dashed broken line as all of the devices of the post-1970 regulatory revolution take effect. Developers who are shut out of the suburbs take their plans for housing and commercial and industrial development elsewhere. The "elsewheres" are indicated by arrows 2, 3, and 4.

One possible refuge for displaced development is indicated by arrow 2, out to the rural areas. These places have some land use regulations, but they are not (yet) of the growth-control variety. Arrow 2a indicates that widely spaced housing developments spring up along with some commercial centers in a pattern that Joel Garreau (1991) creatively identified as "edge cities."

Arrow 3 in figure 8.1 indicates that some developers (and their customers, of course) who are displaced by suburban growth controls head back to the central city. The political economy that I will discuss presently has it that the central city welcomes most development, at least initially, and the result is housing gentrification and commercial redevelopment as indicated by arrow 3a. For most people who are concerned about arrow 2 (excess conversion of rural land to urban uses and sprawl) or who just think suburbs are bad, arrow 3 and the higher K/L are good things.

Arrow 4 of the Rube Goldberg–esque diagram represents developers of housing and firms moving out of the metropolitan area entirely. This outmigration to other regions is the ultimate safety valve on a city's land use policies. But this response also has the cumulative effect of causing the urban area to lose population to other areas. Even if the city does not lose population, growth-control regulations may deter low-income people from living there.

8.2 Land Use Politics: Rural Areas Become Suburban

The reason figure 8.1 has three distinct government types is that their regulatory behaviors are presumed to be different. Previous chapters have alluded to some of these distinctions, but the main model that was being promoted previously was the homevoter hypothesis. Homevoters own their own homes (and not much else) and are acutely aware that the quality of their neighborhood and community services affects the value of their largest asset. Because of this concern and because they typically live in contiguous areas where they are the majority, homevoters rule in the suburbs. As I argued in both chapter 5 (on a broader historical scale) and chapter 7 (at the community level), events of the 1970s made homevoters especially touchy about their environs. This caused the transformation of suburban land use policies from "good-housekeeping" zoning to growth controls. Arrow 1 in figure 8.1, which pushes down the pre-1970s land use intensity, pretty much sums this up.

Arrow 2, which shows the "leapfrog" development to rural areas outside the suburbs, is more complicated. The political life of rural areas differs from the suburbs because the developable land is regarded as a resource by much of the population. For farmers and other owners of large tracts, the option of development is an important form of wealth. For other residents who are not commuters or retired, development itself may increase their locally based incomes. So one would expect that such communities might be more in favor of development that has been pushed their way by suburban exclusion, and evidence indicates they are (Kline and Wichelns 1994; Pendall, Wolanski, and McGovern 2002; Eric Williams 2011).

What surprises me about rural communities is how long they stay pro-development even after a good deal of the land has been converted to what are essentially suburban residences. Newcomers usually outnumber the old-time landowners and their allies within a short period, but the newcomers do not immediately take the reins of government and adopt suburban-style growth controls. The best insight into this forbearance was provided by Jere Daniell, a colleague in Dartmouth's history department. Jere has spent much of his time investigating the history of individual New England towns. His outlet for this research is not publication but local talks to citizens of those towns, who are most often residents active in town affairs, and he listens to what they have to say.

Daniell believes that newcomers have a strong tendency to adopt the mores and traditions of the town they have chosen. This makes them generally respectful of the old-time families and local workers, and this respect allows landowners to have more influence than their numbers might warrant. Rural politics remains pro-development for a longer time than the demographic composition of the populations might otherwise indicate. This view corresponds with Alexander von Hoffman's histories of zoning in Massachusetts towns on which I relied in the previous chapter as well as fine-grained accounts of politics in rural Connecticut by Thomas Rudel (1989) and in Shasta County, California, by Robert Ellickson (1991). Shasta County traditional ranchers were generally respected by newcomers, and the ranchers had more influence on local public affairs than their numbers would seem to warrant.

8.3 East Amwell's Path from Rural Township to Exclusive Suburb

Eventually, however, rural townships on the outskirts of growing metropolitan areas become more like suburbs in their behavior. Often the transformation is caused by a singular event that threatens to accelerate the pace of development, which, in turn, forces suburban-style residents to confront the traditional authority of the more pro-development landowners and their allies. (This scenario contrasts with the incremental adoption of growth controls in Acton, Massachusetts, described in chapter 7 above.) I saw an example of this confrontation at close range as an expert witness for farmland owners in *New Jersey Farm Bureau v. Township of East Amwell*, 380 N.J. Super. 325 (App. Div. 2005). The township is a suburb of Trenton and Princeton, both about 15 miles to the south, but the land is a mixture of hillside forest on the Sourland Mountains and farmland in the Amwell Valley. The hillsides had been downzoned to ten-acre-minimum lot sizes years before, but most of the farmland area was zoned for three-acre lots. This had been increased from one-acre lots in the recent past, but the change did not generate much complaint from landowners because that was generally a size that prospective homeowners were content with in this rural setting.

The galvanizing event was a proposal by Merrill-Lynch in 1997 to build a major research and financial services center in Hopewell, New Jersey, just north of Trenton. (Stephan Schmidt [2008] describes the effect of this and related developments on two nearby townships, whose anti-growth reactions were much like East Amwell's). This center was expected to cause many executives to move to the area and build on the available lots in East Amwell. A local activist, Barbara Wolfe, led the planning board to downzone the farmland to ten-acre-minimum lots. Downzoning for this purpose is typically justified as a means of preserving farmland, but its primary effect is to enhance the value of nonfarming real estate (Walls, Kousky, and Chu 2013). Ms. Wolfe was an avid horsewoman who was concerned that the informal riding trails that landowners permitted would disappear with development. She obtained the support of most of the suburban-oriented residents who lived in East Amwell. They feared that the rural character that they enjoyed would be eroded by more development, even though anticipated development would have been along the lines that most them already enjoyed.

A special anxiety that all New Jersey communities had was the *Mount Laurel* obligations, in which the New Jersey Supreme Court required all municipalities to use their zoning to provide for a minimum percentage of low-income housing. (The case is also discussed in the next chapter.) East Amwell had met its quota at the time, in part through Ms. Wolfe's previous efforts. But the New Jersey Supreme Court's standard was based on the *proportion* of the housing stock that was affordable, not the absolute amount, and not adjusted for location. Any significant growth by East Amwell would require that it go through the painful process of siting more affordable housing.

East Amwell's new zoning sufficiently alienated local farmers that they enlisted the New Jersey Farm Bureau (a branch of a national organization of farmers) to finance litigation against the township. (The Farm Bureau's funds were supplemented by a development-minded landowner who remained in the background.) The new ten-acre zoning, they argued, reduced their land values without providing any compensatory gains in farm value. Although the township did propose "right-to-farm" legislation that would have protected farmers from some nuisance claims, and property taxes were based on below-market agricultural values, the plaintiffs argued that farming had become uneconomical even with reduced taxes and right-to-farm legislation. Most farmers were not eager to develop their land, but the plaintiffs wanted to preserve the option to sell their property for development.

The farmland owners in East Amwell lost their suit to prevent the downzoning. Several years later, Peter Buchsbaum, who had been the farmers' lawyer, sent me a notice of what was being built on the ten-acre lots. A lengthy advertisement for a newly-built home in the *Hunterdon County Democrat* (April 15, 2014) read in part: "This magnificent French Country Manor in East Amwell displays high levels of customization, style and craftsmanship. Situated on ten open, level and professionally landscaped acres with panoramic mountain views, this property is farmland assessed, with close proximity to The Ridge Country Golf Club." No price was listed; as the saying goes, if you have to ask, you can't afford it. "Farmland assessed," by the way, means that the owner gets a tax break.

The ad might suggest that the farmland owners did not fare too badly economically from East Amwell's downzoning, but this particular parcel seems unusual. As in much of rural New Jersey, many acres of farmland in East Amwell have been preserved "in perpetuity" under purchase of development rights. According to studies of New Jersey municipalities by Paul Gottlieb et al. (2012) and Thomas Rudel et al. (2011), East Amwell's large-lot zoning has become the norm and generally suppresses the construction of middle-class housing.

As illustrated by the East Amwell case, rural areas close to expanding cities eventually become just like the suburbs from which developers were originally shut out. Thus a dynamic view of the diagram in figure 8.1 would have to draw successive leaps of remote suburbanization and edge-cities. Indeed, the "inner" edge cities provide the basis for yet farther expansion of

8.4 Big-City Politics: From Pro-development to Suburban Norms?

Arrow 3 in figure 8.1, which illustrates the possible displacement of suburban development back to the central city, suggests another political posture that is different from the suburbs. I have long argued that central cities are more pro-development than their suburbs. Part of the reason for this stance was an inaccurate projection by many central cities in the post–World War II era. Chicago, for example, "overzoned" (meaning it allowed more density than was realistically possible at the time) much of its residential areas in anticipation of population growth that did not occur (Schwieterman, Caspall, and Heron 2006). Its planners had looked at past growth and projected it to the future. But while Chicago's suburbs grew considerably, the inner city itself stagnated because of the lure of the suburbs and because big-city public school quality declined, crime increased, and race relations became more contentious in the 1960s. Developers who wanted to build in Chicago and many other big cities found zoning laws that were much more accommodating than those in the suburbs.

Even without the inertia of outdated, permissive zoning laws, big-city politics gives developers more clout than they had in the suburbs. A larger population requires a larger variety of city services and more complex agencies, which make it more difficult for homevoters to identify which candidates work for their interests. A student paper about a rezoning in Chicago indicated that the local alderman played a key role in helping the developer get what he wanted, and such stories are widespread in other cities as well. Big-city land use issues are more complex and thus more difficult for amateurs to penetrate. City mayors and councilors have a larger electorate to appeal to and so must rely more on producer interest groups such as developers and unions to finance their campaigns. Cities also contain more residents who both work and live within their municipal boundaries, so the employment benefits of development will factor into popular opinion about development.

In other words, homevoters have more political competition in central cities than in the suburbs. Big-city land use policies are well characterized by sociologist Harvey Molotch (1976), whose influential article, "The City as Growth Machine," described an urban political process that was dominated by pro-development interests. The political divide between a "growth machine" in big cities and "growth control" in the suburbs has become the conventional wisdom in land use circles. As an aside, I would note that Molotch and I have more in common than one might think. His 1976 article challenged the sociological view that development was just something that happened without much input from the public sector. His insight was that public actors are critical in modern urban development. The development of my views is similar in that most economists in the 1970s did not think that public regulation had much to do with city development. Like Molotch, I thought that zoning made a big difference; developers were not able to just go out and build what looked most profitable to them. But since most metropolitan development was occurring in the suburbs, the public activity that seemed most important to me was the growing trend of citizen-led opposition to development.

The idea that big cities are dominated by the growth machine has come under attack recently. David Schleicher (2013) and Rick Hills and Schleicher (2011) look at many larger American cities and see a good deal less pro-development activity than my model or Molotch's would lead one to believe. Vicki Been, Josiah Madar, and Simon McDonnell (2014) empirically examined recent development in New York City, which as the nation's largest city, should be a bastion of pro-development forces. Their subtitle asked, "Are Homevoters Overtaking the Growth Machine?" Their answer for large parts of the city is yes. Areas with greater proportions of homeowners (who are actually a minority in the city) were more likely to be downzoned or protected from nonconforming apartment developments.

In a similar vein, Ed Glaeser, a Harvard professor and New York native, asked (with Joseph Gyourko and Raven Saks [2005b]), "Why Is Manhattan So Expensive?" While recognizing that the centers of the biggest cities should have higher housing prices, they found that the cost of adding extra floors to most buildings was far smaller than the economic benefit (expected rents) from doing so. This indicated that something was holding down potential construction that would reduce average rents. Their answer squarely blamed regulatory constraints. Histories of modern zoning changes in Chicago (Schwieterman, Caspall, and Heron 2006) and Los Angeles (Andrew Whittemore 2012) also indicate that their once-robust growth machines are now sputtering, their engines clogged with the same homevoter concerns that animate suburban politics.

The latter two studies indicate that Chicago and Los Angeles became less developer-dominated in the late 1960s and early 1970s, about the same time that the growth-control movement was hitting the suburbs. Growth controls were not so obvious in the bigger cities both because they had been overzoned and because the political apparatus of the growth machine was better entrenched. The other condition that changed in cities was the decline in crime. The current trend is summarized by the back-to-the-city arrow 3 in figure 8.1. It suggests that cities should have gotten some of the displaced development as suburbs adopted growth controls after 1970. But big-city conditions up to about 1990 were not hospitable to residential development. Schools were terrible, race relations worse, and crime rates were soaring. Developers displaced by suburban downzoning were much more likely to head for rural townships than go back to the city to redevelop old neighborhoods.

After 1990, crime rates in all big cities began a steady decline that was not even interrupted by the great recession of 2008. (Crime normally rises in recessions.) I favor the view of Jonathan Klick, John MacDonald, and Thomas Stratmann (2012) that the spread of cell phones was a major cause of the decline since they made reporting and recording of criminal activity in densely populated areas easier. But one need not accept this hypothesis to appreciate that the crime decline is durable and has made big cities more attractive to residents who in former times would have headed for the suburbs (Schwartz, Susin, and Voicu 2003). Big-city schools may also have become somewhat better, and race relations are at least not worse.

These recent trends suggest that the increased regulatory demands in big cities may be caused by the growing influence of upscale homebuyers in recent years. My theme in previous chapters has been that land use regulations are governed largely by the demand side of the housing market. With the growth of homevoters in the biggest cities, the back-to-the-city pressure that my Rube Goldberg–esque diagram suggest needs another outlet. That outlet is suggested by arrow 4, the soaring line that leads out of the picture.

The modern trend in regional outmigration was the centerpiece of the history of zoning in chapter 5. Around the 1970s, the rise in home values caused by inflation made homevoters even more sensitive to the risk of neighborhood change. Zoning was converted from a good-housekeeping device to a growth-control strategy as high-income homeowners seized control from local authorities who had previously balanced developer and landowner interests with neighborhood protection. The new growth-control devices accelerated the increase in home values and spread quickly across metropolitan areas. Indeed, in severely growth-constrained communities, the housing stock began to filter up or gentrify, as wealthier residents moved in (Zorn, Hansen, and Schwartz 1986). This caused the outmigration of the poor. Thus the arrow 4 in figure 8.1 was not a general emigration from a growth-controlled urban area but a largely selective outmigration of lower-income residents. The entire metropolitan area, not just the central city, has become gentrified.

8.5 When Does Suburbanization Become Sprawl?

The picture of sprawl in figure 8.1 started with reference to the solid line drawn with the "good-housekeeping" standard of zoning. (This could also be called the ideal "transect" as described by the new urbanists, but I will stick to the idea of a "baseline" so as not to appropriate their agenda, which is largely critical of traditional zoning [Duany and Talen 2002].) Regulations existed but were not anti-growth. But even if that level of regulation was efficient, there are reasons to believe that the baseline by itself represented an excessively suburbanized metropolitan area. Urban economists think of suburbanization as the product of a trade-off between transportation costs and housing costs. Closer to the center of the city, housing prices will be high but transportation costs—chiefly the time cost of travel—will be lower. Households (or firms) who move farther away get cheaper land (and thus choose more of it) but have to endure high commuting costs. When transportation costs decline, the city will tend to spread out. When the demand for housing increases, chiefly because of rising personal incomes, the city will also spread out.

Suburbanization can be thought of as a decline in overall slope (the gradient) of the solid curve in figure 8.1. Much of this is perfectly natural. As chapter 1 indicated, suburbanization is a worldwide phenomenon in cities both old and new. In the United States, higher incomes and better transportation were largely responsible for reducing the overcrowding of tenement houses in the older cities and preventing overcrowding in the central parts of newer cities. But two types of government subsidies made the process of suburbanization excessive. One was the favorable tax treatment of owner-occupied homes. By not taxing the imputed rent that owners get from their own homes, the income tax system makes housing seem cheaper. Imputed rent is the amount that you would pay to live in your home if someone else owned it (Follain and Melamed 1998). This benefit can, of course, be had in central cities, but the subsidy is generally agreed to cause excessive suburbanization.

The other subsidy is to transportation. Here the subsidy is more subtle and not mainly what critics of automobile transportation point to, which is the government-sponsored construction of highways. Most highway construction was financed by motor fuel taxes, which amount to a rough-and-ready user charge. The real subsidy is the failure to charge users of highways for the congestion they cause other drivers. This is a true external cost (as pointed out in section 7.5) in that people who decide to travel on a certain road at a certain time think only about the speed of the cars in front of them. They do not consider the cost of their decisions on those behind them—the cost being the slowing down they cause as they ease into the lane of a busy expressway during rush hour. This sounds trivial, but when the seconds lost by tapping the brake to avoid hitting the entering vehicle are added up over many vehicles, they can amount to a large number.

The effect of unpriced highway congestion on suburbanization is complex, since it may cause both households and firms to relocate either to the suburbs or to the central city. The consensus from most theoretical and simulation models is that unpriced highway congestion causes excessive suburbanization, but it is not obvious how much particular congestion tolls would compress the city. The most typical policy response to excess automobile driving is to promote low-cost mass transit with even larger subsidies. Projections of ridership of new fixed-rail systems almost never come true, and transit fares are heavily subsidized in almost every system. Urban planners seem to be in the thrall of "A Desire Named Streetcar," as the title of one critical study put it (Don Pickrell 1992). The effects of these alternative modes on overall congestion are estimated by economists to range from nil to modest. (For a review of previous studies and a contrary example, see Michael Anderson [2014].)

What is clearer is that the subsidy to owner-occupied housing does cause excessive suburbanization. The tax benefits of housing cost the government huge amounts in foregone tax revenues (Henry Aaron 1972; Dennis Ventry 2010). The subsidy to mortgage interest rates by government-chartered organizations such as Fannie Mae has a much smaller impact than the failure to treat income from owner-occupied housing like the income from other personal investments. Moreover, the tax subsidy accrues to owner-occupants, so it creates a larger class of investor-homeowners who often oppose new development that would increase the density of their neighborhoods and communities.

This is the down side of the homevoter hypothesis. Homeowners are generally better citizens in that they maintain their properties better, are committed to higher-quality local education, and generally have more social capital than the renter population (DiPasquale and Glaeser 1999). But their large, undiversified asset also drives them to worry excessively about infill developments that would make for less commuting and more convenient homes and jobs for most residents.

8.6 Do Speculators Cause Sprawl?

Another factor that is often said to cause excessively low densities is land speculation. The story, which is an old one (Ernest Fisher 1933), goes like this. Owners of undeveloped land in the suburbs often decline to develop it, even when there is a bona fide builder at hand. The owner speculates that the land's value will be greater if she waits a few years. As a result, the builders bypass the land and erect houses in locations even more remote from urban centers. This pattern of "leapfrog" development is said to contribute to suburban sprawl, and a number of land use regulations—some actually put into practice, such as the Portland program, described below—have been devised to discourage it.

The trouble with this scenario is that it ends too soon. It does not ask whether the land speculator might reasonably assume that the first offer, which he turns down, will be upped by a later developer. The later developer may find it profitable to put up higher-density housing. The eventual pattern is leapfrog-with-infill, in which the infill development has a greater density (Ohls and Pines 1975; David Mills 1981). Thus, successful land speculation ultimately causes less suburban sprawl, not more. There are empirical studies that indicate that later infill development tends to occur at higher densities than it does in neighboring subdivisions (Richard Peiser 1989).

If the later and higher-density builder does not materialize with a better financial offer (which at least compensates for the cost of waiting), the speculator has caused some sprawl. But in that case, the speculator has lost money (in the sense of foregone profits) by waiting too long. Thus, the main way by which land speculators contribute to sprawl is by losing money. This may happen, but poor speculators are soon just plain poor and are driven from the market. Land speculators as a group may also find their socially optimal decision rules distorted by taxes (Daniel McMillen 1990). Income taxes raise interest rates, which makes speculators inclined to sell their land too soon. But this is a problem with all investment decisions, not just land.

Perhaps the strongest evidence that zoning, not the behavior of speculators, causes low density comes from studies of land values. If undeveloped land that has been bypassed by development were simply being held by speculators, its current market value would be nearly equal to that of already developed land. There would, of course, be some cost to subdividing the land, so vacant land held by speculators would be slightly lower in price than land that was already subdivided and ready to sell. However, even when subdivision costs are taken into account, econometric evidence consistently shows that restrictively zoned, undeveloped land in the suburbs of metropolitan areas has a much lower sale value than land on which development has been permitted (James White 1988; Colwell and Sirmans 1993). Buyers of restrictively zoned, undeveloped land are consistently paying less for it than for otherwise comparable land. Such differences can exist only if buyers of the undeveloped land anticipate that there are very large transaction costs to obtaining development permission. Low-density zoning is not a paper tiger, and its existence is pervasive in the suburbs.

There is another, more plausible explanation for how land speculation causes sprawl. Speculators are forward looking not just to future market possibilities, but to political change as well. Owners of developable tracts of land might want to wait several years until high-density development possibilities open up. But they might also anticipate that as nearby tracts are developed, the new residents will change land use regulations in ways that make the higher-density development unfeasible. James Thorson (1997) found that developers in McHenry County, Illinois (near Chicago), anticipated a downzoning (which did in fact come to pass) and subdivided more quickly. As a result of developing sooner, the overall density of their projects was probably lower than they would have chosen later on. In this sense, forward-looking speculators could be said to cause sprawl.

Such a conclusion looks at the wrong cause, however, and does not play through the logical scenario. If the speculators had ignored the signs that their property would be downzoned and held it undeveloped despite the downzoning, the downzoning itself was the obvious cause of sprawl. With that scenario as the baseline from which to judge the speculators' behavior, a decision to develop sooner than was optimal put at least some houses (or other uses) on the ground and thereby accommodated some development that would have been built even farther from the central city.

What surprises me about landowners is how many of them overlook the political signs that a rezoning is imminent. It is perhaps just in the nature of longtime landowners to expect that political conditions will not change much. Land development is an episodic activity, which may discourage the networks of information-sharing that arise in other industries. Manufacturers and retailers, for example, have trade associations whose industry publications and government-affairs specialists keep members up to date on the latest regulatory trends. By contrast, for the farmers and woodlot owners who hold a large fraction of land that is apt to be developed, sale of the land is only a side activity, and usually only a remote possibility as well.

8.7 Land Use Regulation to Combat Sprawl

The way to combat inefficient suburbanization—sprawl—would be to eliminate the subsidies to owner-occupied housing and charge motorists (and mass-transit riders) the full social cost of each mile traveled. This would not eliminate suburbanization, of course, but it would discourage its excesses. The technical means of dealing with congestion are already available in the form of electronic toll devices such as EZ Pass. Taxing the imputed rent of homeowners is more difficult, but simply eliminating the mortgage deduction (or capping it at a reasonable level) would eliminate most of the subsidy. (People who could pay cash for houses would still get a subsidy in the form of an asset whose income is not taxed.) But both of these policies face formidable political barriers. The mortgage subsidy is as popular as Mom and apple pie used to be, and universal electronic tolling raises some nontrivial privacy concerns (Denvil Duncan et al. 2014), so it is worth considering whether land use policies might be adopted to achieve the same goals.

The most ambitious anti-sprawl policy along these lines has been going on in Oregon. Since Portland is by far the state's largest urban area, I will direct attention to it, as have many studies by economists and planners (Knaap and Nelson 1992; Phillips and Goodstein 2000; Grout, Jaeger, and Plantinga 2011). As described briefly in chapter 2, Portland in the early 1970s established an urban growth boundary around its central city and close-in suburbs. Most other cities that drew up urban growth boundaries have to deal with the fact that developers and new homebuyers can leapfrog outside the urban containment district to other, more permissive towns and still be close enough to commute to the city. These adjustments largely undermine the sprawl-prevention purposes of the growth boundary, at least when viewed from a metropolitan perspective. Those who move to the more rural or distant small towns end up buying more housing (because land is cheaper) and commuting longer distances. Purely local growth boundaries seem as likely to cause sprawl as contain it.

Oregon overcame this problem by organizing its growth boundaries by statewide legislation. All of the communities within metropolitan areas were required to be within the growth boundary. Undeveloped land outside of these communities was essentially declared off-limits to development, largely by zoning it exclusively for agriculture. The urban growth boundary was not conceived of as fixed for all time. Adjustments were to be made periodically to accommodate anticipated growth in employment and housing. Local governments did not lose their land use authority, but they were required to develop plans that would accommodate infill development and otherwise develop and redevelop at greater densities than they might have chosen on their own.

The agency that supervised the urban growth boundary and the local government plans is called Metro. Most regional groupings of local governments are federations of the municipalities, with each one having its own representative. The one-municipality, one-vote approach has two problems. The first is that it maintains a local view at the regional level, and this makes it difficult to enforce cooperative agreements. The region might be better off if City A took more of the expected growth or businesses than City B, but the individual constituents in both cities might be opposed to the plan and thus prevent its fruition. If the regional federation is given more substantial powers that might overcome individual holdouts, a second problem arises. Under the U.S. Supreme Court's rulings on one-person, one-vote, such a body would have to be districted in such a way that the larger cities would have more representation than the smaller cities. The smaller suburban cities might find that objectionable and let their state legislators (who are elected by geographically contiguous areas) know that such an arrangement is unacceptable.

Portland's Metro, by contrast, is independently chartered by the state and has a board that is elected by districts that are equal in size (so constitutional representation strictures are not offended), with boundaries that do not correspond to those of any particular local government. Metro thus avoids the local pressures that undermine most urban government federations and, because of its proportional representation, can assume governmental authority over the region. Metro thus has regulatory teeth, and it does enforce the higher-density infill zoning requirements.

8.8 Portland's Growth Boundary Concentrates Development

The representation of Portland's plan is shown in figure 8.2. The solid, downward-sloping base line is the same as that in figure 8.1. It represents what the Portland area would look like if local governments had adopted

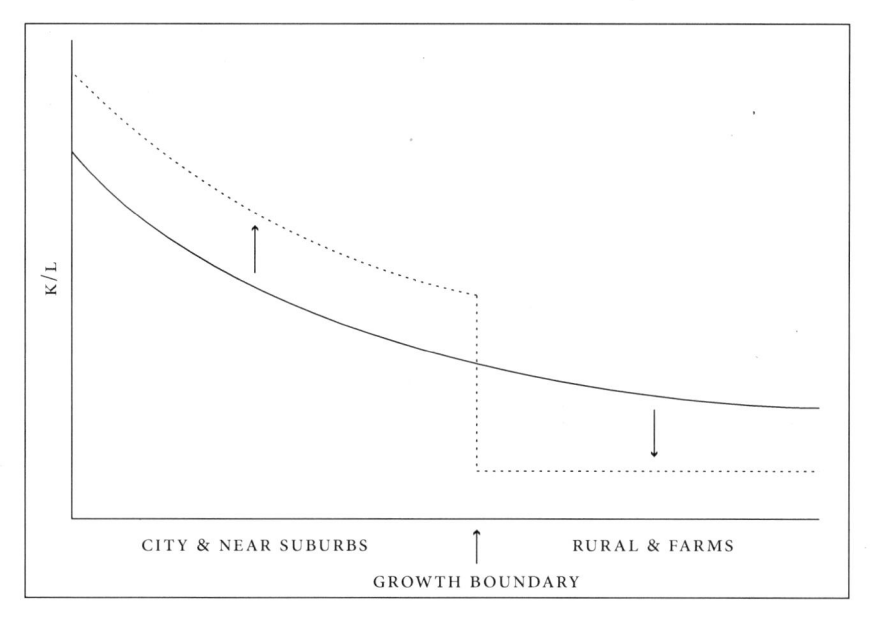

FIGURE 8.2 Portland Growth Boundary

"good-housekeeping" zoning. It is excessively suburbanized not because of local policies but because individuals commute too much (there are no congestion tolls) and because they demand too much housing, since it is a tax-favored asset. Superimposed on this is an urban growth boundary. The boundary includes both the central city (Portland) and its close-in, contiguous suburbs, and so it is farther from the central business district than the central city/suburban boundary in figure 8.1.

The arrows in figure 8.2 do not require much explanation—Rube Goldberg this is not. The capital-to-land ratio outside of the boundary is pushed way down. In most cases, only agricultural and closely related structures are allowed. Farmhouses must be occupied by farmers or farm workers. Inside the boundary, the K/L ratio is pushed upwards. Rail transit has been promoted along with the urban growth boundary.

Portland has the oldest growth boundary of any large urban area, and it has been much studied for its effects on housing prices, transit use, congestion, and sprawl. The studies are surprisingly mixed. Myung-Jin Jun (2004) finds that Portland does not seem less suburbanized, less densely populated, or less dependent on automobiles than a comparison group of similar sized U.S.

metropolitan areas. Yet Portland's boundary is clearly visible from the sky and on the ground—there is development right inside, and farmland outside—and economic studies find that property values are much higher inside than outside the boundary (Grout, Jaeger, and Plantinga 2011). This suggests that the boundary is a serious constraint and that housing is more costly inside than out. Some of the differences in the aforementioned studies could result from time trends. The original growth boundary included a great deal of undeveloped territory, and the plan was to expand it regularly. However, in the early 1990s, authorities decided not to expand the urban growth boundary as much as had been previously projected, and housing prices shot upward (Mildner, Dueker, and Rufolo 1996).

Portland's policy has also had implementation problems. A monopoly on mass transit funds facilitated uncharacteristic corruption in the city's government (Randal O'Toole 2007). Overall housing prices are high for an urban area of its size, which may deter immigrants if it does not reflect higher quality of life (Phillips and Goodstein 2000; Gordon and Richardson 1997). The high prices have a disproportionate effect on low-income residents, an issue that continues to concern many "smart growth" advocates, who otherwise admire Portland's experience. Long distance commuting to Clark County (Vancouver), Washington, which is adjacent to Portland, has also increased, so the leapfrog development that frustrates other urban containment plans is at least partly apparent in Portland. (On a plane headed to Portland in the late 1990s, my home-bound seatmate told me he was moving from his downtown home, where he could walk to work, to a rural location in Clark County so he could enjoy a ranch-like homestead.) And the severe regulations on development outside the urban growth line fueled the property-rights initiatives (described in section 6.13) that roiled land use decisions across the state in the period 2004–2007 and continues to vex the planning establishment.

The controversies about Portland's policy makes one ask how it got adopted and why it persists. Its adoption in the 1970s was the product of a popular xenophobia best expressed by Governor Tom McCall's 1971 declaration, "Come visit us again and again.... But for heaven's sake, don't come here to live" (Walker and Hurley 2011, 8). This unusual political stance reflected popular anxiety that out-of-staters—and they were mostly Californians—were responsible for developments that were thought to be reducing the state's quality of life. Governor McCall's attitude was actually in line with long-standing Oregon sensibilities, some of which evolved from a selective, Tiebout-like sorting of immigrants from the eastern United States. According to Donald Meinig (1986), Oregon was settled by sober-minded farmers and pastoralists who took a dim view of the gold-mining and commercial opportunism of their neighboring territory to the south.

More surprising for a population with many New England ties was voters' willingness to surrender local control of government to Metro. This looks like a serious challenge to the homevoter view of local government. Metro's job is to increase the density of development in communities that at least initially don't want it and in some cases in places where neighbors oppose it. It will not do to explain Metro as an accidental agency that just grew out of hand. Oregon voters have long had the initiative, and they use it regularly. Several initiatives that would have disbanded or severely weakened Metro were advanced but defeated (Ellen Bassett 2009). The only one with any success was Measure 37 in 2004 (discussed earlier in section 6.13), the compensation-for-regulation initiative, and that was largely eviscerated by another initiative just three years afterward. If homevoters are alive in Oregon, they do not seem to dislike Metro all that much.

One possible advantage of Metro over local government is that it helps Portland-area communities cartelize the housing market. By keeping most rural sites off limits to development, it channels homebuyers into the existing area, thus making demand for housing more inelastic and raising existing home values. The down side of this for existing homeowners is that they might be at risk of devaluation from projects that are approved by Metro but that their local government would have rejected. It is possible that most of the required infill projects avoid single-family neighborhoods and so do not provoke homevoter antipathy. Even if they are at occasional risk from unwanted infill, Portland homeowners might regard the higher home values they get from the urban growth boundary as adequate compensation. The odd thing about that argument is that it seems consistent with the "smart growth" justifications for urban growth boundaries.

8.9 The Houston Inclusionary Strategy: Don't Zone at All

The problem addressed by exclusionary zoning is that the suburbs want to zone too strictly. Perhaps one could solve the problem by abandoning zoning altogether. Economists are always looking for "natural experiments" with which to examine the effect of institutional change, and Houston, Texas, almost fits the bill. ("Almost" because Houston's policy is locally chosen, not imposed from without.) Houston does not have zoning, and it never has. Since 1929, Houston has had a planning commission, but the commission's recommendations for zoning have failed five times in citywide advisory referenda, the last in 1993. The city has adopted piecemeal regulations that look like what zoned cities do (off-street parking requirements, historic preservation districts, some developer exactions), but it lacks broad regulations over the use and size of most buildings, which are the essence of American zoning.

Houston's unusual condition has attracted almost as much social science attention as Portland, though Houston visitors seem to be more of the individualistic, libertarian bent than those who regularly visit Portland. A Chicago-area land use lawyer, Bernard Siegan (1972), heard about Houston's lack of zoning—a condition unique among large American cities—and undertook an on-site study to see how it was working out. He concluded that Houston works just fine. The major industrial uses were clustered near transportation hubs and away from residential areas. Most of the suburban (but within-city) residential areas were covered by private covenants, which prevented nonconforming uses and controlled most of the contingencies that zoning would have covered. In the older parts of the city that lacked covenants, entrepreneurs who wanted to start a small business in their homes were not inhibited by zoning rules, and developers were seldom hindered by NIMBYism. Although Siegan's views about property regulation were regarded among the law professoriate as outside of the mainstream, the economists of my acquaintance who live in Houston tend to concur with him that the city does not suffer because of its lack of zoning.

One of the notable byproducts of lack of zoning is Houston's lower housing costs, even when compared with pro-development (but thoroughly zoned) Dallas (Richard Peiser 1981). This is despite the considerable growth of population in Houston (even adjusting for its elastic boundaries). If lack of zoning in Houston is bad for homebuyers, immigrants do not seem to mind too much.

About 20 years ago, a student in my Dartmouth urban economics class, Kihara Kiarie (1996), decided to write an undergraduate honors thesis about Houston. His work took two directions. One was a statistical comparison of "housing price gradients" in Houston and three other sunbelt metropolitan areas, Dallas, Tampa, and Phoenix. The gradient is the percentage change in housing prices as one moves from the center of the city to its suburbs. Urban economists have for years used it as a way to measure the degree of suburbanization. The presumption is that a more centralized city will have a larger (in absolute value—the gradient is presumed to be negative) housing price gradient than a suburbanized city. A more suburbanized city has experienced a relative movement in its population from the center to outer suburbs. Typical housing price gradients in the 1970s ranged from minus .04 in traditionally centralized cities like Boston to minus .02 in newer, more suburbanized cities like Phoenix. The nearly universal trend in housing price gradients is for them to become lower as time passes, representing the steady suburbanization of cities in the United States and most other nations.

Kiarie found that the four sunbelt cities he examined all had small gradients, but Houston stood out as having a *positive* housing price gradient. His census-based measure was value per room of owner occupied housing, so it adjusted for the fact that homes in suburban Houston were newer and had more rooms. He was curious about the source of this anomaly—positive housing price gradients suggest that the center was repelling would-be homeowners—and undertook some fieldwork. He spent time in Houston both interviewing local officials and looking around and photographing downtown conditions. He was especially good at ferreting out information about businesses that were expanding into residential areas. If the boss in the front would not talk to him, he would go around back and talk to the workers on the loading dock.

He found from multiple sources that homeownership in Houston's central area was a risky activity. Businesses were able to expand into residential areas, and residences could themselves be converted to business uses. This was advantageous to the businesses but generally not to the homeowners. In the outer parts of the city, however, private covenants, administered by homeowner associations, controlled this activity. There had been covenants in many of the center city neighborhoods, but their controls had often lapsed over the years because they had not been actively enforced. Kiarie concluded that Houston's positive price gradient was at least in part caused by the lack of what I have called "good-housekeeping" zoning in the center city. (It is not clear that this raises or lowers the capital-to-land ratio in the central part of the city, though, since it may encourage more multi-unit housing and business activity.)

An earlier study of Houston confirms that lack of covenants or zoning is hard on home values there. Janet Furman Speyrer (1989) found two cities, Bellaire and West University Place, that are completely surrounded by

Houston but have their own municipal government. Both of the small cities have zoning, and the neighborhoods of Houston on which they border do not, even though they look very much like those in the small cities. Speyrer collected data on 230 home sales in the area and compared their values by using the usual regression techniques.

Speyrer found that both zoning and covenants added almost 10 percent to the sale value of the homes compared to homes that lacked either covenants or zoning. What this indicates is that establishing covenants in already developed neighborhoods (like those in her sample) was difficult to do. A home that lacked zoning (because it was in Houston) could not easily establish covenants with its neighbors and get a 10 percent capital gain because of the transaction costs of doing so. Saying that covenants are equivalent to zoning looks valid insofar as each adds value to homes. But the difficulty of establishing covenants once neighborhoods are built out suggests that zoning is a cheaper way to add value to neighborhood homes.

8.10 Houston Voters Keep Rejecting Zoning

Why doesn't Houston have zoning? It is truly unique among large American cities. The not entirely satisfactory answer is that its voters do not want zoning. It has been defeated in referenda six times over the last 80 years, most recently in 1993. (The city's planning department's website has a timeline and a brief history, http://www.houstontx.gov/planning/AboutPD/pd_history.html.) Houston both confirms and confutes my theory that zoning is a bottom-up phenomenon. It confirms that land use politics is ultimately decided by the local electorate. Many mayors and other city officials have advocated comprehensive zoning, but Houston's voters keep rejecting it. What challenges my bottom-up theory is this: What makes Houston different from all other American cities? Dallas and all other big cities in Texas have zoning, so the explanation cannot reside in a distinctive Texas culture. Zoning advocates in Houston point to the campaigning against zoning in the referenda by various real estate interests, but such tactics would have been available to real estate and other anti-zoning groups in many other cities, and only Houston lacks zoning. And many real estate interests in Houston favored zoning, so opposition was hardly monolithic.

The answer that seems more reasonable lies in Houston's elastic boundaries and its diverse population of white Anglos (mostly in the in-city suburban areas) and African Americans and Hispanics, who more often live in the central parts of Houston that lack covenants. Examination of election results in 1993 indicated that, somewhat paradoxically, the white Anglos, who most often enjoyed the benefits of protective covenants and private homeowner associations in the suburban areas, were most in favor of adopting citywide zoning (John McDonald 1995). It was lower-income blacks and Hispanics who disproportionately opposed zoning, even though they most often lived in areas the lacked covenants.

McDonald suggests that the voting results are best explained by the concern by inner-city blacks and Hispanics that suburban whites would be in charge of zoning and would use it to their advantage and hold back lower-income people. Empirical studies have shown, for example, that high-income suburbs tend to zone out commerce and industry, while low-income places are more inclined to accept it for its employment, fiscal, and convenience benefits (Evenson and Wheaton 2003). It is not as if minorities do not want any zoning, though. It is clear that their home values would be stabilized with zoning. What they want (I infer) is to be able to adjust zoning to their own needs, not have it dictated by a more affluent majority. It seems likely that if Houston were divided into two cities, center and suburban, in which each had a more homogenous population, both of them would have adopted zoning long ago.

The other explanation for Houston's rejection of zoning is fiscal. Chapters 4 and 5 demonstrated that many cities adopted zoning in order to manage their property tax base. Industrial and commercial invasions of residential areas are hard on the value of homes and hence on the property tax base of the city. (Some of the home devaluation would be offset by higher values of commercial property, but a nuanced study of Massachusetts towns found that overall property values were higher when nonresidential uses were concentrated rather than spread around the community [Lafferty and Frech 1978].) One would expect fiscal pressures to induce Houston's voters to accept more land use regulation.

Houston deals with the erosion of its inner-city tax base by the expedient of annexing the suburban tax base as it grows outward. Cities in Texas can annex unincorporated territory that is within its "extraterritorial jurisdiction," usually within three miles of its current outer boundaries. Houston has done so repeatedly for most of the last century, which has made it the fourth most populous municipality in the nation and the city with the fourth largest land area. (As an urban area, Houston ranks seventh in both categories.) Few cities besides Houston have as much opportunity to use annexation to bail out their fiscal erosion. In its last major annexation, Houston's mayor was explicit about wanting to annex the Kingwood development because it would add $4 million per year in tax revenues (*Houston Chronicle*, October 8, 2006). Even though the state legislature has curtailed some of Houston's annexation ability, it still allows it to annex territory with commercial activity and to appropriate half of the sales taxes.

The irony here is that Houston's ability to annex its suburbs is a power long sought by most urban planners, who regard the fragmentation of metropolitan areas as a setback to rational planning. Houston's experience suggests that a unified city could be so politically divided that it would not muster the political will to undertake much planning. It could also be that by now, Houston voters are proud of their distinctive policy, which is often noted in national news about the city. In the same vein, Portland residents also seem to enjoy the national and international attention to their long-standing urban growth boundary. It is difficult to be too censorious about either city in a nation where most adults have some choice about where to live.

8.11 Sources of the New Exclusionary Zoning

The previous sections addressed the effects of zoning on the distribution of activities within metropolitan areas. This and the following sections deal with a related issue. I opened chapter 5 with a description of a study that indicated that higher housing prices in the Northeast and West Coast were holding back the inter-regional migration that had formerly allowed poor people to seek their fortunes in richer cities. The higher regional housing prices were closely associated with more stringent land use regulation. The resulting redistribution of the U.S. population reflects a new kind of exclusionary zoning. The old one worried—with good reason—about excessive exclusion of the poor from the suburbs. The new exclusion concerns the exclusion of the poor (and much of the middle class) from the high-productivity metropolitan areas of the Northeast and the West Coast.

It should be added that the regional variations in housing prices might not be so good for highly skilled, high-income immigrants, either. They are somewhat less sensitive to high housing prices than the poor, but high housing prices that reflect monopolistic scarcity rather than higher amenities reduce the well-being of the rich as well. If this is the case—a big if—then much of the national wealth disparity that results from regional variations in the housing market may be illusory (Enrico Moretti 2013). The net wealth of late-arriving households in Marin County California or Weston, Massachusetts, is overstated by looking at their home values, since much of that wealth is in land that returns no services. It is like the talisman that must be purchased to enter the club but that otherwise has no use. Having purchased the entrance ticket, its current owners certainly do not want it devalued, as it is a large part of their portfolio. Unlike other forms of capital, however, artificially scarce land does not add to the nation's productivity. It may actually subtract from it by discouraging able workers from moving to high-productivity areas.

The conclusion of chapter 5 hinted at the source of variations in land use regulation among regions of the country. The discussion of politics in the present chapter offers a platform to expand on those hints. My theory about the increasing stringency of land use regulation from chapter 5 was that it results from an interaction of popular demand and institutional supply. Popular demand arose from a drop in intrametropolitan transport costs—the interstate highway system—which made the suburbs more accessible; their construction also galvanized local opponents. The 1970s inflation accelerated the rise in housing prices and made them an object of greater concern to homeowners. Both of these factors were present all over the country; there was no serious regional variation in highway building or inflation.

Other arguably exogenous trends were affecting regions differently. One was the energy crisis of the 1970s, which made a great deal of traditional manufacturing in the "rust belt" uneconomical. I grew up in Bethlehem, Pennsylvania., and within my lifetime Bethlehem Steel's local employment went from about 30,000 to zero. (Incidentally, the city is doing reasonably well: Local officials developed industrial parks for employment in other industries, and the luck of location near Philadelphia and New York provided the demand for its output.) The energy crisis accelerated a long-standing trend away from manufacturing and toward services. Later in the decade, California and Washington State became leaders in computer development. In the 1980s, employment in the finance industry blossomed, and the traditional seats of banking and finance in the Northeast attracted many more highly skilled workers. This was new: A banking career in the 1960s was considered safe and boring and not all that remunerative.

It would help if there were an explanation for why computers gained a foothold in California but lost it in Massachusetts, or why finance did not spread more from New York to Dallas or Denver. My best guess is that reductions in international trade barriers and the opening of formerly Communist countries accelerated the worldwide demand for American computer technology and financial services. The reason these industries remain localized despite housing prices that would deter many potential employees is the power of agglomeration economies. I had underestimated their power in my 1985 book when I suggested that the high housing prices in Silicon Valley would within a decade or two cause the computer industry to relocate to cheaper regions. Wrong. Despite the eager blandishments of other states, the industry remains thoroughly rooted in the San Francisco Bay area, and housing prices have remained so high as to create a local backlash against high-tech employees who are gentrifying San Francisco.

As Donald Meinig's (1986) multivolume work on the geographic history on the United States clearly demonstrates, regional shifts in the centers of American economic growth are not new. But before the 1970s, there seem to have been no significant barriers for internal migrants to relocate to centers of opportunity, save those created by slavery and racial segregation. And the latter institutions play a central role in my explanation for the variations in American land use regulation.

8.12 Regional Variations in Local Governance Affect Zoning

The theory of land use regulation described in chapters 5 and 7 holds that it changes primarily in response to democratic demands. Local voters wanted more protection for their homes as they became more valuable. The political theory advanced in the present chapter has concentrated on the size and location of the unit of government. Big central cities are less paradigms of Molotch's growth machine than they used to be, but they are still closer to it than the suburbs, especially the smaller units that surround most central cities in the northern United States. But suburban government fragmentation does not explain much regional variation. St. Louis and Detroit have fragmented governments, but, given lack of excess demand for locating there, most of them have not bothered to adopt a growth-control regime. And, even more problematic for the small-suburb story, the most severe growth controls developed in California, where larger units of government, often the county, control land use regulation. On my theory that big government units are more responsive to development interests, California should have lagged rather than led the nation in growth control activity.

The answer for the West is the voter initiative. Developers may have been the major players with county and big-city officials in the West, but homevoters held the trump card in the form of the voter initiative. Indeed, the geographic remoteness of the state capital from the majority of the people, which makes it difficult to monitor misbehaving officials, may have been responsible for the origins and spread of the initiative in California and other western states. Western counties are likewise much larger in land area than those east of the 100th meridian, and local voters might also have wanted extra control on political activities there. Many commentators criticize the voter initiative for upsetting land use plans set up by elected officials and professional planners, but that is very much the point in the minds of homevoters.

The South is different from both the North and the West. The South lacks the fragmented local governments that characterize the North, and it uses the voter initiative sparingly and hardly at all on land use matters. I established the latter by searching a summary of 500 zoning entries for "initiative" within the last decade listed by state in the Ballotpedia website (http://ballotpedia.org/wiki/index.php?title=Special:Search&redirs=1&profile=default&search=zoning&limit=500&offset=20), which catalogs state and local plebiscites. The only southern states that had any land use initiatives were Maryland, West Virginia, and Florida, and the number of their initiatives was small compared to other states outside the South. Thus the two major institutional mechanisms by which growth controls get adopted—small democracies and voter initiatives—are lacking in the South.

If the demand for zoning is an expression of popular control, why has the South refrained from developing similar mechanisms by breaking up counties into more autonomous municipalities and enabling the voter initiative for land use measures? The answer is the legacy of slavery and racial segregation, as earlier suggested in section 2.2. Slavery undermined the creation of local institutions because plantation life was self-contained (Gavin Wright 2006). A slave owner who developed new land in Alabama had little use for cooperative white neighbors. He could do most of the work with his slaves. White settlers in Illinois, however, were eager to have cooperative white neighbors, since they relied on local exchanges (both market and informal) to develop and manage their farms and businesses. Settlers in the North were eager to attract immigrants by establishing free local public services. Thus was born the independent local public school district (Fischel 2009b). It was primarily bait for settlers. In the South, all that was necessary to keep order and record property transactions was the county. Local schools and other local institutions were superfluous to men whose major form of property was in portable slaves rather than immobile land.

Local government remained anemic in the South after the Civil War and Reconstruction because whites who controlled the statehouses were concerned that localized black majorities would obtain more political power than whites thought was desirable (Robert Margo 1990). This was especially important once the quality of public education became important in the early twentieth century. Whites wanted access to better schools, including public high school, but did not want to pay for blacks to get better educations. Even when only a small percentage of blacks could vote in local elections, white candidates in close contests could appeal to them for electoral support and thus get some access to public funds (William Link 1992). White majorities in the state legislature forestalled electoral competition by directing funds to whites through the county governments. The county became the default school district for most of the South.

Without schools to control and with a population that mistrusted a large fraction of the rest of the population, popular local government could not get a foothold in the South. After desegregation became effective in the 1960s, administration of the Voting Rights Act discouraged the establishment of the multiple school districts and local governments that would follow (Hiroshi Motomura 1983). The southern county school district was born of segregation and is kept alive by desegregation. A byproduct of that mistrust of black voters is the suppression of local democracy in land use matters. The exception that proves the rule is Florida, which has county government, but perhaps because of a large population with northern origins, does practice voter initiatives. Florida thus has more instances of growth management than one would expect in other southern states (Keith Ihlanfeldt 2007).

In sum, the reason the high-productivity urban areas of the Northeast developed growth controls is that homevoters exercised controls through small, responsive local government. The reason the high-productivity urban areas of the West developed growth controls is that homevoters could control development through the voter initiative. The reason the South did not adopt growth controls when sunbelt manufacturing was expanding is that homevoters had neither responsive local governments nor the voter initiative.

8.13 Evaluating Zoning with Surveys and Statistics

This section will backtrack on the regional variations story to look more carefully at the empirical work that indicates that growth controls are both a local and a regional phenomenon. As the reader may have guessed, quantitative methods are not my forte in economics. My modest skill set probably accounts for popularity of a short monograph for the Lincoln Institute called "Do Growth Controls Matter?" (Fischel 1990). That work explained for people without much statistical training what economists had been up to in several dozen empirical studies done between 1970 and 1990. The overall conclusions were:

1. Zoning did impose both costs and benefits within a community. The studies that found no effect from the nonconforming uses that zoning is supposed to exclude were most often confounded by failure to consider that neighbors may have had some influence on whether a nonconforming use was allowed. Urban spillovers are sufficiently important that political institutions arise to control them effectively, which makes the spillovers themselves difficult to detect.

2. Land subject to downzoning almost always loses value, and nearby homes and businesses usually gain in value. The few works that suggest that downzonings have no effect were concerned with agricultural zoning in areas in which urban development was remote in both time and place. (More recent studies finding these mixed effects in rural areas are those of Kopits, McConnell, and Miles [2012] and Liu and Lynch [2011].)

3. The higher housing prices that result from more stringent zoning could reflect either zoning's benign effects in promoting orderly growth and making the community more attractive or its less benign monopoly effects on housing supply, or, most likely, some combination of the two. Local voters do not care whether their home values are enhanced by monopolistic restrictions or regulations that control external costs.

None of these conclusions has changed much today. What is different is the scope of empirical studies. In previous decades, most studies looked at localized effects of new policies such as the establishment of the California Coastal Zone (Frech and Lafferty 1984) or the effect of new growth policies in particular cities within California (Katz and Rosen 1987). Data about actual land use and what was permitted by regulation were difficult to assemble. More recent studies have taken advantage of the intervening rise in geographic information systems (GIS), so that researchers can determine just what land forms influence house prices. Margaret Walls, Carolyn Kousky, and Ziyan Chu (2013), for example, find that views of farmland enhance residential values more than views of forest lands. The wider availability on the Internet of local prices for housing and (to a much lesser extent) raw land also has facilitated more general explorations. Econometric techniques have likewise developed to test for endogeneity and (to a lesser extent) correct the biases created by the fact that zoning policies are influenced by those who benefit from them.

There are still plenty of local studies that find that zoning raises housing prices. Among the more convincing are those produced by Edward L. Glaeser and Bryce A. Ward (2009) and Jeffrey Zabel and Maurice Dalton (2011), both of which use Boston-area samples and detailed land use information. But the biggest change has come from the development of metropolitan indexes of land use regulation. The best-known of these is the national survey of residential housing prices created by Joseph Gyourko, Albert Saiz, and Anita Summers (2008). They produced the Wharton Residential Land Use Regulation Index (the Wharton Index), which updated and improved an index from an earlier project. They compressed the results of extensive and complex nationwide surveys of planning officials to a single number.

My description of the zoning process in chapter 2, which emphasized the many devices available to regulate land use, makes the Wharton effort seem heroic. I have read many studies that purport to measure the stringency of zoning by focusing on a few variables such as lot size and height limitations, and they seem inadequate to the task of comparing one community's regulations to another. The Wharton group was aware of such problems and undertook a substantial effort to overcome them with multiple data sets and statistical techniques such as factor analysis.

One can quibble with some of the questions on the Wharton Index survey. Officials are asked whether there are annual limits on the number of building permits for housing construction. Questions about how high the limits are relative to the current stock and whether the limits have ever been reached are not asked. But that really is a quibble. A community that would go to the trouble of enacting any limits at all is surely under growth pressure and interested in limiting it. Asking the busy planners to whom the surveys were sent to look up the relevant numbers would surely have reduced the response rate.

Somewhat more serious was the Wharton group's treatment of exactions. Most of their questions regarding the use of land use exactions treated them as being indicators of anti-development activity. I have in previous chapters (especially section 3.26) argued that exactions are a means of reducing the stringency of regulation by allowing developers to compensate the community for relaxing them. Prohibiting exactions would most likely make communities keep stringent regulations in place, a position with which at least one of the Wharton group (Gyourko 1991) seems to agree. But again, the actual use of exactions is probably less important than their very existence. Communities without much development pressure, or those dominated by rural landowners, or those whose fixed costs are spread over so few residents that they welcome new development are not likely to have gone to the trouble of adopting impact fees or other formalized exactions. Byron Lutz (2015) found that New Hampshire communities that were under growth pressure adopted exactions and impact fees (as permitted by state law) as an alternative to just stopping growth.

8.14 The Deeper Problem with Surveys

The Wharton Index is one of several comparative measures of zoning that have been developed in the last two decades or so (Stephen Malpezzi 1996; Raven Saks 2008). The indexes differ in methods and emphasis, but their common finding is that more regulation is closely associated with higher housing prices. Larger metropolitan areas in the Northeast and the West Coast stand out for their higher prices and more thorough regulations in all cases. Other studies using smaller samples but more detailed data from individual metropolitan areas are consistent with this generalization (Mayer and Somerville 2000; Kok, Monkkonen, and Quigley 2014).

The common results raise another issue. These indexes imply that a sample of municipalities within a metropolitan area could be aggregated to a meaningful index of restrictiveness for the metropolitan area as a whole. My skepticism of adding up responses from varied cities and suburbs was the product of my Tiebout view of the world, which sees communities as providing different levels and types of services to attract residents. Eric Heikkila's (1996) examination of Los Angeles suburbs revealed that they were as different from one another as from the central city along many dimensions; I also found this to be the case in the Seattle area (Fischel 2001), as did John McDonald and Daniel McMillen (2004) in Chicago. Besides this, the central city and suburbs have long been at odds over exclusionary zoning. Adding these disparate communities up to make a single metropolitan index did not make sense to me.

Yet regardless of the particulars of the indexes and their level of aggregation, the results seem to defy intrametropolitan variations. There are more heavily regulated metropolitan areas, and they are concentrated in the Northeast and the West Coast. The statistical associations are all the same: The higher the metropolitan regulatory index, the higher the housing prices. Even when one adds measures of topographic restraints (mountains and water bodies), the regulatory barriers still come through (Louis Rose 1989; Albert Saiz 2010). (I would, however, second Thomas Davidoff's [2014] observation that mountains and water bodies stimulate the demand for regulation by homeowners who like nice views and other benefits of proximity to them. It is also likely that developers offer less political resistance to regulation in areas that are costly to build on, like mountainsides and wetlands.)

The common results suggest to me that the particulars of an index do not matter too much. The irrelevance of exactly what one counts is consistent with my view that rising home values themselves create a demand for regulation, which further accelerates the rise in housing prices. The main source of my initial skepticism about the indexes—regulatory variety among municipalities within the metropolitan areas—is overwhelmed by the common trend in regional housing prices and the urge to protect and enhance home values in almost all communities.

8.15 The Agglomeration Problem: Density versus Size

In his popular book, *Triumph of the City,* Edward Glaeser (2011) promotes the economic power of agglomeration economies. His is not just a fan book for urban life. Its theme is that cities themselves should be regarded as economic engines, in the same sense that the modern corporation and the Internet are institutions that facilitate economic growth. Agglomeration economies are to a large extent examples of spontaneous order, but, as Glaeser argues, public policies can enhance or subvert them.

As I mentioned in chapter 1, agglomeration economies come in two flavors, density and size. Density promotes the multifaceted, face-to-face interactions that are required for trust and nuanced communications. Economic and scientific innovations thrive on close communication, to mention only one advantage. Larger size, on the other hand, promotes specialization and the division of labor and refinement of consumption opportunities. Glaeser criticizes national urban policies that hold down both of these dimensions. Undue restrictions on building higher, such as those in New York and Calcutta, are excoriated. Development policies that try to keep rural people from migrating to urban areas are seen as misguided.

I am certainly not going to gainsay Glaeser's views about the virtues of cities. What seems debatable to me is his unifying rationale for action to promote urbanization: It is to deal with global climate change, which is generally regarded as the product of excessive production of carbon dioxide. His analysis is sound, and the evidence in support of urbanization's beneficial effects on reducing greenhouse gases is supportive of his position (William Meyer 2013). Higher-density homes and offices, especially those in multifamily units, use less energy to heat and cool. More important, higher density generally promotes less daily travel, and it is automobile travel especially that contributes to carbon dioxide emissions. (Glaeser concedes that these problems would be best dealt with by a national carbon tax, but I assume he regards this as politically unlikely and so has embraced the second-best approach.) And, as several people have pointed out, the most constricting rules on density seem to be in coastal California, where the climate is conducive to low energy requirements for heating and cooling buildings. If we really want to control greenhouse gasses, a much larger fraction of the American population should live in high-rise condos between the Pacific Coast and the Coast Ranges of California. (Eastward of the Coast Ranges, the climate is not appreciably different from Las Vegas and Phoenix, and the benefits of natural air conditioning are lost.)

The problem with Glaeser's attention to global warming is that it seems to privilege density over size. Density can be achieved without having urban areas grow much at all. Many suburban towns in exclusive areas have adopted plans that increase the density of development. The town of Acton, the archetype of the developing suburb in chapter 7, has cluster zoning that encourages developers to build homes close together, and it has established several urban centers to encourage infill development near existing commercial and transportation nodes. But in most cases, the increased density in one area is offset by decreased density in another. The smaller lots in cluster zones do not relieve the developer of the multi-acre minimum lot sizes. She must arrange to have the unused land preserved from development, usually in perpetuity.

8.16 "Garden Cities of Tomorrow" Would Work if Tomorrow Were 1905

The ideal of small but high density seems to grip much of the planning profession. It manifests itself in the "new urbanism" (discussed in section 2.13), which idealizes high-density mixed uses but at a small scale. The intellectual antecedent of this ideal appears to be the "garden cities" movement, whose chief promoter was Ebenezer Howard (1902). Howard envisioned small-city development that would solve the problems of slums not by pushing people out to rural areas (which he did not idealize) but by building small cities outside of existing urban centers. These cities were to be compact and self-contained in that people were expected to reside, work, shop, and otherwise entertain themselves within their precincts. Self-containment was a necessary bow to transportation constraints in the pre-automobile age. Workers had to walk to work, so jobs had to be nearby. Shoppers did not have cars to haul their purchases, so shopping had to be closely integrated with residences.

Garden cities did not allow for much in the way of agglomeration economies of size. They did have specialized areas, but the general population was expected to live and work in the same small city. There certainly are advantages to such a life. I live in a small town in which I can (and do) walk to work, shopping, and entertainment. It is nice (usually) to have several neighboring homes visible from my own and pleasant to have serendipitous encounters with my neighbors and random pedestrians. But housing urban populations in such towns would lose a great deal of the urban agglomeration advantages that come from a large city. Student-centered liberal arts colleges can thrive in small town environments, but major research universities usually require a sizable city. (The exceptions are those state university campuses that in effect create their own city by virtue of their enormous enrollments.) The agglomeration benefits of a large city cannot be captured by distributing people into a collection of small, compact towns.

On a larger scale, urban growth boundaries such as that of Portland do promote higher densities. The problem with Portland's urban growth boundary is not its ideal of promoting infill and transit-oriented development. It is its inhibition on overall growth. Businesses are deterred from moving to places with high housing prices, however nice the downtown might be, and the exclusion of growth outside the growth boundaries makes business expansion more difficult. To promote the agglomeration economies of size, Portland needs to be more like Atlanta, which grows rapidly but spreads out at what many believe are excessively low densities. The difficulty is that the planning ideals of high-density, transit-oriented development are at odds with the demands of so many households.

Part of the problem is a misperception of the density that can be obtained with single-family development. Suburban development of single-family homes on modest-sized lots will get gross density almost as high as that of most existing central cities. The gross density of Daly City, the suburb adjacent to San Francisco, is 13,000 per square mile, almost as high as that of the city of San Francisco itself (18,000). Daly City, however, was the subject of the scornful song "Little Boxes," which mocked life in the suburbs. I have seen pictures of Daly City offered as the epitome of sprawl, when it is almost exactly the opposite in terms of its intense use of suburban land. No similar song has been written to mock the even smaller boxes of infill condominiums in Ballard, a trendy section of Seattle; indeed, they are praised as the epitome of responsible urban living. Yet only a tiny fraction of the population would demand such small quarters, and then only for a brief period of their lives. If planners want to have a serious effect on urban sprawl, they need to embrace the high-density single-family communities of Daly City, Levittown, and Shaker Heights, along with fashionable downtown apartments and condominiums.

It is evident from privately developed planned communities such as Reston, Virginia, Columbia, Maryland, and Foster City, California, that many suburbanites are willing to live in relatively high-density communities as long as they get good public amenities, especially safety. The gross densities—including all land uses, not just housing—range from about 4,000 (Reston and Columbia at its projected completion) to 7,000 (Foster City) persons per square mile. These are on the order of twice the gross density of the suburban parts of most urbanized areas. At the lower-end density—Reston and Columbia—this implies about two-fifths of an acre per household, which, by the usual rule of thumb that has residential as half of all uses, works out to a net density of one-fifth acre per household.

The relatively high densities of these affluent places might, with further investigation, form a useful benchmark for calculating efficient suburban densities. This is because the developers of privately planned communities have a strong incentive to internalize all spillover effects within their territory (Fischel 1994). That is, developers have to pay attention to both the beneficial and adverse effects of each land use on its neighbors' values because the developers initially own all the property. Without that incentive, public planners may neglect the opportunity cost of open space and low-density development. Furthermore, most of the open spaces of Reston, Columbia, and Foster City are actually open to the public, in contrast to the mostly privately owned open spaces (the backyards) in low-density suburbs.

8.17 Measuring Benefits and Costs of Land Use Regulation: The Zoning Haystack

The case for and against various zoning regimes can be framed by reference to figure 8.3, which I call the zoning haystack. The vertical axis measures the total value of land in a community, counting both developed and undeveloped land. The community has borders expansive enough to be able to internalize both the costs of the necessary nuisances of life such as landfills, commercial establishments, and transportation facilities. It can also internalize most of the benefits of desirable uses such as parks, gardens, and nature preserves. This means that some of the land within its borders can remain relatively undeveloped, and some could be intensively developed. (As a technical note, the vertical axis in figure 8.3 is the cumulative sum of the "marginal benefit" curves in the previous entitlements diagrams in chapter 6 and 7. Articles exploring the community land-value maximization criterion include those by Pines and Weiss [1976], Sonstelie and Portney [1978], Susan Rose-Ackerman [1979], and Jan Brueckner [1983].)

The community considered in figure 8.3 does not have to encompass its entire metropolitan area. If it did, the possibility of monopoly gains would have to be discounted, though in the free-migration, "open city" model, there would be little to monopolize. Having many small governments might also give rise to adverse spillovers on other communities—the noxious factory placed on the downwind border—but I have argued that these are not likely to be important among close neighbors (Fischel 2001). The "haystack" also does not account for the beneficial spillover effects of increased employment on a wider area, though state government officials might be expected to respond to such effects.

The idea behind the horizontal axis of figure 8.3 is to aggregate and summarize the conceptual approaches of chapters 6 and 7. Chapter 6 began with an individualized conflict for specific properties, the hotels in Miami and the Clem development in West Lebanon, New Hampshire. The paradigm for chapter 7 was a larger community, Acton, Massachusetts, and that is the same unit shown in the zoning haystack. What is different in the present diagram is the allowance for a variety of uses, not just residential development. This means that there is value added not just by building more housing, but by

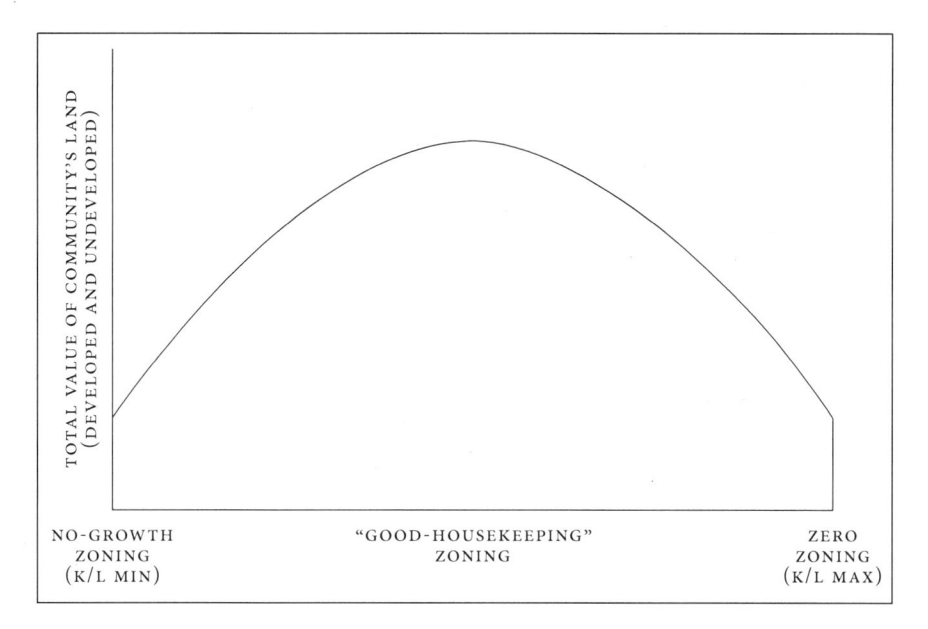

FIGURE 8.3 The Zoning Haystack

[Graph: horizontal axis labeled NO-GROWTH ZONING (K/L MIN), "GOOD-HOUSEKEEPING" ZONING, ZERO ZONING (K/L MAX); vertical axis labeled TOTAL VALUE OF COMMUNITY'S LAND (DEVELOPED AND UNDEVELOPED)]

good planning as well. This idea is embodied by the three approaches to land use regulation indicated on the horizontal axis.

The first is "no-growth" zoning. Its ideal is the status quo of the community before the no-growth policy was adopted. The role of planners is simply to make that work. Its devices include multi-acre minimum lot sizes, exclusive agricultural zoning, and conservation easements. Residential development of any sort is minimized. All new businesses are excluded except perhaps those that serve current neighborhood demands.

The total value of land in the community is not zero in the no-growth regime. Indeed, the value of individual homes and businesses might be comparatively high. In arriving at the total value, however, the enhanced value of existing homes is offset by the diminished value of land that cannot be developed. This is the advantage of using land value as a metric for evaluating planning regimes. Development-minded owners of vacant land do not just consider the demands of those who already live in the community. They have to think about potential residents and businesses, and most of these live outside the community in the larger metropolitan area or in the nation (and other nations) as a whole. Developers do not have an unerring ear for such demands, of course. My only contention is that they, more than established residents, have a stronger incentive to think about the interests of potential residents who are not presently part of the community.

The peak of the zoning haystack occurs in the region I have called the "good-housekeeping" model. It has two qualities: a place for everything, and everything in its place. Like all models, it is a great simplification. It is not necessary to literally have a place for nuclear waste facilities and luxury estates in each community. There can be community specialization that, as long as invidious racial, religious, or ethnic exclusion is forbidden, can create metropolitan areas of interesting mosaics. But it does rule out, or at least make costly to accomplish, land use planning that forbids reasonable expansion of the uses in which it has specialized and those that augment their functions.

The "everything in its place" endorses the traditional separation of uses by zones. Some modern planning theories dismiss this feature of Euclidean zoning. As described in chapter 2, the new urbanism, smart growth, transect zoning, and transit-oriented development (TOD) envision much greater mixing than the standard zoning classifications allow. I think all of these are desirable innovations—in their place. What remains unaddressed in all of them is the need to quell the anxieties by homebuyers that the plans they see when they purchase might be changed without substantial input by themselves or their successors in title. The original impetus to zoning was, I argued at length in chapter 5, the concern by homebuyers that their investment will be degraded by community decisions beyond their control. They fear that zoning by professionals who are beyond their control could push their neighborhood over the top of the haystack and lower the value of their investment.

The value-reducing aspect of modern planning theories is not what it proposes to build but what it prevents being built. Transit-oriented development works fine for people who do not want to own cars (or want one instead of two per household), but it should not come at the expense of traditional neighborhoods in which residences are kept separate from businesses and other potentially incompatible uses. It may be the case that transit-oriented development cannot succeed if people are given the choice between dense and mixed-use housing near the station and single-family neighborhoods. But that argument is its own worst enemy. If a plan can succeed only by limiting the choices of competent adults, it is apt to fail on most liberal criteria for well-being as well on the test of Tiebout migration.

The right side of the haystack is called "zero zoning." It does not entirely lack regulation. Private covenants, community associations, and traditional nuisance law are available, as are social norms and self-help remedies ("Paint me!"). These can produce high-value neighborhoods, but as the experience of communities in the post-automobile but pre-zoning world suggests, this can result in value-reducing developments. The experience of Houston indicates that land values will hardly fall to zero, but Houston has enough ad-hoc land use regulation to make it an imperfect test of the "no-zoning" world. At the close of chapter 1, I made a brief case for the benefits of urban land use regulation. Cities are powerful engines of economic growth, so powerful that there are inevitable pressures to make small compromises in the quality of life, the cumulative effect of which can be corrosive. Without some check on private behavior, the uncoordinated efforts of developers are apt to mix incompatible uses excessively and build too intensively.

8.18 Conclusion: Segregation, Sprawl, and Inequality

In the 1994 edition of their textbook *Urban Economics*, Edwin Mills and Bruce Hamilton wrote, "Beyond a doubt, suburban-zoning provisions are consistent with the demands of most of the people who would live there, even in the absence of zoning regulations" (414). The consensus of economists in the intervening 20 years has shifted away from the view that zoning more or less mirrors what the market would have provided without it. This is not to say that zoning is not the product of popular demand. My thesis in the present book—a position only implicit in the 1985 edition—is that modern zoning regulations of the growth-control variety are the product of political markets that respond to economic concerns. These economic concerns have become paramount because of the enormous importance of home values in most residents' asset portfolios. Over the last fifty years, homes have transformed from domiciles to investments, and residents have been converted from homeowners to homevoters.

American land use regulation causes three major problems. It excessively segregates the population by income and class and, mainly as a result of the first two, also by race; it causes metropolitan areas to be more spread out than is efficient, contributing to excessive commuting, housing consumption, and air pollution; and it inhibits American economic growth and equality by retarding the migration of people to high-productivity urban areas. The next chapter will address reforms that might help solve these problems.

CHAPTER 9

Remedial Strategies for Excess Regulation

This chapter reviews some of the reforms for the excesses of land use regulation. The most-discussed reform is actually the least used: the regulatory takings doctrine. I consider its theoretical virtues, to which I have subscribed, and then offer some reasons that the state courts have been so wary of adopting them. The takings doctrine is likely to remain at the edges of zoning reform because its boundaries are not judicially manageable.

The key to reform is to understand that zoning is not the product of top-down policies. The bottom-up, demand-side sources of zoning and its evolution require reforms that moderate the demand for exclusionary regulation by homeowners. Chief among these is to make homeownership a less important part of the voters' financial portfolios. One way to do this is to reduce the mortgage interest deduction. The deduction induces people with savings to devote too much of it to housing, which in turn makes them overly sensitive to zoning changes.

Reducing transaction costs between developers and local officials is another way to deal with excessive restriction. The legal and cultural barriers to this have diminished in the last 30 years, but transaction costs have been raised by the environmental justice movement and by the Supreme Court's exactions jurisprudence. The most helpful role for the federal government would be to stop providing devices for third parties to intervene in local decisions and thus raise the transaction costs of development.

9.1 Regulatory Takings as a Remedy for Growth Controls

In a 1977 article in the *Yale Law Journal*, Robert Ellickson examined the problem of suburban growth controls through the then-novel application of both economics and law. Ellickson saw the problem as a combination of the success of politics and the failure of law. Residents of suburban communities in which there is plenty of room to grow seize the political apparatus and adopt regulations whose intention is to thwart further development.

This is political success, since the majority gets exactly what it wants. The dark stories of the theory of public choice, in which a small but well-organized faction prevails over majority interests, apply less often in the low-population, upper-income suburban communities that adopt anti-growth regulations. The majoritarian regulations raise the value of existing homes, but they frustrate the aspirations of would-be community residents, developers of homes in the community, and owners of undeveloped land.

Most scholars who analyzed excessive suburban zoning approached it as a problem to be addressed by a higher level of government (Anthony Downs 1973). The states, or, more wishfully, a regional government should take control of land use regulation and make the local governments behave better. Ellickson saw the solution in a different light. He sought a legal approach to remedying exclusionary zoning. Instead of empowering a higher-level government to make municipalities take their share of development, Ellickson saw development-minded landowners as a better locus for the remedy. These landowners should, under Ellickson's theory, be able to collect monetary damages for regulations that defeat projects that would let the community grow.

The novelties of Ellickson's proposal were three: its focus on landowner rights, its remedy of monetary damages, and its adaptation of the old "harm/benefit" rule to modern circumstances to provide a baseline against which compensation should be measured. (I have elaborated on Ellickson's approach in Fischel [1995].) Landowners need rights because they are the economic representatives of people who would like to live and work in the community. Potential residents themselves are poorly organized politically, since most of them do not even know that an opportunity has been denied them. The landowner does not represent their interest *pro bono*, of course. She is in the business of development to make money. But in a competitive market, the price she charges for her services will leave substantial benefits to the buyers. (Economists call this benefit "consumers' surplus," the difference between the maximum they would be willing to pay and the price the market actually charges.) Protecting landowner rights in a competitive market is, Ellickson correctly argued, a good way to protect the rights of would-be residents.

Ellickson's second innovation in the growth-control debate was monetary damages. Landowners often go to court to combat land use regulations, and sometimes they win. The problem is that the courts usually give injunctive remedies, which say in effect, "Do not apply that particular zoning law." This often is no more than a ticket to sue again. The community modifies the law only slightly, or it erects another roadblock farther along in the process, and the developer does not get her project anyway. The problem as Ellickson saw it was that the community faced no penalty for delay. The developer's banker keeps charging her interest on loans used to purchase land, so delay is a big cost to her. Not so for the community. Since maintenance of the status quo is its goal, delay almost always works in its favor.

Monetary damages also can influence the community's choice between taking and regulation. As I proposed in chapter 6, the community can be thought of as a firm that chooses between two inputs—regulation and compensated acquisition—in providing for local public goods such as open space. This choice is influenced heavily by the relative costs of the two means of accomplishing the desired goal. If the cost of regulation is too low compared to acquisition, too much regulation will be chosen.

Ellickson proposed that the Takings Clauses of the U.S. and state constitutions be used as the basis for litigation about suburban growth controls and exclusionary zoning generally. The virtue of the clause is that, unlike other constitutional bases for property rights, the Takings Clause is a right with a remedy attached: "[N]or shall private property be taken for public use without just compensation." If undeveloped land is being pressed into service by the community to promote its collective desire to avoid growth (or, putting it more positively, to preserve open space), this may be a permissible "public use," but it should require just compensation. In other words, if a community is going to downzone a large amount of property, it can do so as long as it pays for the owner's loss in value. The obligation to pay makes the community think very hard about whether downzoning is worthwhile. Facing an out-of-pocket cost would discourage most growth-control schemes that did not meet benefit-cost criteria.

9.2 Resurrecting the "Harm-Benefit" Criterion

Ellickson's third contribution to regulatory takings theory was to update the ancient distinction between noncompensable harm-prevention regulations and fully compensable benefit-extraction regulations (Ernst Freund 1904; Ellickson 1973). This "harm/benefit" test was the traditional border between the police power (meaning government's regulatory authority), which did not require compensation, and the exercise of eminent domain, which clearly did require compensation.

The harm/benefit test suffered two insults over the twentieth century. One was the decline of the common law of nuisance as a remedy for neighborhood disputes. The term "nuisance" always denoted a harmful activity, and so legitimate police-power regulations were easy to identify. They prevented nuisances, and no one thought the perpetrator of a nuisance (read: a harm) ought to be paid not to do it.

The most serious blow to nuisance was the rise of zoning laws in the period 1910–1930. As I argued in chapter 5, zoning was the product of bottom-up demand for protection of residential neighborhoods from the inroads of businesses and apartments whose developers were made footloose by the self-propelled motor truck and bus. But, as my discussion of *Hadacheck v. Los Angeles* (the brickmaker case) in chapter 5 indicated, most businesses and apartments would never have been found to be nuisances in the common law. In upholding zoning laws, the state and federal courts jettisoned the nuisance analogy. As a result, the police power was set adrift from nuisance and harm-prevention. Under zoning, most regulations that reduce the value of developable land do not entail compensation, even when the proposed use cannot be regarded as a nuisance except under the most imaginative stretch of the language.

Language-stretching is the other source of the harm/benefit distinction's demise. Here the demolition was propelled by the economic analysis of law. Valuation in economic theory is both subjective and relativistic. A cost is not just a cost, it is an opportunity cost. The opportunity cost of x is forgoing the benefit of y; the opportunity cost of my writing this chapter is the time that I could be spending with my family on this pleasant weekend. Applied to the law, the concept of opportunity cost caused economists to denigrate the harm/benefit distinction. Preventing a harm is, after all, a social benefit, and foregoing a benefit can likewise be thought of as a harm.

Ellickson attempted to restore the harm/benefit distinction by recasting it in a context that appealed to norms of behavior. Noncompensable harms should be thought of as "subnormal" behavior. Such behavior is to be evaluated not just by what the actor does, but by the context (time and location) in which he does it. The advantage here is that it fights the relativism that undermines the term "harm." An apartment house is not a harm in and of itself. It depends where it is to be built. Constructing one in a neighborhood of single-family homes might be considered subnormal behavior, while building one next to a commuter railway station would not.

Ellickson would thus disallow compensation for developers who proposed something in the context-driven "subnormal" category. The logic of his rule, however, demands that governments that require developers to submit to "supernormal" standards, or those above what their current citizens have imposed on themselves (as evidenced by the type of housing they occupy or by metropolitan-wide norms), should be required to compensate landowners if the authorities choose not to modify the regulations.

Semi-rural communities that are in the path of development and want to downzone their rural land from three- to ten-acre minimum lot size in order to prevent development of homes of the type in which existing residents live would be prime candidates for a regulatory takings suit (Fischel 1995). The burden of regulation often falls on farmland owners who end up with devalued property whose benefits redound to a residential majority (Jesse Richardson 2004; Liu and Lynch 2011). The owners of the undeveloped land would collect monetary damages equal to the devaluation of their land by the downzoning. The community would have the option of rescinding the downzoning (and paying temporary damages for the time they were in place) or paying for the lost development rights and acquiring a permanent easement in them. Ellickson's nuanced application of the takings principle would allow communities to preserve open space, but local taxpayers would have to face the opportunity cost of doing so in most cases.

9.3 The Limited Application of Just Compensation

My review of U.S. Supreme Court decisions in chapter 3 did not mention any applications of the regulatory takings doctrine to suburban growth controls. That is because there are none. This would not have disappointed Ellickson, as he conceived of his principles as being applied by the state courts, not the federal courts. In this respect, Ellickson and the U.S. Supreme

Court seem mostly in agreement, and my discussion in chapter 3 of the problems courts have in obtaining local knowledge would support this hands-off policy. The U.S. Court has provided only the broadest parameters to takings jurisprudence and seems eager for the state courts to decide local land use controversies.

What is more surprising is that the state courts have, if anything, tried to avoid regulatory takings, especially at the local level, in almost all cases. In my 1995 book, I made a distinction (like Ellickson's) between regulations made by local government and by state and national governments. Local governments are more prone to majoritarian abuse of owners of developable land, and land lacks the mobility protection that tempers local regulation of more portable assets. (A more recent exposition of this view is Chris Serkin's [2007].) I did marvel in section 8.2 at how long it takes for newcomers to displace old-timers as exurban land changes from rural to suburban, but the political takeover is almost inevitable.

As Carol Rose (2006) observed in a sympathetic overview, no court of law has accepted this distinction between local and higher-government policies. Regulatory takings has remained a cudgel with which to threaten—without much effect—government initiatives at all levels. A few years ago (actually, more than a decade), Bob Ellickson told me that he knew of no state court that had deployed regulatory takings to rein in growth controls, and my reading of the casebook of which he is the lead author (Ellickson et al. 2013) did not uncover any cases or discussion of such instances. There are state courts that will come to the aid of development-minded landowners—Pennsylvania and Illinois are among the more prominent—but their remedy is injunctive rather than monetary. Sometimes the prevailing plaintiff will be awarded legal fees, but damages for devaluation are very elusive. The U.S. Supreme Court's constitutional floor for regulatory takings—no physical invasion and some scintilla of economic use—has become in effect the ceiling in the state courts.

State courts may be reluctant to embrace regulatory takings for a number of reasons. I will evaluate some of the economic reasons below, but political prudence should be mentioned. As was described in chapter 3, state courts that were hostile to zoning in its early years were sometimes reversed by constitutional amendments that specifically authorized zoning. State judges are also often subject to electoral pressures to which Article III federal judges are immune. The New Jersey Supreme Court began its open-the-suburbs campaign with *Southern Burlington County NAACP v. Township of Mount*

Laurel, 336 A.2d 713 (N.J. 1975). In 1983, the New Jersey court became more aggressive and set up special judicial panels that awarded rezonings to builders who were willing to build a mix of market-rate and low-income housing (456 A.2d 390). David Kirp, John P. Dwyer, and Larry Rosenthal (1995) indicate that the state legislature was strongly disinclined to reappoint Chief Justice Robert Willentz, who had backed the *Mount Laurel* rulings, unless he revised his position and upheld the legislation that in large part undermined the *Mount Laurel* fair-share remedy.

It is also possible that state courts are skittish about regulatory takings for the same reason that the federal courts are. Judges at the state capital are almost as far removed from local controversies as federal judges are. The state judges might reasonably fear that they will be overwhelmed by regulatory takings controversies, especially if they embrace *Penn Central's* "essentially ad hoc, factual inquiries" for deciding even appellate cases (438 U.S. 104 [1978], 124). Whatever else might be muddy about the Supreme Court's regulatory takings jurisprudence, it is clear that it does not want to become the "Universal Board of Zoning Appeals," as Carol Rose (2006) put it. It is quite possible that many state courts shrink from the same prospect.

9.4 The Unloveliness of Liability Rules

It is notable that even when the government offers to pay, the offer is not received happily by property owners. Bethany Berger (2009, 1313) indicated that in the sole instance in which a property owner was compensated under Oregon's Measure 37 (discussed in section 6.14), as an alternative to simply rescinding the regulation, the couple reacted with "fury." They wanted to develop, not to be paid to forego development.

At a much broader level, the idea of compensation was tested by the state of Pennsylvania in its attempt to promote oil and gas exploration by the technique popularly known as "fracking" (Joshua Fershee 2014). Western Pennsylvania is underlain by the Marcellus shale from which vast amounts of natural gas could be extracted using the new technique. Gas developers were concerned that the many independent local governments in Pennsylvania would use local zoning and other regulations to stymie extraction activities. Governor Tom Corbett ran for office with a promise to adopt statewide legislation to overcome this patchwork of yes-no-maybe regulation. The state legislature complied with what looked like the will of the people by enacting Act 13. The legislation provided for an elaborate plan of compensation for localities that hosted fracking operations, but the municipal governments could not use their regulations to ban fracking even in areas that were zoned residential. (The override of residential zoning sounds extreme, but it may have been included to forestall localities that wanted to stop fracking from extending residential zoning to the entire community.)

Instead of gratefully accepting the apparently substantial impact fees (the revenue was twice that of a proposed statewide tax on gas extraction), a large number of Pennsylvania municipalities joined in litigation to overturn Act 13. More surprising was that the Pennsylvania Supreme Court agreed with the municipal plaintiffs. In *Robinson Township v. Commonwealth of Pennsylvania*, 803 A.3d 901 (Pa. 2013), the court overturned almost all of Act 13's provisions, pointing especially to its disregard for local zoning authority. The decision represented an extraordinary about-face by the state court in matters of local government. Like most state courts, Pennsylvania had long regarded municipal governments and their powers as inferior to state legislation. The legal mantra has always been that local governments are "creatures of the state," and the implication was that the state could take back powers that it had delegated to the localities.

The apparent demise (as of this writing) of Pennsylvania's Act 13 should caution calls to adopt a system of impact fees in order to override other forms of zoning. Many economists would agree with Edward Glaeser's (2011) offhanded recommendation in *Triumph of the City* that the land use regulatory process should be replaced with "a simple system of fees, much like congestion tolls, that cover whatever social costs there are from taller buildings and other consequences of increasing urban density" (161). My approval in chapter 3 (and in Fischel 1987) of a relatively unconstrained exactions process as a way to get development done would seem to be largely in line with Glaeser's view.

But there is a substantial difference between an exaction whose schedule and terms are imposed on a community by the state (like those of Pennsylvania's Act 13) and an exaction whose terms are set by the community itself. This difference has to do with the nature of entitlement protection. Section 6.5 reviewed the difference between what scholars call a "property rule" and a "liability rule" as protections of legal entitlements. Property rules allow the owner to refuse to trade or make whatever deal he might want. A liability rule allows the owner to refuse only if the prospective purchaser is unwilling to pay the market value as determined by a third party such as a court or an appraisal board.

What is a little less obvious is that traditional zoning allows municipalities to have property rule protection against those who would seek a change in land use regulations. Communities do not have to exchange their one-acre minimum lot size requirement for cash, no matter how much money or other benefits a would-be developer offers. Indeed, there is often hostility to the very idea of exchange, but that has diminished since the use of air-pollution exchanges in "cap and trade" systems has become widespread. The complaints about Act 13 were not so much about "selling the environment," as might have been heard decades earlier. (The state court did invoke, however, Pennsylvania's hortatory environmental rights clause in its constitution to buttress its decision.) The problem was that required impact fees such as those of Pennsylvania's Act 13 alter local zoning's entitlement protection. Instead of the just-say-no option of a property rule, the municipality is given a just-take-the-money-and-shut-up liability rule.

9.5 The *Kelo* Reaction Shows a Preference for Property Rules

Most people prefer to have property rule protection for their property. Liability rules are accepted grudgingly, as when the action is irreversible (the car was destroyed) or when the government wants the property for public use. The public use requirement for takings was tested by *Kelo v. New London*, 545 U.S. 469 (2005). The city planned to clear a large tract of homes and businesses and sell it to private developers as part of its attempt to retain and attract industry. Ms. Kelo had resisted the taking of her home by eminent domain by New London's redevelopment agency. Eminent domain is the classic case of a liability rule protection for the landowner: Ms. Kelo was entitled to keep her property unless the city paid her the market value of the home, which it was willing to do. Her complaint was that the city was not using her land for a true public use, since the development would ultimately be privately owned, and that she was thus entitled to property rule protection. (She did not say "property rule protection," which is an academic law term, but her insistence on the right to refuse to sell meant exactly that.)

The U.S. Supreme Court held for the city, which reflected its long string of precedents on the matter of public use. The Court defers to legislative determinations of public use in almost all cases, and it has done so for many years. Public use is an area in which state courts are often more aggressive in reviewing legislative determinations than they are in regulatory takings, but the Connecticut courts had also upheld New London's taking with compensation.

The interesting thing about *Kelo* was not the holding but the reaction. What almost all legal scholars saw as a run-of-the-mill decision was greeted by the general public with alarm and indignation. It was, figuratively speaking, a national "Say what? They think it's okay to take a poor lady's little house and hand it over to a private corporation?" Justice Sandra Day O'Connor's caustic dissenting opinion ("Nothing is to prevent the State from replacing any Motel 6 with a Ritz-Carlton, any home with a shopping mall, or any farm with a factory" [546 U.S. at 503]) was widely disseminated, and Suzette Kelo proved to be an angry and effective speaker for the cause of limiting eminent domain. Adverse reaction cut across political parties and most ideological divides. The popular reaction was followed by considerable state legislation, including several voter initiatives, which have narrowed the range of eminent domain activity (Andrew Morriss 2009).

In a few states, voter initiatives were also proposed to expand the scope of compensation for regulatory takings, but these were much less successful. Property rights advocates were somewhat puzzled by this bifurcated response. Among the least likely threats to one's property is to have it taken by eminent domain for something other than a well-settled public use. Hired by a conservative think-tank to investigate eminent domain abuse, attorney Michael Malamut (2000) systematically examined more than 500 cases in the Boston area during the 1990s. He could find nothing more than minor recording and administrative errors in the eminent domain process. Examples of dubious *Kelo*-style takings could not be found. It is not difficult to understand why governments are normally disinclined to use eminent domain when market purchases are feasible. Eminent domain proceedings are costly to the government in terms of direct outlays for appraisers and attorneys, and local political backlash often derails dubious projects (Thomas Merrill 1986). The worst abuses, I have argued, come from projects that are financed by earmarked funds from higher governments and for which local taxpayers are insulated from the costs (Fischel 2004c).

Land use regulation, by contrast, is ubiquitous and has occasioned innumerable complaints among scholars and practitioners about its excesses. Why doesn't the public express similar outrage about regulatory horror stories? The answer may be that most people regard land use regulations as having benefits as well as costs. Zoning regulations enhance property values related to the quiet enjoyment of one's home, which is the sort of property most people own. The enterprise use of property is of interest to relatively few development-minded landowners, and then usually only episodically. The risk of losing one's property to eminent domain is something most people sympathize with, since it involves the loss of quiet enjoyment. Homeowners of all political persuasions felt Suzette Kelo's well-publicized pain, and state legislators and initiative voters responded accordingly if not always coherently (Ilya Somin 2008). (I visited the Kelo site, and her "little pink house" did indeed have a wonderful view of Long Island Sound. My students who looked into the controversy before it reached the U.S. Supreme Court also reported that the city agency itself had doubts about the merits of the redevelopment project, which has subsequently been deemed a failure.)

9.6 Regulatory Takings: A Personal Journey

In 1985 I took a leave of absence from Dartmouth and spent a year teaching economics at the University of California at Santa Barbara. I had just published the first version of this book and was looking for additional projects on land use issues. One of my friends in the economics department there, Perry Shapiro, recommended I visit a friend of his in the UCSB sociology department who was also interested in land use. It was Harvey Molotch, whose views of land use regulation were that they were dominated by the "growth machine" (1976) of pro-development public officials and were as a result way too permissive. My view was quite the opposite. Whatever growth machine had been operating in Santa Barbara and other cities in California seemed to have been stymied by popular initiatives and a court system that had years before turned against development (Hanke and Carbonell 1978; Joseph diMento et al. 1980). It did not sound promising for us to collaborate. (But see my belated appreciation of Molotch's original insight above in section 8.4.) I instead started talking with Perry about an article he had written with two other economists, Lawrence Blume and Daniel Rubinfeld (and Shapiro 1984).

The startling conclusion of their article was that "just compensation" for takings was economically inefficient. The source of inefficiency was a form of moral hazard that is created by the expectation of being compensated. Their scenario involved a landowner who has some idea that a government project might take his land. The landowner has to make a decision as to whether to commit some irreversible (or too costly to remove) capital to the land. If he knows he will not be compensated, he places the investment elsewhere. If he knows that compensation is forthcoming, he makes the investment in the original location, and when the government (with some probability) takes the property, the fixed capital is wasted. That is the inefficiency.

I thought this article might have overlooked some behavioral nuances, and I wanted to write a paper exploring the issue. Shapiro was interested in doing more research on it, too, so we formed a collaboration that resulted in two papers. "A Constitutional Choice Model of Compensation for Takings" (Fischel and Shapiro 1989) backed up the question of compensation to a decision made behind a "veil of ignorance" in the manner of John Rawls (1971). In this theoretical position, prospective rule-makers know that offering compensation might create some inefficiency (as Blume, Rubinfeld, and Shapiro showed), but they also know that the government that springs into existence after the constitutional rules are made might misbehave and not pay enough attention to benefit-cost analysis if it does not have to pay. The rule that falls out of this is that some but not full compensation would be the optimal choice at the constitutional convention. How full the compensation should be could not be derived from the comparative statics model that was mostly Shapiro's brainchild. Our key finding was that whether compensation should be paid depended largely on the expected nature of the government.

In connection with this account, I have been reading Gordon Wood's *Empire of Liberty* (2009), which describes the adoption of the Bill of Rights. At the constitutional convention in Philadelphia, James Madison had been reluctant to give in to calls for a Bill of Rights. Wood explained why Madison (initially) and other delegates to the convention did not favor one. The practical concern was that an enumeration might be construed as implying that those rights not enumerated would not be protected. That I had known, but Wood's deeper explanation for the convention's indifference was that its members saw the new government they were proposing as entirely different from that of Britain and the rest of the world.

The English bill of rights was regarded as a bargain between the king and his subjects. The king held all of the residual power, and any gains of rights for his subjects had to be extracted under duress, as when King John was forced to accept Magna Carta. In America, by contrast, the people ruled already, thought those mostly well-born white men. The Declaration of Independence had it that legitimate governments were those "deriving their just powers from the consent of the governed." The constitutional convention started from the assumption that "we the people" already held all the rights. To enumerate them would be to admit to an adversarial view of government that delegates to the convention did not hold.

Outside the circle of men who met in Philadelphia, however, there was much less confidence in a view of the social compact that might be derided today as "sitting by the fire and singing 'Kumbayah,'" the feel-good camp song. The anti-federalists at the state ratifying conventions took a harder view of human nature. They soon prevailed in that the first Congress adopted most of Madison's proposals for a bill of rights, which he had distilled from hundreds of submissions from the state conventions. The Takings Clause cannot be interpreted without understanding that it reflects at least some level of distrust of the motives of even freely chosen governments.

9.7 Explicating the Michelman Utilitarian Criteria

The other article that we published was "Takings, Insurance, and Michelman: Comments on Economic Interpretations of 'Just Compensation' Law" (Fischel and Shapiro 1988). Even the rhythms of the title were intended to evoke the most famous scholarly essay on takings law, Frank Michelman's "Property, Utility, and Fairness: Comments on the Ethical Foundations of 'Just Compensation' Law" (1967). Like many other famous articles, Michelman's had become a source that was almost ritually cited but seldom examined closely. Our task was to explicate it in economic-utilitarian terms and apply it to the issues of governance and regulation. The idea of just compensation was viewed by Blume and Rubinfeld (and not Shapiro) (1984) as an insurance device. In that role, the takings issue devolved into a question of circumstances in which citizens might not be able to easily obtain private market insurance (including self-insurance) against the risk of losing one's property by takings. The insurance idea was latent in Blume, Rubinfeld, and Shapiro (1984) in that the idea of "moral hazard" was central to the inefficiency caused by the prospect of government compensation for takings.

Our article (Fischel and Shapiro 1988) explicated Michelman's utilitarian criteria to demonstrate that the takings issue was not properly analogous to insurance against more-or-less random hazards. (Michelman had actually said as much [1967, 1217].) Michelman saw just compensation as balancing two types of costs. On the one hand, if the government did not compensate, owners and their sympathizers would endure "demoralization costs," which are the anxieties and disappointments that follow from having one's interests purposely disregarded, plus the collateral inefficiencies that arise from such insecurity. Among such inefficiencies would be premature development by owners who want to put their stakes in the ground and have their projects grandfathered before new regulations take effect, as suggested by David Dana (1995) and Timothy Riddiough (1997) and for which James Thorson

(1997) provides evidence. On the other hand, if government *does* compensate, it endures "settlement costs," which include the transaction costs of eminent domain proceedings, the deadweight loss of increased taxation to pay claims, the costs of winnowing out false claims, and (under Blume, Rubinfeld, and Shapiro's rubric) the moral hazard costs of property owners not taking into account foreseeable losses.

If prospective demoralization costs look like they will be higher than settlement costs, Michelman's utilitarian rule would call for just compensation. In the usual government road-building scenario, the demoralization costs of displacing an owner for the benefit of the public would seem to be high, and the settlement costs look relatively low, so it is easy to justify a rule of almost-invariable compensation for physical invasions by the government. If settlement costs are expected to exceed demoralization costs, as is the case for general regulations prohibiting nuisances, it is unproblematic to deny compensation for an owner's abatement costs in almost all cases. The regulatory world between these two examples is vast and complicated, and navigating it has not been eased by the fact that Michelman (1988) has all but disowned the utilitarian approach of his 1967 article.

9.8 Bad Apples Hit the Takings Issue

I used Michelman's theoretical considerations as the anchor for my 1995 book, *Regulatory Takings*. The fun of writing that book was to investigate actual cases to see how they squared with the theory and with my view that regulatory takings jurisprudence was best (if not exclusively) applied to the excesses of zoning that are addressed in the present book. One of the cases that had always puzzled me was *Miller v. Schoene*, 276 U.S. 272 (1928).

In 1914, Virginia had passed a law requiring that red cedar trees (actually a species of juniper) had to be cut down if they were shown to be a threat to the highly profitable apple-growing industry, which was centered in the Shenandoah Valley. The cedars themselves were not the cause of the damage. A native fungus, popularly called the cedar-apple rust ("rust" from the yellowish color it gave to apple tree leaves), had an unusual life cycle. It spent one part of its life on red cedar trees, which were not harmed by the rust, and then produced spores that were borne by the wind to nearby apple trees. In the apple-tree stage of its life cycle, cedar rust caused serious damage to both the apple crop and the trees themselves. The burgeoning apple industry was being threatened by the rust, and the Virginia legislature (among others) passed a law that resulted in cutting the cedars that were within two miles of an orchard.

Dr. Casper Miller wanted compensation for the ornamental value of the cedars that were cut down on his homestead upon the order of the state entomologist, William J. Schoene. The state demurred, and the Virginia and U.S. Supreme Courts sustained the state's position. It is tempting to treat this as a simple nuisance case. Requiring owners to abate a nuisance normally does not require compensation of any sort. Red cedars, however, were by themselves not nuisances. They tend to grow wild in fence lines and untended fields, but they were (and are) often planted as ornaments and windbreaks. The life cycle of the cedar-apple rust also upsets ordinary conceptions of causation. It was as if you played outdoor music, and its disturbing echo off of your neighbor's house suggests that your neighbor ought to remove her house because of the nuisance it causes. Justice Harlan Fisk Stone reflected on this conundrum and verbally shrugged his shoulders:

> [T]he state was under the necessity of making a choice between the preservation of one class of property and that of the other wherever both existed in dangerous proximity. It would have been none the less a choice if, instead of enacting the present statute, the state, by doing nothing, had permitted serious injury to the apple orchards within its borders to go on unchecked. When forced to such a choice the state does not exceed its constitutional powers by deciding upon the destruction of one class of property in order to save another which, in the judgment of the legislature, is of greater value to the public. (276 U.S. at 279)

An early approach to law and economics founded by Robert Hale is grounded on Stone's "none the less a choice" phrase, which illustrates the relativistic nature of harms and benefits (Barbara Fried 1998). Warren Samuels (1971), who embraced Hale's theories, wrote an article that sparked an exchange with James Buchanan (1972) about the interpretation of *Miller v. Schoene* in law and economics. (Neither was aware of the facts I later uncovered.) My research (done after *Regulatory Takings* was published) found that Justice Stone had overstated the seeming balance of interests of apple growers and cedar owners (Fischel 2007). Apples were the economic backbone of the Shenandoah Valley, and even owners of cedars conceded that they should take precedence (Edmund Fulling 1943). But that leaves the question of why the cedar owners were not compensated for their losses. Here I discovered something of a natural experiment in just compensation law.

The apple orchardists who advanced the cedar-cutting legislation actually had offered compensation for cut cedars. Prior to the adoption of the law, the orchardists had undertaken cedar cutting on their own. They received permission to cut their neighbors' cedars and did the cutting themselves. But holdout problems arose, and to deal with them the apple growers induced the legislature to pass the law that was subsequently challenged and upheld in *Miller v. Schoene*. The surprising thing about the law was that it did allow for compensation for cedar owners. Farming operations that were disrupted were paid for, and the cut cedars were trimmed up for the farmers for use as fence posts. Moreover, owners of cedars who had planted them as windbreaks or ornamentals could go to court to claim additional damages. The funds for these operations, including court-determined compensation, were raised by a special tax on apple orchards, not from general state taxes.

This looks like an ideal system of just compensation. (Buchanan [1972] had recommended just such a system, apparently without knowing that the original law had provided for it.) The orchardists were willing to tax themselves (or use their own labor) to have cedars removed and to pay landowners when compensation was due. The arrangement came undone, however, as many cedar owners who had formerly put no value on their weedy, self-seeded cedars saw that some of their neighbors, who claimed their cedars had ornamental value, were getting good money for allowing their trees to be cut. They thought that they should get some of that money, too. Subsequently, the number of claims for compensation began to mount, and the apple growers began to think that the apple-cedar rust was less of a threat than the rising taxes on their orchards to pay damages.

A wealthy plaintiff named Daniel Kelleher most likely sponsored Casper Miller's litigation seeking an injunction and compensation. The apple growers drew their line in this case and insisted that no compensation was due, despite the language of the statute that they themselves had written. The Virginia Supreme Court agreed with the apples growers, perhaps with a nudge from Governor Harry Byrd, who owned the largest apple orchard in the state. The U.S. Supreme Court sustained the Virginia ruling without indicating anything about the noble but ultimately frustrated effort by the apple growers to do right by their neighbors.

9.9 Just Compensation Statutes and Overentry by Plaintiffs

Miller v. Schoene encapsulates an important difficulty with designing a plan of just compensation. The difficulty is all the more compelling because the orchardists had what looked like a simple problem. There were some distance issues. Should cedars be cut down within one, two, or three miles from the orchards? But that was minor compared to the unanticipated demands for compensation by cedar owners who, as the orchardists knew from long experience, would have been indifferent to or even pleased by having their cedars removed from derelict fields.

I had previously regarded the moral hazard issue as a minor administrative problem (Fischel 1995). State highway builders, for example, try to warn landowners of their plans and sometimes negotiate with them not to build. Urban renewal plans are broadcast with warnings that business owners ought not to expand. (Failure to follow through, however, can create the problem of "planning blight" for neighborhoods in which buildings are abandoned, but the highway or redevelopment does not materialize [Gideon Kanner 1973].) But in the cedar-apple case the moral hazard problem would have sunk the whole program and subjected the apple industry to enormous losses, an outcome almost no one in Virginia wanted.

Sometime back in the late 1980s, John McClaughry, a Vermont state senator with whom I was acquainted, asked for my help in drafting a takings bill for Vermont. John is a libertarian (and no longer a state senator), and he wanted to introduce legislation that would rein in Vermont's extensive regulations on land use. So here was my chance to apply my ideas. It would give them some public voice even if the legislation did not have much chance of passing in a state in which McClaughry was an unusual sport.

I thought about it for a few days and could not come up with a proposal that I was willing to put my name on. One problem was what baseline would be appropriate for determining compensation? Would it apply only to future changes in regulation? But that would validate a vast sea of regulation that had already been applied without the cost-benefit test of the price system. Choosing some date in the past as the baseline for compensation would seem equally arbitrary. It would also add the complication of determining what long-gone regulations actually were, and it would undermine expectations by neighboring property owners who acted in reliance of what they thought were long-settled regulations. (Similar complications had arisen under Minnesota's early attempt to undertake zoning by eminent domain after police-power zoning had been struck down [William Anderson 1927]. Police-power zoning was restored in *State ex. rel. Beery v. Houghton*, 164 Minn. 146 [1925], with the court noting the practical difficulties of compensation schemes.)

The problem of excessive claims might be handled by threshold rules, such as requiring compensation only for losses of at least 50 percent. That, however, seems both arbitrary and subject to manipulation by dividing or aggregating property interests so as to magnify losses. (Robert Ellickson [1996], who is sympathetic to compensation, offers this and other warnings about the hazards of legislative drafting.) There are no doubt scholars and practitioners who can draft takings bills better than I could. In fact, some such bills were adopted as laws in several states (Lynda Butler 1997). Their existence seems to invert the usual story about courts and legislatures, casting the legislatures as more eager protectors of property rights than the courts (Stewart Sterk 2004). In any case, the legislative compensation bills (as opposed to voter initiatives like Oregon's, described in the previous chapter) seem to have had relatively mild effects. Florida adopted a carefully crafted regulatory takings bill in 1995 (as described by its drafters, Powell, Rhodes, and Stengle [1995]). It seems to have generated so little controversy that it was not even mentioned in an extensive study of that state's growth management program (Gregory Ingram et al. 2009).

The more fundamental reason that takings legislation is difficult to craft is that there is so little agreement on what sorts of government action should *not* be considered takings. This is sometimes narrowly cast as the baseline or denominator problem, as in what portion of a landowner's holdings (or even possible holdings) should be counted as having been burdened by a regulation. (This was discussed in section 3.25 under the rubric of "conceptual severance.")

Baseline questions have a more extensive margin, too. I have informally kept a list of takings claims that seem to stretch the boundaries of property and takings. When I was doing research on Amish one-room schools (Fischel 2012b), I came across the name of William Ball, who argued successfully for the Amish's right to forego high school education in *Wisconsin v. Yoder*, 406 U.S. 205 (1972). His support for the Amish's right to educate their children as they pleased was related to his advocacy for Catholic parochial schools. One of Ball's claims was that the taxes that parents of parochial students paid for public schools that their children did not attend was a taking of their property (Shawn Peters 2003). A claim by an anesthesiologist that Medicare's low reimbursements for his services were a taking of his property in his profession actually made it to a federal court of appeals (without succeeding) in *Garelick v. Sullivan*, 987 F. 2d 913 (1993).

A theory with more scholarly backing is "deregulatory takings" by Gregory Sidak and Daniel Spulber (1996). The deregulation of several of the network industries, such as electric power and telephones, left many firms with facilities that were profitable only under a regulatory constraint. Sidak and Spulber argued that there had been an implicit compact between government and the utilities, in which the utilities acceded to some unprofitable service obligations in return for an assurance that their large, fixed investments would not be undermined by future competition. Another creative theory is offered by Chris Serkin (2014), who considers the possibility that governments might be liable for takings damages in cases where it has been passive, as when it allows flooding or global warming, rather than through overt actions.

I raise these examples not because I think they are unreasonable—well, maybe some are a stretch—but because some of them do make sense. Therein lies the problem. The Takings Clause can logically be made to apply to a host of government actions (or inactions). It thereby swallows most of the rest of the U.S. Constitution as well as those of the states, which are, after all, mostly frameworks for self-governance by elected officials rather than by judges. This possibility was most clearly demonstrated by the most famous book-length treatise to advocate an expansive view of the Takings Clause, that of Richard Epstein (1985). His book is, as I have written (Fischel 1995), entirely logical, well-argued, more-or-less historically defensible, and a bracing corrective to shoddy reasoning. It also scares people. Epstein would have the courts review a large fraction of redistributive legislation, including progressive income taxation and the National Labor Relations Act, along with the more traditional property-based police-power regulations. Judges would have to have analytical skills and political nerve that even those favorable to Epstein's point of view do not claim to have (Jay Plager 1995).

It could be argued that anxiety about what would happen under regulatory takings is based on a parade of unlikely hypotheticals. Sidak and Spulber's deregulatory takings and Serkin's liability for nonresponse to global warming have not caught on just yet, so there is not much evidence of how they would be applied. But there are examples suggesting that unexpected expansion of compensation can generate calls for compensation in other areas. During World War II, many Japanese American citizens, native born as well as naturalized, were herded into concentration camps for the duration of the war. Many lost their property during their absence as well as their liberty. In 1988 the United States made a public apology for this gross breach of constitutional liberties. Congress subsequently paid the surviving internees $20,000 in partial compensation for their losses.

The success of Japanese Americans in obtaining some redress suggested to African Americans that they should get some compensation for slavery. The idea had been advanced before, but the example of compensation for the Japanese American internment clearly reenergized the movement and moved it into the mainstream (Eric K. Yamamoto 1999). It is not my point to argue the merits of reparations for slavery. It is only to illustrate the power of the prospect of compensation to energize political movements as well as individual owners. A large-scale movement to pay compensation for land use regulations would not stop at land use.

9.10 "My Hero, Billy Brennan"

I taught an undergraduate seminar in law and economics at Dartmouth for several years. The course was organized around property and land use regulation with an emphasis on regulatory takings. I would have students write papers about some takings controversy and ask them to follow up on what happened afterwards. They had to contact someone from both sides of the issue and evaluate the outcome using both the transaction costs approach of Coase and the normative framework of either Michelman or Epstein.

The curious aspect of the years of reports was how few of my students would come out on the side of the plaintiff landowners. Often I was also convinced by their more searching examination of the facts and the aftermath that just compensation was not warranted. (It was almost never obtained.) But almost as often my students simply thought that the public benefits of the regulation in question were sufficiently important, and the private losses sufficiently minor, that compensation would not have met the Michelman fairness and efficiency criteria. Dartmouth economics students may not be representative of their cohort at large, but if they had any normative biases, I would have expected them to fall toward the development-minded landowner. I feel as if I have been in one of those psychological experiments where everyone else turns the wrong way in the elevator, and you start to think the wrong way is the right way.

With all of these arguments against a regulatory takings doctrine, why not simply abandon it? Its current use hardly meets the normative criteria set out by the many scholars who have addressed the issue. As an economic deterrent against excessive regulation, its effect is modest and, in the case of the Supreme Court's exactions jurisprudence, perhaps perverse in its inhibition of exchanges. Many countries in the rest of the world that rate highly on economic freedom surveys, such as Canada, do not embrace any such doctrine (Rachelle Alterman 2010). It is often remarked that the British Town and Country Planning Act offered at least some compensation for regulatory restrictions despite the lack of any constitutional compulsion to do so. The one country that recently embraced a constitutional measure for regulatory compensation, Switzerland, does not seem to have developed a policy more coherent than that of the United States (Enrico Riva 1984).

Yet abandonment of the doctrine would have adverse consequences. As I concluded in chapter 3, U.S. Supreme Court decisions do not add up to a coherent doctrine, but they do seem to have forestalled some problematic trends among the states that might have proceeded further without them. The fact that land use regulators must prudently look over their shoulders at the possibility of financial consequences keeps the concept of opportunity cost on their minds. It is likely that other forces, such as foregone property tax revenues and political pressures from developers and their allies, are more important reminders of opportunity cost, but sometimes a developer does not have such forces working for her. Sometimes the courts are the only source of redress.

Which brings me to the title of this section. Sometime in the mid-1980s I attended a conference in Chicago about law and land use. I was still learning the nuances of takings law (my 1985 zoning book discussed it in ways that I now find a little embarrassing), and the conference introduced me to some of the legal scholars and practitioners whom I had not previously met. One was Gideon Kanner, who was both a practitioner and an author of vivid commentary, which I had not yet read. Nor did I know then that he was the plaintiff's attorney in several of the landmark takings cases at the Supreme Court. But I formed enough of an impression of him at the conference that when he prefaced a remark with "my hero, Billy Brennan," I thought he was being ironic. (Gideon wrote to me that he cannot recall having used those words, but he provided me with an obituary note in which he honored "Bill Brennan" as "the stand-up guy when the Constitution needed help" [Kanner 1997].) Kanner was what I would call a takings maven, eager to use the command of just compensation to protect property rights against excessive regulation.

Justice William Brennan ("Billy" to his friends) was among the most liberal members of the Court. Brennan seemingly never saw a regulation he did not think was reasonable. A lower court's invocation of the opinion he wrote in *Penn Central v. New York* is an almost sure sign that the complaining property owner has lost.

But Justice Brennan had a principled dedication to a larger mission. This was to preserve the Court's review of state law under the Bill of Rights as incorporated by the Fourteenth Amendment. As I indicated in section 3.21, it was becoming evident in the 1970s and early 1980s that the California Supreme Court was bent on eliminating the just compensation requirement for regulatory takings. The New York Court of Appeals (the state's highest) had also gone over to the California side in *Fred F. French Investing Co. v. City of New York*, 39 N.Y.2d 587 (1976). The issue of whether regulatory takings' sole remedy was injunctive relief, not damages, seemed to have been joined in *San Diego Gas and Electric v. City of San Diego*, 450 U.S. 621 (1981). However, in a five-to-four decision, the Court decided that the case was not ripe for review, as the California court had not issued a final decision that necessarily precluded compensation.

Justice Brennan dissented from the ripeness conclusion of the majority in *San Diego Gas* and went on to indicate why he thought that just compensation, not invalidation alone, was required both for regulatory takings (if they are found) and for traditional exercises of eminent domain, in which title is transferred to the government. (Chief Justice William Rehnquist agreed with the majority that the case was not ripe but indicated his agreement with Brennan's analysis, which made the case a harbinger of decisions to come.) In the process of arguing for a damages remedy, Brennan embraced the language of takings jurisprudence as protecting individuals and tempering government attempts to substitute police powers for eminent domain in phrases that would make him an unironic hero to Gideon Kanner:

> Police power regulations such as zoning ordinances and other land use restrictions can destroy the use and enjoyment of property in order to promote the public good just as effectively as formal condemnation or physical invasion of property. From the property owner's point of view, it may matter little whether his land is condemned or flooded, or whether it is restricted by regulation to use in its natural state, if the effect in both cases is to deprive him of all beneficial use of it. From the government's

point of view, the benefits flowing to the public from preservation of open space through regulation may be equally great as from creating a wildlife refuge through formal condemnation or increasing electricity production through a dam project that floods private property. (450 U.S. at 652, footnote omitted; also reprinted in Berger and Kanner. [1998, 873])

At footnote 26 of his *San Diego Gas* dissent (not the one omitted above), Justice Brennan was even more explicit about the disciplinary benefits of a compensation remedy:

Indeed, land-use planning commentators have suggested that the threat of financial liability for unconstitutional police power regulations would help to produce a more rational basis of decision-making that weighs the costs of restrictions against their benefits.

These considerations, however, were not what primarily motivated the dissent. For Justice Brennan, the California court's attempt to evade the compensation required by Takings Clause would undo more than just the tail end of the Fifth Amendment. He regarded the most important rulings of the Warren Court of the 1960s to be those that applied the Bill of Rights to the states (Brennan 1986). He was not about to let the state courts escape that obligation. Just how the states were to live up to their obligations to take seriously regulatory takings was not, in his opinion, for the U.S. Supreme Court to decide. Brennan had urged the state courts to develop severally a Bill of Rights jurisprudence that would supplement that of the federal courts. But one option for building that body of law was not to dismiss its application entirely.

9.11 Demand-Dampening Reforms and Good Housekeeping

The weaknesses of the regulatory takings doctrine warrant a search for other routes to reform. Those with which I conclude this chapter are derived from my historical and theoretical analysis of what caused zoning to be adopted in the 1910s and to become more stringent in the 1970s. My basic outlook is that zoning is a popular institution, not something handed down by government officials who were out of touch with public opinion. Zoning's most acute advocates are not planners but homeowners. In this respect, I respectfully disagree with one famous line of Justice Brennan's *San Diego Gas* dissent (in the same note 26 above): "After all, if a policeman must know the Constitution, then why not a planner?"

Brennan's assumption seems to be that the difficulty with applying the regulatory takings doctrine is that planners may not know its obligations. My view of the overregulation problem is not based on any failure by planners to know the legal implications of their jobs. That would entail a supply-side view of what drives zoning. Planners already have plenty of access to legal advice. The problem is that the voters who are the source of their continued employment do not want to take to that advice. Public officials and employees who do things their constituents do not like will usually be looking for other jobs after the next election.

It is worth considering again why property owners are concerned about zoning. I have sometimes raised the question of why there is almost no regulation of what kind or quality of motor vehicle can be parked in public lots. Almost no one cares whether the vehicle parked next to theirs is a new Mercedes or a beat-up pickup truck. The reason is that the use is temporary and the person parking has no property rights in a particular space that could be transferred to others. And of course if some people do care, they can "vote with their wheels" to find another space at almost no cost.

In a world of mostly immovable, owner-occupied homes and businesses, people do care about their neighborhoods. Their concern has both positive and negative economic effects. The positive effects are generally called "agglomeration economies," and there are reasons to cultivate them by keeping adverse spillover effects within reasonable bounds. Protective covenants, consolidated ownership, and the "good-housekeeping" version of municipal zoning are ways of managing spillovers. The negative effects of people's caring about their neighbors go under the rubric of racial segregation and exclusionary zoning.

The goal of the "demand-dampening" reforms is to obtain a modern version of the good-housekeeping rule for zoning. It has a place for everything, and everything in its place. Incompatible uses may be separated in exclusive zones or (contrary to old housekeeping theory) sometimes allowed space in modern mixed-use zones. Modern good housekeeping does not allow racial segregation as any part of the "everything in its place" goal, but it should allow, for reasons indicated in chapter 4 (about the benefits of "voting with your feet"), some leeway for communities that are partly stratified by income or other observable determinants of demand for local public goods.

9.12 Housing's Financial Equity as Benefit and Burden

The theme of the *Homevoter Hypothesis*, which also runs through the present book, is that owner-occupied housing forms such a large portion of most people's assets that it makes them hyperaware of local changes that would affect their homes' value. The good thing about this awareness is that it helps overcome the free-rider problem in local affairs. Studies continually confirm that homeowners are better citizens. They have more social capital—in the suburbs, too—than renters (Brueckner and Largey 2008). As on-site managers, homeowners tend to maintain their property better than distant landlords, possibly because they are more immediately aware of the frowns and smiles of their neighbors. Homeownership also insures people against rent increases during inflationary times. Housing equity provides a convenient way for middle-class people to save and smooth their consumption over time by providing a mortgageable asset against which to borrow funds for their children's education, medical emergencies, and retirement activities.

The downside of homeownership is that the good side can go too far. Homeownership fuels the NIMBY syndrome that stymies desirable as well as dubious developments (Voith and Gyourko 2002). The frowns and smiles of one's neighbors can enforce a stultifying conformism. Labor mobility is somewhat inhibited by homeownership and may contribute to unemployment (Blanchflower and Oswald 2013). National policies that worked to extend homeownership to the poor, such as promoting subprime mortgages, contributed to the housing bubble that triggered the great recession of 2008.

There can be little doubt that homeownership is augmented by the treatment of owner-occupied housing in the federal and most state income tax codes. As I explained in section 8.5, the major everyday subsidy to housing is that the income tax collectors do not recognize the "imputed rent" from owner-occupied housing as taxable income. (They actually do recognize it when an employer offers free or reduced-price housing as part of the compensation package for employees, assuming the employees are not required also to use the home for business activities.) If the Internal Revenue Code did tax the net annual value of housing services, then it would be entirely consistent with principles of efficient taxation to allow the owner—the investor—to deduct mortgage interest and property taxes as well as maintenance and depreciation. The current tax code ignores the gross income from imputed rent (mainly return on investment) but also allows deduction of mortgage interest and property taxes (but not maintenance and depreciation).

As a result of this situation, homeownership in the United States grew rapidly after World War II from about 44 percent in 1940 to 62 percent in 1960. At least a quarter of this growth was due to the growth of the federal income tax, whose liabilities on the middle class were modest before the war (Rosen and Rosen 1980). As further evidence that it was the income tax subsidy and not just general affluence that drove homeownership, it is notable that Switzerland does tax the imputed rent of housing, and Germany disallows mortgage interest deductions. The owner-occupancy rate of these two affluent nations are the lowest in Europe (30 percent for Switzerland, 43 for Germany), and far below the 65 percent rate for the United States (Elia Werczbergera 1997).

In chapter 5, however, I argued that it was not homeownership itself that drove the shift from good-housekeeping zoning to growth controls in the 1970s. It was the interaction between inflation and the mortgage deduction that made owning a house more attractive. For those who already had homes, having an even bigger house also became more attractive. The prospect of a capital gain from housing and the ever larger fraction of housing in middle-class investment portfolios made formerly passive homeowners into active promoters of home values.

Inflation has been low for several decades now, and, since the housing market crash of 2007 and the great recession of 2008, home values in many places are lower than they used to be, even in nominal terms. This has probably reduced the expansion rate of growth-control measures. Around 2012 I undertook some web searches for a new zoning device called "neighborhood conservation districts," which I described in section 2.16. These are submunicipal districts that were designed to provide even more neighborhood protections than regular zoning (which still applied) but were less burdensome to homeowners than historic district designations. What I did not mention before was that the web reports about their formation dried up almost completely as of 2007, the year housing prices stopped rising and began to fall in many areas. This is consistent with the idea that growth-control measures are driven by rising housing prices. (See also Baldassare and Wilson 1996.)

There is a second punch line: No evidence exists that any of the neighborhood conservations districts that were previously formed have been disbanded. There seems to be a ratchet effect for most regulatory devices. This may explain why the growth controls established during inflationary decades have not been reversed even after inflation has diminished. Growth controls, like ordinary zoning, have regulations that are hard to let down.

And indeed that is a rational view from the homeowner's position. As I emphasized in section 7.9, the institutions necessary to implement credible growth controls require that they be difficult to undo. Moreover, even in a down market, homevoters still care about the value of their community relative to other communities that homebuyers might shop for.

9.13 Limiting the Federal Income Tax Subsidy to Homeownership

The most obvious policy to dampen demand for regulations is to reduce the federal income tax subsidy to owner-occupied housing. I say reduce or limit the subsidy rather than abolish it. There are benefits to society from homeownership. As already mentioned, solid studies show that owning a home makes for better citizens (Dietz and Haurin 2003). There even seem to be educational benefits to children of parents who live in owner-occupied homes. But almost all of these benefits come from homeownership itself. The magnitude of one's equity in a home (or homes—more on that presently) does not seem to have any effect on the citizenship virtues of homeowning (Glaeser and Shapiro 2002). After all, homes were a smaller fraction of most households' wealth before 1970, and homeownership was high and local social capital was, according to Robert Putnam (2000), even higher. So the key to dampening the demand for growth controls without throwing out the virtues of homeownership is to limit the size of the subsidy. Three possibilities stand out.

First, keep in mind that communal virtues of homeownership accrue almost entirely to owner-*occupied* housing. The tax subsidy should be allowed for only one principal residence. Second and third homes should be treated like any other investment, regardless of whether they are rented out part of the time or kept only for the owners' vacation enjoyment. It is true that vacation homes reduce the tax price of local schools for resort communities (as discussed in section 6.10), but that is no reason for taxpayers in the rest of the nation to subsidize them. Absentee owners of homes will care about fiscal prudence and neighborhood quality of the communities that host their homes, but absentees add little to the everyday social network that year-round occupied housing promotes.

Second, put a cap on the size of the subsidy per household. If the reform is directed toward reducing the mortgage interest deduction, the cap might be something like the mortgage necessary to purchase a starter home in the area. This would still encourage homeownership among people likely to be affected by it but reduce the demand for moving up to or building oversize mansions. If the reform would involve taxing imputed rent (as in Switzerland and Germany), then the tax could be progressive with respect to the size of the home.

Third, restore the tax on capital gains for housing. Such gains would be smaller in any case if the first two reforms were implemented, as housing demand, at least at the high end, would be dampened. But the modern source of NIMBYism and growth controls under my theory is that people became worried about the size of the capital gains that they might get as well as protecting their current investment. A capital gains tax (and allowances for capital losses) would reduce the variance in holding this particular asset and make homeowners a little saner when faced with some neighborhood risks.

Each of these ideas is independent of the other. Any one of them would dampen the demand for additional growth controls. A reduction in the overall level of housing equity in voters' portfolios would make it easier for them to accept—or at least not to oppose—policies such as infill development, low-income housing, and unlovely but necessary land uses such as recycling centers and public utilities. With less to lose, voters would be less opposed to land use change and more inclined to see its benefits when they were positive. It is interesting that Switzerland, which taxes imputed income from owner-occupied housing and has a low homeownership rate, has surprisingly little difficulty in overcoming the NIMBY problem for waste sites, though Frey and Oberholzer-Gee (1997) attribute this to the Swiss fairness-oriented procedures. My suspicion, though, is that such procedures are easier to adopt where homes are less prominent in residents' investment portfolios.

9.14 Taxing Imputed Rent or Limiting the Mortgage Deduction?

I have waffled so far as to whether taxing imputed rent or limiting the mortgage deduction makes more sense. In the absence of administrative difficulties and political acceptability, taxing imputed rent is more attractive. The virtue of the tax on imputed rent is that it applies even if the owner has paid off the mortgage. It makes investing in an owner-occupied house the same as investing in an apartment house or in a factory or in a fleet of trucks, and so it removes those distortions in the capital market that generally favor housing. Its rate can be made to match those on other assets, and it can be made progressive and allow for thresholds to encourage first-time buyers and the like.

But an imputed-rent tax does raise formidable administrative issues. Every homeowner, not just those rich enough to itemize deductions on their federal form, would have to deduct expenses to determine their taxable income. In effect, a majority of the nation's households would have to become small businesses for tax purposes. Taxing imputed rent would require that federal tax collectors acquire considerable knowledge of the value of homes. Tax collection would require some assessment of home values (since rents are not observed). This process would make imputed-rent taxes overlap with the local property tax.

The universality of property taxation means that there is an administrative structure in place almost everywhere, and so local assessors could be enlisted to determine imputed-rent taxes. But enlistment of local assessors would make the federal tax look like a property tax, and property taxes disconnected from local benefits are even more unpopular than other taxes. Having the federal government as a partner in local assessments would create both political and administrative frictions. The use of imputed-rent taxation in Switzerland suggests that these problems are not insuperable, but I confess to not knowing much about the details of European taxation, which are seldom translated to my native language.

Limiting the mortgage deduction is certainly easier to do. Relatively few taxpayers actually itemize deductions right now, and with less mortgage interest to deduct, more people would take the standard deduction. (The standard deduction, however, might also be reduced if its purpose is to approximate average itemized deductions.) Income tax preparation would be simpler for many people. Both the imputed-rent tax and limiting the mortgage deduction would result in substantial increases in federal tax collections, which could be used for debt reduction, new expenditures, or reductions in other taxes. The recent experience of Australia, which adopted and then rescinded a carbon tax after adversely affected parties complained, suggests that some of the additional revenue might wisely be used to placate interest groups like homebuilders and construction unions, which might otherwise seek to scuttle housing tax reform.

Note that the virtues of housing tax reform operate on two planes. The virtue I have emphasized here, because it is novel (but also noticed by Voith and Gyourko [2002]), is that it will help change political behavior. People will be made less crazy by the value of their homes, and they will be less resistant to reasonable land use changes. The reform does that on top of what most other economists emphasize, which is changes in individual economic behavior. Housing tax reform will reduce sprawl by making the trade-off between convenient commuting and cheaper land favor less remote locations. As housing became more costly in the suburbs (where it is mostly owner-occupied), many people would choose to live closer to city jobs. Public transportation would become more viable. Congestion would not necessarily be reduced—time of day tolls that rise during rush-hour are needed for that—but work trips would generally be shorter, and hence external effects like pollution would lessen. And capital markets would have more savings to direct to expansion of businesses and other capital and thus raise wages. It is difficult to think of another tax reform that has as many good things going for it.

9.15 Home Value Insurance and Transaction Cost

Housing-tax reform is a passive idea for reducing sprawl and promoting more sensible regulation generally. A more active idea is home value insurance. I wrote about this in 2001 in the *Homevoter Hypothesis*. In brief, the idea is for promoters of new development to offer nearby homeowners who might object an insurance contract on their home values. If the new development was completed and the insured homeowner found that the price of her home had risen by less than that of comparable homes (the baseline), the insurer would pay the homeowner the difference in value.

An advantage of such a plan is that it gives the developer an incentive to bring his plans to completion in such a way as to reduce the chances of having to pay anything. Zoning itself is a kind of insurance in that nearby homeowners can bring their concerns to the planning and zoning boards and have them impose conditions on the developer. But if those who impose the conditions do not foresee some unpleasant aspect of the development, the nearby homeowners are out of luck. That risk feeds back into homeowners' anxieties and would heighten their opposition in the first place. Under developer-financed insurance, the developer both assuages the homeowners and has an incentive to avoid spillovers that he or the regulators might not have thought of.

I do not want to spend too much time on this idea here, and not just because I have written about it elsewhere (Fischel 2004a). The reason is that I cannot think of many good reasons why developers or enterprising risk managers would not have done this already on their own. There are few collective action barriers to creating markets like this. State insurance regulations are a barrier to large-scale instances of this idea, but this is not a large-scale idea. The home-value insurance I propose is to assuage NIMBYs, and it is usually a small-scale affair.

The large home-value insurance companies that are in existence (or, as of this writing, in receivership) do not address local political opposition at all. They are designed to insure against national or metropolitan housing price fluctuations such as those accounted for the by the boom and bust of the 2001–2008 housing market (Shiller and Weiss 1999). They are also marketed mainly to homeowners themselves. Homeowners in my present perspective need to be given insurance by developers or their allies in order to relent in opposing their proposals. Zoning itself is their insurance policy, and they need to be persuaded to trade it in for something else.

Because of its small and localized scale, it is possible that there are many instances of home value insurance that are offered without getting noticed. The motivating story for how I came up with the homevoter hypothesis came from my experience on the Hanover zoning board. An otherwise reasonable neighbor to a proposed development was raising much more of a fuss than I thought was justified by the project itself. It came to me suddenly that the neighbor was not worried about the expected outcome but the risk that the outcome would turn out badly and adversely affect the value of his largest asset, his owner-occupied home.

A few years later, I was at a social event and found myself talking with the developer who had bought the property in question after the original developer had given up. The successor developer did get his project done to his satisfaction. I asked how he had dealt with the neighbor who had frustrated the previous developer. He said, "No problem. I just gave him an acre of land between my project and his, and he agreed not to oppose my project."

Giving someone a land buffer is not exactly insurance, but the transaction does illustrate that experienced developers (which the original guy was not) may not have much demand to participate in the small-scale insurance market that I had proposed. They have many of ways of dealing with individual objectors. An industry of consultants is now available to help smooth conflicts between individual developers and community residents (Sean Nolon 2009). A more ambitious proposal to deal with homeowners' anxieties by reformulating fusty doctrines in property law is Lee Fennell's *The Unbounded Home* (2008). For more complex negotiations, developers might be willing (or induced) to participate in "Community Benefit Agreements." CBAs designate side-payments and concessions to various interest groups, often including labor unions and housing advocates, and are now frequently used in larger and more regulated cities (Vicki Been 2010). Having many parties at the table may complicate life for developers, but they get some assurance that the list of opponents will not grow indefinitely.

The transaction costs of individual negotiations are likely to be reduced by the foregoing efforts. The real problem arises when whole communities adopt growth-control devices, especially those that, like conservation easements, are intended to be difficult to reverse. Here both the legal and political transaction costs are much larger, and no insurance scheme or clever negotiation strategy is likely to be able to do anything about it. This pessimistic conclusion makes the strategy of housing-tax reform, discussed above, more attractive.

9.16 Does Inclusionary Zoning Lead to General Exclusion?

One of the causes of growth control may be, paradoxically, the movement to open the suburbs to low-income housing. A powerful indicator of this is that the two states with by far the most vigorous efforts to combat exclusionary zoning, Massachusetts and New Jersey, are also the most active in preserving farmland and acquiring open space. In the 1998–2003 period, these two urban states led the nation in voter initiatives to purchase farmland development rights (Kotchen and Powers 2006). Using a different source, Spencer Banzhaf et al. (2006) indicate that between 1997 and 2004, more than 40 percent of all open-space initiatives in the nation took place in New Jersey and Massachusetts. It might be understandable that these two urban, eastern states value farmland preservation more than, say, Nebraska or North Dakota, where farmland is obviously plentiful, but the question of why they lead other urban and eastern states by such a wide margin still needs explanation.

As I mentioned in section 5.19, New Jersey's *Mount Laurel* program has led localities to pull up the gangplank after they had met their obligation. This was almost ordained by the New Jersey Supreme Court in its 1983 ruling. After a community meets its quota, "the Mount Laurel Doctrine will not restrict other measures, including large-lot and open area zoning, that would maintain its beauty and communal character" (*Mount Laurel* II, 456 A.2d at 421). And downzone they did. A study by Stephan Schmidt and Kurt Paulsen asked in its title, "Is Open-Space Preservation a Form of Exclusionary Zoning?" (2009). The very question is sensitive. Most enlightened local leaders would argue that preservation of open space is done for environmental reasons and has nothing to do with exclusionary zoning, which they, of course, regard as something other communities might do but not theirs. Most would deny that there is a trade-off between agricultural and other open-space preservation and affordable housing.

Schmidt and Paulsen's approach to this issue was to conduct three studies in New Jersey, the state with the most strenuous affordable housing mandate (from the *Mount Laurel* cases), as well as a vigorous open-space preservation program funded by state and local sources. The problem with identifying exclusionary motives, as Schmidt and Paulsen well understand, is that they are not transparent. Indeed, there are legal hazards for any municipal official who might admit to such motives. So the detection must proceed indirectly. First, the authors examined the New Jersey statewide vote to fund open-space acquisition. They found that community votes favoring the referendum can be explained as if open space was a "normal good," one which is more frequently purchased in rich communities than in poor. This hardly condemns the communities that favored it, but it does cast doubt on the idea that land was being preserved solely because of its inherent characteristics.

Second, the authors looked at decisions by individual communities to actually acquire open space. Again, it looks as if economic concerns affected the votes, especially those of homeowners, whose assets are most sensitive to the costs and benefits of preservation and exclusion. This sets the stage for the most interesting test, which was to look at those communities that actually paid to discharge their low-income-housing obligations in other communities (as was legal in New Jersey up to 2008). Such communities are surely the best candidates for having a preference for exclusion. Schmidt and Paulsen then got GIS information about the type of land that these communities actually acquired for open space. Instead of acquiring the undeveloped land most likely to be rural in character, this subset of exclusionary communities acquired land that was most likely to be developed for affordable housing, which was land that had public sewerage available.

9.17 *Mount Laurel* Compared to Pennsylvania's Good-Housekeeping Rule

The two states with the most vigorous efforts to open the suburbs to low-income housing are New Jersey and Massachusetts. After 40 years of effort, these two states have achieved some of the highest housing prices in the nation. Defenders of *Mount Laurel* point to the numerous units that have been built under its name. Douglas Massey et al. (2013) examined the new housing project in Mount Laurel itself and pronounced it a resounding success. (One drawback they mentioned, though, was the lack of public transportation in its isolated suburban area.) Massey was also coauthor of a study showing that out-migration from New Jersey was disproportionately represented by low-income families, for which they explicitly blamed high housing prices (Young, Varner, and Massey 2008). A policy that helps a small fraction of the poor—those few who got *Mount Laurel* housing—but induces communities to adopt growth controls that harm a large fraction of the poor requires some rethinking.

My discussion of fiscal zoning in chapter 4 addressed the possibility that residents of most suburban communities are not as hostile to community diversity as the *Mount Laurel* advocates suppose. The demand for what I called "(limited) diversity" seemed evident both in higher education and, more to the point for the present discussion, in the political survival of the Massachusetts legislation that requires that communities accommodate new low-income housing. The "anti-snob zoning act," now more often known by its statutory number, 40B, survived a 2010 initiative to abolish it. Abolition was more popular in the farther suburbs than in big cities, but even if the major cities' votes had been discarded, 40B would still have survived. Given the chance to get the state off their backs in the privacy of the voting booth, suburban voters decided they preferred to subject themselves and neighboring communities to a commitment to accommodate low-income housing.

The Massachusetts standard does not require as much low-income housing as that of New Jersey, which may explain some of the difference between New Jersey voters, who generally dislike *Mount Laurel* (as evidenced by their support for politicians who oppose it), and Massachusetts voters. But the reader may have noticed a paradox in Massachusetts. As I mentioned at the beginning of the preceding section, it appears that Massachusetts towns have adopted the same devices to forestall development that New Jersey has: farmland preservation and open space acquisition. At the state level, Massachusetts voters favor 40B, but at the local level they seem to work against it as vigorously as voters do in New Jersey (Fisher and Marantz 2014).

The difference in political attitudes is probably caused by the source of reform. In New Jersey, reform came down from the state supreme court, whose members are supposed to be isolated from political give and take. In Massachusetts, reform came from the governor and legislature, who are at least somewhat responsive to the people. Moreover, 40B has been modified somewhat over its lifetime. Legislation enjoys more support in democracies than judicial decrees, not least because legislators can more easily modify problematic laws. But support for 40B as a general principle does not mean that it would not be resisted in its specific applications. Americans voted for prohibition of alcoholic beverages in 1920 but spent much effort thereafter searching for a drink.

In recent years I have become intrigued by the retro due process doctrine of the Pennsylvania Supreme Court. The court routinely issues orders to communities to adopt "curative amendments" for zoning rules that it deems outside the pale of proper regulation. Its ideal appears to be what I have called the good-housekeeping model for zoning. The state court has said that communities are generally obliged to zone to accommodate for all reasonable uses, and that includes apartments. It has generally opposed large-lot zoning by suburbs. Although there is some complaining about abuse of the curative amendments to leverage high-income housing projects (Katrin Rowan 2007), at least one economic study found that the Pennsylvania court's doctrine had more benign effects on housing market diversity in Pennsylvania than neighboring New Jersey's self-consciously redistributive zoning reforms (James Mitchell 2004).

The problem with the Pennsylvania approach is that it is almost universally disdained by the planning bar. Its rulings are examples of substantive due process. But that may be a reason why they have not generated much political backlash. Unlike regulatory takings, due process does not cost the local government money, aside from legal fees. The curative amendment makes sure that the rezoning actually happens, but local officials do not have to worry that they will be threatened with possibly baseless litigation designed primarily to extract money from their budgets.

Urban economists likewise have some difficulties with the Pennsylvania court's guiding principle, which is that every community should have land zoned for every use. The municipal specialization that lies at the heart of the Tiebout model would seem not to be allowed in Pennsylvania. And a study of diversity within communities by Howard Pack and Janet R. Pack (1977) found that the state's municipalities indeed displayed an internal heterogeneity that seems inconsistent with the predictions of the Tiebout model. But as I emphasized in chapter 4, internal homogeneity is necessary to make economic models of Tiebout competition mathematically tractable. The priorities of actual communities that want to attract residents may include some measure of diversity in the population.

9.18 Contract Zoning and Environmental Justice

One of the explanations for the difficulty in changing zoning to accommodate new development that I offered in *Economics of Zoning Laws* (1985) was the legal transaction costs of purchasing development rights. "Zoning for sale" was a put-down of many proposals by developers to ease their way through the zoning obstacle course. Courts abetted this hostility with doctrines that undercut what was called "contract zoning."

Hostility to contract zoning seems to have abated considerably in the last quarter century. Communities seem willing to put dollar amounts on rezonings. Courts have increasingly tolerated obvious evasions of the supposed ban on contract zoning (Christopher Serkin 2007). At least some of the greater tolerance for cash exchanges has been the rise of tradable emission permits. Buying and selling "the right to pollute" was once disdained by environmentalists. Now it is eagerly embraced by many such organizations. The fungibility of public environmental entitlements seems to have trickled down to everyday zoning controversies. "Zoning for sale" is no longer a trump card for people opposed to neighborhood change.

The lesser constraints on contract zoning would seem to make local land use outcomes more pro-development. A parallel movement promoting "environmental justice" seems to push in the opposite direction. Pro-development decisions by local governments are second-guessed by both judicial and legislative reviews for their impact on the poor. Some of this concern is promoted by social scientists who view political competition for industry as a destructive "race to the bottom" or, at best, a zero-sum game in which the gains to one community are offset by losses to another (Daniel Ingberman 1995; Daniel Esty 1996). I had argued long ago (Fischel 1975) that even if there were no geographic advantages of one location over another, variation in preferences among residents of communities would justify the competitive process. I proposed that residents see a trade-off between the loss of environmental amenities and the rewards of nearby industry, chiefly a lower tax-price for local public goods, but sometimes more convenient access to jobs and shopping.

Because of ordinary income effects, low-income communities would be more likely to give more weight to the gains from industry than the loss of local environmental amenities. (This is the local analogy to the "environmental Kuznets curve," which holds that richer societies demand better environments.) As long as people are less mobile than industry, an efficient outcome will result in more (not all) industries being located in lower-income communities. Most evidence does indicate that higher-income communities are indeed more leery of commercial and industrial development and adopt regulations to discourage it (William Fox 1981; Evenson and Wheaton 2003). Lower-income communities either developed around preexisting industry or were more inclined to allow it to come into their communities (Been and Gupta 1997). Environmental-justice advocates may take the lesser resistance to industrial development to be political ineptitude or corruption by local officials, but there seems to be little systematic evidence pointing in those directions. Environmental justice, however well intentioned, seems to be imposing a special transaction cost on poor communities who want to get better jobs or reduce the tax price of local school spending and get more of other local public goods.

The more charged issue is whether African Americans have been systematically discriminated against in land use policies. Since African American communities tend to have lower incomes, the evidence for this is complicated by an identification problem. It is further complicated by the fact that disfranchisement of blacks certainly did make them more vulnerable to dumping of problematic land uses in their neighborhoods (Hinds and Ordway 1986). But since voting rights have been restored as a result of the Voting Rights Act of 1965, the argument seems to have lost its punch, and the evidence that African American communities suffer more environmental injuries than otherwise similar non-minority neighborhoods is almost nonexistent (Been and Gupta 1997). Nonetheless, there continue to be special reviews of industrial location on this account, and this should count as an additional (perhaps desirable) transaction cost for locating problematic land uses.

9.19 The Dutiful Dozen

The major novelty of this book has been my view that zoning is a bottom-up institution. Its origins were rooted in the footloose transportation innovations of the early twentieth century, which greatly increased the risks that homeowners would lose the quiet enjoyment of their property as well as much of its value. Zoning was originally protective rather than aggressive with respect to home values. In the 1970s, inflation and further transportation innovations induced the growth-control movement. It is the excesses of that movement that motivate most of the policy recommendations listed below in the order of their importance. I have tried to avoid recommendations that require the implementation of other reforms for them to work, but the order reflects my personal assessment of which seems most important.

1. The major macro efforts that stand some chance of adoption involve reducing the federal tax subsidies to owner-occupied housing. For tax purposes, housing should be treated for like any other investment in terms of both its annual stream of services and its capital gains. Economists should understand that reforms in that direction are not just about getting more revenue and leveling the playing field among types of capital taxation. The housing subsidy is most likely the major political basis for excessive land use regulation. Bringing the inflated owner-occupied housing sector down to earth would moderate the NIMBY syndrome and make public demands for land use regulation more reasonable.

2. The use of conservation easements should be reexamined for their impact on urban structure as well as their environmental benefits. Removal of 50 acres of land from the market forever (that is what "in perpetuity" means, to the apparent surprise of one donor) is probably harmless for 95 percent of the land area in the United States. But where urban development is possible, perpetual easements are the worst form of suburban exclusion, in that they push development to remote areas and increase inefficient sprawl. Even if one does not share Thomas Jefferson's view that "the earth belongs in usufruct to the living" (cited by Julia Mahoney [2004, 574]), one could still agree with Professor Mahoney, who teaches at the law school Mr. Jefferson founded, that the practical problems with perpetual conservation easements make them a dubious gift to future generations.

3. States should rethink the double-veto system of regional growth management. While it has been a major instrument in the anti-development movement, its intellectual rationale is dubious. The idea that local governments adopt land use plans without regard for their neighboring communities is not supported by any systematic evidence. Variety among municipalities should be celebrated, not suppressed.

4. Legal remedies for exclusionary zoning need to take into account which parties are in the better position to enforce them. They should also consider the acceptability of their remedies to local governments. The relative success of Pennsylvania's jurisprudence is that it makes developers allies of low-income-housing advocates instead of (as in New Jersey) objects of taxation to finance low-income housing. Pennsylvania's substantive due-process

approach, which relies on injunctive remedies rather than monetary damages, may be inelegant in theory, but it has the practical virtue of being more acceptable to localities than regulatory takings and their open-ended liabilities.

5. The U.S. Supreme Court should reassess its concern about exactions. It would be helpful to articulate the concern that local governments might adopt regulations just for the purpose of raising revenue that is more properly the role of property taxes. But the courts should be aware that new development can have public impacts that are greater than previous developments that look exactly the same. The sequential nature of most development inevitably means that latecomers will be more burdensome than those that came earlier. This fact-based inquiry is usually better undertaken by state courts and legislatures.

6. Low-income communities should be trusted to make decisions for themselves. The environmental-justice movement should focus its inquiries on whether the local political process in poor or minority communities is working in the same way that it works in more affluent places. Small groups of people in even the richest suburbs often dissent from collective decisions, but that by itself does not warrant outside intervention in their decisions. To apply the same standards to the substance of zoning decisions in low-income communities as high-income communities seems patronizing to the former and raises the transaction costs of their land use negotiations.

7. The federal government should stop abetting parochial growth control schemes with false alarms about running out of farmland and other sky-is-falling issues. It should also limit litigation about environmental issues to parties that have an ongoing stake in the issues. Mostly, though, the federal role should be to leave the states alone.

8. Economists and allied researchers should work to endogenize zoning in their models of housing price determination. Discussion of regulatory reform would be more useful if it was understood that growth controls are not just something that happens because "policymakers" have the wrong information.

9. Reforms should not focus solely on the regions that currently have growth controls. It is not that Massachusetts is more or less virtuous than Indiana. The Midwest will adopt growth controls as soon as there are major immigrations that drive up housing demand.

10. Urban growth boundaries such as those of Portland, Oregon, require a mix of federalism tolerance—it is Oregon's boat to float—and critical eval-

uation before encouraging their establishment elsewhere. Portland seems to have found a means of achieving infill development despite NIMBY sentiment, but its constraining growth boundaries undermine local governments outside the pale and may cartelize the housing market, making the region less attractive and productive than it might be if exurban growth were simply charged its marginal cost.

11. Rent control is always problematical for the housing market insofar as it discourages rental housing supply, but an additional reason to oppose it is that, by reducing the supply of rental housing, it drives more people into the owner-occupied sector (Daniel Fetter 2013) and thus encourages more NIMBYism. While there have been political movements that have cut back on rent control—it is not common in America—this is an instance in which the regulatory takings doctrine might be profitably deployed at the state level.

12. "Make only little plans." My inversion of Daniel Burnham's famous dictum, "Make no little plans," is tongue-in-cheek but cautionary. Large plans are often high-profile targets for people who oppose developments. Modesty in scale often gets things done, not least because many reviews have thresholds that intentionally allow small players more leeway. More particularly, the megaprojects of urban renewal, like that of New London, Connecticut, create holdout situations and adverse publicity that more modest and contingent development can more easily avoid.

9.20 Conclusion

President Harry Truman was said to be impatient about his economic advisors' "on the one hand, on the other hand" approach to policy. He wanted a one-handed economist who would just tell him the answers. But one-handed economists are in short supply, and the laity should be skeptical of those who offer unambiguous advice.

The economic approach to zoning and local government offers plenty of room for the ambidextrous economist. On the one hand, it is a popular institution. This is partly because it is effective. It has protected that risky investment, single-family homes, for almost a century. Local governments have fine-tuned zoning and integrated it with their other powers to make municipal life more efficient and stable. It is an important means of promoting pleasant local environments. Zoning will not wither away, and plans to curtail it by abolition, preemption, or substitution of private alternatives are not likely to succeed.

On the other hand, local land use regulation has a steep downside that needs to be reckoned with. In combination with federal tax policies, it has distorted metropolitan form to create cities that are more spread out than necessary. Its post-1970 incarnations have promoted a maldistribution of income and wealth within the nation as a whole as well as within urban areas. Growth controls have made it more difficult for productive firms to grow, which holds back the American economy as a whole. We need to revisit Robert Frost's question that I quoted at the conclusion of chapter 1 and better figure out "how to crowd and still be kind."

References

Cases

[§§ indicate sections within this book]

Agins v. Tiburon, 447 U.S. 255 (1980). [§§3.14, 3.21, 6.14]
Ambler v. Euclid, 297 F. 307, 316 (1924). [§§3.3, 5.20]
Appeal of Girsh, 263 A.2d 395 (Pa. 1970). [§3.18]
Arlington Heights v. Metropolitan Housing Corp., 429 U.S. 252 (1976). [§§3.13, 3.29]
Belle Terre v. Boraas, 416 U.S. 1 (1974). [§§2.1, 3.17]
Bellevue v. East Bellevue Community Council, 138 Wash.2d 937 (1999). [§2.16]
Bellows Farms v. Acton, 364 Mass. 253 (1973). [§7.2]
Boerne v. Flores, 521 U.S. 507 (1997). [§3.17]
Buchanan v. Warley, 245 U.S. 60 (1917). [§§3.5, 3.6, 3.15, 3.29, 5.19]
Casey v. Warwick Township, 328 A.2d 464 (Pa. 1974). [§3.18]
Coniston v. Village of Hoffman Estates, 844 F.2d 461 (1988). [§3.23]
Coty v. Ramsey Associates, 149 Vt. 451 (1988). [§2.14]
Dolan v. Tigard, 512 U.S. 374 (1994). [§§3.27–3.29]
Eastlake v. Forest City Enterprises, 426 U.S. 668 (1976). [§§3.17, 3.22]
Eubank v. City of Richmond, 226 U.S. 137 (1912). [§2.5]
Euclid v. Ambler, 272 U.S. 365 (1926). [§§2.19, 3.2, 3.3, 3.6, 5.4, 5.7, 5.14, 5.20]
Ex parte Montgomery, 163 Cal. 457 (1912). [§5.12]
Ex parte Quong Wo, 161 Cal. 220 (1911). [§5.12]
First English Evangelical Lutheran Church v. County of Los Angeles, 482 U.S. 304 (1987). [§§3.21, 3.29]
Forty-Five Twenty-Five v. Fontainebleau, 114 So. 2d 357 (Fla. App. 1959). [§6.3]
Fred F. French Investing Co. v. City of New York, 39 N.Y.2d 587 (1976). [§9.10]
Garelick v. Sullivan, 987 F. 2d 913 (1993). [§9.9]
Goldblatt v. Hempstead, 369 U.S. 590 (1962). [§3.17]

Goreib v. Fox, 274 U.S. 603 (1927). [§3.8]
Hadacheck v. Los Angeles, 239 U.S. 394 (1915). [§§5.11, 5.12, 9.2]
Hall v. Santa Barbara, 833 F.2d 1270 (9th Cir. 1986). [§6.14]
HFH v. Superior Court of Los Angeles County, 542 P.2d 237 (Cal. 1976). [§3.22]
Kelo v. City of New London, 545 U.S. 469 (2005). [§§6.5, 9.5]
Koontz v. St. Johns River Water Management District, 568 U.S. ___, 133 S.Ct. 2586 (2013). [§§3.27–3.29]
Lingle v. Chevron USA Inc., 544 U.S. 528 (2005). [§3.14]
Loretto v. Teleprompter, 458 U.S. 419 (1982). [§§3.20, 3.29]
Louisville & Nashville Railroad v. Barber Asphalt Paving, 197 U.S. 430 (1905). [§3.28]
Lucas v. South Carolina Coastal Council, 505 U.S. 1003 (1992). [§§3.24, 3.25, 3.29, 6.14]
Lumund v. Rutherford, 73 A.2d 545 (N.J. 1950). [§3.4]
McCord v. Bond, 165 S.E. 590 (Ga. 1932). [§3.4]
Miller v. Schoene, 276 U.S. 272 (1928). [§§9.8, 9.9]
Moore v. City of East Cleveland, 431 U.S. 494 (1977). [§3.17]
Mount Laurel cases: See *Southern Burlington County NAACP v. Mount Laurel*, 336 A.2d 713 (1975).
Nectow v. Cambridge, 260 Mass. 441 (1927). [§3.10]
Nectow v. Cambridge, 277 U.S. 183 (1928). [§§3.8–3.11, 3.13, 3.23]
New Jersey Farm Bureau v. Township of East Amwell, 380 N.J. Super. 325 (App. Div. 2005). [§8.3]
Nollan v. California Coastal Commission, 483 U.S. 825 (1987). [§§3.26–3.29]
Oxford Construction v. Orange, 137 A. 545 (1927). [§3.4]
Palazzolo v. Rhode Island, 533 U.S. 606 (2001). [§§3.22, 3.29]
Penn Central Transportation Co. v. New York City, 438 U.S. 104 (1978). [§§3.20, 3.21, 3.29, 9.3, 9.10]
Pennsylvania Coal v. Mahon, 260 U.S. 393 (1922). [§§3.14, 3.28]
Plessy v. Ferguson, 163 U.S. 537 (1896). [§3.5]
Pruneyard Shopping Center v. Robbins, 153 Cal. Rptr. 854 (1979). [§3.15]
Robinson Township v. Commonwealth of Pennsylvania, 803 A.3d 901 (Pa. 2013). [§9.4]
San Antonio Independent School District v. Rodriguez, 411 U.S. 1 (1973). [§3.13]
San Diego Gas and Electric v. San Diego, 450 U.S. 621 (1981). [§§3.18, 9.10]
Seattle Title Trust Co. v. Roberge, 278 U.S. 116 (1928). [§2.16]
Serrano v. Priest, 135 Cal. Rptr. 345 (1976). [§4.16]
Shelley v. Kramer, 334 U.S. 1 (1948). [§§3.6, 5.19]
Sierra-Tahoe Preservation Council v. Tahoe Regional Planning Agency, 535 U.S. 302 (2002). [§3.25]
Simplex v. Newington, 145 N.H. 727 (2001). [§2.5]
Southern Burlington County NAACP v. Mount Laurel, 336 A.2d 713 (N.J. 1975) ("*Mount Laurel I*"); 456 A.2d 390 (N.J. 1983) ("*Mount Laurel II*"). [§§3.13, 5.19, 8.3, 9.3, 9.16]
Spur Industries v. Del Webb Development, 494 P.2d 700 (1972). [§2.14]
State ex. rel. Beery v. Houghton, 164 Minn. 146 (1925). [§9.9]
United States v. Causby, 328 U.S. 256 (1946). [§3.20]
Vulcan Material Co. v. Griffith, 114 S.E.2d 29 (Ga. 1960). [§3.4]
Warth v. Seldin, 422 U.S. 490 (1974). [§§3.13, 3.17, 3.29]
Williamson County v. Hamilton Bank, 473 U.S. 172 (1984). [§§3.23, 3.29]
Wisconsin v. Yoder, 406 U.S. 205 (1972). [§9.9]
Yee v. Escondido, 503 U.S. 519 (1992). [§§3.20, 6.14]
Yick Wo v. Hopkins, 118 U.S. 356 (1886). [§5.12]

Young v. American Mini Theaters, 427 U.S. 50 (1976). [§3.17]
Zahn v. Board of Public Works of Los Angeles, 274 U.S. 325 (1927). [§3.8]

Secondary Sources

[§§ indicate sections within this book]

Aaron, Henry. 1972. *Shelter and Subsidies: Who Benefits from Federal Housing Policies?* Washington, DC: Brookings Institution. [§8.5]

Adelaja, Adesoji O., and Keith Friedman. 1999. "Political Economy of Right to Farm." *Journal of Agricultural and Applied Economics* 31: 565–579. [§2.14]

Advisory Commission on Regulatory Barriers to Affordable Housing. 1991. *"Not In My Back Yard": Removing Barriers to Affordable Housing.* Washington, DC: U.S. Department of Housing and Urban Development. [§5.14]

Alpern, Andrew, and Seymour Durst. 1984. *Holdouts!* New York: McGraw-Hill. [§6.5]

Alterman, Rachelle, ed. 2010. *Takings International: A Comparative Perspective on Land Use Regulations and Compensation Rights.* Chicago: American Bar Association. [§9.10]

Altshuler, Alan A., and Jose A. Gómez Ibáñez, with Arnold M. Howitt. 1993. *Regulation for Revenue: The Political Economy of Land Use Exactions.* Cambridge, MA: Lincoln Institute of Land Policy. [§3.26]

American Civic Association. 1920. *Zoning as an Element in City Planning, and for Protection of Property Values, Public Safety, and Public Health.* Washington, DC: American Civic Association. [§§5.6, 5.11]

Anderson, John E., and Richard W. England. 2014. *Use-Value Assessment of Rural Land in the United States.* Cambridge, MA: Lincoln Institute of Land Policy. [§1.5]

Anderson, Michael L. 2014. "Subways, Strikes, and Slowdowns: The Impacts of Public Transit on Traffic Congestion." *American Economic Review* 104: 2763–2796. [§8.5]

Anderson, Michelle W. 2012. "Sprawl's Shepherd: The Rural County." *California Law Review* 100: 365–380. [§§2.2, 4.14, 5.9, 5.10]

Anderson, Nathan B. 2006. "Beggar Thy Neighbor? Property Taxation of Vacation Homes." *National Tax Journal* 54: 757–780. [§6.12]

———. 2011. "No Relief: Tax Prices and Property Tax Burdens." *Regional Science and Urban Economics* 41: 537–549. [§6.12]

Anderson, William. 1927. "Zoning in Minnesota: Eminent Domain vs. Police Power." *National Municipal Review* 16: 624–629. [§9.9]

Angel, Shlomo, Jason Parent, Daniel L. Civco, and Alejandro M. Blei. 2012. *Atlas of Urban Expansion.* Cambridge MA: Lincoln Institute of Land Policy. [§1.4]

Angel, Shlomo, Stephen Sheppard, and Daniel Civco. 2005. *The Dynamics of Global Urban Expansion.* Transport and Urban Development Department. Washington DC: The World Bank. [§1.4]

Arkes, Hadley. 1994. *The Return of George Sutherland: Restoring a Jurisprudence of Natural Rights.* Princeton, NJ: Princeton University Press. [§3.3]

Arnott, Richard J., and Joseph E. Stiglitz. 1979. "Aggregate Land Rents, Expenditures on Public Goods, and Optimal City Size." *Quarterly Journal of Economics* 93: 471–500. [§1.6]

Arrow, Kenneth J. 1951. *Social Choice and Individual Values.* New York: Wiley. [§6.11]

Asabere, Paul K. 2014. "The Value of Homes in Cluster Development Residential Districts: The Relative Significance of the Permanent Open Spaces Associated with Clusters." *Journal of Real Estate Finance and Economics* 48: 244–255. [§2.1]

Ausubel, Jesse H., Iddo K. Wernick, and Paul E. Waggoner. 2013. "Peak Farmland and the Prospect for Land Sparing." *Population and Development Review* 38: 221–242. [§1.11]

Autor, David, H., Christopher J. Palmer, and Parag A. Pathak. 2012. "Housing Market Spillovers: Evidence from the End of Rent Control in Cambridge Massachusetts." Working paper No. w18125. National Bureau of Economic Research. [§2.8]

Babcock, Richard F. 1966. *The Zoning Game*. Madison: University of Wisconsin Press. [§§2.0, 5.14, 5.18]

Babcock, Richard F., and Charles Siemon. 1985. *The Zoning Game Revisited*. Cambridge, MA: Lincoln Institute of Land Policy. [§3.29]

Baker, Newman F. 1927. *Legal Aspects of Zoning*. Chicago: University of Chicago Press. [§3.3]

Baldassare, Mark, and Georgeanna Wilson. 1996. "Changing Sources of Suburban Support for Growth Controls." *Urban Studies* 33: 459–471. [§9.12]

Banner, Stuart. 2011. *American Property: A History of How, Why, and What We Own*. Cambridge, MA: Harvard University Press. [§2.8]

Banzhaf, H. Spencer, and Nathan Lavery. 2010. "Can the Land Tax Help Curb Urban Sprawl? Evidence from Growth Patterns in Pennsylvania." *Journal of Urban Economics* 67: 169–179. [§1.6]

Banzhaf, H. Spencer, Wallace Oates, James N. Sanchirico, David Simpson, and Randall Walsh. 2006. "Voting for Conservation: What Is the American Electorate Revealing?" *Resources* (Winter): 7–12. [§9.16]

Barrows, Robert G. 1983. "Beyond the Tenement: Patterns of American Urban Housing, 1870–1930." *Journal of Urban History* 9: 395–420. [§5.10]

Bartholomew, Harland. 1939. "Nonconforming Uses Destroy the Neighborhood." *Land Economics* 15: 96–97. [§5.11]

Bassett, Ellen M. 2009. "Framing the Oregon Land Use Debate: An Exploration of Oregon Voters' Pamphlets, 1970–2007." *Journal of Planning Education and Research* 29: 157–197. [§8.8]

Baum-Snow, Nathaniel. 2007. "Did Highways Cause Suburbanization?" *Quarterly Journal of Economics* 122: 775–805. [§5.22]

Been, Vicki. 1994. "Locally Undesirable Land Uses in Minority Neighborhoods: Disproportionate Siting or Market Dynamics?" *Yale Law Journal* 103: 1383–1422. [§5.21]

———. 2010. "Community Benefits Agreements: A New Local Government Tool or Another Variation on the Exactions Theme?" *University of Chicago Law Review* 77: 5–35. [§§3.28, 9.15]

Been, Vicki, and Francis Gupta. 1997. "Coming to the Nuisance or Going to the Barrios? A Longitudinal Analysis of Environmental Justice Claims." *Ecology Law Quarterly* 24: 1–56. [§9.18]

Been, Vicki, Josiah Madar, and Simon McDonnell. 2014. "Urban Land-Use Regulation: Are Homevoters Overtaking the Growth Machine?" *Journal of Empirical Legal Studies* 11: 227–265. [§§3.1, 5.16, 8.4]

Berger, Bethany R. 2009. "What Owners Want and Governments Do: Evidence from the Oregon Experiment." *Fordham Law Review* 78: 1281–1330. [§§3.19, 6.13, 6.15, 9.4]

Berger, Michael M. 1992. "Amortization as 'Just Compensation': If It Works for Billboards, Can Office Buildings Be Far Behind?" *Institute on Planning, Zoning and Eminent Domain*. New York: Matthew Bender and Company. [§2.4]

Berger, Michael M., and Gideon Kanner. 1998. "The Need for Takings Law Reform: A View from the Trenches." *Santa Clara Law Review* 38: 837–884. [§9.10]

———. 2004. "Shell Game! You Can't Get There from Here: Supreme Court Ripeness Jurisprudence in Takings Cases at Long Last Reaches the Self-Parody Stage." *Urban Lawyer* 36: 671–712. [§3.23]

Bernstein, David E. 1998. "Philip Sober Controlling Philip Drunk: *Buchanan v. Warley* in Historical Perspective." *Vanderbilt Law Review* 51: 797–879. [§3.5]

Berry, Christopher. 2001. "Land Use Regulation and Residential Segregation: Does Zoning Matter?" *American Law and Economics Review* 3: 251–274. [§5.19]

Black, Duncan. 1948. "On the Rationale of Group Decision-Making." *Journal of Political Economy* 56: 23–34. [§§6.10, 6.11]

Black, Duncan, Robert Albert Newing, Iain McLean, Alistair McMillan, and Burt L. Monroe. 1958. *The Theory of Committees and Elections*. Cambridge, UK: Cambridge University Press. [§6.11]

Blanchflower, David G., and Andrew J. Oswald. 2013. "Does High Home-Ownership Impair the Labor Market?" Working paper No. w19079. National Bureau of Economic Research. [§9.12]

Blume, Lawrence E., and Daniel L. Rubinfeld. 1984. "Compensation for Takings." *California Law Review* 72: 569–628. [§9.7]

Blume, Lawrence E., Daniel L. Rubinfeld, and Perry Shapiro. 1984. "The Taking of Land: When Should Compensation Be Paid?" *Quarterly Journal of Economics* 99: 71–92. [§§3.20, 9.6, 9.7]

Bogart, Dan, and Gary Richardson. 2008. "Institutional Adaptability and Economic Development: The Property Rights Revolution in Britain, 1700 to 1830." Working paper No. w13757. National Bureau of Economic Research. [§1.8]

Bollens, Scott A. 1992. "State Growth Management: Intergovernmental Frameworks and Policy Objectives." *Journal of the American Planning Association* 58: 454–466. [§2.13]

Bond, Horace Mann. 1934. *The Education of the Negro in the American Social Order*. New York: Octagon Books, 1966. (Reprint of 1934 edition). [§2.2]

Borcherding, Thomas, and Robert Deacon. 1972. "The Demand for the Services of Non-Federal Governments." *American Economic Review* 62: 891–901. [§6.12]

Bosselman, Fred. 1973. "Can the Town of Ramapo Pass a Law to Bind the Rights of the Whole World?" *Florida State University Law Review* 1: 234–265. [§4.6]

Bosselman, Fred P., and David Callies. 1971. *The Quiet Revolution in Land Use Control*. Washington, DC: Council on Environmental Quality. [§§2.1, 5.21]

Bosselman, Fred P., David Callies, and John Banta. 1973. *The Taking Issue*. Washington, DC: Council on Environmental Quality. [§3.25]

Bourassa, Steven C. 2009. "The Political Economy of Land Value Taxation." In *Land Value Taxation: Theory, Evidence, and Practice*, ed. Richard Dye and Richard England. Cambridge, MA: Lincoln Institute of Land Policy. [§1.6]

Boustan, Leah Platt. 2010. "Was Postwar Suburbanization 'White Flight'? Evidence from the Black Migration." *Quarterly Journal of Economics* 125: 417–443. [§5.16]

———. 2012. "School Desegregation and Urban Change: Evidence from City Boundaries." *American Economic Journal: Applied Economics* 4: 85–108. [§5.16]

Bowman, John H., and John L. Mikesell. 1988. "Uniform Assessment of Agricultural Property for Taxation: Improvements from System Reform." *Land Economics* 64: 28–36. [§1.5]

Boyd, Marie. 2013. "Zoning for Apartments: A Study of the Role of Law in the Control of Apartment Houses in New Haven, Connecticut, 1912–1932." *Pace Law Review* 33: 600–684. [§5.7]

Boyer, M. Christine. 1983. *Dreaming the Rational City: The Myth of American City Planning.* Cambridge, MA: MIT Press. [§§5.6–5.8]

Brennan, William J., Jr. 1986. "The Bill of Rights and the States: The Revival of State Constitutions as Guardians of Individual Rights." *New York University Law Review* 61: 535–553. [§9.10]

Briffault, Richard. 1990. "Our Localism: Part I—The Structure of Local Government Law." *Columbia Law Review* 90: 1–115. [§2.1]

Brooks, Richard O. 1974. *New Towns and Communal Values: A Case Study of Columbia, Maryland.* New York: Praeger. [§2.15]

Brownstone, David, and Arthur DeVany. 1991. "Zoning, Returns to Scale, and the Value of Undeveloped Land." *Review of Economics and Statistics* 73: 699–704.

Brueckner, Jan K. 1983. "Property Value Maximization and Public Sector Efficiency." *Journal of Urban Economics* 14: 1–15. [§8.17]

Brueckner, Jan K., and Ann G. Largey. 2008. "Social Interaction and Urban Sprawl." *Journal of Urban Economics* 64: 18–34. [§9.12]

Bruegmann, Robert. 2005. *Sprawl: A Compact History.* Chicago: University of Chicago Press. [§§1.4, 1.8]

Brunner, Eric J., James Murdoch, and Mark Thayer. 2002. "School Finance Reform and Housing Values: Evidence from the Los Angeles Metropolitan Area." *Public Finance and Management* 2: 535–565. [§4.16]

Brunner, Eric J., and Jon Sonstelie. 2006. "California's School Finance Reform: An Experiment in Fiscal Federalism." In *The Tiebout Model at Fifty*, ed. William A. Fischel. Cambridge, MA: Lincoln Institute of Land Policy. [§4.16]

Bryden, David P. 1977. "The Impact of Variances: A Study of Statewide Zoning." *Minnesota Law Review* 61: 769–840. [§2.5]

Buchanan, James M., 1972. "Politics, Property and the Law: An Alternative Interpretation of *Miller et al. v. Schoene.*" *Journal of Law and Economics* 15: 439–452. [§9.8]

Buchanan, James M., and Charles J. Goetz. 1972. "Efficiency Limits of Fiscal Mobility: An Assessment of the Tiebout Model." *Journal of Public Economics* 1: 25–43. [§4.4]

Burchfield, Marcy, Henry G. Overman, Diego Puga, and Matthew A. Turner. 2006. "Causes of Sprawl: A Portrait from Space." *Quarterly Journal of Economics* 121: 351–397. [§§1.1, 2.9]

Burge, Gregory S., Arthur C. Nelson, and John Matthews. 2007. "Effects of Proportionate-Share Impact Fees." *Housing Policy Debate* 18: 679–710. [§3.26]

Burnes, Daria, David Neumark, and Michelle J. White. 2011. "Fiscal Zoning and Sales Taxes: Do Higher Sales Taxes Lead to More Retailing and Less Manufacturing?" Working paper no. 16932. National Bureau of Economic Research. [§4.16]

Butler, Lynda L. 1997. "The Politics of Takings: Choosing the Appropriate Decisionmaker." *William and Mary Law Review* 38: 749–807. [§9.9]

Calabrese, Stephen M., Dennis N. Epple, and Richard E. Romano. 2012. "Inefficiency from Metropolitan Political and Fiscal Decentralization: Failures of Tiebout Competition." *Review of Economic Studies* 79: 1081–1111. [§4.10]

Calabresi, Guido. 1961. "Some Thoughts on Risk Distribution and the Law of Torts." *Yale Law Journal* 70: 499–553. [§6.4]

Calabresi, Guido, and A. Douglas Melamed. 1972. "Property Rules, Liability Rules, and Inalienability: One View of the Cathedral." *Harvard Law Review* 85: 1089–1128. [§§2.7, 6.5]

Callies, David L. 1994a. "The Quiet Revolution Revisited: A Quarter Century of Progress." *Urban Lawyer* 26: 197–213. [§§2.13, 7.12]

———. 1994b. *Preserving Paradise: Why Regulation Won't Work*. Honolulu: University of Hawai'i Press. [§3.25]

———. 1999. "Regulatory Takings and the Supreme Court: How Perspectives on Property Rights Have Changed from *Penn Central* to *Dolan*, and What State and Federal Courts Are Doing About It." *Stetson Law Review* 28: 567–576. [§3.20]

———. 2010. *Regulating Paradise: Land Use Controls in Hawaii*, 2nd ed. Honolulu: University of Hawai'i Press. [§3.25]

Callies, David L., Nancy C. Neuffer, and Carlito P. Caliboso. 1991. "Ballot Box Zoning: Initiative, Referendum and the Law." *Washington University Journal of Urban and Contemporary Law* 39: 53–98. [§§3.17, 3.22]

Campbell, Colin D. 1969. "Social Insurance in the United States: A Program in Search of an Explanation." *Journal of Law and Economics* 1: 249–265. [§4.16]

Caplan, Bryan D. 2007. *The Myth of the Rational Voter: Why Democracies Choose Bad Policies*. Princeton, NJ: Princeton University Press. [§6.11]

Caplin, Andrew, Sewin Chan, Charles Freeman, and Joseph Tracy. 1997. *Housing Partnerships: A New Approach to a Market at a Crossroads*. Cambridge, MA: MIT Press. [§5.10]

Cappel, Andrew J. 1991. "A Walk Along Willow: Patterns of Land Use Coordination in Pre-Zoning New Haven (1870–1926)." *Yale Law Journal* 101: 617–642. [§§5.5, 5.7]

Caro, Robert A. 1974. *The Power Broker: Robert Moses and the Fall of New York*. New York: Knopf. [§5.22]

Carruthers, John I. 2001. "Evaluating the Effectiveness of Regulatory Growth Management Programs." *Journal of Planning Education and Research* 21: 391–405. [§3.16]

Case, Karl E. 2007. "The Value of Land in the United States: 1975–2005." In *Land Policies and Their Outcomes*, ed. Gregory K. Ingram and Yu-Hung Hong. Cambridge, MA: Lincoln Institute of Land Policy. [§5.15]

Case, Karl E., and Robert J. Shiller. 1990. "Forecasting Prices and Excess Returns in the Housing Market." *Real Estate Economics* 18: 253–273. [§5.1]

Cashin, Sheryll D. 1999. "Localism, Self-Interest, and the Tyranny of the Favored Quarter: Addressing the Barriers to New Regionalism." *Georgetown Law Journal* 88: 1985–2048. [§5.19]

Cheape, Charles W. 1980. *Moving the Masses: Urban Public Transit in New York, Boston, and Philadelphia, 1880–1912*. Cambridge, MA: Harvard University Press. [§5.5]

Cheney, Charles H. 1920. "Zoning in Practice." *National Municipal Review* 9: 31–43. [§5.8]

Cheung, Ron. 2008. "The Interaction Between Public and Private Governments: An Empirical Analysis." *Journal of Urban Economics* 63: 885–901. [§4.16]

Cion, Richard M. 1966. "Accommodation Par Excellence: The Lakewood Plan." In *Metropolitan Politics: A Reader*, ed. Michael N. Danielson. Boston: Little, Brown. [§§2.18, 5.9]

Claeys, Eric R. 2003. "Takings, Regulations, and Natural Property Rights." *Cornell Law Review* 88: 1549–1671. [§3.18]

Clawson, Marion. 1968. *The Land System of the United States: An Introduction to the History and Practice of Land Use and Land Tenure.* Lincoln: University of Nebraska Press. [§1.7]

Clingemeyer, James C. 1993. "Distributive Politics, Ward Representation, and the Spread of Zoning." *Public Choice* 77: 725–738. [§2.16]

Clowney, Stephen. 2005. "A Walk Along Willard: A Revised Look at Land Use Coordination in Pre-Zoning New Haven." *Yale Law Journal* 115: 116–184. [§5.5]

———. 2007. "An Empirical Look at Churches in the Zoning Process." *Yale Law Journal* 116: 859–868. [§§2.12, 3.17]

Coase, Ronald H. 1960. "The Problem of Social Cost." *Journal of Law and Economics* 3: 1–44. [§§4.1, 6.3, 6.4]

———. 1972. "Durability and Monopoly." *Journal of Law and Economics* 15: 143–149. [§§1.9, 7.9]

———. 1988. *The Firm, the Market, and the Law.* Chicago: University of Chicago Press. [§6.4]

Colwell, Peter F., and C. F. Sirmans. 1993. "A Comment on Zoning, Returns to Scale, and the Value of Undeveloped Land." *Review of Economics and Statistics* 75: 783–786. [§8.6]

Cooley, Thomas M. 1868. *A Treatise on the Constitutional Limitations Which Rest Upon the Legislative Power of the State of the American Union.* Boston: Little, Brown. [§3.2]

Coons, John E., William H. Clune III, and Stephen D. Sugarman. 1969. "Educational Opportunity: A Workable Constitutional Test for State Financial Structures." *California Law Review* 57: 305–421. [§5.19]

Cord, Steven B. 1983. "Taxing Land More than Buildings: The Record in Pennsylvania." *Proceedings of the Academy of Political Science* 35: 172–179. [§1.6]

Cordes, Joseph J., and Burton A. Weisbrod. 1979. "Government Behavior in Response to Compensation Requirements." *Journal of Public Economics* 11: 47–58. [§6.16]

———. 1985. "When Government Programs Create Inequities: A Guide to Compensation Policies." *Journal of Policy Analysis and Management* 4: 178–195. [§6.16]

Costonis, John J. 1974. *Space Adrift: Landmark Preservation and the Market Place.* Urbana: University of Illinois Press. [§§3.20, 4.6]

Coyle, Dennis J. 1993. *Property Rights and the Constitution: Shaping Society Through Land Use Regulation.* Albany: State University of New York Press. [§3.2]

Cronon, William. 1991. *Nature's Metropolis: Chicago and the Great West.* New York: W. W. Norton. [§5.4]

Cudahy, Brian J. 1990. *Cash, Tokens and Transfers: A History of Urban Mass Transit in North America.* New York: Fordham University Press. [§5.5]

Cullen, Julie Berry, and Steven Levitt. 1999. "Crime, Urban Flight, and the Consequences for Cities." *Review of Economics and Statistics* 81: 159–169. [§5.16]

Cullingworth, J. Barry. 2002. *The Political Culture of Planning: American Land Use Planning in Comparative Perspective.* New York: Routledge. [§2.2]

Dain, Amy. 2005. *Residential Land-Use Regulation in Eastern Massachusetts.* Cambridge, MA: Pioneer Institute and Rappaport Institute, Harvard University. [§2.1]

Dana, David A. 1995. "Natural Preservation and the Race to Develop." *University of Pennsylvania Law Review* 143: 655–708. [§9.7]

Danielson, Michael N. 1976. *The Politics of Exclusion.* New York: Columbia University Press. [§5.10]

Davidoff, Thomas. 2013. "Supply Elasticity and the Housing Cycle of the 2000s." *Real Estate Economics* 41: 793–813. [§7.14]

———. 2014. "Supply Constraints Are Not Valid Instrumental Variables for Home Prices Because They Are Correlated with Many Demand Factors." Available at SSRN: http://ssrn.com/abstract=2400833 or http://dx.doi.org/10.2139/ssrn.2400833. [§8.14]

Dehring, Carolina A., and Craig Depken. 2010. "Sharing the Burden of Water Supply Protection." *Regulation* 33(1): 36–40. [§6.14]

Demsetz, Harold. 1969. "Information and Efficiency: Another Viewpoint." *Journal of Law and Economics* 12: 1–22. [§6.4]

Deutsch, Stuart L. 1984. "Antitrust Challenges to Local Zoning and Other Land Use Controls." *Chicago-Kent Law Review* 60: 60–88. [§7.8]

Dietz, Robert D., and Donald R. Haurin. 2003. "The Social and Private Micro-Level Consequences of Homeownership." *Journal of Urban Economics* 54: 401–450. [§9.13]

Dillon, John F. 1871. *Commentaries on the Law of Municipal Corporations.* Boston: Little, Brown. [§3.2]

DiMento, Joseph F., Michael D. Dozier, Steven L. Emmons, Donald G. Hagman, Christopher Kim, Karen Greenfield-Sanders, Paul F. Waldau, and Jay A. Woollacott. 1980. "Land Development and Environmental Control in the California Supreme Court: The Deferential, the Preservationist, and the Preservationist-Erratic Eras." *UCLA Law Review* 27: 859–1066. [§§3.2, 3.21, 5.13, 9.6]

DiPasquale, Denise, and Edward L. Glaeser. 1999. "Incentives and Social Capital: Are Homeowners Better Citizens?" *Journal of Urban Economics* 45: 354–384. [§8.5]

Donald, David Herbert. 1995. *Lincoln.* New York: Simon and Schuster. [§1.7]

Downs, Anthony. 1957. *An Economic Theory of Democracy.* New York: Harper and Row. [§6.11]

———. 1973. *Opening Up the Suburbs: An Urban Strategy for America.* New Haven, CT: Yale University Press. [§§2.6, 9.1]

———. 1994. *New Visions for Metropolitan America.* Washington, DC: Brookings Institution. [§§1.10, 2.13, 4.10]

Dresch, Marla, and Steven M. Sheffrin. 1997. *Who Pays for Development Fees and Exactions?* San Francisco: Public Policy Institute of California. [§4.16]

Duany, Andres, Elizabeth Plater-Zyberk, and Jeff Speck. 2001. *Suburban Nation: The Rise of Sprawl and the Decline of the American Dream.* New York: Macmillan. [§2.13]

Duany, Andres, and Emily Talen. 2002. "Transect Planning." *Journal of the American Planning Association* 68: 245–266. [§§2.3, 8.5]

Dukeminier, Jesse, Jr., and Clyde L. Stapleton. 1962. "The Zoning Board of Adjustment: A Case Study in Misrule." *Kentucky Law Journal* 50: 273–350. [§2.5]

Dumm, Randy E., G. Stacy Sirmans, and Greg T. Smersh. 2012. "Building Code, Wind Contours, and House Prices." *Journal of Real Estate Research* 34: 73–98. [§2.8]

Duncan, Denvil, Venkata Nadella, Ashley Bowers, Stacey Giroux, and John D. Graham. 2014. "Bumpy Designs: Impact of Privacy and Technology Costs on Support for Road Mileage User Fees." *National Tax Journal* 67: 497–504. [§8.7]

Dunham, Allison. 1959. "Flood Control via the Police Power." *University of Pennsylvania Law Review* 107: 1098–1132. [§6.14]

Dyble, Louise N. 2007. "Revolt Against Sprawl: Transportation and the Origins of the Marin County Growth-Control Regime." *Journal of Urban History* 34: 38–66. [§5.23]

Dye, Richard F., and Daniel P. McMillen. 2007. "Teardowns and Land Values in the Chicago Metropolitan Area." *Journal of Urban Economics* 61: 45–64. [§1.6]

Eagle, Steven J. 1998. "The 1997 Regulatory Takings Quartet: Retreating from the 'Rule of Law.'" *New York Law School Law Review* 42: 345–406. [§3.22]

———. 2011. "The Parcel and Then Some: Unity of Ownership and the Parcel as a Whole." *Vermont Law Review* 36: 550–601. [§3.25]

———. 2014. "The Four-Factor *Penn Central Regulatory* Takings Test." *Penn State Law Review* 118: 601–646. [§3.20]

Ebel, Robert D., and John E. Petersen, eds. 2012. *Oxford Handbook of State and Local Government Finance.* New York: Oxford University Press. [§4.3]

Elkharrat, Simon J. 2012. "'But It Wasn't My Fault!' The Scope of the Zoning Estoppel Doctrine." *Cardozo Law Review* 34: 1999–2030. [§4.7]

Ellickson, Robert C. 1973. "Alternatives to Zoning: Covenants, Nuisance Rules, and Fines as Land Use Controls." *University of Chicago Law Review* 40: 681–78. [§§2.14, 3.24, 5.8, 6.4, 9.2]

———. 1977. "Suburban Growth Controls: An Economic and Legal Analysis." *Yale Law Journal* 86: 385–511. [§§3.18, 6.13, 7.8, 9.1]

———. 1982. "Cities and Homeowners Associations." *University of Pennsylvania Law Review* 130: 1519–1580. [§2.1]

———. 1989. "Bringing Culture and Human Frailty to Rational Actors: A Critique of Classical Law-and-Economics." *Chicago-Kent Law Review* 65: 23–65. [§5.20]

———. 1991. *Order without Law.* Cambridge, MA: Harvard University Press. [§§4.1, 5.6, 8.2]

———. 1996. "Takings Legislation: A Comment." *Harvard Journal of Law and Public Policy* 20: 75–84. [§9.9]

———. 1998. "New Institutions for Old Neighborhoods." *Duke Law Journal* 48: 75–110. [§§2.16, 3.17]

Ellickson, Robert C., Vicki Been, Roderick Hills Jr., and Christopher Serkin. 2013. *Land Use Controls, Cases and Materials*, 4th ed. New York: Wolter Kluwer. [§§2.5, 2.6, 2.11, 3.0, 3.2, 3.17, 3.23, 3.27, 9.3]

Ellickson, Robert C., and A. Dan Tarlock. 1981. *Land Use Controls: Cases and Materials.* Boston: Little, Brown. [§3.28]

Elliott, Donald L. 2008. *A Better Way to Zone.* Washington, DC: Island Press. [§2.19]

Ely, James W., Jr. 1992. *The Guardian of Every Other Right: A Constitutional History of Property Rights.* New York: Oxford University Press. [§§1.8, 3.14]

Ely, John Hart. 1980. *Democracy and Distrust: A Theory of Judicial Review.* Cambridge, MA: Harvard University Press. [§3.18]

Epstein, Richard A. 1985. *Takings: Private Property and the Power of Eminent Domain.* Cambridge, MA: Harvard University Press. [§§5.12, 6.13, 9.9]

———. 2007. "*Coniston Corp v. Village of Hoffman Hills*: How to Make Procedural Due Process Disappear." *University of Chicago Law Review* 74: 1689–1703. [§3.23]

Esty, Daniel C. 1996. "Revitalizing Environmental Federalism." *Michigan Law Review* 95: 570–653. [§§5.21, 9.18]

Evans, Lawrence B. 1921. "The Constitutional Convention of Massachusetts." *American Political Science Review* 15: 214–232. [§§3.9, 5.14]

Evenson, Bengte, and William C. Wheaton. 2003. "Local Variation in Land Use Regulations." *Brookings-Wharton Papers on Urban Affairs* 2003: 221–260. [§§7.3, 8.10, 9.18]

Fennell, Lee Anne. 2001. "Beyond Exit and Voice: User Participation in the Production of Local Public Goods." *Texas Law Review* 80: 1–87. [§5.19]

———. 2009. *The Unbounded Home: Property Values Beyond Property Lines.* New Haven, CT: Yale University Press. [§9.15]

Fennell, Lee Anne, and Eduardo M. Peñalver. 2013. "Exactions Creep." *Supreme Court Review* 2013: 287–358. [§3.27]

Fershee, Joshua P. 2014. "Facts, Fiction, and Perception in Hydraulic Fracturing: Illuminating Act 13 and Robinson Township v. Commonwealth of Pennsylvania." *West Virginia Law Review* 116: 869–913. [§9.4]

Fetter, Daniel K. 2013. "The Home Front: Rent Control and the Rapid Wartime Increase in Home Ownership." Working paper No. w19604. National Bureau of Economic Research. [§9.19]

Fischel, William A. 1975. "Fiscal and Environmental Considerations in the Location of Firms in Suburban Communities." In *Fiscal Zoning and Land Use Controls*, ed. Edwin S. Mills and Wallace E. Oates. Lexington, MA: Heath-Lexington Books. [§§4.9, 9.18]

———. 1978. "A Property Rights Approach to Municipal Zoning." *Land Economics* 54: 64–81. [§7.4]

———. 1979. "Determinants of Voting on Environmental Quality: A Study of a New Hampshire Pulp Mill Referendum." *Journal of Environmental Economics and Management* 6: 107–118. [§6.7]

———. 1982. "The Urbanization of Agricultural Land: A Review of the National Agricultural Lands Study." *Land Economics* 58: 236–259. [§1.1]

———. 1985. *The Economics of Zoning Laws: A Property Rights Approach to American Land Use Controls.* Baltimore, MD: Johns Hopkins University Press. [§§5.1, 5.15, 6.7, 8.1, 8.11, 8.18, 9.10, 9.18]

———. 1987. "The Economics of Land Use Exactions: A Property Rights Analysis." *Law and Contemporary Problems* 50: 101–113. [§9.4]

———. 1989a. "Centralized Control: Do We Want a Double-Veto System?" *Journal of the American Planning Association* 55: 205–206. [§2.13]

———. 1989b. "Did *Serrano* Cause Proposition 13?" *National Tax Journal* 42: 465–474. [§4.16]

———. 1990. *Do Growth Controls Matter?* Cambridge, MA: Lincoln Institute of Land Policy. [§§5.15, 8.13]

———. 1991. "Exploring the Kozinski Paradox: Why Is More Efficient Regulation a Taking of Property?" *Chicago-Kent Law Review* 67: 865–912. [§6.14]

———. 1992. "Property Taxation and the Tiebout Model: Evidence for the Benefit View from Zoning and Voting." *Journal of Economic Literature* 30: 171–177. [§§4.8, 4.16]

———. 1994. "Zoning, Nonconvexities, and T. Jack Foster's City." *Journal of Urban Economics* 35: 175–181. [§8.16]

———. 1995. *Regulatory Takings: Law, Economics, and Politics.* Cambridge, MA: Harvard University Press. [§§2.12, 3.21, 3.22, 3.27, 3.28, 3.29, 5.15, 5.25, 6.13, 6.14, 9.1–9.3, 9.8, 9.9]

———. 1996. "The Political Economy of Just Compensation: Lessons from the Military Draft for the Takings Issue." *Harvard Journal of Law and Public Policy* 20: 23–63. [§6.16]

———. 2001. *The Homevoter Hypothesis.* Cambridge, MA: Harvard University Press. [§§2.2, 2.18, 3.1, 3.2, 3.4, 3.12, 4.12, 4.14, 5.9, 5.10, 5.21, 5.24, 6.10, 6.13, 8.14, 8.17, 9.12, 9.15]

———. 2004a. "An Economic History of Zoning and a Cure for Its Exclusionary Effects." *Urban Studies* 41: 317–340. [§§3.11, 5.22, 9.15]

———. 2004b. "Did John Serrano Vote for Proposition 13? A Reply to Stark and Zasloff, 'Tiebout and Tax Revolts: Did *Serrano* Really Cause Proposition 13?'" *UCLA Law Review* 51: 887–932. [§4.16]

———. 2004c. "The Political Economy of Public Use in *Poletown*: How Federal Grants Encourage Excessive Use of Eminent Domain." *Michigan State Law Review* 2004: 929–955. [§9.5]

———. 2005. "Politics in a Dynamic View of Land-Use Regulations: Of Interest Groups and Homevoters." *Journal of Real Estate Finance and Economics* 31: 397–403. [§3.17]

———. 2006. "Why Voters Veto Vouchers: Public Schools and Community-Specific Social Capital." *Economics of Governance* 7: 109–132. [§5.10]

———. 2007. "The Law and Economics of Cedar-Apple Rust: State Action and Just Compensation in *Miller v. Schoene*." *Review of Law and Economics* 3: 133–195. [§9.8]

———. 2009a. "*Serrano* and Proposition 13: The Importance of Asking the Right Question." In *After the Tax Revolt: California's Proposition 13 Turns Thirty*, ed. Jack Citrin and Isaac W. Martin. Berkeley: Berkeley Public Policy Press, Institute of Governmental Studies, University of California. [§4.16]

———. 2009b. *Making the Grade: The Economic Evolution of American School Districts*. Chicago: University of Chicago Press. [§§2.2, 4.12, 4.13, 5.2, 8.12]

———. 2012a. "Neighborhood Conservation Districts: The New Belt and Suspenders of Municipal Zoning." *Brooklyn Law Review* 78: 339–354. [§2.16]

———. 2012b. "Do Amish One-Room Schools Make the Grade? The Dubious Data of *Wisconsin v. Yoder*." *University of Chicago Law Review* 79: 107–129. [§9.9]

———. 2014. "Not by the Hand of Horace Mann: How the Quest for Land Value Created the American School System." In *Education, Land, and Location*, ed. Gregory K. Ingram and Daphne A. Kenyon. Cambridge, MA: Lincoln Institute of Land Policy. [§5.2]

Fischel, William A., and Perry Shapiro. 1988. "Takings, Insurance, and Michelman: Comments on Economic Interpretations of 'Just Compensation' Law." *Journal of Legal Studies* 17: 269–293. [§9.7]

———. 1989. "A Constitutional Choice Model of Compensation for Takings." *International Review of Law and Economics* 9: 115–128. [§9.6]

Fischler, Raphael. 1998a. "Health, Safety, and the General Welfare: Markets, Politics, and Social Science in Early Land-Use Regulation and Community Design." *Journal of Urban History* 24: 675–719. [§§5.3, 5.4, 5.20]

———. 1998b. "The Metropolitan Dimension of Early Zoning: Revisiting the 1916 New York City Ordinance." *Journal of the American Planning Association* 64: 170–188. [§§5.7, 5.8]

Fisher, Ernest M. 1933. "Speculation in Suburban Lands." *American Economic Review* 23: 152–162. [§8.6]

Fisher, Glenn W. 1996. *The Worst Tax? A History of the Property Tax in America*. Lawrence: University of Kansas Press. [§4.13]

Fisher, Lynn M., and Nicholas J. Marantz. 2014. "Can State Law Combat Exclusionary Zoning? Evidence from Massachusetts." *Urban Studies* [online June 12, 2014]. [§§4.11, 9.17]

Fogel, Robert W. 2004. *The Escape from Hunger and Premature Death, 1700–2100: Europe, America, and the Third World*. Cambridge, UK: Cambridge University Press. [§1.11]

Fogelson, Robert M. 2005. *Bourgeois Nightmares: Suburbia 1870–1930*. New Haven, CT: Yale University Press. [§§4.14, 5.8]

Follain, James R., and Lisa Sturman Melamed. 1998. "The False Messiah of Tax Policy: What Elimination of the Home Mortgage Interest Deduction Promises and a Careful Look at What It Delivers." *Journal of Housing Research* 9: 179–200. [§8.5]

Fox, William F. 1981. "Fiscal Differentials and Industrial Location: Some Empirical Evidence." *Urban Studies* 18: 105–111. [§9.18]

Frantz, Douglas, and Catherine Collins. 1999. *Celebration, U.S.A.* New York: Holt. [§4.15]

Frech, H. E., III, and Ronald N. Lafferty. 1984. "The Effect of the California Coastal Commission on Housing Prices." *Journal of Urban Economics* 16: 105–23. [§8.13]

Freund, Ernst. 1904. *The Police Power: Public Policy and Constitutional Rights.* Chicago: Callahan. [§9.2]

———. 1929. "Some Inadequately Discussed Problems of the Law of City Planning and Zoning." *Illinois Law Review* 24: 135–149. [§§4.6, 5.14]

Frey, Bruno S., and Felix Oberholzer-Gee. 1997. "The Cost of Price Incentives: An Empirical Analysis of Motivation Crowding-Out." *American Economic Review* 87: 746–755. [§9.13]

Frey, H. Thomas. 1983. "Expansion of Urban Areas in the United States: 1960–1980." Economic Research Service Staff Report AGES830615. Washington, DC: U.S. Department of Agriculture. [§1.1]

Fried, Barbara H. 1998. *The Progressive Assault on Laissez Faire: Robert Hale and the First Law and Economics Movement.* Cambridge, MA: Harvard University Press. [§9.8]

Frieden, Bernard J. 1979. *The Environmental Protection Hustle.* Cambridge, MA: MIT Press. [§§5.21, 7.12]

Frug, Gerald E. 1999. *City Making: Building Communities Without Building Walls.* Princeton, NJ: Princeton University Press. [§3.13]

Frug, Gerald E., and David J. Barron. 2008. *City Bound: How States Stifle Urban Innovation.* Ithaca, NY: Cornell University Press. [§5.21]

Fulling, Edmund H. 1943. "Plant Life and the Law of Man. IV. Barberry, Currant and Gooseberry, and Cedar Control." *Botanical Review* 9: 483–592. [§9.8]

Galvan, Sara C. 2005. "Gone Too Far: Oregon's Measure 37 and the Perils of Over-Regulating Land Use." *Yale Law and Policy Review* 23: 587–600. [§§6.13, 6.15]

Ganong, Peter, and Daniel Shoag. 2013. "Why Has Regional Income Convergence in the U.S. Declined?" Working paper No. RWP12-028. Harvard Kennedy School. [§§1.10, 5.1, 5.25]

Gardner, Royal C. 2011. *Lawyers, Swamps, and Money: U.S. Wetland Law, Policy, and Politics.* Washington, DC: Island Press. [§§2.5, 2.11, 3.28]

Gardner, Todd. 2001. "The Slow Wave: The Changing Residential Status of Cities and Suburbs in the United States, 1850–1940." *Journal of Urban History* 27: 293–312. [§5.5]

Garnett, Nicole S. 2013. "Redeeming Transect Zoning." *Brooklyn Law Review* 78: 571–588. [§§2.3, 2.19]

Garreau, Joel. 1991. *Edge City: Life on the New Frontier.* New York: Doubleday. [§8.1]

Gates, Paul W. 1968. *History of Public Land Law Development.* Washington, DC: U.S. Government Printing Office. [§3.2]

George, Henry. 1879. *Progress and Poverty.* New York: Appleton. [§§1.6, 4.2]

Gillette, Clayton P. 2001. "Regionalization and Interlocal Bargains." *New York University Law Review* 76: 190–271. [§5.21]

Gisler, Erin B. 2009. "Land Trusts in the Twenty-First Century: How the Tax Abuse and Corporate Governance Threaten the Integrity of Charitable Land Preservation." *Santa Clara Law Review* 49: 1123–1151. [§2.17]

Glaeser, Edward L. 1996. "The Incentive Effects of Property Taxes on Local Governments." *Public Choice* 89: 93–111. [§4.3]

———. 1998. "Are Cities Dying?" *Journal of Economic Perspectives* 12: 139–160. [§1.3]

———. 2011. *Triumph of the City: How Our Greatest Invention Makes Us Richer, Smarter, Greener, Healthier, and Happier*. New York: Penguin Press. [§§1.3, 5.1, 8.15, 9.4]

Glaeser, Edward L., and Joshua Gottlieb. 2006. "Urban Resurgence and the Consumer City." *Urban Studies* 8: 1275–1299. [§5.16]

Glaeser, Edward L., and Joseph Gyourko. 2003. "The Impact of Zoning on Housing Affordability." *Economic Policy Review* 9(2): 21–39. [§7.9]

Glaeser, Edward L., Joseph Gyourko, and Albert Saiz. 2008. "Housing Supply and Housing Bubbles." *Journal of Urban Economics* 64: 198–217. [§7.14]

Glaeser, Edward L., Joseph E. Gyourko, and Raven E. Saks. 2005a. "Why Have Housing Prices Gone Up?" *American Economic Review (Papers and Proceedings)* 95: 329–333. [§4.15]

———. 2005b. "Why Is Manhattan So Expensive? Regulation and the Rise in Housing Prices." *Journal of Law and Economics* 48: 331–369. [§8.4]

Glaeser, Edward L., and Matthew E. Kahn. 2001. "Decentralized Employment and the Transformation of the American City." *Brookings-Wharton Papers on Urban Affairs*: 1–63. [§5.18]

Glaeser, Edward L., Hedi D. Kallal, Jose A. Scheinkman, and Andrei Shleifer. 1992. "Growth in Cities." *Journal of Political Economy* 100: 1126–1154. [§5.25]

Glaeser, Edward L., Jed Kolko, and Albert Saiz. 2001. "Consumer City." *Journal of Economic Geography* 1: 27–50. [§4.14]

Glaeser, Edward L., and Jesse M. Shapiro. 2002. "The Benefits of the Home Mortgage Interest Deduction." Working paper No. w9284. National Bureau of Economic Research. [§9.13]

Glaeser, Edward L., and Kristina Tobio. 2008. "The Rise of the Sunbelt." *Southern Economic Journal* 74: 610–643. [§5.15]

Glaeser, Edward L., and Bryce A. Ward. 2009. "The Causes and Consequences of Land Use Regulation: Evidence from Greater Boston." *Journal of Urban Economics* 65: 265–278. [§§5.3, 7.3, 8.13]

Glatt, John. 2013. *The Prince of Paradise*. New York: St. Martin's Press. [§§6.5, 6.6]

Goodchild, Robin, and Richard Munton. 1985. *Development and the Landowner: An Analysis of the British Experience*. London: Allen and Unwin. [§1.8]

Gordon, Peter, and Harry W. Richardson. 1997. "Are Compact Cities a Desirable Planning Goal?" *Journal of the American Planning Association* 63: 95–106. [§8.8]

Gottlieb, Paul D., Anthony O'Donnell, Thomas Rudel, Karen O'Neill, and Melanie McDermott. 2012. "Determinants of Local Housing Growth in a Multi-Jurisdictional Region, along with a Test for Nonmarket Zoning." *Journal of Housing Economics* 21: 296–309. [§§7.13, 8.3]

Gramlich, Edward M., and Daniel L. Rubinfeld. 1982. "Micro Estimates of Public Spending Demand Functions and Tests of the Tiebout and Median-Voter Hypotheses." *Journal of Political Economy* 90: 536–560. [§6.12]

Greenbaum, Robert T., and Jim Landers. 2014. "The Tiff over TIF: A Review of the Literature Examining the Effectiveness of Tax Increment Financing." *National Tax Journal* 67: 655–674. [§4.9]

Greenstone, Michael, Rick Hornbeck, and Enrico Moretti. 2010. "Identifying Agglomeration Spillovers: Evidence from Winners and Losers of Large Plant Openings." *Journal of Political Economy* 118: 536–598. [§4.9]

Grout, Cyrus A., William K. Jaeger, and Andrew J. Plantinga. 2011. "Land-Use Regulations and Property Values in Portland, Oregon: A Regression Discontinuity Design Approach." *Regional Science and Urban Economics* 41: 98–107. [§§8.7, 8.8]

Gyourko, Joseph. 1991. "Impact Fees, Exclusionary Zoning, and the Density of New Development." *Journal of Urban Economics* 30: 242–256. [§§3.26, 8.13]

Gyourko, Joseph, Christopher Mayer, and Todd Sinai. 2013. "Superstar Cities." *American Economic Journal: Economic Policy* 5: 167–199. [§5.1]

Gyourko, Joseph, Albert Saiz, and Anita Summers. 2008. "A New Measure of the Local Regulatory Environment for Housing Markets: The Wharton Residential Land Use Regulatory Index." *Urban Studies* 45: 693–729. [§§5.1, 8.13]

Gyourko, Joseph, and Richard Voith. 1992. "Local Market and National Components in House Price Appreciation." *Journal of Urban Economics* 32: 52–69. [§5.15]

Haar, Charles M. 1953. "Zoning for Minimum Standards: The *Wayne Township* Case." *Harvard Law Review* 66: 1051–1063. [§5.14]

———. 1955. "In Accordance with a Comprehensive Plan." *Harvard Law Review* 68: 1154–1175. [§2.6]

———. 1996. *Suburbs under Siege*. Princeton, NJ: Princeton University Press. [§5.19]

Haar, Charles M., and Michael A. Wolf. 2002. "*Euclid* Lives: The Survival of Progressive Jurisprudence." *Harvard Law Review* 115: 2158–2203. [§5.2]

Hall, Joshua. 2006. "Fiscal Competition and Tax Instrument Choice: The Role of Income Inequality." *Economics Bulletin* 8: 1–8. [§4.3]

Hamilton, Bruce W. 1975. "Zoning and Property Taxation in a System of Local Governments." *Urban Studies* 12: 205–211. [§4.4]

———. 1982. "Wasteful Commuting." *Journal of Political Economy* 90: 1035–1053. [§5.18]

Hanford, A. Chester. 1926. *Problems in Municipal Government*. Chicago: A. W. Shaw. [§5.7]

Hanke, Steve H., and Armando J. Carbonell. 1978. "Democratic Methods of Defining Property Rights: A Study of California's Coastal Zone. *Water Supply and Management* 2: 483–487. [§9.6]

Hart, John F. 1996. "Colonial Land Use Law and Its Significance for Modern Takings Doctrines." *Harvard Law Review* 109: 1252–1300. [§5.4]

Hart, John Fraser. 2001. "Half a Century of Cropland Change." *Geographical Review* 91: 525–543. [§1.1]

Haurin, Donald R., and David Brasington. 1996. "School Quality and Real House Prices: Inter- and Intrametropolitan Effects." *Journal of Housing Economics* 5: 351–368. [§4.13]

Heikkila, Eric. 1996. "Are Municipalities Tieboutian Clubs?" *Regional Science and Urban Economics* 26: 203–226. [§8.14]

Henderson, J. Vernon. 1980. "Community Development: The Effects of Growth and Uncertainty." *American Economic Review* 70: 894–910. [§§2.15, 7.6]

Heyman, Ira M., and Thomas K. Gihool. 1964. "The Constitutionality of Imposing Increased Community Costs on New Suburban Residents Through Subdivision Exactions." *Yale Law Journal* 73: 1119–1157. [§5.15]

Higginbotham, A. Leon, Jr., F. Michael Higginbotham, and S. Sandile Ngcobo. 1990. "De Jure Housing Segregation in the United States and South Africa: The Difficult Pursuit for Racial Justice." *University of Illinois Law Review* 1990: 763–877. [§3.6]

Hilber, Christian A. L., and Christopher Mayer. 2009. "Why Do Households Without Children Support Local Public Schools? Linking House Price Capitalization to School Spending." *Journal of Urban Economics* 65: 74–90. [§§4.15, 5.10]

Hilber, Christian A. L., and Frédéric Robert-Nicoud. 2013. "On the Origins of Land Use Regulations: Theory and Evidence from U.S. Metro Areas." *Journal of Urban Economics* 75: 29–43. [§7.5]

Hills, Roderick M., Jr., and David Schleicher. 2010. "The Steep Costs of Using Noncumulative Zoning to Preserve Land for Urban Manufacturing." *University of Chicago Law Review* 77: 249–273. [§2.3]

———. 2011. "Balancing the Zoning Budget." *Case Western Reserve Law Review* 62: 81–134. [§§2.6, 8.4]

———. 2014. "City Replanning." George Mason Law & Economics Research Paper 14–32. [§§2.6, 4.0]

Hinds, Dudley S., and Nicholas Ordway. 1986. "The Influence of Race on Rezoning Decisions: Equality of Treatment in Black and White Census Tracts, 1955–1980." *Review of Black Political Economy* 14: 51–63. [§9.18]

Hirsch, Werner Z. 1988. "An Inquiry into Effects of Mobile Home Park Rent Controls." *Journal of Urban Economics* 24: 212–226. [§3.20]

Hirt, Sonia. 2012. "Mixed Use by Default: How the Europeans (Don't) Zone." *Journal of Planning Literature* 27: 375–393. [§§2.19, 4.6, 4.8]

———. 2014. *Zoned in the USA: The Origins and Implications of American Land-Use Regulation*. Ithaca, NY: Cornell University Press. [§2.3]

Hochman, Harold M., and James D. Rodgers. 1969. "Pareto Optimal Redistribution." *American Economic Review* 59: 542–557. [§4.11]

Holderness, Clifford. 1998. "Standing." *New Palgrave Dictionary of Economics and the Law*. London: Macmillan. [§2.11]

Holland, Daniel M., ed. 1970. *The Assessment of Land Value*. Madison: University of Wisconsin Press. [§1.6]

Holzer, Harry J., Keith R. Ihlanfeldt, and David L. Sjoquist. 1994. "Work, Search, and Travel Among White and Black Youth." *Journal of Urban Economics* 35: 320–345. [§5.18]

Howard, Ebenezer. 1902. *Garden Cities of To-Morrow*. London: Swan Sonnenschein. [§8.16]

Hoxby, Caroline M. 1999. "The Productivity of Schools and Other Local Public Goods Producers." *Journal of Public Economics* 74: 1–30. [§6.11]

———. 2000. "Benevolent Colluders? The Effects of Antitrust Action on College Financial Aid and Tuition." Working paper No. 7754. National Bureau of Economic Research. [§§4.11, 7.11]

Hubbard, F. Patrick. 2007. "The Impact of *Lucas* on Coastal Development: Background Principles, the Public Trust Doctrine, and Global Warming." *Southeastern Environmental Law Journal* 16: 65–82. [§3.24]

Ihlanfeldt, Keith R. 2007. "The Effect of Land Use Regulation on Housing and Land Prices." *Journal of Urban Economics* 61: 420–435. [§8.12]

Ingberman, Daniel E. 1995. "Siting Noxious Facilities: Are Markets Efficient?" *Journal of Environmental Economics and Management* 29: S-20–S-33. [§§5.21, 9.18]

Ingram, Gregory K., Armando Carbonell, Yu-Hung Hong, and Anthony Flint. 2009. *Smart Growth Policies*. Cambridge, MA: Lincoln Institute of Land Policy. [§§2.13, 9.9]

Jackson, Kenneth T. 1972. "Metropolitan Government Versus Political Autonomy: Politics on the Crabgrass Frontier." In *Cities in American History*, ed. Kenneth T. Jackson and Stanley Schultz. New York: Knopf. [§5.9]

Jacobs, Jane. 1961. *The Death and Life of Great American Cities*. New York: Random House. [§2.3]

———. 1969. *The Economy of Cities*. New York: Random House. [§1.3]

Jansen, Brian N., and Edwin S. Mills. 2013. "Distortions Resulting from Residential Land Use Controls in Metropolitan Areas." *Journal of Real Estate Finance and Economics* 20: 193–202. [§7.14]

Joondeph, Bradley W. 1995. "The Good, the Bad, and the Ugly: An Empirical Analysis of Litigation-Prompted School Finance Reform." *Santa Clara Law Review* 35: 763–824. [§5.19]

Jun, Myung-Jin. 2004. "The Effects of Portland's Urban Growth Boundary on Urban Development Patterns and Commuting." *Urban Studies* 41: 1333–1348. [§8.8]

Kahn, Matthew E., and John G. Matsusaka. 1997. "Demand for Environmental Goods: Evidence from Voting Patterns on California Initiatives." *Journal of Law and Economics* 40: 137–173. [§7.13]

Kane, Thomas J., Stephanie K. Riegg, and Douglas O. Staiger. 2006. "School Quality, Neighborhoods, and Housing Prices." *American Law and Economics Review* 8: 183–212. [§5.16]

Kang, Sung Hoon, Mark Skidmore, and Laura Reese. 2012. "The Effects of Changes in Property Tax Rates and School Spending on Residential and Business Property Value Growth." *Real Estate Economics* 42: 351–363. [§4.13]

Kanner, Gideon. 1973. "Condemnation Blight: Just How Just Is Just Compensation?" *Notre Dame Lawyer* 48: 765–810. [§9.9]

———. 1997. "Justice Brennan's Grand Conservative Moment." *National Law Journal*, August 11. A21. [§9.10]

Karr, Ronald D. 1981. "The Evolution of an Elite Suburb: Community Structure and Control in Brookline, Massachusetts, 1770–1900." Ph.D. dissertation, Boston University. [§5.6]

Katz, Lawrence, and Kenneth Rosen. 1987. "The Interjurisdictional Effects of Growth Controls on Housing Prices." *Journal of Law and Economics* 30: 149–160. [§§7.13, 8.13]

Kayden, Jerold S. 1991. "Zoning for Dollars: New Rules for an Old Game? Comments on the *Municipal Art Society* and *Nollan* Cases." *Washington University Journal of Urban and Contemporary Law* 39: 3–51. [§3.28]

———. 2000. "National Land-Use Planning in America: Something Whose Time Has Never Come." *Washington University Journal of Law and Policy* 3: 445–472. [§2.12]

Kent, David L. 1993. "The Presumption in Favor of Granting Zoning Variances." *New Hampshire Bar Journal* 34: 29–34. [§2.5]

Kenyon, Daphne A., Adam H. Langley, and Bethany P. Paquin. 2012. *Rethinking Property Tax Incentives for Business*. Policy Focus Report. Cambridge, MA: Lincoln Institute of Land Policy. [§4.9]

Kiarie, Kihara R. 1996. "The Effects of the Lack of Zoning on Urban Structure in Houston." Undergraduate honors thesis, Economics Department, Dartmouth College. [§8.9]

Kinkade, Brent S. 1992. "Municipal Antitrust Immunity after *City of Columbia v. Omni Outdoor Advertising*." *Washington Law Review* 67: 479–500. [§7.8]

Kirp, David L., John P. Dwyer, and Larry Rosenthal. 1995. *Our Town: Race, Housing, and the Soul of Suburbia*. New Brunswick, NJ: Rutgers University Press. [§9.3]

Klick, Jonathan, John MacDonald, and Thomas Stratmann. 2012. "Mobile Phones and Crime Deterrence: An Underappreciated Link." In *Handbook of Law and Economics: Criminal Law*, ed. Aron Harel and Keith Hylton. Northampton, MA: Edward Elgar. [§8.4]

Kline, Jeffrey, and Dennis Wichelns. 1994. "Using Referendum Data to Characterize Public Support for Purchasing Development Rights to Farmland." *Land Economics* 70: 223–233. [§§5.20, 8.2]

Knaap, Gerrit, and Arthur C. Nelson. 1992. *The Regulated Landscape: Lessons on State Land Use Planning from Oregon.* Cambridge, MA: Lincoln Institute of Land Policy. [§8.7]

Knack, Ruth E. 1996. "Return to Euclid." *Planning* 62: 4–9. [§2.6]

Knauss, Norman L. 1933. *Zoned Municipalities in the United States.* Washington, DC: U.S. National Bureau of Standards. [§5.4]

Kneebone, Elizabeth, and Steven Raphael. 2011. *City and Suburban Crime Trends in Metropolitan America.* Washington, DC: Brookings Institution. [§5.16]

Kok, Nils, Paavo Monkkonen, and John M. Quigley. 2014. "Land Use Regulations and the Value of Land and Housing: An Intra-Metropolitan Analysis." *Journal of Urban Economics* 81: 136–148. [§8.14]

Kolnick, Kathy A. 2008. "Order Before Zoning: Land Use Regulation in Los Angeles, 1880–1915." PhD dissertation, University of Southern California. [§§2.4, 5.11–5.14]

Komesar, Neil K. 2001. *Law's Limits: The Rule of Law and the Supply and Demand of Rights.* Cambridge, UK: Cambridge University Press. [§§3.25, 3.29]

Kopits, Elizabeth, Virginia McConnell, and Daniel Miles. 2012. "Lot Size, Zoning, and Household Preferences." *Housing Policy Debate* 22: 153–173. [§8.13]

Korngold, Gerald. 2001. "The Emergence of Private Land Use Controls in Large-Scale Subdivisions: The Companion Story to *Village of Euclid v. Ambler Realty Co.*" *Case Western Reserve Law Review* 51: 617–643. [§§3.6, 5.5, 5.8]

———. 2007. "Solving the Contentious Issues of Private Conservation Easements: Promoting Flexibility for the Future and Engaging the Public Land Use Process." *Utah Law Review* 2007: 1039–1084. [§2.17]

———. 2012. "Governmental Conservation Easements: A Means to Advance Efficiency, Freedom from Coercion, Flexibility, and Democracy." *Brooklyn Law Review* 78: 467–520. [§2.17]

Kotchen, Matthew J., and Shawn M. Powers. 2006. "Explaining the Appearance and Success of Voter Referenda for Open-Space Conservation." *Journal of Environmental Economics and Management* 52: 373–390. [§9.16]

Kraybill, Donald B. 2001. *The Riddle of Amish Culture.* Baltimore, MD: Johns Hopkins University Press. [§3.1]

Krefetz, Sharon Perlman. 2001. "Impact and Evolution of the Massachusetts Comprehensives Permits and Zoning Appeals Act: Thirty Years of Experience with a State Legislative Effort to Overcome Exclusionary Zoning." *Western New England Law Review* 22: 381–430. [§§4.11, 7.9]

Krier, James E., and Stewart J. Schwab. 1995. "Property Rules and Liability Rules: The Cathedral in Another Light." *New York University Law Review* 70: 440–483. [§6.5]

Kurban, Haydar, Ryan M. Gallagher, and Joseph J. Persky. 2012. "Estimating Local Redistribution Through Property-Tax-Funded Public School Systems." *National Tax Journal* 65: 629–652. [§4.13]

Ladd, Helen (Principal Author), Ben Chinitz and Dick Netzer, eds. 1998. *Local Government Tax and Land Use Policies in the United States: Understanding the Links.* Cheltenham, UK: Edward Elgar. [§4.8]

Lafferty, Ronald N., and H. E. Frech III. 1978. "Community Environment and the Market Value of Single Family Homes: The Effect of the Dispersion of Land Uses." *Journal of Law and Economics* 2: 381–394. [§8.10]

Landemore, Hélène. 2012. *Democratic Reason: Politics, Collective Intelligence, and the Rule of the Many.* Princeton, NJ: Princeton University Press. [§6.11]

Larkin, Jack. 1988. *The Reshaping of Everyday Life, 1790–1840.* New York: Harper & Row. [§5.4]

Lazarus, Richard J. 1992. "Pursuing 'Environmental Justice': The Distributional Effects of Environmental Protection." *Northwestern University Law Review* 87: 787–857. [§5.21]

Lees, Martha A. 1994. "Preserving Property Values—Preserving Proper Homes—Preserving Privilege—The Pre-Euclid Debate over Zoning for Exclusively Private Residential Areas, 1916–1926." *University of Pittsburgh Law Review* 56: 367–439. [§§5.7, 5.20]

Lehman, Tim. 1995. *Public Values, Private Lands: Farmland Preservation Policy, 1933–1985.* Chapel Hill: University of North Carolina Press. [§§1.1, 2.12]

LeRoy, Stephen F., and Jon Sonstelie. 1983. "Paradise Lost and Regained: Transportation Innovation, Income and Residential Location." *Journal of Urban Economics* 13: 67–89. [§5.5]

Levine, Jonathan C. 2006. *Zoned Out: Regulation, Markets, and Choices in Transportation and Metropolitan Land-Use.* Washington, DC: Resources for the Future. [§4.0]

Levinson, Daryl J. 2000. "Making Governments Pay: Markets, Politics, and the Allocation of Constitutional Costs." *University of Chicago Law Review* 67: 345–420. [§§3.19, 6.13]

Levinson, Marc. 2006. *The Box: How the Shipping Container Made the World Smaller and the World Economy Bigger.* Princeton, NJ: Princeton University Press. [§5.18]

Lewis, Paul G. 2001. "Retail Politics: Local Sales Taxes and the Fiscalization of Land Use." *Economic Development Quarterly* 15: 21–35. [§4.3]

Libecap, Gary D., and Dean Lueck. 2011. "The Demarcation of Land and the Role of Coordinating Property Institutions." *Journal of Political Economy* 119: 426–467. [§1.7]

Libecap, Gary D., Dean Lueck, and Trevor O'Grady. 2011. "Large-Scale Institutional Changes: Land Demarcation in the British Empire." *Journal of Law and Economics* 54(4): S295–S327. [§1.7]

Liebmann, George W. 1993. "Devolution of Power to Community and Block Associations." *Urban Lawyer* 25: 335–383. [§2.16]

Link, William A. 1992. *The Paradox of Southern Progressivism, 1880–1930.* Chapel Hill: University of North Carolina Press. [§8.12]

Linklater, Andro. 2002. *Measuring America: How an Untamed Wilderness Shaped the United States and Fulfilled the Promise of Democracy.* New York: Walker. [§1.7]

Listokin, David, and David B. Hattis. 2005. "Building Codes and Housing." *Cityscape* 8: 21–67. [§2.8]

Liu, Xiangping, and Lori Lynch. 2011. "Do Zoning Regulations Rob Rural Landowners' Equity?" *American Journal of Agricultural Economics* 93: 1–25. [§§8.13, 9.2]

Longtin, James. 1975. "Avoiding and Defending Constitutional Attacks on Land Use Regulations (Including Inverse Condemnation)." *NIMLO Municipal Law Review* 38B: 175–193. [§3.18]

Lovelady, Adam. 2008. "Broadened Notions of Historic Preservation and the Role of Neighborhood Conservation Districts." *Urban Lawyer* 40: 147–183. [§2.16]

Lubove, Roy. 1969. *Twentieth-Century Pittsburgh: Government, Business, and Environmental Change.* New York: Wiley. [§5.22]

Lucas, David. 1995. *Lucas vs. the Green Machine: Landmark Supreme Court Property Rights Decision by the Man Who Won It Against the Odds.* Charleston, SC: Alexander Books. [§6.14]

Lutz, Byron. 2015. "Quasi-Experimental Evidence on the Connection between Property Taxes and Residential Capital Investment." *American Economic Journal: Economic Policy* 7: 300–330. [§§4.14, 7.11, 8.13]

MacDonald, James M. 2011. *Why Are Farms Getting Larger? The Case of the United States.* Washington DC: United States Department of Agriculture, Economic Research Service. [§1.9]

Madry, Alan R. 2007. "Judging *Ziervogel*: The Twisted Path of Recent Zoning Variance Decisions in Wisconsin." *Marquette Law Review* 91: 485–534. [§2.5]

Mahoney, Julia D. 2004. "The Illusion of Perpetuity and the Preservation of Privately Owned Lands." *Natural Resources Journal* 44: 573–600. [§9.19]

Malamut, Michael. 2000. *The Power to Take: The Use of Eminent Domain in Massachusetts.* Boston: Pioneer Institute for Public Policy Research. [§9.5]

Malpezzi, Stephen. 1996. "Housing Prices, Externalities, and Regulation in U.S. Metropolitan Areas." *Journal of Housing Research* 7: 209–241. [§8.14]

Mandelker, Daniel R. 1976. "The Role of the Local Comprehensive Plan in Land Use Regulation." *Michigan Law Review* 74: 899–973. [§2.6]

———. 2011. "Housing Quotas for People with Disabilities: Legislating Exclusion." *Urban Lawyer* 43: 915–947. [§2.12]

Margo, Robert A. 1990. *Race and Schooling in the South, 1880–1950: An Economic History.* Chicago: University of Chicago Press. [§8.12]

Martin, Isaac. 2006. "Does School Finance Litigation Cause Taxpayer Revolt? *Serrano* and Proposition 13." *Law and Society Review* 40: 525–557. [§4.16]

Massey, Douglas S., Len Albright, Rebecca Casciano, Elizabeth Derickson, and David N. Kinsey. 2013. *Climbing Mount Laurel: The Struggle for Affordable Housing and Social Mobility in an American Suburb.* Princeton, NJ: Princeton University Press. [§9.17]

Massey, Douglas S., and Jonathan Rothwell. 2009. "The Effect of Density Zoning on Racial Segregation in U.S. Urban Areas." *Urban Affairs Review* 44: 779–806. [§3.6]

Mayer, Christopher J., and C. Tsuriel Somerville. 2000. "Land Use Regulation and New Construction." *Regional Science and Urban Economics* 30: 639–662. [§8.14]

McChesney, Fred S. 2001. "Rent Seeking and Rent Extraction." In *The Elgar Companion to Public Choice,* ed. William Shugart and Laura Razzolini. Northampton, MA: Edward Elgar. [§3.28]

McDonald, John F. 1995. "Houston Remains Unzoned." *Land Economics* 71: 137–140. [§8.10]

McDonald, John F., and Daniel P. McMillen. 2004. "Determinants of Suburban Development Controls: A Fischel Expedition." *Urban Studies* 41: 341–361. [§8.14]

McKenzie, Robert D. 1933. *The Metropolitan Community.* New York: McGraw-Hill. [§5.4]

McMichael, Stanley L., and Robert F. Bingham. 1923. *City Growth and Values.* Cleveland: Stanley McMichael Publishing Organization. [§5.7]

McMillen, Daniel P. 1990. "The Timing and Duration of Development Tax Rate Increases." *Journal of Urban Economics* 28: 1–18. [§8.6]

McMillen, Daniel P., and John F. McDonald. 1993. "Could Zoning Have Increased Land Values in Chicago?" *Journal of Urban Economics* 33: 167–188. [§5.5]

———. 2002. "Land Values in a Newly Zoned City." *Review of Economics and Statistics* 84: 62–72. [§5.7]

Meadows, Donella H. 1991. *The Global Citizen*. Washington, DC: Island Press. [§5.20]

Meck, Stuart. 1996. "Model Planning and Zoning Enabling Legislation: A Short History." *Modernizing State Planning Statutes: The Growing Smart Working Papers* 1: 1–18. [§4.5]

Meinig, Donald W. 1986. *The Shaping of America: A Geographical Perspective on 500 Years of History*. New Haven, CT: Yale University Press. [§§8.8, 8.11]

Meltzer, Rachel, and Ron Cheung. 2013. "Homeowners Associations and the Demand for Local Land Use Regulation." *Journal of Regional Science* 53: 511–534. [§§2.15, 2.16]

Merrill, Thomas W. 1986. "The Economics of Public Use." *Cornell Law Review* 72: 61–116. [§9.5]

———. 2010. "Direct Voting by Property Owners." *University of Chicago Law Review* 77: 275–310. [§2.16]

Merrill, Thomas W., and Henry E. Smith. 2000. "Optimal Standardization in the Law of Property: The Numerus Clausus Principle." *Yale Law Journal* 110: 1–70. [§6.4]

Metzenbaum, James. 1930. *The Law of Zoning*. New York: Baker, Voorhis. [§5.14]

Meyer, William B. 2013. *The Environmental Advantages of Cities: Countering Commonsense Antiurbanism*. Cambridge, MA: MIT Press. [§8.15]

Michelman, Frank I. 1967. "Property, Utility, and Fairness: Comments on the Ethical Foundations of 'Just Compensation' Law." *Harvard Law Review* 80: 1165–1258. [§§5.11, 9.7]

———. 1988. "Takings, 1987." *Columbia Law Review* 88: 1600–1629. [§9.7]

Mieszkowski, Peter. 1972. "The Property Tax: An Excise Tax or a Profits Tax?" *Journal of Public Economics* 1: 73–96. [§4.4]

Mieszkowski, Peter, and Edwin S. Mills. 1993. "The Causes of Metropolitan Suburbanization." *Journal of Economic Perspectives* 7: 135–147. [§5.16]

Mieszkowski, Peter, and George R. Zodrow. 1989. "Taxation and the Tiebout Model: The Differential Effects of Head Taxes, Taxes on Land Rents, and Property Taxes." *Journal of Economic Literature* 27: 1098–1146. [§§4.4, 4.8]

Mildner, Gerald C., Kenneth J. Dueker, and Anthony M. Rufolo. 1996. *Impact of the Urban Growth Boundary on Metropolitan Housing Markets*. Portland, OR: Portland State University Center for Urban Studies. [§§2.9, 8.8]

Miller, Gary J. 1981. *Cities by Contract: The Politics of Municipal Incorporation*. Cambridge, MA: MIT Press. [§5.9]

Mills, David E. 1981. "Growth, Speculation and Sprawl in a Monocentric City." *Journal of Urban Economics* 10: 201–226. [§8.6]

Mills, Edwin S. 1979. "Economic Analysis of Urban Land-Use Controls." In *Current Issues in Urban Economics*, ed. Peter Mieszkowski and Mahlon Straszheim. Baltimore, MD: Johns Hopkins University Press. [§5.15]

Mills, Edwin S., and Bruce W. Hamilton. 1994. *Urban Economics*, 5th ed. Glenview, IL: Scott, Foresman. [§8.18]

Mitchell, James L. 2004. "Will Empowering Developers to Challenge Exclusionary Zoning Increase Suburban Housing Choice?" *Journal of Policy Analysis and Management* 23: 119–134. [§§3.13, 5.25, 9.17]

Mohl, Raymond A. 2004. "Stop the Road: Freeway Revolts in American Cities." *Journal of Urban History* 30: 674–706. [§§2.11, 5.22]

Molotch, Harvey. 1976. "The City as a Growth Machine: Toward a Political Economy of Place." *American Journal of Sociology* 82: 309–332. [§§4.14, 8.4, 9.6]

Monkkonen, Eric H. 1988. *America Becomes Urban: The Development of United States Cities and Towns, 1780–1980*. Berkeley: University of California Press. [§6.13]

———. 1995. *The Local State: Public Money and American Cities*. Stanford, CA: Stanford University Press. [§6.13]

Moore, Kathryn L. 2011. "The Lexington-Fayette Urban County Board of Adjustment: Fifty Years Later." *Kentucky Law Journal* 100: 435–529. [§§2.5, 2.18]

Moretti, Enrico. 2012. *The New Geography of Jobs*. Boston: Houghton Mifflin Harcourt. [§§5.1, 5.25]

———. 2013. "Real Wage Inequality." *American Economic Journal: Applied Economics* 5: 65–103. [§§5.1, 8.11]

Morriss, Andrew P. 1995. "'This State Will Soon Have Plenty of Laws': Lessons from One Hundred Years of Codification in Montana." *Montana Law Review* 56: 359–450. [§3.2]

———. 2009. "Symbol or Substance? An Empirical Assessment of State Responses to *Kelo*." *Supreme Court Economic Review* 17: 237–278. [§9.5]

Moses, Leon, and Harold F. Williamson Jr. 1967. "The Location of Economic Activity in Cities." *American Economic Review* 57: 211–222. [§5.6]

Motomura, Hiroshi. 1983. "Preclearance under Section Five of the Voting Rights Act." *North Carolina Law Review* 61: 189–246. [§8.12]

Munro, William B. 1931. "A Danger Spot in the Zoning Movement." *Annals of the American Academy of Political and Social Sciences* 155: 202–206. [§5.7]

Musgrave, Richard A. 1939. "The Voluntary Exchange Theory of Public Economy." *Quarterly Journal of Economics* 53: 213–237. [§6.7]

National Agricultural Lands Study. 1981. *Final Report*. Washington, DC: U.S. Government Printing Office. [§1.1]

National Commission on Urban Problems. 1968. *Building the American City*. New York: Praeger. [§5.14]

[*National Municipal Review*]. 1927. "Editorial Comment." *National Municipal Review* 16 (June): 353. [§3.4]

Nechyba, Thomas. J. 2001. "The Benefit View and the New View: Where Do We Stand, Twenty-Five Years into the Debate?" In *Property Taxation and Local Government Finance*, ed. Wallace E. Oates. Cambridge, MA: Lincoln Institute of Land Policy. [§4.4]

Nelson, Robert H. 1977. *Zoning and Property Rights*. Cambridge, MA: MIT Press. [§2.18]

———. 1999. "Privatizing the Neighborhood: A Proposal to Replace Zoning with Private Collective Property Rights to Existing Neighborhoods." *George Mason Law Review* 7: 827–880. [§2.16]

———. 2005. *Private Neighborhoods and the Transformation of Local Government*. Washington, DC: Urban Institute. [§2.15]

Nguyen, Mai Thi. 2007. "Local Growth Control at the Ballot Box: Real Effects or Symbolic Politics?" *Journal of Urban Affairs* 29: 129–147. [§3.17]

Nolon, Sean F. 2009. "The Lawyer as Process Advocate: Encouraging Collaborative Approaches to Controversial Development Decisions." *Pace Environmental Law Review* 27: 103–150. [§9.15]

Nye, Joseph S., Philip Zelikow, and David C. King. 1997. *Why People Don't Trust Government.* Cambridge, MA: Harvard University Press. [§5.17]

Oates, Wallace E. 1969. "The Effects of Property Taxes and Local Public Spending on Property Values: An Empirical Study of Tax Capitalization and the Tiebout Hypothesis." *Journal of Political Economy* 77: 957–971. [§§4.4, 4.15, 5.10]

———. 2005. "Property Taxation and Local Public Spending: The Renter Effect." *Journal of Urban Economics* 57: 419–431. [§6.10]

Oates, Wallace E., and Robert M. Schwab. 1997. "The Impact of Urban Land Taxation: The Pittsburgh Experience." *National Tax Journal* 50: 1–22. [§1.6]

Ohls, James C., and David Pines. 1975. "Discontinuous Urban Development and Economic Efficiency." *Land Economics* 51: 224–234. [§8.6]

Ortalo-Magné, Francois, and Andrea Prat. 2014. "On the Political Economy of Urban Growth: Homeownership Versus Affordability." *American Economic Journal—Microeconomics* 6: 154–181. [§§5.0, 7.5]

O'Toole, Randal. 2007. "Debunking Portland: The City that Doesn't Work." *Cato Policy Analysis* 596: 1–24. [§8.8]

Owley, Jessica. 2011. "Changing Property in a Changing World: A Call for the End of Perpetual Conservation Easements." *Stanford Environmental Law Journal* 30: 121–173. [§2.17]

Pack, Howard, and Janet R. Pack. 1977. "Metropolitan Fragmentation and Suburban Homogeneity." *Urban Studies* 14: 191–201. [§§4.10, 9.17]

Paulsen, Kurt. 2013. "The Effects of Growth Management on the Spatial Extent of Urban Development, Revisited." *Land Economics* 89: 193–210. [§2.13]

Pauly, Mark V. 1973. "Income Redistribution as a Local Public Good." *Journal of Public Economics* 2: 35–58. [§4.11]

Peiser, Richard B. 1981. "Land Development Regulation: A Case Study of Dallas and Houston, Texas." *AREUEA Journal* 9: 397–417. [§8.9]

———. 1989. "Density and Urban Sprawl." *Land Economics* 65: 193–204. [§§1.1, 8.6]

Peñalver, Eduardo M. 2004. "Is Land Special? The Unjustified Preference for Real Property in Regulatory Takings Law." *Ecology Law Quarterly* 31: 227–287. [§3.1]

Pendall, Rolf, Jonathan Martin, and William B. Fulton. 2002. *Holding the Line: Urban Containment in the United States.* Washington, DC: Brookings Institution. [§2.9]

Pendall, Ronald, M. Wolanski, and Douglas McGovern. 2002. "Property Rights in State Legislatures: Rural-Urban Differences in Support for State Anti-Taking Bills." *Journal of Rural Studies* 18: 19–33. [§§5.10, 8.2]

Persky, Joseph. 1990. "Suburban Income Inequality: Three Theories and a Few Facts." *Regional Science and Urban Economics* 20: 125–137. [§4.10]

Peters, Shawn F. 2003. *The Yoder Case: Religious Freedom, Education, and Parental Rights.* Lawrence: University Press of Kansas. [§9.9]

Peterson, George E., and Harvey Yampolsky. 1975. *Urban Development and the Protection of Metropolitan Farmland.* Washington, DC: Urban Institute. [§5.20]

Phillips, Justin, and Eban Goodstein. 2000. "Growth Management and Housing Prices: The Case of Portland, Oregon." *Contemporary Economic Policy* 18: 334–344. [§§8.7, 8.8]

Pickrell, Don H. 1992. "A Desire Named Streetcar: Fantasy and Fact in Rail Transit Planning." *Journal of the American Planning Association* 58: 158–176. [§8.5]

Pidot, Jeff. 2005. *Reinventing Conservation Easements.* Cambridge, MA: Lincoln Institute of Land Policy. [§2.17]

Piketty, Thomas. 2014. *Capital in the Twenty-first Century.* Cambridge, MA: Harvard University Press. [§1.10]

Pines, David, and Yoram Weiss. 1976. "Land Improvement Projects and Land Values." *Journal of Urban Economics* 3: 1–13. [§8.17]

Pittsburgh Committee on Taxation. 1916. *Report of the Committee on Taxation Study to Council of the City of Pittsburgh, Pennsylvania.* Pittsburgh. [§4.3]

Plager, Jay. 1995. "Takings Law and Appellate Decision Making." *Environmental Law* 25: 161–169. [§§3.0, 9.9]

Plotkin, Sidney. 1987. *Keep Out: The Struggle for Land Use Control.* Berkeley: University of California Press. [§2.12]

Plotnick, Robert D., and Richard F. Winters. 1985. "A Politico-Economic Theory of Income Redistribution." *American Political Science Review* 79: 458–473. [§4.11]

Plott, Charles R., and Kathryn Zeiler. 2005. "The Willingness to Pay–Willingness to Accept Gap." *American Economic Review* 95: 530–545. [§6.17]

Pollakowski, Henry O., and Susan M. Wachter. 1990. "The Effects of Land-Use Constraints on Housing Prices." *Land Economics* 66: 315–324. [§7.9]

Pollard, W. L. 1931. "Outline of the Law of Zoning in the United States." *Annals of the American Academy of Political and Social Science* 155(2): 15–33. [§§2.3, 5.12]

Pomeroy, Adam R. 2012. "*Penn Central* After 35 Years: A Three Part Balancing Test or a One Strike Rule?" *Federal Circuit Bar Journal* 22: 677–706. [§3.20]

Popper, Frank. 1988. "Understanding American Land Use Regulation Since 1970." *Journal of the American Planning Association* 54: 291–301. [§5.21]

Porter, Douglas R. 2008. *Managing Growth in America's Communities*, 2nd ed. Washington, DC: Island Press. [§2.13]

Poterba, James M. 1984. "Tax Subsidies to Owner-Occupied Housing: An Asset-Market Approach." *Quarterly Journal of Economics* 99: 729–752. [§§5.24, 7.11]

Poutvaara, Panu, and Andreas Wagener. 2006. "The Economic Costs and the Political Allure of Conscription." Discussion paper No. 106. Helsinki Center of Economic Research. [§6.16]

———. 2011. "The Political Economy of Conscription." In *Handbook on the Political Economy of War*, ed. Christopher J. Coyne and Rachel Mathers. Northampton, MA: Edward Elgar. [§6.16]

Powell, David L., Robert M. Rhodes, and Dan R. Stengle. 1995. "A Measured Step to Protect Private Property Rights." *Florida State University Law Review* 23: 255–314. [§9.9]

Power, Garrett. 1983. "Apartheid Baltimore Style: The Residential Segregation Ordinances of 1910–1913." *Maryland Law Review* 42: 289–328. [§§3.5, 3.6]

President's Commission on Housing. 1982. *Report.* Washington, DC: U.S. Government Printing Office. [§5.14]

President's Committee on Urban Housing. 1969. *A Decent Home: The Report of the President's Committee on Urban Housing.* Washington, DC: U.S. Government Printing Office. [§5.14]

Protash, William, and Mark Baldassare. 1983. "Growth Policies and Community Status: A Test and Modification of Logan's Theory." *Urban Affairs Review* 18: 397–412. [§5.19]

Pugh, Donna, and Alexander Lucas. 2012. "Fighting Dirty: The New Frontier of Competitors' Conduct in Zoning Disputes." *Zoning and Planning Law Report* 35(11): 1–12. [§7.8]

Putnam, Robert D. 2000. *Bowling Alone: The Collapse and Revival of American Community.* New York: Simon and Schuster. [§9.13]

Quigley, John M. 2007. "Regulation and Property Values in the United States: The High Cost of Monopoly." In *Land Policies and Their Outcomes*, ed. Gregory K. Ingram and Yu-Hung Hong. Cambridge, MA: Lincoln Institute of Land Policy. [§7.8]

Rabin, Jack, W. Bartley Hildreth, and Gerald Miller. 1989. *Handbook of Public Administration*, 2nd ed. New York: Marcel Dekker. [§4.13]

Radin, Margaret J. 1988. "The Liberal Conception of Property: Cross Currents in the Jurisprudence of Takings." *Columbia Law Review* 88: 1667–1696. [§3.25]

Rawls, John. 1971. *A Theory of Justice.* Cambridge, MA: Belknap Press. [§9.6]

Reichman, Uriel. 1976. "Residential Private Governments: An Introductory Survey." *University of Chicago Law Review* 43: 253–306. [§§2.15, 7.6]

Reilly, William K., ed. 1973. *The Use of Land: A Citizens Policy Guide to Urban Growth.* New York: Thomas Crowell. [§2.6]

Reps, John W. 1965. *The Making of Urban America: A History of City Planning in the United States.* Princeton, NJ: Princeton University Press. [§5.4]

Revell, Keith D. 1992. "Regulating the Landscape: Real Estate Values, City Planning, and the 1916 Zoning Ordinance." In *The Landscape of Modernity: New York City, 1900–1940*, ed. David Ward and Oliver Zunz. Baltimore: Johns Hopkins University Press. [§5.11]

———. 1999. "The Road to *Euclid v. Ambler*: City Planning, State Building, and the Changing Scope of the Police Power." *Studies in American Political Development* 13: 50–145. [§5.14]

Richards, J. Gregory. 1982. "Zoning for Direct Social Control." *Duke Law Journal* 1982: 761–845. [§2.1]

Richardson, Jesse J., Jr. 2004. "Downzoning, Fairness and Farmland Protection." *Journal of Land Use and Environmental Law* 19: 59–90. [§9.2]

Richardson, Jesse J., Meghan Z. Gough, and Robert Puentes. 2003. *Is Home Rule the Answer? Clarifying the Influence of Dillon's Rule on Growth Management.* Washington, DC: Center on Urban and Metropolitan Policy, Brookings Institution. [§3.2]

Riddiough, Timothy J. 1997. "The Economic Consequences of Regulatory Taking Risk on Land Value and Development Activity." *Journal of Urban Economics* 41: 56–77. [§9.7]

Riva, Enrico. 1984. "Regulatory Takings in American Law and 'Material Expropriation' in Swiss Law: A Comparison of the Applicable Standards." *Urban Lawyer* 16: 425–458. [§9.10]

Rockoff, Jonah E. 2010. "Local Response to Fiscal Incentives in Heterogeneous Communities." *Journal of Urban Economics* 68: 138–147. [§6.12]

Rose, Carol M. 1984. "New Models for Local Land Use Decisions." *Northwestern University Law Review* 79: 1155–1171. [§3.12]

———. 1989. "The Ancient Constitution vs. the Federalist Empire: Anti-Federalism from the Attack on Monarchism to Modern Localism." *Northwestern University Law Review* 84: 74–105. [§3.2]

———. 2004. "The Story of *Shelley v. Kraemer*." In *Property Stories*, ed. Gerald Korngold and Andrew P. Morriss. New York: Foundation Press. [§3.6]

———. 2006. "What Federalism Tells Us About Takings Jurisprudence." *UCLA Law Review* 54: 1681–1701. [§9.3]

Rose, Louis A. 1989. "Urban Land Supply: Natural and Contrived Restrictions." *Journal of Urban Economics* 25: 325–345. [§§7.11, 8.14]

Rose-Ackerman, Susan. 1979. "Market Models of Local Government: Exit, Voting, and the Land Market." *Journal of Urban Economics* 6: 319–337. [§8.17]

Rosen, Harvey S., and Kenneth T. Rosen. 1980. "Federal Taxes and Homeownership: Evidence from Time Series." *Journal of Political Economy* 88: 59–75. [§9.12]

Rosen, Kenneth T., and Mitchel Resnick. 1980. "The Size Distribution of Cities: An Examination of the Pareto Law and Primacy." *Journal of Urban Economics* 8: 165–186. [§1.3]

Rosenberg, Gerald K. 1991. *The Hollow Hope: Can Courts Bring About Social Change?* Chicago: University of Chicago Press. [§3.6]

Ross, Justin M. 2013. "Are Community-Nuisance Fiscal Zoning Arrangements Undermined by State Property Tax Reforms? Evidence from Nuclear Power Plants and School Finance Equalization." *Land Economics* 89: 449–465. [§5.19]

Ross, Justin M., Joshua C. Hall, and William G. Resh. 2014. "Frictions in Polycentric Administration with Noncongruent Borders: Evidence from Ohio School District Class Sizes." *Public Administration Research and Theory* 24: 623–649. [§4.12]

Rothwell, Jonathan T. 2009. "The Origins of Zoning: Rural Settlements vs. Urbanization." Available at SSRN: http://ssrn.com/abstract=1422737. [§5.3]

———. 2012. *Housing Costs, Zoning, and Access to High-Scoring Schools*. Washington, DC: Brookings Institution. [§1.10]

Rowan, Katrin C. 2007. "Anti-Exclusionary Zoning in Pennsylvania: A Weapon for Developers, a Loss for Low Income Pennsylvanians." *Temple Law Review* 80: 1271–1304. [§9.17]

Ruane, Kathleen A. 2012. *The Siting of Wireless Communications Facilities: An Overview of Federal, State, and Local Law*. Washington, DC: Congressional Research Service. [§2.12]

Rudel, Thomas K. 1989. *Situations and Strategies in American Land-Use Planning*. Cambridge, UK: Cambridge University Press. [§§4.14, 5.6, 7.3, 8.2]

Rudel, Thomas K., Karen O'Neill, Karen, Paul Gottlieb, Melanie McDermott, and Colleen Hatfield. 2011. "From Middle to Upper Class Sprawl? Land Use Controls and Changing Patterns of Real Estate Development in Northern New Jersey." *Annals of the Association of American Geographers* 101: 609–624. [§§5.25, 8.3]

Rueben, Kim, and Sheila Murray. 2008. "Racial Disparities in Education Finance: Going Beyond Equal Revenues." Brookings Discussion paper No. 29. [§5.19]

Sager, Lawrence G. 1969. "Tight Little Islands: Exclusionary Zoning, Equal Protection, and the Indigent." *Stanford Law Review* 21: 767–800. [§§3.17, 5.19]

Saiz, Albert. 2010. "The Geographic Determinants of Housing Supply." *Quarterly Journal of Economics* 125: 1253–1296. [§§7.11, 8.14]

Saks, Raven E. 2008. "Job Creation and Housing Construction: Constraints on Metropolitan Area Employment Growth." *Journal of Urban Economics* 64: 178–195. [§§5.1, 8.14]

Salkin, Patricia E. 2012. "The Quiet Revolution and Federalism: Into the Future." *John Marshall Law Review* 45: 253–305. [§2.12]

Salkin, Patricia E., and Amy Lavine. 2008. "Genesis of RLUIPA and Federalism: Evaluating the Creation of a Federal Statutory Right and Its Impact on Local Government." *Urban Lawyer* 40: 195–267. [§3.17]

Salvino, Robert, Michael T. Tasto, and Geoffrey K. Turnbull. 2012. "A Direct Test of Direct Democracy: New England Town Meetings." *Applied Economics* 44: 2393–2402. [§4.12]

Samuels, Warren J. 1971. "Interrelations Between Legal and Economic Processes." *Journal of Law and Economics* 24: 435–450. [§9.8]

Samuelson, Paul A. 1954. "The Pure Theory of Public Expenditures." *Review of Economics and Statistics* 36: 387–389. [§§4.10, 6.7]

Sanjek, Roger. 1998. *The Future of Us All: Race and Neighborhood Politics in New York City*. Ithaca, NY: Cornell University Press. [§2.4]

Sax, Joseph L. 1993. "Property Rights and the Economy of Nature: Understanding *Lucas v. South Carolina Coastal Council*." *Stanford Law Review* 45: 1433–1455. [§3.24]

Saxer, Shelley R. 1998. "Zoning Away First Amendment Rights." *Washington University Journal of Urban and Contemporary Law* 53: 1–111. [§3.15]

Schaeffer, K. H., and Elliott Sklar. 1975. *Access for All: Transportation and Urban Growth*. Harmondsworth, UK: Penguin Books. [§5.6]

Schelling, Thomas C. 1971. "Dynamic Models of Segregation." *Journal of Mathematical Sociology* 1: 143–186. [§4.11]

Schiller, Suzanne I. 2000. "Petition and Protest: How to Deal with Expressive Activity." *National Real Estate Investor*, July 1. http://nreionline.com/mag/security-petition-and-protest-how-deal-expressive-activity. [§3.15]

Schleicher, David. 2013. "City Unplanning." *Yale Law Journal* 122: 1670–1737. [§§5.16, 8.4]

Schmidt, Benno C., Jr. 1982. "Principle and Prejudice: The Supreme Court and Race in the Progressive Era. Part 1: The Heyday of Jim Crow." *Columbia Law Review* 82: 444–524. [§3.5]

Schmidt, Stephan. 2008. "From Pro-Growth to Slow-Growth in Suburban New Jersey." *Journal of Planning Education and Research* 27: 306–318. [§8.3]

Schmidt, Stephan, and Kurt Paulsen. 2009. "Is Open-Space Preservation a Form of Exclusionary Zoning? The Evolution of Municipal Open-Space Policies in New Jersey." *Urban Affairs Review* 4: 92–118. [§§5.25, 9.16]

Schoen, Robert, Young J. Kim, Constance A. Nathanson, Nan Marie Astone, and Jason Fields. 1997. "Why Do Americans Want Children?" *Population and Development Review* 23: 333–358. [§4.13]

Schuetz, Jenny. 2008. "Guarding the Town Walls: Mechanisms and Motives for Restricting Multifamily Housing in Massachusetts." *Real Estate Economics* 36: 555–586. [§5.3]

Schuetz, Jenny, Rachel Meltzer, and Vicki Been. 2011. "Silver Bullet or Trojan Horse? The Effects of Inclusionary Zoning on Local Housing Markets." *Urban Studies* 48: 297–329. [§7.10]

Schwartz, Amy Ellen, Scott Susin, and Ioan Voicu. 2003. "Has Falling Crime Driven New York City's Real Estate Boom?" *Journal of Housing Research* 14: 101–135. [§8.4]

Schwieterman, Joseph P., Dana M. Caspall, and Jane Heron. 2006. *The Politics of Place: A History of Zoning in Chicago*. Chicago: Lake Claremont Press. [§§5.9, 5.13, 8.4]

Serkin, Christopher. 2007. "Local Property Law: Adjusting the Scale of Property Protection." *Columbia Law Review* 107: 883–948. [§§9.3, 9.18]

———. 2009. "Existing Uses and the Limits of Land Use Regulation." *New York University Law Review* 84: 1222–1291. [§§2.4, 5.11, 5.13]

———. 2010. "Entrenching Environmentalism: Private Conservation Easements over Public Land." *University of Chicago Law Review* 77: 341–366. [§§2.14, 7.9]

———. 2014. "Passive Takings: The State's Affirmative Duty to Protect Property." *Michigan Law Review* 113: 345–404. [§9.9]

Shiller, Robert J., and Allan N. Weiss. 1999. "Home Equity Insurance." *Journal of Real Estate Finance and Economics* 19: 21–47. [§§5.10, 9.15]

Sidak, J. Gregory, and Daniel F. Spulber. 1996. "Deregulatory Takings and Breach of the Regulatory Contract." *New York University Law Review* 71: 851–999. [§9.9]

Siegan, Bernard H. 1972. *Land Use Without Zoning.* Lexington, MA: Lexington Books. [§§5.8, 8.9]

Silva, Fabio, and Jon C. Sonstelie. 1995. "Did *Serrano* Cause a Decline in School Spending?" *National Tax Journal* 48: 199–215. [§6.12]

Simon, Julian L., and Seymour Sudman. 1982. "How Much Farmland Is Being Converted to Urban Use?" *International Regional Science Review* 7: 257–272. [§1.1]

Skidmore, Mark, and Michael Peddle. 1998. "Do Development Impact Fees Reduce the Rate of Residential Development?" *Growth and Change* 29: 383–400. [§3.26]

Skinner, Jonathan S. 1994. "Housing and Saving in the United States." In *Housing Markets in the U.S. and Japan*, ed. Yukio Noguchi and James Poterba. Chicago: University of Chicago Press. [§5.24]

Somerville, C. Tsuriel. 1999. "The Industrial Organization of Housing Supply: Market Activity, Land Supply and the Size of Homebuilder Firms." *Real Estate Economics* 27: 669–694. [§§1.9, 7.13]

Somin, Ilya. 2008. "The Limits of Backlash: Assessing the Political Response to *Kelo*." *Minnesota Law Review* 93: 2100–2178. [§9.5]

Sonstelie, Jon C., and Paul R. Portney. 1978. "Profit Maximizing Communities and the Theory of Local Public Expenditures." *Journal of Urban Economics* 5: 263–277. [§§7.4, 8.17]

Span, Henry. 2001. "How the Courts Should Fight Exclusionary Zoning." *Seton Hall Law Review* 32: 1–107. [§3.13]

Speyrer, Janet Furman. 1989. "The Effect of Land Use Restrictions on the Market Value of Single Family Homes in Houston." *Journal of Real Estate Finance and Economics* 2: 117–130. [§8.9]

Spry, John. 2005. "The Effects of Fiscal Competition on Local Property and Income Tax Reliance." *Topics in Economic Analysis and Policy* 5: 1–19. [§4.3]

Staley, Samuel R. 2001. "Ballot-Box Zoning, Transaction Costs, and Urban Growth." *Journal of the American Planning Association* 67: 25–37. [§§3.17, 6.9]

[*Stanford Law Review*]. 1955. "Note: The Elimination of Nonconforming Uses." *Stanford Law Review* 7: 415–421. [§5.11]

Stark, Kirk, and Jonathan Zasloff. 2003. "Tiebout and Tax Revolts: Did *Serrano* Really Cause Proposition 13?" *UCLA Law Review* 50: 801–858. [§4.16]

Steffens, Lincoln. 1904. *The Shame of the Cities.* New York: McClure, Phillips. [§2.18]

Stein, Gregory M. 2012. "The Modest Impact of *Palazzolo v. Rhode Island*." *Vermont Law Review* 36: 675–730. [§3.22]

Sterk, Stewart E. 1985. "Freedom from Freedom of Contract: The Enduring Value of Servitude Restrictions." *Iowa Law Review* 70: 615–662. [§2.15]

———. 1987. "Neighbors in American Land Law." *Columbia Law Review* 87: 55–104. [§6.6]

———. 2004. "The Federalist Dimension of Regulatory Takings Jurisprudence." *Yale Law Journal* 114: 203–271. [§9.9]

———. 2011. "Structural Obstacles to Settlement of Land Use Disputes." *Boston University Law Review* 91: 227–272. [§§2.11, 7.12]

Stigler, George J. 1966. *The Theory of Price*, 3rd ed. New York: Macmillan. [§6.3]

Surowiecki, James. 2004. *The Wisdom of Crowds.* New York: Doubleday. [§6.11]

Swift, Earl. 2011. *The Big Roads: The Untold Story of the Engineers, Visionaries, and Trailblazers Who Created the American Superhighways.* Boston: Houghton Mifflin Harcourt. [§5.22]

Talen, Emily. 2012. *City Rules: How Regulations Affect Urban Form*. Washington, DC: Island Press. [§2.1]

Tarr, Joel A. 1996. *The Search for the Ultimate Sink: Urban Pollution in Historical Perspective*. Akron, OH: University of Akron Press. [§5.4]

Teaford, Jon C. 1979. *City and Suburb: The Political Fragmentation of Metropolitan America, 1850–1970*. Baltimore, MD: Johns Hopkins University Press. [§§2.2, 5.9, 7.12]

———. 1997. *Post-Suburbia: Government and Politics in the Edge Cities*. Baltimore, MD: Johns Hopkins University Press. [§§5.9, 5.10, 5.18, 5.21]

Thibodeau, Thomas. 1992. *Residential Real Estate Prices 1974–1983: From the Standard Metropolitan Area Annual Housing Surveys*. Mount Pleasant, MI: Blackstone. [§5.1]

Thompson, Barton H., Jr. 1997. "The Endangered Species Act: A Case Study in Takings and Incentives." *Stanford Law Review* 49: 601–676. [§2.11]

Thorson, James A. 1996. "An Examination of the Monopoly Zoning Hypothesis." *Land Economics* 72: 43–55. [§7.11]

———. 1997. "The Effect of Zoning on Housing Construction." *Journal of Housing Economics* 6: 81–91. [§§8.6, 9.7]

Tideman, T. Nicolaus. 1969. "Three Approaches to Improving Urban Land Use." Ph.D. dissertation, University of Chicago. [§5.21]

Tiebout, Charles M. 1956. "A Pure Theory of Local Expenditures." *Journal of Political Economy* 64: 416–424. [§§4.4, 6.10, 7.4, 7.13]

Toll, Seymour. 1969. *Zoned American*. New York: Grossman. [§§5.4, 5.7]

U.S. Bureau of the Census. 1975. *Historical Statistics of the United States, Colonial Times to 1970*. Washington, DC: U.S. Department of Commerce. [§§5.6, 5.18]

U.S. Department of Agriculture, Natural Resources Conservation Service. 2007. *National Resources Inventory*. Washington, DC: U.S. Department of Agriculture.

Van Kampen, Carol. 1977. "From Dairy Valley to Chino: An Example of Urbanization in Southern California's Dairy Land." *California Geographer* 17: 39–48. [§4.15]

Veiller, Lawrence. 1916. "Districting by Municipal Regulation." *Proceedings of the Eighth National Conference on City Planning*. New York: National Conference on City Planning. [§§5.11, 5.13]

Ventry, Dennis J. 2010. "The Accidental Deduction: A History and Critique of the Tax Subsidy for Mortgage Interest." *Law and Contemporary Problems* 73: 233–284. [§8.5]

Voith, Richard, and Joseph Gyourko. 2002. "Capitalization of Federal Taxes, the Relative Price of Housing, and Urban Form: Density and Sorting Effects." *Regional Science and Urban Economics* 32: 673–690. [§§9.12, 9.14]

Von Hoffman, Alexander. 1996. "Weaving Urban Fabric: Nineteenth-Century Patterns of Residential Real Estate Development in Outer Boston." *Journal of Urban History* 22: 191–230. [§§5.5, 5.10]

———. 2006. *Creating an Anti-Growth Regulatory Regime: A Case from Greater Boston*. Cambridge, MA: Rappaport Institute for Greater Boston. [§§7.1, 7.13]

———. 2010a. *To Preserve and Protect: Land Use Regulations in Weston, Massachusetts*. Cambridge, MA: Joint Center for Housing Studies, Harvard University. [§§4.3, 5.4, 7.1]

———. 2010b. *Wrestling with Growth in Acton, Massachusetts: The Possibilities and Limits of Progressive Planning*. Cambridge, MA: Rappaport Institute for Greater Boston. [§§7.1, 7.2, 7.3]

Wagner, Kevin M. 2010. "Rewriting the Guarantee Clause: Justifying Direct Democracy in the Constitution." *Willamette Law Review* 47: 67–100. [§3.22]

Walker, Peter A., and Patrick Hurley. 2011. *Planning Paradise: Politics and Visioning of Land Use in Oregon*. Tucson: University of Arizona Press. [§8.8]

Walls, Margaret, Carolyn Kousky, and Ziyan Chu. 2013. "Is What You See What You Get? The Value of Natural Landscape Views." Resources for the Future Discussion paper, 13–25. [§§8.3, 8.13]

Warner, Deborah Jean, and Robert B. Ariail. 1995. *Alvan Clark & Sons, Artists in Optics*. Richmond, VA: Willmann-Bell and the Smithsonian Institution. [§§3.8, 3.11]

Warner, Sam Bass. 1962. *Streetcar Suburbs: The Process of Growth in Boston, 1870–1900*. New York: Atheneum. [§5.5]

———. 1972. *The Urban Wilderness: A History of the American City*. New York: Harper & Row. [§§5.4, 5.7]

Weber, Rachel, Saurav Dev Bhattaa, and David Merriman. 2007. "Spillovers from Tax Increment Financing Districts: Implications for Housing Price Appreciation." *Regional Science and Urban Economics* 37: 259–281. [§4.9]

Weiss, Marc A. 1987. *The Rise of the Community Builders: The American Real Estate Industry and Urban Land Planning*. New York: Columbia University Press. [§§5.4, 5.8, 5.13, 7.6]

Werczbergera, Elia. 1997. "Home Ownership and Rent Control in Switzerland." *Housing Studies* 12: 337–353. [§9.12]

Wheaton, William C. 1977. "Income and Urban Residence: An Analysis of Consumer Demand for Location." *American Economic Review* 67: 620–631. [§5.18]

Wheeler, Michael. 1994. "Negotiating NIMBYs: Learning from the Failure of the Massachusetts Siting Law." *Yale Journal on Regulation* 11: 241–291. [§2.13]

White, Gilbert F. [1945]. "Human Adjustment to Floods." In *Geography, Resources, and Environment*, Volume 1, ed. Robert W. Kates and Ian Burton. Chicago: University of Chicago Press, 1986. [original PhD dissertation University of Chicago 1945] [§6.14]

White, James R. 1988. "Large Lot Zoning and Subdivision Costs: A Test." *Journal of Urban Economics* 23: 370–384. [§8.6]

Whittemore, Andrew H. 2012. "Zoning Los Angeles: A Brief History of Four Regimes." *Planning Perspectives* 27: 393–415. [§§5.14, 8.4]

Wickwar, W. Hardy. 1970. *The Political Theory of Local Government*. Columbia, SC: University of South Carolina Press. [§3.1]

Wilkerson, Isabel. 2010. *The Warmth of Other Suns: The Epic Story of America's Great Migration*. New York: Random House. [§5.1]

Williams, Eric J. 2011. *The Big House in a Small Town: Prisons, Communities, and Economics in Rural America*. Santa Barbara, CA: ABC-CLIO. [§§4.9, 8.2]

Williams, Joan C. 1986. "The Constitutional Vulnerability of American Local Government: The Politics of City Status in American Law." *Wisconsin Law Review* 1986: 83–153. [§3.2]

Williams, Norman, Jr. 1974. *American Land Planning Law*. St. Paul, MN: West. [§§2.11, 3.13, 3.16, 5.17, 5.19, 5.21]

———. 1982. "Planning Law in the 1980s: What Do We Know About It?" *Vermont Law Review* 7: 205–247. [§§5.14, 5.19]

Wittman, Donald. 1980. "First Come, First Served: An Economic Analysis of 'Coming to the Nuisance.'" *Journal of Legal Studies* 9: 557–568. [§2.14]

Wolf, Michael Allan. 2008. *The Zoning of America: Euclid v. Ambler*. Lawrence, KS: University Press of Kansas. [§3.3]

Wolff, Edward N. 1983. "The Size Distribution of Household Disposable Wealth in the United States." *Review of Income and Wealth* 29: 125–146. [§1.10]

Wood, Gordon S. 2009. *Empire of Liberty: A History of the Early Republic, 1789–1815.* Oxford, UK: Oxford University Press. [§9.6]

Worley, William S. 1990. *J. C. Nichols and the Shaping of Kansas City: Innovation in Planned Residential Communities.* Columbia: University of Missouri Press. [§5.8]

Wright, Gavin. 2006. *Slavery and American Economic Development.* Baton Rouge: Louisiana State University Press. [§8.12]

Xie, Feng, and David Levinson. 2010. "How Streetcars Shaped Suburbanization: A Granger Causality Analysis of Land Use and Transit in the Twin Cities." *Journal of Economic Geography* 10: 453–470. [§5.5]

Yamamoto, Eric K. 1999. "Racial Reparations: Japanese American Redress and African American Claims." *Boston College Third World Law Journal* 19: 477–523. [§9.9]

Young, Cristobal, Charles Varner, and Douglas S. Massey. 2008. *Trends in New Jersey Migration: Housing, Employment, and Taxation.* Princeton, NJ: Policy Research Institute of Woodrow Wilson School of Public Affairs, Princeton University. [§§5.1, 9.17]

Zabel, Jeffrey, and Maurice Dalton. 2011. "The Impact of Minimum Lot Size Regulations on House Prices in Eastern Massachusetts." *Regional Science and Urban Economics* 41: 571–583. [§§7.3, 8.13]

Zodrow, George R. 2001. "Reflections on the New View and the Benefit View of the Property Tax." In *Property Taxation and Local Government Finance*, ed. Wallace E. Oates. Cambridge, MA: Lincoln Institute of Land Policy. [§4.4]

———. 2007. "The Property Tax Incidence Debate and the Mix of State and Local Finance of Local Public Expenditures." *CESifo Economic Studies* 53: 495–521. [§§4.4, 4.8]

Zorn, Peter M., David E. Hansen, and Seymour I. Schwartz. 1986. "Mitigating the Price Effects of Growth Control: A Case Study of Davis, California." *Land Economics* 62: 47–57. [§8.4]

Index

Legal cases and authors cited are indexed in the References

Acton (Massachusetts), 261–268, 271, 276, 287–288, 294, 321, 324
Ambler Realty Company, 74–76, 82
American Farmland Trust, 1, 3–4
Amish, Old Order, 71
Ancient lights, legal doctrine of, 220, 222–223, 225, 227, 229, 231
Anti-growth organizations, interstate highway construction and, 208–210
Anti-snob zoning act (Massachusetts), 96, 150–151, 361–362
Apartheid zoning, 79, 81
Apartments, regulations restricting, 104–105, 113, 133, 168, 173, 177–178, 198, 264
Apple industry in Virginia, regulatory takings and, 341–343
Arlington (Massachusetts), 262, 286
Arrow impossibility theorem, 246
Article 60 (Massachusetts zoning amendment), 85
Assessors: land tax and, 15–16, 132; real property tax and 15, 143, 356
Australia, carbon tax and, 356

Balancing test for takings, 107, 109, 340
Ballard, consolidation with Seattle, 323
Ballot-box zoning, 102–103, 112, 128, 242
BART (Bay Area Transit System), 212
Bassett, Edward (zoning pioneer), 137, 168, 179, 186
Battersby, Sarah (geographer), 152
"Beggar-thy-neighbor" syndrome, 207
Bellaire (Texas), 309–310
Berra, Yogi (Yankee philosopher), 166
Bethlehem (Pennsylvania), 313
Bettman, Alfred (zoning pioneer), 76, 78, 137, 168
Bill of Rights, 73, 92; adoption of, 339–340; regulatory takings and, 349–350
Blackburn, Elizabeth (Dartmouth student), 106
Boston, development of suburbs surrounding, 172–173
Boulder (Colorado), growth boundary, 47
Brennan, William, opinion in *Penn Central Transportation Co. v. New York City*, 107, 108; *San Diego Gas* dissent, 105, 348–351
Brookline (Massachusetts), 174

401

Buchsbaum, Peter (New Jersey attorney), 295
Building codes, 46–47
Burnham, Daniel (Chicago planner), 367
Buses, effect on residential districts, 175, 178, 216
Byrd, Harry, (Virginia governor) 343

California: development of Dairy Valley, 158–159; freeway revolts, 210–212, 258; judicial anti-development stance, 217; Proposition 13, 161–162; voter initiatives and zoning in, 314–315. *See also individual cities*
California Coastal Commission, 55, 125, 127
California Coastal Zone, 317–318
California Supreme Court, 73, 98, 105, 161, 188–189, 217, 349; standoff with U.S. Supreme Court, 109–111
Cambridge (Massachusetts): introduction of zoning in, 85–86; *Nectow v. Cambridge*, 85–91
Capital, property tax as tax on, 136
Capital gains: from housing, 213, 217; taxing housing, 355
Capital markets, housing tax reform and, 355, 357
Capital-to-land ratio, 9; in metropolitan sprawl, 290, 291–292; Portland growth boundaries and, 305
Capitalization: property-tax, 159–160; undeveloped land and delayed, 157–158; zoning and housing prices and, 159, 250
Carbon tax, 321, 356
Categorical regulation, zoning and, 48
Cattle, Scottish Highland, 142–143
Cattle trespass example, 130–131, 141
Cedar rust, 341–343
Celebration (Florida), 159, 273
Cell-phone tower placement regulations, 53
Cell phones and crime reduction, 298
Central business district (CBD), 290, 291
"Character of the neighborhood," 38, 63

Chicago: adoption of zoning in, 173, 176–177; growth controls in, 297–298; overzoning in, 296; population of, 7; suburban development, 182
Church of St. Martin in the Fields, 11–12
Churches, zoning and, 54, 103
Cities: annexation of rural areas/suburbs by, 33, 34, 181–182, 311–312; back-to-the-city migrants and growth controls, 197; consumer, 157; edge, 292; fiscal zoning and, 156–158; outmigration from, 292; transition from prodevelopment to suburban norms, 296–299
Citizen power, rise of, 205, 206–207, 216–217
City Beautiful Movement, 170–171, 177
City of Industry (Los Angeles County), 169–170
City planners, 41–43, 137
City planning, 66
City size, urban agglomeration and, 6–10
Civil rights law, exclusionary zoning and, 201–203
Civitas (New York organization), 142
Clark, Alvan (telescope builder), 84–85, 87, 90–91
Clark, Alvan Graham (son), 84–85, 87, 90–91
Clark, George (son), 84–85, 87, 90–91
Clean Air Act, 51, 260
Clean Water Act, 49–51
Clem, David (developer), 238–242, 283
Cluster zoning, 31, 265; conservation easements and, 65; development density and, 321
Coase theorem, 123, 225–228, 231, 259; free-riding and, 237; newcomer fees and, 275; public goods and, 236–237; transaction costs and, 229–230
Columbia (Maryland), 323–324
Commerce Clause, Clean Water Act and, 50
Common-law adjudication, cross-state similarities in zoning and, 72–73
Community Benefit Agreements (CBAs), 358–359
Community character, as amenity, 268

Community development: in Acton, 262–268; congestion and political control of, 270–272; exclusionary spread to neighboring towns, 285–286; Goldilocks dilemma, 272–274; homeowners and zoning, 274–276; monopoly zoning, 276–283; Tiebout-style model, 268–270
Community heterogeneity: desire for limited, 149–152, 281; lack of zoning in Houston and, 310–311; Tiebout-Hamilton model and, 147–149
Community size, optimal, 271–274
Compensation: fracking, 334–335, 336; highways and, 258–259; for land use regulation, 250–251; Oregon Measure 37, 250–251, 253–254, 255–258, 307, 334. *See also* Just compensation
Conceptual severance, 117, 345
Conditional use permit, 38
Condorcet, Nicolas de (voting theories), 246, 247
Congestion, community development and optimal community size, 270–272
Conservation easements, 57, 64–66, 265, 288; impact on urban structure, 365; monopoly zoning and, 280
Conservation land purchases, 265, 280
Consumers' surplus, 237, 330
Contract zoning, 363
Cooley, Thomas M. (pro-local jurist), 73, 78
Corbett, Thomas M. (Pennsylvania governor), 334
Cost of community development, 268–270. *See also* Transaction costs
Cost regulation, regulatory takings and, 123–125
Council on Affordable Housing (New Jersey), 96
County, as unit of local government, 5, 33, 34
Covenants, 29, 139; developers demand for zoning to supplement, 178–180; protective, 59–61. *See also* Private covenants
Crime rates: decline in urban areas, 298; effect on suburbs, 197
Cropland, percent of U.S. land in, 3, 4

Cubberley, Elwood (education leader), 167
Cumulative zoning, 35, 88
Curative amendments for zoning (Pennsylvania), 105, 362

Dairy Valley (California), 158–159
Daly City (California), 323
Damages, injunctive relief *vs.*, 104
Daniell, Jere (Dartmouth historian), 293
Dartmouth College undergraduate research, x, 99, 103, 106, 144, 247, 296, 308–309, 338, 347
Day, William (Supreme Court Justice), 79
Deadweight loss, 132, 142–144; property rule protection and, 233
Declaration of Independence, 339
Deed records, 29
Del Webb (developer), 57–58, 286
Demoralization costs, just compensation and, 340–341
Density: agglomeration economies and, 320–322; Portland's growth boundaries and, 322–323; smart growth and, 56. *See also* Population density
Deregulatory takings, 346
Developers: clout in cities, 296; demand for zoning and, 171; demand for zoning to supplement covenants, 178–180; environmental reviews and, 285; exactions and impact fees and, 275; home value insurance and, 357–359; optimal community size and, 272–274; private covenants and, 59–61; rezoning and, 43–44; subdivision regulations and, 44–46; wetlands regulation and, 50–51; zoning in Acton and, 262–263, 266–268
Developers' cases, 100
Development: holistic projects, 144–147; infill, 56, 301, 367; leapfrog, 47, 56, 301; rate of, 4–5; zoning as means of controlling, 30–31
Dillon's rule, 73
Diminishing returns, law of, 25–26
Diversity. *See* Community heterogeneity
Dodgson, Charles (voting paradox), 246

Dolan, Frances (takings plaintiff), 120
Double-veto system, 54–57, 62, 68, 206, 216, 284, 365
Douglas, William O. (Supreme Court Justice), 102
Downzoning, 35–36, 264; economic effect of, 317; metropolitan sprawl from, 290–292; regulatory takings and, 332; in rural area, 294
Due process: *Euclid v. Ambler* and, 76; procedural, 92–93; substantive, 92, 93–94, 104–105; takings and, 97; zoning and, 92–94; zoning litigation and, 92–94

Earth Day, 204
Easements, 29; conservation, 57, 64–66, 265, 280, 288, 365
East Amwell (New Jersey), 293–296
Economic development, urban density and, 11–12
Economic inequality, suburbanization and, 202–203
Economic progress, role of cities in, 9
Economic rent, 12
Eden Roc Hotel (Miami Beach), 219–228, 231, 232–235
Edge cities, 292
Edgeworth box, 254
Efficiency: of land tax, 15; liability rule protection and, 234–235
Eisenhower, Dwight, and Interstate Highway System, 209
Ellickson, Robert, 69; cattle trespass example, 130–131, 141, 293; growth controls, 329; just compensation, 250; monopolistic zoning, 277; *Nolan/Dolan* test, 121; personal associations, 102; regulation of subnormal activities, 103; regulatory takings, 104, 250, 329–333; sublocal governing structures, 63; takings legislation, 345
Eminent domain, 30, 331; highway rights of way and, 258–259; holdouts and, 232; *Kelo v. New London*, 336–338; zoning by, 344–345

Eminent Domain Clause, 92
Employment: development and, 145; shift to suburbs, 199–201, 216
Encyclopedia of Cleveland History, 81–82
Endangered Species Act, 49, 51
Energy crisis of 1970, regional effects of, 313
Entitlements: Coase theorem and, 227–228; Pareto optimal and transaction costs, 228–230; protection of, 232–233; sunlight, 219–222, 219–228
Environmental Impact Statement (EIS), 101, 285
Environmental impact studies, 49–51
Environmental justice movement, 207, 363–364, 366
Environmental Kuznets curve, 363–364
Environmental legislation: development proposal review and, 285; *Lucas* ruling and, 117–118
Environmental movement, interstate highway construction and, 208–210
Environmental Protection Agency (EPA), 50
Environmental racism, 207
Environmentalism, as ideology for exclusion, 203–205, 216
Equal Protection Clause: *Euclid v. Ambler* and, 76; zoning and, 102; zoning litigation and, 92, 94–96
Euclid (Ohio): durability of zoning in, 81–82; master plan, 42
Euclidean zoning, 67–68, 326
Europe: feudalism and planning in, 20–22; suburbanization in, 21–22
Exactions, 275–276, 287; regulatory takings and, 118–120; subdivision, 45; taxes *vs.*, 119; treatment of, in Wharton Index, 319
Exactions cases, 118–120, 328, 366
Excess burden of tax, 132
Exclusionary zoning: civil-rights law and suburban, 201–203; demand for, 198–199, 216–217; environmentalism as ideology for, 203–205, 216; equal protection clause and, 94–96; inequality and, 24; national migration and income convergence and,

164–167; New Jersey Supreme Court and, 73; ngram for, 195; open space preservation and, 359–360; racial zoning, 78–79; sources of, 312–314; spread of, 285–286. *See also* Growth controls
Exclusive-use zones, 35
EZ Pass, 303

Fair Housing Act, 52
Fair share formulas, 43
Fannie Mae, 300
Farmland: concentration of ownership, 23; downzoning of, 294–295; as percent of U.S. land, 3; supply and demand for, 14
Farmland preservation, 5, 51, 205, 264, 295, 361, 366
Federal commissions, housing prices and, 193
Federal flood insurance regulations, 52
Federal government: growth controls and, 366; land-use regulations and, 51–54
Federal government property, NEPA and, 49
Federal Housing Administration (FHA), 192
Fee simple ownership, 20
Fetcher bills, 124
Feudalism, European planning and, 20–22
Fifth Amendment, 69–70, 92
First Amendment, 98
First-in-time, first-in-right principle, 58, 188, 190
Fiscal zoning, 138–140; community heterogeneity and, 147–149; development and redevelopment and, 144–147, 161; rural areas and big cities, 156–158; school children and, 153–156; school districts and, 152–153; use of, 140–142
Floods, use of regulation to control damage from, 252–253
Floor area ratios (FAR), 31
Florida: Celebration, 159, 273; regulatory takings bill, 345; sunlight entitlements, 219–228; voter initiatives in, 316
Fontainebleau Hotel (Miami Beach), 219–228, 231, 232–235

Ford, Henry, 168, 174
Ford Motor Company, 86, 87, 90
Forests, percent of U.S. land in, 3, 4
Form-based zoning, 35
40B (anti-snob zoning law), 96, 150–151, 361–362
Foster City (California), 323–324
Fourteenth Amendment, 92, 113; *Buchanan v. Warley* and, 79, 81; review of state law by Supreme Court and, 349; zoning and, 73–74. *See also* Equal Protection Clause
Fracking, compensation for, 334–335, 336
Free riders: Coase theorem and, 237; homeownership and, 352; public goods and, 243; Tiebout model and, 135
Free speech, property rights and, 98–100
Freeway revolts, 210–212, 258
Friedman, Milton (economist), 194–195, 227
Frost, Robert, 26, 368

Garden cities movement, 322–324
GDP per capita, urban density and, 11
General welfare: due process and, 93; equal protection clause and, 93
Gentrification, urban, 292, 299, 314
Geographic information systems (GIS): measuring population density using, 6; zoning studies and, 318
Geographic mobility, economic and social mobility and, 165
Geographical inclusiveness, due process and, 93
George, Henry (reformer), 15, 131
Georgia: *McCord v. Bond*, 78; *Vulcan Material Co. v. Griffith*, 77–78
Germany, origins of zoning in, 172, 353
Global warming, urbanization and, 321
Goldberg, Rube (cartoonist), 290
Goldilocks dilemma, 272–274
Good housekeeping land-use regulations, 192–193; in central city, 291; demand-dampening reforms and, 351; in Pennsylvania, 360–362; in zoning haystack, 325, 326

Good School Realty (Acton, Mass.), 266
Google Earth, 21, 89, 251
Government: cartel creation by higher, 283–285; effect of compensation on behavior of, 249–259
Government land ownership, 18–20
Government subsidies, suburbanization and, 299–301, 303
Grand Central Terminal, 106–109
Grandfathering for preexisting nonconforming uses, 36–38, 190, 192, 341–343
Grapes of Wrath (Steinbeck), 164
Grassland pasture and range, percent of U.S. land in, 3, 4
"Great migration," (African-American) 164–167
Grid system of land survey, 18, 19
Group-home regulations, 52–53
Growth boundaries, 47–48, 303–307, 322–323, 366–367
Growth controls, 55, 163; citizen participation in Acton and, 263–265; explanations for rise of, 197–199; factors leading to, 217; federal government and, 366; freeway revolts and, 210–212; homevoters and suburban, 292; housing prices and, 159, 353–354; interstate highway construction and, 208–210; ngram for, 195; regional variation in local government and institution of, 314–316; remedies for (*see* Remedial strategies for excess regulation); restricting development through, 202–203. *See also* Exclusionary zoning; Monopoly zoning
Growth machine (Harvey Molotch), 296–298, 314, 338

Habitability codes, 46–47
Hadacheck, John C. (brick maker), 186–187, 189–190
Hail, Christopher, Cambridge (Massachusetts) building records of, 84
Handicapped access regulations, 52
Hanover (New Hampshire), zoning in, 29, 39–40, 358

Harm/benefit rule, regulatory takings and, 329–330, 331–332
Hawaii, preservation regulations, 117
Heckscher, August (New York parks commissioner), 142
Height limitations, 29, 30–31, 59, 134, 138, 142, 169
Henry George theorem, 15
Hierarchical pyramid of land use, 35–36, 183
Historic districts, 61–64, 103, 140, 144
Historic preservation, 106–109
Hoffman Estates, Village of (Illinois), 114
Holdouts, property rule/liability rule distinction and, 230–234
Holmes, Oliver Wendell, 98, 147
Homebuilding industry, 23, 286
Homeowners: concern about nonconforming neighbors and demand for zoning, 175–178; as dominant factor in local politics, 156, 182–185; land use regulation and interests of, 71–72; planners vs., 185–188; takeover of zoning by, 274–276
Homeownership: growth of, 353; NIMBY-ism and, 352; support for zoning and, 169–170
Homes, politics and value of owner-occupied, 184–185
Homevoters, 163, 242–245; downside of, 300–301; exclusionary zoning in suburbs and, 292; inflation and rise of, 212–215, 217; urban, 298–299
Hoover, Herbert, 137, 179
Housing codes, 46–47
Housing equity, advantages and disadvantages of, 352–354
Housing gentrification, in central city, 292, 299
Housing market: cartelization of, 283; Portland growth boundaries and cartelization of, 307
Housing price gradients, in sunbelt cities, 308–309
Housing price inflation: migration and, 166; monopoly growth controls and, 282–283

Housing prices: endogenization of zoning in models of, 366; federal commissions on, 193; growth control measures and rising, 353–354; Houston, 308–310; land use regulation and, 159–160, 165–166, 318, 319–320; national surveys of, 318–320; ngram for, 195; persistence of high, 287–288; regional variation in, 196–197, 217–128, 312–313; regulatory constraints and high urban, 297; urban area size and, 7–8

Houston, 310–312; lack of zoning in, 307–312, 327

Illinois, injunctive remedies in, 333. *See also* Chicago
Impact fees, 45, 119, 161, 275, 287, 319
Impossibility theorem, Arrow's, 246
Imputed rent, taxing, 355–357
Incentive zoning, 124
Inclusionary zoning, 359–360; in Houston, 307–312; monopoly power and, 280–282
Income convergence, exclusionary zoning and, 164–167
Income taxes, 134–135; monopoly growth controls and, 282–283
Index of land use regulation, 318–320
Indian Hills (Ohio), 106
Industrial zones, 190–191
Industry: Cambridge zoning and, 86–89, 90; demand for zoning to regulate placement of, 177–178; interstate highways and relocation of, 199–201, 216; motorized vehicles and expansion into residential neighborhoods, 91
Inequality: land use regulation and, 24–25, 327; suburbanization and economic, 202–203
Infill development, 56, 301, 367
Inflation: effect on housing as investment, 163; effect on zoning, 196; home mortgage deduction and, 353; monopoly growth controls and, 282–283; rise of homevoters and, 212–215, 217
Information, as transaction cost, 230

Injunctive remedies for excessive land-use regulation, 333; damages remedy *vs.*, 104
Internal-circle rule for minimum lot size, 31
Internal Revenue Service, conservation easements and, 64, 65–66
Interstate highway system: anti-growth organizations and, 208–210; compensation and, 258–259; NEPA and, 50; relocation of industry and, 199–201, 216; suburbanization and, 299–300, 303
Investment-backed expectations standard, 107–108
Isoquant diagram, for physical acquisition and regulation, 251–252

Jackson, Henry (U.S. Senator), 51
Jacobs, Jane (urban theorist), 9, 35, 50, 67
Jefferson, Thomas, 365
Jitney bus, 175
Joint Center for Housing Studies (Harvard University), 262
Jones Beach (New York), 212
Judicial supervision of land use regulation: California-federal standoff, 109–111; due process and, 92–94; environmental legislation and, 117–118; equal protection and, 94–96; exactions, 118–120, 328, 366; free speech and property rights, 98–100; historic preservation, 106–109; just compensation, 105–106; local governments prevailing in court, 101–103; neighbors' cases, 100–101; regulatory takings, 104–125; Takings Clause and, 96–98. *See also* State courts; U.S. Supreme Court
Jury theorem, Condorcet's, 246–247
Just compensation, 259; eminent domain and, 232; inefficiency of, 338–339; liability rules and, 334–336; limited application of, 332–334; property rules and, 336–338; regulatory takings and, 332–334, 338–350; statutes, 344–347; takings and, 338–350; zoning litigation and, 92. *See also* Compensation; Takings Clause

Kanner, Gideon (eminent domain lawyer), 348–349
Kansas City residential development, 179
Kelleher, Daniel (takings plaintiff), 343
Kelo, Suzette (eminent domain activist), 336–338
Keynes, John Maynard (economist), 194–195
Kiarie, Kihara (Dartmouth student), 308–309
Koontz, Coy (takings plaintiff), 121–122, 127
Kozinski paradox, 254–255

Land: litigation and immobility of, 70–71; monopoly zoning and "waste," 279–280; supply and demand for, 13–15
Land ownership: concentration of, 23–24; government, 18–20; inequality and, 24–25
Land rent, 12–15, 24; monopoly returns and, 23–24
Land sales, in U.S. vs. Europe, 20–21
Land speculation, sprawl and, 301–303
Land taxes, 12–15, 131–132, 132; efficiency and, 15; split rate system, 16–17
Land use, major classes in U.S., 3–4
Land use exactions. See Exactions
Land use law: Clean Water Act, 49–51; NEPA, 49–51
Land use litigation: environmental legislation and, 205; housing prices and, 165–166. See also Judicial supervision of land use regulation; individual cases
Land use patterns, pre-zoning era, 172–175
Land use regulation: benefits and costs of, 324–327; choices between acquisition and, 251–256; to combat sprawl, 303–307; federal government, 51–54; inequality and, 24–25, 327; litigation regarding (see Judicial supervision of land-use regulation; Litigation about land use regulation; individual cases); political internalization of cost of, 253–254; problems of, 327; resolution of conflict regarding, 70–72; sprawl and excessive, 5; as substitute for taxation, 251–256

Land values, using zoning to devalue property, 91
Landowners: erosion of status of, 266–267; exactions fees and, 275–276; regulatory takings and rights of, 329–330, 332; unhappiness with compensation to forgo development, 334–336
Lapidus, Morris (hotel architect), 231
Large-lot zoning, 280, 294–295
Lawyers: criticism of variances by, 39–40, 115, 141; role in zoning, 44, 69, 170, 202, 264;
Leapfrog development, 47, 56, 301
Least cost avoider, 229
Legislation, administrative decisions vs., 93–94
Levittown (New York), 323
Liability rule/property rule distinction, 230–234, 335–336
Liability rules, 234–235, 334–336
Limited community diversity, demand for, 149–152, 281
Lincoln, Abraham, 19
Lindsey, John (New York mayor), 232
Litigation about land use regulation, 70–72. See also individual cases; Judicial supervision of land use regulation
"Little Boxes" (satirical song), 2, 323
Liu, Emily (Dartmouth student), 99
Local government: fiscal zoning and, 140; free riders and, 243; growth controls in Northeast and, 316; litigation outcomes in favor of, 101–103; median voters and, 243–249; regulatory takings and, 333; in South, 315–316; zoning and, 32–34, 48, 66; zoning and regional variation in, 314–316; zoning as police power of, 29–30
Local government structure, zoning behavior and, 282–283
Local knowledge, evaluation of land use cases and, 126–127
Local norms, zoning exceptions and, 141–142
London, Church of St. Martin in the Fields, 11–12

Los Angeles: early zoning, 163; growth controls, 297–298; industrial and commercial zones, 190–191; planners *vs.* homeowners in, 185–188; population, 7
Louisiana Purchase, 18
Louisville (Kentucky), racial zoning in, 78–79, 81
Low-income communities, environmental justice and, 363–364, 366
Low-income housing: growth management regulations and, 202–203; in Massachusetts, 96, 150–151, 359, 360, 361–362; in New Jersey (*Mount Laurel* remedy), 202, 203, 217, 259, 294–295, 333–334, 334, 359–362, 365; in Pennsylvania, 365–366
Low-income people: criticism of zoning for excluding, 193; exclusionary zoning and migration of, 164–167; outmigration from cities, 298–299
Lucas, David (takings plaintiff), 115–116, 255
LULUs (locally unwanted land uses), 56
Lyme Properties, 238, 242

Madison, James, 339–340
Magna Carta, 339
Malthus, Thomas Robert, 25
Malthus's paradox, 25–26
Mann, Horace (school reformer), 167
Marginal benefit (MB) curve, sunlight entitlements and, 222–227
Marin County, growth control and, 110, 211–212
Massachusetts: Article 60, 85; 40B (anti-snob zoning law), 96, 150–151, 359, 360, 361–362; farmland preservation and open space acquisition in, 361; *Nectow v. Cambridge,* 82–91; varieties of zoning constraints, 31; wetlands protection and growth restriction, 265, 266
Massachusetts Institute of Technology (MIT), 86, 87, 89–90
Master plans, 41–43, 159, 240, 273
McCall, Tom (Oregon governor), 306
McClaughry, John (Vermont legislator), 344
McHenry County (Illinois), 302

Meadows, Donella (environmentalist), 204–205
Measure 37 (Oregon), 250–251, 253–254, 255–258, 307, 334
Measure 49 (Oregon), 257–258
Median voters, 219, 243–245, 247; evidence for model, 247–249; tax price and, 259
Merger solution, 228
Merrill-Lynch, New Jersey development of, 294
Metes and bounds survey, 18–19
Metro (Oregon agency), 304, 307
Metropolitan federations, 55
Metropolitan fragmentation, zoning and, 180–182
Metropolitan indexes of land use regulation, 318–320
Metropolitan sprawl: diagram of, 290–292; housing tax reform and, 357; land use regulation and, 303–307, 327; speculators as cause of, 301–303; suburbanization as cause of, 299–301; transformation of rural areas into suburbs, 292–296
Metropolitan Statistical Area (MSA), 5–6
Metzenbaum, James (Euclid attorney), 76, 168, 193
Miami Beach (Florida), legal entitlements to sunlight, 219–228
Michelman utilitarian criteria, 340–341
Micropolitan Statistical Area (μSA), 5–6
Migration: effect of exclusionary zoning on national, 164–167; from low-income regions to higher-income regions, 25; to Sunbelt, 218
Military draft, compensation and, 258–259
Miller, Casper (takings plaintiff), 342, 343
Minimum house-size rules, 193
Minimum lot size, 28, 30–31, 105, 215, 265, 294, 318
Minneapolis and St. Paul Metropolitan Council, 55
Minnesota: tax policy changes, 248–249; zoning by eminent domain, 344–345
Misrule, zoning boards of adjustment and, 39–40

Mixed-use development, spillover effects, 236–238
Mixed-use zoning, 35, 67, 139
Model T Ford, zoning development and, 174–175
Molotch, Harvey ("Growth Machine" author), 296–297, 338
Monetary damages, regulatory takings and, 329, 330. *See also* Compensation; Just compensation
Monopoly land ownership, 23–24
Monopoly power: of homebuilders, 286; source of, 282–283
Monopoly zoning, 276–279; inclusionary zoning and, 280–282; "waste" land and, 279–280
Moral hazard, takings issue and, 340, 344
Mortgage interest deduction: reform of, 328, 352–359, 365; sprawl and, 300, 303; zoning and reduction in, 328
Moses, Robert (New York planner), 209, 212
Motorized vehicles, land use regulation and introduction of, 91, 168, 174–175, 183–184
Mount Laurel obligations (New Jersey), 202, 203, 217, 259, 294–295, 359–362, 365
Moving to the nuisance, 57–58
Moving-to-the-taking argument, 111–112
Mufson, Harry (hotel owner), 231, 233, 235
Murray Hill (New York neighborhood), 178

National Agricultural Lands Study (NALS), 3
National Association for the Advancement of Colored People (NAACP), 79, 100
National defense, percent of U.S. land in, 3
National Environmental Policy Act (NEPA), 49–51, 204, 205
National Labor Relations Board, 93
Nature Conservancy, 64
Nectow, Saul (zoning plaintiff), 82–83, 85, 86–87
Neighborhood conservation districts, 63–64, 353–534
Neighborhood effects, 60–61
Neighborhood empowerment, environmental laws and, 205, 206–207, 216–217

Neighbors' cases, 100–101
New Haven (Connecticut): adoption of zoning 176; pre-zoning development, 173, 174
New Jersey: exclusionary zoning and, 73, 95–96; *Lumund v. Rutherford*, 77; minimum house-size rules, 193; *Mount Laurel* requirements, 202, 203, 217, 259, 294–295, 333–334, 359–362, 365; *Oxford Construction v. Orange*, 77; *Southern Burlington County NAACP v. Mount Laurel*, 95–96
New urbanism, 55–56, 322, 326
New York City: demand for zoning, 177–178; development in, 297; early zoning in, 136, 163, 170, population, 7
Newcomers, deference to longtime residents/landowners from, 266–267, 293
Nexus requirement, 120–121, 122–123
Ngrams, 194–197
Nichols, J. C. (developer), 179
NIMBYism, 195; home value insurance and, 358; homeownership and, 352; homevoters and, 249; Houston and, 308; inclusionary zoning and, 281; mortgage interest deduction reform and, 365; "Quiet Revolution" and, 205–207; rent control and, 367
Noerr-Pennington doctrine, 278
Nollan, Pat (takings plaintiff), 127
Nollan/Dolan standard, 121–122, 124
Nonconforming uses: grandfathering of, 36–38; persistence of, 191–192; termination of, 186–188, 189–190
Non-distorting tax, 15
Norcross Construction Company, 86
Northeast (U.S. region): government structure and zoning in, 282; housing prices in, 165, 196, 217–218, 282, 286, 312, 319
Novack, Ben (hotel owner), 230–231, 235
Nuisance law, 57–58, 139; grandfathering and, 36–37; zoning and, 188–189, 331
Numerus clausus principle, 230

O'Connor, Sandra Day (Supreme Court Justice), 337

"Offer-ask" disparity, 259–260
Ohio, *Euclid v. Ambler,* 67, 74–77, 81–82, 101, 171, 177, 204
Olmstead, Frederick Law, Jr. (planner), 137
Open-meeting laws, 285
Open space preservation: cluster zoning and, 31; as exclusionary zoning, 359–360; in Massachusetts, 361; smart growth and, 56
Opportunity costs: harm/benefit distinction and, 331; land-use regulation and, 158, 253, 254–256; regulatory takings and, 123
Optimal community size, 271–274
Oregon: Measure 37, 250–251, 253–254, 255–258; Measure 49, 257–258; statewide regional land use commission, 54, 304, 307
Orford (New Hampshire), 142–143
Ottenbacher, Jacob (baker), 184
Overlapping generations model, 163
Overlay zones, 67
Overzoning, 296

Parcel as a whole, 117
Pareto optimality, 228–230
Pareto superior, 228
Penn Central doctrine, 115, 116, 123, 127
Pennsylvania: *Appeal of Girsh,* 104–105; compensation for fracking, 334–335, 336; curative amendments for zoning, 362; good-housekeeping rule, 360–362; injunctive remedies, 333; judicial attempt to slow suburban exclusion, 217; low-income housing in, 365–366; as pro-developer state, 73; split rate system in, 16–17
"Perfect" zoning, 136
Permit moratoria, 34
Physical invasion standard, 108–109
Pine Barrens Commission, 55
Pittsburgh, 16, 17, 134, 208
Placement/positioning requirements, 29, 31
Planned Unit Development (PUD), 45, 67
Planners, 66; homeowners *vs.,* 185–188
Planning blight, 344

Planning boards, 41–43, 93–94; rezoning and, 43–44
Plebiscites, zoning and, 242. *See also* Ballot-box zoning; Voter initiatives
Point Reyes National Seashore, 212
Polaroid Corporation, 86
Police power: *Hadacheck* decision and, 188; zoning as, 29–30
Political control of community development, 270–272
Political dominance of homeowners in suburbs, 182–185
Political resolution of conflict regarding land use, 71–72
Politics: lack of zoning in Houston and, 310–312; in rural areas, 293; transition from prodevelopment to suburban norms in cities, 296–299; of zoning, 27, 66
Population density: measuring, 5–6; proximity effects and, 8–9. *See also* Density
Population distribution in U.S., skewed, 7–8
Portland (Oregon): growth boundaries, 47–48, 303–307, 322–323, 366–367; housing price and urban area size, 7–8
Preemptive regulation, zoning and, 48
Private community associations, 57
Private covenants, 57, 59–61; in early suburbs, 173; in Houston residential areas, 308, 309–310; racial segregation and, 80–81, 201; zoning *vs.,* 60–61
Privately developed planned communities, 323–324
Procedural due process, 92–93
Property rights, free speech and, 98–100
Property rules, 233; *Kelo v. New London* and, 336–338; liability rule *vs.,* 230–234, 335–336
Property tax abatements, 145
Property-tax capitalization, 159–160
Property taxes, 15, 16–17; deadweight loss of, 142–144; incentive-compatible, 132–135; negotiated relief from, 146; "new view" of, 135–136; schools and, 152–156, 161–162; as tax, 129, 160–162; zoning and, 131–132, 134–136. *See also* Fiscal zoning

Proposition 13 (California initiative), 161–162
Protective covenants, 59–61
Proximity effect, urban area size and, 8–9
Public goods: free riders and, 243; tax price and, 243–245, 247–249; transaction costs of, 236–238
Public Land Survey, 18–20
Public law, 130

"Quiet Revolution," 30, 206–207

Race: discrimination in land use policies and, 364; geographic pattern of local governments and, 34; zoning and segregation of, 78–79, 201–202
Racial zoning, 78–79, 201–202; private covenants as substitutes for, 80–81
Railroad construction, 209
Rainfall, geographic pattern of local governments and, 33
Rank-size rule, 7
Rational ignorance, 245–246
Real property, 15
Reddy, Smita (Dartmouth student), 99
Redevelopment: in central city, 292; fiscal zoning and, 144–147
Regional governments: excessive suburban zoning and, 329; zoning control and, 283–284
Regional growth management, double-veto system and, 54–57, 62, 68, 206, 216, 284, 365
Regional land use commission, 54–55, 304, 365
Regional planning organizations, 267–268
Regional variation in housing prices, 165, 196, 217–218, 282, 286, 312–313, 319
Regional variation in zoning, 289–290
Regionalism, "Quiet Revolution," 206–207
Regulatory takings: California and, 109–111; as check on zoning enthusiasm, 105–106; difficulty of moving cases to federal courts, 112–114; exactions and, 118–120; federal standard for, 114–115; fiscal opportunism and, 123–125; harm/benefit rule and, 329–330, 331–332; just compensation and, 332–334, 338–350; liability rules, 334–336; Michelman utilitarian criteria, 340–341; property rules and, 335–338; as remedy for growth controls, 328, 329–330; Rhode Island and, 111–112; state legislation on, 344–347; superseding substantive due process, 104–105; tax price and, 249–251; U.S. Supreme Court and, 106–109, 125–128, 348–351; William Brennan and, 348–351
Rehnquist, William (Chief Justice), 349
Religious Freedom Restoration Act, 53
Religious Land Use and Institutionalized Persons Act (RLUIPA), 53–54, 103
Remedial strategies for excess regulation: demand-dampening reforms, 350–351; home value insurance, 357–359; recommended reforms, 364–367; reform of mortgage interest deduction, 328, 352–359; regulatory takings (*see* Regulatory takings); transaction cost reduction, 328; transaction costs, 357–359
Rent, land, 12–15
Rent controls, 242, 254, 367; housing codes and, 46–47
Renters, political influence of, 243, 271
Reparations for slavery, 346–347
Residential neighborhoods: motorized vehicles and expansion of industrial sites into, 91; zoning and concern about nonconforming neighbors, 175–178
Residential private government, 59–60, 159, 273
Reston (Virginia), 323–324
Reynolds, Malvina ("Little Boxes"), 2
Rezoning, 43–44; ballot-box, 112; curative orders for, 105; to devalue property, 91; imminent signs of, 302–303; neighbors and, 240–242; transaction costs of public goods and, 236–238; West Lebanon case study, 238–240
Rhode Island, *Palazzolo v. Rhode Island*, 111–112
Right to farm laws, 57–58, 190, 295
Riis, Jacob (housing reformer), 11

Road-frontage requirements, 31
Roberts, John G., Jr., (Chief Justice) 118
Rough proportionality test, 120–121, 122–123
Running with the land, 241–242
Rural areas: fiscal zoning and, 156–158; landowner skepticism of zoning in, 157; political life of, 293; transformation into suburban/urban areas, 1–5, 158–160, 292–296
Rural landowners, diminishing political clout of, 253–254, 267
Rural transportation, percent of U.S. land in, 3
Russian Tea Room (holdout example), 232

Sales taxes, 133, 162
Samuelson efficiency conditions, 147
San Francisco, 7–8, 323
Scalia, Antonin (Supreme Court Justice), 116
Schoene, William J. (Virginia entomologist), 342
School children, fiscal zoning and, 153–156
School districts, fiscal zoning and, 152–153
School financing: inequalities in, 202; property taxes and, 161–162
Segregation, land use regulation and, 327
Servitudes, 59
Settlement costs, just compensation and, 341
Shaker Heights (Ohio), 323
Shapiro, Perry (Santa Barbara economist), 338–339, 340, 341
Shasta County (California), 293
Sierra Club, 55, 208
Silicon Valley, 314
Site visits, zoning variances and, 39, 115
Size, agglomeration economies and, 9, 320–321
Skyscrapers, 8–9, 142, 169, 186
Slavery: legacy of, 315–316; reparations for, 347
Smart growth, 195, 306, 326; double veto and, 54–57
Smart sprawl, 11
South (U.S. region): development of local government in, 34; government structure and zoning in, 282; lack of political mechanisms favoring growth controls in, 315; migration to, 218; school financing model, 152–153
South Carolina, *Lucas v. South Carolina Coastal Council*, 115–116, 127–128, 255
South Royalton (Vermont), 56
Speculators, sprawl and, 301–303
Spite fences, 234–235
Split rate system (for property tax), 16–17
Spot zoning, 42, 94, 240
Sprawl, 5. *See also* Metropolitan sprawl
Standard State Zoning Enabling Act (SZEA), 72, 76, 179, 192; effect of, 136–138; fiscal zoning and, 138–140
State courts: cross-state similarities on zoning, 72–74; difficulty of moving land use cases to federal courts, 112–114; litigation about land use regulation, 70–72; regulatory takings and, 109–112, 332–334
States: just compensation statutes, 344–347; Standard State Zoning Enabling Act and, 137. *See also individual states*
Statistics, evaluation of zoning using, 317–319
Steinbeck, John (author), 164
Stone, Harlan Fiske (Supreme Court Justice), 342
Street-car suburbs, 172–174
Subdivision exactions, 45
Subdivision regulations, 44–46; zoning *vs.*, 45–46
Substantive due process, 92, 93–94, 365; superseded by regulatory takings, 104–105
Suburbanization: density and, 323–324; economic inequality and, 202–203; in Europe, 21–22; process of, 4, 5; rate of, 197–198, 199; as sprawl, 299–301; as worldwide phenomenon, 10–12
Suburbs: adoption of zoning and, 33; annexation by cities and, 181–182; community heterogeneity and, 148–149; development of (*see* Community development); in diagram of metropolitan

Suburbs (cont.)
sprawl, 291; homevoters in, 156–157; interstate highways and shift in jobs to, 199–201, 216; nonconforming neighbors and demand for zoning, 176–178; political dominance of homeowners in, 182–185; school quality and home values in, 155; spread of zoning to, 171, 172–174; street-car, 172–174; transformation of rural areas into, 292–296
Sunlight entitlements, 219–222; Coase theorem and, 225–228; valuing, 222–225
Supply and demand for land, 13–15
Surveys: evaluation of zoning using, 317–319; problems with, 319–320
Sutherland, George (Supreme Court Justice), 76–77, 78, 82, 168, 177
Switzerland, takings law in, 348, 353, 355

Takings Clause, 69–70, 92, 96–98; distrust of government and, 339–340; due process and, 97; *Euclid v. Ambler* and, 76; growth controls and litigation using, 330; superceding substantive due process, 104–105; tax price and, 249–251. *See also* Regulatory takings
Tax incentives, 146
Tax increment financing (TIF), 145–146
Tax price, 243–245; Measure 37 and, 256–258; median voters and, 247–249; regulatory takings and, 249–251; response of voters to, 259
Tax rate, tax price *vs.*, 244
Tax subsidy, to owner-occupied housing, 300, 303
Tax treatment, of conservation easements, 64, 65–66
Taxes: capital gains, 355; definition of, 160; exactions *vs.*, 119; Houston's erosion of inner city tax base, 311–312; on imputed rent, 355–357; income, 134–135, 282–283; property, 15; substitution of regulation for, 251–256. *See also* Land taxes; Mortgage interest deduction; Property taxes
Telecommunications Act of 1996, 53

Tenth Amendment, 92
Texas, public land survey, 18
Tiebout model, 268–270, 286; community heterogeneity and, 147–149
Time consistency, 61
Tipping point, affordable housing percentages and, 151
Town and County Planning Act (Britain), 348
Townships, 18, 19
Tradable emissions, 260, 363
Transaction costs, 228–230; home value insurance and, 357–359; liability rule protection and, 234–235; of public goods, 236–238; reducing, 328
Transect zoning, 35, 67, 326
Transferrable development rights (TDRs), 67, 107
Transit-oriented development (TOD), 35, 326
Transportation: effect of interstate highways, 199–201, 216; housing tax reform and public, 357; suburbanization and government subsidies to, 299–300, 303. *See also* Interstate highway system
Transportation changes: development of zoning and, 168; separation of home from work and, 183–184
Trucks, effect on residential districts, 174–175
Truman, Harry, 208, 367
Twain, Mark, 12

Undeveloped land, delayed capitalization and, 157–158
Uniformity requirements, 139
United States: classes of land use, 3–4; land sales in, 20
U.S. Army Corps of Engineers, 50, 51
U.S. census definitions of urban areas, 5–6
U.S. Department of Agriculture, 3
U.S. Department of Housing and Urban Development, 193

U.S. Supreme Court: cross-state similarities regarding zoning and, 73–74; exactions

cases, 119–128, 276, 328, 366; procedural barriers to getting takings cases into federal court, 113–114; on racial zoning *(Buchanan v. Warley)*, 78–79, 81; regulatory takings and, 106–111, 111–112, 115–116, 125–128; standoff with California courts over just compensation, 109–111; Takings Clause and, 97–98, 104–105, 332–333;
Upzoning, 36
Urban agglomeration, city size and, 6–10
Urban areas: percent of U.S. land in, 3; U.S. census definitions of, 5–6
Urban Clusters, 6
Urban density: GDP per capita and, 11; reduced, as worldwide phenomenon, 10–12
Urban land trends, 10–12
Urban Place, 6
Urban spillovers, 317
Urbanization, 1–5, 321
Urbanized Area (UA), 6; population rank and size of 25 largest, 7
Use limitations, 30
Utilitarian criteria, 340–341

Valuations, of rights to build/sunlight entitlements, 219–225
Vanderbilt, Cornelius (railroad builder), 108
Vanderbilt family (Fifth Avenue residences), 177–178
Variances, 32, 38–41, 94, 141; *Lucas v. South Carolina Coastal Council*, 115–116, 118
Vermont: double-veto structure, 206; statewide regional land use commission, 54; takings bill, 344–345
Vermont Law School, 56
Virginia, *Miller v. Schoene*, 341–344
Virginia Military District, 19–20
von Hoffman, Alexander (urban historian), 262
Voter initiatives: effect on zoning in West, 289, 314–315; in Florida, 316; regulatory takings compensation and, 337
Voting behavior, 245–247; median voters, 243–245, 247–249

Voting Rights Act of 1965, 316, 364
Voting rules, municipal and private communities, 61, 273

Wages, urban area size and, 8
Walmart, 44, 278
Walpole (New Hampshire) pulp mill, 236
Walt Disney Company (Celebration, Florida, developer), 159
Wealth: housing as source of, 214, 217; regional variation in housing prices and, 312–313
Webb, Del (developer), 57–58, 286
Wellesley (Massachusetts), 277
West (U.S. region): development of local government in, 33; government structure and zoning in, 282; housing prices in, 165, 196, 217–218, 282, 286, 312, 319; school financing model, 153; urban growth boundaries in, 47–48, 303–307, 322–323, 366–367
West Lebanon (New Hampshire), rezoning case study, 238–242
West University Place (Texas), 309–310
Westenhaver, David (*Euclid* judge), 76, 81, 204
Weston (Massachusetts), 262, 265; adoption of zoning, 171; property taxes in, 133–134
Wetlands regulation, 50–51; Clean Water Act and, 50; growth restrictions and, 265, 266
Wharton Residential Land Use Regulation Index (the Wharton Index), 318–319
Willentz, Robert (New Jersey jurist), 334
Wolfe, Barbara (East Amwell activist), 294
Worker productivity, urban area size and, 8
Wright, Frank Lloyd, 10
Wyoming, 145

Zero zoning, in zoning haystack, 325, 326–327
Zombie zoning, 64–66
Zoning: basic rules of, 28–32; beginnings of, 163; cause of early, 163; contract, 363; control of development and, 30–31;

Zoning (cont.)
criticism of, 192–193; cross-state similarities in, 72–74; defined, 28; demand for, 170–172, 215–217; democratization of adoption of, 198–199; due process and, 92–94; effect of trucks and buses on demand for, 174–178; effects of, 163–164; Euclidean, 67–68; evaluation of using surveys and statistics, 317–319; federal land-use regulations, 51–54; fiscal (*see* Fiscal zoning); good housekeeping through growth controls, 192–197, 261–263; grandfathering and restrictive, 37–38; hierarchical pyramid of land use, 35–36; higher housing prices and, 318, 319–320; homeownership and, 169–170, 274–276; impersonal nature of, 31–32; inflation effect and, 196; limited community heterogeneity and, 149–152; local government and, 66; as local initiative, 48; management of property tax base by, 17; metropolitan fragmentation and, 180–182; micromanagement of development and, 142–144; nuisance law and, 188–189; "perfect," 136; as police power, 29–30; political nature of, 27, 66; popular evolution of, 27; private covenants *vs.*, 60–61; property taxes and, 131–132, 134–136; racial (*see* Racial zoning); recommended reforms in, 364–367; regional variation in, 289–290; regional variations in local governance and, 314–316; relevance of, 130–131; rezoning, 43–44; rural-to-urban transition and, 158–160; simplified zoning map, 28–29; subdivision regulations, 44–46; as supplement to covenants, 178–180; supply and demand for, 168–169; transect, 35, 67, 326; type of local government involved in, 32–34; zombie, 64–66. *See also* Exclusionary zoning; Fiscal zoning; Monopoly zoning; Standard State Zoning Enabling Act (SZEA)

Zoning authority, SZEA and, 138–139

Zoning board, 38–41, 140

Zoning board of adjustment/zoning board of appeals, 38–41 137, 140, 141, 207

"Zoning budget" (Hills and Schleicher), 43

Zoning exceptions, 141–142

Zoning haystack (diagram), 324–237

About the Author

Photo by Janice G. Fischel

Bill Fischel has taught economics at Dartmouth College since 1973, when he received his PhD from Princeton after receiving his BA from Amherst College. He also occupies the Robert C. 1925 and Hilda Hardy Chair in Legal Studies, although he does not have a law degree. Fischel's scholarship focuses on local government, especially land use regulation and property taxation. He is the author of *The Economics of Zoning Laws* (Johns Hopkins, 1985), *Regulatory Takings* (Harvard, 1995), *The Homevoter Hypothesis* (Harvard, 2001), and *Making the Grade* (Chicago, 2009), which is about the economic development of school districts. Fischel is also the editor of *The Tiebout Model at Fifty: Essays in Public Economics in Honor of Wallace Oates* (Lincoln Institute, 2006).

Bill has served on the Hanover, NH, zoning board and on the board of directors of the Lincoln Institute of Land Policy. He and his wife Janice are both natives of Bethlehem, Pennsylvania. They have spent sabbatical leaves from Dartmouth on the West Coast at Berkeley, Davis, and Santa Barbara, California, and at the University of Washington in Seattle. Bill enjoys cross-country skiing, snowshoeing, and mountain biking. He and Janice like to visit cities when they travel, and they pay special attention to local architecture and the sites of famous land use controversies.

ABOUT THE
LINCOLN INSTITUTE OF LAND POLICY

The Lincoln Institute of Land Policy seeks to improve quality of life through the effective use, taxation, and stewardship of land. A nonprofit private operating foundation whose origins date to 1946, the Lincoln Institute researches and recommends creative approaches to land as a solution to economic, social, and environmental challenges. Through education, training, publications, and events, we integrate theory and practice to inform public policy decisions worldwide. With locations in Cambridge, Washington, Phoenix, and Beijing, we organize our work in seven major areas: Planning and Urban Form, Valuation and Taxation, International and Institute-Wide Initiatives, Latin America and the Caribbean, People's Republic of China, the Babbitt Center for Land and Water Policy, and the Center for Community Investment.

LINCOLN INSTITUTE OF LAND POLICY

113 Brattle Street
Cambridge, MA 02138-3400 USA

Phone: 1-617-661-3016 or 1-800-526-3873
Fax: 1-617-661-7235 or 1-800-526-3944
Email: help@lincolninst.edu
Web: www.lincolninst.edu